Java Programming

Fifth Edition

Joyce Farrell

COURSE TECHNOLOGY
CENGAGE Learning™

Australia • Brazil • Japan • Korea • Mexico • Singapore • Spain • United Kingdom • United States

COURSE TECHNOLOGY
CENGAGE Learning™

Java Programming, Fifth Edition
Joyce Farrell

Executive Editor: Marie Lee

Acquisitions Editor: Amy Jollymore

Managing Editor: Tricia Coia

Development Editor: Dan Seiter

Editorial Assistant:
Julia Leroux-Lindsey

Marketing Manager: Bryant Chrzan

Content Project Manager:
Heather Furrow

Art Director: Marissa Falco

Cover Designer: Bruce Bond

Cover Photo: TBD

Manufacturing Coordinator:
Julio Esperas

Proofreader: Andrea Schein

Indexer: Elizabeth Cunningham

Compositor: International Typesetting
and Composition

Microsoft® is a registered trademark of the Microsoft Corporation.

ISBN-13: 978-0-3245-9951-0

ISBN-10: 0-3245-9951-X

Course Technology
25 Thomson Place
Boston, MA 02210
USA

Cengage Learning is a leading provider of customized learning solutions with office locations around the globe, including Singapore, the United Kingdom, Australia, Mexico, Brazil, and Japan. Locate your local office at:
www.international.cengage.com/region

Cengage Learning products are represented in Canada by Nelson Education, Ltd.

To learn more about Course Technology, visit
www.cengage.com/coursetechnology
Purchase any of our products at your local bookstore or at our preferred online store **www.ichapters.com**

Printed in the United States of America
2 3 4 5 6 7 12 11 10

BRIEF CONTENTS

CONTENTS

CONTENTS

CONTENTS

CONTENTS

CONTENTS

CONTENTS

CONTENTS

CONTENTS

CONTENTS

CONTENTS

CONTENTS

CONTENTS

CONTENTS

PREFACE

Java Programming, Fifth Edition provides the beginning programmer with a guide to developing applications using the Java programming language. Java is popular among professional programmers because it can be used to build visually interesting graphical user interface (GUI) and Web-based applications. Java also provides an excellent environment for the beginning programmer—a student quickly can build useful programs while learning the basics of structured and object-oriented programming techniques.

This textbook assumes that you have little or no programming experience. This book provides a solid background in good object-oriented programming techniques and introduces object-oriented terminology using clear, familiar language. The writing is nontechnical and emphasizes good programming practices. The examples are business examples; they do not assume a mathematical background beyond high-school business math. In addition, the examples illustrate only one or two major points; they do not contain so many features that you become lost following irrelevant and extraneous details. The explanations in this textbook are written clearly in straightforward sentences so that native and non-native English speakers alike can master the programming concepts. Complete, working code examples appear frequently in each chapter; these examples help the student make the transition from the theoretical to the practical. The code presented in each chapter is also provided on disk, so that students can easily run the programs and experiment with changes to them.

ORGANIZATION AND COVERAGE

Java Programming, Fifth Edition presents Java programming concepts, enforcing good style, logical thinking, and the object-oriented paradigm. Objects are covered right from the beginning, earlier than in many other textbooks. You create your first Java program in Chapter 1. Chapters 2, 3, and 4 increase your understanding of how data, classes, objects, and methods interact in an object-oriented environment.

Chapters 5 and 6 explore input and repetition structures, which are the backbone of programming logic and essential to creating useful programs in any language. You learn the special considerations of string and array manipulation in Chapters 7 and 8.

Chapters 9, 10, and 11 thoroughly cover inheritance (the object-oriented concept that allows you to develop new objects quickly by adapting the features of existing ones) and exception handling (the object-oriented approach to handling errors). Both are important concepts in object-oriented design. Chapter 12 provides information on handling files so you can permanently store and retrieve program output.

Chapters 13 and 14 introduce GUI `Swing` components—Java's visually pleasing, user-friendly widgets—and their layout managers. Chapters 15 and 16 show you ways to provide interactive excitement using graphics, applets, images, and sound.

In every chapter, *Java Programming, Fifth Edition* follows the text explanation with a "You Do It" section that contains step-by-step exercises to illustrate the concepts just learned, reinforcing the student's understanding and allowing concepts to be better retained. Creating the programs in the step-by-step examples also provides students with a successful experience in the language; finishing the examples provides them with models for their own creations.

The student using *Java Programming, Fifth Edition* builds applications from the bottom up, rather than starting with existing objects. This facilitates a deeper understanding of the concepts used in object-oriented programming, and engenders appreciation for the existing objects students use as their knowledge of the language advances. When students complete this book, they will know how to modify and create simple Java programs and will have the tools to create more complex examples. They also will have a fundamental knowledge of object-oriented programming, which will serve them well in advanced Java courses or in studying other object-oriented languages such as C++, C#, and Visual Basic.

FEATURES

Java Programming, Fifth Edition is a superior textbook because it also includes the following features:

- » **Objectives:** Each chapter begins with a list of objectives so you know the topics that will be presented in the chapter. In addition to providing a quick reference to topics covered, this feature provides a useful study aid.

- » **Notes:** These highlighted tips provide additional information—for example, an alternative method of performing a procedure, another term for a concept, background information on a technique, or a common error to avoid.

- » **Figures:** Each chapter contains many figures. Code figures are most frequently 25 lines or less, illustrating one concept at a time. Frequently placed screen shots show exactly how program output appears.

NEW! » **Callouts in more figures:** Callouts have been added to many figures to help students focus on the points emphasized in the text. Some icons contain the words "Don't Do It" to emphasize when an example illustrates a practice not to emulate.

- » **Color:** The code figures in each chapter contain all Java keywords in brown. This helps students identify keywords more easily, distinguishing them from programmer-selected names.

- » **Files:** The Student Disk holds more than 180 files that contain the code presented in the figures in each chapter. Students can run the code for themselves, view the output, and make changes to the code to observe the effects.

NEW! » **Two Truths and a Lie:** A new quiz reviews each chapter section, with answers provided. This quiz contains three statements from the preceding section of text—two statements are true and one is false. Over the years, students have requested answers to problems, but we have hesitated to distribute them in case instructors want to use problems as assignments or test questions. These true-false mini-quizzes provide students with immediate feedback as they read, without "giving away" answers to the existing multiple-choice and programming problem questions.

- » **You Do It:** In each chapter, step-by-step exercises help the student create multiple working programs that emphasize the logic a programmer uses in choosing statements to include. This section provides a means for students to achieve success on their own—even those in online or distance learning classes.

NEW! » **Don't Do It:** This section at the end of each chapter summarizes common mistakes and pitfalls that plague new programmers while learning the current topic.

» **Key Terms:** Each chapter includes a list of newly introduced vocabulary, shown in the order of appearance in the text. The list of key terms provides a mini-review of the major concepts in the chapter.

» **Summaries:** Following each chapter is a summary that recaps the programming concepts and techniques covered in the chapter. This feature helps students check their understanding of the main points in each chapter.

» **Review Questions:** Each chapter includes 20 multiple-choice questions that serve as a review of chapter topics.

» **Exercises:** Each chapter concludes with meaningful programming exercises that provide additional practice of the skills and concepts learned in the chapter. These exercises vary in difficulty and are designed to allow exploration of logical programming concepts.

» **Game Zone:** Each chapter provides one or more exercises in which the student creates interactive games using the programming techniques learned up to that point; 70 game programs are suggested in the book. The games are fun to create and play; writing them motivates students to master the necessary programming techniques. Students might exchange completed game programs with each other, suggesting improvements and discovering alternate ways to accomplish tasks.

» **Tough Questions:** Each chapter includes two or more fairly difficult, and often open-ended, questions **NEW!** that are typical of what an applicant might encounter in a technical job interview. Some questions involve coding; others might involve research.

» **Up for Discussion:** Each chapter concludes with a few thought-provoking questions concerning programming in general or Java in particular. The questions can be used to start classroom or online discussions, or to develop and encourage research, writing, and language skills.

» **Glossary:** This edition includes a glossary that contains definitions for all key terms in the book, **NEW!** presented in alphabetical order.

» **Appendix on javadoc:** This edition includes a new appendix on creating javadoc comments. **NEW!**

» **Other pedagogical improvements:** This edition introduces the following pedagogical improvements: **NEW!**

  » The `Scanner` class is introduced in Chapter 2 to facilitate user keyboard entry in programs.

  » Programming examples provide earlier and more consistent use of named constants.

  » Clearer distinction between troublesome concepts is provided—for example, argument vs. parameter and static vs. nonstatic.

  » The `String` chapter focuses on `StringBuilder` instead of `StringBuffer` because `StringBuilder` is more efficient. However, it is emphasized that the two classes are used in exactly the same way.

  » The GUI chapters have been completely rewritten and moved later in the book, which makes it easier for instructors who want to cover the concepts of inheritance and polymorphism first. Similarly, applet coverage has been removed from the GUI chapters, which makes it easier for instructors who want to cover GUI topics first.

  » Applets have been moved to the last chapter in the book, reflecting their diminished popularity as a business tool.

» **Quality:** Every program example in the book, as well as every exercise and game solution, was tested by the author and then tested again by a Quality Assurance team using Java Standard Edition (SE) 6, the most recent version available. (The external version number used by Sun Microsystems is 6.0; the internal version number is 1.6.0. For more information on the features of the JDK, visit *http://java.sun.com*.)

» **CD-ROM included with book:** The CD that comes with this book includes the following items:

  » Sun Microsystems Java SE 6, the Java language, compiler, and runtime environment

  » The jGRASP integrated development environment for Java

  » Code files for all Java program examples contained in the text

TEACHING TOOLS

The following supplemental materials are available when this book is used in a classroom setting. All of the teaching tools available with this book are provided to the instructor on a single CD.

» **Electronic Instructor's Manual:** The Instructor's Manual that accompanies this textbook includes additional instructional material to assist in class preparation, including items such as Sample Syllabi, Chapter Outlines, Technical Notes, Lecture Notes, Quick Quizzes, Teaching Tips, Discussion Topics, and Key Terms.

» **ExamView®:** This textbook is accompanied by ExamView, a powerful testing software package that allows instructors to create and administer printed, computer (LAN-based), and Internet-based exams. ExamView includes hundreds of questions that correspond to the topics covered in this text, enabling students to generate detailed study guides that include page references for further review. The computer-based and Internet testing components allow students to take exams at their computers, and they save the instructor time by grading each exam automatically.

» **PowerPoint Presentations:** This book comes with Microsoft PowerPoint slides for each chapter. These are included as a teaching aid for classroom presentation, to make available to students on the network for chapter review, or to be printed for classroom distribution. Instructors can add their own slides for additional topics they introduce to the class.

» **Solution Files:** Solutions to "You Do It" exercises and all end-of-chapter exercises are provided on the Instructor Resources CD and on the Course Technology Web site at *www.course.com*. The solutions are password protected.

  Annotated solutions are provided for the multiple-choice Review Questions. For example, if students are likely to debate answer choices, or not understand the choice deemed to be the correct one, a rationale is provided.

» **Distance Learning:** Course Technology is proud to present online test banks in WebCT and Blackboard to provide the most complete and dynamic learning experience possible. Instructors are encouraged to make the most of the course, both online and offline. For more information on how to access the online test bank, contact your local Course Technology sales representative.

ACKNOWLEDGEMENTS

I would like to thank all of the people who helped to make this book a reality, especially Dan Seiter, Development Editor. Dan's suggestions and attention to detail made this a superior book, and his sense of humor made writing it practically painless.

Thanks also to Tricia Coia, Managing Editor; and Heather Furrow, Content Project Manager. I am lucky to work with Tricia and Heather; they are dedicated to producing quality instructional materials.

Thanks to Serge Palladino, John Freitas, and Chris Scriver of the Quality Assurance Department.

Thank you to Dick Grant of Seminole Community College, Sanford, Florida. He provided important technical and pedagogical suggestions based on his classroom use of this book. He possesses the rare combination of excellent teacher and programmer, and he made this book more accurate and more useful to students.

I am also grateful to the many other reviewers who provided comments and encouragement during this book's development, including Karlyn Barilovits, Kaplan University; Kay Chen, Bucks County Community College; Roman Erenshteyn, Goldey-Beacom College; Jeff Hedrington, University of Phoenix-Online; and Aaron Jagers, Louisiana Technical College.

Thanks, too, to my husband, Geoff, who supports me every step of the way. Finally, this book is dedicated to our lifelong friends, George and Mary Profeta.

Joyce Farrell

READ THIS BEFORE YOU BEGIN

The following information will help you as you prepare to use this textbook.

TO THE USER OF THE DATA FILES

To complete the steps and projects in this book, you need data files that have been created specifically for this book. Your instructor will provide the data files to you. You also can obtain the files electronically from the Course Technology Web site by connecting to *www.course.com* and then searching for this book title. Note that you can use a computer in your school lab or your own computer to complete the exercises in this book.

USING YOUR OWN COMPUTER

To use your own computer to complete the steps and exercises, you need the following:

» **Software:** Java SE 6, available from *http://java.sun.com*. (Although almost all of the examples in this book will work with earlier versions of Java, this book was created using Java 6.) The book clearly points out the few cases when an example does not work with earlier versions of Java. You also need a text editor, such as Notepad. A few exercises ask you to use a browser, such as Internet Explorer.

» **Hardware:** To install Java on your computer, the Java Web site suggests at least a Pentium III 500-MHz system with 512 MB of memory and at least 850 MB of disk space. A Pentium IV 1.4-GHz system with 1 GB of memory and 1 GB of disk space is recommended.

» **Data Files:** You cannot complete all the chapters and projects in this book using your own computer unless you have the data files. You can get the data files from your instructor, or you can obtain the data files electronically from the Course Technology Web site by connecting to *www.course.com* and then searching for this book title.

The following material is provided on the CD that comes with this book:

» Sun Microsystems Java SE 6, the Java language, compiler, and runtime environment
» Sun Microsystems Java Application Programming Interface (API) Specification, official documentation for the Java programming language
» The jGRASP integrated development environment for Java
» Code files for all Java program examples contained in the text

VISIT OUR WORLD WIDE WEB SITE
Additional materials designed especially for this book might be available for your course. Periodically search *www.course.com* for more details and updates.

1

CREATING YOUR FIRST JAVA CLASSES

In this chapter, you will:

Learn about programming
Be introduced to object-oriented programming concepts
Learn about Java
Analyze a Java application that uses console output
Add comments to a Java class
Save, compile, run, and modify a Java application
Create a Java application using GUI output
Correct errors and find help

LEARNING ABOUT PROGRAMMING

A computer **program** is a set of instructions that you write to tell a computer what to do. Computers are constructed from circuitry that consists of small on/off switches, so you could create a computer program by writing something along the following lines:

```
first switch—on
second switch—off
third switch—off
fourth switch—on
```

> **» NOTE**
> Programmers often say that machine language consists of 1s and 0s. What they mean is that you can use 1s and 0s to represent on and off switches.

Your program could go on and on, for several thousand switches. A program written in this style is written in **machine language**, which is the most basic circuitry-level language. For this reason, machine language is a **low-level programming language**, or one that corresponds closely to a computer processor's circuitry. The problems with this approach lie in keeping track of the many switches involved in programming any worthwhile task and in discovering the errant switch or switches if the program does not operate as expected. In addition, the number and location of switches vary from computer to computer, which means that you would need to customize a machine language program for every type of machine on which you want the program to run.

> **» NOTE**
> In every high-level programming language, the names of memory locations cannot include spaces.

Fortunately, programming has evolved into an easier task because of the development of high-level programming languages. A **high-level programming language** allows you to use a vocabulary of reasonable terms, such as "read," "write," or "add," instead of the sequences of on and off switches that perform these tasks. High-level languages also allow you to assign intuitive names to areas of computer memory, such as "hoursWorked" or "rateOfPay," rather than having to remember the memory locations (switch numbers) of those values. Java is a high-level programming language.

Each high-level language has its own **syntax**, or rules of the language. For example, depending on the specific high-level language, you might use the verb "print" or "write" to produce output. All languages have a specific, limited vocabulary and a specific set of rules for using that vocabulary. When you are learning a computer programming language, such as Java, C++, or Visual Basic, you really are learning the vocabulary and syntax rules for that language.

Using a programming language, programmers write a series of **program statements**, similar to English sentences, to carry out the tasks they want the program to perform. After the program statements are written, high-level language programmers use a computer program called a **compiler** or **interpreter** to translate their language statements into machine code. A compiler translates an entire program before carrying out the statement, or **executing** it, whereas an interpreter translates one program statement at a time, executing a statement as soon as it is translated. Compilers and interpreters issue one or more error messages each time they encounter an invalid program statement—that is, a statement containing a **syntax error**, or misuse of the language. Subsequently, the programmer can correct the error and attempt another translation by compiling or interpreting the program again. Locating and repairing all syntax errors is part of the process of **debugging** a program—freeing the program of all errors. Whether you use a compiler or interpreter often depends on the programming language you use—for example, C++ is a compiled language and Visual Basic is an interpreted language. Each type of translator has its supporters—programs written in compiled languages execute more quickly, whereas programs written in interpreted languages are easier to develop and debug. Java uses the best of both technologies—a compiler to translate your programming statements and an interpreter to read the compiled code line by line at run time.

> **》NOTE**
> You will learn more about debugging Java programs later in this chapter.

In addition to learning the correct syntax for a particular language, a programmer also must understand computer programming logic. The **logic** behind any program involves executing the various statements and procedures in the correct order to produce the desired results. Although you begin to debug a program by correcting all the syntax errors, it is not fully debugged until you have also fixed all logical errors. For example, you would not write statements to tell the computer program to process data until the data had been properly read into the program. Similarly, you might be able to use a computer language's syntax correctly, but fail to end up with a logically constructed, workable program. Examples of logical errors include multiplying two values when you meant to divide them, or producing output prior to obtaining the appropriate input. Tools that will help you visualize and understand logic are presented in Chapter 5.

> **》NOTE** Programmers call some logical errors **semantic errors**. For example, if you misspell a programming-language word, you commit a syntax error, but if you use a correct word in the wrong context, you commit a semantic error.

»TWO TRUTHS AND A LIE: LEARNING ABOUT PROGRAMMING

1. Unlike a low-level programming language, a high-level programming language allows you to use a vocabulary of reasonable terms instead of the sequences of on and off switches that perform the corresponding tasks.

2. A compiler executes each program statement as soon as it is translated, whereas an interpreter translates all of a program's statements before executing any.

3. A syntax error occurs when you misuse a language; locating and repairing all syntax errors is part of the process of debugging a program.

The false statement is #2. A compiler translates an entire program before carrying out any statements, whereas an interpreter translates one program statement at a time, executing a statement as soon as it is translated.

INTRODUCING OBJECT-ORIENTED PROGRAMMING CONCEPTS

Two popular approaches to writing computer programs are procedural programming and object-oriented programming.

PROCEDURAL PROGRAMMING

»NOTE
Procedures are also called modules, methods, functions, and subroutines. Users of different programming languages tend to use different terms. Java programmers most frequently use the term "method."

Procedural programming is a style of programming in which sets of operations are executed one after another in sequence. It involves using your knowledge of a programming language to create names for computer memory locations that can hold values—for example, numbers and text—in electronic form. The named computer memory locations are called **variables** because they hold values that might vary. For example, a payroll program written for a company might contain a variable named rateOfPay. The memory location referenced by the name rateOfPay might contain different values (a different value for every employee of the company) at different times. During the execution of the payroll program, each value stored under the name rateOfPay might have many operations performed on it—the value might be read from an input device, the value might be multiplied by another variable representing hours worked, and the value might be printed on paper. For convenience, the individual operations used in a computer program are often grouped into logical units called **procedures**. For example, a series of four or five comparisons and calculations that together determine a person's federal withholding tax value might be grouped as a procedure named calculateFederalWithholding. A procedural program defines the variable memory locations and then **calls** a series of procedures to input, manipulate, and output the values stored in those locations. A single procedural program often contains hundreds of variables and thousands of procedure calls.

OBJECT-ORIENTED PROGRAMMING

Object-oriented programming is an extension of procedural programming in which you take a slightly different approach to writing computer programs. Writing **object-oriented programs** involves creating classes, creating objects from those classes, and creating **applications**, which are stand-alone executable programs that use those objects. After being created, classes can be reused over and over again to develop new programs. Thinking in an object-oriented manner involves envisioning program components as objects that belong to classes and are similar to concrete objects in the real world; then, you can manipulate the objects and have them interrelate with each other to achieve a desired result.

If you've ever used a computer that uses a command-line operating system (such as DOS), and if you've also used a graphical user interface (GUI), such as Windows, then you are familiar with one of the differences between procedural and object-oriented programs. If you want to move several files from a floppy disk to a hard disk, you can type a command at a prompt or command line, or you can use a mouse in a graphical environment to accomplish the task. The difference lies in whether you issue a series of commands, in sequence, to move the three files, or you drag icons representing the files from one screen location to another, much as you would physically move paper files from one file cabinet to another in your office. You can move the same three files using either operating system, but the GUI system allows you to manipulate the files like their real-world paper counterparts. In other words, the GUI system allows you to treat files as objects.

Understanding how object-oriented programming differs from traditional procedural programming requires understanding three basic concepts:

» Encapsulation as it applies to classes as objects
» Inheritance
» Polymorphism

> **NOTE**
> Do not assume that all object-oriented programs are written to use GUI objects—they are not. However, the difference between command-line and GUI operating systems provides an analogy that helps you envision object-oriented concepts.

You can remember these three concepts by remembering the acronym *PIE*, as shown in Figure 1-1.

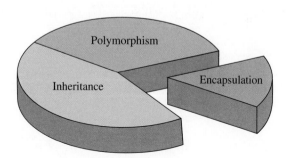

Figure 1-1 The three major features of object-oriented programming

UNDERSTANDING OBJECTS, CLASSES, AND ENCAPSULATION

Objects, both in the real world and in object-oriented programming, are made up of attributes and methods. **Attributes** are the characteristics that define an object; the values contained in attributes differentiate objects of the same class from one another. For example, some of your automobile's attributes are its make, model, year, and purchase price. Other attributes include whether the automobile is currently running, its gear, its speed, and whether it is dirty. All automobiles possess the same attributes, but not, of course, the same values for those attributes. Similarly, your dog has the attributes of its breed, name, age, and

> **NOTE**
> In object-oriented programming grammar, an object is equivalent to a noun and an attribute is an adjective. Methods are similar to verbs.

»»NOTE
When you learn a programming language such as Java, you learn to work with two types of classes: those that have already been developed by the language's creators and your own new, customized classes.

whether his shots are current. The values of the attributes of an object are also referred to as the object's **state**.

In object-oriented terminology, a **class** is a term that describes a group or collection of objects with common properties. A **class definition** describes what attributes its objects will have and what those objects will be able to do. An **instance** of a class is an existing object of a class. Therefore, your red Chevrolet `Automobile` with the dent is an instance of the class that is made up of all automobiles, and your Akita `Dog` named Ginger is an instance of the class that is made up of all dogs. Thinking of items as instances of a class allows you to apply your general knowledge of the class to individual members of the class. A particular instance of a class takes its attributes from the general category. If your friend purchases an `Automobile`, you know it has a model name, and if your friend gets a `Dog`, you know the dog has a breed. You might not know the current state of your friend's `Automobile`— for example, its current speed, or the status of her `Dog`'s shots—but you do know what attributes exist for the `Automobile` and `Dog` classes. Similarly, in a GUI operating environment, you expect each component to have specific, consistent attributes, such as a button being clickable or a window being closable, because each component gains these attributes as a member of the general class of GUI components. Figure 1-2 shows the relationship of some `Dog` objects to the `Dog` class.

»»NOTE
In the same way that a blueprint exists before any houses are built from it, and a recipe exists before any cookies are baked from it, so does a class exist before any objects are instantiated from it.

»»NOTE By convention, programmers using Java begin their class names with an uppercase letter. Thus, the class that defines the attributes and methods of an automobile would probably be named `Automobile`, and the class for dogs would probably be named `Dog`. However, following this convention is not required to produce a workable program.

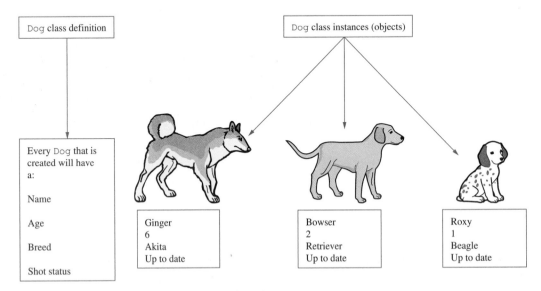

Figure 1-2 A class definition and some objects created from it

Besides attributes, objects can use methods to accomplish tasks. A **method** is a self-contained block of program code, similar to a procedure. An `Automobile`, for example, can move forward and backward. It also can be filled with gasoline or be washed. Some methods can ascertain certain attributes, such as the current speed of an `Automobile` and the status of its gas tank. Similarly, a `Dog` can walk or run, eat food, and get a bath, and there are methods to determine how hungry the `Dog` is or what its name is. GUI operating system components can be maximized, minimized, and dragged.

Like procedural programs, object-oriented programs have variables (attributes) and procedures (methods), but the attributes and methods are encapsulated into objects that are then used much like real-world objects. **Encapsulation** refers to the hiding of data and methods within an object. Encapsulation provides the security that keeps data and methods safe from inadvertent changes. Programmers sometimes refer to encapsulation as using a "black box," or a device that you can use without regard to the internal mechanisms. A programmer can access and use the methods and data contained in the black box but cannot change them.

If an object's methods are well written, the user is unaware of the low-level details of how the methods are executed, and the user must simply understand the interface or interaction between the method and the object. For example, if you can fill your `Automobile` with gasoline, it is because you understand the interface between the gas pump nozzle and the vehicle's gas tank opening. You don't need to understand how the pump works mechanically or where the gas tank is located inside your vehicle. If you can read your speedometer, it does not matter how the displayed figure is calculated. As a matter of fact, if someone produces a superior, more accurate speed-determining device and inserts it in your `Automobile`, you don't have to know or care how it operates, as long as your interface remains the same. The same principles apply to well-constructed objects used in object-oriented programs.

UNDERSTANDING INHERITANCE AND POLYMORPHISM

An important feature of object-oriented programs is **inheritance**—the ability to create classes that share the attributes and methods of existing classes, but with more specific features. For example, `Automobile` is a class, and all `Automobile` objects share many traits and abilities. `Convertible` is a class that inherits from the `Automobile` class; a `Convertible` is a type of `Automobile` that has and can do everything a "plain" `Automobile` does—but with an added mechanism for and an added ability to lower its top. (In turn, `Automobile` inherits from the `Vehicle` class.) `Convertible` is not an object—it is a class. A specific `Convertible` is an object—for example, `my1967BlueMustangConvertible`.

> **» NOTE**
> Chapters 9 and 10 provide more information about inheritance and polymorphism, and how they are implemented in Java.

Inheritance helps you understand real-world objects. For example, the first time you encounter a `Convertible`, you already understand how the ignition, brakes, door locks, and other `Automobile` systems work. You need to be concerned only with the attributes and methods that are "new" with a `Convertible`. The advantages in programming are the same—you can build new classes based on existing classes and concentrate on the specialized features you are adding.

A final important concept in object-oriented terminology is **polymorphism**. Literally, polymorphism means "many forms"—it describes the feature of languages that allows the same word or symbol to be interpreted correctly in different situations based on the context. For

»NOTE
When you see a plus sign (+) between two numbers, you understand they are being added. When you see it carved in a tree between two names, you understand that the names are linked romantically. Because the symbol has diverse meanings based on context, it is polymorphic.

example, in English the verb "run" means different things if you use it with "a footrace," a "business," or "a computer." You understand the meaning of "run" based on the other words used with it. Object-oriented programs are written so that the most useful verbs, such as "print" or "save," work differently based on their context. The advantages of polymorphism will become more apparent when you begin to create GUI applications containing features such as windows, buttons, and menu bars. In a GUI application, it is convenient to remember one method name, such as `setColor` or `setHeight`, and have it work correctly no matter what type of object you are modifying.

»TWO TRUTHS AND A LIE: INTRODUCING OBJECT-ORIENTED PROGRAMMING CONCEPTS

1. An instance of a class is a created object that possesses the attributes and methods described in the class definition.
2. Encapsulation protects data by hiding it within an object.
3. Polymorphism is the ability to create classes that share the attributes and methods of existing classes, but with more specific features.

The false statement is #3. Inheritance is the ability to create classes that share the attributes and methods of existing classes, but with more specific features; polymorphism describes the ability to use one term to cause multiple actions.

LEARNING ABOUT JAVA

»NOTE
When programmers call the JVM "hypothetical," they don't mean it doesn't exist. Instead, they mean it is not a physical entity created from hardware, but is composed only of software.

Java was developed by Sun Microsystems as an object-oriented language for general-purpose business applications and for interactive, Web-based Internet applications. Some of the advantages that have made Java so popular in recent years are its security features and the fact that it is **architecturally neutral**, which means that you can use Java to write a program that will run on any platform (operating system).

Java can be run on a wide variety of computers because it does not execute instructions on a computer directly. Instead, Java runs on a hypothetical computer known as the **Java Virtual Machine (JVM)**.

»NOTE
Interactive applications are those in which a user communicates with a program by using an input device such as the keyboard or a mouse.

Figure 1-3 shows the Java environment. Programming statements written in a high-level programming language are called **source code**. When you write a Java program, you first construct the source code using a text editor such as Notepad. The statements are saved in a file; then, the Java compiler converts the source code into a binary program of **bytecode**. A program called the **Java interpreter** then checks the bytecode and communicates with the operating system, executing the bytecode instructions line by line within the Java Virtual Machine. Because the Java program is isolated from the operating system, the Java program is also insulated from the particular hardware on which it is run. Because of this insulation, the JVM provides security against intruders accessing your computer's hardware through the operating system. Therefore, Java is more secure than other languages. Another advantage provided by the JVM means less work for programmers—when using other programming languages, software vendors usually have to produce multiple versions of the same product (a Windows version, Macintosh version, UNIX version, Linux version, and so on) so all users can run the program. With Java, one program version will run on all these platforms.

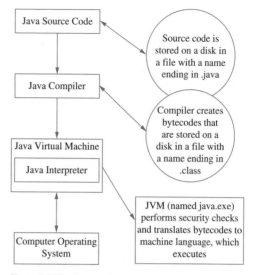

Figure 1-3 The Java environment

Java is also simpler to use than many other object-oriented languages. Java is modeled after C++. Although neither language is easy to read or understand on first exposure, Java does eliminate some of the most difficult-to-understand features in C++, such as pointers and multiple inheritance.

JAVA PROGRAM TYPES

You can write two kinds of programs using Java. Programs that are embedded in a Web page are called Java **applets**. Stand-alone programs are called Java **applications**. Java applications can be further subdivided into **console applications**, which support character output to a computer screen in a DOS window, for example, and **windowed applications**, which create a GUI with elements such as menus, toolbars, and dialog boxes. Console applications are the easiest applications to create; you start using them in the next section.

»TWO TRUTHS AND A LIE: LEARNING ABOUT JAVA

1. Java was developed to be architecturally neutral, which means that anyone can build an application without extensive study.
2. After you write a Java program, the compiler converts the source code into a binary program of bytecode.
3. Java programs that are embedded in a Web page are called applets, while stand-alone programs are called Java applications.

The false statement is #1. Java was developed to be architecturally neutral, which means that you can use Java to write a program that will run on any platform.

ANALYZING A JAVA APPLICATION THAT USES CONSOLE OUTPUT

At first glance, even the simplest Java application involves a fair amount of confusing syntax. Consider the application in Figure 1-4. This program is written on seven lines, and its only task is to print "First Java application" on the screen.

NOTE Some programmers prefer to reserve the term "print" for output that is produced on paper; they use "display" when referring to screen output. Because Java uses the `print()` and `println()` methods to display output on the screen, this book will use the term "print" to mean screen output.

```java
public class First
{
    public static void main(String[] args)
    {
        System.out.println("First Java application");
    }
}
```

Figure 1-4 The `First` class

UNDERSTANDING THE STATEMENT THAT PRINTS THE OUTPUT

The statement `System.out.println("First Java application");` does the actual work in this program. Like all Java statements, this one ends with a semicolon.

The text "First Java application" is a **literal string** of characters; that is, it is a series of characters that will appear in output exactly as entered. Any literal string in Java is written between double quotation marks. Figure 1-5 labels this string and the other parts of the statement.

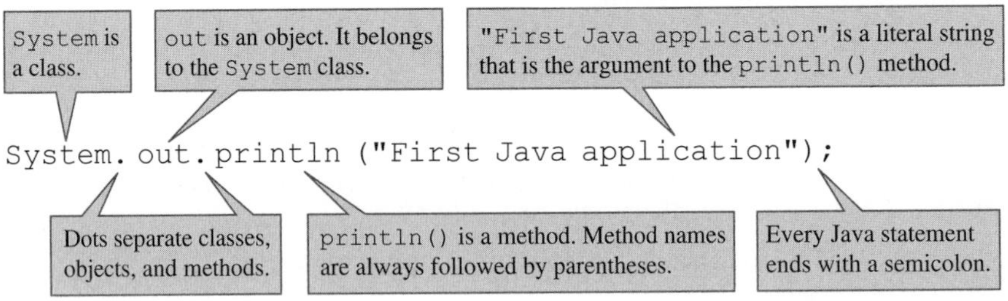

System is a class.

out is an object. It belongs to the System class.

"First Java application" is a literal string that is the argument to the println() method.

`System. out. println ("First Java application");`

Dots separate classes, objects, and methods.

println() is a method. Method names are always followed by parentheses.

Every Java statement ends with a semicolon.

Figure 1-5 Anatomy of a Java statement

NOTE The dots (periods) in `System.out.println` are used to separate the names of the class, object, and method. You will use this same class-dot-object-dot-method format repeatedly in your Java programs.

The string "First Java application" appears within parentheses because the string is an argument to a method, and arguments to methods always appear within parentheses. **Arguments** are pieces of information that are sent into, or **passed** to, a method, usually because the method requires the information to perform its task or carry out its purpose. As an example, consider placing a catalog order with a company that sells sporting goods. Processing a catalog order is a method that consists of a set of standard procedures—recording the order, checking the availability of the item, pulling the item from the warehouse, and so on. Each catalog order also requires a set of data items, such as which item number you are ordering and the quantity of the item desired; these data items can be considered the order's argument. If you order two of item 5432 from a catalog, you expect different results than if you order 1,000 of item 9008. Likewise, if you pass the argument "Happy Holidays" to a Java method, you expect different results than if you pass the argument "First Java application".

>> **NOTE** The `println()` method requires only one argument. Later in this chapter, you will learn about a method named `showMessageDialog()` that requires two arguments. Other methods require more.

Within the statement `System.out.println("First Java application");`, the method to which you are passing `"First Java application"` is named `println()`. The `println()` method prints a line of output on the screen and positions the insertion point on the next line, so that any subsequent output appears on a new line.

Within the statement `System.out.println("First Java application");`, *out* is an object. The `out` object represents the screen. Several methods, including `println()`, are available with the `out` object. Of course, not all objects have a `println()` method (for instance, you can't print to a keyboard, to your `Automobile`, or to your `Dog`), but the creators of Java assume you frequently want to display output on a screen. Therefore, the `out` object was created and endowed with the method named `println()`.

>> **NOTE** The `print()` method is very similar to the `println()` method. With `println()`, after the message prints, the insertion point appears on the following line. With `print()`, the insertion point does not advance to a new line; it remains on the same line as the output.

Within the statement `System.out.println("First Java application");`, *System* is a class. Therefore, `System` defines the attributes of a collection of similar "System" objects, just as the `Dog` class defines the attributes of a collection of similar `Dog` objects. One of the `System` objects is `out`. (You can probably guess that another object is *in* and that it represents an input device.) The `out` object refers to the **standard output device** for a system, normally the monitor.

The statement that prints the string "First Java application" cannot stand alone; it is embedded within a class, as shown in Figure 1-4.

UNDERSTANDING THE First CLASS

Everything that you use within a Java program must be part of a class. When you write `public class First`, you are defining a class named `First`. You can define

>> **NOTE**
When you call a method, you always use parentheses following the method name. In this book you will learn about many methods that require arguments between their parentheses, and many others for which you leave the parentheses empty.

>> **NOTE**
You can use the `println()` method with no arguments when you want to print a blank line.

>> **NOTE**
Method names usually are referenced followed by their parentheses, as in `println()`, so that you can distinguish method names from variable names.

>> **NOTE**
Java is case sensitive; the class named `System` is a completely different class from one named `system`, `SYSTEM`, or even `sYsTeM`.

a Java class using any name or **identifier** you need, as long as it meets the following requirements:

» A class name must begin with a letter of the English alphabet, a non-English letter (such as α or π), an underscore, or a dollar sign. A class name cannot begin with a digit.

» A class name can contain only letters, digits, underscores, or dollar signs.

» A class name cannot be a Java reserved keyword, such as `public` or `class`. (See Table 1-1 for a list of reserved keywords.)

» A class name cannot be one of the following values: `true`, `false`, or `null`. These are not keywords (they are primitive values), but they are reserved and cannot be used.

NOTE
Java is based on **Unicode**, which is an international system of character representation. The term "letter" indicates English-language letters as well as characters from Arabic, Greek, and other alphabets. You can learn more about Unicode in Appendix B.

abstract	double	int	strictfp
assert	else	interface	super
boolean	enum	long	switch
break	extends	native	synchronized
byte	final	new	this
case	finally	package	throw
catch	float	private	throws
char	for	protected	transient
class	goto	public	try
const	if	return	void
continue	implements	short	volatile
default	import	static	while
do	instanceof		

Table 1-1 Java reserved keywords

NOTE
You should follow established conventions for Java so your programs will be easy for other programmers to interpret and follow. This book uses established Java programming conventions.

It is a Java standard, although not a requirement, to begin class identifiers with an uppercase letter and employ other uppercase letters as needed to improve readability. Table 1-2 lists some valid and conventional class names that you could use when writing programs in Java. Table 1-3 provides some examples of class names that *could* be used in Java (if you use these class names, the class will compile) but that are unconventional and not recommended. Table 1-4 provides some class name examples that are illegal.

NOTE
Using an uppercase letter to begin an identifier and to start each new word in an identifier is known as **Pascal casing**.

Class Name	Description
Employee	Begins with an uppercase letter
UnderGradStudent	Begins with an uppercase letter, contains no spaces, and emphasizes each new word with an initial uppercase letter
InventoryItem	Begins with an uppercase letter, contains no spaces, and emphasizes the second word with an initial uppercase letter
Budget2011	Begins with an uppercase letter and contains no spaces

Table 1-2 Some valid class names in Java

Class Name	Description
Undergradstudent	New words are not indicated with initial uppercase letters; difficult to read
Inventory_Item	Underscore is not commonly used to indicate new words
BUDGET2011	Using all uppercase letters is not common

Table 1-3 Legal but unconventional and nonrecommended class names in Java

Class Name	Description
An employee	Space character is illegal
Inventory Item	Space character is illegal
class	class is a reserved word
2011Budget	Class names cannot begin with a digit
phone#	# symbol is illegal

Table 1-4 Some illegal class names in Java

In Figure 1-4 (and again in Figure 1-6), the line `public class First` is the class header; it contains the keyword `class`, which identifies `First` as a class. The reserved word `public` is an access modifier. An **access modifier** defines the circumstances under which a class can be accessed and the other classes that have the right to use a class. Public access is the most liberal type of access; you will learn about public and other types of access in Chapter 3.

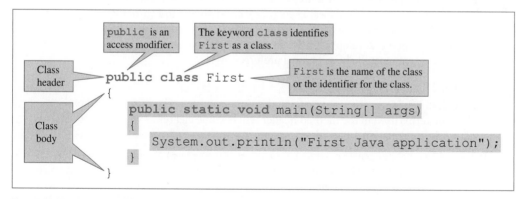

Figure 1-6 The parts of a typical class

After the class header, you enclose the contents of a class within curly braces ({ and }). A class can contain any number of data items and methods. In Figure 1-4 (and again in Figure 1-6), the class `First` contains only one method within its curly braces. The name of the method is `main()`, and the `main()` method, like the `println()` method, contains its own set of parentheses.

The `main()` method in the `First` class contains only one statement—the statement that uses the `println()` method.

》NOTE In general, whitespace is optional in Java. **Whitespace** is any combination of nonprinting characters; for example, spaces, tabs, and carriage returns (blank lines). However, you cannot use whitespace within any identifier or keyword. You can insert whitespace between words or lines in your program code by typing spaces, tabs, or blank lines because the compiler ignores these extra spaces. You use whitespace to organize your program code and make it easier to read.

For every opening curly brace ({) in a Java program, there must be a corresponding closing curly brace (}). The placement of the opening and closing curly braces is not important to the compiler. For example, the following method is executed in exactly the same way as the one shown in Figure 1-4. The only difference is that the layout of the method is different—the line breaks occur in different locations.

```
public static void main(String[] args) {
    System.out.println("First Java application");
}
```

》NOTE The indent style in which curly braces are aligned and each occupies its own line is called the **Allman style**, named for Eric Allman, a programmer who popularized the style. The indent style in which the opening brace follows the header line is known as the **K & R style**, named for Kernighan and Ritchie, who wrote the first book on the C programming language.

Many Java programmers prefer to write code using the style shown in this example, with the opening curly brace for the method at the end of the method header line. This format saves a vertical line of type in the saved source code file. Others feel that code in which you vertically align each pair of opening and closing curly braces (as shown in Figure 1-4) is easier to read. Either style is acceptable, and both produce workable Java programs. When you write your own code, you should develop a consistent style. When you get a job as a Java programmer, your organization most likely will have a preferred style.

UNDERSTANDING THE `main()` METHOD

The method header for the `main()` method is quite complex. The meaning and purpose of each of the terms used in the method header will become clearer as you complete this textbook; a brief explanation will suffice for now.

In the method header `public static void main(String[] args)`, the word `public` is an access modifier, just as it is when you use it to define the `First` class. In Java, the reserved keyword **static** means that a method is accessible and usable even though no objects of the class exist. Of course, other classes eventually might have their own, different `main()` methods. (Figure 1-7 shows the parts of the `main()` method.)

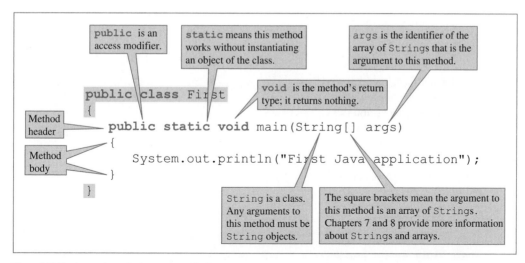

```
                                                                  args is the identifier of the
    public is an          static means this method                array of Strings that is the
    access modifier.      works without instantiating             argument to this method.
                          an object of the class.

                                              void is the method's return
    public class First                        type; it returns nothing.
    {
         public static void main(String[] args)

         {
             System.out.println("First Java application");
         }
    }
                                      String is a class.    The square brackets mean the argument to
                                      Any arguments to       this method is an array of Strings.
                                      this method must be    Chapters 7 and 8 provide more information
                                      String objects.        about Strings and arrays.
```

Method header

Method body

Figure 1-7 The parts of a typical `main()` method

In English, the word "void" means empty. When the keyword **void** is used in the `main()` method header, it does not indicate that the `main()` method is empty, but rather that the `main()` method does not return any value when it is called. This doesn't mean that `main()` doesn't produce output—in fact, the method in Figure 1-4 (and in Figure 1-7) does. It only means that the `main()` method does not send any value back to any other method that might use it. You will learn more about return values in Chapter 3.

Not all classes have a `main()` method; in fact, many do not. All Java *applications*, however, must include a class containing a public method named `main()`, and most Java applications have additional classes and methods. When you execute a Java application, the JVM always executes the `main()` method first.

In the method header `public static void main(String[] args)`, the contents between the parentheses, `(String[] args)`, represent the type of argument that can be passed to the `main()` method, just as the string `"First Java application"` is an argument passed to the `println()` method. `String` is a Java class that can be used to hold character strings. The identifier `args` is used to hold any `String` objects that might be sent to the `main()` method. The `main()` method could do something with those arguments, such as print them, but in Figure 1-4, the `main()` method does not actually use the `args` identifier. Nevertheless, you must place an identifier within the `main()` method's parentheses. The identifier does not need to be named `args`—it could be any legal Java identifier—but the name `args` is traditional.

>> **NOTE**
When you refer to the `String` class in the `main()` method header, the square brackets indicate an array of `String` objects. You will learn more about the `String` class and arrays in Chapters 7 and 8.

>> **NOTE** You won't pass any arguments to the `main()` method in this book, but when you run a program, you could. Even though you pass no arguments, the `main()` method must contain `String[]` and a legal identifier (such as `args`) within its parentheses.

The simple application shown in Figure 1-4 has many pieces to remember. However, for now you can use the Java code shown in Figure 1-8 as a shell, in which you replace `AnyClassName` with a class name you choose and the line `/******/` with any statements that you want to execute.

```
public class AnyClassName
{
    public static void main(String[] args)
    {
        /******/
    }
}
```

Figure 1-8 Shell code

»TWO TRUTHS AND A LIE: ANALYZING A JAVA APPLICATION THAT USES CONSOLE OUTPUT

1. In the method header `public static void main(String[] args)`, the word `public` is an access modifier.
2. In the method header `public static void main(String[] args)`, the word `static` means that a method is accessible and usable, even though no objects of the class exist.
3. In the method header `public static void main(String[] args)`, the word `void` means that the `main()` method is an empty method.

The false statement is #3. In the method header `public static void main(String[] args)`, the word `void` means that the `main()` method does not return any value when it is called.

ADDING COMMENTS TO A JAVA CLASS

As you can see, even the simplest Java class requires several lines of code and contains somewhat perplexing syntax. Large applications that perform many tasks include much more code, and as you write larger applications it becomes increasingly difficult to remember why you included steps or how you intended to use particular variables. Documenting your program code helps you remember why you wrote lines of code the way you did. **Program comments** are nonexecuting statements that you add to a program for the purpose of documentation. Programmers use comments to leave notes for themselves and for others who might read their programs in the future. At the very least, your Java class files should include comments indicating the author, the date, and the class's name or function. The best practice dictates that you also include a brief comment to describe the purpose of each method you create within a class.

»NOTE
As you work through this book, add comments as the first three lines of every file. The comments should contain the class name and purpose, your name, and the date. Your instructor might ask you to include additional comments.

Comments can also be useful when you are developing an application. If a program is not performing as expected, you can comment out various statements and subsequently run the program to observe the effect. When you **comment out** a statement, you turn it into a comment so the compiler does not translate and the JVM does not execute its command. This can help you pinpoint the location of errant statements in malfunctioning programs.

There are three types of comments in Java:

» **Line comments** start with two forward slashes (//) and continue to the end of the current line. A line comment can appear on a line by itself or at the end (and to the right) of a line following executable code. Line comments do not require an ending symbol.

» **Block comments** start with a forward slash and an asterisk (/*) and end with an asterisk and a forward slash (*/). A block comment can appear on a line by itself, on a line before executable code, or on a line after executable code. Block comments can also extend across as many lines as needed.

» **Javadoc** comments are a special case of block comments. They begin with a forward slash and two asterisks (/**) and end with an asterisk and a forward slash (*/). You can use javadoc comments to generate documentation with a program named javadoc. Appendix E teaches you how to create javadoc comments.

Figure 1-9 shows how comments are used in code. In this example, the only statement that executes is the `System.out.println("Hello");` statement; everything else (all the shaded parts) is a comment.

»NOTE
The forward slash (/) and the backslash (\) characters often are confused, but they are two distinct characters. You cannot use them interchangeably.

»NOTE
The Java Development Kit (JDK) includes the javadoc tool, which you can use when writing programs in Java. The tool produces HTML pages that describe classes and their contents.

```
// Demonstrating comments
/* This shows
   that these comments
   don't matter */
System.out.println("Hello"); // This line executes
   // up to where the comment started
/* Everything but the println()
   is a comment */
```

Figure 1-9 A program segment containing several comments

»TWO TRUTHS AND A LIE: ADDING COMMENTS TO A JAVA CLASS

1. Line comments start with two forward slashes (//) and end with two backslashes (//); they can extend across as many lines as needed.

2. Block comments start with a forward slash and an asterisk (/*) and end with an asterisk and a forward slash (*/); they can extend across as many lines as needed.

3. Javadoc comments begin with a forward slash and two asterisks (/**) and end with an asterisk and a forward slash (*/); they are used to generate documentation with a program named javadoc.

The false statement is #1. Line comments start with two forward slashes (//) and continue to the end of the current line; they do not require an ending symbol.

SAVING, COMPILING, RUNNING, AND MODIFYING A JAVA APPLICATION

SAVING A JAVA CLASS

» NOTE
Appendix A contains important information on saving, compiling, and running a Java application.

When you write a Java class, you must save it using some storage medium; for example, a disk, CD, or USB device. In Java, if a class is public (that is, if you use the public access modifier before the class name), you must save the class in a file with exactly the same name and a .java extension. For example, the First class must be stored in a file named First.java. The class name and filename must match exactly, including the use of uppercase and lowercase characters. If the extension is not .java, the Java compiler does not recognize the file as containing a Java class.

COMPILING A JAVA CLASS

After you write and save an application, two steps must occur before you can view the application's output.

1. You must compile the class you wrote (called the source code) into bytecode.
2. You must use the Java interpreter to translate the bytecode into executable statements.

To compile your source code from the command line, your prompt should show the folder or directory where your program file is stored. Then, you type javac followed by the name of the file that contains the source code. For example, to compile a file named First.java, you type the following and then press Enter:

```
javac First.java
```

There will be one of three outcomes:

» You receive a message such as 'javac' is not recognized as an internal or external command, operable program or batch file.
» You receive one or more program language error messages.
» You receive no messages, which means that the application compiled successfully.

> » NOTE When compiling, if the source code file is not in the current path, you can type a full path with the filename. For example:
>
> ```
> javac c:\java\MyClasses\Chapter.01\First.java
> ```
>
> In a DOS environment, you can change directories using the cd command. For example, to change from the current directory to a subdirectory named MyClasses, you type cd MyClasses and press Enter. Within any directory, you can back up to the root directory by typing cd\ and pressing Enter.

If you receive an error message that the command is not recognized, it might mean one of the following:

» You misspelled the command `javac`.

» You misspelled the filename.

» You are not within the correct subfolder or subdirectory on your command line.

» Java was not installed properly. (See Appendix A for information on installation.)

If you receive a programming language error message, there are one or more syntax errors in the source code. Recall that a syntax error is a programming error that occurs when you introduce typing errors into your program or use the programming language incorrectly. For example, if your class name is `first` (with a lowercase "f") in the source code but you saved the file as First.java (with an uppercase "F"), when you compile the application you'll receive an error message, such as `class first is public, should be declared in a file named first.java` because "first" and "First" are not the same in a case-sensitive language. If this error occurs, you must reopen the text file that contains the source code and make the necessary corrections.

If you receive no error messages after compiling the code in a file named First.java, the application compiled successfully, and a file named First.class is created and saved in the same folder as the application text file. After a successful compile, you can run the class file on any computer that has a Java language interpreter.

RUNNING A JAVA APPLICATION

To run the `First` application from the command line, you type the following:

```
java First
```

Figure 1-10 shows the application's output in the command window. In this example, you can see that the `First` class is stored in a folder named Java on the C drive.

Figure 1-10 Output of the `First` application

MODIFYING A JAVA CLASS

After viewing the application output, you might decide to modify the class to get a different result. For example, you might decide to change the `First` application's output from `First Java application` to the following:

```
My new and improved
Java application
```

To produce the new output, first you must modify the text file that contains the existing class. You need to change the literal string that currently prints, and then add an additional text string. Figure 1-11 shows the class that changes the output.

```
public class First
{
   public static void main(String[] args)
   {
      System.out.println("My new and improved");
      System.out.println("Java application");
   }
}
```

Figure 1-11 First class containing modified output from original version

The changes to the First class include the addition of the statement System.out.println ("My new and improved"); and the removal of the word "First" from the string in the other println() statement. However, if you make changes to the file as shown in Figure 1-11, save the file, and execute the program by typing java First at the command line, you will not see the new output—you will see the old output without the added line. Even though you save a text file containing the modified source code for a class, it is the compiled class in the already-compiled class file that executes. After you save the file named First.java, the old compiled version of the class with the same name is still stored on your computer. Before the new source code will execute, you must do the following:

1. Save the file with the changes (using the same filename).

2. Compile the class with the javac command. (Actually, you are *re*compiling the class.)

3. Interpret the class bytecode and execute the class using the java command.

Figure 1-12 shows the new output.

Figure 1-12 Execution of modified First class

> **NOTE** When you complete these steps, the original version of the compiled file with the .class extension is replaced, and the new application executes. The original version no longer exists. When you modify a class, you must decide whether you want to retain the original version. If you do, you must give the new version a new class and filename.

CREATING A JAVA APPLICATION USING GUI OUTPUT

Besides allowing you to use the `System` class to produce command window output, Java provides built-in classes that produce GUI output. For example, Java contains a class named **JOptionPane** that allows you to produce dialog boxes. A **dialog box** is a GUI object resembling a window in which you can place messages you want to display. Figure 1-13 shows a class named `FirstDialog`. The `FirstDialog` class contains many elements that are familiar to you; only the two shaded lines are new.

```
import javax.swing.JOptionPane;
public class FirstDialog
{
    public static void main(String[] args)
    {
        JOptionPane.showMessageDialog(null, "First Java dialog");
    }
}
```

Figure 1-13 The `FirstDialog` class

> **»NOTE** In older versions of Java, any application that used a `JOptionPane` dialog was required to end with a `System.exit(0);` statement or the application would not terminate. You can add this statement to your programs, and they will work correctly, but it is not necessary.

In Figure 1-13, the first shaded line is an `import` statement. You use an **import statement** when you want to access a built-in Java class that is contained in a group of classes called a **package**. To use the `JOptionPane` class, you must import the package named `javax.swing.JOptionPane`.

> **»NOTE** Any `import` statement you use must be placed outside of any class you write in a file. You will learn more about `import` statements in general, and the `javax.swing` packages in particular, as you continue to study Java.

> **»NOTE** You do not need to use an `import` statement when you use the `System` class (as with the `System.out.println()` method) because the `System` class is contained in the package `java.lang`, which is automatically imported in every Java program. You *could* include the statement `import java.lang;` at the top of any file in which you use the `System` class, but you are not required to do so.

> **»NOTE**
> Earlier in this chapter, you learned that `true`, `false`, and `null` are all reserved words that represent values.

The second shaded statement in the `FirstDialog` class in Figure 1-13 uses the `showMessageDialog()` method that is part of the `JOptionPane` class. Like the `println()` method that is used for console output, the `showMessageDialog()` method is followed by a set of parentheses. However, whereas the `println()` method requires only one argument between its parentheses to produce an output string, the `showMessageDialog()` method requires two arguments. When the first argument to `showMessageDialog()` is `null`, as it is in the class in Figure 1-13, it means the output message box should be placed in the center of the screen. The second argument, after the comma, is the string that should be output.

> **»NOTE**
> You will learn more about dialog boxes, including how to position them in different locations and how to add more options to them, in Chapter 2.

When a user executes the `FirstDialog` class, the dialog box in Figure 1-14 is displayed. The user must click the OK button or the Close button to dismiss the dialog box.

> **»NOTE**
> Whenever a method requires multiple arguments, the arguments are always separated with commas.

Figure 1-14 Output of the `FirstDialog` application

»TWO TRUTHS AND A LIE: CREATING A JAVA APPLICATION USING GUI OUTPUT

1. A dialog box is a GUI object resembling a window in which you can place messages you want to display.
2. You use an `append` statement when you want to access a built-in Java class that is contained in a group of classes called a package.
3. Different methods can require different numbers of arguments.

The false statement is #2. You use an `import` statement when you want to access a built-in Java class that is contained in a group of classes called a package.

CORRECTING ERRORS AND FINDING HELP

Frequently, you might make typing errors as you enter Java statements into your text editor. When you issue the command to compile the class containing errors, the Java compiler produces one or more error messages. The exact error message that appears varies depending on the compiler you are using. In the `First` class (shown in Figure 1-4), if you mistype the `System.out.println()` code using a lowercase "s" in System (as `system.out.println("First Java Application");`), an error message similar to the one shown in Figure 1-15 is displayed. The first line of the error message displays the name of the file in which the error was found (First.java), the line number in which it was found (5), and the nature of the error ("package system does not exist"). The next line identifies the location of the error. This is a **compile-time error**, or one in which the compiler detects a violation of language syntax rules and is unable to translate the source code to machine code. In this case, the compiler cannot find a symbol named `system` (with a lowercase initial letter) because Java is a case-sensitive programming language.

Figure 1-15 Error message generated when program contains "system" instead of "System"

When you compile a class, the compiler reports as many errors as it can find so that you can fix as many errors as possible. Sometimes, one error in syntax causes multiple error messages that normally would not be errors if the first syntax error did not exist. Consider the `ErrorTest` class shown in Figure 1-16. The class contains a single error—the comment that starts in the second line is never closed. However, when you attempt to compile this class, you receive two error messages, as shown in Figure 1-17.

```
public class ErrorTest
/*   This class prints a test message
{
   public static void main(String[] args)
   {
      System.out.println("Test");
   }
}
```

Figure 1-16 The `ErrorTest` class with an unclosed comment

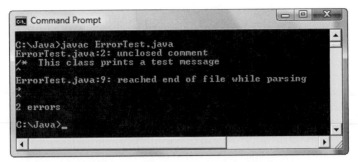

Figure 1-17 Error messages generated by `ErrorTest` application in Figure 1-16

> **»NOTE** In Figure 1-17, notice that the line number where the error was detected appears as part of the error message. For example, "ErrorTest.java:2: unclosed comment" means that the comment that is unclosed begins in line 2 of the file. Also, a caret appears below the location where Java detected the error—in this case, at the opening slash of the comment. When the compiler reports a line number in an error message, you can start to look at the indicated location. Frequently, however, the actual error you made is not precisely where Java first noticed it—only nearby. A compile-time error message indicates the spot where the program could go no further.

> **»NOTE**
> You also will receive the error message "reached end of file while parsing" if you omit a program's closing curly brace.

The first error message in Figure 1-17 correctly identifies the unclosed comment. The second error message is more confusing: "reached end of file while parsing". **Parsing** is the process the compiler uses to divide your source code into meaningful portions; the message means that the compiler was in the process of analyzing the code when the end of the file was encountered prematurely. If you repair the first error by closing off the comment and then save and recompile the class, both error messages disappear. The second message is generated only as a side effect of the unfinished comment. When you compile a class and view a list of errors, correct the errors that make sense to you and then recompile; sometimes, when you correct an error or two, several others disappear. On the other hand, sometimes when you fix a compile-time error and recompile a program, new error messages are generated. That's because when you fix the first error, the compiler can proceed beyond that point and possibly discover new errors.

> **»NOTE**
> A logic error is a type of **run-time error**—an error not detected until the program asks the computer to do something wrong, or even illegal, while executing.

Of course, no programmer intends to type a program containing syntax errors, but when you do, the compiler finds them all for you. A second kind of error occurs when the syntax of the program is correct and the program compiles but produces incorrect results when you execute it. This type of error is a **logic error**, which is usually more difficult to find and resolve. In the `First` class in Figure 1-4, typing the executable statement as `System.out.println("Frst Java Application");` does not produce an error. The compiler does not find the spelling error of "Frst" instead of "First"; the code is compiled and the JVM can execute the statements. Other examples of logic errors include multiplying two values when you meant to add, printing one copy of a report when you meant to print five, or forgetting to produce a requested count of the number of times an event has occurred. Errors of this type must be detected by carefully examining the program output. It is the responsibility of the program author to test programs and find any logic errors. Good programming practice stresses programming structure and development that helps minimize errors.

In addition, each chapter in this book contains four exercises in which you get the opportunity to locate and correct syntax and logic errors. Programmers call the process of correcting all these errors "debugging" a program.

> **» NOTE** The process of fixing computer errors has been known as debugging since a large moth was found wedged into the circuitry of a mainframe computer at Harvard University in 1945. See these Web sites for interesting details and pictures: *www.jamesshuggins.com/h/tek1/first_computer_bug.htm* and *www.history.navy.mil/photos/images/h96000/ h96566kc.htm.*

As you write Java programs, you can frequently consult this book as well as other Java documentation. A great wealth of helpful material exists at the Sun Microsystems Web site, *http://java.sun.com.* Of particular value is the Java application programming interface, more commonly referred to as the **Java API**. The Java API is also called the Java class library; it contains information about how to use every prewritten Java class, including lists of all the methods you can use with the classes.

Also of interest at the *java.sun.com* Web site are frequently asked questions (**FAQ**s) that provide brief answers to many common questions about Java software and products. You can also find several versions of the Java Development Kit (**JDK**) that you can download for free. Versions are available for Windows, Linux, and Solaris operating systems. You can search and browse documentation online or you can download the documentation file for the JDK and install it on your computer. After it is installed, you can search and browse documentation locally.

> **» NOTE** The JDK is an **SDK**—a software development kit that includes tools used by programmers.

A downloadable Java tutorial titled "The Java Tutorial: A practical guide for programmers" with hundreds of complete working examples is available from *http://java.sun.com/docs/ books/tutorial/.* The tutorial is organized into trails—groups of lessons on a particular subject. You can start the tutorial at the beginning and navigate sequentially to the end, or jump from one trail to another. As you study each chapter in this book, you are encouraged to make good use of these support materials.

» TWO TRUTHS AND A LIE: CORRECTING ERRORS AND FINDING HELP

1. When you compile a program, sometimes one error in syntax causes multiple error messages.
2. When you compile a program, sometimes multiple syntax errors cause only one error message.
3. Syntax errors are more difficult to find and resolve than logic errors.

The false statement is #3. Logic errors are usually more difficult to find and resolve than syntax errors. The compiler locates all syntax errors, but logic errors can be eliminated only through careful examination of your program and its output.

YOU DO IT

YOUR FIRST APPLICATION

Now that you understand the basics of an application written in Java, you are ready to enter your first Java application into a text editor. It is a tradition among programmers that the first program you write in any language produces "Hello, world!" as its output. You will create such a program now. You can use any text editor, such as Notepad, TextPad, or any other text-processing program.

NOTE
It is best to use the simplest available text editor when writing Java programs. Multifeatured word-processing programs save documents as much larger files because of all the built-in features, such as font styles and margin settings, which you do not need in your Java programs.

To write your first Java application:

1. Start any text editor (such as Notepad or TextPad), and then open a new document, if necessary.
2. Type the class header as follows:

   ```
   public class Hello
   ```

   In this example, the class name is `Hello`. You can use any valid name you want for the class. If you choose Hello, you always must refer to the class as Hello, and not as hello, because Java is case sensitive.
3. Press **Enter** once, type **{**, press **Enter** again, and then type **}**. You will add the `main()` method between these curly braces. Although it is not required, it is good practice to place each curly brace on its own line and to align opening and closing curly brace pairs with each other. Using this format makes your code easier to read.
4. As shown in the shaded portion of Figure 1-18, add the `main()` method header between the curly braces, and then type a set of curly braces for `main()`.

```
public class Hello
{
   public static void main(String[] args)
   {
   }
}
```

Figure 1-18 The `main()` method shell for the `Hello` class

5. Next add the statement within the `main()` method that will produce the output, "Hello, world!". Use Figure 1-19 as a guide for adding the shaded `println()` statement to the `main()` method.

```
public class Hello
{
   public static void main(String[] args)
   {
      System.out.println("Hello, world!");
   }
}
```

Figure 1-19 Complete `Hello` class

6. Save the application as **Hello.java**. Make certain that the file extension is .java. If it is not, the compiler for Java does not recognize the file as an application it can compile.

7. Go to the command-line prompt for the drive and folder or subdirectory in which you saved Hello.java. At the command line, type:

```
javac Hello.java
```

8. When the compile is successful, execute your application by typing **java Hello** at the command line. The output should appear on the next line, as shown in Figure 1-20.

Figure 1-20 Output of `Hello` application

ADDING COMMENTS TO A CLASS

In this exercise, you add comments to your `Hello.java` application and save it as a new class named `Hello2`.

To add comments to your application and save it as a new class:

1. Position the insertion point at the top of the file that contains the `Hello` class, press **Enter** to insert a new line, press the **Up arrow** key to go to that line, and then type the following comments at the top of the file. Press **Enter** after typing each line. Insert your name and today's date where indicated.

```
// Filename Hello2.java
// Written by <your name>
// Written on <today's date>
```

2. Scroll to the end of the line `public class Hello`, change the class name to **Hello2**, press **Enter**, and then type the following block comment:

```
/*  This class demonstrates the use of the println()
method to print the message Hello, world!  */
```

3. Save the file as **Hello2.java**. The file must be named Hello2.java because the class name is Hello2.

4. Go to the command-line prompt for the drive and folder or subdirectory in which you saved Hello2.java, and type the following command to compile the program:

```
javac Hello2.java
```

>> **NOTE** If you receive an error message when you compile or run the program, look in the section "Saving, Compiling, Running, and Modifying a Java Application" to find its cause and then make the necessary corrections. Save the file again and then repeat Step 4 until your application compiles successfully.

5. When the compile is successful, execute your application by typing **java Hello2** at the command line. The output should appear on the next line, as shown in Figure 1-21.

Figure 1-21 Successful compilation and execution of `Hello2` application

»NOTE After the application compiles successfully, a file named Hello2.class is created and stored in the same folder as the Hello2.java file. If your application compiled without error but you receive an error message, such as "Exception in thread 'main' java.lang.NoClassDefFoundError," when you try to execute the application, you probably do not have your class path set correctly. See Appendix A for details.

»NOTE When you run a Java application using the `java` command, do not add the .class extension to the filename. If you type `java First`, the interpreter looks for a file named First.class. If you type `java First.class`, the interpreter incorrectly looks for a file named First.class.class.

MODIFYING A CLASS

Next, you modify your Hello2 class, but to retain the Hello2 file, you save the modified file as the Hello3 class.

To change the Hello2 class to the Hello3 class and rerun the application:

1. Open the file **Hello2.java** in your text editor. Change both the comment name and the class name to **Hello3**.

2. Add the following statement below the statement that prints "Hello, world!":

```
System.out.println("I'm ready for Java programming!");
```

Be certain to type the semicolon at the end of the statement and use the correct case.

»NOTE
If you receive compile errors, return to the Hello3.java file in the text editor, fix the errors, and then repeat Step 3 until the class compiles successfully.

3. Save the file as **Hello3.java**. Then, at the command line, compile the file by typing the following command:

```
javac Hello3.java
```

4. Interpret and execute the class by typing the command **java Hello3**. Your output should look like Figure 1-22.

Figure 1-22 Output of Hello3 application

CREATING A DIALOG BOX

Next, you write a Java application that produces output in a dialog box.

To create an application that produces a dialog box as output:

1. Open a new file in your text editor. Type comments similar to the following, inserting your own name and today's date where indicated.

```
// Filename HelloDialog.java
// Written by <your name>
// Written on <today's date>
```

2. Enter the import statement that allows you to use the JOptionPane class:

```
import javax.swing.JOptionPane;
```

3. Enter the HelloDialog class:

```
public class HelloDialog
{
    public static void main(String[] args)
    {
        JOptionPane.showMessageDialog(null, "Hello,
            world!");
    }
}
```

4. Save the file as **HelloDialog.java**. Compile the class using the command **javac HelloDialog.java**. If necessary, eliminate any syntax errors, resave the file, and recompile. Then execute the program using the command **java HelloDialog**. The output appears as shown in Figure 1-23.

Figure 1-23 Output of HelloDialog application

5. Click **OK** to dismiss the dialog box.

DON'T DO IT

At the end of each chapter, a Don't Do It list will alert you to common mistakes made by beginning programmers.

» Don't forget that in Java, a public file's name must match the name of the class it contains. For example, if a file is named Program1.java, you can't simply rename it Program1BackUp.java and expect it to compile unless you change the class name within the file.

» Don't confuse the names *parentheses*, *braces*, *brackets*, *curly braces*, *square brackets*, and *angle brackets*. When you are writing a program or performing some other computerized task and someone tells you, "Now, type some braces," you might want to clarify which term is meant. Table 1-5 summarizes these punctuation marks.

Punctuation	Name	Typical use in Java	Alternate names
( )	Parentheses	Follows method names as in `println()`.	Parentheses can be called *round brackets*, but such usage is unusual.
{ }	Curly braces	A pair surrounds a class body, a method body, and a block of code. When you learn about arrays in Chapter 8, you will find that curly braces also surround lists of array values.	Curly braces might also be called *curly brackets*.
[ ]	Square brackets	A pair signifies an array. Arrays are covered in Chapter 8.	Square brackets might be called *box brackets* or *square braces*.
< >	Angle brackets	A pair of angle brackets surrounds HTML tags, as you will learn in Chapter 16. In Java, a pair is also used with generic arguments in parameterized classes.	When angle brackets appear with nothing between them, they are called a *chevron*.

Table 1-5 Braces and brackets used in Java

» Don't forget to end a block comment. Every /* must have a corresponding */, even if it is several lines later. It's harder to make a mistake with line comments (those that start with //), but remember that nothing on the line after the // will execute.

» Don't forget that Java is case sensitive.

» Don't forget to end every statement with a semicolon, but *not* to end class or method headers with a semicolon.

» Don't forget to recompile a program to which you have made changes. It can be very frustrating to fix an error, run a program, and not understand why you don't see evidence of your changes. The reason might be that the .class file does not contain your changes because you forgot to recompile.

» Don't panic when you see a lot of compiler error messages. Often, fixing one will fix several.

» Don't think your program is perfect when all compiler errors are eliminated. Only by running the program multiple times and carefully examining the output can you be assured that your program is logically correct.

KEY TERMS

A computer **program** is a set of instructions that you write to tell a computer what to do.

A program written in circuitry-level language, as a series of on and off switches, is written in **machine language**.

A **low-level programming language** is written to correspond closely to a computer processor's circuitry.

A **high-level programming language** allows you to use a vocabulary of reasonable terms, such as "read," "write," or "add," instead of the sequences of on and off switches that perform these tasks.

Syntax is the rules of the language.

Program statements are similar to English sentences; they carry out the tasks that programs perform.

A **compiler**, or **interpreter**, is a program that translates language statements into machine code.

Executing a statement means to carry it out.

A **syntax error** is a programming error that occurs when you introduce typing errors into your program or use the programming language incorrectly. A program containing syntax errors will not compile.

The process of **debugging** a program frees it of all errors.

The **logic** behind any program involves executing the various statements and procedures in the correct order to produce the desired results.

Semantic errors occur when you use a correct word in the wrong context in program code.

Procedural programming is a style of programming in which sets of operations are executed one after another in sequence.

Variables are named computer memory locations that hold values that might vary.

Procedures are sets of operations performed by a computer program.

A procedural program **calls** a series of procedures to input, manipulate, and output values.

Writing **object-oriented programs** involves creating classes, creating objects from those classes, and creating applications that use those objects. Thinking in an object-oriented manner involves envisioning program components as objects that are similar to concrete objects in the real world; then, you can manipulate the objects to achieve a desired result.

An **application** is a stand-alone, executable program.

Objects are instances of a class; they are made up of attributes and methods.

Attributes are the characteristics that define an object as part of a class.

The values of the attributes of an object are also referred to as its **state**.

In object-oriented terminology, a **class** is a term that describes a group or collection of objects with common properties.

A **class definition** describes what attributes its objects will have and what those objects will be able to do.

An **instance** of a class is an existing object of a class.

A **method** is a self-contained block of program code, similar to a procedure.

Encapsulation refers to the hiding of data and methods within an object.

Inheritance is the ability to create classes that share the attributes and methods of existing classes, but with more specific features.

Polymorphism describes the feature of languages that allows the same word to be interpreted correctly in different situations based on the context.

Java was developed by Sun Microsystems as an object-oriented language used both for general-purpose business applications and for interactive, Web-based Internet applications.

Java is **architecturally neutral**, which means that you can use it to write a program that runs on any platform (operating system).

The **Java Virtual Machine (JVM)** is a hypothetical (software-based) computer on which Java runs.

Interactive applications are those in which a user communicates with a program by using an input device.

Source code consists of programming statements written in a high-level programming language.

Bytecode consists of programming statements that have been compiled into binary format.

A program called the **Java interpreter** checks the bytecode and communicates with the operating system, executing the bytecode instructions line by line within the Java Virtual Machine.

"Write once, run anywhere" (WORA) is a slogan developed by Sun Microsystems to describe the ability of one Java program version to work correctly on multiple platforms.

Java programs that are embedded in a Web page are called Java **applets**.

Stand-alone Java programs are called Java **applications**.

Console applications support character output to a computer screen in a DOS window.

Windowed applications create a graphical user interface (GUI) with elements such as menus, toolbars, and dialog boxes.

A **literal string** is a series of characters that appear exactly as entered. Any literal string in Java appears between double quotation marks.

Arguments are information passed to a method so it can perform its task.

Sending arguments to a method is called **passing** them.

The **standard output device** is normally the monitor.

An **identifier** is a name of a program component such as a class, object, or variable.

Unicode is an international system of character representation.

Using an uppercase letter to begin an identifier and starting each new word in an identifier is known as **Pascal casing**.

An **access modifier** defines the circumstances under which a class can be accessed and the other classes that have the right to use a class.

Whitespace is any combination of nonprinting characters; for example, spaces, tabs, and carriage returns (blank lines).

The **Allman style** is the indent style in which curly braces are aligned and each occupies its own line; it is named for Eric Allman, a programmer who popularized the style.

The **K & R style** is the indent style in which the opening brace follows the header line; it is named for Kernighan and Ritchie, who wrote the first book on the C programming language.

The reserved keyword `static` means that a method is accessible and usable even though no objects of the class exist. Of course, other classes eventually might have their own, different `main()` methods.

The keyword `void`, when used in a method header, indicates that the method does not return any value when it is called.

Program comments are nonexecuting statements that you add to a Java file for the purpose of documentation.

When you **comment out** a statement, you turn it into a comment so the compiler will not execute its command.

Line comments start with two forward slashes (//) and continue to the end of the current line. Line comments can appear on a line by themselves or at the end of a line following executable code.

Block comments start with a forward slash and an asterisk (/*) and end with an asterisk and a forward slash (*/). Block comments can appear on a line by themselves, on a line before executable code, or on a line after executable code. Block comments can also extend across as many lines as needed.

A special case of block comments are **javadoc** comments. They begin with a forward slash and two asterisks (/**) and end with an asterisk and a forward slash (*/). You can use javadoc comments to generate documentation with a program named javadoc.

A **clean build** is created when you delete all previously compiled versions of a class before compiling again.

The Java class named `JOptionPane` allows you to produce dialog boxes.

A **dialog box** is a GUI object resembling a window in which you can place messages you want to display.

You use an **import statement** when you want to access a built-in Java class that is contained in a package.

A **package** contains a group of built-in Java classes.

A **compile-time error** is one in which the compiler detects a violation of language syntax rules and is unable to translate the source code to machine code.

Parsing is the process the compiler uses to divide source code into meaningful portions for analysis.

A **logic error** occurs when a program compiles successfully but produces an error during execution.

A **run-time error** occurs when a program compiles successfully but does not execute.

The **Java API** is the application programming interface, a collection of information about how to use every prewritten Java class.

FAQs are frequently asked questions.

The **JDK** is the Java Development Kit.

An **SDK** is a software development kit, or a set of tools useful to programmers.

CHAPTER SUMMARY

» A computer program is a set of instructions that tells a computer what to do. You can write a program using a high-level programming language, which has its own syntax, or rules of the language. After you write a program, you use a compiler, or interpreter, to translate the language statements into machine code.

» Writing object-oriented programs involves creating classes, creating objects from those classes, and creating applications—stand-alone executable programs that use those objects, which are similar to concrete objects in the real world. Object-oriented programming languages support encapsulation, inheritance, and polymorphism.

» A program written in Java is run on a standardized hypothetical computer called the Java Virtual Machine (JVM). When your class is compiled into bytecode, an interpreter within the JVM subsequently interprets the bytecode and communicates with your operating system to produce the program results.

» Everything that you use within a Java program must be part of a class; the contents of all classes are contained within opening and closing curly braces. Methods within classes hold statements. All Java programming statements end with a semicolon. Periods (called dots) are used to separate classes, objects, and methods in program code. All Java applications must have a method named main(). Most Java applications have additional methods.

» Program comments are nonexecuting statements that you add to a file for the purpose of documentation. Java provides you with three types of comments: line comments, block comments, and javadoc comments.

» To compile your source code from the command line, type `javac` followed by the name of the file that contains the source code. When you compile your source code, the compiler creates a file with a .class extension. You can run the .class file on any computer that has a Java language interpreter by entering the `java` command followed by the name of the class file. When you modify a class, you must recompile it for the changes to take effect.

» Java provides you with built-in classes that produce GUI output. For example, Java contains a class named `JOptionPane` that allows you to produce dialog boxes.

» To avoid and minimize syntax and logic errors, you must enter code carefully and closely examine your program's output.

REVIEW QUESTIONS

1. The most basic circuitry-level computer language, which consists of on and off switches, is _____ .

   a. a high-level language   c. Java

   b. machine language   d. C++

2. Languages that let you use a vocabulary of descriptive terms, such as "read," "write," or "add," are known as _____ languages.

   a. high-level   c. procedural

   b. machine   d. object-oriented

3. The rules of a programming language constitute its _____ .

   a. objects   c. format

   b. logic   d. syntax

4. A _____ translates high-level language statements into machine code.

   a. programmer   c. compiler

   b. syntax detector   d. decipherer

5. Named computer memory locations are called _____ .

   a. compilers   c. addresses

   b. variables   d. appellations

6. The individual operations used in a computer program are often grouped into logical units called _____ .

   a. procedures   c. constants

   b. variables   d. logistics

7. Envisioning program components as objects that are similar to concrete objects in the real world is the hallmark of _____ .

   a. command-line operating systems   c. object-oriented programming

   b. procedural programming   d. machine languages

8. The values of an object's attributes also are known as its _____ .

   a. states   c. methods

   b. orientations   d. procedures

9. An instance of a class is a(n) _____ .

   a. object   c. method

   b. procedure   d. class

10. Java is architecturally _____ .

   a. specific   c. neutral

   b. oriented   d. abstract

11. You must compile classes written in Java into _____ .

   a. bytecode   c. javadoc statements

   b. source code   d. object code

12. All Java programming statements must end with a _____ .

   a. period   c. semicolon

   b. comma   d. closing parenthesis

13. Arguments to methods always appear within _____ .

   a. parentheses   c. single quotation marks

   b. double quotation marks   d. curly braces

14. In a Java program, you must use _____ to separate classes, objects, and methods.

   a. commas   c. dots

   b. semicolons   d. forward slashes

15. All Java applications must have a method named _____ .

   a. `method()`   c. `java()`

   b. `main()`   d. `Hello()`

16. Nonexecuting program statements that provide documentation are called _____ .
    a. classes   c. comments
    b. notes   d. commands

17. Java supports three types of comments: _____ , _____ , and javadoc.
    a. line, block   c. constant, variable
    b. string, literal   d. single, multiple

18. After you write and save a Java application file, you _____ it.
    a. interpret and then compile   c. compile and then resave
    b. interpret and then execute   d. compile and then interpret

19. The command to execute a compiled Java application is _____ .
    a. run   c. javac
    b. execute   d. java

20. You save text files containing Java source code using the file extension _____ .
    a. .java   c. .txt
    b. .class   d. .src

EXERCISES

1. For each of the following Java identifiers, note whether it is legal or illegal:
   a. weeklySales   g. abcdefghijklmnop
   b. last character   h. 23jordan
   c. class   i. my_code
   d. MathClass   j. 90210
   e. myfirstinitial   k. year2010budget
   f. phone#   l. abffraternity

2. Name at least three attributes that might be appropriate for each of the following classes:
   a. TelevisionSet
   b. EmployeePaycheck
   c. PatientMedicalRecord

3. Name at least three objects that are members of each of the following classes:
   a. Politician
   b. SportingEvent
   c. Book

4. Name at least three classes to which each of these objects might belong:

   a. `mickeyMouse`

   b. `myDogSpike`

   c. `bostonMassachusetts`

5. Write, compile, and test a class that prints your first name on the screen. Save the class as **Name.java**.

6. Write, compile, and test a class that prints your full name, street address, city, state, and zip code on three separate lines on the screen. Save the class as **Address.java**.

7. Write, compile, and test a class that displays the following pattern on the screen:

```
    X
   XXX
  XXXXX
 XXXXXXX
    X
```

   Save the class as **Tree.java**.

8. Write, compile, and test a class that prints your initials on the screen. Compose each initial with five lines of initials, as in the following example:

```
        J       FFFFFF
        J       F
        J       FFFF
   J    J       F
   JJJJJJ       F
```

   Save the class as **Initial.java**.

9. Write, compile, and test a class that prints all the objectives listed at the beginning of this chapter. Save the class as **Objectives.java**.

10. Write, compile, and test a class that displays the following pattern on the screen:

```
    *
   * *
  * * *
   * *
    *
```

   Save the class as **Diamond.java**.

11. Write, compile, and test a class that uses the command window to display the following statement about comments:

    "Program comments are nonexecuting statements you add to a file for the purpose of documentation."

    Also include the same statement in three different comments in the class; each comment should use one of the three different methods of including comments in a Java class. Save the class as **Comments.java**.

12. Modify the Comments.java program in Exercise 11 so that the statement about comments is displayed in a dialog box. Save the class as **CommentsDialog.java**.

13. From 1925 through 1963, Burma Shave advertising signs appeared next to highways all across the United States. There were always four or five signs in a row containing pieces of a rhyme, followed by a final sign that read "Burma Shave." For example, one set of signs that has been preserved by the Smithsonian Institution reads as follows:

    ```
    Shaving brushes
    You'll soon see 'em
    On a shelf
    In some museum
    Burma Shave
    ```

    Find a classic Burma Shave rhyme on the Web. Write, compile, and test a class that produces a series of four dialog boxes so that each displays one line of a Burma Shave slogan in turn. Save the class as **BurmaShave.java**.

14. Write a Java application to display an attractive layout of the information in a typical business card. Data items in a typical business card include a name, address, city, state, zip code, home phone number, and work phone number. Save the class as **CardLayout.java**.

DEBUGGING EXERCISES

Each of the following files in the Chapter.01 folder on your Student Disk has syntax and/ or logic errors. In each case, determine the problem and fix the errors. After you correct the errors, save each file using the same filename preceded with Fix. For example, DebugOne1.java will become FixDebugOne1.java.

a. DebugOne1.java   c. DebugOne3.java

b. DebugOne2.java   d. DebugOne4.java

GAME ZONE

In 1952, A.S. Douglas wrote his University of Cambridge Ph.D. dissertation on human-computer interaction, and created the first graphical computer game—a version of Tic-Tac-Toe. The game was programmed on an EDSAC vacuum-tube mainframe computer. The first computer game is generally assumed to be "Spacewar!", developed in 1962 at

>> **NOTE**
When you change a filename, remember to change every instance of the class name within the file so that it matches the new filename. In Java, the filename and class name must always match.

MIT; the first commercially available video game was "Pong," introduced by Atari in 1973. In 1980, Atari's "Asteroids" and "Lunar Lander" became the first video games to be registered in the U. S. Copyright Office. Throughout the 1980s, players spent hours with games that now seem very simple and unglamorous; do you recall playing "Adventure," "Oregon Trail," "Where in the World is Carmen Sandiego?," or "Myst"?

Today, commercial computer games are much more complex; they require many programmers, graphic artists, and testers to develop them, and large management and marketing staffs are needed to promote them. A game might cost many millions of dollars to develop and market, but a successful game might earn hundreds of millions of dollars. Obviously, with the brief introduction to programming you have had in this chapter, you cannot create a very sophisticated game. However, you can get started.

For games to hold your interest, they almost always include some random, unpredictable behavior. For example, a game in which you shoot asteroids loses some of its fun if the asteroids follow the same, predictable path each time you play the game. Therefore, generating random values is a key component in creating the most interesting computer games.

Appendix D contains information on generating random numbers. To fully understand the process, you must learn more about Java classes and methods. However, for now, you can copy the following statement to generate and use a dialog box that displays a random number between 1 and 10:

```
JOptionPane.showMessageDialog(null,"The number is "  +
   (1 + (int)(Math.random() * 10)));
```

Write a Java application that displays two dialog boxes in sequence. The first asks you to think of a number between 1 and 10. The second displays a randomly generated number; the user can see whether his or her guess was accurate. (In future chapters you will improve this game so that the user can enter a guess and the program can determine whether the user was correct. If you wish, you also can tell the user how far off the guess was, whether the guess was high or low, and provide a specific number of repeat attempts.) Save the file as **RandomGuess.java**.

TOUGH QUESTIONS

Achieving success at a job interview involves being able to think on your feet, but you can still be prepared. The Tough Questions section at the end of each chapter will present questions that an interviewer might ask at a technical job interview. A particular question might have several good answers. If you can't think of an answer right away, try doing some research on the Web or in other Java books.

1. Describe Java and how it differs from other programming languages.

2. What is the difference between a compiler and an interpreter? Which does Java use? Why?

3. What are the conventions for naming classes and variables in Java? What are the advantages to using these conventions?

4. Can you store two public Java classes in the same file? How do you know?

UP FOR DISCUSSION

Up for Discussion questions are designed to probe your attitudes and opinions about topics that are relevant to computer programmers and other business professionals.

1. Have you written programs in any programming language before starting this book? If so, what do you think the advantages and disadvantages of using Java will be? If not, how difficult do you think writing programs will be compared to other new skills you have mastered?

2. Using the Web, try to discover which computer game is the most popular one ever sold. Have you played this game? Would you like to? What makes this game so appealing?

3. Obviously, learning Java is useful to a Computer Information Systems major. List several other major courses of study and discuss how programming skills might be useful to them.

4. Most programming texts encourage students to use many comments in their programs. Many students feel that writing program comments is a waste of time. What is your opinion? Why? Are there circumstances under which you would take the opposite stance?

2

USING DATA WITHIN A PROGRAM

In this chapter, you will:

Use constants and variables
Learn about the `int` data type
Display data
Write arithmetic statements
Use the Boolean data type
Learn about floating-point data types
Understand numeric-type conversion
Work with the `char` data type
Use the `Scanner` class to accept keyboard input
Use the `JOptionPane` class for GUI input

JAVA ON THE JOB, SCENE 2

How are you doing with your first programs?" asks Lynn Greenbrier during a coffee break. "OK, I think," you reply, with just a bit of doubt in your voice. "I sure wish I could do some calculations, though," you continue. "Writing code that only prints the output I coded using `println()` statements isn't exactly what I had in mind when I considered a job in programming."

"Well then," Lynn replies, "let's start learning how Java uses different data types to perform arithmetic and other kinds of calculations."

USING CONSTANTS AND VARIABLES

You can categorize data items as constant or variable. A data item is **constant** when its value cannot be changed while a program is running; a data item is variable when its value might change. For example, when you include the following statement in a Java class, the number 459 is a constant:

```
System.out.println(459);
```

» NOTE

Besides using literal constants, you can use named constants. You will learn about these later in this chapter.

Every time an application containing the constant 459 is executed, the value 459 prints. Programmers refer to the number 459 as a **literal constant** because its value is taken literally at each use.

On the other hand, you can set up a data item as a variable. A **variable** is a named memory location that you can use to store a value. A variable can hold only one value at a time, but the value it holds can change. For example, if you create a variable named `ovenTemperature`, it might hold 0 when the application starts, later be altered to hold 350, and still later be altered to hold 400.

» NOTE

You might also hear programmers refer to a value such as 459 as a **numeric constant**. That means simply that 459 is a number, as opposed to an alphabetic character or string of characters. The value 459 is an unnamed numeric constant because it does not have an identifier.

Whether a data item is variable or constant, in Java it always has a data type. An item's **data type** describes the type of data that can be stored there, how much memory the item occupies, and what types of operations can be performed on the data. Java provides for eight primitive types of data. A **primitive type** is a simple data type. The eight types are described in Table 2-1.

Keyword	Description
byte	Byte-length integer
short	Short integer
int	Integer
long	Long integer
float	Single-precision floating point
double	Double-precision floating point
char	A single character
boolean	A Boolean value (true or false)

Table 2-1 Java primitive data types

The eight primitive data types are called "primitive" because they are simple and uncompli-cated. Primitive types also serve as the building blocks for more complex data types, called **reference types**. The classes you will begin creating in Chapter 3 are examples of reference types.

DECLARING VARIABLES

You name variables using the same naming rules for legal class identifiers. Basically, variable names must start with a letter and cannot be any reserved keyword. You must declare all variables you want to use in a class, and you must declare them before you can use them. A **variable declaration** is a statement that reserves a named memory location and includes the following:

» A data type that identifies the type of data that the variable will store

» An identifier that is the variable's name

» An optional assignment operator and assigned value, if you want a variable to contain an initial value

» An ending semicolon

Variable names conventionally begin with lowercase letters to distinguish them from class names. However, like class names, variable names can begin with either an uppercase or a lowercase letter.

> **»NOTE** Beginning an identifier with a lowercase letter and capitalizing subsequent words within the identifier is a style known as **camel casing**. An identifier such as `lastName` resembles a camel because of the uppercase "hump" in the middle.

For example, the following declaration creates a variable of type `int` named `myAge` and assigns it an initial value of 25:

```
int myAge = 25;
```

This declaration is a complete statement that ends in a semicolon. The equal sign (=) is the **assignment operator**. Any value to the right of the equal sign is assigned to the variable on the left of the equal sign. An assignment made when you declare a variable is an **initialization**; an assignment made later is simply an **assignment**. Thus, `int myAge = 25;` initializes `myAge` to 25, and a subsequent statement `myAge = 42;` might assign a new value to the variable.

Note that the expression `25 = myAge` is illegal; you cannot assign an identifying name to a literal. The assignment operator has right-to-left associativity. **Associativity** refers to the order in which values are used with operators.

> **»NOTE** An identifier that can appear on the left side of an assignment statement is sometimes referred to as an **lvalue**. A numeric constant like 25 is not an lvalue; it is only an **rvalue**, or an item that can appear only on the right side of an assignment statement. A variable can be used as an lvalue or an rvalue, but a numeric constant can only be an rvalue.

> **»NOTE**
> The value of a reference type is actually a memory address. When you declare a `Scanner` object later in this chapter, you will use the value of a reference.

> **»NOTE**
> The Java program-ming language is a **strongly typed language**, or one in which all variables must be declared before they can be used.

> **»NOTE**
> The assignment operator means "is assigned the value of the following expression." In other words, the state-ment `myAge = 25` can be read as "myAge is assigned the value of the following expres-sion: 25."

> **»NOTE**
> The associativity of every operator is either right-to-left or left-to-right.

The following variable declaration also declares a variable of type int named myAge, but no value is assigned at the time of creation:

```
int myAge;
```

You can declare multiple variables of the same type in separate statements on different lines. For example, the following statements declare two variables—the first variable is named myAge and its value is 25. The second variable is named yourAge and its value is 19.

```
int myAge = 25;
int yourAge = 19;
```

You also can declare two (or more) variables of the same type in a single statement by separating the variable declarations with a comma and placing the declarations in the same line, as shown in the following statement:

```
int myAge = 25, yourAge = 19;
```

Another option is to declare two (or more) variables of the same type in a single statement, separating the variable declarations with a comma, but placing them on different lines, as shown in the following three-line statement:

```
int myAge = 25,
    yourAge = 19,
    grandpasAge = 87;
```

Even though this example covers three lines in your editor, it is a single Java statement, ending with a semicolon.

You can declare as many variables in a statement as you want, as long as the variables are the same data type. However, if you want to declare variables of different types, you must use a separate statement for each type. The following statements declare two variables of type int (myAge and yourAge) and two variables of type double (mySalary and yourSalary):

```
int myAge, yourAge;
double mySalary, yourSalary;
```

DECLARING NAMED CONSTANTS

A variable is a named memory location for which the contents can change. If a named location's value should not change during the execution of a program, you can create it to be a **named constant**. A named constant is similar to a variable in that it has a data type, a name, and a value. A named constant differs from a variable in several ways:

» In its declaration statement, the data type of a named constant is preceded by the keyword **final**.

» A named constant can be assigned a value only once, and then it can never be changed. Usually you initialize a named constant when you declare it; if you do not initialize it at declaration, it is known as a **blank final**.

» Although it is not a requirement, named constants conventionally are given identifiers using all uppercase letters, using underscores as needed to separate words.

For example, each of the following defines a named constant:

```
final int NUMBER_OF_DEPTS = 20;
final double PI = 3.14159;
final double TAX_RATE = 0.015;
final string COMPANY = "ABC Manufacturing";
```

You can use each of these named constants anywhere you can use a variable of the same type, except on the left side of an assignment statement. In other words, after they receive their initial values, named constants are rvalues.

A constant always has the same value within a program, so you might wonder why you cannot use the actual, literal value. For example, why not code 20 when you need the number of departments in a company rather than going to the trouble of creating the NUMBER_OF_DEPTS named constant? There are several good reasons to use the named constant rather than the literal one:

» The number 20 is more easily recognized as the number of departments if it is associated with an identifier. Using named constants makes your programs easier to read and understand.

» If the number of departments in your organization changes, you would change the value of NUMBER_OF_DEPTS at one location within your program—where the constant is defined—rather than searching for every use of 20 to change it to a different number. Being able to make the change at one location saves you time, and prevents you from missing a reference to the number of departments.

» Even if you are willing to search for every instance of 20 in a program to change it to the new department number value, you might inadvertently change the value of one instance of 20 that is being used for something else, such as a payroll deduction value.

» Using named constants reduces typographical errors. For example, if you must include 20 at several places within a program, you might inadvertently type 10 for one of the instances.

» When you use a named constant in an expression, it stands out as separate from a variable. For example, in the following statement, it is easy to see which elements are variable and which are constant because the constants have been named conventionally:

```
double payAmount = hoursWorked * STD_PAY_RATE -
    numDependents * DEDUCTION;
```

» NOTE Some programmers refer to the use of a literal numeric constant, such as 20, as using a **magic number**—a value that does not have immediate, intuitive meaning or a number that cannot be explained without additional knowledge. These programmers prefer that you use a named variable or constant in place of every numeric value. For example, you might write a program that uses the value 7 several times, or you might use constants such as DAYS_IN_WEEK and NUM_RETAIL_OUTLETS that both hold the value 7 but more clearly describe its purpose. Avoiding magic numbers helps provide internal documentation for your programs.

» NOTE Although many programmers use named constants to stand for most of the constant values in their programs, many make an exception when using 0 or 1.

PITFALL: FORGETTING THAT A VARIABLE HOLDS ONE VALUE AT A TIME

Each constant can hold only one value for the duration of its program; each variable can hold just one value at a time. Suppose you have two variables, x and y, and x holds 2 and y holds 10. Suppose further that you want to switch their values so that x holds 10 and y holds 2. You cannot simply make an assignment such as x = y because then both variables will hold 10, and the 2 will be lost. Similarly, if you make the assignment y = x, then both variables will hold 2, and the 10 will be lost. The solution is to declare and use a third variable, as in the following sequence of events:

```
z = x;
x = y;
y = z;
```

In this example, the third variable, z, is used as a temporary holding spot for one of the original values. The variable z is assigned the value of x, so z becomes 2. Then the value of y, 10, is assigned to x. Finally, the 2 held in z is assigned to y. The extra variable is used because as soon as you assign a value to a variable, any value that was previously in the memory location is gone.

»TWO TRUTHS AND A LIE: USING CONSTANTS AND VARIABLES

1. A variable is a named memory location that you can use to store a value; it can hold only one value at a time, but the value it holds can change.
2. An item's data type determines what legal identifiers can be used to describe variables and whether the variables can occupy memory.
3. A variable declaration is a statement that reserves a named memory location and includes a data type, an identifier, an optional assignment operator and assigned value, and an ending semicolon.

The false statement is #2. An item's data type describes the type of data that can be stored, how much memory the item occupies, and what types of operations can be performed on the data. The data type does not alter the rules for a legal identifier, and the data type does not determine whether variables can occupy memory—all variables occupy memory.

LEARNING ABOUT THE int DATA TYPE

In Java, you use variables of type **int** to store (or hold) integers; an **integer** is a whole number without decimal places. A variable of type int can hold any whole number value from –2,147,483,648 to +2,147,483,647. When you assign a value to an int variable, you do not type any commas; you type only digits and an optional plus or minus sign to indicate a positive or negative integer.

The types **byte**, **short**, and **long** are all variations of the integer type. You use a byte or a short if you know a variable will need to hold only small values, so you can save space in memory. You use a long if you know you will be working with very large values. Table 2-2 shows the upper and lower value limits for each of these types. It is important to choose appropriate types for the variables you will use in an application. If you attempt to assign a value that is too large for the data type of the variable, the compiler issues an error message and the application does not execute. If you choose a data type that is larger than you need, you waste memory. For example, a personnel application might use a `byte` variable for number of dependents (because a limit of 127 is more than enough), a `short` for hours worked in a month (because 127 isn't enough), and an `int` for an annual salary (because even though a limit of 32,000 might be large enough for your salary, it isn't enough for the CEO's). If your application uses a literal constant integer, such as 932, the integer is an `int` by default. If you need to use a constant higher than 2,147,483,647, you must follow the number with the letter L to indicate `long`. For example, `long mosquitosInTheNorthWoods = 2444555888L;` stores a number that is greater than the maximum limit for the `int` type. You can type either an uppercase or lowercase L to indicate the `long` type, but the uppercase L is preferred to avoid confusion with the number 1. You need no special notation to store a numeric constant in a `byte` or a `short`.

> **»NOTE** Because integer constants, such as 18, are type `int` by default, the examples in this book almost always declare a variable as type `int` when the variable's purpose is to hold a whole number. That is, even if the expected value is less than 127, such as `hoursWorkedToday`, this book will declare the variable to be an `int`. If you are writing an application in which saving memory is important, you might choose to declare the same variable as a `byte`.

> **»NOTE** In other programming languages, the format and size of primitive data types might depend on the platform on which a program is running. In contrast, Java consistently specifies the size and format of its primitive data types.

Type	Minimum Value	Maximum Value	Size in Bytes
byte	−128	127	1
short	−32,768	32,767	2
int	−2,147,483,648	2,147,483,647	4
long	−9,223,372,036,854,775,808	9,223,372,036,854,775,807	8

Table 2-2 Limits on integer values by type

»TWO TRUTHS AND A LIE: LEARNING ABOUT THE int DATA TYPE

1. A variable of type `int` can hold any whole number value from approximately negative two billion to positive two billion.

2. When you assign a value to an `int` variable, you do not type any commas; you type only digits and an optional plus or minus sign to indicate a positive or negative integer.

3. You can use the data types `byte` or `short` to hold larger values than can be accommodated by an `int`.

The false statement is #3. You use a `long` if you know you will be working with very large values; you use a `byte` or a `short` if you know a variable will need to hold only small values.

DISPLAYING DATA

»NOTE
When a method like `println()` can accept different argument types, the method is *overloaded*. When a method is overloaded, it means there are multiple versions with the same name that can be used with a variety of options. You will learn about overloaded methods in Chapter 4.

You can display a variable or a constant in a `print()` or `println()` statement alone or in combination with a string. For example, the `NumbersPrintln` class shown in Figure 2-1 declares an integer `billingDate`, which is initialized to 5. In the first shaded statement, the value of `billingDate` is sent alone to the `print()` method; in the second shaded statement, `billingDate` is combined with, or **concatenated** to, a `String`. In Java, when a numeric variable is concatenated to a `String` using the plus sign, the entire expression becomes a `String`. The `println()` method can accept either a number or a `String`, so both statements work. The output of the application shown in Figure 2-1 appears in Figure 2-2.

```
public class NumbersPrintln
{
    public static void main(String[] args)
    {
        int billingDate = 5;
        System.out.print("Bills are sent on the ");
        System.out.print(billingDate);
        System.out.println("th");
        System.out.println("Next bill: October " +
            billingDate);
    }
}
```

Figure 2-1 NumbersPrintln class

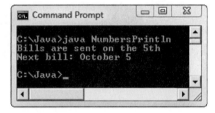

Figure 2-2 Output of `NumbersPrintln` application

> **»NOTE** Later in this chapter, you will learn that a plus sign (+) between two numeric values indicates an addition operation. However, when you place a string on one or both sides of a plus sign, concatenation occurs. In Chapter 1, you learned that *polymorphism* describes the feature of languages that allows the same word or symbol to be interpreted correctly in different situations based on the context. The plus sign is polymorphic in that it indicates concatenation when used with strings but addition when used with numbers.

The program in Figure 2-1 uses the command line, but you also can use a dialog box to display values. The `JOptionPane.showMessageDialog()` method, however, will not accept a single numeric value as its display argument; it requires a `String`. Figure 2-3 shows a `NumbersDialog` class that uses the `showMessageDialog()` method twice to display an integer declared as `creditDays` and initialized to 30. In each shaded statement in the class, the numeric variable is concatenated to a `String`. In the first shaded statement, the `String` is empty; the empty `String` is created by typing a set of quotes with nothing between them. Even this empty `String`, or **null String**, is enough to make the entire expression a `String`, so the application produces the two dialog boxes shown in Figures 2-4 and 2-5. The first dialog box shows just the value 30; after it is dismissed by clicking OK, the second dialog box appears.

```
import javax.swing.JOptionPane;
public class NumbersDialog
{
    public static void main(String[] args)
    {
        int creditDays = 30;
        JOptionPane.showMessageDialog(null,"" + creditDays);
        JOptionPane.showMessageDialog
            (null, "Every bill is due in " + creditDays + " days");
    }
}
```

Figure 2-3 NumbersDialog class

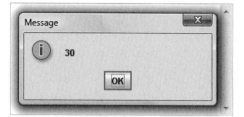

Figure 2-4 First dialog box created by NumbersDialog application

Figure 2-5 Second dialog box created by NumbersDialog application

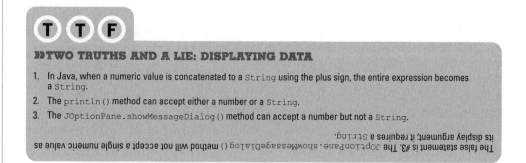

»TWO TRUTHS AND A LIE: DISPLAYING DATA

1. In Java, when a numeric value is concatenated to a String using the plus sign, the entire expression becomes a String.
2. The println() method can accept either a number or a String.
3. The JOptionPane.showMessageDialog() method can accept a number but not a String.

The false statement is #3. The JOptionPane.showMessageDialog() method will not accept a single numeric value as its display argument; it requires a String.

WRITING ARITHMETIC STATEMENTS

Table 2-3 describes the five standard arithmetic operators for integers. You use **arithmetic operators** to perform calculations with values in your programs. A value used on either side of an operator is an **operand**. For example, in the expression 45 + 2, the numbers 45 and 2 are operands. The arithmetic operators are examples of **binary operators**, so named because they require two operands.

»NOTE
You will learn about the Java shortcut arithmetic operators in Chapter 6.

»NOTE
When you perform paper-and-pencil division, you divide first to determine a remainder. In Java, you do not need to perform a division operation before you can perform a remainder operation. A remainder operation can stand alone.

Operator	Description	Example
+	Addition	45 + 2, the result is 47
−	Subtraction	45 − 2, the result is 43
*	Multiplication	45 * 2, the result is 90
/	Division	45/2, the result is 22 (not 22.5)
%	Remainder (modulus)	45 % 2, the result is 1 (that is, 45/2 = 22 with a remainder of 1)

Table 2-3 Integer arithmetic operators

»NOTE
In arithmetic, you might be used to indicating multiplication with an X (as in 45 X 2), a dot (as in 45 • 2), or parentheses (as in 45(2)). None of these formats works in Java; you must use an asterisk to perform multiplication (as in 45 * 2).

The operators / and % deserve special consideration. When you perform **integer division**, whether the two operators used in the arithmetic expression are integer constants or integer variables, the result is an integer. In other words, any fractional part of the result is lost. For example, the result of 45/2 is 22, even though the result is 22.5 in a mathematical expression. The percent sign is the **remainder operator**. When you use the remainder operator with two integers, the result is an integer with the value of the remainder after division takes place—the result of 45 % 2 is 1 because 2 "goes into" 45 twenty-two times with a remainder of 1. Other examples of division and remainder operations include the following:

»NOTE
The remainder operator is also called the **modulus operator**, or sometimes just **mod**.

» 39/5 is 7 because 5 goes into 39 seven whole times. Similarly, 38/5, 37/5, 36/5, and 35/5 all evaluate to 7.

» 39 % 5 is 4 because 5 goes into 39 seven times with a remainder of 4.

» 36/4 is 9, as you would expect.

» 36 % 4 is 0 because there is no remainder when 4 is divided into 36.

When you combine mathematical operations in a single statement, you must understand both associativity and precedence. The associativity of arithmetic operators with the same precedence is left-to-right. In a statement such as `answer = x + y + z;`, the x and y are added first, producing a temporary result, and then z is added to the temporary sum. After the sum is computed, the result is assigned to `answer`.

»NOTE
Later in this chapter, you will learn about values that contain decimal places. Unlike with integer division, you do not lose the fractional part of the result if at least one of the operands in a division operation is a floating-point data type.

Operator precedence refers to the rules for the order in which parts of a mathematical expression are evaluated. The multiplication, division, and remainder operators have the same precedence. Their precedence is higher than that for the addition and subtraction operators. Addition and subtraction have the same precedence. In other words, multiplication, division, and remainder always take place from left to right prior to addition or subtraction in an expression. For example, the following statement assigns 14 to `result`:

```
int result = 2 + 3 * 4;
```

The multiplication operation (3 * 4) occurs before adding 2. You can override normal operator precedence by putting the operation to perform first in parentheses. The following statement assigns 20 to `result`:

```
int result = (2 + 3) * 4;
```

The addition within the parentheses takes place first, and then the intermediate result (5) is multiplied by 4. When multiple pairs of parentheses are used in a statement, the innermost expression surrounded by parentheses is evaluated first. For example, the value of the following expression is 46:

```
2 * (3 + (4 * 5))
```

First, 4 * 5 evaluates to 20, and then 3 is added, giving 23. Finally, the value is multiplied by 2, giving 46.

Remembering that *, /, and % have the same precedence is important in arithmetic calculations. These operations are performed from left to right, regardless of the order in which they appear. For example, the value of the following expression is 9:

```
25 / 8 * 3
```

First, 25 is divided by 8. The result is 3 because with integer division, you lose any remainder. Then 3 is multiplied by 3, giving 9. If you assumed that * was performed before /, you would calculate an incorrect answer.

» NOTE
You will learn more about operator precedence in Chapter 5.

WRITING ARITHMETIC STATEMENTS EFFICIENTLY

You can make your programs operate more efficiently if you avoid unnecessary repetition of arithmetic statements. For example, suppose you know the values for an employee's hourly pay and pay rate and you want to compute state and federal withholding tax based on known rates. You could write two statements as follows:

```
stateWithholding = hours * rate * STATE_RATE;
federalWithholding = hours * rate * FED_RATE;
```

With this approach, you perform the multiplication of `hours * rate` twice. It is more efficient to perform the calculation once, as follows:

```
grossPay = hours * rate;
stateWithholding = grossPay * STATE_RATE;
federalWithholding = grossPay * FED_RATE;
```

The time saved is very small, but these savings would be more important if the calculation was more complicated or if it was repeated many times in a program. As you think about the programs you write, remain on the lookout for ways to improve efficiency by avoiding duplication of operations.

» TWO TRUTHS AND A LIE: WRITING ARITHMETIC STATEMENTS

1. The arithmetic operators are examples of unary operators, which are so named because they perform one operation at a time.
2. The value of 66 % 2 is 0.
3. In Java, operator precedence dictates that multiplication, division, and remainder always take place prior to addition or subtraction in an expression.

The false statement is #1. The arithmetic operators are examples of binary operators, which are so named because they require two operands.

USING THE BOOLEAN DATA TYPE

Boolean logic is based on true-or-false comparisons. Whereas an `int` variable can hold millions of different values (at different times), a **Boolean variable** can hold only one of two values—`true` or `false`. The following statements declare and assign appropriate values to Boolean variables:

```
boolean isItPayday = false;
boolean areYouBroke = true;
```

»NOTE
A relational operator sometimes is called a **comparison operator**.

You can also assign values based on the result of comparisons to Boolean variables. Java supports six relational operators that are used to make comparisons. A **relational operator** compares two items; an expression that contains a relational operator has a Boolean value. Table 2-4 describes the relational operators.

»NOTE
You will learn about other Boolean operators in Chapter 5.

Operator	Description	True example	False example
<	Less than	3 < 8	8 < 3
>	Greater than	4 > 2	2 > 4
==	Equal to	7 == 7	3 == 9
<=	Less than or equal to	5 <= 5	8 <= 6
>=	Greater than or equal to	7 >= 3	1 >= 2
!=	Not equal to	5 != 6	3 != 3

Table 2-4 Relational operators

»NOTE
When you use "Boolean" as an adjective, as in "Boolean operators," you usually begin with an uppercase B because the data type is named for Sir George Boole, the founder of symbolic logic, who lived from 1815 to 1864. The Java data type "boolean," however, begins with a lowercase "b."

When you use any of the operators that have two symbols (==, <=, >=, or !=), you cannot place any whitespace between the two symbols. You also cannot reverse the order of the symbols. That is, =<, =>, and =! are all invalid operators.

Legal declaration statements might include the following statements, which compare two values directly:

```
boolean isSixBigger = (6 > 5);
   // Value stored would be true
boolean isSevenSmallerOrEqual = (7 <= 4);
   // Value stored would be false
```

»NOTE
Although you can use any legal identifier for Boolean variables, they are easily identified as Boolean if you use a form of "to be" (such as "is" or "are") as part of the variable name, as in `isSixBigger`.

The Boolean expressions are more meaningful when variables (that have been assigned values) are used in the comparisons, as in the following examples. In the first statement, the `hours` variable is compared to a constant value of 40. If the `hours` variable is not greater than 40, the expression evaluates to `false`. In the second statement, the `income` variable must be greater than 100,000 for the expression to evaluate to `true`. In the third statement, two variables are compared to determine the value of `isFirstScoreHigher`:

```
boolean isOvertimePay = (hours > 40);
boolean isTaxBracketHigh = (income > 100000);
boolean isFirstScoreHigher = (score1 > score2);
```

LEARNING ABOUT FLOATING-POINT DATA TYPES

A **floating-point** number contains decimal positions. Java supports two floating-point data types: `float` and `double`. A **float** data type can hold floating-point values of up to six or seven significant digits of accuracy. A **double** data type requires more memory than a `float`, and can hold 14 or 15 significant digits of accuracy. The term **significant digits** refers to the mathematical accuracy of a value. For example, a `float` given the value 0.324616777 displays as 0.324617 because the value is accurate only to the sixth decimal position. Table 2-5 shows the minimum and maximum values for each floating-point data type.

> **»NOTE** A `float` given the value 324616777 displays as 3.24617e+008, which means approximately 3.24617 times 10 to the 8th power, or 324617000. The `e` in the displayed value stands for exponent; the +008 means the true decimal point is eight positions to the right of where it is displayed, indicating a very large number. (A negative number would indicate that the true decimal point belongs to the left, indicating a very small number.) This format is called **scientific notation**. The large value contains only six significant digits.

Type	Minimum	Maximum	Size in Bytes
float	$-3.4 * 10^{38}$	$3.4 * 10^{38}$	4
double	$-1.7 * 10^{308}$	$1.7 * 10^{308}$	8

Table 2-5 Limits on floating-point values

Just as an integer constant, such as 178, is a value of type `int` by default, a floating-point constant, such as 18.23, is a `double` by default. To store a value explicitly as a `float`, you can type the letter F after the number, as in the following:

```
float pocketChange = 4.87F;
```

You can type either a lowercase or an uppercase F. You also can type D (or d) after a floating-point constant to indicate it is a `double`, but even without the D, the value will be stored as a `double` by default.

> **»NOTE** A programmer might choose to store a value as a `float` instead of a `double` to save memory. However, if high levels of accuracy are needed, such as in graphics-intensive software, the programmer might choose to use a `double`, opting for high accuracy over saved memory.

> **»NOTE** A value written as $3.4 * 10^{38}$ indicates that the value is 3.4 multiplied by 10 to the 38th power, or 10 with 38 trailing zeros—a very large number.

> **»NOTE** A value stored in a `double` is a **double-precision floating-point number**; a value in a `float` is a **single-precision floating-point number**.

»NOTE
In Java, when you use the % operator with floating-point values, the result is the remainder from a rounded division.

As with `int` values, you can perform the mathematical operations of addition, subtraction, multiplication, and division with floating-point numbers. You also can perform remainder operations using floating-point values, but it is seldom useful to do so.

»TWO TRUTHS AND A LIE: LEARNING ABOUT FLOATING-POINT DATA TYPES

1. Java supports two floating-point data types: `float` and `double`. The `double` data type requires more memory and can hold more significant digits.

2. A floating-point constant, such as 5.6, is a `float` by default.

3. As with integers, you can perform the mathematical operations of addition, subtraction, multiplication, and division with floating-point numbers.

The false statement is #2. A floating-point constant, such as 5.6, is a `double` by default.

UNDERSTANDING NUMERIC-TYPE CONVERSION

When you perform arithmetic with variables or constants of the same type, the result of the operation retains the same type. For example, when you divide two `int`s, the result is an `int`, and when you subtract two `double`s, the result is a `double`. Often, however, you might want to perform mathematical operations on operands with unlike types.

When you perform arithmetic operations with operands of unlike types, Java chooses a unifying type for the result. The **unifying type** is the type to which all operands in an expression are converted so that they are compatible with each other. Java performs an **implicit conversion**; that is, it automatically converts nonconforming operands to the unifying type. The following list shows the order for establishing unifying types between values:

»NOTE
Implicit conversions are called **promotions**.

1. `double`

2. `float`

3. `long`

4. `int`

»NOTE
Boolean values cannot be converted to another type. In some languages, such as C++, Boolean values are actually numbers. However, this is not the case in Java.

When two unlike types are used in an expression, the unifying type is the one with the lower number in this list. In other words, the operand that is a type that has a higher number in this list is converted to the type of the one that has a lower number. For example, the addition of a `double` and an `int` results in a `double`, and the subtraction of a `long` from a `float` results in a `float`.

For example, assume that an `int`, `hoursWorked`, and a `double`, `payRate`, are defined and then multiplied as follows:

```
int hoursWorked = 37;
double payRate = 6.73;
double grossPay = hoursWorked * payRate;
```

The result of the multiplication is a `double` because when a `double` and an `int` are multiplied, the `int` is promoted to the higher-ranking unifying type `double`—the type with the lower number in the preceding list. Therefore, assigning the result to `grossPay` is legal. The following code will not compile because Java does not allow the loss of precision that occurs if you try to store the calculated `double` result in an `int`:

```
int hoursWorked = 37;
double payRate = 6.73;
int grossPay = hoursWorked * payRate;
```

You can explicitly (or purposely) override the unifying type imposed by Java by performing a type cast. **Type casting** forces a value of one data type to be used as a value of another type. To perform a type cast, you use a **cast operator**, which is created by placing the desired result type in parentheses. Using a cast operator is an **explicit conversion**. The cast operator is followed by the variable or constant to be cast. For example, a type cast is performed in the following code:

```
double bankBalance = 189.66;
float weeklyBudget = (float) bankBalance / 4;
   // weeklyBudget is 47.415, one-fourth of bankBalance
```

In this example, the `double` value `bankBalance` / 4 is converted to a `float` before it is stored in `weeklyBudget`. Without the conversion, the statement that assigns the result to `weeklyBudget` would not compile. Similarly, a cast from a `float` to an `int` occurs in this code segment:

```
float myMoney = 47.82f;
int dollars = (int) myMoney;
   // dollars is 47, the integer part of myMoney
```

In this example, the `float` value `myMoney` is converted to an `int` before it is stored in the integer variable named `dollars`. When the `float` value is converted to an `int`, the decimal place values are lost.

> **NOTE** It is easy to lose data when performing a cast. For example, the largest `byte` value is 127 and the largest `int` value is 2,147,483,647, so the following statements produce distorted results:
>
> ```
> int anOkayInt = 200;
>
> byte aBadByte = (byte)anOkayInt;
> ```

> **NOTE** A `byte` is constructed from eight 1s and 0s, or binary digits. The first binary digit, or bit, holds a 0 or 1 to represent positive or negative. The remaining seven bits store the actual value. When the integer value 200 is stored in the `byte` variable, its large value consumes the eighth bit, turning it into a 1, and forcing the `aBadByte` variable to appear to hold the value –72, which is inaccurate and misleading.

You do not need to perform a cast when assigning a value to a higher unifying type. For example, when you write a statement such as the following, Java automatically promotes the integer constant 10 to be a `double` so that it can be stored in the `payRate` variable:

```
double payRate = 10;
```

> **NOTE**
> The data types `char`, `short`, and `byte` all are promoted to `int` when used in statements with unlike types. If you perform a calculation with any combination of `char`, `short`, and `byte` values, the result is an `int` by default. For example, if you add two `bytes`, the result is an `int`, not a `byte`.

> **NOTE**
> The cast operator is more completely called the **unary cast operator**. Unlike a binary operator that requires two operands, a **unary operator** uses only one operand. The unary cast operator is followed by its operand.

> **NOTE**
> The cast operator does not permanently alter any data's type; the alteration is only for the duration of the current operation.

> **NOTE**
> The word "cast" is used in a similar fashion when referring to molding metal, as in "cast iron." In a Java arithmetic cast, a value is "molded" into a different type.

However, for clarity, if you want to assign 10 to payRate, you might prefer to write the following:

```
double payRate = 10.0;
```

The result is identical to the result when you assign the literal integer 10 to the double variable.

»TWO TRUTHS AND A LIE: UNDERSTANDING NUMERIC-TYPE CONVERSION

1. When you perform arithmetic operations with operands of unlike types, you must make an explicit conversion to a unifying type.
2. Summing a double, int, and float results in a double.
3. You can explicitly override the unifying type imposed by Java by performing a type cast; type casting forces a value of one data type to be used as a value of another type.

The false statement is #1. When you perform arithmetic operations with operands of unlike types, Java performs an implicit conversion to a unifying type.

WORKING WITH THE char DATA TYPE

You use the **char** data type to hold any single character. You place constant character values within single quotation marks because the computer stores characters and integers differently. For example, the following are typical character declarations:

```
char myMiddleInitial = 'M';
char myGradeInChemistry = 'A';
char aStar = '*';
```

A character can be any letter—uppercase or lowercase. It might also be a punctuation mark or digit. A character that is a digit is represented in computer memory differently than a numeric value represented by the same digit. For example, the following two statements are legal:

```
char aCharValue = '9';
int aNumValue = 9;
```

If you display each of these values using a println() statement, you see a 9. However, only the numeric value, aNumValue, can be used to represent the value 9 in arithmetic statements.

The following two statements are legal, but unless you understand their meanings, they might produce undesirable results:

```
char aCharValue = 9;
int aNumValue = '9';
```

If these variables are used in the following println() statement, then the resulting output produces a blank for aCharValue and the number 57 for aNumValue:

```
System.out.println("aCharValue is " + aCharValue +
    "aNumValue is " + aNumValue);
```

»NOTE
You can use a char variable in arithmetic statements, but its value might not be what you intended. For example, the value of '7' is 55, the value of '8' is 56, and the value of '9' is 57.

The unexpected values are Unicode values. Every computer stores every character it uses as a number; every character is assigned a unique numeric code using Unicode. Table 2-6 shows some Unicode decimal values and their character equivalents. For example, the character 'A' is stored using the value 65 and the character 'B' is stored using the value 66.

Dec	Char	Dec	Char	Dec	Char	Dec	Char
0	nul	32		64	@	96	`
1	soh ^A	33	!	65	A	97	a
2	stx ^B	34	"	66	B	98	b
3	etx ^C	35	#	67	C	99	c
4	eot ^D	36	$	68	D	100	d
5	enq ^E	37	%	69	E	101	e
6	ack ^F	38	&	70	F	102	f
7	bel ^G	39	'	71	G	103	g
8	bs ^H	40	(	72	H	104	h
9	ht ^I	41	)	73	I	105	i
10	lf ^J	42	*	74	J	106	j
11	vt ^K	43	+	75	K	107	k
12	ff ^L	44	,	76	L	108	l
13	cr ^M	45	-	77	M	109	m
14	so ^N	46	.	78	N	110	n
15	si ^O	47	/	79	O	111	o
16	dle ^P	48	0	80	P	112	p
17	dc1 ^Q	49	1	81	Q	113	q
18	dc2 ^R	50	2	82	R	114	r
19	dc3 ^S	51	3	83	S	115	s
20	dc4 ^T	52	4	84	T	116	t
21	nak ^U	53	5	85	U	117	u
22	syn ^V	54	6	86	V	118	v
23	etb ^W	55	7	87	W	119	w
24	can ^X	56	8	88	X	120	x
25	em ^Y	57	9	89	Y	121	y
26	sub ^Z	58	:	90	Z	122	z
27	esc	59	;	91	[	123	{
28	fs	60	<	92	\	124		
29	gs	61	=	93	]	125	}
30	rs	62	>	94	^	126	~
31	us	63	?	95	_	127	del

Table 2-6 Unicode values 0 through 127 and their character equivalents

NOTE
Appendix B contains more information on Unicode.

NOTE
A numeric constant can be stored as a character, but you cannot store an alphabetic letter in a numeric-type variable.

A variable of type char can hold only one character. To store a string of characters, such as a person's name, you must use a data structure called a String. In Java, **String** is a built-in class that provides you with the means for storing and manipulating character strings. Unlike single characters, which use single quotation marks, string constants are written between double quotation marks. For example, the expression that stores the name Audrey as a string in a variable named firstName is:

```
String firstName = "Audrey";
```

NOTE
You will learn more about strings and the String class in Chapter 7.

You can store any character—including nonprinting characters such as a backspace or a tab—in a char variable. To store these characters, you can use an **escape sequence**, which always begins with a backslash followed by a character—the pair represents a single character.

For example, the following code stores a newline character and a tab character in the `char` variables `aNewLine` and `aTabChar`:

```
char aNewLine = '\n';
char aTabChar = '\t';
```

In the declarations of `aNewLine` and `aTabChar`, the backslash and character pair acts as a single character; the escape sequence serves to give a new meaning to the character. That is, the literal characters in the preceding code have different values from the "plain" characters 'n' or 't'. Table 2-7 describes some common escape sequences that you can use with command window output in Java.

NOTE
When you display values within `JOptionPane` dialog boxes rather than in a command window, the escape sequences '\n' (newline), '\"' (double quote), and '\\' (backslash) operate as expected within a `JOptionPane` object, but '\t', '\b', and '\r' do not work in the GUI environment.

Escape Sequence	Description
\b	Backspace; moves the cursor one space to the left
\t	Tab; moves the cursor to the next tab stop
\n	Newline or linefeed; moves the cursor to the beginning of the next line
\r	Carriage return; moves the cursor to the beginning of the current line
\"	Double quotation mark; prints a double quotation mark
\'	Single quotation mark; prints a single quotation mark
\\	Backslash; prints a backslash character

Table 2-7 Common escape sequences

```
public class HelloThereNewLine
{
   public static void main(String[] args)
   {
      System.out.println("Hello\nthere");
   }
}
```

Figure 2-6 `HelloThereNewLine` class

When you want to produce console output on multiple lines in the command window, you have two options: You can use the newline escape sequence, or you can use the `println()` method multiple times. For example, Figures 2-6 and 2-7 both show classes that produce the same output: "Hello" on one line and "there" on another. The version you choose to use is up to you. The example in Figure 2-6 is more efficient—both from a typist's point of view because the text `System.out.println` appears only once, and from the compiler's point of view because the `println()` method is called only once. The example in Figure 2-7, however, might be easier to read and understand. When programming in Java, you will find occasions when each of these approaches makes sense.

```
public class HelloTherePrintlnTwice
{
    public static void main(String[] args)
    {
        System.out.println("Hello");
        System.out.println("there");
    }
}
```

Figure 2-7 HelloTherePrintlnTwice class

》TWO TRUTHS AND A LIE: WORKING WITH THE char DATA TYPE

1. You use the char data type to hold any single character; you place constant character values within single quotation marks.

2. To store a string of characters, you use a data structure called a Text; string constants are written between parentheses.

3. An escape sequence always begins with a backslash followed by a character; the pair represents a single character.

The false statement is #2. To store a string of characters, you use a data structure called a String; string constants are written between double quotation marks.

USING THE Scanner CLASS FOR KEYBOARD INPUT

In Chapter 1, you learned how to display output on the monitor using the System.out object. The System.out object refers to the standard output device, which usually is the monitor. Frequently you also want to create interactive programs that accept input from a user. To do so, you can use the System.in object, which refers to the **standard input device** (normally the keyboard).

You can use the print() and println() methods to display many data types; for example, you can use them to display a double, int, or String. The System.in object is not as flexible; it is designed to read only bytes. That's a problem, because you often want to accept data of other types. Fortunately, the designers of Java have created a class named Scanner that makes the System.in object more flexible.

To create a Scanner object and connect it to the System.in object, you write a statement similar to the following:

```
Scanner inputDevice = new Scanner(System.in);
```

The portion of the statement to the left of the assignment operator, Scanner inputDevice, declares an object of type Scanner with the programmer-chosen name inputDevice, in exactly the same way that int x declares an integer with the programmer-chosen name x.

»NOTE
In Chapter 4, you
will learn that the
second part of the
Scanner state-
ment calls a spe-
cial method in the
prewritten
Scanner class
called a construc-
tor; it constructs a
new Scanner
object. You also will
learn more about
the Java keyword
new in Chapters 3
and 4.

The portion of the statement to the right of the assignment operator, new Scanner(System.in), creates a Scanner object that is connected to the System.in object. In other words, the created Scanner object is connected to the default input device. The keyword new is required by Java; you will use it whenever you create objects that are more complex than the simple data types.

The assignment operator in the Scanner declaration statement assigns the value of the new object—that is, its memory address—to the inputDevice object in the program.

A Scanner object breaks its input into units called **tokens**, separating them when it encounters whitespace. The resulting tokens can then be converted into values of different types using the various class methods. Table 2-8 summarizes some of the most useful methods that read different data types from the default input device. Each retrieves a value from the keyboard and returns it as the appropriate data type. The appropriate method executes, retrieving data when a user presses an appropriate whitespace key at the keyboard. The nextLine() method does not retrieve data until the user presses Enter; the other methods retrieve data when the user presses Enter, the spacebar, or the tab key.

»NOTE
In addition to the
methods listed
in Table 2-8, the
Scanner class con-
tains methods called
nextByte(),
nextFloat(),
nextLong(), and
nextShort() that
work as you would
expect.

Method	Description
nextDouble()	Retrieves input as a double
nextInt()	Retrieves input as an int
nextLine()	Retrieves the next line of data and returns it as a String
next()	Retrieves the next complete token as a String

Table 2-8 Selected Scanner class methods

»NOTE
The Scanner class
does not contain
a nextChar()
method. To retrieve
a single character
from the keyboard,
you can use the
nextLine()
method and then
use the charAt()
method. Chapter 7
provides more
details about the
charAt() method.

Figure 2-8 contains a program that uses two of the Scanner class methods. The program reads a string and an integer from the keyboard and displays them. The Scanner class is used in the four shaded statements in the figure.

» The first shaded statement is import java.util.Scanner;. This statement imports the package necessary to use the Scanner class.

» The second shaded statement declares a Scanner object named inputDevice.

» The third shaded statement uses the nextLine() method to retrieve a line of text from the keyboard and store it in the name variable.

» The last shaded statement uses the nextInt() method to retrieve an integer from the keyboard and store it in the age variable.

»NOTE Java programmers would say that the Scanner methods *return* the appropriate value. That also means that the value of the method is the appropriate value, and that you can assign the returned value to a variable, display it, or use it in other legal statements. In Chapter 3, you will learn how to write your own methods that return values.

Figure 2-9 shows a typical execution of the program.

```
import java.util.Scanner;
public class GetUserInfo
{
    public static void main(String[] args)
    {
        String name;
        int age;
        Scanner inputDevice = new Scanner(System.in);
        System.out.print("Please enter your name >> ");
        name = inputDevice.nextLine();
        System.out.print("Please enter your age >> ");
        age = inputDevice.nextInt();
        System.out.println("Your name is " + name +
            " and you are " + age + " years old.");
    }
}
```

> Repeating as output what a user has entered as input is called **echoing the input.** Echoing input is a good programming practice; it helps eliminate misunderstandings when the user can visually confirm what was entered.

Figure 2-8 The GetUserInfo class

»NOTE
The print() statements that appear before each input statement are examples of prompts. A **prompt** is a displayed message for the user that requests and describes input. Programs would work without prompts, but they would not be as user-friendly.

»NOTE
Each prompt in the GetUserInfo class ends with a space. This is not required; it just separates the words in the prompt from the user's input value on the screen, improving readability.

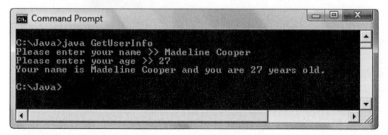

```
C:\Java>java GetUserInfo
Please enter your name >> Madeline Cooper
Please enter your age >> 27
Your name is Madeline Cooper and you are 27 years old.

C:\Java>
```

Figure 2-9 Typical execution of the GetUserInfo program

PITFALL: USING nextLine() FOLLOWING ONE OF THE OTHER Scanner INPUT METHODS

You can encounter a problem when you use one of the numeric Scanner class retrieval methods or the next() method before you use the nextLine() method. Consider the program in Figure 2-10. It is identical to the one in Figure 2-8, except that the user is asked for an age before being asked for a name. Figure 2-11 shows a typical execution.

```
import java.util.Scanner;
public class GetUserInfo2
{
    public static void main(String[] args)
    {
        String name;
        int age;
        Scanner inputDevice = new Scanner(System.in);
        System.out.print("Please enter your age >> ");
        age = inputDevice.nextInt();
        System.out.print("Please enter your name >> ");
        name = inputDevice.nextLine();
        System.out.println("Your name is " +
            name + " and you are " + age +
            " years old.");
    }
}
```

»DON'T DO IT

If you accept numeric input prior to string input, the string input is ignored unless you take special action.

Figure 2-10 The `GetUserInfo2` class

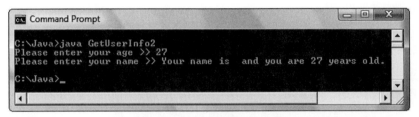

Figure 2-11 Typical execution of the `GetUserInfo2` program

In Figure 2-11, the user is prompted correctly for an age. However, after the user enters an age and the prompt for the name is displayed, the program does not pause to let the user enter a name. Instead, the program proceeds directly to the output statement, which does not contain a valid name, as you can see in Figure 2-11.

When you type characters using the keyboard, they are stored temporarily in a location in the memory called the **keyboard buffer**. All keystrokes are stored, including the Enter key. The problem occurs because of a difference in the way the `nextLine()` method and the other `Scanner` retrieval methods work. The `nextLine()` method reads data up to the Enter key character. When you ask for data with a method such as `nextLine()`, `nextInt()`, or `nextDouble()`, any leading whitespace characters are discarded, and a token is retrieved up to the next whitespace entry. However, `nextLine()` does not ignore leading whitespace; so, for example, when a numeric input method leaves the Enter keypress in the input buffer, and is followed by a call to `nextLine()`, the `nextLine()` method accepts the Enter key that followed the number as its input, and needs no additional input from the user.

The solution to the problem is simple. After any numeric or `next()` input, you can add an extra `nextLine()` method call that will retrieve the abandoned Enter key character. Then, if string input follows, the program will execute smoothly. Figure 2-12 shows a program that contains just one change from Figure 2-10—the addition of the shaded statement that retrieves the abandoned Enter key character from the input buffer. Although you could assign the Enter key to a character variable, there is no need to do so. When you accept an entry and discard it without using it, programmers say that the entry is **consumed**. The diagram in Figure 2-12 shows how the first call to nextInt() accepts the integer, the call to nextLine() accepts the Enter key that follows the integer entry, and the second nextLine() call accepts both the entered name and the Enter key that follows it. Figure 2-13 shows that the revised program executes correctly.

```java
import java.util.Scanner;
public class GetUserInfo3
{
    public static void main(String[] args)
    {
        String name;
        int age;
        Scanner inputDevice = new Scanner(System.in);
        System.out.print("Please enter your age >> ");
        age = inputDevice.nextInt();
        inputDevice.nextLine();
        System.out.print("Please enter your name >> ");
        name = inputDevice.nextLine();
        System.out.println("Your name is " + name +
            " and you are " + age + " years old.");
    }
}
```

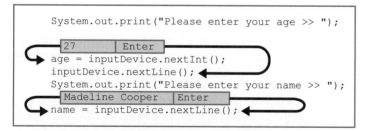

Figure 2-12 The GetUserInfo3 class and a diagram of how the input keys are consumed

Figure 2-13 Typical execution of the GetUserInfo3 program

»NOTE
When you write programs that accept user input, there is a risk that the user will enter the wrong type of data. For example, if you include a nextInt() method call in your program, but the user types an alphabetic character, an error will occur and your program will stop running. You will learn to handle this type of error in Chapter 11.

USING THE JOptionPane CLASS FOR GUI INPUT

In Chapter 1, you learned how to display output at the command line and how to create GUI message boxes to display String objects. Earlier in this chapter, you learned to accept input from the keyboard at the command line. You can also accept input in a GUI dialog box using the JOptionPane class.

Two dialog boxes that can be used to accept user input are:

» InputDialog—Prompts the user for text input

» ConfirmDialog—Asks the user a question, providing buttons that the user can click for Yes, No, and Cancel responses

USING INPUT DIALOG BOXES

An **input dialog box** asks a question and provides a text field in which the user can enter a response. You can create an input dialog box using the **showInputDialog() method**. Six overloaded versions of this method are available, but the simplest version uses a single argument that is the prompt you want to display within the dialog box. The showInputDialog() method returns a String that represents a user's response; this means that you can assign the showInputDialog() method to a String variable and the variable will hold the value that the user enters.

For example, Figure 2-14 shows an application that creates an input dialog box containing a prompt for a first name. When the user executes the application, types "Audrey", then clicks the OK button or presses Enter on the keyboard, the response String will contain "Audrey". The response String can then be used like any other String object. For example, in the application in Figure 2-14, the response is concatenated with a welcoming message and displayed in a message dialog box. Figure 2-15 shows the dialog box containing a user's response, and Figure 2-16 shows the resulting output message box.

```
import javax.swing.JOptionPane;
public class HelloNameDialog
{
    public static void main(String[] args)
    {
        String result;
        result = JOptionPane.showInputDialog(null, "What is your name?");
        JOptionPane.showMessageDialog(null, "Hello, " + result + "!");
    }
}
```

Figure 2-14 The `HelloNameDialog` class

Figure 2-15 Input dialog box of the `HelloNameDialog` application

Figure 2-16 Output of the `HelloNameDialog` application

Within the `JOptionPane` class, an overloaded version of the `showInputDialog()` method allows the programmer flexibility in controlling the appearance of the input dialog box. The version of `showInputDialog()` that requires four arguments can be used to display a title in the dialog box title bar and a message that describes the type of dialog box. The four arguments to `showInputDialog()` include:

» The parent component, which is the screen component, such as a frame, in front of which the dialog box will appear. If this argument is null, the dialog box is centered on the screen.

» The message the user will see before entering a value. Usually this message is a `String`, but it actually can be any type of object.

» The title to be displayed in the title bar of the input dialog box.

» A class field describing the type of dialog box; it can be one of the following: `ERROR_MESSAGE`, `INFORMATION_MESSAGE`, `PLAIN_MESSAGE`, `QUESTION_MESSAGE`, or `WARNING_MESSAGE`.

For example, when the following statement executes, it displays the input dialog box shown in Figure 2-17.

```
JOptionPane.showInputDialog(null,
    "What is your area code?",
    "Area code information",
    JOptionPane.QUESTION_MESSAGE);
```

Figure 2-17 An input dialog box with a `String` in the title bar and a question mark icon

Note that the title bar displays "Area code information," and the dialog box shows a question mark icon.

The `showInputDialog()` method returns a `String` object, which makes sense when you consider that you might want a user to type any combination of keystrokes into the dialog box. However, when the value that the user enters is intended to be used as a number, as in an arithmetic statement, the returned `String` must be converted to the correct numeric type. Earlier in this chapter, you learned how to cast a value from one data type to another. However, casting data only works with primitive data types—`double`, `int`, `char`, and so on— not with class objects (that are reference types) such as a `String`. To convert a `String` to an `integer` or `double`, you must use methods from the built-in Java classes `Integer` and `Double`. Each primitive type in Java has a corresponding class contained in the `java.lang` package; like most classes, the names of these classes begin with uppercase letters. These classes are called **type-wrapper classes**. They include methods that can process primitive-type values.

Figure 2-18 shows a `SalaryDialog` application that contains two `String` objects—`wageString` and `dependentsString`. Two `showInputDialog()` methods are called, and the answers are stored in the declared `String`s. The shaded statements in Figure 2-18 show how the `String`s are converted to numeric values using methods from the type-wrapper classes `Integer` and `Double`. The `double` value is converted using the `Double.parseDouble()` method, and the integer is converted using the `Integer.parseInt()` method. Figure 2-19 shows a typical execution of the application.

>> **NOTE**
The term **parse** means to break into component parts. Grammarians talk about "parsing a sentence"— deconstructing it so as to describe its grammatical components. Parsing a `String` converts it to its numeric equivalent.

>> **NOTE** Remember that in Java, the reserved keyword `static` means that a method is accessible and usable even though no objects of the class exist. You can tell that the method `Double.parseDouble()` is a `static` method, because the method name is used with the class name `Double`—no object is needed. Similarly, you can tell that `Integer.parseInt()` is also a `static` method.

```
import javax.swing.JOptionPane;
public class SalaryDialog
{
   public static void main(String[] args)
   {
      String wageString, dependentsString;
      double wage, weeklyPay;
      int dependents;
      final double HOURS_IN_WEEK = 37.5;
      wageString = JOptionPane.showInputDialog(null,
         "Enter employee's hourly wage", "Salary dialog 1",
         JOptionPane.INFORMATION_MESSAGE);
      weeklyPay = Double.parseDouble(wageString) *HOURS_IN_WEEK;
      dependentsString = JOptionPane.showInputDialog(null,
         "How many dependents?", "Salary dialog 2",
         JOptionPane.QUESTION_MESSAGE);
      dependents = Integer.parseInt(dependentsString);
      JOptionPane.showMessageDialog(null, "Weekly salary is $" +
         weeklyPay + "\nDeductions will be made for " +
         dependents + " dependents");
   }
}
```

Figure 2-18 The SalaryDialog class

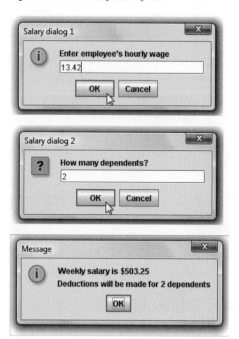

Figure 2-19 Sample execution of the SalaryDialog application

USING CONFIRM DIALOG BOXES

Sometimes, the input you want from a user does not have to be typed from the keyboard. When you present simple options to a user, you can offer buttons that the user can click to confirm a choice. A **confirm dialog box** displays the options Yes, No, and Cancel; you can create one using the **showConfirmDialog() method** in the JOptionPane class. Four overloaded versions of the method are available; the simplest requires a parent component (which can be null) and the String prompt that is displayed in the box. The showConfirmDialog() method returns an integer containing one of three possible values: JOptionPane.YES_OPTION, JOptionPane.NO_OPTION, or JOptionPane.CANCEL_OPTION. Figure 2-20 shows an application that asks a user a question. The shaded statement displays the dialog box shown in Figure 2-21 and stores the user's response in the integer variable named selection.

```
import javax.swing.JOptionPane;
public class AirlineDialog
{
   public static void main(String[] args)
   {
      int selection;
      boolean isYes;
      selection = JOptionPane.showConfirmDialog(null,
         "Do you want to upgrade to first class?");
      isYes = (selection == JOptionPane.YES_OPTION);
      JOptionPane.showMessageDialog(null,
         "You responded " + isYes);
   }
}
```

Figure 2-20 The AirlineDialog class

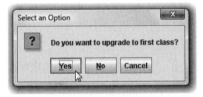

Figure 2-21 The confirm dialog box displayed by the AirlineDialog application

After a value is stored in selection, a Boolean variable named isYes is set to the result when selection and JOptionPane.YES_OPTION are compared. If the user has selected the Yes button in the dialog box, this variable is set to true; otherwise, the variable is set to false. Finally, the true or false result is displayed. Figure 2-22 shows the result when a user clicks the Yes button in the dialog box.

Figure 2-22 Output of AirlineDialog application when user clicks Yes

You can also create a confirm dialog box with five arguments, as follows:

» The parent component, which can be null
» The prompt message
» The title to be displayed in the title bar
» An integer that indicates which option button will be shown (It should be one of the class variables YES_NO_CANCEL_OPTION or YES_NO_OPTION.)
» An integer that describes the kind of dialog box (It should be one of the class variables ERROR_MESSAGE, INFORMATION_MESSAGE, PLAIN_MESSAGE, QUESTION_MESSAGE, or WARNING_MESSAGE.)

When the following statement is executed, it displays a confirm dialog box, as shown in Figure 2-23:

```
JOptionPane.showConfirmDialog(null,
    "A data input error has occurred. Continue?",
    "Data input error", JOptionPane.YES_NO_OPTION,
    JOptionPane.ERROR_MESSAGE);
```

» NOTE
Confirm dialog boxes provide more practical uses when your applications can make decisions based on the users' responses. In Chapter 5, you will learn how to make decisions within programs.

Note that the title bar displays "Data input error," the Yes and No buttons appear, and the dialog box shows the error message, "A data input error has occurred. Continue?" It also displays the octagonal ERROR_MESSAGE icon.

Figure 2-23 Confirm dialog box with title, Yes and No buttons, and error icon

» TWO TRUTHS AND A LIE: USING THE JOptionPane CLASS FOR GUI INPUT

1. You can create an input dialog box using the showInputDialog() method; the method returns a String that represents a user's response.

2. Casting data only works with primitive data types, and not with reference types such as String. You must use methods from the Java classes Integer and Double when you want to convert a dialog box's returned values to numbers.

3. A confirm dialog box can be created using the showConfirmDialog() method in the JOptionPane class; a confirm dialog box displays the options Accept, Reject, and Escape.

The false statement is #3. A confirm dialog box displays the options Yes, No, and Cancel.

YOU DO IT

WORKING WITH NUMERIC VALUES

In this section, you will write an application to declare and display numeric values.

To declare and display an integer value in an application:

1. Open a new document in your text editor.

2. Create a class header and an opening and closing curly brace for a new class named **DemoVariables** by typing the following:

```
public class DemoVariables
{
}
```

3. Position the insertion point after the opening curly brace, press **Enter**, press the **spacebar** several times to indent the line, and then type the following main() method and its curly braces:

```
public static void main(String[] args)
{
}
```

> **NOTE** Some programmers use the Tab key to indent lines; others use spaces. Tabs can pose a problem when your code is opened in an editor that is configured differently from the one in which you wrote the source code originally. This book will use three spaces as the standard indentation, but you might prefer two, four, or five spaces in your programs.

> **NOTE**
> You can declare variables at any point within a method prior to their first use. However, it is common practice to declare variables first in a class, and to place executable statements after them.

4. Position the insertion point after the opening curly brace in the main() method, press **Enter**, press the **spacebar** several times to indent the line, and then type the following to declare a variable of type int named entry with a value of 315:

```
int entry = 315;
```

> **NOTE**
> When your output contains a literal string such as "The entry is", you can type a space before the closing quotation mark so there is a space between the end of the literal string and the value that prints.

5. Press **Enter** at the end of the entry declaration statement, indent the line appropriately, and then type the following two output statements. The first statement uses the print() method to output "The entry is " and leaves the insertion point on the same output line. The second statement uses the println() method to output the value of entry and advances the insertion point to a new line:

```
System.out.print("The entry is ");
System.out.println(entry);
```

6. Save the file as **DemoVariables.java**.

7. Compile the file from the command line by typing **javac DemoVariables.java**. If necessary, correct any errors, save the file, and then compile again.

8. Execute the application from the command line by typing **java DemoVariables**. The command window output is shown in Figure 2-24.

Figure 2-24 Output of the DemoVariables application

ACCEPTING USER DATA

A program that displays the same value each time it executes is not as useful as one that can accept and display a user's entered value.

To accept user data in the application:

1. Return to the **DemoVariables.java** file in the text editor. Rename the class **DemoVariables2**. Immediately save the file as **DemoVariables2.java**.

2. At the top of the file, as the first line, type the statement that will allow you to use the Scanner class for data entry:

```
import java.util.Scanner;
```

3. Remove the value assigned to entry so that the declaration becomes:

```
int entry;
```

4. After the declaration of entry, add a declaration for a Scanner object that can be used to accept data entry from the keyboard:

```
Scanner keyBoard = new Scanner(System.in);
```

5. On the next two lines, add a prompt that asks the user to enter an integer and write the statement that accepts the user's entry:

```
System.out.print("Enter an integer ");
entry = keyBoard.nextInt();
```

6. Save the application, then compile it by typing **javac DemoVariables2.java** at the command line. If necessary, correct any errors, save the file, and then compile again.

7. Execute the application by typing **java DemoVariables2**. When the prompt appears on the screen, enter an integer. Figure 2-25 shows a typical execution.

Figure 2-25 Output of the DemoVariables2 application

>> NOTE
When you modify a file by changing its class name, it is a good idea to save the file with the corresponding new name immediately. Otherwise, it is easy to forget that you have not saved the changes, and when you choose *Save*, you inadvertently write over the previous file version with the old class name.

8. Execute the program several times using different values, including negative numbers, and confirm that the program works as expected. Then execute the program and type an invalid entry; for example, a letter of the alphabet. Figure 2-26 shows the error messages generated when the user types something other than an integer.

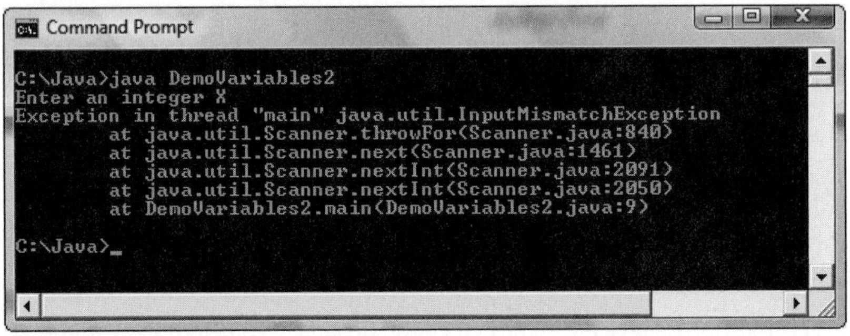

Figure 2-26 Error messages generated when the user enters an "X" into the `DemoVariables2` program

As you write Java programs in this chapter and the next few chapters, you are likely to make similar data-entry mistakes. The messages in Figure 2-26 might look intimidating, but you should remember two points:

» First, if you read the messages carefully, you will find they provide some useful information. The last line of the message indicates that the problem occurred in line 9 of the `DemoVariables2` program. In the source code file, line 9 is the one that attempts to get the next integer from the keyboard. This provides a clue that a problem occurred with data entry.

» Second, you can ignore the messages and simply rerun the program. When you enter valid data, the program will work as expected—you haven't "broken" anything.

PERFORMING ARITHMETIC

In the next steps, you will accept an additional value into your program and perform arithmetic operations on the entered values.

To add another variable and perform arithmetic:

1. Open the **DemoVariables2.java** text file, and rename the class **DemoVariables3**. Immediately save it as **DemoVariables3.java**.

2. After the declaration of `entry`, add a declaration for a second variable:

```
int anotherEntry;
```

3. Following the existing statements that prompt for and receive a value for `anotherEntry`, add two statements that prompt for and receive the newly declared integer:

```
System.out.print("Enter another integer ");
anotherEntry = keyBoard.nextInt();
```

4. At the end of the `main()` method, after the statement that displays the value of `entry` and just before the closing curly brace for the method, add statements that display the second entered value:

```
System.out.print("The other entry is ");
System.out.println(anotherEntry);
```

5. Add some statements that perform arithmetic operations on the two entered values.

```
System.out.println(entry + " plus " +
    anotherEntry + " is " + (entry + anotherEntry));
  System.out.println(entry + " minus " +
      anotherEntry + " is " + (entry - anotherEntry));
  System.out.println(entry + " times " +
      anotherEntry + " is " + (entry * anotherEntry));
  System.out.println(entry + " divided by " +
      anotherEntry + " is " + (entry / anotherEntry));
  System.out.println("The remainder is " +
      (entry % anotherEntry));
```

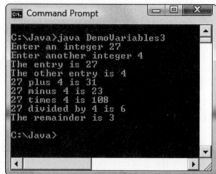

6. Save the file, then compile and test the application several times using different input values. A typical execution is shown in Figure 2-27. Make sure you execute the program a few times using negative values for one or both of the integers. Notice that the remainder value is affected only by the sign of the first operand in the remainder statement, and not by the second.

Figure 2-27 Output of the `DemoVariables3` application

EXPERIMENTING WITH JAVA PROGRAMS

Next, you will experiment with the program you have created to get a better understanding of variables and arithmetic.

To get a better understanding of Java:

1. Open the **DemoVariables3.java** file in your text editor and change the class name to **DemoVariables4**. Immediately save the file as **DemoVariables4.java**.

2. Remove the parentheses surrounding `entry + anotherEntry` in the statement that displays the sum of the two input values. Save, compile, and execute the program. What is the output?

3. Open the **DemoVariables3.java** file in your text editor (not DemoVariables4.java) and change the class name to **DemoVariables5**. Immediately save the file as **DemoVariables5.java**.

4. Remove the parentheses surrounding `entry * anotherEntry` in the statement that displays the product of the two input values. Save, compile, and execute the program. What is the significant difference between this example and the one from Step 2? Why?

5. Open the **DemoVariables3.java** file in your text editor and change the class name to **DemoVariables6**. Immediately save the file as **DemoVariables6.java**.

6. Change the data types of the two variables to `double`. Change the two prompts to ask the user for a `double` instead of an integer. Change the two instances of `nextInt()` to `nextDouble()`. Save, compile, and execute the program several times, entering floating-point values when prompted. Notice the slight imprecisions that occur with floating-point arithmetic. Study the remainder figure and see if you can determine what it means. Execute the program and enter integers, and notice that the program works appropriately.

7. Open the **DemoVariables3.java** file in your text editor and change the class name to **DemoVariables7**. Immediately save the file as **DemoVariables7.java**.

8. Following the two existing variable declarations, declare a `String` as follows:

```
String name;
```

9. Just before the closing curly brace for the `main()` method, add the following statements that prompt a user for a name, accept it, and display it:

```
System.out.print("Enter your name ");
  name = keyBoard.nextLine();
  System.out.println("Goodbye, " + name);
```

10. Save, compile, and execute the program. After you enter the requested integers and the arithmetic results are displayed, you are not given the chance to enter a name. That's because the `nextLine()` method accepts the Enter key that remained in the input buffer after the last number was entered. To remedy the situation, add the following statement after the statement that gets the last number:

```
keyBoard.nextLine();
```

11. Save, compile, and execute the program. This time, you are able to enter a name and the program ends as expected.

DON'T DO IT

» Don't attempt to assign a literal constant floating-point number, such as 2.5, to a `float` without following the constant with an uppercase or lowercase F. By default, constant floating-point values are `doubles`.

» Don't forget precedence rules when you write statements that contain multiple arithmetic operations. For example, `score1 + score2 / 2` does not compute the average of two scores. Instead, it adds half of `score2` to `score1`. To compute the average, you would write `(score1 + score2) / 2`.

» Don't forget that integer division results in an integer, dropping any fractional part. For example, 1 / 2 is not equal to 0.5; it is equal to 0.

» Don't attempt to assign a constant decimal value to an integer using a leading 0. For example, if you declare `int num = 021;` and then display `num`, you will see 17. The leading 0 indicates that the value is in base 8 (octal), so its value is two 8s plus one 1. In the decimal system, 21 and 021 mean the same thing, but not in Java.

» Don't use a single equal sign (=) in a Boolean comparison for equality. The operator used for equivalency is composed of two equal signs (==).

» Don't try to store a string of characters, such as a name, in a `char` variable. A `char` variable can hold only a single character.

» Don't forget that when a `String` and a numeric value are concatenated, the resulting expression is a string. For example, `"X" + 2 + 4` results in `"X24"`, *not* `"X6"`. If you want the result to be `"X6"`, you can use the expression `"X" + (2 + 4)`.

» Don't forget to consume the Enter key after numeric input using the `Scanner` class when a `nextLine()` method call follows.

» Don't forget to use the appropriate `import` statement when using the `Scanner` or `JOptionPane` class.

KEY TERMS

A data item is **constant** when it cannot be changed during the execution of an application.

A **literal constant** is a value that is taken literally at each use.

A **variable** is a named memory location that you can use to store a value.

An item's **data type** describes the type of data that can be stored there, how much memory the item occupies, and what types of operations can be performed on the data.

A **numeric constant** is a number whose value is taken literally at each use.

A **primitive type** is a simple data type. Java's primitive types are `byte`, `short`, `int`, `long`, `float`, `double`, `char`, and `boolean`.

Reference types are complex data types that are constructed from primitive types.

A **variable declaration** is a statement that reserves a named memory location.

A **strongly typed language** is one in which all variables must be declared before they can be used.

Camel casing is a style in which an identifier begins with a lowercase letter and subsequent words within the identifier are capitalized.

The **assignment operator** is the equal sign (=); any value to the right of the equal sign is assigned to the variable on the left of the equal sign.

An **initialization** is an assignment made when you declare a variable.

An **assignment** is the act of providing a value for a variable.

Associativity refers to the order in which operands are used with operators.

An **lvalue** is an expression that can appear on the left side of an assignment statement.

An **rvalue** is an expression that can appear only on the right side of an assignment statement.

A **garbage value** is the unknown value stored in an uninitialized variable.

A **named constant** is a memory location whose declaration is preceded by the keyword `final`, and whose value cannot change during program execution.

The keyword **final** precedes named constants.

A **symbolic constant** is a named constant.

A **blank final** is a `final` variable that has not yet been assigned a value.

A **magic number** is a value that does not have immediate, intuitive meaning or a number that cannot be explained without additional knowledge. Unnamed constants are magic numbers.

The data type **int** is used to store integers.

An **integer** is a whole number without decimal places.

The **byte** data type holds very small integers, from –128 to 127.

The **short** data type holds small integers, from –32,768 to 32,767.

The **long** data type holds very large integers, from –9,223,372,036,854,775,808 to 9,223,372,036,854,775,807.

A value can be combined with, or **concatenated** to, another value.

An empty `String` created by typing a set of quotes with nothing between them is called a **null String**.

You use **arithmetic operators** to perform calculations with values in your applications.

An **operand** is a value used in an arithmetic statement.

Binary operators require two operands.

Integer division is the operation in which one integer value is divided by another; the result contains no fractional part.

The **remainder operator** is the percent sign; when it is used with two integers, the result is an integer with the value of the remainder after division takes place.

The remainder operator is also called the **modulus operator**, or sometimes just **mod**.

Operator precedence is the rules for the order in which parts of a mathematical expression are evaluated.

A **Boolean variable** can hold only one of two values—`true` or `false`.

A **relational operator** compares two items; an expression that contains a relational operator has a Boolean value.

A **comparison operator** is another name for a relational operator.

A **floating-point** number contains decimal positions.

A **float** data type can hold a floating-point value of up to six or seven significant digits of accuracy.

A **double** data type can hold a floating-point value of up to 14 or 15 significant digits of accuracy.

The term **significant digits** refers to the mathematical accuracy of a value.

Scientific notation is a display format that more conveniently expresses large or small numeric values; a multidigit number is converted to a single-digit number and multiplied by 10 to a power.

A **double-precision floating-point number** is stored in a double.

A **single-precision floating-point number** is stored in a float.

A **unifying type** is a single data type to which all operands in an expression are converted.

An **implicit conversion** is the automatic transformation of one data type to another.

Promotion is an implicit conversion.

Type casting forces a value of one data type to be used as a value of another type.

A **cast operator** performs an explicit-type conversion; it is created by placing the desired result type in parentheses before the expression to be converted.

An **explicit conversion** is the data-type transformation caused using a cast operator.

The **unary cast operator** is a more complete name for the cast operator that performs explicit conversions.

A **unary operator** uses only one operand.

The **char** data type is used to hold any single character.

String is a built-in Java class that provides you with the means for storing and manipulating character strings.

An **escape sequence** begins with a backslash followed by a character; the pair represents a single character.

The **standard input device** normally is the keyboard.

A **token** is a unit of data; the Scanner class separates input into tokens.

A **prompt** is a message that requests and describes user input.

Echoing the input means to repeat the user's entry as output so the user can visually confirm the entry's accuracy.

The **keyboard buffer** is a small area of memory where keystrokes are stored before they are retrieved into a program.

The **type-ahead buffer** is the keyboard buffer.

To **consume** an entry is to retrieve and discard it without using it.

An **input dialog box** asks a question and provides a text field in which the user can enter a response.

You can create an input dialog box using the **showInputDialog() method**.

Type-wrapper classes, contained in the `java.lang` package, include methods that can process primitive-type values.

To **parse** means to break into component parts.

A **confirm dialog box** displays the options Yes, No, and Cancel; you can create one using the **showConfirmDialog() method** in the `JOptionPane` class.

CHAPTER SUMMARY

» Data is constant when it cannot be changed after a class is compiled; data is variable when it might change. Variables are named memory locations in which programs store values. You must declare all variables you want to use in a program by providing a data type and a name. Java provides for eight primitive types of data: `boolean`, `byte`, `char`, `double`, `float`, `int`, `long`, and `short`.

» A named constant is a memory location that holds a value that can never be changed; it is preceded by the keyword `final`.

» A variable of type `int` can hold any whole number value from –2,147,483,648 to +2,147,483,647. The types `byte`, `short`, and `long` are all variations of the integer type.

» You can display variable or constant values using `System.out.print()` and `println()` statements as well as by using dialog boxes.

» There are five standard arithmetic operators for integers: +, –, *, /, and %.

» Operator precedence is the order in which parts of a mathematical expression are evaluated. Multiplication, division, and remainder always take place prior to addition or subtraction in an expression. Right and left parentheses can be added within an expression when exceptions to this rule are required. When multiple pairs of parentheses are added, the innermost expression surrounded by parentheses is evaluated first.

» A `boolean`-type variable can hold a `true` or `false` value. Java supports six relational operators: >, <, ==, >=, <=, and !=.

» A floating-point number contains decimal positions. Java supports two floating-point data types: `float` and `double`.

» When you perform mathematical operations on unlike types, Java implicitly converts the variables to a unifying type. You can explicitly override the unifying type imposed by Java by performing a type cast.

» You use the `char` data type to hold any single character. You type constant character values in single quotation marks. You type `String` constants that store more than one character between double quotation marks. You can store some characters using an escape sequence, which always begins with a backslash.

» You can use the `Scanner` class and the `System.in` object to accept user input from the keyboard. Several methods are available to convert input to usable data, including `nextDouble()`, `nextInt()`, and `nextLine()`.

» You can accept input using the `JOptionPane` class. The `showInputDialog()` method returns a `String`, which must be converted to a number using a type-wrapper class before you can use it as a numeric value.

REVIEW QUESTIONS

1. When data cannot be changed after a class is compiled, the data is _____ .

   a. constant

   b. variable

   c. volatile

   d. mutable

2. Which of the following is not a primitive data type in Java?

   a. `boolean`

   b. `byte`

   c. `int`

   d. `sector`

3. Which of the following elements is not required in a variable declaration?

   a. a type

   b. an identifier

   c. an assigned value

   d. a semicolon

4. The assignment operator in Java is _____ .

   a. `=`

   b. `==`

   c. `:=`

   d. `::`

5. Assuming you have declared `shoeSize` to be a variable of type `int`, which of the following is a valid assignment statement in Java?

   a. `shoeSize = 9;`

   b. `shoeSize = 9.5;`

   c. `shoeSize = '9';`

   d. `shoeSize = "nine";`

6. Which of the following data types can store a value in the least amount of memory?

   a. `short`

   b. `long`

   c. `int`

   d. `byte`

7. The remainder operator _____ .

   a. is represented by a forward slash

   b. provides the remainder of integer division

   c. provides the quotient of integer division

   d. Answers b and c are correct.

8. According to the rules of operator precedence, when division occurs in the same arithmetic statement as _____, the division operation always takes place first.

    a. multiplication   c. subtraction

    b. remainder   d. Answers a and b are correct.

9. A Boolean variable can hold _____ .

    a. any character   c. any decimal number

    b. any whole number   d. the value `true` or `false`

10. The "equal to" relational operator is _____ .

    a. =   c. !=

    b. ==   d. !!

11. The value 137.68 can be held by a variable of type _____ .

    a. `int`   c. `double`

    b. `float`   d. Two of the preceding answers are correct.

12. When you perform arithmetic with values of diverse types, Java _____ .

    a. issues an error message

    b. implicitly converts the values to a unifying type

    c. requires you to explicitly convert the values to a unifying type

    d. requires you to perform a cast

13. If you attempt to add a `float`, an `int`, and a `byte`, the result will be a(n) _____ .

    a. `float`   c. `byte`

    b. `int`   d. error message

14. You use a _____ to explicitly override an implicit type.

    a. mistake   c. format

    b. type cast   d. type set

15. In Java, what is the value of 3 + 7 * 4 + 2?

    a. 21   c. 42

    b. 33   d. 48

16. Which assignment is correct in Java?

    a. `int value = (float) 4.5;`   c. `double value = 2.12;`

    b. `float value = 4 (double);`   d. `char value = 5c;`

17. Which assignment is correct in Java?

    a. `double money = 12;`   c. `double money = 12.0d;`

    b. `double money = 12.0;`   d. all of the above

18. Which assignment is correct in Java?

    a. `char aChar = 5;`   c. `char aChar = '*';`

    b. `char aChar = "W";`   d. Two of the preceding answers are correct.

19. An escape sequence always begins with a(n) _____ .

    a. e   c. backslash

    b. forward slash   d. equal sign

20. Which Java statement produces the following output?

    w

    xyz

    a. `System.out.println("wxyz");`

    b. `System.out.println("w" + "xyz");`

    c. `System.out.println("w\nxyz");`

    d. `System.out.println("w\nx\ny\nz");`

EXERCISES

1. What is the numeric value of each of the following expressions as evaluated by Java?

    a. 4 + 6 * 3   g. 16 % 2

    b. 6 / 3 * 7   h. 17 % 2

    c. 18 / 2 + 14 / 2   i. 28 % 5

    d. 16 / 2   j. 28 % 5 * 3 + 1

    e. 17 / 2   k. (2 + 3) * 4

    f. 28 / 5   l. 20 / (4 + 1)

2. What is the value of each of the following Boolean expressions?

a. 4 > 1

b. 5 <= 18

c. 43 >= 43

d. 2 == 3

e. 2 + 5 == 7

f. 3 + 8 <= 10

g. 3 != 9

h. 13 != 13

i. -4 != 4

j. 2 + 5 * 3 == 21

3. Choose the best data type for each of the following so that no memory storage is wasted. Give an example of a typical value that would be held by the variable and explain why you chose the type you did.

a. your age

b. the U.S. national debt

c. your shoe size

d. your middle initial

4. a. Write a Java class that declares variables to represent the length and width of a room in feet. Assign appropriate values to the variables—for example, `length` = 15 and `width` = 25. Compute and display the floor space of the room in square feet (area = length * width). Display explanatory text with the value—for example, `The floor space is 375 square feet`. Save the class as **Room.java**.

   b. Convert the `Room` class to an interactive application. Instead of assigning values to the length and width variables, accept them from the user as input. As output, echo the user's entries as well as displaying the floor space. Save the revised class as **Room2.java**.

5. a. Write a Java class that declares variables to represent the length and width of a room in feet and the price of carpeting per square foot in dollars and cents. Assign appropriate values to the variables. Compute and display, with explanatory text, the cost of carpeting the room. Save the class as **Carpet.java**.

   b. Convert the `Carpet` class to an interactive application. Instead of assigning values to the length, width, and price variables, accept them from the user as input. Save the revised class as **Carpet2.java**.

6. a. Write a class that declares a variable named `minutes`, which holds minutes worked on a job, and assign a value. Display the value in hours and minutes; for example, 197 minutes becomes 3 hours and 17 minutes. Be sure to use a named constant where appropriate. Save the class as **Time.java**.

   b. Write an interactive version of the `Time` class that accepts the minutes worked from a user. Save the class as **Time2.java**.

7. Write a class that declares variables to hold your three initials. Display the three initials with a period following each one, as in J.M.F. Save the class as **Initials.java**.

8. Write a class that prompts a student for the number of credit hours in which the student is enrolled, and the amount of money spent on books. Display, with a full explanation, the student's total fees. The total is $85 per credit hour, plus the amount for books, plus a $65 athletic fee. Save the class as **Fees.java**.

9. Write a class that accepts a user's hourly rate of pay and the number of hours worked. Display the user's gross pay, the withholding tax (15% of gross pay), and the net pay (gross pay – withholding). Save the class as **Payroll.java**.

10. Write a class that calculates and displays the conversion of an entered number of dollars into currency denominations—20s, 10s, 5s, and 1s. Save the class as **Dollars.java**.

11. Write a program that accepts a temperature in Fahrenheit from a user and converts it to Celsius by subtracting 32 from the Fahrenheit value and multiplying the result by 5/9. Display both values. Save the class as **FahrenheitToCelsius.java**.

12. Travel Tickets Company sells tickets for airlines, tours, and other travel-related services. Because ticket agents frequently mistype long ticket numbers, Travel Tickets has asked you to write an application that indicates invalid ticket number entries. The class prompts a ticket agent to enter a six-digit ticket number. Ticket numbers are designed so that if you drop the last digit of the number, then divide the number by 7, the remainder of the division will be identical to the last dropped digit. This process is illustrated in the following example:

Step 1	Enter the ticket number; for example, 123454.
Step 2	Remove the last digit, leaving 12345.
Step 3	Determine the remainder when the ticket number is divided by 7. In this case, 12345 divided by 7 leaves a remainder of 4.
Step 4	Assign the Boolean value of the comparison between the remainder and the digit dropped from the ticket number.
Step 5	Display the result—`true` or `false`—in a message box.

Accept the ticket number from the agent and verify whether it is a valid number. Test the application with the following ticket numbers:

» 123454; the comparison should evaluate to `true`

» 147103; the comparison should evaluate to `true`

» 154123; the comparison should evaluate to `false`

Save the program as **TicketNumber.java**.

>> NOTE
When you change a filename, remember to change every instance of the class name within the file so that it matches the new filename. In Java, the filename and class name must always match.

DEBUGGING EXERCISES

Each of the following files in the Chapter.02 folder on your Student Disk has syntax and/or logic errors. In each case, determine the problem and fix the application. After you correct the errors, save each file using the same filename preceded with Fix. For example, DebugTwo1.java will become FixDebugTwo1.java.

a. DebugTwo1.java   c. DebugTwo3.java

b. DebugTwo2.java   d. DebugTwo4.java

GAME ZONE

Mad Libs® is a children's game in which they provide a few words that are then incorporated into a silly story. The game helps children understand different parts of speech because they are asked to provide specific types of words. For example, you might ask a child for a noun, another noun, an adjective, and a past-tense verb. The child might reply with such answers as "table," "book," "silly," and "studied." The newly created Mad Lib might be:

Mary had a little *table*

Its *book* was *silly* as snow

And everywhere that Mary *studied*

The *table* was sure to go.

Create a Mad Lib program that asks the user to provide at least four or five words, and then create and display a short story or nursery rhyme that uses them. Save the file as **MadLib.java**.

TOUGH QUESTIONS

1. In a single sentence, describe the relationship between *associativity* and *precedence*.

2. Write Java statements that would round a numeric value to the nearest whole number. You cannot use a prewritten `round()` method.

3. Suppose you need to display the last digit of a four-digit number. You can use the remainder operator (%) to extract the remainder when the number is divided by 10. Suppose the "%" key is broken on your computer, but the program must be written immediately. What would you do?

4. Write a series of Java statements that interchange the values of two numeric variables without using a third variable.

5. In many programming languages, a named constant must be assigned a value when it is declared. This isn't true in Java. Provide some examples of how this restriction might be advantageous.

UP FOR DISCUSSION

1. What advantages are there to requiring variables to have a data type?

2. Some programmers use a system called Hungarian notation when naming their variables. What is Hungarian notation, and why do many object-oriented programmers feel it is not a valuable style to use? What do you think?

3. Some languages do not require explicit type casting when you want to perform an unlike assignment, such as assigning a `double` to an `int`. Instead, the type casting is performed automatically, the fractional part of the `double` is lost, and the whole number portion is simply stored in the `int` result. Are there any reasons this approach is superior or inferior to the way Java works? Which do you prefer?

4. Did you have a favorite computer game when you were growing up? Do you have one now? How are they similar and how are they different? Did you have a favorite board game? What does it have in common with your favorite computer game?

3

USING METHODS, CLASSES, AND OBJECTS

In this chapter, you will:

Create methods with no parameters, a single parameter, and multiple parameters

Create methods that return values

Learn about class concepts

Create a class

Create instance methods in a class

Declare objects and use their methods

Organize classes

Begin to understand how to use constructors

Understand that classes are data types

JAVA ON THE JOB, SCENE 3

"How do you feel about programming so far?" asks your new mentor, Lynn Greenbrier, who is head of computer programming for Event Handlers Incorporated.

"It's fun," you reply. "It's great to see programs actually work, but I still don't understand what the other programmers are talking about when they mention 'object-oriented programming.' I *think* everything is an object, and objects have methods, but I'm not really clear on this whole thing at all."

"Well then," Lynn says, "let me explain methods, classes, and objects."

CREATING METHODS WITH ZERO, ONE, AND MULTIPLE PARAMETERS

A **method** is a program module that contains a series of statements that carry out a task. To execute a method, you **invoke** or **call** it from another method; the **calling method** makes a **method call**, which invokes the **called method**. Any class can contain an unlimited number of methods, and each method can be called an unlimited number of times.

> **»NOTE**
> The statements within a method execute only if and when the method is called. Devices you own might contain features you never use. For example, you might use a DVR to play movies, but never to record TV programs, or you might never use the "defrost" option on your microwave oven. Similarly, a class might contain any number of methods that are never called from a particular application.

Some methods require that data be sent to them when they are called. Data items you use in a call to a method are called **arguments**. When the method receives them, they are called **parameters**. The simplest methods you can invoke don't require any data items to be sent to them from the calling method, nor do they send any data back to the calling method (called **returning a value**). Consider the simple First class that you saw in Chapter 1, shown in Figure 3-1.

```
public class First
{
    public static void main(String[] args)
    {
        System.out.println("First Java application");
    }
}
```

Figure 3-1 The First class

> **»NOTE**
> Although there are differences, if you have used other programming languages, you can think of methods as being similar to procedures, functions, or subroutines.

Suppose you want to add three lines of output to this application to display your company's name and address. You can simply add three new println() statements, but instead you might choose to create a separate method to display the three new lines.

There are two major reasons to create a separate method to display the three address lines. First, the main() method remains short and easy to follow because main() contains just one statement to call the method, rather than three separate println() statements to perform the work of the method. What is more important is that a method is easily reusable. After you create the name and address method, you can use it in any application that needs the company's name and address. In other words, you do the work once, and then you can use the method many times.

A method must include the following:

» A declaration (or header or definition)
» An opening curly brace
» A body
» A closing curly brace

»NOTE Using a method name to contain or encapsulate a series of statements is an example of the feature that programmers call **abstraction**. Consider abstract art, in which the artist tries to capture the essence of an object without focusing on the details. Similarly, when programmers employ abstraction, they use a general method name in a module rather than list all the detailed activities that will be carried out by the method.

The **method declaration** is the first line, or **header**, of a method. It contains the following:

» Optional access modifiers
» The return type for the method
» The method name
» An opening parenthesis
» An optional list of method parameters (you separate multiple parameters with commas)
» A closing parenthesis

The access modifier for a Java method can be any of the following modifiers: `public`, `private`, `protected`, or, if left unspecified, `package`. Most often, methods are given `public` access. Endowing a method with `public` access means that any class can use it. In addition, like `main()`, any method that can be used without instantiating an object requires the keyword modifier `static`.

»NOTE Classes can contain instance methods and class methods. Instance methods operate on an object, and do not use the `static` keyword. Class methods do not need an object instance in order to be used. These methods use the `static` keyword. You will learn about these concepts when you create objects later in this chapter.

You can write the `nameAndAddress()` method shown in Figure 3-2. According to its declaration, the method is `public` and `static`, meaning any class can use it and no objects need to be created. Like the `main()` method you have been using in your Java applications, the `nameAndAddress()` method returns nothing, so its return type is `void`. The method receives nothing, so its parentheses are empty. Its body, consisting of three `println()` statements, appears within curly braces.

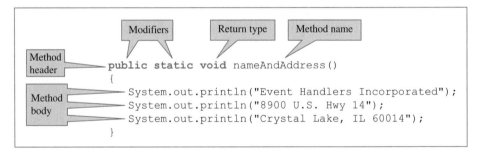

Figure 3-2 The `nameAndAddress()` method

>> **NOTE** Some methods you have used contain parameters within their parentheses. For example, when you write a `main()` method in a class, the parentheses in its header surround a parameter (`String[] args`), and when you use the `println()` method, its parentheses usually contain text information you want to print. That information becomes a parameter to the `println()` method. Unlike those two methods, the `nameAndAddress()` method header shown here does not contain any parameters within its parentheses. You will write methods that accept parameters later in this chapter.

>> **NOTE**
The order in which you place methods' bodies in a class has no bearing on the order in which the methods are called. Any method in a file might call any of the other methods in any order and any number of times. The order in which you call methods does make a difference in how an application executes.

You can place a method within the class that will use it, but it must be outside of any other methods. In other words, you cannot place a method within another method. Figure 3-3 shows the two locations where you can place additional methods within the `First` class—within the curly braces of the class, but outside of (either before or after) any other methods.

>> **NOTE** Methods can never overlap. That is, no method can be placed within another method, and no method can start before another method has ended. Method calls lie within other methods, but the called method (header and body) is always placed outside the calling method. A called method is placed before the header or after the closing brace of the calling method, or in a totally different class.

>> **NOTE**
The `main()` method executes first in an application, no matter where you physically place the `main()` method within its class. Remember that every application must contain a `main()` method, but each Java class is not required to contain one.

```
public class First
{
   // You can place additional methods here, before main()
   public static void main(String[] args)
   {
      System.out.println("First Java application");
   }
   // You can place additional methods here, after main()
}
```

Figure 3-3 Placement of methods within a class

If you want the `main()` method in the `First` class to call the `nameAndAddress()` method, you simply use the `nameAndAddress()` method's name as a statement within the body of `main()`. Figure 3-4 shows the complete application. In this application, `main()` performs two actions. First, it calls the `nameAndAddress()` method, and then it prints "First Java application".

```
public class First
{
   public static void main(String[] args)
   {
      nameAndAddress();
      System.out.println("First Java application");
   }
   public static void nameAndAddress()
   {
      System.out.println("Event Handlers Incorporated");
      System.out.println("8900 U.S. Hwy 14");
      System.out.println("Crystal Lake, IL 60014");
   }
}
```

Figure 3-4 First class with main() calling nameAndAddress()

Figure 3-5 shows the output from the execution of the application shown in Figure 3-4. Because the main() method calls the nameAndAddress() method before it prints the phrase "First Java application", the name and address appear first in the output.

Figure 3-5 Output of the First application, including the nameAndAddress() method

The full name of the nameAndAddress() method is First.nameAndAddress();. The full name includes the class name, a dot, and the method name. When you use the nameAndAddress() method within its own class, you do not need to use the full name (although you can); the method name alone is enough. However, if you want to use the nameAndAddress() method in another class, the compiler does not recognize the method unless you use the full name, writing it as First.nameAndAddress();. This format notifies the new class that the method is located in the First class. You have used similar syntax (including a class name, dot, and method name) when calling the JOptionPane.showMessageDialog() method.

>> **NOTE** First.nameAndAddress() includes only a class name and a method name (separated by a dot) because nameAndAddress() is a static method—one that is used with the class name, without an object. Using System.out.println() includes a class name, an object name, and a method name (using a dot to separate each) because println() is not a static method, but is an instance method. You will learn more about instance methods later in this chapter.

>> **NOTE** Think of the class name as the family name. Within your own family, you might refer to an activity as "the family reunion," but outside the family people need to use a surname as well, as in "the Anderson family reunion." Similarly, within a class a method name alone is sufficient, but outside the class you need to use the fully qualified name.

>> **NOTE** Each of two different classes can have its own method named nameAndAddress(). Such a method in the second class would be entirely distinct from the identically named method in the first class. Two classes in an application cannot have the same name.

CREATING METHODS THAT REQUIRE A SINGLE PARAMETER

»NOTE
At any call, the
println() method
can receive any
one of an infinite
number of argu-
ments—"Hello",
"Goodbye", or any
other String.
No matter what
message is sent
to println(), the
message is dis-
played correctly.
If the println()
method could not
accept arguments,
it would not be
practical
to use it within
applications.

Some methods require information to be sent in from the outside. If a method could not receive your communications, you would have to write an infinite number of methods to cover every possible situation. (Remember that these communications are called *arguments* when you send them and *parameters* when the method receives them.) As a real-life example, when you make a restaurant reservation, you do not need to employ a different method for every date of the year at every possible time of day. Rather, you can supply the date and time as information to the person who carries out the method. The method, recording the reserva-tion, is then carried out in the same manner, no matter what date and time are supplied. In a program, if you design a method to square numeric values, it makes sense to design a square() method that you can supply with an argument that represents the value to be squared, rather than having to develop a square1() method (that squares the value 1), a square2() method (that squares the value 2), and so on. To call a square() method, you might write a statement like square(17); or square(86);.

»NOTE
Hidden implemen-
tation methods are
often referred to as
existing in a **black
box**. Many every-
day devices are
black boxes—that
is, you can use
them without under-
standing how they
work. For example,
most of us use tele-
phones, television
sets, and automo-
biles without under-
standing much
about their internal
mechanisms.

An important principle of object-oriented programming is the notion of **implementation hiding**, the encapsulation of method details within a class. That is, when you make a request to a method, you don't know the details of how the method is executed. For example, when you make a real-life restaurant reservation, you do not need to know how the reservation is actually recorded at the restaurant—perhaps it is written in a book, marked on a large chalk-board, or entered into a computerized database. The implementation details don't concern you as a client, and if the restaurant changes its methods from one year to the next, the change does not affect your use of the reservation method—you still call and provide your name, a date, and a time. With well-written object-oriented programming methods, using implementation hiding means that a method that calls another must know the name of the called method, what type of information to send, and what type of return data to expect, but the program does not need to know how the method works internally. In other words, the calling method needs to understand only the **interface** to the called method. The interface is the only part of a method that the method's client sees or with which it interacts. In addition, if you substitute a new or revised method implementation, as long as the interface to the method does not change, you won't need to make any changes in any methods that call the altered method.

> **»NOTE** As an example of how professional programmers use implementation hiding, you can visit the Java Web site at *http://java.sun.com* to see the interfaces for thousands of prewritten methods that reside in the Java prewritten classes. You are not allowed to see the code inside these methods; you only see their interfaces, which is all you need to be able to use them.

When you write the method declaration for a method that can receive a parameter, you begin by defining the same elements as with methods that do not accept parameters—optional access modifiers, the return type for the method, and the method name. In addition, you must include the following items within the method declaration parentheses:

» The parameter type
» A local name for the parameter

For example, the declaration for a public method named `predictRaise()` that displays a person's salary plus a 10% raise could be written as follows:

```
public static void predictRaise(double moneyAmount)
```

You can think of the parentheses in a method declaration as a funnel into the method—parameters listed there contain data that is "dropped into" the method. A parameter accepted by a method can be any data type, including the primitive types, such as `int`, `double`, `char`, and so on; it also can be a class type.

>> **NOTE** In addition to accepting parameters that are primitive types, a method can accept a class type. If a class named `Customer` exists, a method might accept an instance of `Customer` as a parameter, as in `public void approveCredit(Customer oneCustomer)`. In other words, a method can accept anything from a simple `int` to a complicated `Customer` that contains 20 data fields. You will learn more about class types later in this chapter.

The parameter `double moneyAmount` within the parentheses indicates that the `predictRaise()` method will receive a value of type `double`, and that within the method, the passed value representing a salary will be known as `moneyAmount`. Figure 3-6 shows a complete method.

```
public static void predictRaise(double moneyAmount)
{
    double newAmount;
    final double RAISE = 1.10;
    newAmount = moneyAmount * RAISE;
    System.out.println("With raise, salary is " + newAmount);
}
```
Parameter type
Parameter identifier that is local to the method

Figure 3-6 The `predictRaise()` method

The `predictRaise()` method is a `void` method because it does not need to return any value to any other method that uses it—its only function is to receive the `moneyAmount` value, multiply it by the `RAISE` constant (1.10, which results in a 10% salary increase), and then display the result.

>> **NOTE** The phrases "void method" and "method of type void" mean the same thing. Both phrases refer to a method that has a return type of `void`.

Within a program, you can call the `predictRaise()` method by using either a constant value or a variable as an argument. Thus, both `predictRaise(472.25);` and `predictRaise(mySalary);` invoke the `predictRaise()` method correctly, assuming that `mySalary` is declared as a `double` variable and is assigned an appropriate value in the calling method. You can call the `predictRaise()` method any number of times, with a different constant or variable argument each time. Each of these arguments becomes known as `moneyAmount` within the method. The identifier `moneyAmount` represents a variable that holds any `double` value passed into the `predictRaise()` method; `moneyAmount` holds a copy of the value passed to it.

It is interesting to note that if the value used as an argument in the method call to `predictRaise()` is a variable, it might possess the same identifier as `moneyAmount` or a different one, such as mySalary. For example, the code in Figure 3-7 shows three calls to the predictRaise() method, and Figure 3-8 shows the output. One call uses a constant, 400.00. The other two use variables—one with the same name as moneyAmount and the other with a different name, mySalary. The identifier moneyAmount is simply a placeholder while it is being used within the predictRaise() method, no matter what name it "goes by" in the calling method. The parameter moneyAmount is a **local variable** to the predictRaise() method; that is, it is known only within the boundaries of the method.

```
public class DemoRaise
{
   public static void main(String[] args)
   {
      double mySalary = 200.00;
      double moneyAmount = 800.00;
      System.out.println("Demonstrating some raises");
      predictRaise(400.00);
      predictRaise(mySalary);
      predictRaise(moneyAmount);
   }
   public static void predictRaise(double moneyAmount)
   {
      double newAmount;
      final double RAISE = 1.10;
      newAmount = moneyAmount * RAISE;
      System.out.println("With raise, salary is " + newAmount);
   }
}
```

Figure 3-7 The DemoRaise class with a main() method that uses the predictRaise() method three times

>>**NOTE** Recall that the final modifier makes RAISE constant. Because moneyAmount is not altered within the predictRaise() method in Figure 3-7, you could also make it constant by declaring the method header as public static void predictRaise(final double moneyAmount). There would be no difference in the program's execution, but declaring a parameter as final means it cannot be altered within the method. Someone reading your program would be able to see that the parameter is not intended to change.

>>**NOTE**
Notice the output in Figure 3-8. Floating-point arithmetic is always imprecise. If you do not like the appearance of the numbers in this output, you can use the techniques described in Appendix C to format your output to a specific number of decimal places.

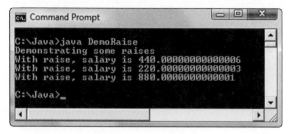

Figure 3-8 Output of the DemoRaise application

Within the `predictRaise()` method in Figure 3-7, if you later decide to change the way in which the 10% raise is calculated—for example, by changing the value of RAISE to 0.10 and coding the following—no method that uses the `predictRaise()` method will ever know the difference:

```
newAmount = moneyAmount + (moneyAmount * RAISE);
```

The calling method passes a value for moneyAmount into `predictRaise()` and then a correct calculated result appears on the screen.

Each time the `predictRaise()` method in Figure 3-7 executes, a moneyAmount variable is redeclared—that is, a new memory location large enough to hold a double is set up and named moneyAmount. Within the `predictRaise()` method, moneyAmount holds a copy of whatever value is passed into the method by the `main()` method. When the `predictRaise()` method ends, at the closing curly brace, the local moneyAmount variable ceases to exist. After the raise is calculated in the method, if you placed a statement such as the following within `predictRaise()`, it would make no difference:

```
moneyAmount = 100000;
```

That is, if you change the value of moneyAmount after you have used it in the calculation within `predictRaise()`, it affects nothing else. The memory location that holds moneyAmount is released at the end of the method, and if you change its value within the method, it does not affect any value in the calling method. In particular, there wouldn't be any change in the variable named moneyAmount in the `main()` method; that variable, even though it has the same name as the locally declared parameter in the method, is a different variable with its own memory address, and is totally different from the one in the `predictRaise()` method.

CREATING METHODS THAT REQUIRE MULTIPLE PARAMETERS

A method can require more than one parameter. You can pass multiple arguments to a method by listing the arguments within the call to the method and separating them with commas. For example, rather than creating a `predictRaise()` method that adds a 10% raise to every person's salary, you might prefer to create a method to which you can pass two values—the salary to be raised as well as a percentage figure by which to raise it. Figure 3-9 shows a method that uses two such parameters.

```
public static void predictRaiseUsingRate(double money, double rate)
{
    double newAmount;
    newAmount = money * (1 + rate);
    System.out.println("With raise, new salary is " + newAmount);
}
```

Figure 3-9 The `predictRaiseUsingRate()` method that accepts two parameters

> **NOTE**
> If you pass a named constant to a method and the accepting parameter is not defined as final, then the parameter within the method is not constant. Conversely, if you pass a variable to a method that declares the accepting parameter to be final, then the value in the method is a constant.

> **NOTE**
> When a variable ceases to exist at the end of a method, programmers say the variable "goes out of scope."

> **NOTE**
> Note that a declaration for a method that receives two or more parameters must list the type for each parameter separately, even if the parameters have the same type.

»NOTE
If two method parameters are the same type—for example, two doubles—passing arguments to a method in the wrong order results in a logical error; that is, the program does compile and execute, but it probably produces incorrect results. If a method expects parameters of diverse types, passing arguments in the wrong order constitutes a syntax error, and the program does not compile.

In Figure 3-9, two parameters (double money and double rate) appear within the parentheses in the method header. A comma separates each parameter, and each parameter requires its own declared type (in this case, both are double) as well as its own identifier. When values are passed to the method in a statement such as predictRaiseUsingRate(mySalary, promisedRate);, the first value passed is referenced as money within the method, and the second value passed is referenced as rate. Therefore, arguments passed to the method must be passed in the correct order. The call predictRaiseUsingRate(200.00, 0.10); results in output representing a 10% raise based on a $200.00 salary amount (or $220.00), but predictRaiseUsingRate(0.10, 200.00); results in output representing a 20,000% raise based on a salary of 10 cents (or $20.10).

You can write a method so that it takes any number of parameters in any order. However, when you call a method, the arguments you send to a method must match in order—both in number and in type—the parameters listed in the method declaration. A method's **signature** is the combination of the method name and the number, types, and order of arguments. A method call must match the called method's signature.

Thus, a method to compute an automobile salesperson's commission amount might require arguments such as an integer dollar value of a car sold, a double percentage commission rate, and a character code for the vehicle type. The correct method executes only when three arguments of the correct types are sent in the correct order. Figure 3-10 shows a class containing a three-parameter method and a main() method that calls it twice, once using variable arguments and again using constant arguments. Figure 3-11 shows the output of the application.

```java
public class ComputeCommission
{
    public static void main(String[] args)
    {
        char vType = 'S';
        int value = 23000;
        double commRate = 0.08;
        computeCommission(value, commRate, vType);
        computeCommission(40000, 0.10, 'L');
    }
    public static void computeCommission(int value,
        double rate, char vehicle)
    {
        double commission;
        commission = value * rate;
        System.out.println("\nThe " + vehicle +
            " type vehicle is worth $" + value);
        System.out.println("With " + (rate * 100) +
            "% commission rate, the commission is $" +
            commission);
    }
}
```

Figure 3-10 The ComputeCommission class

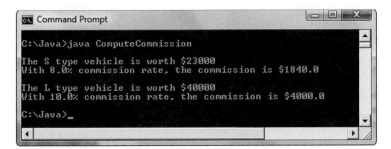

Figure 3-11 Output of the ComputeCommission application

» NOTE
The arguments in a method call are often referred to as **actual parameters**. The variables in the method declaration that accept the values from the actual parameters are **formal parameters**.

» **NOTE** When you look at Java applications, you might see methods that appear to be callable in multiple ways. For example, you can use System.out.println() with no arguments to print a blank line, or with a String argument to print the String. You can use the method with different argument lists only because multiple versions of the method have been written, each taking a specific set of arguments. The ability to execute different method implementations by altering the argument used with the method name is known as *method overloading*, a concept you will learn about in the next chapter.

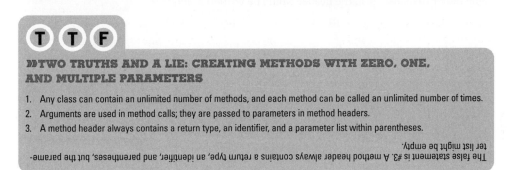

» **TWO TRUTHS AND A LIE: CREATING METHODS WITH ZERO, ONE, AND MULTIPLE PARAMETERS**

1. Any class can contain an unlimited number of methods, and each method can be called an unlimited number of times.
2. Arguments are used in method calls; they are passed to parameters in method headers.
3. A method header always contains a return type, an identifier, and a parameter list within parentheses.

The false statement is #3. A method header always contains a return type, an identifier, and parentheses, but the parameter list might be empty.

CREATING METHODS THAT RETURN VALUES

A method ends when any of the following events takes place:

» The method completes all of its statements. You have seen methods like this in the last section.

» The method throws an exception. You will learn about exceptions in Chapter 11.

» The method reaches a return statement. A **return statement** causes a method to end and the program's logic to return to the calling method. Also, a return statement frequently sends a value back to the calling method.

The return type for a method can be any type used in Java, which includes the primitive types int, double, char, and so on, as well as class types (including class types you create). Of course, a method can also return nothing, in which case the return type is void.

A method's return type is known more succinctly as a **method's type**. For example, the declaration for the `nameAndAddress()` method shown earlier in Figure 3-4 is written `public static void nameAndAddress()`. This method is `public` and it returns no value, so it is type `void`. A method that returns `true` or `false`, depending on whether an employee worked overtime hours, might be declared as:

```
public boolean workedOvertime()
```

This method returns a Boolean value, so it is type `boolean`.

> **▶▶NOTE** In addition to returning one of the primitive types, a method can return a class type. If your application contains a class named `BankLoan`, a method might return an instance of a `BankLoan`, as in `public BankLoan approvalProcess()`. In other words, a method can return anything from a simple `int` to a complicated `BankLoan` that is composed of 20 data fields. You will learn more about class types later in this chapter.

The `predictRaise()` method shown earlier produces output, but does not return any value, so its return type is `void`. If you want to create a method to return the new, calculated salary value rather than display it, the header would be written as follows:

```
public static double predictRaise(double moneyAmount)
```

Figure 3-12 shows this method.

```
public static double predictRaise(double moneyAmount)
{
    double newAmount;
    final double RAISE = 1.10;
    newAmount = moneyAmount * RAISE;
    return newAmount;
}
```

Figure 3-12 The `predictRaise()` method returning a `double`

> **▶▶NOTE**
> A method can return, at most, one value. The value can be a primitive data type, such as `int`, `char`, or `double`, or it can be a class type.

Notice the shaded return type `double` that precedes the method name in the `predictRaise()` method header in Figure 3-12. Also notice the shaded `return` statement that is the last statement within the method. The `return` statement causes a value to be sent from a called method back to the calling method. In this case, the value stored in `newAmount` is sent back to any method that calls the `predictRaise()` method. A method's declared return type must match the type of the value used in the `return` statement; if it does not, the class does not compile.

> **▶▶NOTE** All methods except `void` methods require a `return` statement that returns a value of the appropriate type. You can place a `return` statement in a `void` method that is simply the word `return` followed by a semicolon. However, most Java programmers do not include a `return` statement when nothing is returned from a method.

You cannot place any statements after a method's `return` statement. Such statements are **unreachable statements** because the logical flow leaves the method at the `return` statement. An unreachable statement can never execute, and it causes a compiler error.

NOTE
Unreachable statements are also called **dead code**.

If a method returns a value, then when you call the method, you normally use the returned value, although you are not required to do so. For example, when you invoke the `predictRaise()` method, you might want to assign the returned value (also called the method's value) to a `double` variable named `myNewSalary`, as in the following statement:

```
myNewSalary = predictRaise(mySalary);
```

The `predictRaise()` method returns a `double`, so it is appropriate to assign the method's returned value to a `double` variable.

NOTE
A method can contain multiple `return` clauses if they are embedded in a decision. However, no other statements can be placed after the last `return` clause. You will learn about decision making in Chapter 5.

Alternatively, you can choose to use a method's returned value directly, without storing it in any variable. When you use a method's value, you use it in the same way you would use any variable of the same type. For example, you can print a return value in a statement such as the following:

```
System.out.println("New salary is " + calculateRaise(mySalary));
```

In the preceding statement, the call to the `calculateRaise()` method is made from within the `println()` method call. Because `calculateRaise()` returns a `double`, you can use the method call `calculateRaise()` in the same way that you would use any simple `double` value. As another example, you can perform arithmetic with a method's return value, as in the following statement:

```
spendingMoney = calculateRaise(mySalary) - expenses;
```

CALLING A METHOD FROM ANOTHER METHOD

You can call a method from within another method. For example, you can call `println()` or `nextInt()` from a method. As another example, the `predictRaise()` method in Figure 3-12 can be called from a `main()` method. Similarly, the `predictRaise()` method could call other methods. For example, if a company's raise calculation was based on a complicated formula, you might want to store parts of the calculation in different methods that all were called from `predictRaise()`. After you have written the shaded method, the `predictRaise()` method might look like the version shown in Figure 3-13.

```
public static double predictRaise(double moneyAmount)
{
    double newAmount;
    double bonusAmount;
    final double RAISE = 1.10;
    newAmount = moneyAmount * RAISE;
    bonusAmount = calculateBonus(newAmount);
    newAmount = newAmount + bonusAmount;
    return newAmount;
}
```

Figure 3-13 The `predictRaise()` method calling other methods

In the version of the method in Figure 3-13, you can see a shaded call to a new method named `calculateBonus()`. From this method, you do not know how `calculateBonus()` works. Assuming a program that contains this method compiles without error, you only know that the `calculateBonus()` method accepts a `double` as a parameter (because `newAmount` is passed into it) and that it must return either a `double` or a type that can automatically be promoted to a `double` (because the result is stored in `bonusAmount`). In other words, the method acts as a black box.

»TWO TRUTHS AND A LIE: CREATING METHODS THAT RETURN VALUES

1. The return type for a method can be any type used in Java, including `int`, `double`, and `void`.
2. A method's declared return type must match the type of the value used in the parameter list.
3. You cannot place a method within another method, but you can call a method from within another method.

The false statement is #2. A method's declared return type must match the type of the value used in the `return` statement.

LEARNING ABOUT CLASS CONCEPTS

When you think in an object-oriented manner, everything is an object, and every object is a member of a class. You can think of any inanimate physical item as an object—your desk, your computer, and the building in which you live are all called objects in everyday conversation. You can also think of living things as objects—your houseplant, your pet fish, and your sister are objects. Events are also objects—the stock purchase you made, the mortgage closing you attended, and a graduation party that was held in your honor are all objects.

»NOTE
Programmers also use the phrase "is-a" when talking about inheritance relationships. You will learn more about inheritance in Chapters 9 and 10.

Everything is an object, and every object is a member of a more general class. Your desk is a member of the class that includes all desks, and your pet fish a member of the class that contains all fish. An object-oriented programmer would say that your desk is an instance of the `Desk` class and your fish is an instance of the `Fish` class. These statements represent **is-a relationships**—that is, relationships in which the object "is a" concrete example of the class. Expressing an is-a relationship is correct only when you refer to the object and the class in the proper order. You can say, "My oak desk with the scratch on top *is a* `Desk` and my goldfish named Moby *is a* `Fish`." You don't define a `Desk` by saying, "A `Desk` *is an* oak desk with a scratch on top," or explain what a `Fish` is by saying, "A `Fish` *is a* goldfish named Moby," because both a `Desk` and a `Fish` are much more general. The difference between a class and an object parallels the difference between abstract and concrete. An object is an **instantiation** of a class, or one tangible example of a class. Your goldfish, my guppy, and the zoo's shark each constitute one instantiation of the `Fish` class.

»NOTE
Everything is an object—even a class.

The concept of a class is useful because of its reusability. Objects gain their attributes from their classes, and all objects have predictable attributes because they are members of certain classes. For example, if you are invited to a graduation party, you automatically know many things about the object (the party). You assume there will be a starting time, a certain number of guests, some quantity of food, and some kind of gifts. You understand what a party entails because of your previous knowledge of the `Party` class of which all parties are members. You don't know the number of guests, what food will be served, or what gifts will be received at this particular party, but you understand that because all parties have guests and refreshments, this one must too. Because you understand the general characteristics of a `Party`, you anticipate different behaviors than if you plan to attend a `TheaterPerformance` object or a `DentalAppointment` object.

In addition to their attributes, objects have methods associated with them, and every object that is an instance of a class is assumed to possess the same methods. For example, for all `Party` objects, at some point you must set the date and time. In a program, you might name these methods `setDate()` and `setTime()`. Party guests need to know the date and time and might use methods named `getDate()` and `getTime()` to find out the date and time of any `Party` object.

Your graduation party, then, might have the identifier `myGraduationParty`. As a member of the `Party` class, `myGraduationParty`, like all `Party` objects, might have data methods `setDate()` and `setTime()`. When you use them, the `setDate()` and `setTime()` methods require arguments, or information passed to them. For example, statements such as `myGraduationParty.setDate("May 12")` and `myGraduationParty.setTime("6 P.M.")` invoke methods that are available for the `myGraduationParty` object. When you use an object and its methods, think of being able to send a message to the object to direct it to accomplish some task—you can tell the `Party` object named `myGraduationParty` to set the date and time you request. Even though `yourAnniversaryParty` is also a member of the `Party` class, and even though it also has access to `setDate()` and `setTime()` methods, the arguments you send to `yourAnniversaryParty` methods will be different from those you send to `myGraduationParty` methods. Within any object-oriented program, you are continuously making requests to objects' methods and often including arguments as part of those requests.

In addition, some methods used in an application must return a message or value. If one of your party guests uses the `getDate()` method, the guest hopes that the method will respond with the desired information. Similarly, within object-oriented programs, methods are often called upon to return a piece of information to the source of the request. For example, a method within a `Payroll` class that calculates the federal withholding tax might return a tax amount in dollars and cents, and a method within an `Inventory` class might return `true` or `false`, depending on the method's determination of whether an item is at the reorder point.

With object-oriented programming, sometimes you create classes so that you can instantiate objects from them, and other times you create classes to run as applications; the application classes frequently instantiate objects that use the objects of other classes (and their data and their methods). Sometimes you write classes that do both. The same programmer does not need to write every class he or she uses. Often, you will write programs that use classes created by others; similarly, you might create a class that others will use to instantiate objects within their own applications. You can call an application or class that instantiates objects of another prewritten class a **class client** or **class user**.

>> **NOTE** You can identify a class that is an application because it contains a `public static void main()` method. The `main()` method is the starting point for any application. You will write and use many classes that do not contain a `main()` method—these classes can be used by other classes that are applications or applets. (You will learn about applets in Chapter 16.)

>> **NOTE**
The data components of a class are often referred to as the **instance variables** of that class. Also, class data attributes are often called **fields** to help distinguish them from other variables you might use.

>> **NOTE**
Method names that begin with "get" and "set" are very typical. You will learn more about get and set methods in the next section.

>> **NOTE**
The `System` class that you have used to produce output in the Command Prompt window provides an example of using a class that was written by someone else. You did not have to create it or its object's `println()` method; both were created for you by Java's creators.

>> **NOTE**
A Java application can contain only one method with the header `public static void main(String[] args)`. If you write a class that imports another class, and both classes have a `main()` method, your application will not compile.

So far, you've learned that object-oriented programming involves objects that send messages to other objects requesting they perform tasks, and that every object belongs to a class. Understanding classes and how objects are instantiated from them is the heart of object-oriented thinking.

»TWO TRUTHS AND A LIE: LEARNING ABOUT CLASS CONCEPTS

1. A class is an instantiation of many objects.
2. Objects gain their attributes and methods from their classes.
3. An application or class that instantiates objects of another prewritten class is a class client.

The false statement is #1. An object is one instantiation of a class.

CREATING A CLASS

When you create a class, you must assign a name to the class, and you must determine what data and methods will be part of the class. Suppose you decide to create a class named `Employee`. One instance variable of `Employee` might be an employee number, and two necessary methods might be a method to set (or provide a value for) the employee number and another method to get (or retrieve) that employee number. To begin, you create a class header with three parts:

» An optional access modifier
» The keyword `class`
» Any legal identifier you choose for the name of your class

»NOTE
You will learn about extended classes in Chapter 9.

For example, a header for a class that represents an employee might be:

```
public class Employee
```

»NOTE
You can use the following class modifiers when defining a class: `public`, `final`, `abstract`, or `strictfp`. You will use the `public` modifier for most of your classes. You use the other modifiers only under special circumstances.

The keyword `public` is a class modifier. Classes that are `public` are accessible by all objects, which means that public classes can be **extended**, or used as a basis for any other class. The most liberal form of access is `public`. Making access `public` means that if you develop a good `Employee` class, and someday you want to develop two classes that are more specific, `SalariedEmployee` and `HourlyEmployee`, then you do not have to start from scratch. Each new class can become an extension of the original `Employee` class, inheriting its data and methods.

After writing the class header `public class Employee`, you write the body of the `Employee` class between a set of curly braces. The body contains the data fields and methods for the class. Figure 3-14 shows the shell for the `Employee` class.

```
public class Employee
{
// Data fields (instance variables) and methods go here
}
```

Figure 3-14 The `Employee` class shell

Data fields are variables you declare within a class, but outside of any method. When you eventually create, or instantiate, objects from a class, each will have its own copy of each non-static data field you declare. For example, to allow each `Employee` to have its own employee number, you can declare an employee number that will be stored as an integer simply by typing `int empNum;` within the curly braces of the `Employee` class (but not within any method). However, programmers frequently include an access modifier for each of the class fields, and so you would declare the `empNum` as follows:

```
private int empNum;
```

You have already learned that Java supports four distinct access levels for member variables and methods: `private`, `protected`, `public`, and, if left unspecified, `package`. Most fields are `private`, which provides the highest level of security. Assigning **private access** to a field means that no other classes can access the field's values, and only methods of the same class are allowed to set, get, or otherwise use private variables. The principle used in creating private access is sometimes called **information hiding** and is an important component of object-oriented programs. A class's private data can be changed or manipulated only by a class's own methods and not by methods that belong to other classes. In contrast to fields, most class methods are `public`, not `private`. The resulting private data/public method arrangement provides a means for you to control outside access to your data—only a class's nonprivate methods can be used to access a class's private data. The situation is similar to hiring a public receptionist to sit in front of your private office and control which messages you receive (perhaps deflecting trivial or hostile ones) and which messages you send (perhaps checking your spelling, grammar, and any legal implications). The way in which the nonprivate methods are written controls how you use the private data.

> **NOTE**
> To help you determine whether a data field should be `static` or not, you can ask yourself how many times it occurs. If it occurs once per class, it is `static`, but if it occurs once per object, it is not `static`.

> **NOTE**
> The first release of Java (1.0) supported five access levels—the four listed previously plus `private protected`. The `private protected` access level is not supported in versions of Java higher than 1.0; you should not use it in your Java programs.

> **NOTE** Data fields are most often `private` and not `static`. Only rarely is a data field made `public`. A class's fields are made `static` only when you do not want each object to have its own copy of the field. You will learn more about how and why to create `static` and nonstatic class members in the next section.

> **NOTE** Data fields are most frequently made `public` when they are both `static` and `final`—that is, when a class contains a nonchanging value that you want to use without being required to create an object. For example, the Java `Math` class contains a `public` field called `PI` that you can use without instantiating a `Math` object. You will learn about the `Math` class in Chapter 4.

The Employee class developed to this point appears in Figure 3-15. It defines a public class named Employee, with one field, which is a private integer named empNum.

```
public class Employee
{
    private int empNum;
}
```

Figure 3-15 The Employee class with one field

»TWO TRUTHS AND A LIE: CREATING A CLASS

1. A class header contains an optional access modifier, the keyword class, and an identifier.
2. When you instantiate objects, each has its own copy of each static data field in the class.
3. Most fields in a class are private, and most methods are public.

The false statement is #2. When you instantiate objects, each has its own copy of each nonstatic data field in the class.

CREATING INSTANCE METHODS IN A CLASS

Besides data, classes contain methods. For example, one method you need for an Employee class that contains an empNum is the method to retrieve (or return) any Employee's empNum for use by another class. A reasonable name for this method is getEmpNum(), and its declaration is public int getEmpNum() because it will have public access, return an integer (the employee number), and possess the identifier getEmpNum(). Figure 3-16 shows the complete getEmpNum() method.

```
public int getEmpNum()
{
    return empNum;
}
```

Figure 3-16 The getEmpNum() method

The getEmpNum() method contains just one statement: the statement that accesses the value of the private empNum field.

Notice that, unlike the class methods you created earlier in this chapter, the getEmpNum() method does not employ the static modifier. The keyword static is used for classwide methods, but not for methods that "belong" to objects. If you are creating a program with a main() method that you will execute to perform some task, many of your methods will be static so you can call them from within main() without creating objects. However, if you are creating a class from which objects will be instantiated, most methods will probably be nonstatic because you will associate the methods with individual objects. For example, the getEmpNum() method must be nonstatic because it returns a different empNum value for every Employee object you ever create. **Nonstatic methods**, those methods used with object instantiations, are called **instance methods**.

Understanding when to declare fields and methods as static and nonstatic is a challenge for new programmers. Table 3-1 provides a summary.

Static	Nonstatic
In Java, `static` is a keyword. It also can be used as an adjective.	There is no keyword for nonstatic items. When you do not explicitly declare a field or method to be static, then it is nonstatic by default.
Static fields in a class are called class fields.	Nonstatic fields in a class are called instance variables.
Static methods in a class are called class methods.	Nonstatic methods in a class are called instance methods.
When you use a static field or method, you do not use an object; for example: `JOptionPane.showDialog();`	When you use a nonstatic field or method, you must use an object; for example: `System.out.println();`
When you create a class with a static field and instantiate 100 objects, only one copy of that field exists in memory.	When you create a class with a nonstatic field and instantiate 100 objects, then 100 copies of that field exist in memory.
When you create a static method in a class and instantiate 100 objects, only one copy of the method exists in memory and the method does not receive a `this` reference.	When you create a nonstatic method in a class and instantiate 100 objects, only one copy of the method exists in memory, but the method receives a `this` reference that contains the address of the object currently using it.
Static class variables are not instance variables. The system allocates memory to hold class variables once per class, no matter how many instances of the class you instantiate. The system allocates memory for class variables the first time it encounters a class, and every instance of a class shares the same copy of any static class variables.	Instance fields and methods are nonstatic. The system allocates a separate memory location for each nonstatic field in each instance.

Table 3-1 Comparison of `static` and nonstatic

▶▶NOTE
You will learn about the `this` reference in Chapter 4.

When a class contains data fields, you want a means to assign values to them. For an `Employee` class with an `empNum` field, you need a method with which to set the `empNum`. Figure 3-17 shows a method named `setEmpNum()` that sets the value of an `Employee`'s `empNum`. The method is a `void` method because there is no need to return any value to a calling method. The method receives an integer, locally called `emp`, to be assigned to `empNum`.

```
public void setEmpNum(int emp)
{
    empNum = emp;
}
```

Figure 3-17 The `setEmpNum()` method

Figure 3-18 shows the complete `Employee` class containing one private data field and two public methods, all of which are nonstatic. This class becomes the model for a new data type named `Employee`; when `Employee` objects are eventually created, each will have its own `empNum` field, and each will have access to two methods—one that provides a value for its `empNum` field and another that retrieves the value stored there.

```
public class Employee
{
    private int empNum;
    public int getEmpNum()
    {
        return empNum;
    }
    public void setEmpNum(int emp)
    {
        empNum = emp;
    }
}
```

Figure 3-18 The `Employee` class with one field and two methods

When you create a class like `Employee`, you can compile it, and you should to locate typographical errors. However, you cannot execute the class because it does not contain a `main()` method. A class like `Employee` is intended to be used as a data type for objects within other applications, as you will see in the next section.

»TWO TRUTHS AND A LIE: CREATING INSTANCE METHODS IN A CLASS

1. The keyword `static` is used with classwide methods, but not for methods that "belong" to objects.
2. When you create a class from which objects will be instantiated, most methods are nonstatic because they are associated with individual objects.
3. Static methods are instance methods.

The false statement is #3. Nonstatic methods are instance methods; static methods are class methods.

DECLARING OBJECTS AND USING THEIR METHODS

Declaring a class does not create any actual objects. A class is just an abstract description of what an object will be like if any objects are ever actually instantiated. Just as you might understand all the characteristics of an item you intend to manufacture long before the first item rolls off the assembly line, you can create a class with fields and methods long before you instantiate any objects that are members of that class.

A two-step process creates an object that is an instance of a class. First, you supply a type and an identifier—just as when you declare any variable—and then you allocate computer memory for that object. For example, you might define an integer as `int someValue;` and you might define an `Employee` as follows:

```
Employee someEmployee;
```

In this statement, `someEmployee` stands for any legal identifier you choose to represent an `Employee`.

When you declare an integer as `int someValue;`, you notify the compiler that an integer named `someValue` will exist, and you reserve computer memory for it at the same time. When you declare the `someEmployee` instance of the `Employee` class, you are notifying the compiler that you will use the identifier `someEmployee`. However, you are not yet setting aside computer memory in which the `Employee` named `someEmployee` might be stored— that is done automatically only for primitive-type variables. To allocate the needed memory for an object, you must use the **new operator**. Two statements that actually set aside enough memory to hold an `Employee` are as follows:

```
Employee someEmployee;
someEmployee = new Employee();
```

NOTE
You first learned about the `new` operator when you created a `Scanner` object in Chapter 2.

You can also define and reserve memory for `someEmployee` in one statement, as in the following:

```
Employee someEmployee = new Employee();
```

In this statement, `Employee` is the object's type (as well as its class), and `someEmployee` is the name of the object. In this statement, `someEmployee` becomes a **reference to the object**—the name for a memory address where the object is held. The equal sign is the assignment operator, so a value is being assigned to `someEmployee`. The `new` operator is allocating a new, unused portion of computer memory for `someEmployee`. The value that the statement is assigning to `someEmployee` is a memory address at which `someEmployee` is to be located. You do not need to be concerned with what the actual memory address is—when you refer to `someEmployee`, the compiler locates it at the appropriate address for you.

NOTE
Every object name is also a reference— that is, a computer memory location. In Chapter 2, you learned that a class like `Employee` is a *reference type*.

The final portion of the statement after the `new` operator, `Employee()`, with its parentheses, looks suspiciously like a method name. In fact, it is the name of a method that constructs an `Employee` object. The `Employee()` method is a **constructor**, a special type of method that

NOTE
You will learn to write constructors later in this chapter.

creates and initializes objects. You can write your own constructor, but when you don't write a constructor for a class, Java writes one for you, and the name of the constructor is always the same as the name of the class whose objects it constructs.

After an object has been instantiated, its methods can be accessed using the object's identifier, a dot, and a method call. For example, Figure 3-19 shows an application that instantiates two `Employee` objects. The two objects, `clerk` and `driver`, each use the `setEmpNum()` and `getEmpNum()` method one time. The `DeclareTwoEmployees` application can use these methods because they are public, and it must use them with an `Employee` object because the methods are not static. Figure 3-20 shows the output of the application.

»NOTE
The program in Figure 3-19 assumes that the Employee.java file is stored in the same folder as the application. If the `Employee` file was stored in a different folder, you would need an import statement at the top of the file, similar to the ones you use for the `Scanner` and `JOptionPane` classes.

```java
public class DeclareTwoEmployees
{
   public static void main(String[] args)
   {
      Employee clerk = new Employee();
      Employee driver = new Employee();
      clerk.setEmpNum(345);
      driver.setEmpNum(567);
      System.out.println("The clerk's number is " +
         clerk.getEmpNum() + " and the driver's number is " +
         driver.getEmpNum());
   }
}
```

Figure 3-19 The `DeclareTwoEmployees` class

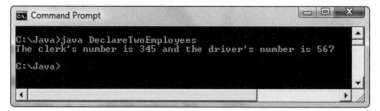

Figure 3-20 Output of the `DeclareTwoEmployees` application

UNDERSTANDING DATA HIDING

Within the `DeclareTwoEmployees` class, you must use the public methods `setEmpNum()` and `getEmpNum()` to be able to set and retrieve the value of the `empNum` field for each `Employee` because you cannot access the private `empNum` field directly. For example, the following statement would not be allowed:

```java
clerk.empNum = 789;
```

This statement generates the error message "empNum has private access in Employee", meaning you cannot access empNum from the DeclareTwoEmployees class. If you made empNum public instead of private, a direct assignment statement would work, but you would violate an important principle of object-oriented programming—that of data hiding using encapsulation. Data fields should usually be private, and a client application should be able to access them only through the public interfaces—that is, through the class's public methods. However, you might reasonably ask, "When I write an application, if I *can't* set an object's data field directly, but I *can* set it using a public method, what's the difference? The field value is set either way!" Actually, the setEmpNum() method in the Employee class in Figure 3-18 *does* accept any integer value you send into it. However, you could rewrite the setEmpNum() method to prevent invalid data from being assigned to an object's data fields. For example, perhaps your organization has rules for valid employee ID numbers—they must be no fewer than five digits, or they must start with a 9, for instance—or perhaps you calculate a check-digit that is appended to every employee ID number. The statements that enforce these requirements would be part of the setEmpNum() method.

>>NOTE Checking a value for validity requires decision making. You will begin to learn about making decisions in Java in Chapter 5.

>>NOTE A check-digit is a number appended to a field, typically an ID number or account number. The check-digit ensures that the number is valid. For example, an organization might use five-digit employee ID numbers in which the fifth digit is calculated by dividing the first four by 7 and taking the remainder. As an example, if the first four digits of your ID number are 7235, then the fifth digit is 4, the remainder when you divide the first four digits by 7. So the five-digit ID becomes 72354. Later, if you make a mistake and enter your ID into a company application as 82354, the application would divide the first four digits, 8235, by 7. The remainder is not 4, and the ID would be found invalid.

Similarly, a get method might control how a value is retrieved. Perhaps you do not want clients to have access to part of an employee's ID number, or perhaps you always want to add a company code to every ID before it is returned to the client. Even when a field has no data value requirements or restrictions, making data private and providing public set and get methods establishes a framework that makes such modifications easier in the future.

>>NOTE You will not necessarily write set and get methods for every field in a class; there are some fields that clients will not be allowed to alter. Some fields will simply be assigned values, and some field values might be calculated from the values of others.

>>TWO TRUTHS AND A LIE: DECLARING OBJECTS AND USING THEIR METHODS

1. When you declare an object, you give it a name and set aside enough memory for the object to be stored.
2. An object name is a reference; it holds a memory address.
3. When you don't write a constructor for a class, Java creates one for you; the name of the constructor is always the same as the name of its class.

The false statement is #1. When you declare an object, you are not yet setting aside computer memory in which the object is stored; to allocate the needed memory for an object, you must use the new operator.

ORGANIZING CLASSES

Most classes you create have more than one data field and more than two methods. For example, in addition to requiring an employee number, an `Employee` needs a last name, a first name, and a salary, as well as methods to set and get those fields. Figure 3-21 shows how you could code the data fields for `Employee`.

```
public class Employee
{
   private int empNum;
   private String empLastName;
   private String empFirstName;
   private double empSalary;
   // Methods will go here
}
```

Figure 3-21 An `Employee` class with several data fields

> **NOTE**
> A unique identifier is one that should have no duplicates within an application. For example, an organization might have many employees with the last name Johnson or a weekly salary of $400.00, but there is only one employee with employee number 128.

Although there is no requirement to do so, most programmers place data fields in some logical order at the beginning of a class. For example, `empNum` is most likely used as a unique identifier for each employee (what database users often call a **primary key**), so it makes sense to list the employee number first in the class. An employee's last name and first name "go together," so it makes sense to store these two `Employee` components adjacently. Despite these common-sense rules, you have a lot of flexibility in how you position your data fields within any class.

Because there are two `String` components in the current `Employee` class, they might be declared within the same statement, such as `private String empLastName, empFirstName;`. However, it is usually easier to identify each `Employee` field at a glance if the fields are listed vertically.

You can place a class's data fields and methods in any order within a class. For example, you could place all the methods first, followed by all the data fields, or you could organize the class so that several data fields are followed by methods that use them, then several more data fields are followed by the methods that use them. This book will follow the convention of placing all data fields first so that you can see their names and data types before reading the methods that use them.

Even if the only methods created for the `Employee` class include one `set` method and one `get` method for each instance variable, eight methods are required. Consider an employee record for most organizations and you will realize that many more fields are often required (such as address, phone number, hire date, number of dependents, and so on), as well as many more methods. Finding your way through the list can become a formidable task. For ease in locating class methods, many programmers store them in alphabetical order. Other programmers arrange values in pairs of "get" and "set" methods, an order that also results in functional groupings. Figure 3-22 shows how the complete class definition for an `Employee` might appear.

```
public class Employee
{
    private int empNum;
    private String empLastName;
    private String empFirstName;
    private double empSalary;
    public int getEmpNum()
    {
        return empNum;
    }
    public void setEmpNum(int emp)
    {
        empNum = emp;
    }
    public String getEmpLastName()
    {
        return empLastName;
    }
    public void setEmpLastName(String name)
    {
        empLastName = name;
    }
    public String getEmpFirstName()
    {
        return empFirstName;
    }
    public void setEmpFirstName(String name)
    {
        empFirstName = name;
    }
    public double getEmpSalary()
    {
        return empSalary;
    }
    public void setEmpSalary(double sal)
    {
        empSalary = sal;
    }
}
```

Figure 3-22 The `Employee` class with several data fields and corresponding methods

The `Employee` class is still not a particularly large class, and each of its methods is very short, but it is already becoming quite difficult to manage. It certainly can support some well-placed comments, as shown in Figure 3-23.

```
// Employee.java holds employee data
// Programmer: Lynn Greenbrier
// Date: September 24, 2011
public class Employee
{
    // private data members:
    private int empNum;
    private String empLastName;
    private String empFirstName;
    private double empSalary;

    // public mutator and accessor methods:
    public int getEmpNum()
    {
        return empNum;
    }
    public void setEmpNum(int emp)
    {
        empNum = emp;
    }
    // ...and so on
```

Figure 3-23 Start of `Employee` class with data fields, methods, and comments

»TWO TRUTHS AND A LIE: ORGANIZING CLASSES

1. You can place a class's fields first within the class, followed by methods.
2. You can place a class's methods first within the class, followed by fields.
3. Although you can and should place comments in a Java application, you should not use them in a class from which objects will be instantiated.

The false statement is #3. You can place comments in any Java class, whether it is an application or not.

AN INTRODUCTION TO USING CONSTRUCTORS

When you create a class, such as `Employee`, and instantiate an object with a statement such as the following, you are actually calling the `Employee` class constructor that is provided by default by the Java compiler:

```
Employee chauffeur = new Employee();
```

A constructor establishes an object; a **default constructor** is one that requires no arguments. A default constructor is created automatically by the Java compiler for any class you create whenever you do not write your own constructor.

When the prewritten, default constructor for the `Employee` class is called, it establishes one `Employee` object with the identifier provided. The automatically supplied default constructor provides the following specific initial values to an object's data fields:

» Numeric fields are set to 0 (zero).

» Character fields are set to Unicode '\u0000'.

» Boolean fields are set to `false`.

» Fields that are objects themselves (for example, `String` fields) are set to `null` (or empty).

If you do not want each field in an object to hold these default values, or if you want to perform additional tasks when you create an instance of a class, you can write your own constructor. Any constructor you write must have the same name as the class it constructs, and constructors cannot have a return type. Normally, you declare constructors to be public so that other classes can instantiate objects that belong to the class.

»NOTE
You never provide a return type for a constructor—not even `void`.

For example, if you want every `Employee` object to have a starting salary of $300.00 per week, you could write the constructor for the `Employee` class that appears in Figure 3-24. Any `Employee` object instantiated will have an `empSalary` field value equal to 300.00, and the other `Employee` data fields will contain the default values.

```
public Employee()
{
    empSalary = 300.00;
}
```

Figure 3-24 The `Employee` class constructor

»NOTE
The `Employee` class constructor in Figure 3-24 takes no parameters. You will learn about constructors that take parameters in the next chapter.

»NOTE Even if you do not initialize an object's field, it always contains the default value listed previously, and even though you might want the field to hold the default value, you still might prefer to explicitly initialize the field for clarity. For example, if an `Employee` class contains an integer field named `yearsOnTheJob`, you might choose to place a statement in a constructor such as `yearsOnTheJob = 0;`. Although the `int` field would be initialized to 0 anyway, the explicit assignment allows anyone reading the constructor to clearly understand your intentions.

You can write any Java statement in a constructor. Although you usually have no reason to do so, you could print a message from within a constructor or perform any other task.

You can place the constructor anywhere inside the class, outside of any other method. Typically, a constructor is placed with the other methods. Often, programmers list the constructor first because it is the first method used when an object is created.

»NOTE
You are never required to write a constructor for a class; Java provides you with a default version if the class contains no explicit constructor.

»NOTE
A class can contain multiple constructors. You will learn how to overload constructors in the next chapter.

»TWO TRUTHS AND A LIE: AN INTRODUCTION TO USING CONSTRUCTORS

1. In Java, you cannot write a default constructor; it must be supplied for you automatically.

2. The automatically supplied default constructor sets all numeric fields to 0, character fields to Unicode '\u0000', Boolean fields to false, and fields that are object references to `null`.

3. When you write a constructor, it must have the same name as the class it constructs, and it cannot have a return type.

The false statement is #1. A default constructor is one that takes no parameters. If you do not create a constructor for a class, Java creates a default constructor for you. However, you can create a default constructor that replaces the automatically supplied one.

»NOTE
When you write a constructor for a class, you no longer receive the automatically written version.

UNDERSTANDING THAT CLASSES ARE DATA TYPES

The classes that you create become data types. Java has eight built-in primitive data types such as int and double. You do not have to define those types; the creators of Java have already done so. For example, when the int type was first created, the programmers who designed it had to think of the following:

Q: What shall we call it?

A: int.

Q: What are its attributes?

A: An int is stored in four bytes; it holds whole number values.

Q: What methods are needed by int?

A: A method to assign a value to a variable (for example, num = 32;).

Q: Any other methods?

A: Some operators to perform arithmetic with variables (for example, num + 6;).

Q: Any other methods?

A: Of course, there are even more attributes and methods of an int, but these are a good start.

Your job in constructing a new data type is similar. If you need a class for employees, you should ask:

Q: What shall we call it?

A: Employee.

Q: What are its attributes?

A: It has an integer ID number, a String last name, and a double salary.

Q: What methods are needed by Employee?

A: A method to assign values to a member of this class (for example, one Employee's ID number is 3232, her last name is "Walters", and her salary is 30000).

Q: Any other methods?

A: A method to display data in a member of this class (for example, display one Employee's data).

Q: Any other methods?

A: Probably, but this is enough to get started.

When you declare a primitive-type object, you provide its type and an identifier. When you declare an object from one of your classes, you do the same. After each exists, you can use them in very similar ways. For example, suppose you declare an int named myInt and an Employee named myEmployee. Then each can be passed into a method, returned from a method, or assigned to another object of the same data type.

For example, Figure 3-25 shows a program in which the main() method uses two other methods. One method accepts an Employee as a parameter, and the other returns an Employee. (The Employee class is defined in Figure 3-22.) You can see in this sample program that an Employee is passed into and out of methods just like a primitive object would be. Classes are not mysterious; they are just new data types that you invent.

```
import java.util.Scanner;
class MethodsThatUseAnEmployee
{
   public static void main (String args[])
   {
      Employee myEmployee;
      myEmployee = getEmployeeData();
      displayEmployee(myEmployee);
   }
   public static Employee getEmployeeData()
   {
      Employee tempEmp = new Employee();
      int id;
      double sal;
      Scanner input = new Scanner(System.in);
      System.out.print("Enter employee ID ");
      id = input.nextInt();
      tempEmp.setEmpNum(id);
      System.out.print("Enter employee salary ");
      sal = input.nextDouble();
      tempEmp.setEmpSalary(sal);
      return tempEmp;
   }
   public static void displayEmployee(Employee anEmp)
   {
      System.out.println("\nEmployee #" + anEmp.getEmpNum() +
         " Salary is " + anEmp.getEmpSalary());
   }
}
```

Figure 3-25 The `MethodsThatUseAnEmployee` application

»NOTE Notice in the application in Figure 3-25 that the `Employee` declared in the `main()` method is not constructed there. An `Employee` is constructed in the `getEmployeeData()` method and passed back to the `main()` method, where it is assigned to the `myEmployee` reference. The `Employee` constructor could have been called in `main()`, but the values assigned would have been overwritten after the call to `getEmployeeData()`.

**»TWO TRUTHS AND A LIE: UNDERSTANDING
THAT CLASSES ARE DATA TYPES**

1. When you declare a primitive variable or instantiate an object from a class, you provide both a type and an identifier.
2. Unlike a primitive variable, an instantiated object cannot be passed into or returned from a method.
3. The address of an instantiated object can be assigned to a declared reference of the same type.

The false statement is #2. An instantiated object can be passed into or returned from a method.

YOU DO IT

CREATING A STATIC METHOD THAT REQUIRES NO ARGUMENTS AND RETURNS NO VALUES

Event Handlers Incorporated assists its clients in planning and hosting social events and business meetings. In this section, you will create a new class named `SetUpSite`, which you will eventually use to set up one `EventSite` object that represents the site where an event can be held. For now, the class will contain a `main()` method and a `statementOfPhilosophy()` method for Event Handlers Incorporated.

To create the `SetUpSite` class:

1. Open a new document in your text editor.

2. Type the following shell class to create a `SetUpSite` class and an empty `main()` method:

```
public class SetUpSite
{
    public static void main(String[] args)
    {
    }
}
```

3. Between the curly braces of the `main()` method, type the following:

```
statementOfPhilosophy();
```

This statement calls a method named `statementOfPhilosophy()`.

4. Place the `statementOfPhilosophy()` method outside the `main()` method, just before the closing curly brace for the `SetUpSite` class code:

```
public static void statementOfPhilosophy()
{
    System.out.println("Event Handlers Incorporated is");
    System.out.println("dedicated to making your event");
    System.out.println("a most memorable one.");
}
```

5. Save the file as **SetUpSite.java**.

6. At the command line, compile the application by typing **javac SetUpSite.java**.

   If you receive any error messages, you must correct their cause. For example, Figure 3-26 shows the error message received when `println()` is spelled incorrectly once within the SetUpSite.java file. Notice the message indicates that the file is SetUpSite.java, the line on which the error occurs is line 10, and the error is "cannot find symbol", followed by the name of the symbol that the compiler does not understand: "symbol: method prinln(java.lang.String)".

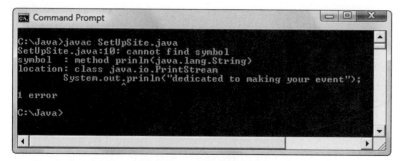

Figure 3-26 Error message received when `println` is incorrectly spelled

To help you, Java tells you where the error might be: "location: class java.io.PrintStream"; Java assumes the error is in the `PrintStream` class because you are using the `System.out` object, which it knows is a `PrintStream` object, and the compiler can't find a method with the name `prinln()` there. The compiler displays the offending line, and a caret appears just below the point at which the compiler could proceed no further. When you view this error message, you should notice the misspelling of the `println()` method name. To correct the spelling error, return to the SetUpSite.java file, fix the mistake, save the file, and then compile it again.

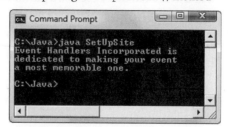

Figure 3-27 Output of the `SetUpSite` application

7. Execute the application using the command **java SetUpSite**. Your output should look like Figure 3-27.

CALLING A STATIC METHOD FROM ANOTHER CLASS

Next, you will see how to call the `statementOfPhilosophy()` method from a method within another class.

To call a static method from a method within another class:

1. First, open a new document in your text editor, and then enter the following class in which the `main()` method calls the `statementOfPhilosophy()` method that resides in a different class:

```java
public class TestStatement
{
    public static void main(String[] args)
    {
        System.out.println("Calling method from another class");
        SetUpSite.statementOfPhilosophy();
    }
}
```

»NOTE
If you want one class to call a method of another class, both classes should reside in the same folder. If they are not saved in the same folder, when you compile the calling class, your compiler issues the error message "cannot find symbol" and the symbol it names is the missing class you tried to call.

2. Save the file as **TestStatement.java**. Compile the application with the command **javac TestStatement.java**.

3. Execute the application with the command **java TestStatement**. Your output should look like Figure 3-28.

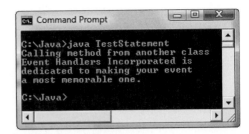

Figure 3-28 Output of the `TestStatement` application

CREATING A STATIC METHOD THAT ACCEPTS ARGUMENTS AND RETURNS VALUES

Next, you will add a method to the `SetUpSite` class; the new method both receives a parameter and returns a value. The purpose of the method is to accept the current year and calculate how long Event Handlers Incorporated has been in business.

To add a method that receives a parameter and returns a value:

1. Open the **SetUpSite.java** file in the text editor, and then change the class name to **SetUpSite2**. Immediately save the file as **SetUpSite2**.

2. Add three integer declarations as the first statements following the opening curly brace of the `main()` method. One is a constant that holds the year Event Handlers Incorporated was established. The other two are variables that hold the current year, which will be entered by a user, and the age of the organization, which will be calculated from the other two values.

```
final int FOUNDED_YEAR = 1977;

int currentYear;

int age;
```

3. As the first line in the file, add an import statement that will allow the use of the `Scanner` class:

```
import java.util.Scanner;
```

> **»NOTE** Instead of importing *the* Scanner class to provide console input, you could substitute JOptionPane and include program statements that provide GUI input. The input process can use other techniques too, such as getting data from a storage device—you will learn about file input in Chapter 12. The concept of input (getting data into memory from the outside) is the same no matter what specific technique or type of hardware device you use.

4. In the `main()` method, following the constant and variable declarations, add the statement that associates a `Scanner` object with the `System.in` object:

```
Scanner input = new Scanner(System.in);
```

5. In the `main()` method, after the call to the `statementOfPhilosophy()` method, add a prompt for the current year and the statement that retrieves it from the keyboard:

```
System.out.print("Enter the current year as a four-digit number ");
currentYear = input.nextInt();
```

6. Following the input statement, add a call to a method that will receive the founding and current years as parameters and that will return the age of the organization:

```
age = calculateAge(FOUNDED_YEAR, currentYear);
```

7. Type the following to print information about the number of years the company has been in business:

```
System.out.println("Founded in " + FOUNDED_YEAR);
System.out.println("Serving you for " + age + " years ");
```

8. Now you will write the `calculateAge()` method. Position the insertion point after the closing brace of the `statementOfPhilosophy()` method, press **Enter** to start a new line before the closing brace of the program, and then enter the `calculateAge()` method as follows:

```
public static int calculateAge(int originYear, int currDate)
{
    int years;
    years = currDate - originYear;
    return years;
}
```

The `calculateAge()` method receives two integer values. Note that the names `originYear` and `currDate` do not possess the same identifiers as the arguments passed in from the `main()` method, although they could. Notice also that the method declaration indicates an `int` value will be returned. The `calculateAge()` method performs the necessary subtraction and returns the difference to the calling function.

>> **NOTE** The `calculateAge()` method is static because no `SetUpSite2` objects need to be created to use it; it is a class method.

9. Save the file (as **SetUpSite2.java**), compile it, and correct any errors. Execute the application and confirm that the results are correct. Figure 3-29 shows the output.

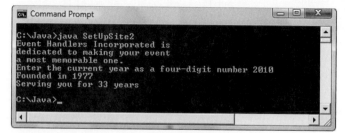

Figure 3-29 Output of the `SetUpSite2` application

CREATING A CLASS THAT CONTAINS INSTANCE FIELDS AND METHODS

Next, you will create a class to store information about event sites for Event Handlers Incorporated.

To create the class:

1. Open a new document in your text editor.

2. Type the following class header and the curly braces to surround the class body:

```
public class EventSite
{
}
```

3. Type **private int siteNumber;** between the curly braces to insert the private data field that will hold an integer site number for each event site used by the company.

4. Within the `EventSite` class's curly braces and after the declaration of the `siteNumber` field, enter the following `getSiteNumber()` method to return the site number to any calling class:

```
public int getSiteNumber()
{
    return siteNumber;
}
```

5. Add the following method to the file after the final curly brace for the `getSiteNumber()` method, but prior to the closing curly brace for the `EventSite` class:

```
public void setSiteNumber(int n)
{
    siteNumber = n;
}
```

The argument *n* represents any number sent to this method.

» NOTE
Notice that the methods in the `EventSite` class are not static. That means they must be used with an `EventSite` object.

6. Save the file as **EventSite.java**, compile it, and then correct any syntax errors. (You cannot run this file as a program because it does not contain a `public static main()` method.) The complete class appears in Figure 3-30.

```
public class EventSite
{
    private int siteNumber;
    public int getSiteNumber()
    {
        return siteNumber;
    }
    public void setSiteNumber(int n)
    {
        siteNumber = n;
    }
}
```

Figure 3-30 The `EventSite` class

CREATING A CLASS THAT INSTANTIATES OBJECTS OF ANOTHER CLASS

Next, you will modify the `SetUpSite2` application so that it instantiates an `EventSite` object.

To instantiate an object:

1. Open the **SetUpSite2.java** file. Change the class name to **SetUpSite3**, then immediately save the file as **SetUpSite3.java**.

2. Following the `Scanner` declaration within the `main()` method, add a statement that declares and allocates memory for a new `EventSite` object named `oneSite`:

   ```
   EventSite oneSite = new EventSite();
   ```

3. Just below the newly entered declaration for `oneSite`, add an integer declaration as follows:

   ```
   int siteNum;
   ```

4. Below the statements that prompt for and receive the year, add statements that prompt for and receive the site number:

   ```
   System.out.print("Enter the event site number ");

   siteNum = input.nextInt();
   ```

5. Next, call the method `setSiteNumber()` to set the site number for `oneSite`:

   ```
   oneSite.setSiteNumber(siteNum);
   ```

6. After the statement that prints the age of the company, enter the statement that displays the site number by calling the `getSiteNumber()` method from within the `println()` method:

   ```
   System.out.println("The site number is " +
   oneSite.getSiteNumber());
   ```

7. Save the program file (as **SetUpSite3.java**) and compile the program by typing **javac SetUpSite3.java**.

8. Execute the program by typing **java SetUpSite3**. Enter values appropriately when you are prompted. Figure 3-31 shows a typical execution.

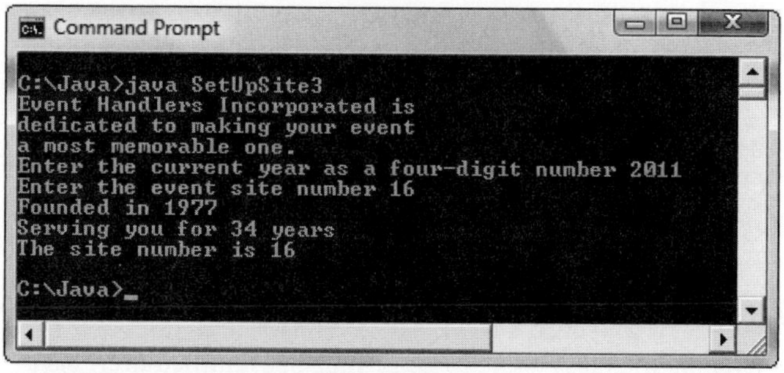

```
C:\Java>java SetUpSite3
Event Handlers Incorporated is
dedicated to making your event
a most memorable one.
Enter the current year as a four-digit number 2011
Enter the event site number 16
Founded in 1977
Serving you for 34 years
The site number is 16

C:\Java>
```

Figure 3-31 Typical execution of the `SetUpSite3` application

ADDING A CONSTRUCTOR TO A CLASS

Next, you will add a default constructor to the `EventSite` class and demonstrate that it is called automatically when you instantiate an `EventSite` object.

To add a constructor to the `EventSite` class:

1. Open the **EventSite.java** file in your text editor.

2. Following the declaration of the `siteNumber` field, insert the following default constructor function that sets any `EventSite siteNumber` to 999 upon construction:

```java
public EventSite()
{
    siteNumber = 999;
}
```

3. Save the file (as **EventSite.java**), compile it, and correct any errors.

4. Open a new text file and create a test class named `TestConstructor` using the code shown in Figure 3-32.

```java
public class TestConstructor
{
    public static void main(String[] args)
    {
        EventSite oneSite = new EventSite();
        System.out.println("Site number " +
            onesite.getSiteNumber());
    }
}
```

Figure 3-32 The `TestConstructor` application

5. Save the file as **TestConstructor.java**, compile the file, and correct any syntax errors. Execute the program to confirm that when the `oneSite` object of type `EventSite` is declared, the automatically called constructor assigns the appropriate initial value, as shown in Figure 3-33.

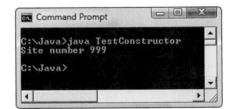

Figure 3-33 Output of the `TestConstructor` application

CREATING A MORE COMPLETE CLASS

In the next steps, you will add data fields and methods to the `EventSite` class to make it more complete.

To make a more complete class:

1. Open the **EventSite.java file**. Change the class name to `MyEventSite`. Immediately save the file as **MyEventSite.java**.

2. Add two more fields to the class—a `double` that holds the hourly fee for using the event site and a `String` that is the name of the site. For example, the Grand Ballroom might cost $100 an hour. Add get and set methods for each new field.

3. Modify the `EventSite` constructor name to the name of the new class. Add statements that initialize the new fields to appropriate default values.

4. Save the file, compile it, and correct any errors.

5. Write a program named `TestMyEventSite` that demonstrates that each method and the constructor all work correctly. Save the file as **TestMyEventSite.java**.

DON'T DO IT

» Don't place a semicolon at the end of a method header. After you get used to putting semicolons at the end of every statement, it's easy to start putting them in too many places. Method headers never end in a semicolon.

» Don't think "default constructor" means only the automatically supplied constructor. Although a class's automatically supplied constructor is a default constructor, so is any constructor you create that accepts no parameters.

» Don't think that a class's methods must accept its own fields' values as parameters or return values to its own fields. When a class contains both fields and methods, each method has direct access to every field within the class.

» Don't create a class method that has a parameter with the same identifier as a class field—yet. If you do, you will only be allowed to access the local variable within the method, and will not be able to access the field. You will be able to use the same identifier and still access both values after you read Chapter 4. For now, make sure that the parameter in any class method has a different identifier from any class field.

KEY TERMS

A **method** is a program module that contains a series of statements that carry out a task.

When you **invoke** or **call** a method, you execute it.

The **calling method** makes a **method call** that invokes the **called method**.

Arguments are data items sent to methods in a method call.

Parameters are the data items received by a method.

Returning a value sends a data value from a called method back to the calling method.

Abstraction is the programming feature that allows you to use a method name to encapsulate a series of statements.

The **method declaration** is the first line, or **header**.

Access modifiers are also called **access specifiers**.

Implementation hiding is a principle of object-oriented programming that describes the encapsulation of method details within a class.

A **black box** is a device you can use without understanding how it works.

The **interface** to a method includes the method's return type, name, and arguments. It is the part that a client sees and uses.

A **local variable** is known only within the boundaries of a method.

A method's **signature** is the combination of the method name and the number, types, and order of arguments.

Actual parameters are the arguments in a method call.

Formal parameters are the variables in a method declaration that accept the values from actual parameters.

A `return` **statement** ends a method, and frequently sends a value from a called method back to the calling method.

A **method's type** is its return type.

Unreachable statements are those that cannot be executed because the logical path can never encounter them; an unreachable statement causes a compiler error.

Unreachable statements are also called **dead code**.

An **is-a relationship** is the relationship between an object and the class of which it is a member.

An **instantiation** of a class is an object; in other words, it is one tangible example of a class.

The **instance variables** of a class are its data components.

Fields are data variables declared in a class outside of any method.

A **class client** or **class user** is an application or class that instantiates objects of another prewritten class.

Classes can be **extended**, or used as a basis for any other class.

Assigning **private access** to a field means that no other classes can access the field's values, and only methods of the same class are allowed to set, get, or otherwise use private variables.

Information hiding is the object-oriented programming principle used when creating private access for data fields; a class's private data can be changed or manipulated only by a class's own methods, and not by methods that belong to other classes.

Nonstatic methods, those methods used with object instantiations, are called **instance methods**.

Mutator methods set values.

Accessor methods retrieve values.

The `new` **operator** allocates the memory needed to hold an object.

A **reference to an object** is the name for a memory address where the object is held.

A **constructor** is a method that establishes an object.

A **primary key** is a unique identifier for data within a database.

A **default constructor** is one that is created automatically by the Java compiler.

An **abstract data type** is a type whose implementation is hidden and accessed through its public methods.

A **programmer-defined data type** is one that is created by a programmer and not built into the language.

CHAPTER SUMMARY

» A method is a series of statements that carry out a task. Methods must include a declaration (or header or definition), an opening curly brace, a body, and a closing curly brace. A method declaration contains optional access modifiers, the return type for the method, the method name, an opening parenthesis, an optional list of parameters, and a closing parenthesis.

» When you write the method declaration for a method that can receive a parameter, you need to include the parameter type and a local name for the parameter within the method declaration parentheses. You can call a method within a program using either a constant value or a variable as an argument.

» You can pass multiple arguments to methods by listing the arguments separated by commas within the call to the method. The arguments you send to the method must match (both in number and in type) the parameters listed in the method declaration.

» The return type for a method (the method's type) can be any Java type, including `void`. You use a `return` statement to send a value back to a calling method.

» Methods can call other methods.

» Objects have attributes and methods associated with them. Class instance methods that are used with objects are nonstatic. You can send messages to objects using their methods.

» A class header contains an optional access modifier, the keyword `class`, and any legal identifier you choose for the name of your class.

» The instance variables, or fields, of a class are placed as statements within the class's curly braces. Fields and methods used with object instantiations are nonstatic.

» Declaring a class does not create any actual objects; you must instantiate any objects that are members of a class. To create an object that is an instance of a class, you supply a type and an identifier, and then you allocate computer memory for that object using the `new` operator.

» With well-written object-oriented programming methods, using implementation hiding, or the encapsulation of method details within a class, means that the calling method needs to understand only the interface to the called method. In this case, the calling method only needs to know the name of the called method, what type of information to send it, and what type of return data to expect.

» Programmers can organize their classes in many ways. Fields can be placed before or after methods, and methods can be placed in any logical order.

» A constructor establishes an object and provides specific initial values for the object's data fields. A constructor always has the same name as the class of which it is a member. By default, numeric fields are set to 0 (zero), character fields are set to Unicode '\u0000', Boolean fields are set to `false`, and object type fields are set to `null`.

» A class is an abstract, programmer-defined data type.

REVIEW QUESTIONS

1. In Java, methods must include all of the following except _____ .

   a. a declaration   c. curly braces

   b. a call to another method   d. a body

2. All method declarations contain _____ .

   a. the keyword `static`   c. arguments

   b. one or more explicitly named access modifiers   d. parentheses

3. A `public static` method named `computeSum()` is located in `classA`. To call the method from within `classB`, use the statement _____ .

   a. `computeSum(classB);`

   b. `classB(computeSum());`

   c. `classA.computeSum();`

   d. You cannot call `computeSum()` from within `classB`.

4. Which of the following method declarations is correct for a `static` method named `displayFacts()` if the method receives an `int` argument?

   a. `public static int displayFacts()`

   b. `public void displayFacts(int data)`

   c. `public static void displayFacts(int data)`

   d. Two of these are correct.

5. The method with the declaration `public static int aMethod(double d)` has a method type of _____ .

   a. `static`   c. `double`

   b. `int`   d. You cannot determine the method type.

6. Which of the following is a correct call to a method declared as `public static void aMethod(char code)`?

   a. `void aMethod();`   c. `aMethod(char 'M');`

   b. `void aMethod('V');`   d. `aMethod('Q');`

7. A method is declared as `public static void showResults(double d, int i)`. Which of the following is a correct method call?

   a. `showResults(double d, int i);`   c. `showResults(4, 99.7);`

   b. `showResults(12.2, 67);`   d. Two of these are correct.

8. The method with the declaration `public static char procedure(double d)` has a method type of _____ .

   a. `public`   c. `char`

   b. `static`   d. `double`

9. The method `public static boolean testValue(int response)` returns _____ .

   a. a `boolean` value   c. no value

   b. an `int` value   d. You cannot determine what is returned.

10. Which of the following could be the last legally coded line of a method declared as `public static int getVal(double sum)`?

    a. `return;`   c. `return 2.3;`

    b. `return 77;`   d. Any of these could be the last coded line of the method.

11. The nonstatic data components of a class often are referred to as the _____ of that class.

    a. access types   c. methods

    b. instance variables   d. objects

12. Objects contain methods and data items, which are also known as _____ .

    a. fields   c. themes

    b. functions   d. instances

13. You send messages or information to an object through its _____ .

    a. fields   c. classes

    b. methods   d. type

14. A program or class that instantiates objects of another prewritten class is a(n) _____ .
    a. class client
    b. superclass
    c. object
    d. patron

15. The body of a class is always written _____ .
    a. in a single line, as the first statement in a class
    b. within parentheses
    c. between curly braces
    d. as a method call

16. Most class data fields are _____ .
    a. `private`
    b. `public`
    c. `static`
    d. `final`

17. The concept of allowing a class's private data to be changed only by a class's own methods is known as _____ .
    a. structured logic
    b. object orientation
    c. information hiding
    d. data masking

18. Suppose you declare an object as `Book thisBook;`. Before you store data in `thisBook`, you _____ .
    a. also must explicitly allocate memory for it
    b. need not explicitly allocate memory for it
    c. must explicitly allocate memory for it only if it has a constructor
    d. can declare it to use no memory

19. If a class is named `Student`, the class constructor name is _____ .
    a. any legal Java identifier
    b. any legal Java identifier that begins with S
    c. `StudentConstructor`
    d. `Student`

20. If you use the automatically supplied default constructor when you create an object, _____ .
    a. numeric fields are set to 0 (zero)
    b. character fields are set to blank
    c. Boolean fields are set to `true`
    d. All of these are true.

EXERCISES

1. Create an application named `TestMethods` whose `main()` method holds two integer variables. Assign values to the variables. In turn, pass each value to methods named `displayIt()`, `displayItTimesTwo()`, and `displayItPlusOneHundred()`. Create each method to perform the task its name implies. Save the application as **TestMethods.java**.

2. a. Create an application named `Numbers` whose `main()` method holds two integer variables. Assign values to the variables. Pass both variables to methods named `sum()` and `difference()`. Create the methods `sum()` and `difference()`; they compute the sum of and difference between the values of two arguments, respectively. Each method should perform the appropriate computation and display the results. Save the application as **Numbers.java**.

   b. Add a method named `product()` to the `Numbers` class. The `product()` method should compute the multiplication product of two integers, but not display the answer. Instead, it should return the answer to the calling method, which displays the answer. Save the application as **Numbers2.java**.

3. Create a class named `Eggs`. Its `main()` method holds an integer variable named `eggs` to which you will assign a value entered by a user at the keyboard. Create a method to which you pass `eggs`. The method displays the eggs in dozens; for example, 50 eggs is 4 full dozen (with 2 eggs remaining). Save the application as **Eggs.java**.

4. a. Create a class named `Exponent`. Its `main()` method accepts an integer value from a user at the keyboard, and in turn passes the value to a method that squares the number (multiplies it by itself) and to a method that cubes the number (multiplies it by itself twice). The `main()` method prints the results. Create the two methods that, respectively, square and cube an integer that is passed to them, returning the calculated value. Save the application as **Exponent.java**.

   b. Modify the Exponent program so that the cubing method calls the square method, then multiplies that result by the numbers to calculate the cubed value that it returns. Save the application as **Exponent2.java**.

5. Create an application that contains a method that computes the final price for a sales transaction and returns that value to a calling method. The `sale()` method requires three arguments: product price, salesperson commission rate, and customer discount rate. A product's final price is the original price plus the commission amount minus the discount amount; the customer discount is taken as a percentage of the total price after the salesperson commission has been added to the original price. Write a `main()` method that prompts the user for the price of an item, the salesperson's commission expressed as a percentage, and the customer discount expressed as a percentage. Save the application as **Calculator.java**.

6. Write an application that displays the result of dividing two numbers and displays any remainder. The `main()` method prompts the user for values and sends them to the

dividing method; the dividing method performs the calculation and displays the results. Save the application as **Divide.java**.

7. Write an application that calculates and displays the weekly salary for an employee. The `main()` method prompts the user for an hourly pay rate, regular hours, and overtime hours. Create a separate method to calculate overtime pay, which is regular hours times the pay rate plus overtime hours times 1.5 times the pay rate; return the result to the `main()` method to be displayed. Save the program as **Salary.java**.

8. Write an application that calculates and displays the amount of money a user would have if his or her money could be invested at 5% interest for one year. Create a method that prompts the user for the starting value of the investment and returns it to the calling program. Call a separate method to do the calculation and return the result to be displayed. Save the program as **Interest.java**.

9. a. Create a class named `Pizza`. Data fields include a `String` for toppings (such as pepperoni), an integer for diameter in inches (such as 12), and a `double` for price (such as 13.99). Include methods to get and set values for each of these fields. Save the class as **Pizza.java**.

   b. Create an application named `TestPizza` that instantiates one `Pizza` object and demonstrates the use of the `Pizza` set and get methods. Save this application as **TestPizza.java**.

10. a. Create a class named `Student`. A `Student` has fields for an ID number, number of credit hours earned, and number of points earned. (For example, many schools compute grade point averages based on a scale of 4, so a three-credit-hour class in which a student earns an A is worth 12 points.) Include methods to assign values to all fields. A `Student` also has a field for grade point average. Include a method to compute the grade point average field by dividing points by credit hours earned. Write methods to display the values in each `Student` field. Save this class as **Student.java**.

    b. Write a class named `ShowStudent` that instantiates a `Student` object from the class you created and assign values to its fields. Compute the `Student` grade point average, and then display all the values associated with the `Student`. Save the application as **ShowStudent.java**.

    c. Create a constructor for the `Student` class you created. The constructor should initialize each `Student`'s ID number to 9999, his or her points earned to 12, and credit hours to 3 (resulting in a grade point average of 4.0). Write a program that demonstrates that the constructor works by instantiating an object and displaying the initial values. Save the application as **ShowStudent2.java**.

11. a. Create a class named `Checkup` with fields that hold a patient number, two blood pressure figures (systolic and diastolic), and two cholesterol figures (LDL and HDL). Include methods to get and set each of the fields. Include a method named `computeRatio()` that divides LDL cholesterol by HDL cholesterol and displays the result. Include an additional method named `explainRatio()` that explains that HDL

is known as "good cholesterol" and that a ratio of 3.5 or lower is considered optimum. Save the class as **Checkup.java**.

b. Create a class named `TestCheckup` whose `main()` method declares four `Checkup` objects. Call a `getData()` method four times. Within the method, prompt a user for values for each field for a `Checkup`, and return a `Checkup` object to the `main()` method where it is assigned to one of `main()`'s `Checkup` objects. Then, in `main()`, pass each `Checkup` object in turn to a `showValues()` method that displays the data. Blood pressure values are usually displayed with a slash between the systolic and diastolic numbers. (Typical blood pressure values are 110/78 or 130/90.) With the cholesterol figures, display the explanation of the cholesterol ratio calculation. (Typical cholesterol values are 100 and 40 or 180 and 70.) Save the application as **TestCheckup.java**.

12. a. Create a class named `Invoice` that contains fields for an item number, name, quantity, price, and total cost. Create instance methods that set the item name, quantity, and price. Whenever the price or quantity is set, recalculate the total (price times quantity). Also include a `displayLine()` method that displays the item number, name, quantity, price, and total cost. Save the class as **Invoice.java**.

b. Create a class named `TestInvoice` whose `main()` method declares three `Invoice` items. Create a method that prompts the user for and accepts values for the item number, name, quantity, and price for each `Invoice`. Then display each completed object. Save the application as **TestInvoice.java**.

DEBUGGING EXERCISES

Each of the following files saved in the Chapter.03 folder on your Student Disk has syntax and/or logic errors. In each case, determine and fix the problem. After you correct the errors, save each file using the same filename preceded with Fix. For example, DebugThree1.java will become FixDebugThree1.java.

a. DebugThree1.java
c. DebugThree3.java

b. DebugThree2.java
d. DebugThree4.java

> **NOTE**
> When you change a filename, remember to change every instance of the class name within the file so that it matches the new filename. In Java, the filename and class name must always match.

GAME ZONE

1. Playing cards are used in many computer games, including versions of such classics as Solitaire, Hearts, and Poker. Design a `Card` class that contains a character data field to hold a suit ('s' for spades, 'h' for hearts, 'd' for diamonds, or 'c' for clubs) and an integer data field for a value from 1 to 13. (When you learn more about string handling in Chapter 7, you can modify the class to hold words for the suits, such as "spades" or "hearts," as well as words for some of the values—for example, "ace" or "king".) Include get and set methods for each field. Save the class as **Card.java**.

Write an application that randomly selects two playing cards and prints their values. Simply assign a suit to each of the cards, but generate a random number for each card's value. Appendix D contains information on generating random numbers. To fully understand the process, you must learn more about Java classes and methods. However, for now, you can copy the following statements to generate a random number between 1 and 13 and assign it to a variable:

```
final int CARDS_IN_SUIT = 13;

myValue = ((int)(Math.random() * 100) % CARDS_IN_SUIT + 1);
```

After you learn about decision making in Chapter 5, you will be able to have the game determine the higher card. For now, just observe how the card values change as you execute the program multiple times. Save the application as **PickTwoCards.java**.

2. Computer games often contain different characters or creatures. For example, you might design a game in which alien beings possess specific characteristics such as color, number of eyes, or number of lives. Design a character for a game, creating a class to hold at least three attributes for the character. Include methods to get and set each of the character's attributes. Save the file as **MyCharacter.java**. Then write an application in which you create at least two characters. In turn, pass each character to a display method that prints the character's attributes. Save the application as **TwoCharacters.java**.

TOUGH QUESTIONS

1. Describe some situations in which passing arguments to a method in the wrong order would not cause any noticeable errors.

2. Suppose you have created a class named `Employee`. Further suppose that you have an application that declares the following:

```
final Employee myEmployee = new Employee();
```

Can `myEmployee`'s fields be altered?

3. Describe a chicken using a programming analogy. (This question is purposely vague. Be creative.)

4. Consider the real-life class named `StateInTheUnitedStates`. What are some real-life attributes of this class that are static attributes, and what attributes are instance attributes? Create another example of a real-life class and discuss what its static and instance members might be.

5. Can you think of any circumstances in which program comments would be a detriment?

UP FOR DISCUSSION

1. One of the advantages to writing a program that is subdivided into methods is that such a structure allows different programmers to write separate methods, thus dividing the work. Would you prefer to write a large program by yourself, or to work on a team in which each programmer produces one or more modules? Why?

2. In this chapter, you learned that hidden implementations are often said to exist in a black box. What are the advantages to this approach in both programming and real life? Are there any disadvantages?

4

MORE OBJECT CONCEPTS

In this chapter, you will:

Learn about blocks and scope
Overload a method
Learn about ambiguity
Send arguments to constructors
Overload constructors
Learn about the this reference
Use static variables
Use constant fields
Use automatically imported, prewritten constants
   and methods
Use the explicitly imported prewritten class
   GregorianCalendar
Learn about composition
Learn about nested and inner classes

Lynn Greenbrier, your mentor at Event Handlers Incorporated, pops her head into your cubicle on Monday morning. "How's the programming going?" she asks.

"I'm getting the hang of using objects," you tell her, "but I want to create lots of objects, and it seems like I will need so many methods for the classes I create that it will be very hard to keep track of them." You pause for a moment and add, "And all these `set` methods are driving me crazy. I wish an object could just start with values."

"Anything else bothering you?" Lynn asks.

"Well," you reply, "since you asked, shouldn't some objects and methods that are commonly needed by many programmers already be created for me? I can't be the first person who ever thought about taking a square root of a number or calculating a billing date for 10 days after service."

"You're in luck," Lynn says. "Java's creators have already thought about these things. Let me tell you about some of the more advanced things you can do with your classes."

UNDERSTANDING BLOCKS AND SCOPE

Within any class or method, the code between a pair of curly braces is called a **block**. For example, the method shown in Figure 4-1 contains two blocks. The first block contains another, so it is an example of an **outside block** (also called an **outer block**). It begins immediately after the method declaration and ends at the end of the method. The second block (shaded in Figure 4-1) is called the **inside block** or **inner block**. It is contained within the second set of curly braces and contains two executable statements: the declaration of `anotherNumber` and a `println()` statement. The inside block is **nested**, or contained entirely within, the outside block. A block can exist entirely within another block or entirely outside and separate from another block, but blocks can never overlap. For example, if a method contains two opening curly braces, indicating the start of two blocks, the next closing curly brace always closes the inner (second) block—it cannot close the outer block because that would make the blocks overlap. Another way to state this concept is that whenever you encounter a closing brace that ends a block, it always closes the most recently started block.

If you declare a variable in one program that you write, you cannot refer to that variable in another program (although you can declare another variable with the same name in the new program). Similarly, when you declare a variable within a block, you cannot refer to that variable outside the block. The portion of a program within which you can refer to a variable is the variable's **scope**. A variable comes into existence, or **comes into scope**, when you declare it. A variable ceases to exist, or **goes out of scope**, at the end of the block in which it is declared.

> **》NOTE**
> Although you can create as many variables and blocks as you need within any program, it is not wise to do so without a reason. The use of unnecessary variables and blocks increases the likelihood of improper use of variable names and scope.

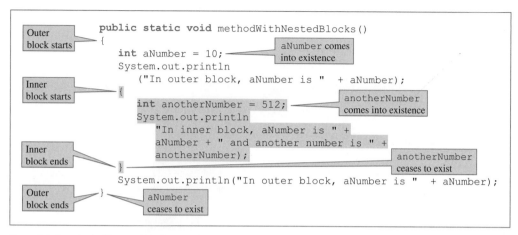

Figure 4-1 A method with nested blocks

In the `methodWithNestedBlocks()` method shown in Figure 4-1, the variable `aNumber` exists from the point of its declaration until the end of the method. This means `aNumber` exists both in the outer block and in the inner block and can be used anywhere in the method. The variable `anotherNumber` comes into existence within the inner block; `anotherNumber` goes out of scope when the inner block ends and cannot be used beyond its block. Figure 4-2 shows the output when the method in Figure 4-1 is called from another method.

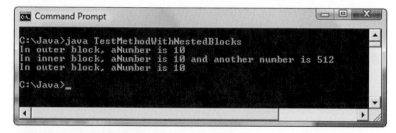

Figure 4-2 Output produced by application that uses `methodWithNestedBlocks()`

Figure 4-3 shows a method that contains some shaded, invalid statements. The first assignment, `aNumber = 75;`, is invalid because `aNumber` has not been declared yet. Similarly, the statements that attempt to assign 489 and 165 to `anotherNumber` are invalid because `anotherNumber` has not been declared yet. After `anotherNumber` is declared, it can be used for the remainder of the block, but the statement that attempts to assign 34 to it is outside the block in which `anotherNumber` was declared. The last shaded statement in Figure 4-3, `aNumber = 29;`, does not work because it falls outside the block in which `aNumber` was declared; it actually falls outside the entire `methodWithInvalidStatements()` method.

> **» NOTE**
> You are not required to vertically align the opening and closing braces for a block, but your programs are much easier to read if you do.

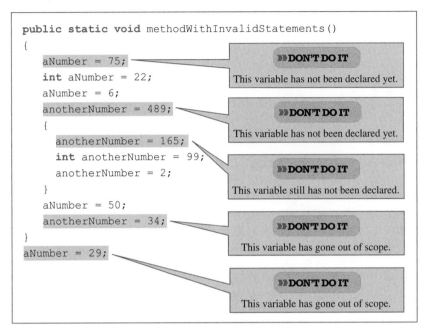

Figure 4-3 The `methodWithInvalidStatements()` method

Within a method, you can declare a variable with the same name multiple times, as long as each declaration is in its own nonoverlapping block. For example, the two declarations of variables named `someVar` in Figure 4-4 are valid because each variable is contained within its own block. The first instance of `someVar` has gone out of scope before the second instance comes into scope.

```
                    public static void twoDeclarations()
                    {
                        {
                            int someVar = 7;
                            System.out.println(someVar);
                        }
                        {
                            int someVar = 845;
                            System.out.println(someVar);
                        }
                    }
```

> **»» DON'T DO IT**
> Don't declare blocks for no reason. A new block starts here only to demonstrate scope.

> This variable will go out of scope at the next closing curly brace.

> This variable is totally different from the one in the previous block.

Figure 4-4 The `twoDeclarations()` method

You cannot declare the same variable name more than once within a block, even if a block contains other blocks. When you declare a variable more than once in a block, you are attempting to **redeclare the variable**—an illegal action. For example, in Figure 4-5, the second declaration of aValue causes an error because you cannot declare the same variable twice within the outer block of the method. By the same reasoning, the third declaration of aValue is also invalid, even though it appears within a new block. The block that contains the third declaration is entirely within the outside block, so the first declaration of aValue has not gone out of scope.

```
public static void invalidRedeclarationMethod()
{
   int aValue = 35;
   int aValue = 44;          ▶▶DON'T DO IT
   {                         Invalid redeclaration of
                             aValue in the same block
      int anotherValue = 0;
      int aValue = 10;       ▶▶DON'T DO IT
   }                         Invalid redeclaration of
}                            aValue in the inner block
                             of the same block
```

Figure 4-5 The invalidRedeclarationMethod()

Although you cannot declare a variable twice within the same block, you can declare a variable within one method of a class and use the same variable name within another method of the class. In this case, the variable declared inside each method resides in its own location in computer memory. When you use the variable's name within the method in which it is declared, it takes precedence over, or **overrides**, any other variable with the same name in another method. In other words, a locally declared variable always masks or hides another variable with the same name elsewhere in the class.

For example, consider the class in Figure 4-6. In the main() method of the OverridingVariable class, aNumber is declared and assigned the value 10. When the program calls firstMethod(), a new variable is declared with the same name but with a different memory address and a new value. The new variable exists only within firstMethod(), where it is displayed holding the value 77. After firstMethod() executes and the logic returns to the main() method, the original aNumber is displayed, containing 10. When aNumber is passed to secondMethod(), a copy is made within the method. This copy has the same identifier as the original aNumber, but a different memory address. So, within secondMethod(), when the value is changed to 862 and displayed, it has no effect on the original variable in main(). When the logic returns to main() after secondMethod(), the original value is displayed again. Examine the output in Figure 4-7 to understand the sequence of events.

▶▶NOTE
Object-oriented programmers also use the term "override" when a child class contains a field or method that has the same name as one in the parent class. You will learn more about inheritance in Chapters 9 and 10.

```
public class OverridingVariable
{
    public static void main(String[] args)          aNumber is declared
    {                                                in main().
        int aNumber = 10;
        System.out.println("In main(), aNumber is " + aNumber);          Whenever
        firstMethod();                                                   aNumber is
        System.out.println("Back in main(), aNumber is " + aNumber);     used in main(),
        secondMethod(aNumber);                                           it retains its
        System.out.println("Back in main() again, aNumber is " + aNumber);   value of 10.
    }
    public static void firstMethod()          This aNumber resides at a
    {                                         different memory address than the
        int aNumber = 77;                     one in main(). It is declared
        System.out.println("In firstMethod(), aNumber is "    locally in this method.
            + aNumber);
    }
    public static void secondMethod(int aNumber)          This aNumber also resides
    {                                                     at a different memory
        System.out.println("In secondMethod(), at first " +     address than the one in
            "aNumber is " + aNumber);                           main(). It is declared
        aNumber = 862;                                          locally in this method.
        System.out.println("In secondMethod(), after an assignment " +
            "aNumber is " + aNumber);
    }
}
```

Figure 4-6 The OverridingVariable class

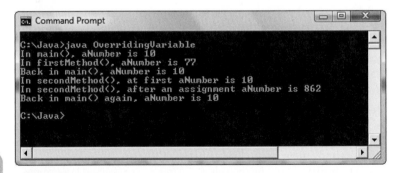

Figure 4-7 Output of the OverridingVariable application

NOTE You are familiar with local names overriding names defined elsewhere. If someone in your household is named "Eric," and someone in the house next door is named "Eric," members of your household who talk about "Eric" are referring to the local version. They would add a qualifier such as "Eric Johnson" or "Eric next door" to refer to the nonlocal version.

When they have the same name, variables within methods of a class also override the class's variables. Figure 4-8 shows an Employee class that contains two instance variables and three void methods. The setValues() method provides values for the two class instance fields. Whenever the method named methodThatUsesInstanceAttributes() is used with an Employee object, the instance values for empNum and empPayRate are used. However, when the other method, methodThatUsesLocalVariables(), is used with an Employee object, the local variable values within the method, 33333 and 555.55, override the class's instance variables. Figure 4-9 shows a short application that declares an Employee object and uses each method; Figure 4-10 shows the output.

```
public class Employee
{
    private int empNum;
    private double empPayRate;
    public void setValues()
    {
        empNum = 111;
        empPayRate = 22.22;
    }
    public void methodThatUsesInstanceAttributes()
    {
        System.out.println("Employee number is " + empNum);
        System.out.println("Pay rate is " + empPayRate);
    }
    public void methodThatUsesLocalVariables()
    {
        int empNum = 33333;
        double empPayRate = 555.55;
        System.out.println("Employee number is " + empNum);
        System.out.println("Pay rate is " + empPayRate);
    }
}
```

Figure 4-8 The Employee class

```
public class TestEmployeeMethods
{
    public static void main(String[] args)
    {
        Employee aWorker = new Employee();
        aWorker.setValues();
        aWorker.methodThatUsesInstanceAttributes();
        aWorker.methodThatUsesLocalVariables();
    }
}
```

Figure 4-9 The TestEmployeeMethods application

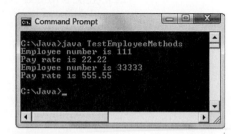

Figure 4-10 Output of the TestEmployeeMethods application

When you write programs, you might choose to avoid confusing situations that arise when you give the same name to a class's instance field and to a local method variable. But, if you do use the same name, be aware that within the method, the method's local variable overrides the instance variable.

It is important to understand the impact that blocks and methods have on your variables. Variables and fields with the same names represent different memory locations when they are declared within different scopes. After you understand the scope of variables, you can more easily locate the source of many errors within your programs.

》》TWO TRUTHS AND A LIE: UNDERSTANDING BLOCKS AND SCOPE

1. A variable ceases to exist, or goes out of scope, at the end of the block in which it is declared.
2. You cannot declare the same variable name more than once within a block, even if a block contains other blocks.
3. A class's instance variables override locally declared variables with the same names that are declared within the class's methods.

The false statement is #3. When they have the same name, variables within methods of a class override a class's instance variables.

OVERLOADING A METHOD

Overloading involves using one term to indicate diverse meanings, or writing multiple methods with the same name but with different arguments. When you use the English language, you over-load words all the time. When you say "open the door," "open your eyes," and "open a computer file," you are talking about three very different actions using very different methods and producing very different results. However, anyone who speaks English fluently has no trouble understanding your meaning because the verb *open* is understood in the context of the noun that follows it.

When you overload a Java method, you write multiple methods with a shared name. The compiler understands your meaning based on the arguments you use with the method. For example, suppose you create a class method to apply a simple interest rate to a bank balance. The method is named `calculateInterest()`; it receives two `double` arguments—the bal-ance and the interest rate—and displays the multiplied result. Figure 4-11 shows the method.

```
public static void calculateInterest(double bal, double rate)
{
   double interest;
   interest = bal * rate;
   System.out.println("Simple interest on $" + bal +
      " at  " + rate + "% rate is " + interest);
}
```

Figure 4-11 The `calculateInterest()` method with two `double` arguments

NOTE The `calculateInterest()` method in Figure 4-11 can receive integer arguments, even though it is defined as needing `double` arguments, because `int`s are promoted or cast automatically to `double`s, as you learned in Chapter 2.

When an application calls the `calculateInterest()` method and passes two `double` values, as in `calculateInterest(1000.00, 0.04)`, the interest is calculated correctly as 4% of $1000.00. Assume, however, that different users want to calculate interest using different argument types. Some users who want to indicate an interest rate of 4% might use 0.04; others might use 4 and assume that it means 4%. When the `calculateInterest()` method is called with the arguments $1000.00 and 0.04, the interest is calculated correctly as 40.00. When the method is called using $1000.00 and 4, the interest is calculated incorrectly as 4000.00.

A solution for the conflicting use of numbers to represent parameter values is to overload the `calculateInterest()` method. For example, in addition to the `calculateInterest()` method shown in Figure 4-11, you could add the method shown in Figure 4-12.

Notice the data type for `rate`

```
public static void calculateInterest(double bal, int rate)
{
   double interest, rateAsPercent;
   rateAsPercent = rate / 100.0;
   interest = bal * rateAsPercent;
   System.out.println("Simple interest on $" +
      bal + " at  " + rate + "% rate is " +
      interest);
}
```

Dividing by 100.0 converts `rate` to its decimal equivalent

Figure 4-12 The `calculateInterest()` method with a `double` argument and an `int` argument

NOTE Note the `rateAsPercent` figure is calculated by dividing by 100.0 and not by 100. If two integers are divided, the result is a truncated integer; dividing by a `double` 100.0 causes the result to be a `double`. Alternatively, you could use an explicit cast such as `rateAsPercent = (double)rate / 100.0`.

If an application calls the method `calculateInterest()` using two `double` arguments—for example, `calculateInterest(1000.00, 0.04)`—the first version of the method, the one shown in Figure 4-11, executes. However, if an integer is used as the second parameter in a call to `calculateInterest()`—as in `calculateInterest(1000.00, 4)`—the second version of the method, the one shown in Figure 4-12, executes. In this second example, the whole number rate figure is correctly divided by 100.0 before it is used to determine the interest earned.

Of course, you could use methods with different names to solve the dilemma of producing an accurate interest figure—for example, `calculateInterestUsingDouble()` and `calculateInterestUsingInt()`. However, it is easier and more convenient for programmers who use your methods to remember just one method name that they can use in the form that is most appropriate for their programs. It is convenient to be able to use one reasonable name for tasks that are functionally identical except for the argument types that can be passed to them. The compiler knows which method version to call based on the passed arguments.

»TWO TRUTHS AND A LIE: OVERLOADING A METHOD

1. When you overload Java methods, you write multiple methods with a shared name.
2. When you overload Java methods, the methods are called using different arguments.
3. Instead of overloading methods, it is preferable to write methods with unique identifiers.

The false statement is #3. Overloading methods is preferable to using unique identifiers because it is convenient for programmers to use one reasonable name for tasks that are functionally identical, except for the argument types that can be passed to them.

LEARNING ABOUT AMBIGUITY

When an application contains just one version of a method, you can call the method using a parameter of the correct data type, or one that can be promoted to the correct data type. For example, consider the simple method shown in Figure 4-13.

```
public static void simpMeth(double d)
{
    System.out.println("Method receives double parameter");
}
```

Figure 4-13 The `simpMeth()` method with a `double` parameter

If you write an application in which you declare `doubleValue` as a `double` variable and `intValue` as an `int` variable (as shown in Figure 4-14), either method call `simpMeth(doubleValue);` or `simpMeth(intValue);` results in the output "Method receives double parameter". When you call the method with the `double` argument, the method works as expected. When you call the method with the integer argument, the integer is cast as (or promoted to) a `double`, and the method also works. The output is shown in Figure 4-15.

```
public class CallSimpMeth
{
    public static void main(String[] args)
    {
        double doubleValue = 45.67;
        int intValue = 17;
        simpMeth(doubleValue);
        simpMeth(intValue);
    }
    public static void simpMeth(double d)
    {
        System.out.println("Method receives double parameter");
    }
}
```

Figure 4-14 The `CallSimpMeth` application that calls `simpMeth()` with a `double` and an integer

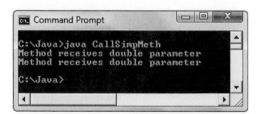

Figure 4-15 Output of the `CallSimpMeth` application

»NOTE Note that if the method with the declaration `void simpMeth(double d)` did not exist, but the declaration `void simpMeth(int i)` did exist, then the method call `simpMeth(doubleValue);` would fail. Although an `int` can be promoted to a `double`, a `double` cannot become an `int`. This makes sense if you consider the potential loss of information when a `double` value is reduced to an integer.

When you properly overload a method, you can call it providing different argument lists, and the appropriate version of the method executes. Within the application in Figure 4-14, if you add a second overloaded `simpMeth()` method that takes an integer parameter (as shown in Figure 4-16, with the new method shaded), the output changes when you call `simpMeth(intValue);`. Instead of promoting an integer argument to a `double`, the compiler recognizes a more exact match for the method call that uses the integer argument, so it calls the version of the method that produces the output "Method receives integer parameter". Figure 4-17 shows the output.

```
public class CallSimpMethAgain
{
    public static void main(String[] args)
    {
        double doubleValue = 45.67;
        int intValue = 17;
        simpMeth(doubleValue);
        simpMeth(intValue);
    }
    public static void simpMeth(double d)
    {
        System.out.println("Method receives double parameter");
    }
    public static void simpMeth(int d)
    {
        System.out.println("Method receives integer parameter");
    }
}
```

Figure 4-16 The CallSimpMethAgain application that calls simpMeth() with a double and an integer

Figure 4-17 Output of the CallSimpMethAgain application

When you overload methods, you risk creating an **ambiguous** situation—one in which the compiler cannot determine which method to use. Consider the following overloaded calculateInterest() method declarations:

```
public static void calculateInterest(int bal, double rate)
public static void calculateInterest(double bal, int rate)
    // Notice rate type
```

> **▶▶ NOTE**
> An overloaded method is not ambiguous on its own—it only becomes ambiguous if you create an ambiguous situation. A program containing a potentially ambiguous situation will run problem-free if you do not make any ambiguous method calls.

A call to calculateInterest() with an int and a double argument (in that order) executes the first version of the method, and a call to calculateInterest() with a double and an int argument executes the second version of the method. With each of these calls, the compiler can find an exact match for the arguments you send. However, if you call calculateInterest() using two integer arguments, as in calculateInterest(300, 6);, an ambiguous situation arises because there is no exact match for the method call. Because two integers can be promoted to an integer and a double (thus matching the first version of the overloaded method), or to a double and an integer (thus matching the second version), the compiler does not know which version of the calculateInterest() method to use and the program does not compile.

It is important to note that you can overload methods correctly by providing different parameter lists for methods with the same name. Methods with identical names that have identical parameter lists but different return types are not overloaded—they are illegal. For example, the following two methods are ambiguous:

```
int   aMethod(int x)
void aMethod(int x)
```

The compiler determines which of several versions of a method to call based on the arguments in the method call. If those two methods existed within a class, when the method call aMethod(17); was made, the compiler would not know which method to execute because both methods take an integer parameter.

>> **NOTE**
The compiler determines which version of a method to call by the method's signature. In Chapter 3, you learned that a method's signature is the combination of the method name and the number, types, and order of parameters.

>> **TWO TRUTHS AND A LIE: LEARNING ABOUT AMBIGUITY**

1. When it is part of the same program as void myMethod(int age, String name), the following method would be ambiguous: void myMethod(String name, int age).
2. When it is part of the same program as void myMethod(int age, String name), the following method would be ambiguous: String myMethod(int zipCode, String address).
3. When it is part of the same program as void myMethod(int age, String name), the following method would be ambiguous: void myMethod(int x, String y).

The false statement is #1. A method that accepts an int parameter followed by a String is not ambiguous with one that accepts the parameters in the reverse order.

SENDING ARGUMENTS TO CONSTRUCTORS

In Chapter 3, you learned that Java automatically provides a constructor when you create a class. You also learned that you can write your own constructor, and that you often do so when you want to ensure that fields within classes are initialized to some appropriate default value. In Chapter 3, you learned about automatically provided default constructors that do not require arguments, and you learned that you can also write a custom default constructor. However, when you write your own constructors, they can receive parameters. Such parameters are often used to initialize data fields for an object.

>> **NOTE**
If the keyword final appears in a method's parameter list, it is ignored when determining ambiguity. In other words, two methods with the headers void aMethod(int x) and void aMethod(final int x) are ambiguous.

For example, consider the Employee class with just one data field, shown in Figure 4-18. Its constructor assigns 999 to the empNum of each potentially instantiated Employee object. Anytime an Employee object is created using a statement such as Employee partTimeWorker = new Employee();, even if no other data-assigning methods are ever used, you ensure that the partTimeWorker Employee, like all Employee objects, will have an initial empNum of 999.

```java
public class Employee
{
    private int empNum;
    Employee()
    {
        empNum = 999;
    }
}
```

Figure 4-18 The Employee class with its constructor that initializes empNum field

>> **NOTE**
You can use a setEmpNum() method to assign values to individual Employee objects after construction, but a constructor assigns the values at the time of creation.

Alternatively, you might choose to create `Employee` objects with initial `empNum` values that differ for each `Employee`. To accomplish this when the object is instantiated, you can pass an employee number to the constructor. Figure 4-19 shows an `Employee` class that contains a constructor that receives a parameter. With this constructor, an argument is passed using a statement such as the following:

```java
Employee partTimeWorker = new Employee(881);
```

```java
public class Employee
{
    private int empNum;
    Employee(int num)
    {
        empNum = num;
    }
}
```

Figure 4-19 The `Employee` class with its constructor that accepts a value

When the constructor executes, the integer within the method call (881) is passed to `Employee()` as the parameter `num`, which is assigned to the `empNum` within the constructor.

When you create an `Employee` class with a constructor such as the one shown in Figure 4-19, every `Employee` object you create must have an integer argument in its constructor call. In other words, with this new version of the class, the following statement no longer works:

```java
Employee partTimeWorker = new Employee();
```

After you write a constructor for a class, you no longer receive the automatically provided default constructor. If a class's only constructor requires an argument, you must provide an argument for every object of the class that you create.

> **» NOTE** In Chapter 2, you learned that Java casts variables to a unifying type when you perform arithmetic with unlike types. In a similar way, Java can promote one data type to another when you pass a parameter to a method. For example, if a method has a `double` parameter and you pass in an integer, it is promoted to a `double`. Recall that the order of promotion is `double`, `float`, `long`, and `int`. Any type in this list can be promoted to any type that precedes it.

» TWO TRUTHS AND A LIE: SENDING ARGUMENTS TO CONSTRUCTORS

1. A default constructor is one that is automatically created.
2. When you write a constructor, it can be written to receive parameters or not.
3. If a class's only constructor requires an argument, you must provide an argument for every object of the class that you create.

The false statement is #1. A default constructor is one that takes no arguments. The constructor that is automatically created when you do not write your own version is a default constructor, but so is one that you write to take no arguments.

OVERLOADING CONSTRUCTORS

If you create a class from which you instantiate objects, Java automatically provides you with a constructor. If you create your own constructor, the automatically created constructor no longer exists. Therefore, after you create a constructor that takes a parameter, you no longer have the option of using the automatic constructor that requires no parameters.

Fortunately, as with any other method, you can overload constructors. Overloading constructors provides you with a way to create objects with or without initial arguments, as needed. For example, in addition to using the provided constructor shown in Figure 4-19, you can create a second constructor for the Employee class; Figure 4-20 shows an Employee class that contains two constructors. When you use this class to create an Employee object, you have the option of creating the object either with or without an initial empNum value. When you create an Employee object with the statement Employee aWorker = new Employee();, the constructor with no parameters is called, and the Employee object receives an initial empNum value of 999. When you create an Employee object with Employee anotherWorker = new Employee(7677);, the constructor version that requires an integer is used, and the anotherWorker Employee receives an initial empNum of 7677.

```java
public class Employee
{
    private int empNum;
    Employee(int num)
    {
        empNum = num;
    }
    Employee()
    {
        empNum = 999;
    }
}
```

Figure 4-20 The Employee class that contains two constructors

>> **NOTE** You can use constructor arguments to initialize field values, but you can also use arguments for any other purpose. For example, you could use the presence or absence of an argument simply to determine which of two possible constructors to call, yet not make use of the argument within the constructor. As long as the constructor parameter lists differ, there is no ambiguity about which constructor to call.

>> **TWO TRUTHS AND A LIE: OVERLOADING CONSTRUCTORS**

Assume that the following statement in a Java program works correctly:

    Chair myChair = new Chair();

1. The Chair class has a default constructor.
2. You can be sure that the Chair class does not have overloaded constructors.
3. The Chair class might have a constructor with the following header:

    Chair(int legs)

The false statement is #2. The Chair class might have overloaded constructors. This statement happens to use the default constructor, but there could be others.

LEARNING ABOUT THE this REFERENCE

When you start creating classes, they can become large very quickly. Besides data fields, each class can have many methods, including several overloaded versions. On paper, a single class might require several pages of coded statements.

When you instantiate an object from a class, memory is reserved for each instance field in the class. For example, if a class contains 20 data fields, when you create one object from that class, enough memory is reserved to hold the 20 values for that object. When you create 200 objects of the same class, the computer reserves enough memory for 4,000 data fields—20 for each of the 200 objects. In many applications, the computer memory requirements can become substantial. Fortunately, it is not necessary to store a separate copy of each variable and method for each instantiation of a class.

Usually, you want each instantiation of a class to have its own data fields. If an Employee class contains fields for employee number, name, and salary, every individual Employee object needs a unique number, name, and salary value. (When you want each object to have a unique field value, you do not define the field as static.) However, when you create a method for a class, any object can use the same method. Whether the method performs a calculation, sets a field value, or constructs an object, the instructions are the same for each instantiated object. Not only would it take an enormous amount of memory to store a separate copy of each method for every object created from a class, but memory would also be wasted because you would be storing identical copies of methods—that is, each copy of the method would have the same contents for each object. Luckily, in Java just one copy of each method in a class is stored, and all instantiated objects can use that copy.

When you use a nonstatic method, you use the object name, a dot, and the method name—for example, aWorker.getEmpNum();. When you execute the aWorker.getEmpNum() method, you are running the general, shared Employee class getEmpNum() method; aWorker has access to the method because aWorker is a member of the Employee class. However, within the getEmpNum() method, when you access the empNum *field*, you access aWorker's private, individual copy of the empNum field. Many Employee objects might exist, but just one copy of the method exists no matter how many Employees there are—so when you call aWorker.getEmpNum();, the compiler must determine *whose* copy of the empNum value should be returned by the single getEmpNum() method.

» NOTE
When you pass a reference, you pass a memory address.

The compiler accesses the correct object's field because you implicitly pass a reference to aWorker to the getEmpNum() method. A **reference** is an object's memory address. The reference is implicit because it is automatically understood without actually being written. The reference to an object that is passed to any object's nonstatic class method is called the **this reference**; this is a reserved word in Java. For example, the two getEmpNum() methods shown in Figure 4-21 perform identically. The first method simply uses the this reference without you being aware of it; the second method uses the this reference explicitly.

```
public int getEmpNum()
{
    return empNum;
}
public int getEmpNum()
{
    return this.empNum;
}
```

Figure 4-21 Two versions of the getEmpNum() method, with and without an explicit this reference

Usually, you neither want nor need to refer to the `this` reference within the methods you write, but the `this` reference is always there, working behind the scenes, so that the data field for the correct object can be accessed.

On a few occasions, you must use the `this` reference to make your classes work correctly; one example is shown in the `Student` class in Figure 4-22. Within the constructor for this class, the parameter names `stuNum` and `gpa` are identical to the class field names. Within the constructor, `stuNum` and `gpa` refer to the locally declared names, not the class field names. The statement `stuNum = stuNum` accomplishes nothing—it assigns the local variable value to itself. The client application in Figure 4-23 attempts to create a `Student` object with an ID number of 111 and a grade point average of 3.5, but Figure 4-24 shows the output. The values are not assigned; instead, they are just zeroes.

»NOTE
Recall that methods associated with individual objects are instance methods. Only instance methods implicitly receive a `this` reference. In other words, only nonstatic methods receive a `this` reference.

```java
public class Student
{
    private int stuNum;
    private double gpa;
    public Student(int stuNum, double gpa)
    {
        stuNum = stuNum;
        gpa = gpa;
    }
    public void showStudent()
    {
        System.out.println("Student #" + stuNum +
            " gpa is " + gpa);
    }
}
```

»DON'T DO IT
All four variables used in these two statements are the local versions declared in the method's parameter list. The fields are never accessed.

Figure 4-22 A `Student` class whose constructor does not work as expected

```java
public class TestStudent
{
    public static void main(String[] args)
    {
        Student aPsychMajor = new Student(111, 3.5);
        aPsychMajor.showStudent();
    }
}
```

Figure 4-23 The `TestStudent` class that instantiates a `Student` object

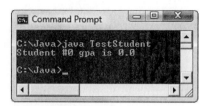

Figure 4-24 Output of the `TestStudent` application

Figure 4-25 shows a modified Student class. The only difference between this class and the one in Figure 4-22 is the explicit use of the this reference within the constructor. When the this reference is used with a field name in a class method, the reference is to the class field instead of to the local variable declared within the method. When the TestStudent application uses this new version of the Student class, the output appears as expected, as shown in Figure 4-26.

```
public class Student
{
    private int stuNum;
    private double gpa;
    public Student(int stuNum, double gpa)
    {
        this.stuNum = stuNum;
        this.gpa = gpa;
    }
    public void showStudent()
    {
        System.out.println("Student #" + stuNum +
            " gpa is " + gpa);
    }
}
```

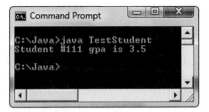

Figure 4-25 The Student class using the explicit this reference within the constructor

Figure 4-26 Output of the TestStudent application using the new version of the Student class

USING THE this REFERENCE TO MAKE OVERLOADED CONSTRUCTORS MORE EFFICIENT

Suppose you create a student class with data fields for a student number and a grade point average. Further suppose you want four overloaded constructors as follows:

» A constructor that accepts an int and a double and assigns them the student number and grade point average, respectively

» A constructor that accepts a double and assigns it to the grade point average. Every student number is initialized to 999.

» A constructor that accepts an int and assigns it to the student number. Every grade point average is initialized to 0.0.

» A default constructor that assigns 999 to every student number and 0.0 to every grade point average

Figure 4-27 shows the class. Although this class works, and allows Students to be constructed in four different ways, there is a lot of repetition within the constructors.

You can make the code in Figure 4-27 more efficient and less error-prone by calling one constructor version from the others. To do so, you use the this reference from one constructor version to call another version. Figure 4-28 shows how the Student class can be rewritten.

```
public class Student
{
    private int stuNum;
    private double gpa;
    Student(int num, double avg)
    {
        stuNum = num;
        gpa = avg;
    }
    Student(double avg)
    {
        stuNum = 999;
        gpa = avg;
    }
    Student(int num)
    {
        stuNum = num;
        gpa = 0.0;
    }
    Student()
    {
        stuNum = 999;
        gpa = 0.0;
    }
}
```

Figure 4-27 Student class with four constructors

```
public class Student
{
    private int stuNum;
    private double gpa;
    Student(int num, double avg)
    {
        stuNum = num;
        gpa = avg;
    }
    Student(double avg)
    {
        this(999, avg);
    }
    Student(int num)
    {
        this(num, 0.0);
    }
    Student()
    {
        this(999, 0.0);
    }
}
```

Figure 4-28 The Student class using this in three of four constructors

By writing each constructor to call one master constructor, you save coding and reduce the chance for errors. For example, if code is added later to ensure that all student ID numbers are three digits, or that no grade point average is greater than 4.0, the code will be written only in the two-parameter version of the constructor, and all the other versions will use it.

> **» NOTE**
> Testing a variable to ensure it falls within the proper range of values requires decision making. Chapter 5 covers this topic.

> **» NOTE**
> If you call this() from a constructor, it must be the first statement within the constructor.

> **» NOTE**
> You cannot call this() from other methods in a class; you can only call it from constructors.

»TWO TRUTHS AND A LIE: LEARNING ABOUT THE this REFERENCE

1. Usually, you want each instantiation of a class to have its own nonstatic data fields, but each object does not need its own copy of most methods.

2. When you use a nonstatic method, the compiler accesses the correct object's field because you implicitly pass an object reference to the method.

3. The this reference is supplied automatically in classes; you cannot use it explicitly.

The false statement is #3. Usually, you neither want nor need to refer to the this reference within the methods you write, but you can use it—for example, when there are conflicts between identifiers for fields and local variables.

USING static VARIABLES

In Chapter 3, you learned that methods you create to use without objects are static. For example, the main() method in a program and the methods that main() calls without an object reference are static. You also learned that most methods you create within a class are nonstatic—they are methods that you associate with individual objects. Static methods do not have a this reference because they have no object associated with them; therefore, they are called **class methods**.

You can also create **class variables**, which are variables that are shared by every instantiation of a class. Whereas instance variables in a class exist separately for every object you create, there is only one copy of each static, class variable per class. For example, consider the BaseballPlayer class in Figure 4-29. The BaseballPlayer class contains a static field named count, and two nonstatic fields named number and battingAverage. The BaseballPlayer constructor sets values for number and battingAverage and increases the count by one. In other words, every time a BaseballPlayer object is constructed, it contains individual values for number and battingAverage, and the count field contains a count of the number of existing objects and is shared by all BaseballPlayer objects.

```java
public class BaseballPlayer
{
    private static int count = 0;
    private int number;
    private double battingAverage;
    public BaseballPlayer(int id, double avg)
    {
        number = id;
        battingAverage = avg;
        count = count + 1;
    }
    public void showPlayer()
    {
        System.out.println("Player #" + number +
            " batting average is " + battingAverage +
            " There are " + count + " players");
    }
}
```

Figure 4-29 The BaseballPlayer class

The TestPlayer class in Figure 4-30 is an application that declares two BaseballPlayer objects, displays them, and then creates a third BaseballPlayer object and displays it. When you examine the output in Figure 4-31, you can see that by the time the first two objects are declared, the count value that they share is 2. Whether count is accessed using the aCatcher object or the aShortstop object, the count is the same. After the third object is declared, its count value is 3, as is the value of count associated with the previously declared aCatcher object. In other words, because the static count variable is incremented within the class constructor, each object has access to the total number of objects that currently exist. No matter how many BaseballPlayer objects are eventually instantiated, each refers to the single count field.

```java
public class TestPlayer
{
   public static void main(String[] args)
   {
      BaseballPlayer aCatcher = new BaseballPlayer(12, .218);
      BaseballPlayer aShortstop = new BaseballPlayer(31, .385);
      aCatcher.showPlayer();
      aShortstop.showPlayer();
      BaseballPlayer anOutfielder = new BaseballPlayer(44, .505);
      anOutfielder.showPlayer();
      aCatcher.showPlayer();
   }
}
```

Figure 4-30 The TestPlayer class

> **»NOTE**
> Methods declared as static cannot access instance variables, but instance methods can access both static and instance variables.

Figure 4-31 Output of the TestPlayer application

»TWO TRUTHS AND A LIE: USING static VARIABLES

1. Methods declared as static receive a this reference that contains a reference to the object associated with them.
2. Methods declared as static are called class methods.
3. Class variables are variables that are shared by every instantiation of a class.

The false statement is #1. Static methods do not have a this reference because they have no object associated with them.

USING CONSTANT FIELDS

In Chapter 2, you learned to create named constants by using the keyword `final`. Sometimes a data field in a class should be constant. For example, you might want to store a school ID value that is the same for every `Student` object you create, so you declare it to be static. In addition, if you want the value for the school ID to be fixed so that all `Student` objects use the same ID value—for example, when applying to scholarship-granting organizations or when registering for standardized tests—you might want to make the school ID unalterable. As with ordinary variables, you use the keyword `final` with a field to make its value unalterable after construction. For example, the class in Figure 4-32 contains the symbolic constant `SCHOOL_ID`. Because it is static, all objects share a single memory location for the field, and because it is `final`, it cannot change during program execution.

```java
public class Student
{
    private static final int SCHOOL_ID = 12345;
    private int stuNum;
    private double gpa;
    public Student(int stuNum, double gpa)
    {
        this.stuNum = stuNum;
        this.gpa = gpa;
    }
    public void showStudent()
    {
        System.out.println("Student #" + stuNum +
            " gpa is " + gpa);
    }
}
```

Figure 4-32 The `Student` class containing a symbolic constant

▶▶NOTE
Fields that are `final` also can be initialized in a `static` initialization block. For more details about this technique, see *http://java.sun.com*.

A nonstatic `final` field's value can be set in the class constructor. For example, you can set it using a constant, or you can set it using a parameter passed into the constructor. However, after construction, you cannot change a `final` field's value.

▶▶NOTE You can use the keyword `final` with methods or classes. When used in this manner, `final` indicates limitations placed on inheritance. You will learn more about inheritance in Chapters 9 and 10.

▶▶NOTE Fields declared to be `static` are not always `final`. If you want to create a field that all members of the class can access, but the field value changes, then it is `static` but not `final`. Similarly, `final` fields are not always `static`. If you want each object created from a class to contain its own final value, you would not declare the field to be `static`.

Figure 4-33 illustrates how two declared Student objects would look in memory. After each object is constructed, it has its own stuNum and gpa, but the objects share the only copy of SCHOOL_ID.

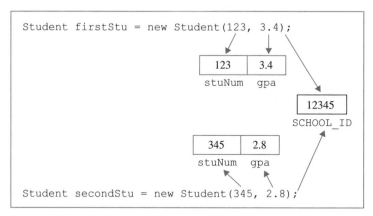

Figure 4-33 Illustration of two Student objects in memory

»TWO TRUTHS AND A LIE: USING CONSTANT FIELDS

1. A static field's value is shared by every object of that class.
2. A final field's value is shared by every object of a class.
3. A final static field's value is shared by every object of a class.

The false statement is #2. A final field's value can be assigned only once, but it is not shared by every object unless it is also static.

USING AUTOMATICALLY IMPORTED, PREWRITTEN CONSTANTS AND METHODS

Often you will need to create classes from which you will instantiate objects. You can create an Employee class with fields appropriate for describing employees in your organization and their functions, and an Inventory class with fields appropriate for whatever type of item you manufacture. However, many classes are commonly used by a wide variety of programmers. Rather than have each Java programmer "reinvent the wheel," the creators of Java have produced nearly 500 classes for you to use in your programs.

You have already used several of these prewritten classes; for example, you have used the `System` and `JOptionPane` classes to produce output. Each of these classes is stored in a **package**, or a **library of classes**, which is simply a folder that provides a convenient grouping for classes. Many Java packages are available only if you explicitly name them within your program; for example, when you use `JOptionPane`, you must import the `javax.swing` package into your program. However, the group that contains classes such as `System` is used so frequently that it is available automatically to every program you write. The package that is implicitly imported into every Java program is named **java.lang**. The classes it contains are **fundamental classes**, or basic classes, as opposed to the **optional classes** that must be explicitly named.

The class `java.lang.Math` contains constants and methods that you can use to perform common mathematical functions. All of the constants and methods in the `Math` class are `static`—they are class variables and class methods. For example, a commonly used constant is `PI`. Within the `Math` class, the declaration for `PI` is as follows:

```
public final static double PI = 3.14159265358979323846;
```

Notice that `PI` is:

» `public`, so any program can access it directly

» `final`, so it cannot be changed

» `static`, so only one copy exists and you can access it without declaring a `Math` object

» `double`, so it holds a floating-point value

> **»NOTE** For mathematicians, another useful constant is E, which represents the base of natural logarithms. Its definition is as follows:
> ```
> public final static double E = 2.7182818284590452354;
> ```

You can use the value of `PI` within any program you write by referencing the full package path in which `PI` is defined; for example, you can calculate the area of a circle using the following statement:

```
areaOfCircle = java.lang.Math.PI * radius * radius;
```

However, the `java.lang` package is imported automatically into your programs, so if you simply reference `Math.PI`, Java recognizes this code as a shortcut to the full package path. Therefore, the preferred (and simpler) statement is the following:

```
areaOfCircle = Math.PI * radius * radius;
```

In addition to constants, many useful methods are available within the `Math` class. For example, the `Math.max()` method returns the larger of two values, and the method `Math.abs()` returns the absolute value of a number. The statement `largerValue = Math.max(32, 75);` results in `largerValue` assuming the value 75, and the statement `posVal = Math.abs(-245);` results in `posVal` assuming the value 245. Table 4-1 lists some common `Math` class methods.

Method	Value That the Method Returns
abs(x)	Absolute value of *x*
acos(x)	Arc cosine of *x*
asin(x)	Arc sine of *x*
atan(x)	Arc tangent of *x*
atan2(x, y)	Theta component of the polar coordinate (r, theta) that corresponds to the Cartesian coordinate x, y
ceil(x)	Smallest integral value not less than *x* (ceiling)
cos(x)	Cosine of *x*
exp(x)	Exponent, where *x* is the base of the natural logarithms
floor(x)	Largest integral value not greater than *x*
log(x)	Natural logarithm of *x*
max(x, y)	Larger of *x* and *y*
min(x, y)	Smaller of *x* and *y*
pow(x, y)	*x* raised to the *y* power
random()	Random double number between 0.0 and 1.0
rint(x)	Closest integer to *x* (*x* is a double, and the return value is expressed as a double)
round(x)	Closest integer to *x* (where *x* is a float or double, and the return value is an int or long)
sin(x)	Sine of *x*
sqrt(x)	Square root of *x*
tan(x)	Tangent of *x*

Table 4-1 Common Math class methods

>> **NOTE**
Because all constants and methods in the Math class are classwide (that is, static), there is no need to create an instance of the Math class. You cannot instantiate objects of type Math because the constructor for the Math class is private and your programs cannot access the constructor.

>> **NOTE** Unless you are a mathematician, you won't use many of these Math class methods, and it is unwise to do so unless you understand their purposes. For example, because the square root of a negative number is undefined, if you display the result after the method call imaginaryNumber = Math.sqrt(-12);, you see NaN. **NaN** stands for "Not a Number."

>> **TWO TRUTHS AND A LIE: USING AUTOMATICALLY IMPORTED, PREWRITTEN CONSTANTS AND METHODS**

1. The creators of Java have produced nearly 500 classes for you to use in your programs.
2. Java packages are available only if you explicitly name them within your program.
3. The implicitly imported java.lang package contains fundamental Java classes.

The false statement is #2. Many Java packages are available only if you explicitly name them within your program, but others are automatically imported.

USING AN EXPLICITLY IMPORTED PREWRITTEN CLASS AND ITS METHODS

Java contains hundreds of classes, only a few of which—those in the `java.lang` package—are included automatically in the programs you write. To use any of the other prewritten classes, you must use one of three methods:

» Use the entire path with the class name.

» Import the class.

» Import the package that contains the class you are using.

For example, the `java.util` class package has useful classes containing methods that deal with dates and times. Within this package, one of the defined classes is named `GregorianCalendar`.

> **NOTE** The Gregorian calendar is the calendar you use to keep track of time. It was instituted on October 15, 1582, and is named for Pope Gregory XIII, who was instrumental in the calendar's adoption. For dates that fall before the Gregorian cutover date, the GregorianCalendar class uses the Julian calendar. The only difference between the two calendars is the leap-year rule. The Julian calendar specifies leap years every four years, whereas the Gregorian calendar omits century years that are not divisible by 400, such as 1900 and 2100.

> **NOTE** Dates obtained using GregorianCalendar are historically accurate only from March 1, 4 A.D. onward, when modern Julian calendar rules were adopted. Before this date, leap-year rules were applied irregularly, and before 45 B.C. the Julian calendar did not exist. Obviously, these constraints are not a problem for most business applications.

You can instantiate an object of type `GregorianCalendar` from this class by using the full class path, as in the following:

```
java.util.GregorianCalendar myAnniversary = new
    java.util.GregorianCalendar();
```

Alternatively, when you include `import java.util.GregorianCalendar;` as the first line in your program, you can shorten the declaration of `myAnniversary` to this:

```
GregorianCalendar myAnniversary = new
    GregorianCalendar();
```

An `import` statement allows you to abbreviate lengthy class names by notifying the Java program that when you use `GregorianCalendar`, you mean the `java.util.GregorianCalendar` class. If you use `import` statements, you must place them before any executing statement in your Java file. That is, within a Java class file, you can have a blank line or a comment line—but nothing else—prior to an `import` statement.

> **NOTE** `GregorianCalendar` is not a reserved word; it is a class you are importing. If you do not want to import the Java utility's `GregorianCalendar` class, you are free to write your own `GregorianCalendar` class.

An alternative to importing a class is to import an entire package of classes. You can use the asterisk (*) as a **wildcard symbol**, which indicates that it can be replaced by any set of characters.

In a Java `import` statement, you use a wildcard symbol to represent all the classes in a package. Therefore, the `import` statement `import java.util.*;` imports the `GregorianCalendar` class and any other `java.util` classes as well. There is no disadvantage to importing the extra classes, and you will most commonly see the wildcard method in professionally written Java programs. However, you have the alternative of importing each class you need individually. Importing each class by name, without wildcards, can be a form of documentation; this technique specifically shows which parts of the package are being used.

> **»NOTE** You cannot use the Java-language wildcard exactly like a DOS or UNIX wildcard because you cannot import all the Java classes with `import java.*;`. The Java wildcard works only with specific packages such as `import java.util.*;` or `import java.lang.*;`. Also, note that the * in an `import` statement imports all of the classes in a package, but not other packages that are within the imported package.

> **»NOTE** The `import` statement does not move the entire imported class or package into your program, as its name implies. Rather, it simply notifies the program that you will be using the data and method names that are part of the imported class or package.

Seven constructors are available for `GregorianCalendar` objects. These constructors are overloaded, requiring different argument lists when they are called, in exactly the same way that constructors for your own classes can be overloaded. The default constructor for the `GregorianCalendar` class creates a calendar object containing the current date and time in the default locale (time zone) that has been set for your computer. You can use other constructors to specify:

- » `year, month, date`
- » `year, month, date, hour, minute`
- » `year, month, date, hour, minute, second`
- » `Locale`
- » `TimeZone`
- » `TimeZone, Locale`

You can create a default `GregorianCalendar` object with a statement such as the following:

```
GregorianCalendar today = new GregorianCalendar();
```

Alternatively, you can create a `GregorianCalendar` object using one of the overloaded constructors—for example:

```
GregorianCalendar myGraduationDate = new GregorianCalendar(2012,5,24);.
```

> **»NOTE** As you read this discussion of the `GregorianCalendar` class, go to *http://java.sun.com*, select API Specifications, select the version of Java with which you are working, and choose `GregorianCalendar` from the list of available classes. The online Java documentation provides valuable information about the data fields and methods that are available with every built-in class. This section discusses the `GregorianCalendar` class as an example of an interesting class, but you can apply what you learn here to any Java class; the techniques for importing and using any class are the same.

> **»NOTE** Notice that the `import` statement ends with a semi-colon. In particular, C++ programmers, who use include statements at the tops of their files, are likely to make the mistake of omitting this punctuation in Java.

> **»NOTE** Your own classes are included in applications because of your `classpath` settings. See Appendix A for more information on `classpath`.

> **»NOTE** `TimeZone` and `Locale` are also Java classes. They, respectively, contain information about the time zone and the locale where the application is being used.

Specific data field values, such as the day, month, and year, can be retrieved from a `GregorianCalendar` object by using a class `get()` method and specifying what you want as an argument. You could retrieve the day of the year (for example, February 1 is the 32nd day of the year) with the following statement:

```
int dayOfYear = today.get(GregorianCalendar.DAY_OF_YEAR);
```

The `GregorianCalendar get()` method always returns an integer. Some of the possible arguments to the `get()` method are shown in Table 4-2.

Arguments	Values Returned by `get()`
DAY_OF_YEAR	A value from 1 to 366
DAY_OF_MONTH	A value from 1 to 31
DAY_OF_WEEK	SUNDAY, MONDAY, . . . SATURDAY, corresponding to values from 1 to 7
YEAR	The current year; for example, 2010
MONTH	JANUARY, FEBRUARY, . . . DECEMBER, corresponding to values from 0 to 11
HOUR	A value from 1 to 12; the current hour in the A.M. or P.M.
AM_PM	A.M. or P.M., which correspond to values from 0 to 1
HOUR_OF_DAY	A value from 0 to 23 based on a 24-hour clock
MINUTE	The minute in the hour, a value from 0 to 59
SECOND	The second in the minute, a value from 0 to 59
MILLISECOND	The millisecond in the second, a value from 0 to 999

Table 4-2 Some possible arguments to and returns from the `GregorianCalendar get()` method

> **NOTE** Notice that the month values in the `GregorianCalendar` class are values from 0 to 11. Thus, January is month 0, February is month 1, and so on.

As an example of how to use a `GregorianCalendar` object, Figure 4-34 shows an `AgeCalculator` application. In this class, a default `GregorianCalendar` object named `now` is created. The user is prompted for a birth year, the current year is extracted from the `now` object using the `get()` method, and the user's age this year is calculated by subtracting the birth year from the current year. Figure 4-35 shows the output when a user born in 1984 runs the application in 2010.

```
import java.util.*;
import javax.swing.*;
public class AgeCalculator
{
    public static void main(String[] args)
    {
        GregorianCalendar now = new GregorianCalendar();
        int nowYear;
        int birthYear;
        int yearsOld;
        birthYear = Integer.parseInt
            (JOptionPane.showInputDialog(null,
            "In what year were you born?"));
        nowYear = now.get(GregorianCalendar.YEAR);
        yearsOld = nowYear - birthYear;
        JOptionPane.showMessageDialog(null,
            "This is the year you become " + yearsOld +
            " years old");
    }
}
```

Figure 4-34 The `AgeCalculator` application

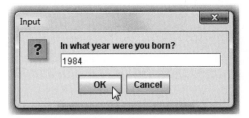
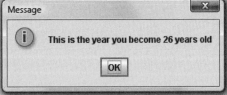

Figure 4-35 Execution of the `AgeCalculator` application

»TWO TRUTHS AND A LIE: USING AN EXPLICITLY IMPORTED PREWRITTEN CLASS AND ITS METHODS

1. To use most Java prewritten classes, you must use the entire path with the class name, import the class, or import the package that contains the class you are using.

2. The `java.util` class package contains many useful classes that let you work with dates and times.

3. When you use an `import` statement, it must be the first statement in a Java file.

The false statement is #3. When you use `import` statements, you must place them before any executing statement in your Java file, but you can have a blank line or a comment line prior to an `import` statement.

UNDERSTANDING COMPOSITION

A class can contain other objects as data members. **Composition** describes the relationship between classes when an object of one class is a data field within another class. When you use an object as a data member of another object, you must remember to supply values for the contained object if it has no default constructor.

For example, you might create a class named NameAndAddress that stores name and address information. Such a class could be used for employees, customers, students, or anyone else who has a name and address. Figure 4-36 shows a NameAndAddress class. The class contains three fields, all of which are set by the constructor. A display() method displays the name and address information on three lines.

```
public class NameAndAddress
{
    private String name;
    private String address;
    private int zipCode;
    public NameAndAddress(String nm, String add, int zip)
    {
        name = nm;
        address = add;
        zipCode = zip;
    }
    public void display()
    {
        System.out.println(name);
        System.out.println(address);
        System.out.println(zipCode);
    }
}
```

Figure 4-36 The NameAndAddress class

Suppose you want to create a School class that holds information about a school. Instead of declaring fields for the School's name and address, you could use the NameAndAddress class. The relationship created is sometimes called a **has-a relationship** because one class "has an" instance of another. Figure 4-37 shows a School class in which the shaded data member is a NameAndAddress object.

```
public class School
{
    private NameAndAddress nameAdd;
    private int enrollment;
    public School(String name, String add, int zip, int enrolled)
    {
        nameAdd = new NameAndAddress(name, add, zip);
        enrollment = enrolled;
    }
    public void display()
    {
        System.out.println("The school is at");
        nameAdd.display();
        System.out.println("Enrollment is " + enrollment);
    }
}
```

Figure 4-37 The School class

> **NOTE** If the NameAndAddress class contained a default constructor, then you could use the following statement within the School constructor:
>
> ```
> nameAdd = new NameAndAddress();
> ```

As Figure 4-37 shows, the School constructor requires four pieces of data. Within the constructor, three of the items—the name, address, and zip code—are passed to the NameAndAddress constructor to provide values for the appropriate fields. The fourth constructor parameter (the school's enrollment) is a standard, simple parameter that is assigned to the School class enrollment field.

In the School class display method, the NameAndAddress object's display() method is called to display the school's name and address. The enrollment figure is displayed afterward. Figure 4-38 shows a simple program that instantiates one School object. Figure 4-39 shows the execution.

```
public class SchoolDemo
{
    public static void main(String[] args)
    {
        School mySchool = new School("Audubon Elementary",
            "3500 Hoyne", 60618, 350);
        mySchool.display();
    }
}
```

Figure 4-39 Output of the SchoolDemo program

Figure 4-38 The SchoolDemo program

A BRIEF LOOK AT NESTED AND INNER CLASSES

Every class you have studied so far has been stored in its own file, and the filename has always matched the class name. In Java, you can create a class within another class and store them together; such classes are **nested classes**. The containing class is the **top-level class**. There are four types of nested classes:

» `static` **member classes**. A `static` member class has access to all static methods of the top-level class.

» **Nonstatic member classes**, also known as **inner classes**. This type of class requires an instance; it has access to all data and methods of the top-level class.

» **Local classes**, which are local to a block of code

» **Anonymous classes**, which are local classes that have no identifier

The most common reason to nest a class inside another is because the inner class is used only by the top-level class; in other words, it is a "helper class" to the top-level class. Being able to package the classes together makes their connection easier to understand and their code easier to maintain.

For example, consider a `RealEstateListing` class used by a real estate company to describe houses that are available for sale. The class might contain separate fields for a listing number, the price, the street address, and the house's living area. As an alternative, you might decide that although the listing number and price "go with" the real estate listing, the street address and living area really "go with" the house. So you might create an inner class like the one in Figure 4-40.

```
public class RealEstateListing
{
    private int listingNumber;
    private double price;
    private HouseData houseData;
    public RealEstateListing(int num, double price, String address,
        int sqFt)
    {
        listingNumber = num;
        this.price = price;
        houseData = new HouseData(address, sqFt);
    }
    public void display()
    {
        System.out.println("Listing number #" + listingNumber +
            "  Selling for $" + price);
        System.out.println("Address: " + houseData.streetAddress);
        System.out.println(houseData.squareFeet + " square feet");
    }
    private class HouseData
    {
        private String streetAddress;
        private int squareFeet;
        public HouseData(String address, int sqFt)
        {
            streetAddress = address;
            squareFeet = sqFt;
        }
    }
}
```

Figure 4-40 The `RealEstateListing` class

>> **NOTE**   Notice that the inner class in Figure 4-40 is a `private` class. You don't have to make an inner class `private`, but doing so keeps its members hidden from outside classes. If you wanted a class's members to be accessible, you would not make it an inner class. An inner class can access its top-level class's fields and methods, even if they are `private`, and an outer class can access its inner class's members.

You usually will not want to create inner classes. For example, if you made the `HouseData` class a regular class (as opposed to an inner class) and stored it in its own file, you could use it with composition in other classes—perhaps a `MortgageLoan` class or an `Appraisal` class. As it stands, it is usable only in the class in which it now resides. You probably will not create nested classes frequently, but you will see them implemented in some built-in Java classes.

YOU DO IT

DEMONSTRATING SCOPE

In this section, you will create a method with several blocks to demonstrate block scope.

To demonstrate block scope:

1. Start your text editor, and then open a new document, if necessary.

2. Type the first few lines for a class named `DemoBlock`:

```
public class DemoBlock
{
    public static void main(String[] args)
```

3. Add a statement that displays the purpose of the program:

```
System.out.println("Demonstrating block scope");
```

4. On a new line, declare an integer named x, assign the value 1111 to it, and display its value:

```
int x = 1111;
System.out.println("In first block x is " + x);
```

5. Begin a new block by typing an opening curly brace on the next line. Within the new block, declare another integer named y, and display x and y. The value of x will be 1111 and the value of y will be 2222:

```
{
    int y = 2222;
    System.out.println("In second block x is " + x);
    System.out.println("In second block y is " + y);
}
```

6. On the next line, begin another new block. Within this new block, declare a new integer with the same name as the integer declared in the previous block; then display x and y. The value of y will be 3333. Call a method named `demoMethod()`, and display x and y again. Even though you will include statements within `demoMethod()` that assign different values to x and y, the x and y displayed here will still be 1111 and 3333:

```
{
    int y = 3333;
    System.out.println("In third block x is " + x);
    System.out.println("In third block y is " + y);
    demoMethod();
    System.out.println("After method x is " + x);
    System.out.println("After method block y is " + y);
}
```

7. On a new line after the end of the block, type the following:

```
System.out.println("At the end x is " + x);
```

This last statement in the `main()` method displays the value of x, which is still 1111. Type a closing curly brace.

8. Finally, enter the following `demoMethod()` that creates its own x and y variables, assigns different values, and then displays them:

```
public static void demoMethod()
{
    int x = 8888, y = 9999;
    System.out.println("In demoMethod x is " + x);
    System.out.println("In demoMethod block y is " + y);
}
```

9. Type the final closing curly brace, and then save the file as **DemoBlock.java**. At the command prompt, compile the file by typing the command **javac DemoBlock.java**. If necessary, correct any errors and compile again.

10. Run the program by typing the command **java DemoBlock**. Your output should look like Figure 4-41. Make certain you understand how the values of x and y are determined in each line of output.

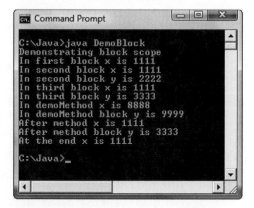

Figure 4-41 Output of the `DemoBlock` application

11. To gain a more complete understanding of blocks and scope, change the values of x and y in several locations throughout the program, and try to predict the exact output before resaving, recompiling, and rerunning the program.

OVERLOADING METHODS

Next, you will overload methods to display event dates for Event Handlers Incorporated. The methods take one, two, or three integer arguments. If there is one argument, it is the month, and the event is scheduled for the first day of the given month in the year 2011. If there are two arguments, they are the month and the day in the year 2011. Three arguments represent the month, day, and year.

> **»NOTE** In addition to creating your own class to store dates, you can use the built-in Java class `GregorianCalendar` to handle dates. This exercise provides you with an understanding of how some of the built-in class was constructed.

To create an application that calls an `overloadDate()` method that can take one, two, or three arguments:

1. Open a new file in your text editor.

2. Begin the following `DemoOverload` class, with three integer variables and three calls to an `overloadDate()` method:

```
public class DemoOverload
{
   public static void main(String[] args)
   {
      int month = 6, day = 24, year = 2010;
      overloadDate(month);
      overloadDate(month, day);
      overloadDate(month, day, year);
   }
```

3. Create the following `overloadDate()` method that requires one parameter:

```
public static void overloadDate(int mm)
{
   System.out.println("Event date " + mm + "/1/2011");
}
```

4. Create the following `overloadDate()` method that requires two parameters:

```
public static void overloadDate(int mm, int dd)
{
   System.out.println("Event date " + mm + "/" +  dd + "/2011");
}
```

5. Create the following `overloadDate()` method that requires three parameters:

```
public static void overloadDate(int mm, int dd, int yy)
{
   System.out.println("Event date " + mm + "/" +  dd + "/" + yy);
}
```

6. Type the closing curly brace for the `DemoOverload` class.

7. Save the file as **DemoOverload.java**.

8. Compile the program, correct any errors, recompile if necessary, and then execute the program. Figure 4-42 shows the output. Notice that whether you call the `overloadDate()` method using one, two, or three arguments, the date prints correctly because you have successfully overloaded the `overloadDate()` method.

Figure 4-42 Output of the `DemoOverload` application

CREATING A CONSTRUCTOR THAT REQUIRES AN ARGUMENT

To demonstrate a constructor that requires an argument when called, you will use a new version of the `EventSite` class you created in Chapter 3.

To alter a constructor to require an argument:

1. Open a new file in your text editor and type the `EventSite` class shown in Figure 4-43. To save typing, you can open the MyEventSite.java file you created in Chapter 3 and make some changes. Change the class name to `EventSite` and change the constructor name to match, as shown in the shaded portions of Figure 4-43. You might also need to modify the field names, method names, and default values you selected for the `fee` and `name` fields to make your class match the one in Figure 4-43 exactly. Recall that the class contains three data fields (`siteNumber`, `usageFee`, and `name`) and a `get` and `set` method for each field. The version in Figure 4-43 also contains a constructor that initializes the `siteNumber` field to 999, the fee to 0, and the `name` to "XXX". Save the file as **EventSite.java**.

2. Add a new constructor to the class. The new constructor requires an `int` parameter that is used as the site number. This constructor should also set the fee to 0 and the manager name to "XXX", so instead of rewriting those statements, call the default constructor prior to using the `int` parameter as the site number:

```java
public EventSite(int siteNum)
{
    this();
    siteNumber = siteNum;
}
```

```java
public class EventSite
{
    private int siteNumber;
    private double fee;
    private String name;
    public EventSite()
    {
        siteNumber = 999;
        fee = 0;
        name = "XXX";
    }
    public int getSiteNumber()
    {
        return siteNumber;
    }
    public void setSiteNumber(int n)
    {
        siteNumber = n;
    }
    public double getFee()
    {
        return fee;
    }
    public void setFee(double n)
    {
        fee = n;
    }
    public String getName()
    {
        return name;
    }
    public void setName(String n)
    {
        name = n;
    }
}
```

Figure 4-43 The `EventSite` class

3. Save the file as **EventSite.java**, and then compile and correct any errors.

4. Open a new text file to create a short application that demonstrates the constructors at work. Type the following code:

```
public class DemoConstructor
{
    public static void main(String[] args)
    {
        EventSite site1 = new EventSite();
        EventSite site2 = new EventSite(678);
        display(site1);
        display(site2);
    }
}
```

5. Just before the closing curly brace for the class, add the display() method that main() calls. The method accepts an EventSite object and displays its details:

```
public static void display(EventSite site)
{
    System.out.println("\nEvent site #" + site.getSiteNumber() +
        "\nFee is $" + site.getFee() +
        "\nName of site is " + site.getName());
}
```

6. Save the file as **DemoConstructor.java**, and then compile and test the program. The output appears in Figure 4-44.

7. On your own, create another overloaded constructor for the EventSite class. This constructor requires a site number, a fee, and a manager name as arguments. Write an application to demonstrate that your constructor works as expected, and save the application as **DemoConstructor2.java**.

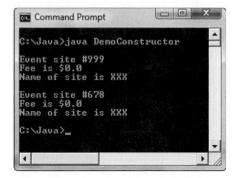

Figure 4-44 Output of DemoConstructor program

USING AN EXPLICITLY IMPORTED PREWRITTEN CLASS

Next, you will construct a program using the GregorianCalendar class and some of the arguments to the GregorianCalendar get() method.

To write a program that uses the GregorianCalendar **class:**

1. Open a new file in your text editor.

2. For the first line in the file, type the following:

```
import java.util.*;
```

3. On the next lines, begin the class by typing the class header, the opening brace, the main() method header, and its opening brace, as follows:

```
public class CalendarDemo
{
    public static void main(String[] args)
    {
```

4. Declare a GregorianCalendar object named now that holds information about the current date and time. Then create a series of output statements that display a variety of GregorianCalendar fields containing information about the date:

```
GregorianCalendar now = new GregorianCalendar();
System.out.println("YEAR: " + now.get(Calendar.YEAR));
System.out.println("MONTH: " + now.get(Calendar.MONTH));
System.out.println("WEEK_OF_YEAR: " +
    now.get(Calendar.WEEK_OF_YEAR));
System.out.println("WEEK_OF_MONTH: " +
    now.get(Calendar.WEEK_OF_MONTH));
System.out.println("DATE: " + now.get(Calendar.DATE));
System.out.println("DAY_OF_MONTH: " +
    now.get(Calendar.DAY_OF_MONTH));
System.out.println("DAY_OF_YEAR: " +
    now.get(Calendar.DAY_OF_YEAR));
System.out.println("DAY_OF_WEEK: " +
    now.get(Calendar.DAY_OF_WEEK));
```

5. Add more statements that display information about the current time, as follows:

```
System.out.println("AM_PM: " +
    now.get(Calendar.AM_PM));
System.out.println("HOUR: " + now.get(Calendar.HOUR));
System.out.println("HOUR_OF_DAY: " +
    now.get(Calendar.HOUR_OF_DAY));
System.out.println("MINUTE: " +
    now.get(Calendar.MINUTE));
System.out.println("SECOND: " +
    now.get(Calendar.SECOND));
System.out.println("MILLISECOND: " +
    now.get(Calendar.MILLISECOND));
```

6. Add the closing curly brace for the main() method and the closing curly brace for the class.

7. Save the file as **CalendarDemo.java**. Compile and execute the program. Figure 4-45 shows the output from the program when it is executed a little after 4 p.m. on Friday, June 24, 2011. Notice that the month of June is represented by 5—the month values in the GregorianCalendar are 0 through 11. When you display month values in your own programs, you might choose to add 1 to any value before displaying it, so that users see month numbers to which they are accustomed.

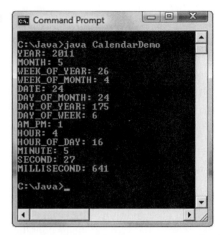

Figure 4-45 Output of the CalendarDemo application

CREATING AN INTERACTIVE APPLICATION WITH A TIMER

Next, you will use the GregorianCalendar class to create an application that outputs a user's response time to a question.

To create a timed interactive application:

1. Open a new file in your text editor and type the following two import statements. You need the JOptionPane class to use the showConfirmDialog() method, and you need the java.util package to use the GregorianCalendar class:

```
import javax.swing.JOptionPane;
import java.util.*;
```

2. Begin the DialogTimer application as follows. Declare variables named milli1, milli2, sec1, and sec2. These will be used to compute time1 and time2 from calendar objects created at the beginning and end of the program. You then use time1 and time2 to compute a timeDifference. Also declare a constant to hold the number of milliseconds in a second:

```
public class DialogTimer
{
    public static void main(String[] args)
    {
        int time1, time2, milli1, milli2, sec1,
            sec2, timeDifference;
        final int MILLISECSINSECOND = 1000;
```

3. Instantiate a `GregorianCalendar` object and retrieve its `MILLISECOND` and `SECOND` values. Compute a `time1` value by multiplying the current `sec1` value by 1000 and adding it to the current `milli1` value:

```
GregorianCalendar before = new GregorianCalendar();
milli1 = before.get(GregorianCalendar.MILLISECOND);
sec1 = before.get(GregorianCalendar.SECOND);
time1 = MILLISECSINSECOND * sec1 + milli1;
```

4. Display a dialog box that asks the user to make a difficult choice:

```
JOptionPane.showConfirmDialog(null, "Is stealing ever justified? ");
```

5. Next, create a new `GregorianCalendar` object. This statement does not execute until the user provides a response for the dialog box, so the time variables contain different values from the first `GregorianCalendar` object created:

```
GregorianCalendar after = new GregorianCalendar();
milli2 = after.get(GregorianCalendar.MILLISECOND);
sec2 = after.get(GregorianCalendar.SECOND);
time2 = MILLISECSINSECOND * sec2 + milli2;
```

6. Compute the difference between the times and display the result in a dialog box.

```
timeDifference = time2 - time1;
JOptionPane.showMessageDialog(null,"It took " +
    timeDifference + " milliseconds for you to answer");
```

7. Add two closing curly braces—one for the method and the other for the class—and then save the file as **DialogTimer.java**.

8. Compile and execute the program. When the question appears, choose a response. The second output looks like Figure 4-46; the actual time displayed varies depending on how long you wait before selecting an answer.

Figure 4-46 Output of the `DialogTimer` application

9. The output in the `DialogTimer` application is accurate only when the first and second `GregorianCalendar` objects are created during the same minute. For example, if the first object is created a few seconds before a new minute starts, and the second object is created a few seconds after the new minute starts, the second `SECOND` value appears to be much lower than the first one. On your own, modify the `DialogTimer` application to rectify this discrepancy. Save the file as **DialogTimer2.java**.

DON'T DO IT

» Don't try to use a variable that is out of scope.

» Don't assume that a constant is still a constant when passed to a method's parameter. If you want a parameter to be constant within a method, you must use `final` in the parameter list.

» Don't overload methods by giving them different return types. If their identifiers and parameter lists are the same, then two methods are ambiguous no matter what their return types are.

» Don't think that *default constructor* means only the automatically supplied version. A constructor with no parameters is a default constructor, whether it is the one that is automatically supplied or one you write.

» Don't forget to write a default constructor for a class that has other constructors if you want to be able to instantiate objects without using arguments.

KEY TERMS

A **block** is the code between a pair of curly braces.

An **outside block**, or **outer block**, contains another block.

An **inside block**, or **inner block**, is contained within another block.

An inside block is **nested** within an outside block.

A variable's **scope** is the portion of a program within which you can refer to the variable.

A variable comes into existence, or **comes into scope**, when you declare it.

A variable ceases to exist, or **goes out of scope**, at the end of the block in which it is declared.

To **redeclare a variable** is to attempt to declare it twice—an illegal action.

A variable **overrides** another with the same name when it takes precedence over the other variable.

Overloading involves using one term to indicate diverse meanings, or writing multiple methods with the same name but with different arguments.

An **ambiguous** situation is one in which the compiler cannot determine which method to use.

A **reference** is an object's memory address.

The **this reference** is a reference to an object that is passed to any object's nonstatic class method.

Class methods are static methods that do not have a `this` reference (because they have no object associated with them).

Class variables are static variables that are shared by every instantiation of a class.

A **package** is a library of classes.

A **library of classes** is a folder that provides a convenient grouping for classes.

The package that is implicitly imported into every Java program is named **`java.lang`**.

The **fundamental classes** are basic classes contained in the `java.lang` package that are automatically imported into every program you write.

The **optional classes** reside in packages that must be explicitly imported into your programs.

NaN is a three-letter abbreviation for "Not a number."

A **wildcard symbol** is an asterisk—a symbol used to indicate that it can be replaced by any set of characters. In a Java `import` statement, you use a wildcard symbol to represent all the classes in a package.

Composition describes the relationship between classes when an object of one class is a data field within another class.

A **has-a relationship** is a relationship based on composition.

Nested classes are classes contained in other classes.

The **top-level class** is the containing class in nested classes.

A **`static` member class** is a type of nested class that has access to all `static` methods of its top-level class.

Nonstatic member classes, also known as **inner classes**, are nested classes that require an instance.

Local classes are a type of nested class that are local to a block of code.

Anonymous classes are nested, local classes that have no identifier.

CHAPTER SUMMARY

» A variable's scope is the portion of a program within which you can reference that variable. A block is the code between a pair of curly braces. Within a method, you can declare a variable with the same name multiple times, as long as each declaration is in its own nonoverlapping block. If you declare a variable within a class and use the same variable name within a method of the class, the variable used inside the method takes precedence over (or overrides, or masks) the first variable.

» Overloading involves writing multiple methods with the same name but different argument lists. Methods that have identical argument lists but different return types are not overloaded; they are illegal.

» When you overload methods, you risk creating an ambiguous situation—one in which the compiler cannot determine which method to use. Constructors can receive arguments and be overloaded. If you explicitly create a constructor for a class, the automatically created constructor no longer exists.

» When you write your own constructors, they can receive parameters. Such parameters are often used to initialize data fields for an object. After you write a constructor for a class, you no longer receive the automatically provided default constructor. If a class's only constructor requires an argument, you must provide an argument for every object of the class that you create.

» You can overload constructors just as you can other methods.

» You store separate copies of data fields for each object, but just one copy of each method. Within nonstatic methods, data fields for the correct object are accessed because you implicitly pass a `this` reference to class methods. Static methods do not have a `this` reference because they have no object associated with them; static methods are also called class methods.

» Static class variables are variables that are shared by every instantiation of a class.

» When a field in a class is `static`, it is shared by each instantiation; when it is `final` it cannot change.

» Java contains nearly 500 prewritten classes that are stored in packages, which are folders that provide convenient groupings for classes. The package that is implicitly imported into every Java program is named `java.lang`. The classes it contains are the fundamental classes, as opposed to the optional classes, which must be explicitly named. The class `java.lang.Math` contains constants and methods that can be used to perform common mathematical functions.

» An `import` statement allows you to abbreviate lengthy class names by notifying the Java program that when you use class names, you are referring to those within the imported class. Any `import` statement you use must be placed before any executing statement in your file. An alternative to importing a class is to import an entire package of classes. To do so, you can use the asterisk (*) as a wildcard symbol to represent all the classes in a package.

» The `GregorianCalendar` class is the calendar generally used in the Western world; it has a number of `get()` methods to define and manipulate dates and time.

» A class can contain other objects as data members. Composition describes the relationship between classes when an object of one class is a data field within another class.

» You can create nested classes that are stored in the same file. The most common reason to nest a class inside another is because the inner class is used only by the outer or top-level class; in other words, it is a "helper class" to the top-level class.

REVIEW QUESTIONS

1. The code between a pair of curly braces in a method is a _____ .

   a. function   c. brick

   b. block   d. sector

2. When a block exists within another block, the blocks are _____ .

   a. structured   c. sheltered

   b. nested   d. illegal

3. The portion of a program within which you can reference a variable is the variable's _____ .

   a. range   c. domain

   b. space   d. scope

4. You can declare variables with the same name multiple times _____ .

   a. within a statement

   b. within a block

   c. within a method

   d. You never can declare multiple variables with the same name.

5. If you declare a variable as an instance variable within a class, and you declare and use the same variable name within a method of the class, then within the method, _____ .

   a. the variable used inside the method takes precedence

   b. the class instance variable takes precedence

   c. the two variables refer to a single memory address

   d. an error will occur

6. A method variable will _____ a class variable with the same name.

   a. acquiesce to   c. override

   b. destroy   d. alter

7. Nonambiguous, overloaded methods must have the same _____ .

   a. name   c. parameter names

   b. number of parameters   d. types of parameters

8. If a method is written to receive a `double` parameter, and you pass an integer to the method, then the method will _____ .

   a. work correctly; the integer will be promoted to a `double`

   b. work correctly; the integer will remain an integer

   c. execute, but any output will be incorrect

   d. not work; an error message will be issued

9. A constructor _____ parameters.

   a. can receive   c. must receive

   b. cannot receive   d. can receive a maximum of 10

10. A constructor _____ overloaded.

   a. can be   c. must be

   b. cannot be   d. is always automatically

11. Usually, you want each instantiation of a class to have its own copy of _____ .

    a. the data fields   c. both of the above

    b. the class methods   d. none of the above

12. If you create a class that contains one method, and instantiate two objects, you usually store _____ for use with the objects.

    a. one copy of the method

    b. two copies of the method

    c. two different methods containing two different `this` references

    d. data only (the methods are not stored)

13. The `this` reference _____ .

    a. can be used implicitly   c. must not be used implicitly

    b. must be used implicitly   d. must not be used

14. Methods that you reference with individual objects are _____ .

    a. `private`   c. `static`

    b. `public`   d. `nonstatic`

15. Variables that are shared by every instantiation of a class are _____ .

    a. class variables   c. `public` variables

    b. `private` variables   d. illegal

16. The keyword `final` used with a variable declaration indicates _____ .

    a. the end of the program

    b. a `static` field

    c. a symbolic constant

    d. that no more variables will be declared in the program

17. Java classes are stored in a folder or _____ .

    a. packet   c. bundle

    b. package   d. gaggle

18. Which of the following statements determines the square root of a number and assigns it to the variable `s`?

    a. `s = sqrt(number);`   c. `number = sqrt(s);`

    b. `s = Math.sqrt(number);`   d. `number = Math.sqrt(s);`

19. A GregorianCalendar object can be created with one of seven constructors. This means that the constructors _____ .

    a. override each other   c. are overloaded

    b. are ambiguous   d. all of the above

20. The GregorianCalendar class get() method always returns a(n) _____ .

    a. day of the week   c. integer

    b. date   d. GregorianCalendar object

EXERCISES

1. a. Create a class named Commission that includes three variables: a double sales figure, a double commission rate, and an int commission rate. Create two overloaded methods named computeCommission(). The first method takes two double parameters representing sales and rate, multiplies them, and then displays the results. The second method takes two parameters: a double sales figure and an integer commission rate. This method must divide the commission rate figure by 100.0 before multiplying by the sales figure and displaying the commission. Supply appropriate values for the variables, and write a main() method that tests each overloaded method. Save the file as **Commission.java**.

   b. Add a third overloaded method to the Commission application you created in Exercise 1a. The third overloaded method takes a single parameter representing sales. When this method is called, the commission rate is assumed to be 7.5% and the results are displayed. To test this method, add an appropriate call in the Commission program's main() method. Save the application as **Commission2.java**.

2. Create a class named Pay that includes five double variables that hold hours worked, rate of pay per hour, withholding rate, gross pay, and net pay. Create three overloaded computeNetPay() methods. When computeNetPay() receives values for hours, pay rate, and withholding rate, it computes the gross pay and reduces it by the appropriate withholding amount to produce the net pay. (Gross pay is computed as hours worked multiplied by pay per hour.) When computeNetPay() receives two parameters, they represent the hours and pay rate, and the withholding rate is assumed to be 15%. When computeNetPay() receives one parameter, it represents the number of hours worked, the withholding rate is assumed to be 15%, and the hourly rate is assumed to be 5.85. Write a main() method that tests all three overloaded methods. Save the application as **Pay.java**.

3. a. Create a class named Household that includes data fields for the number of occupants and the annual income, as well as get and set methods for each field. In addition, create a default constructor that automatically sets the occupants field to 1 and the income field to 0. Save this file as **Household.java**. Create an application named

TestHousehold that demonstrates each method works correctly. Save the file as **TestHousehold.java**.

b. Create an additional overloaded constructor for the Household class you created in Exercise 3a. This constructor receives an integer parameter and assigns the value to the occupants field. Add any needed statements to TestHousehold to ensure that the overloaded constructor works correctly, save it, and then test it.

c. Create a third overloaded constructor for the Household class you created in Exercises 3a and 3b. This constructor receives two parameters, the values of which are assigned to the occupants and income fields, respectively. Alter the TestHousehold application to demonstrate that each version of the constructor works properly. Save the application, and then compile and test it.

4. Create a class named Box that includes integer data fields for length, width, and height. Create three constructors that require one, two, and three parameters, respectively. When one argument is passed to the constructor, assign it to length, assign zeros to height and width, and print "Line created". When two arguments are used, assign them to length and width, assign zero to height, and print "Rectangle created". When three arguments are used, assign them to the three variables and print "Box created". Save this file as **Box.java**. Create an application named TestBox that demonstrates each method works correctly. Save the application as **TestBox.java**.

5. Create a class named Shirt with data fields for collar size and sleeve length. Include a constructor that takes parameters for each field. Also include a final, static String named MATERIAL and initialize it to "cotton". Write an application named TestShirt to instantiate three Shirt objects with different collar sizes and sleeve lengths, and then display all the data, including material, for each shirt. Save both the **Shirt.java** and **TestShirt.java** files.

6. a. Create a class named Circle with fields named radius, diameter, and area. Include a constructor that sets the radius to 1 and calculates the other two values. Also include methods named setRadius() and getRadius(). The setRadius() method not only sets the radius, it also calculates the other two values. (The diameter of a circle is twice the radius, and the area of a circle is pi multiplied by the square of the radius.) Save the class as **Circle.java**.

b. Create a class named TestCircle whose main() method declares several Circle objects. Using the setRadius() method, assign one Circle a small radius value and assign another a larger radius value. Do not assign a value to the radius of the third circle; instead, retain the value assigned at construction. Display all the values for all the Circle objects. Save the application as **TestCircle.java**.

7. Write a Java application that uses the Math class to determine the answers for each of the following:

a. The square root of 30

b. The sine and cosine of 100

c. The value of the floor, ceiling, and round of 44.7

d. The larger and the smaller of the character K and the integer 70

e. A random number between 0 and 10 (*Hint*: The `random()` method returns a value between 0 and 1; you want a number that is 10 times larger.)

Save the application as **MathTest.java**.

8. Write an application to calculate how many days it is from today until the first day of next summer (assume that this date is June 21). Save the file as **Summer.java**.

9. Write an application to calculate how many days it is from today until the end of the current year. Save the file as **YearEnd.java**.

10. a. Create a `CollegeStudent` class. The class contains data fields that hold a student's first name, last name, enrollment date, and projected graduation date, using `GregorianCalendar` objects for each date. Provide `get()` and `set()` methods for each field. Also provide a constructor that requires first and last names and enrollment date, and sets the projected graduation date to exactly four years after enrollment. Save the class as **CollegeStudent.java**.

   b. Create an interactive application that prompts the user for data for two `CollegeStudent` objects. Prompt the user for first name, last name, enrollment month, enrollment day, and enrollment year for each `CollegeStudent`, and then instantiate the objects. Display all the values, including projected graduation dates. Save the application as **TestCollegeStudent.java**.

11. In Deep Water Associates operates a business that offers a variety of services to customers who own swimming pools, including cleaning and filling pools. Write a program that calculates the price of a service call. The price includes a set $75 fee for cleaning plus an additional fee based on the amount of time it will take to fill a customer's pool with water. Table 4-3 provides the necessary parameters for estimating the price (based on the fill-up time) for a pool. Write an application that prompts the user for the length, width, and depth of a pool, and calculates the service and fill-up price. Save the application as **Swimming.java**.

Parameter	Explanation
Fee for cleaning	$75
Pool volume in cubic feet	length * width * average depth, all in feet
Gallons per cubic foot	7.5
Pool capacity in gallons	volume * gallons per cubic foot
Rate of flow	50 gallons per minute
Minutes per hour	60
Fee per hour for filling	$8

Table 4-3 Parameters for estimating pool fill-up price

DEBUGGING EXERCISES

Each of the following files in the Chapter.04 folder on your Student Disk has syntax and/or logic errors. In each case, determine the problem and fix the program. After you correct the errors, save each file using the same filename preceded with Fix. For example, save DebugFour1.java as FixDebugFour1.java.

a. DebugFour1.java

b. DebugFour2.java

c. DebugFour3.java and DebugBox.java

d. DebugFour4.java

GAME ZONE

1. Dice are used in many games. One die can be thrown to randomly show a value from 1 to 6. Design a `Die` class that can hold an integer data field for a value (from 1 to 6). Include a constructor that randomly assigns a value to a die object. Appendix D contains information on generating random numbers. To fully understand the process, you must learn more about Java classes and methods. However, for now, you can copy the following statement to generate a random number between 1 and 6 and assign it to a variable. Using this statement assumes you have assigned appropriate values to the static constants:

    ```
    value = ((int)(Math.random() * 100) % HIGHEST_DIE_VALUE +
        LOWEST_DIE_VALUE);
    ```

    Also include a method in the class to return a die's value. Save the class as **Die.java**.

    Write an application that randomly "throws" two dice and displays their values. After you learn about decision making in Chapter 5, you will be able to have the game determine the higher die. For now, just observe how the values change as you execute the program multiple times. Save the application as **TwoDice.java**.

2. Using the `Die` class, write an application that randomly "throws" five dice for the computer and five dice for the player. Display the values and then, by observing the results, decide who wins based on the following hierarchy of `Die` values. (The computer will not decide the winner; the player will determine the winner based on observation.) Any higher combination beats a lower one; for example, five of a kind beats four of a kind.

    » five of a kind

    » four of a kind

    » three of a kind

    » a pair

    After you learn about decision making in Chapter 5, you will be able to make the program determine whether you or the computer had the better roll, and after you learn about arrays in Chapter 8, you will be able to make the determination more efficient. For now, just observe how the values change as you execute the program multiple times. Save the application as **FiveDice.java**.

TOUGH QUESTIONS

1. Give an example of a situation in which you would want a class's field to be `final` but not `static`. Give another example of when you would want a field to be `static` but not `final`.

2. Suppose class A contains a `main()` method that instantiates an object of class B. Can class B also have a `main()` method? Explain your answer.

3. Can a single class contain two `main()` methods? Explain your answer.

UP FOR DISCUSSION

1. In this chapter, you learned about prewritten classes such as `Math` and `GregorianCalendar`. Explore the Java documentation at *http://java.sun.com* and find at least three other built-in classes you think would be useful. Describe these classes and discuss the types of applications in which you would employ them.

2. So far, the Game Zone sections at the ends of the chapters in this book have asked you to create extremely simple games that rely on random number generation. However, most computer games are far more complex. If you are not familiar with them, find descriptions of the games Grand Theft Auto and Stubbs the Zombie. Why are some people opposed to these games? Do you approve of playing them? Would you impose any age restrictions on players?

5

MAKING DECISIONS

In this chapter, you will:

Learn about decision making
Make decisions with the if and if...else structures
Use multiple statements in an if or if...else structure
Nest if and if...else statements
Use AND and OR operators
Learn to make accurate and efficient decisions
Use the switch statement
Use the conditional and NOT operators
Learn about precedence

JAVA ON THE JOB, SCENE 5

Lynn Greenbrier asks, "Why are you frowning?"

"It's fun writing programs," you tell her, "but I don't think my programs can do much yet. When I use programs written by other people, I can respond to questions and make choices. And other people's programs keep running for a while—the programs I write finish as soon as they start."

"You're disappointed because the programs you've written so far simply carry out a sequence of steps," Lynn says. "You need to learn about decision-making structures."

UNDERSTANDING DECISION MAKING

When computer programmers write programs, they rarely just sit down at a keyboard and begin typing. Programmers must plan the complex portions of programs using paper and pencil. Programmers often use **pseudocode**, a tool that helps them plan a program's logic by writing plain English statements. Using pseudocode requires that you write down the steps needed to accomplish a given task. You write pseudocode in everyday language, not the syntax used in a programming language. In fact, a task you write in pseudocode does not have to be computer-related. If you have ever written a list of directions to your house—for example, (1) go west on Algonquin Road, (2) turn left on Roselle Road, (3) enter expressway heading east, and so on—you have written pseudocode. A **flowchart** is similar to pseudocode, but you write the steps in diagram form, as a series of shapes connected by arrows.

>>NOTE You learned the difference between a program's logic and its syntax in Chapter 1.

Some programmers use a variety of shapes to represent different tasks in their flowcharts, but you can draw simple flowcharts that express very complex situations using just rectangles and diamonds. You use a rectangle to represent any unconditional step and a diamond to represent any decision. For example, Figure 5-1 shows a flowchart describing driving directions to a friend's house. The logic in Figure 5-1 is an example of a logical structure called a **sequence structure**—one step follows another unconditionally. A sequence structure might contain any number of steps, but when one task follows another with no chance to branch away or skip a step, you are using a sequence.

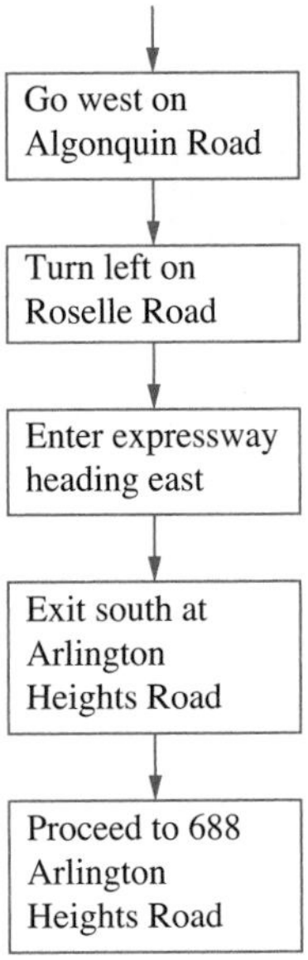
Go west on Algonquin Road
Turn left on Roselle Road
Enter expressway heading east
Exit south at Arlington Heights Road
Proceed to 688 Arlington Heights Road

Figure 5-1 Flowchart of a series of sequential steps

Sometimes, logical steps do not follow in an unconditional sequence—some tasks might or might not occur based on decisions you make. Using diamond shapes, flowchart creators draw paths to alternative courses of action starting from the sides of the diamonds. Figure 5-2 shows a flowchart describing directions in which the execution of some steps depends on decisions.

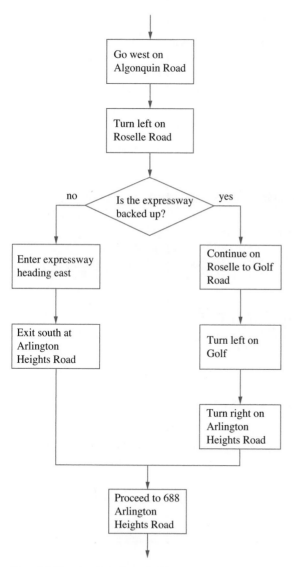

Figure 5-2 Flowchart including a decision

MAKING DECISIONS

Figure 5-2 shows a **decision structure**—one that involves choosing between alternative courses of action based on some value within a program. For example, the program that produces your paycheck can make decisions about the proper amount to withhold for taxes, the program that guides a missile can alter its course, and a program that monitors your blood pressure during surgery can determine when to sound an alarm. Making decisions is what makes computer programs seem "smart."

When reduced to their most basic form, all computer decisions are yes-or-no decisions. That is, the answer to every computer question is "yes" or "no" (or "true" or "false," or "on" or "off"). This is because computer circuitry consists of millions of tiny switches that are either "on" or "off," and the result of every decision sets one of these switches in memory. The values `true` and `false` are **Boolean values**; every computer decision results in a Boolean value. Thus, internally, a program you write never asks, for example, "What number did the user enter?" Instead, the decisions might be "Did the user enter a 1?" "If not, did the user enter a 2?" "If not, did the user enter a 3?"

>> NOTE
Sir George Boole lived from 1815 to 1864. He developed a type of linguistic algebra, based on 0s and 1s, the three most basic operations of which were (and still are) AND, OR, and NOT. All computer logic is based on his discoveries.

>> NOTE
In Chapter 2 you learned that Boolean variables are a type that can hold `true` or `false`.

>> TWO TRUTHS AND A LIE: UNDERSTANDING DECISION MAKING

1. Pseudocode and flowcharts are both tools that are used to check the syntax of computer programs.
2. In a sequence structure, one step follows another unconditionally.
3. In a decision structure, alternative courses of action are chosen based on a Boolean value.

The false statement is #1. Pseudocode and flowcharts are both tools that help programmers plan a program's logic.

MAKING DECISIONS WITH THE `if` AND `if...else` STRUCTURES

>> NOTE
Traditionally, flowcharts use diamond shapes to hold decisions and rectangles to represent actions. Even though input and output statements represent actions, many flowchart creators prefer to show them in parallelograms; this book follows that convention.

In Java, the simplest statement you can use to make a decision is the **if statement**. For example, suppose you have declared an integer variable named someVariable, and you want to print a message when the value of someVariable is 10. The following is the `if` statement that makes the decision to print. Note that the double equal sign (==) is used to determine equality; it is Java's **equivalency operator**. Figure 5-3 shows a diagram of the logic expressed in this statement.

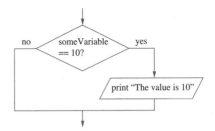

Figure 5-3 Decision structure illustrating an `if` statement

```
if(someVariable == 10)
    System.out.println ("The value is 10");
```

190

In this example, if `someVariable` holds the value 10, the Boolean value of the expression `someVariable == 10` is `true`, and the subsequent `println()` statement executes. If the value of the expression `someVariable == 10` is `false`, the `println()` statement does not execute. Either way, the program continues with the statement that follows the `if` statement.

An `if` statement always includes parentheses. Within the parentheses, you can place any Boolean expression. Most often you use a comparison that includes a relational operator (`==, < >, <=, >=,` or `!=`). However, you can use any expression that evaluates as true or false, such as a simple `boolean` variable or a method that returns a `boolean` value.

» NOTE
You learned about the relational operators in Chapter 2.

PITFALL: MISPLACING A SEMICOLON IN AN `if` STATEMENT

In a Java `if` statement, the Boolean expression, such as `(someVariable == 10)`, must appear within parentheses. Notice that there is no semicolon at the end of the first line of the `if` statement `if (someVariable == 10)` because the statement does not end there. The statement ends after the `println()` call, so that is where you type the semicolon. You could type the entire `if` statement on one line and it would execute correctly; however, the two-line format for the `if` statement is more conventional and easier to read, so you usually type `if` and the Boolean expression on one line, press Enter, and then indent a few spaces before coding the action that will occur if the Boolean expression evaluates as `true`. Be careful—if you use the two-line format and type a semicolon at the end of the first line, as in the example shown in Figure 5-4, the results might not be what you intended.

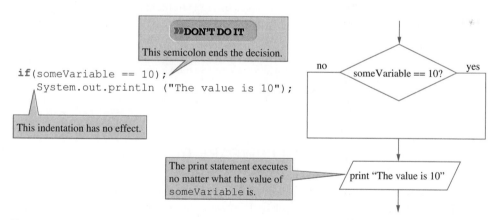

Figure 5-4 Logic that executes when an extra semicolon is inserted at the end of the first line of an `if` statement

When the `if` expression in Figure 5-4 is evaluated, the statement that executes when the tested expression evaluates as `true` is an **empty statement**—it contains only a semicolon. Whether the tested expression evaluates as `true` or `false`, the decision is over immediately, and execution continues with the next independent statement that prints a message. In this case, because of the incorrect semicolon, the `if` statement accomplishes nothing.

PITFALL: USING THE ASSIGNMENT OPERATOR
INSTEAD OF THE EQUIVALENCY OPERATOR

» NOTE
The expression
`if(x = true)`
will compile only if
`x` is a `boolean`
variable, because it
would be legal to
assign `true` to `x`.
However, such a
statement would be
useless because
the decision could
never be `false`.

Another common programming error occurs when a programmer uses a single equal sign rather than the double equal sign when attempting to determine equivalency. The expression `someVariable = 10` does not compare `someVariable` to 10; instead, it attempts to assign the value 10 to the `someVariable` variable. When the expression containing the single equal sign is part of an `if` statement, the assignment is illegal. The confusion arises in part because the single equal sign is used within Boolean expressions in `if` statements in many other programming languages, such as COBOL, Pascal, and BASIC. Adding to the confusion, Java programmers use the word *equals* when speaking of equivalencies. For example, you might say, "If `someVariable` *equals* 10 . . .".

An alternative to using a Boolean expression, such as `someVariable == 10`, is to store the Boolean expression's value in a Boolean variable. For example, if `isValueTen` is a Boolean variable, then the following statement compares `someVariable` to 10 and stores `true` or `false` in `isValueTen`:

```
isValueTen = (someVariable == 10);
```

Then, you can write the `if` as:

```
if(isValueTen)
    System.out.println("The value is 10");
```

This adds an extra step to the program, but makes the `if` statement more similar to an English-language statement.

> **» NOTE** When comparing a variable to a constant, some programmers prefer to place the constant to the left of the comparison operator, as in `10 == someVariable`. This practice is a holdover from other programming languages, such as C++, in which an accidental assignment might be made when the programmer types the assignment operator (a single equal sign) instead of the comparison operator (the double equal sign). In Java, the compiler does not allow you to make a mistaken assignment in a Boolean expression.

PITFALL: ATTEMPTING TO COMPARE OBJECTS
USING THE RELATIONAL OPERATORS

You can use the standard relational operators (==, <, >, <=, >=, and !=) to compare the values of primitive data types such as `int` and `double`. However, you cannot use <, >, <=, or >= to compare objects; a program containing such comparisons will not compile. You can use the equals and not equals comparisons (== and !=) with objects, but when you use them, you compare the objects' memory addresses instead of their values. Recall that every object name is a reference; the equivalency operators compare objects' references. In other words, == only yields `true` for two objects when they refer to the same object in memory, not when they are different objects with the same value. To compare the values of objects, you should write specialized methods. You will learn more about this in Chapters 7 and 10.

THE if...else STRUCTURE

Consider the following statement:

```
if(someVariable == 10)
    System.out.println("The value is 10");
```

Such a statement is sometimes called a **single-alternative if** because you only perform an action, or not, based on one alternative; in this example, you print a statement when someVariable is 10. Often, you require two options for the course of action following a decision. A **dual-alternative if** is the decision structure you use when you need to take one or the other of two possible courses of action. For example, you would use a dual-alternative if structure if you wanted to display one message when the value of someVariable is 10 and a different message when it is not. In Java, the **if...else statement** provides the mechanism to perform one action when a Boolean expression evaluates as true, and to perform a different action when a Boolean expression evaluates as false. For example, the code in Figure 5-5 displays one of two messages. In this example, when the value of someVariable is 10, the message "The value is 10" is printed. When someVariable is any other value, the program prints the message "No, it's not".

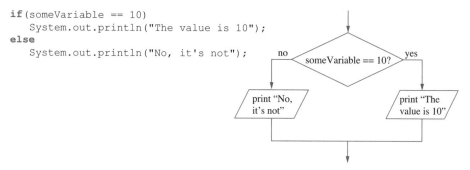

```
if(someVariable == 10)
    System.out.println("The value is 10");
else
    System.out.println("No, it's not");
```

Figure 5-5 An if...else structure

>>NOTE
In an if...else statement, the statement that executes when the tested expression is true ends with a semicolon, as does the statement that executes when the tested expression is false.

When you execute an if...else statement, only one of the resulting actions takes place depending on the evaluation of the Boolean expression following the if. Each statement, the one following the if and the one following the else, is a complete statement, so each ends with a semicolon.

>>NOTE
You can code an if without an else, but it is illegal to code an else without an if.

>>TWO TRUTHS AND A LIE: MAKING DECISIONS WITH THE if AND if...else STRUCTURES

1. In a Java if statement, the keyword if is followed by a Boolean expression within parentheses.
2. In a Java if statement, a semicolon follows the Boolean expression.
3. When determining equivalency in Java, you use a double equal sign.

The false statement is #2. In a Java if statement, a semicolon ends the statement. It is used following the action that should occur if the Boolean expression is true. If a semicolon follows the Boolean expression, then the body of the if statement is empty.

USING MULTIPLE STATEMENTS IN AN `if` OR `if...else` STRUCTURE

Often, you want to take more than one action following the evaluation of a Boolean expression within an `if` statement. For example, you might want to print several separate lines of output or perform several mathematical calculations. To execute more than one statement that depends on the evaluation of a Boolean expression, you use a pair of curly braces to place the dependent statements within a block. For example, the program segment shown in Figure 5-6 determines whether an employee has worked more than the value of a `FULL_WEEK` constant; if so, the program computes regular and overtime pay.

```
if(hoursWorked  >  FULL_WEEK)
{
    regularPay = FULL_WEEK * rate;
    overtimePay = (hoursWorked - FULL_WEEK) * OT_RATE * rate;
}
```

The `if` structure ends here.

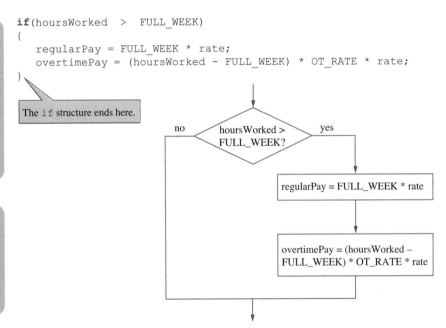

Figure 5-6 An `if` structure that determines pay

When you place a block within an `if` statement, it is crucial to place the curly braces correctly. For example, in Figure 5-7, the curly braces have been omitted. Within the code segment in Figure 5-7, when `hoursWorked > FULL_WEEK` is true, `regularPay` is calculated and the `if` expression ends. The next statement that computes `overtimePay` executes every time the program runs, no matter what value is stored in `hoursWorked`. This last statement does not depend on the `if` statement; it is an independent, stand-alone statement. The indentation might be deceiving; it looks as though two statements depend on the `if` statement, but indentation does not cause statements following an `if` statement to be dependent. Rather, curly braces are required if multiple statements must be treated as a block.

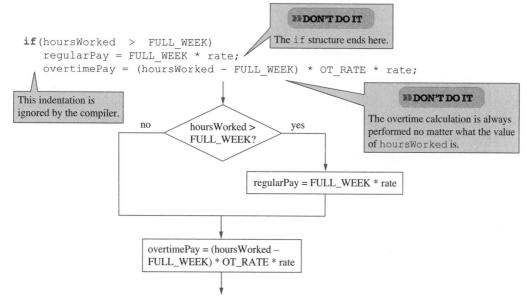

Figure 5-7 Erroneous overtime pay calculation with missing curly braces

Because the curly braces are missing, regardless of whether hoursWorked is more than FULL_WEEK, the last statement in Figure 5-7 is a new stand-alone statement that is not part of the if, and so it executes.

In Figure 5-7, if the hoursWorked value is FULL_WEEK or less, then the regularPay calculation does not execute (it executes only if hoursWorked is greater than FULL_WEEK), but the separate overtimePay statement does. If hoursWorked is 30, for example, and FULL_WEEK is 40, then the program calculates the value of overtimePay as a negative number (because 30 minus 40 results in –10). Therefore, the output is incorrect. Correct blocking is crucial to achieving valid output.

Just as you can block statements to depend on an if, you can also block statements to depend on an else. Figure 5-8 shows an application that contains an if structure with two dependent statements and an else with two dependent statements. The program executes the final println() statement without regard to the hoursWorked variable's value; it is not part of the if structure. Figure 5-9 shows the output from two executions of the program. In the first execution, the user entered 39 for the hoursWorked value and 20.00 for rate; in the second execution, the user entered 42 for hoursWorked and 20.00 for rate.

```java
import java.util.Scanner;
public class Payroll
{
  public static void main(String[] args)
  {
    double rate;
    double hoursWorked;
    double regularPay;
    double overtimePay;
    final int FULL_WEEK = 40;
    final double OT_RATE = 1.5;
    Scanner keyboard = new Scanner(System.in);
    System.out.print("How many hours did you work this week? ");
    hoursWorked = keyboard.nextDouble();
    System.out.print("What is your regular pay rate? ");
    rate = keyboard.nextDouble();
    if(hoursWorked > FULL_WEEK)
    {
      regularPay = FULL_WEEK * rate;
      overtimePay = (hoursWorked - FULL_WEEK) * OT_RATE * rate;
    }
    else
    {
      regularPay = hoursWorked * rate;
      overtimePay = 0.0;
    }
    System.out.println("Regular pay is " +
      regularPay + "\nOvertime pay is " + overtimePay);
  }
}
```

Figure 5-8 Payroll application containing an if and else with blocks

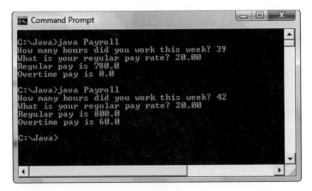

Figure 5-9 Output of the Payroll application

When you block statements, you must remember that any variable you declare within a block is local to that block. For example, the following code segment contains a variable named `sum` that is local to the block following the `if`. The last `println()` statement causes an error because the `sum` variable is not recognized:

```
if(a == b)
{
    int sum = a + b;
    System.out.println
        ("The two variables are equal");
}
System.out.println("The sum is " + sum);
```

»DON'T DO IT

The `sum` variable is not recognized here.

»TWO TRUTHS AND A LIE: USING MULTIPLE STATEMENTS IN AN if OR if...else STRUCTURE

1. To execute more than one statement that depends on the evaluation of a Boolean expression, you use a pair of curly braces to place the dependent statements within a block.

2. Indentation can be used to cause statements following an `if` statement to depend on the evaluation of the Boolean expression.

3. When you declare a variable within a block, it is local to that block.

The false statement is #2. Indentation does not cause statements following an `if` statement to be dependent; curly braces are required if multiple statements must be treated as a block.

NESTING if AND if...else STATEMENTS

Within an `if` or an `else`, you can code as many dependent statements as you need, including other `if` and `else` structures. Statements in which an `if` structure is contained inside another `if` structure are commonly called **nested if statements**. Nested `if` statements are particularly useful when two conditions must be met before some action is taken.

For example, suppose you want to pay a $50 bonus to a salesperson only if the salesperson sells at least three items that total at least $1000 in value during a specified time. Figure 5-10 shows the logic and the code to solve the problem.

Notice that there are no semicolons in the `if` statement code shown in Figure 5-10 until after the `bonus = SALES_BONUS;` statement. The expression `itemsSold >= MIN_ITEMS` is evaluated first. Only if this expression is `true` does the program evaluate the second Boolean expression, `totalValue >= MIN_VALUE`. If that expression is also `true`, the bonus assignment statement executes and the `if` structure ends.

```
final int MIN_ITEMS = 3;
final int MIN_VALUE = 1000;
final int SALES_BONUS = 50;
bonus = 0;

if(itemsSold >= MIN_ITEMS)
   if(totalValue >= MIN_VALUE)
      bonus = SALES_BONUS;
```

The Boolean expression in each if statement must be true for the bonus assignment to be made.

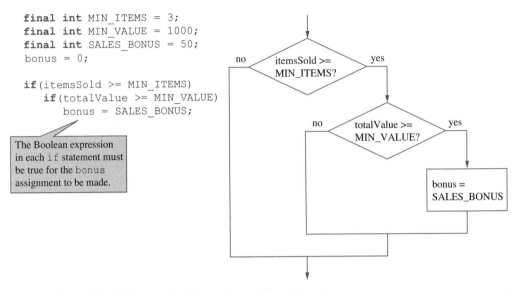

Figure 5-10 Determining whether to assign a bonus using nested if statements

When you use nested if statements, you must pay careful attention to placement of any else clauses. For example, suppose you want to distribute bonuses on a revised schedule, as shown in Figure 5-11. If the salesperson does not sell at least three items, you want to give a $10 bonus. If the salesperson sells at least three items whose combined value is less than $1000, the bonus is $25. If the salesperson sells at least three items whose combined value is at least $1000, the bonus is $50.

```
final int MIN_ITEMS = 3;
final int MIN_VALUE = 1000;
final int LARGE_BONUS = 50;
final int MEDIUM_BONUS = 25;
final int SMALL_BONUS = 10;

bonus = 0;

if(itemsSold >= MIN_ITEMS)
   if(totalValue >= MIN_VALUE)
      bonus = LARGE_BONUS;
   else
      bonus = MEDIUM_BONUS;
else
   bonus = SMALL_BONUS;
```

The last else goes with the first if.

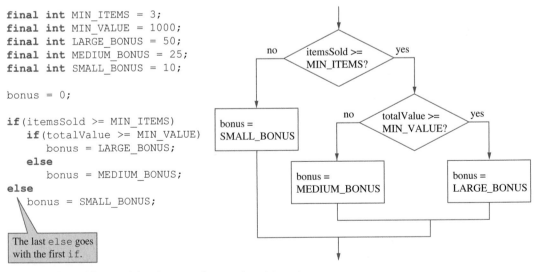

Figure 5-11 Determining one of three bonuses using nested if statements

As Figure 5-11 shows, when one `if` statement follows another, the first `else` clause encountered is paired with the most recent `if` encountered. The complete nested `if...else` structure fits entirely within the `if` portion of the outer `if...else` statement. No matter how many levels of `if...else` statements are needed to produce a solution, the `else` statements are always associated with their `if`s on a "first in-last out" basis.

>> TWO TRUTHS AND A LIE: NESTING `if` AND `if...else` STATEMENTS

1. Statements in which an `if` structure is contained inside another `if` structure are commonly called nested `if` statements.

2. When one `if` statement follows another, the first `else` clause encountered is paired with the first `if` that occurred before it.

3. A complete nested `if...else` structure always fits entirely within either the `if` portion or the `else` portion of its outer `if...else` statement.

The false statement is #2. When one `if` statement follows another, the first `else` clause encountered is paired with the most recent `if` encountered.

USING LOGICAL AND and OR OPERATORS

For an alternative to some nested `if` statements, you can use the **logical AND operator** between two Boolean expressions to determine whether both are `true`. The AND operator is written as two ampersands (`&&`). For example, the two statements shown in Figure 5-12 work exactly the same way. In each case, the `itemsSold` variable is tested, and if it is at least the minimum number of items required for a bonus, the `totalValue` is tested. If `totalValue` is at least the minimum required value, the bonus is set to `SALES_BONUS`.

```
if(itemsSold >= MIN_ITEMS)
   if(totalValue >= MIN_VALUE)
      bonus = SALES_BONUS;

if(itemsSold >= MIN_ITEMS && totalValue >= MIN_VALUE)
   bonus = SALES_BONUS;
```

Figure 5-12 Code for bonus-determining decision using the `&&` operator

It is important to note that when you use the `&&` operator, you must include a complete Boolean expression on each side. If you want to set a bonus to $400 when a `saleAmount` is both over $1000 and under $5000, the correct statement is:

```
if(saleAmount > 1000 && saleAmount < 5000)
   bonus = 400;
```

»NOTE For clarity, many programmers prefer to surround each Boolean expression that is part of a compound Boolean expression with its own set of parentheses. For example:

```
if((saleAmount > 1000) && (saleAmount < 5000))
   bonus = 400;
```

Use this format if it is clearer to you.

Even though the `saleAmount` variable is intended to be used in both parts of the AND expression, the following statement is incorrect and does not compile because there is not a complete expression on both sides of the `&&`:

»DON'T DO IT

This statement will not compile because it does not have a Boolean expression on each side of the &&.

```
if(saleAmount > 1000 && < 5000)
   bonus = 400;
```

The expressions in each part of an AND expression are evaluated only as much as necessary to determine whether the entire expression is `true` or `false`. This feature is called **short-circuit evaluation**. With the AND operator, both Boolean expressions must be `true` before the action in the statement can occur. (The same is true for nested `if`s, as you can see in Figure 5-10.) If the first tested expression is `false`, the second expression is never evaluated, because its value does not matter. For example, if `a` is not greater than `LIMIT` in the following `if` statement, then the evaluation is complete because there is no need to evaluate whether `b` is greater than `LIMIT`.

```
if(a > LIMIT && b > LIMIT)
   System.out.println("Both are greater than " + LIMIT);
```

You are never required to use the AND operator because using nested `if` statements always achieves the same result, but using the AND operator often makes your code more concise, less error-prone, and easier to understand.

»NOTE
The two vertical lines used in the OR operator are sometimes called "pipes." The pipe appears on the same key as the backslash on your keyboard.

With the AND operator, both Boolean expressions that surround the operator must be `true` before the action in the statement can occur. When you want some action to occur even if only one of two conditions is `true`, you can use nested `if` statements, or you can use the **conditional OR operator**, which is written as `||`.

For example, if you want to give a 10% discount to any customer who satisfies at least one of two conditions—buying at least 5 items or buying any number of items that total at least $3000 in value—you can write the code using either of the ways shown in Figure 5-13.

```
final int MIN_ITEMS = 5;
final double MIN_VALUE = 3000.00;
final double DISCOUNT = 0.10;
double discountRate = 0;

if(itemsBought >= MIN_ITEMS)
   discountRate = DISCOUNT;
else
    if(itemsValue >= MIN_VALUE)
       discountRate = DISCOUNT;
```

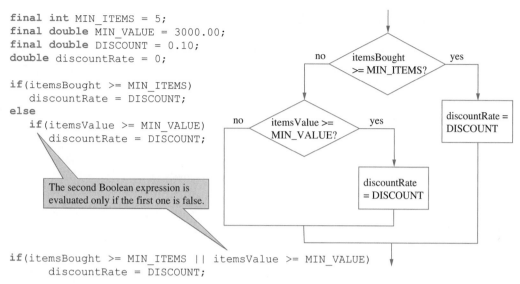

The second Boolean expression is evaluated only if the first one is false.

```
if(itemsBought >= MIN_ITEMS || itemsValue >= MIN_VALUE)
       discountRate = DISCOUNT;
```

Figure 5-13 Determining the customer's discount when the customer needs to meet only one of two criteria

As with the AND operator, the OR operator uses short-circuit evaluation. In other words, because only one of the Boolean expressions in an OR must be true to cause the dependent statements to execute, if the expression to the left of the || is true, then there is no need to evaluate the expression to the right of the ||.

>>**NOTE** A common use of the OR operator is to decide to take action whether a character variable is either the uppercase or lowercase version of a letter. For example, in the following statement, the subsequent action occurs whether the `selection` variable holds an uppercase or lowercase A:

```
if(selection == 'A' || selection == 'a')
   System.out.println("You chose option A");
```

>>**TWO TRUTHS AND A LIE: USING LOGICAL AND and OR OPERATORS**

1. The AND operator is written as two ampersands (`&&`) and the OR operator is written as two pipes (`||`).

2. When you use the `&&` and `||` operators, you must include a complete Boolean expression on each side.

3. When you use an AND or OR operator, each Boolean expression that surrounds the operator is always tested in order from left to right.

The false statement is #3. The expressions in each part of an AND or OR expression are evaluated only as much as necessary to determine whether the entire expression is `true` or `false`. For example, in an AND expression, if the first Boolean value is false, the second expression is not tested. In an OR expression, if the first Boolean value is true, the second expression is not tested. This feature is called short-circuit evaluation.

MAKING ACCURATE AND EFFICIENT DECISIONS

When new programmers must make a range check, they often introduce incorrect or ineffi-cient code into their programs. A **range check** is a series of statements that determine within which of a set of ranges a value falls. Consider a situation in which salespeople can receive one of three possible commission rates based on their sales. For example, a sale totaling $1000 or more earns the salesperson an 8% commission, a sale totaling $500 through $999 earns 6% of the sale amount, and any sale totaling $499 or less earns 5%. Using three separate if statements to test single Boolean expressions might result in some incorrect commission assignments. For example, examine the code shown in Figure 5-14.

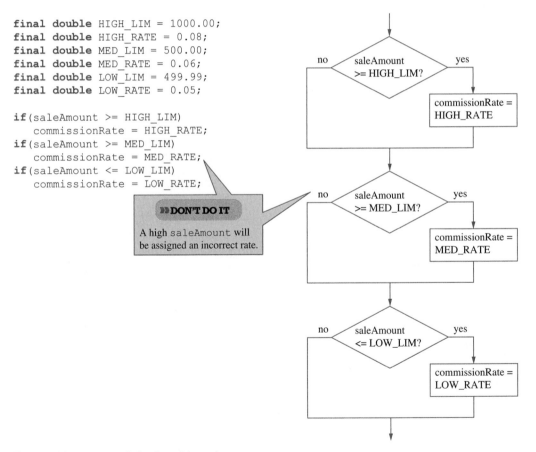

```
final double HIGH_LIM = 1000.00;
final double HIGH_RATE = 0.08;
final double MED_LIM = 500.00;
final double MED_RATE = 0.06;
final double LOW_LIM = 499.99;
final double LOW_RATE = 0.05;

if(saleAmount >= HIGH_LIM)
    commissionRate = HIGH_RATE;
if(saleAmount >= MED_LIM)
    commissionRate = MED_RATE;
if(saleAmount <= LOW_LIM)
    commissionRate = LOW_RATE;
```

»DON'T DO IT

A high saleAmount will be assigned an incorrect rate.

Figure 5-14 Incorrect commission-determining code

Using the code shown in Figure 5-14, when a saleAmount is $5000, for example, the first if statement executes and the Boolean expression (saleAmount >= HIGH_LIM) evaluates as true, so HIGH_RATE is correctly assigned to commissionRate. However, when a saleAmount is $5000, the next if expression, (saleAmount >= MED_LIM), also evaluates as true, so the commissionRate, which was just set to HIGH_RATE, is incorrectly reset to MED_RATE.

A partial solution to this problem is to use an else statement following the first evaluation, as shown in Figure 5-15.

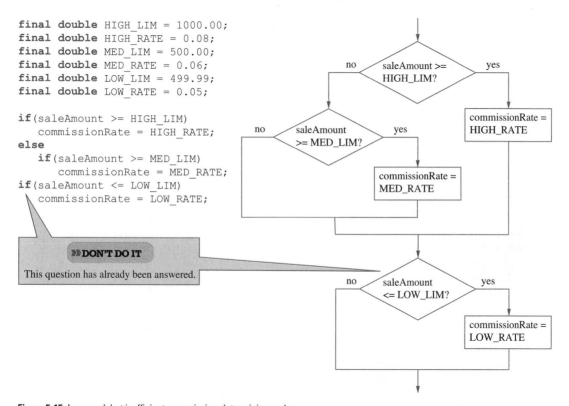

```
final double HIGH_LIM = 1000.00;
final double HIGH_RATE = 0.08;
final double MED_LIM = 500.00;
final double MED_RATE = 0.06;
final double LOW_LIM = 499.99;
final double LOW_RATE = 0.05;

if(saleAmount >= HIGH_LIM)
    commissionRate = HIGH_RATE;
else
    if(saleAmount >= MED_LIM)
        commissionRate = MED_RATE;
if(saleAmount <= LOW_LIM)
    commissionRate = LOW_RATE;
```

» DON'T DO IT

This question has already been answered.

Figure 5-15 Improved, but inefficient, commission-determining code

With the new code in Figure 5-15, when the saleAmount is $5000, the expression (saleAmount >= HIGH_LIM) is true and the commissionRate becomes HIGH_RATE; then the entire if structure ends. When the saleAmount is not greater than or equal to $1000 (for example, $800), the first if expression is false and the else statement executes and correctly sets the commissionRate to MED_RATE.

The code shown in Figure 5-15 works, but it is somewhat inefficient. When the saleAmount is any amount over LOW_RATE, either the first if sets commissionRate to HIGH_RATE for amounts that are at least $1000, or its `else` sets `commissionRate` to `MED_RATE` for amounts that are at least $500. In either of these two cases, the Boolean value tested in the next statement, `if(saleAmount <= LOW_LIM)`, is always `false`, so `commissionRate` is set correctly. However, it was unnecessary to ask the `LOW_LIM` question.

After you know that `saleAmount` is not at least `MED_LIM`, rather than asking `if(saleAmount <= LOW_LIM)`, it's easier, more efficient, and less error prone to use an `else`. If the `saleAmount` is not at least `HIGH_LIM` and is also not at least `MED_LIM`, it must by default be less than or equal to `LOW_LIM`. Figure 5-16 shows this improved logic.

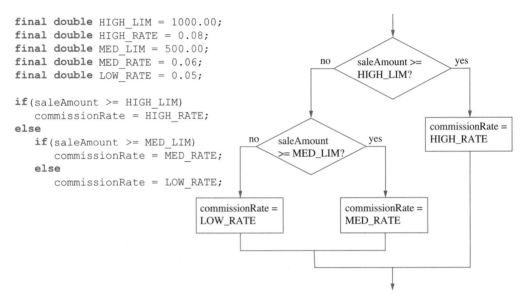

```
final double HIGH_LIM = 1000.00;
final double HIGH_RATE = 0.08;
final double MED_LIM = 500.00;
final double MED_RATE = 0.06;
final double LOW_RATE = 0.05;

if(saleAmount >= HIGH_LIM)
    commissionRate = HIGH_RATE;
else
    if(saleAmount >= MED_LIM)
        commissionRate = MED_RATE;
    else
        commissionRate = LOW_RATE;
```

Figure 5-16 Improved and efficient commission-determining logic

Within a nested `if...else`, like the one shown in Figure 5-16, it is most efficient to ask the question that is most likely to be true first. In other words, if you know that most `saleAmount` values are high, compare `saleAmount` to `HIGH_LIM` first. That way, you most frequently avoid asking multiple questions. If, however, you know that most `saleAmounts` are small, you should ask `if(saleAmount < LOW_LIM)` first. The code shown in Figure 5-17 results in the same commission value for any given `saleAmount`, but is more efficient when most `saleAmount` values are small.

```
final double HIGH_RATE = 0.08;
final double MED_LIM = 1000.00;
final double MED_RATE = 0.06;
final double LOW_LIM = 500.00;
final double LOW_RATE = 0.05;

if(saleAmount < LOW_LIM)
    commissionRate = LOW_RATE;
else
    if(saleAmount < MED_LIM)
        commissionRate = MED_RATE;
    else
        commissionRate = HIGH_RATE;
```

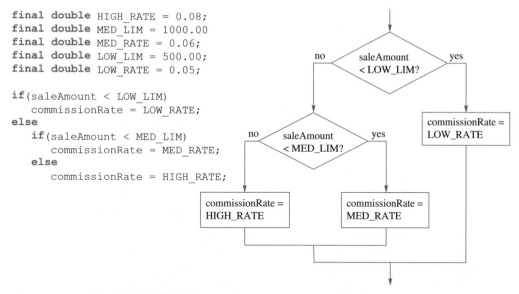

Figure 5-17 Commission-determining code asking about the smallest `saleAmount` first

> **»NOTE** In Figure 5-17, notice that the comparisons use the < operator instead of <=. That's because a `saleAmount` of $1000.00 should result in a `HIGH_RATE` and a `saleAmount` of $500.00 should result in a `MED_RATE`. If you wanted to use <= comparisons, then you could change the `MED_LIM` and `LOW_LIM` cutoff values to 999.99 and 499.99, respectively.

USING AND and OR APPROPRIATELY

Beginning programmers often use the AND operator when they mean to use OR, and often use OR when they should use AND. Part of the problem lies in the way we use the English language. For example, your boss might request, "Print an error message when an employee's hourly pay rate is under $5.85 and when an employee's hourly pay rate is over $60." You define $5.85 as a named constant `LOW` and $60 as `HIGH`. However, because your boss used the word "and" in the request, you might be tempted to write a program statement like the following:

```
if(payRate < LOW && payRate > HIGH)
    System.out.println("Error in pay rate");
```

»DON'T DO IT
This message can never print.

However, as a single variable, no `payRate` value can ever be both below 5.85 and over 60 at the same time, so the print statement can never execute, no matter what value the `payRate` has. In this case, you must write the following code to print the error message under the correct circumstances:

```
if(payRate < LOW || payRate > HIGH)
    System.out.println("Error in pay rate");
```

Similarly, your boss might request, "Print the names of those employees in departments 1 and 2." Because the boss used the word "and" in the request, you might be tempted to write the following:

```
if(department == 1 && department == 2)
   System.out.println("Name is: " + name);
```

However, the variable `department` can never contain both a 1 and a 2 at the same time, so no employee name will ever be printed, no matter what department the employee is in.

» TWO TRUTHS AND A LIE: MAKING ACCURATE AND EFFICIENT DECISIONS

1. A range check is a series of statements that determine within which of a set of ranges a value falls.

2. When you must make a series of decisions in a program, it is most efficient to first ask the question that is most likely to be true.

3. The statement `if(payRate < 6.00 && payRate > 50.00)` can be used to select `payRate` values that are very high or very low.

The false statement is #3. The statement `if(payRate < 6.00 && payRate > 50.00)` cannot be used to make a selection because no value for `payRate` can be both below 6.00 and above 50.00 at the same time.

USING THE `switch` STATEMENT

By nesting a series of `if` and `else` statements, you can choose from any number of alternatives. For example, suppose you want to print a student's class year based on a stored number. Figure 5-18 shows one possible implementation of the program.

```
if(year == 1)
   System.out.println("Freshman");
else
   if(year == 2)
      System.out.println("Sophomore");
   else
      if(year == 3)
         System.out.println("Junior");
      else
         if(year == 4)
            System.out.println("Senior");
         else
            System.out.println("Invalid year");
```

Figure 5-18 Determining class status using nested `if` statements

An alternative to using the series of nested `if` statements shown in Figure 5-18 is to use the `switch` statement. The **switch statement** is useful when you need to test a single variable against a series of exact integer or character values. The `switch` structure uses four keywords:

» `switch` starts the structure and is followed immediately by a test expression enclosed in parentheses.

» `case` is followed by one of the possible values for the test expression and a colon.

» `break` optionally terminates a `switch` structure at the end of each case.

» `default` is optionally used prior to any action that should occur if the test variable does not match any case.

Figure 5-19 shows the `case` structure used to print the four school years.

```
int year;
// Get year value from user input, or simply by assigning
switch (year)
{
    case 1:
        System.out.println ("Freshman");
        break;
    case 2:
        System.out.println ("Sophomore");
        break;
    case 3:
        System.out.println ("Junior");
        break;
    case 4:
        System.out.println ("Senior");
        break;
    default:
        System.out.println ("Invalid year");
}
```

Figure 5-19 Determining class status using a `switch` statement

»NOTE
You are not required to list the `case` values in ascending order, as shown in Figure 5-19, although doing so often makes a statement easier to understand. Logically, it is most efficient to list the most common case first, instead of the case with the lowest value.

»NOTE
Besides `int` and `char`, you can use a `switch` statement to test values of types `byte` and `short`, which hold smaller integer values.

The `switch` structure shown in Figure 5-19 begins by evaluating the `year` variable shown in the `switch` statement. If the year is equal to the first `case` value, which is 1, the statement that prints "Freshman" executes. The `break` statement bypasses the rest of the `switch` structure, and execution continues with any statement after the closing curly brace of the `switch` structure.

If the `year` variable is not equivalent to the first `case` value of 1, the next `case` value is compared, and so on. If the `year` variable does not contain the same value as any of the `case` statements, the `default` statement or statements execute.

You can leave out the `break` statements in a `switch` structure. However, if you omit the `break` and the program finds a match for the test variable, all the statements within the `switch` statement execute from that point forward. For example, if you omit each `break` statement in the code shown in Figure 5-19, when the year is 3, the first two cases are bypassed, but "Junior", "Senior", and "Invalid year" all print. You should intentionally omit the `break` statements if you want all subsequent cases to execute after the test variable is matched.

You do not need to write code for each case in a `case` statement. For example, suppose that the supervisor for departments 1, 2, and 3 is "Jones", but other departments have different supervisors. In that case, you might use the code in Figure 5-20.

```java
int department;
String supervisor;
// Statements to get department
switch(department)
{
    case 1:
    case 2:
    case 3:
        supervisor = "Jones";
        break;
    case 4:
        supervisor = "Staples";
        break;
    case 5:
        supervisor = "Tejano";
        break:
    default:
        System.out.println("Invalid department code");
}
```

Figure 5-20 Using empty `case` statements so the same result occurs in multiple cases

> **»NOTE** When several `char` variables must be checked and you want to ignore whether they are uppercase or lowercase, one frequently used technique employs empty `case` statements, as in the following example:
>
> ```java
> switch(departmentCode)
> {
>     case 'a':
>     case 'A':
>         departmentName = "Accounting";
>         break;
>     case 'm':
>     case 'M':
>         departmentName = "Marketing";
>         break;
> // and so on
> ```

You are never required to use a `switch` structure; you can always achieve the same results with nested `if` statements. The `switch` structure is simply convenient to use when there are several alternative courses of action that depend on a single integer or character variable.

In addition, it makes sense to use `switch` only when there are a reasonable number of specific matching values to be tested. For example, if every sale amount from $1 to $500 requires a 5% commission, it would not be reasonable to test every possible dollar amount using the code in Figure 5-21. Because 500 different dollar values result in the same commission, one test—`if(saleAmount <= 500)`—is far more reasonable than listing 500 separate cases.

```
switch(saleAmount)
{
    case 1:
        commRate = 0.05;
        break;
    case 2:
        commRate = 0.05;
        break;
    case 3:
        commRate = 0.05;
        break;
 // ...and so on for several hundred more cases
}
```

>> **DON'T DO IT**

This structure is too repetitive.

Figure 5-21 Inefficient use of the `switch` statement

>>TWO TRUTHS AND A LIE: USING THE `switch` **STATEMENT**

1. When you must make more decisions than Java can support, you use a `switch` statement instead of nested `if...else` statements.

2. The `switch` statement is useful when you need to test a single variable against a series of exact integer or character values.

3. A `break` statement bypasses the rest of its `switch` structure, and execution continues with any statement after the closing curly brace of the `switch` structure.

The false statement is #1. By nesting a series of `if` and `else` statements, you can choose from any number of alternatives. The `switch` statement is just a more convenient way of expressing nested `if...else` statements when the tested value is an integer or character.

USING THE CONDITIONAL AND NOT OPERATORS

Besides using `if` statements and `case` structures, Java provides one more way to make decisions. The **conditional operator** requires three expressions separated with a question mark and a colon, and is used as an abbreviated version of the `if...else` structure. As with the `switch` structure, you are never required to use the conditional operator; it is simply a convenient shortcut. The syntax of the conditional operator is:

```
testExpression ? trueResult : falseResult;
```

The first expression, testExpression, is a Boolean expression that is evaluated as true or false. If it is true, the entire conditional expression takes on the value of the expression following the question mark (trueResult). If the value of the testExpression is false, the entire expression takes on the value of falseResult.

For example, suppose you want to assign the smallest price to a sale item. Let the variable a be the advertised price and the variable b be the discounted price on the sale tag. The expression for assigning the smallest cost is:

```
smallerNum = (a < b) ? a : b;
```

When evaluating the expression a < b, where a is less than b, the entire conditional expression takes the value of a, which is then assigned to smallerNum. If a is not less than b, the expression assumes the value of b, and b is assigned to smallerNum.

You could achieve the same results with the following if...else structure:

```
if(a < b)
    smallerNum = a;
else
    smallerNum = b;
```

The advantage of using the conditional operator is the conciseness of the statement.

USING THE NOT OPERATOR

You use the **NOT operator**, which is written as the exclamation point (!), to negate the result of any Boolean expression. Any expression that evaluates as true becomes false when preceded by the NOT operator, and accordingly, any false expression preceded by the NOT operator becomes true.

For example, suppose a monthly car insurance premium is $200 if the driver is age 25 or younger and $125 if the driver is age 26 or older. Each of the following if...else statements correctly assigns the premium values:

```
if(age <= 25)
    premium = 200;
else
    premium = 125;

if(!(age <= 25))
    premium = 125;
else
    premium = 200;

if(age >= 26)
    premium = 125;
else
    premium = 200;

if(!(age >= 26))
    premium = 200;
else
    premium = 125;
```

The statements with the NOT operator are somewhat harder to read, particularly because they require the double set of parentheses, but the result of the decision-making process is the same in each case. Using the NOT operator is clearer when the value of a Boolean variable is tested. For example, a variable initialized as `boolean oldEnough = (age >= 25);` can become part of the relatively easy-to-read expression `if(!oldEnough)....`

>>**TWO TRUTHS AND A LIE: USING THE CONDITIONAL AND NOT OPERATORS**

1. The conditional operator is used as an abbreviated version of the `if...else` structure and requires two expressions separated with an exclamation point.

2. The NOT operator is written as the exclamation point (`!`).

3. The value of any false expression becomes true when preceded by the NOT operator.

The false statement is #1. The conditional operator requires three expressions separated with a question mark and a colon.

UNDERSTANDING PRECEDENCE

You can combine as many AND or OR operators as you need to make a decision. For example, if you want to award bonus points (defined as BONUS) to any student who receives a perfect score on any of four quizzes, you might write a statement like the following:

```
if(score1 == PERFECT || score2 == PERFECT ||
    score3 == PERFECT || score4 == PERFECT)
        bonus = BONUS;
else
    bonus = 0;
```

In this case, if at least one of the score variables is equal to the PERFECT constant, the student receives the bonus points. Although you can combine any number of AND or OR operators, special care must be taken when you combine them. You learned in Chapter 2 that operations have higher and lower precedences, and an operator's precedence makes a difference in how an expression is evaluated. For example, within an arithmetic expression, multiplication and division are always performed prior to addition or subtraction. Table 5-1 shows the precedence of the operators you have used so far.

Precedence	Operator(s)	Symbol(s)
Highest	Logical NOT	!
Intermediate	Multiplication, division, modulus	* / %
	Addition, subtraction	+ -
	Relational	> < >= <=
	Equality	== !=
	Logical AND	&&
	Logical OR	||
	Conditional	?:
Lowest	Assignment	=

Table 5-1 Operator precedence for operators used so far

In general, the order of precedence agrees with common algebraic usage. For example, in any mathematical expression, such as x = a + b, the arithmetic is done first and the assignment is done last, as you would expect. The relationship of && and || might not be as obvious. The AND operator is always evaluated before the OR operator. For example, consider the program segments shown in Figure 5-22. These code segments are intended to be part of an insurance company program that determines whether an additional premium should be charged to a driver who meets both of the following criteria:

» Has more than two traffic tickets or is under 25 years old

» Is male

» NOTE
You can remember the precedence of the AND and OR operators by remembering that they are evaluated in alphabetical order.

```
// Assigns extra premiums incorrectly
if(trafficTickets > 2 || age < 25 && gender == 'M')
    extraPremium = 200;
// Assigns extra premiums correctly
if((trafficTickets > 2 || age < 25) && gender == 'M')
    extraPremium = 200;
```

Figure 5-22 Some comparisons using && and ||

Consider a 30-year-old female driver with three traffic tickets; according to the stated criteria, she should not be assigned the extra premium because she is not male. With the first if statement in Figure 5-22, the AND operator takes precedence over the OR operator, so age < 25 && gender == 'M' is evaluated first. The value is false because age is not less than 25, so the expression is reduced to trafficTickets > 2 or false. Because the value of the tickets variable is greater than 2, the entire expression is true, and $200 is assigned to extraPremium, even though it should not be.

In the second `if` statement shown in Figure 5-22, parentheses have been added so the OR operator is evaluated first. The expression `trafficTickets > 2 || age < 25` is true because the value of `trafficTickets` is 3. So the expression evolves to `true && gender== 'M'`. Because gender is not 'M', the value of the entire expression is `false`, and the `extraPremium` value is not assigned 200, which is correct.

The following two conventions are important to keep in mind:

» The order in which you use operators makes a difference.

» You can always use parentheses to change precedence or make your intentions clearer.

» TWO TRUTHS AND A LIE: UNDERSTANDING PRECEDENCE

1. Assume p, q, and r are all Boolean variables that have been assigned the value `true`. After the following statement executes, the value of p is still `true`.

   `p = !q || r;`

2. Assume p, q, and r are all Boolean variables that have been assigned the value `true`. After the following statement executes, the value of p is still `true`.

   `p = !(!q && !r);`

3. Assume p, q, and r are all Boolean variables that have been assigned the value `true`. After the following statement executes, the value of p is still `true`.

   `p = !(q || !r);`

The false statement is #3. If p, q, and r are all Boolean variables that have been assigned the value `true`, then after p = !(q || !r); executes, the value of p is `false`. First p is evaluated as `true`, so the entire expression within the parentheses is `true`. The leading NOT operator reverses that result to `false` and assigns it to p.

YOU DO IT

USING AN `if...else`

In this section, you will start writing a program for Event Handlers Incorporated that determines which employee will be assigned to manage a client's scheduled event. To begin, you will prompt the user to answer a question about the event type, and then the program will display the name of the manager who handles such events. There are two event types: private events, handled by Dustin Britt, and corporate events, handled by Carmen Lindsey.

To write a program that chooses between two managers:

1. Open a new text file, and then enter the first lines of code to create a class named `ChooseManager`. You will import the `Scanner` class so that you can use keyboard input. The class will contain a `main()` method that performs all the work of the class:

```
import java.util.Scanner;
public class ChooseManager
{
    public static void main(String[] args)
    {
```

2. On new lines, declare the variables and constants this application will use. You will ask the user to enter an integer `eventType`. The values of the event types and the names of the managers for private and corporate events are stored as symbolic constants; the chosen manager will be assigned to the `chosenManager` string:

```
int eventType;
String chosenManager;
final int PRIVATE_CODE = 1;
final int CORPORATE_CODE = 2;
final String PRIV_MANAGER = "Dustin Britt";
final String CORP_MANAGER = "Carmen Lindsey";
```

3. Define the input device, then add the code that prompts the user to enter a 1 or 2 depending on the event type being scheduled, and accept the response:

```
Scanner input = new Scanner(System.in);
System.out.println("What type of event are you scheduling?");
System.out.print("Enter " + PRIVATE_CODE + " for private, " +
    CORPORATE_CODE + " for corporate... ");
eventType = input.nextInt();
```

4. Use an `if...else` statement to choose the name of the manager to be assigned to the `chosenManager` string, as follows:

```
if(eventType == PRIVATE_CODE)
    chosenManager = PRIV_MANAGER;
else
    chosenManager = CORP_MANAGER;
```

5. Display the chosen code and corresponding manager's name:

```
System.out.println("You entered " + eventType);
System.out.println("Manager for this event will be " +
    chosenManager);
```

6. Type the two closing curly braces to end the `main()` method and the `ChooseManager` class.

7. Save the program as **ChooseManager.java**, and then compile and run the program. Confirm that the program selects the correct manager when you choose 1 for a private event or 2 for a corporate event. For example, Figure 5-23 shows the output when the user enters 1 for a private event.

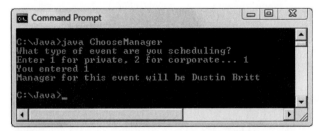

Figure 5-23 Output of the `ChooseManager` application after user enters 1

8. Rerun the ChooseManager program and enter an invalid item, such as 3. The manager selected is Carmen Lindsey because the program tests only for an entered value of 1 or not 1. Modify the program to display an error message when the entered value is not 1 or 2. Rename the class **ChooseManager2** and save the file as **ChooseManager2.java**.

CREATING AN Event CLASS TO USE IN A DECISION-MAKING APPLICATION

Next, you will create an Event class. The class will be used by Event Handlers Incorporated to store data about a planned event. Each Event object includes three data fields: the type of event, the name of the manager for the event, and the hourly rate charged for handling the event. The Event class also contains a get and set method for each field.

To create the Event class:

1. Open a new text file and type the class header for the Event class, followed by declarations for the three data fields:

```
public class Event
{
    private int typeOfEvent;
    private double rate;
    private String manager;
```

2. Create three get methods; each returns one of the data fields in the Event class:

```
public int getType()
{
    return typeOfEvent;
}
public double getRate()
{
    return rate;
}
public String getManager()
{
    return manager;
}
```

3. Also add three set methods; each sets a single data field:

```
public void setType(int eventType)
{
    typeOfEvent = eventType;
}
public void setRate(double eventRate)
{
    rate = eventRate;
}
public void setManager(String managerName)
{
    manager = managerName;
}
```

4. Type the closing curly brace for the class.

5. Save the file as **Event.java**, then compile the file and correct any errors.

WRITING AN APPLICATION THAT USES THE Event CLASS

Now that you have created an Event class, you will create a CreateEventObject application. You will prompt the user for an event type, and then select both a manager and a rate for the Event based on the selected type. Private events are managed by Dustin Britt and cost $47.99 per hour. Corporate events are managed by Carmen Lindsey and cost $75.99 per hour. Events held by nonprofit organizations are managed by Robin Armenetti and cost $40.99 per hour. After the user selects an event type, you will instantiate an Event object containing appropriate event data.

To create an application that uses the Event class:

1. Open a new file in your text editor and type the following to begin the CreateEventObject class:

```
import java.util.Scanner;
public class CreateEventObject
{
    public static void main(String[] args)
    {
```

2. Add variables and constants that will be used in the program as follows:

```
int eventType;
String chosenManager = "";
double chosenRate = 0;
Event scheduledEvent = new Event();
final int PRIVATE_CODE = 1;
final int CORPORATE_CODE = 2;
final int NONPROFIT_CODE = 3;
final String PRIVATE_MANAGER = "Dustin Britt";
final String CORP_MANAGER = "Carmen Lindsey";
final String NONPROFIT_MANAGER = "Robin Armenetti";
final double PRIVATE_RATE = 47.99;
final double CORP_RATE = 75.99;
final double NONPROFIT_RATE = 40.99;
boolean choiceIsGood = true;
```

3. Declare a Scanner object to be used for input, prompt the user for an event type, and read it in:

```
Scanner input = new Scanner(System.in);
System.out.println("What type of event are you scheduling?");
System.out.print("Enter " + PRIVATE_CODE + " for private, " +
    CORPORATE_CODE + " for corporate, or " + NONPROFIT_CODE +
    " for nonprofit... ");
eventType = input.nextInt();
```

4. Write a decision that selects the correct manager and rate based on the user's choice. Because two statements execute when the user selects 1, 2, or 3, the statements must be blocked using curly braces. If the user does not enter 1, 2, or 3, set the Boolean variable choiceIsGood to false:

```
if(eventType == PRIVATE_CODE)
{
   chosenManager = PRIVATE_MANAGER;
   chosenRate = PRIVATE_RATE;
}
else
   if(eventType == CORPORATE_CODE)
   {
      chosenManager = CORP_MANAGER;
      chosenRate = CORP_RATE;
   }
   else
      if(eventType == NONPROFIT_CODE)
      {
         chosenManager = NONPROFIT_MANAGER;
         chosenRate = NONPROFIT_RATE;
      }
      else
         choiceIsGood = false;
```

5. If the user made a valid choice, set values for the three fields that are contained in the scheduled Event object. Otherwise, display an error message:

```
if(choiceIsGood)
{
   scheduledEvent.setType(eventType);
   scheduledEvent.setManager(chosenManager);
   scheduledEvent.setRate(chosenRate);
}
else
   System.out.println("You entered " + eventType +
      " which is invalid.");
```

6. To confirm that the Event was created properly, display the Event object's fields:

```
System.out.println("Scheduled event:");
System.out.println("Type: " + scheduledEvent.getType() +
   " Manager: " + scheduledEvent.getManager() + " Rate: " +
   scheduledEvent.getRate() + " per hour");
```

7. Add a closing curly brace for the main() method and another for the class.

8. Save the application as **CreateEventObject.java**. Compile and run the program several times with different input at the prompt. Confirm that the output shows the correct event manager, type, and rate based on your response to the prompt. (If your response is an invalid event type, then the default values for the event should appear.) Figure 5-24 shows two executions of the program.

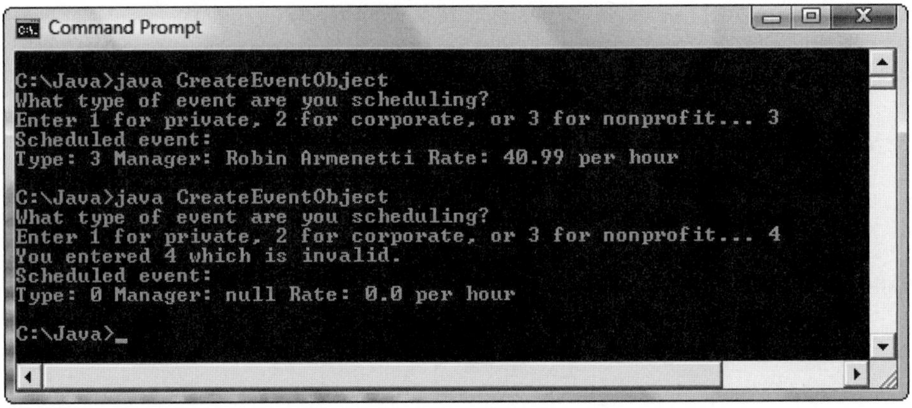

Figure 5-24 Output of the `CreateEventObject` application after the user enters 3 and then 4

9. Experiment with the program by removing the initialization values for `chosenManager` and `chosenRate`. When you compile the program, you receive error messages for the `setManager()` and `setRate()` statements that `chosenManager` and `chosenRate` might not have been initialized. The compiler determines that the values for those variables are set based on `if` statements, and so, depending on the outcome, they might never have been given valid values. Replace the initialization values for the variables to make the program compile successfully.

10. Experiment with the program by removing the initialization value for the Boolean variable `choiceIsGood`. When you compile the program, you receive an error message that the variable might never have been initialized. Because the variable is set to `false` only under certain conditions (an invalid event-type entry), the compiler determines that the variable might not have a usable value. Replace the initialization value and recompile the program to make it work correctly.

USING THE `switch` STATEMENT

Next, you will modify the `CreateEventObject` program to convert the nested `if` statements to a `switch` structure.

To convert the `CreateEventObject` decision-making process to a `switch` structure:

1. If necessary, open the **CreateEventObject.java** file and change the class name to **CreateEventObjectSwitch**. Immediately save the file as **CreateEventObjectSwitch.java**.

2. Delete the `if...else` statements that currently determine which number the user entered, and then replace them with the following `switch` structure:

```
switch(eventType)
{
    case PRIVATE_CODE:
        chosenManager = PRIVATE_MANAGER;
        chosenRate = PRIVATE_RATE;
        break;
    case CORPORATE_CODE:
        chosenManager = CORP_MANAGER;
        chosenRate = CORP_RATE;
        break;
    case NONPROFIT_CODE:
        chosenManager = NONPROFIT_MANAGER;
        chosenRate = NONPROFIT_RATE;
        break;
    default:
        choiceIsGood = false;
}
```

3. Save the file, compile, and test the application. Make certain the correct output appears when you enter 1, 2, 3, or any invalid number as keyboard input.

DON'T DO IT

» Don't ignore subtleties in boundaries used in decision making. For example, selecting employees who make less than $20 an hour is different from selecting employees who make $20 an hour or less.

» Don't use the assignment operator instead of the comparison operator when testing for equality.

» Don't insert a semicolon after the Boolean expression in an `if` statement; insert the semicolon after the entire statement is completed.

» Don't forget to block a set of statements with curly braces when several statements depend on the `if` or the `else` statement.

» Don't forget to include a complete Boolean expression on each side of an `&&` or `||` operator.

» Don't try to use a `switch` structure to test anything other than an integer or character value.

» Don't forget a `break` statement if one is required by the logic of your `switch` structure.

» Don't use the standard relational operators to compare objects; use them only with the built-in Java types. In Chapter 7, you will learn how to compare `Strings` correctly, and in Chapter 10 you will learn how to compare other objects.

KEY TERMS

Pseudocode is a tool that helps programmers plan a program's logic by writing plain English statements.

A **flowchart** is a tool that helps programmers plan a program's logic by writing the steps in diagram form, as a series of shapes connected by arrows.

A **sequence structure** is a logical structure in which one step follows another unconditionally.

A **decision structure** is a logical structure that involves choosing between alternative courses of action based on some value within a program.

`True` or `false` values are **Boolean values**; every computer decision results in a Boolean value.

In Java, the simplest statement you can use to make a decision is the `if` **statement**; you use it to write a single-alternative decision.

The **equivalency operator** (==) compares values and returns `true` if they are equal.

An **empty statement** contains only a semicolon.

A **single-alternative** `if` is a decision structure that performs an action, or not, based on one alternative.

A **dual-alternative** `if` is a decision structure that takes one of two possible courses of action.

In Java, the `if...else` **statement** provides the mechanism to perform one action when a Boolean expression evaluates as `true`, and to perform a different action when a Boolean expression evaluates as `false`.

Statements in which an `if` structure is contained within another `if` structure commonly are called **nested** `if` **statements**.

You can use the **logical AND operator** between Boolean expressions to determine whether both are `true`. The AND operator is written as two ampersands (`&&`).

Short-circuit evaluation describes the feature of the AND and OR operators in which evaluation is performed only as far as necessary to make a final decision.

You can use the **conditional OR operator** between Boolean expressions to determine whether either expression is `true`. The OR operator is written as two pipes (`||`).

A **range check** is a series of statements that determine within which of a set of ranges a value falls.

The `switch` **statement** uses up to four keywords to test a single variable against a series of exact integer or character values. The keywords are `switch`, `case`, `break`, and `default`.

The **conditional operator** requires three expressions separated with a question mark and a colon, and is used as an abbreviated version of the `if...else` structure.

You use the **NOT operator**, which is written as an exclamation point (`!`), to negate the result of any Boolean expression.

CHAPTER SUMMARY

» Making a decision involves choosing between two alternative courses of action based on some value within a program.

» You can use the `if` statement to make a decision based on a Boolean expression that evaluates as `true` or `false`. If the Boolean expression enclosed in parentheses within an `if` statement is `true`, the subsequent statement or block executes. A single-alternative `if` performs an action based on one alternative; a dual-alternative `if`, or `if...else`, provides the mechanism for performing one action when a Boolean expression is `true` and a different action when the expression is `false`.

» To execute more than one statement that depends on the evaluation of a Boolean expression, you use a pair of curly braces to place the dependent statements within a block. Within an `if` or an `else` statement, you can code as many dependent statements as you need, including other `if` and `else` statements.

» Nested `if` statements are particularly useful when two conditions must be met before some action occurs.

» You can use the AND operator (`&&`) within a Boolean expression to determine whether two expressions are both `true`. You use the OR operator (`||`) when you want to carry out some action even if only one of two conditions is `true`.

» New programmers frequently cause errors in their `if` statements when they perform a range check incorrectly or inefficiently, or when they use the wrong operator with AND and OR.

» You use the `switch` statement to test a single variable against a series of exact integer or character values.

» The conditional operator requires three expressions, a question mark, and a colon, and is used as an abbreviated version of the `if...else` statement. You use the NOT operator (`!`) to negate the result of any Boolean expression.

» Operator precedence makes a difference in how expressions are evaluated. You can always use parentheses to change precedence or make your intentions clearer.

REVIEW QUESTIONS

1. The logical structure in which one instruction occurs after another with no branching is a _____ .

   a. sequence   c. loop
   b. selection   d. case

2. Which of the following is typically used in a flowchart to indicate a decision?

   a. square   c. diamond
   b. rectangle   d. oval

3. Which of the following is not a type of `if` statement?

   a. single-alternative `if`   c. reverse `if`
   b. dual-alternative `if`   d. nested `if`

4. A decision is based on a(n) _____ value.

   a. Boolean   c. definitive

   b. absolute   d. convoluted

5. In Java, the value of `(4 > 7)` is _____ .

   a. 4   c. `true`

   b. 7   d. `false`

6. Assuming the variable `q` has been assigned the value 3, which of the following statements prints XXX?

   a. `if(q > 0) System.out.println("XXX");`

   b. `if(q > 7); System.out.println("XXX");`

   c. Both of the above statements print XXX.

   d. Neither of the above statements prints XXX.

7. What is the output of the following code segment?

```
t = 10;
if(t > 7)
{
    System.out.print("AAA");
    System.out.print("BBB");
}
```

   a. AAA   c. AAABBB

   b. BBB   d. nothing

8. What is the output of the following code segment?

```
t = 10;
if(t > 7)
    System.out.print("AAA");
    System.out.print("BBB");
```

   a. AAA   c. AAABBB

   b. BBB   d. nothing

9. What is the output of the following code segment?

```
t = 7;
if(t > 7)
    System.out.print("AAA");
    System.out.print("BBB");
```

   a. AAA   c. AAABBB

   b. BBB   d. nothing

10. When you code an `if` statement within another `if` statement, as in the following, then the `if` statements are _____ .

```
if(a > b)
    if(c > d)x = 0;
```

a. notched   c. nested

b. nestled   d. sheltered

11. The operator that combines two conditions into a single Boolean value that is `true` only when both of the conditions are `true`, but is `false` otherwise, is _____ .

a. $$ c. ||

b. !!   d. &&

12. The operator that combines two conditions into a single Boolean value that is `true` when at least one of the conditions is `true` is _____ .

a. $$ c. ||

b. !!   d. &&

13. Assuming a variable `f` has been initialized to 5, which of the following statements sets `g` to 0?

a. `if(f > 6 || f == 5) g = 0;`

b. `if(f < 3 || f > 4) g = 0;`

c. `if(f >= 0 || f < 2) g = 0;`

d. All of the above statements set `g` to 0.

14. Which of the following groups has the lowest operator precedence?

a. relational   c. addition

b. equality   d. logical OR

15. Which of the following statements correctly prints the names of voters who live in district 6 and all voters who live in district 7?

a. `if(district == 6 || 7)`
   `System.out.println("Name is " + name);`

b. `if(district == 6 || district == 7)`
   `System.out.println("Name is " + name);`

c. `if(district = 6 && district == 7)`
   `System.out.println("Name is " + name);`

d. two of these

16. Which of the following prints "Error" when a student ID is less than 1000 or more than 9999?

    a. `if(stuId < 1000) if(stuId > 9999)`
       `System.out.println("Error");`

    b. `if(stuId < 1000 && stuId > 9999)`

       `System.out.println("Error");`

    c. `if(stuId < 1000)`
          `System.out.println("Error");`
       `else if(stuId > 9999)`
          `System.out.println("Error");`

    d. Two of these are correct.

17. You can use the _____ statement to terminate a `switch` structure.

    a. `switch`   c. `case`

    b. `end`   d. `break`

18. The `switch` argument within a `switch` structure requires a(n) _____ .

    a. integer value   c. `double` value

    b. character value   d. integer or character value

19. Assuming a variable `w` has been assigned the value 15, what does the following statement do?

    `w == 15 ? x = 2 : x = 0;`

    a. assigns 15 to `w`   c. assigns 0 to `x`

    b. assigns 2 to `x`   d. nothing

20. Assuming a variable `y` has been assigned the value 6, the value of `!(y < 7)` is _____ .

    a. 6   c. `true`

    b. 7   d. `false`

EXERCISES

1. a. Write an application that prompts the user for a checking account balance and a savings account balance. Display the message "Checking account balance is low" if the checking account balance is less than $10. Display the message "Savings account balance is low" if the savings account balance is less than $100. Save the file as **Balance.java**.

   b. Modify the application in Exercise 1a to display an additional message, "Both accounts are dangerously low", if both fall below the specified limits. Save the file as **Balance2.java**.

2. a. Write an application for a furniture company; the program determines the price of a table. Ask the user to choose 1 for pine, 2 for oak, or 3 for mahogany. The output is the name of the wood chosen as well as the price of the table. Pine tables cost $100, oak tables cost $225, and mahogany tables cost $310. If the user enters an invalid wood code, set the price to 0. Save the file as **Furniture.java**.

   b. Add a prompt to the application you wrote in Exercise 2a to ask the user to specify a (1) large table or a (2) small table, but only if the wood selection is valid. Add $35 to the price of any large table, and add nothing to the price for a small table. Display an appropriate message if the size value is invalid and assume the price is for a small table. Save the file as **Furniture2.java**.

3. a. Write an application for a college's admissions office. Prompt the user for a student's numeric high school grade point average (for example, 3.2) and an admission test score from 0 to 100. Print the message "Accept" if the student has any of the following:

   » A grade point average of 3.0 or above and an admission test score of at least 60
   » A grade point average below 3.0 and an admission test score of at least 80

   If the student does not meet either of the qualification criteria, print "Reject". Save the file as **Admission.java**.

   b. Modify the application in Exercise 3a so that if a user enters a grade point average under 0 or over 4.0, or a test score under 0 or over 100, an error message appears instead of the "Accept" or "Reject" message. Save the file as **Admission2.java**.

4. Create a class named CheckingAccount with data fields for an account number and a balance. Include a constructor that takes arguments for each field. The constructor sets the balance to 0 if it is below the required $200.00 minimum for an account. Also include a method that displays account details, including an explanation if the balance was reduced to 0. Write an application named TestAccount in which you instantiate two CheckingAccount objects, prompt the user for values for the account number and balance, and display the values of both accounts. Save both the **CheckingAccount.java** and **TestAccount.java** files.

5. a. Write an application that prompts an employee for an hourly pay rate and hours worked. Compute gross pay (hours times rate), withholding tax, and net pay (gross pay minus withholding tax). Withholding tax is computed as a percentage of gross pay based on the following:

Gross Pay ($)	Withholding (%)
Up to and including 300.00	10
300.01 and up	12

   Save the file as **ComputeNet.java**.

b. Modify the application you created in Exercise 5a using the following withholding percentage ranges:

Gross Pay ($)	Withholding (%)
0 to 300.00	10
300.01 to 400.00	12
400.01 to 500.00	15
500.01 and over	20

Save the file as **ComputeNet2.java**.

6. Write an application that prompts the user for two integers and then prompts the user to enter an option as follows: 1 to add the two integers, 2 to subtract the second integer from the first, 3 to multiply the integers, and 4 to divide the first integer by the second. Display an error message if the user enters an option other than 1–4 or if the user chooses the divide option but enters 0 for the second integer. Otherwise, display the results of the arithmetic. Save the file as **Calculate.java**.

7. a. Write an application for a lawn-mowing service. The lawn-mowing season lasts 20 weeks. The weekly fee for mowing a lot under 4,000 square feet is $25. The fee for a lot that is 4,000 square feet or more, but under 600 square feet, is $35 per week. The fee for a lot that is 6,000 square feet or over is $50 per week. Prompt the user for the length and width of a lawn, and then print the weekly mowing fee, as well as the 20-week seasonal fee. Save the file as **Lawn.java**.

b. To the Lawn application you created in Exercise 7a, add a prompt that asks the user whether the customer wants to pay (1) once, (2) twice, or (3) 20 times per year. If the user enters 1 for once, the fee for the season is simply the seasonal total. If the customer requests two payments, each payment is half the seasonal fee plus a $5 service charge. If the user requests 20 separate payments, add a $3 service charge per week. Display the number of payments the customer must make, each payment amount, and the total for the season. Save the file as **Lawn2.java**.

8. Write an application that recommends a pet for a user based on the user's lifestyle. Prompt the user to enter whether he or she lives in an apartment, house, or dormitory (1, 2, or 3) and the number of hours the user is home during the average day. The user will select an hour category from a menu: (1) 18 or more; (2) 10–17; (3) 8–9; (4) 6–7; or (5) 0–5. Print your recommendation based on the following table:

Residence	Hours Home	Recommendation
House	18 or more	Pot-bellied pig
House	10 to 17	Dog
House	Fewer than 10	Snake
Apartment	10 or more	Cat
Apartment	Fewer than 10	Hamster
Dormitory	6 or more	Fish
Dormitory	Fewer than 6	Ant farm

Save the file as **PetAdvice.java**.

9. a. Write an application that displays a menu of three items in a restaurant as follows:

   (1) Cheeseburger   4.99

   (2) Pepsi   2.00

   (3) Chips   0.75

   Prompt the user to choose an item using the number (1, 2, or 3) that corresponds to the item, or to enter 0 to quit the application. After the user makes the first selection, if the choice is 0, display a bill of $0. Otherwise, display the menu again. The user should respond to this prompt with another item number to order or 0 to quit. If the user types 0, display the cost of the single requested item. If the user types 1, 2, or 3, add the cost of the second item to the first, and then display the menu a third time. If the user types 0 to quit, display the total cost of the two items; otherwise, display the total for all three selections. Save the file as **FastFood.java**.

   b. Modify the application in Exercise 9a so that if the user makes a menu selection he or she has already made, ignore the selection—that is, do not add a second price for the same item to the total. The user is still allowed only three entries. Save the file as **FastFood2.java**.

10. a. Create a class named `Invoice` that holds an invoice number, balance due, and three fields representing the month, day, and year that the balance is due. Create a constructor that accepts values for all five data fields. Within the constructor, assign each argument to the appropriate field with the following exceptions:

    » If an invoice number is less than 1000, force the invoice number to 0.

    » If the month field is less than 1 or greater than 12, force the month field to 0.

    » If the day field is less than 1 or greater than 31, force the day field to 0.

    » If the year field is less than 2009 or greater than 2015, force the year field to 0.

    In the `Invoice` class, include a display method that displays all the fields on an `Invoice` object. Save the file as **Invoice.java**.

   b. Write an application containing a `main()` method that declares several `Invoice` objects, proving that all the statements in the constructor operate as specified. Save the file as **TestInvoice.java**.

   c. Modify the constructor in the `Invoice` class so that the day is not greater than 31, 30, or 28, depending on the month. For example, if a user tries to create an invoice for April 31, force it to April 30. Also, if the month is invalid, and thus forced to 0, also force the day to 0. Save the modified `Invoice` class as **Invoice2.java**. Then modify the `TestInvoice` class to create `Invoice2` objects. Create enough objects to test every decision in the constructor. Save this file as **TestInvoice2.java**.

11. Use the Web to locate the lyrics to the traditional song "The Twelve Days of Christmas." The song contains a list of gifts received for the holiday. The list is cumulative so that as each "day" passes, a new verse contains all the words of the previous verse, plus a new item. Write an application that displays the words to the song starting with any day the user enters. (Hint: Use a `switch` statement with `cases` in descending day order and without any `break` statements so that the lyrics for any day repeat all the lyrics for previous days.) Save the file as **TwelveDays.java**.

12. Barnhill Fastener Company runs a small factory. The company employs workers who are paid one of three hourly rates depending on skill level:

Skill Level	Hourly Pay Rate ($)
1	17.00
2	20.00
3	22.00

   Each factory worker might work any number of hours per week; any hours over 40 are paid at one and one-half times the usual rate.

   In addition, workers in skill levels 2 and 3 can elect the following insurance options:

Option	Explanation	Weekly Cost to Employee ($)
1	Medical insurance	32.50
2	Dental insurance	20.00
3	Long-term disability insurance	10.00

   Also, workers in skill level 3 can elect to participate in the retirement plan at 3% of their gross pay.

   Write an interactive Java payroll application that calculates the net pay for a factory worker. The program prompts the user for skill level and hours worked, as well as appropriate insurance and retirement options for the employee's skill level category. The application displays: (1) the hours worked, (2) the hourly pay rate, (3) the regular pay for

40 hours, (4) the overtime pay, (5) the total of regular and overtime pay, and (6) the total itemized deductions. If the deductions exceed the gross pay, display an error message; otherwise, calculate and display (7) the net pay after all the deductions have been subtracted from the gross. Save the file as **Pay.java**.

DEBUGGING EXERCISES

Each of the following files in the Chapter.05 folder on your Student Disk has syntax and/or logic errors. In each case, determine the problem and fix the program. After you correct the errors, save each file using the same filename preceded with Fix. For example, save DebugFive1.java as FixDebugFive1.java.

a. DebugFive1.java

b. DebugFive2.java

c. DebugFive3.java

d. DebugFive4.java

GAME ZONE

1. In Chapter 1, you created a class called RandomGuess. In this game, players guess a number, the application generates a random number, and players determine whether they were correct. Now that you can make decisions, modify the application so it allows a player to enter a guess before the random number is displayed, and then displays a message indicating whether the player's guess was correct, too high, or too low. Save the file as **RandomGuess2.java**. (After you finish Chapter 6, you will be able to modify the application so that the user can continue to guess until the correct answer is entered.)

2. Create a lottery game application. Generate three random numbers (see Appendix D for help in doing so), each between 0 and 9. Allow the user to guess three numbers. Compare each of the user's guesses to the three random numbers and display a message that includes the user's guess, the randomly determined three-digit number, and the amount of money the user has won as follows:

Matching Numbers	Award ($)
Any one matching	10
Two matching	100
Three matching, not in order	1000
Three matching in exact order	1,000,000
No matches	0

Make certain that your application accommodates repeating digits. For example, if a user guesses 1, 2, and 3, and the randomly generated digits are 1, 1, and 1, do not give the user credit for three correct guesses—just one. Save the file as **Lottery.java**.

3. In Chapter 3, you created a `Card` class. Modify the `Card` class so the `setValue()` method does not allow a `Card`'s value to be less than 1 or higher than 13. If the argument to `setValue()` is out of range, assign 1 to the `Card`'s value.

   In Chapter 3, you also created a `PickTwoCards` application that randomly selects two playing cards and displays their values. In that application, all `Card` objects were arbitrarily assigned a suit represented by a single character, but they could have different values, and the player observed which of two `Card` objects had the higher value. Now, modify the application so the suit and the value are both chosen randomly. Using two `Card` objects, play a very simple version of the card game War. Deal two `Cards`—one for the computer and one for the player—and determine the higher card, then display a message indicating whether the cards are equal, the computer won, or the player won. (Playing cards are considered equal when they have the same value, no matter what their suit is.) For this game, assume the Ace (value 1) is low. Make sure that the two `Cards` dealt are not the same `Card`. For example, a deck cannot contain more than one `Card` representing the 2 of Spades. If two cards are chosen to have the same value, change the suit for one of them. Save the application as **War.java**. (After you learn about arrays in Chapter 8, you will be able to create a more sophisticated War game in which you use an entire deck without repeating cards.)

4. In Chapter 4, you created a `Die` class from which you could instantiate an object containing a random value from 1–6. You also wrote an application that randomly "throws" two dice and displays their values. Modify the application so it determines whether the two dice are the same, the first has a higher value, or the second has a higher value. Save the application as **TwoDice2.java**.

5. In the game Rock Paper Scissors, two players simultaneously choose one of three options: rock, paper, or scissors. If both players choose the same option, then the result is a tie. However, if they choose differently, the winner is determined as follows:

   » Rock beats scissors, because a rock can break a pair of scissors.

   » Scissors beats paper, because scissors can cut paper.

   » Paper beats rock, because a piece of paper can cover a rock.

   Create a game in which the computer randomly chooses rock, paper, or scissors. Let the user enter a number 1, 2, or 3, each representing one of the three choices. Then, determine the winner. Save the application as **RockPaperScissors.java**. (In Chapter 7, you will modify the game so that the user enters a string for "rock", "paper", and "scissors", rather than just entering a number.)

TOUGH QUESTIONS

1. What is a quick way to determine whether a value is even or odd?

2. What is the output of the following code?

```
public static void main(String args[])
{
    int num = 5;
    if(num > 0)
        System.out.println("true");
    else;
        System.out.println("false");
}
```

3. What is the output of the following code?

```
int x = 5;
boolean isNumBig = (x > 100);
if(isNumBig = true)
    System.out.println("Number is big");
else
    System.out.println("Number is not big");
```

4. What is the output of the following code?

```
public static void main(String args[])
{
    if(thisMethod() && thatMethod())
        System.out.println("Goodbye");
}
public static boolean thisMethod()
{
    System.out.println("Hello");
    return false;
}
public static boolean thatMethod()
{
    System.out.println("How are you?");
    return true;
}
```

5. Rewrite the following method to work exactly the same way as it does now, using as few words as possible in the method body:

```
public static boolean interesting(boolean value)
{
    if(value == true)
    {
        if(value == false)
            value = false;
        else
            value = true;
    }
```

```
        else
            if(value == false)
                value = false;
            else
                value = true;
        return value;
    }
```

6. What is the output of the following code, assuming that `department` = 1?

```
switch(department)
{
    case 3:
        System.out.println("Manufacturing");
    case 1:
        System.out.println("Accounting");
    case 2:
        System.out.println("Human Resources");
}
```

UP FOR DISCUSSION

1. In this chapter, you learned how computer programs make decisions. Insurance companies use programs to make decisions about your insurability as well as the rates you will be charged for health and life insurance policies. For example, certain preexisting conditions may raise your insurance premiums considerably. Is it ethical for insurance companies to access your health records and then make insurance decisions about you?

2. Job applications are sometimes screened by software that makes decisions about a candidate's suitability based on keywords in the applications. For example, when a help-wanted ad lists "management experience," the presence of those exact words might determine which résumés are chosen for further scrutiny. Is such screening fair to applicants?

3. Medical facilities often have more patients waiting for organ transplants than there are available organs. Suppose you have been asked to write a computer program that selects which of several candidates should receive an available organ. What data would you want on file to use in your program, and what decisions would you make based on the data? What data do you think others might use that you would not use?

6

LOOPING

In this chapter, you will:

Learn about the loop structure
Use a `while` loop
Use shortcut arithmetic operators
Use a `for` loop
Learn how and when to use a `do...while` loop
Learn about nested loops
Understand how to improve loop performance

LEARNING ABOUT THE LOOP STRUCTURE

If making decisions is what makes programs seem smart, looping is what makes programs seem powerful. A **loop** is a structure that allows repeated execution of a block of statements. Within a looping structure, a Boolean expression is evaluated. If it is true, a block of statements called the **loop body** executes and the Boolean expression is evaluated again. As long as the expression is true, the statements in the loop body continue to execute. When the Boolean evaluation is false, the loop ends. Figure 6-1 shows a diagram of the logic of a loop.

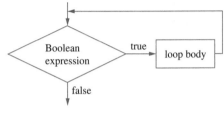

Figure 6-1 Flowchart of a loop structure

In Java, you can use several mechanisms to create loops. In this chapter, you will learn to use three types of loops:

» A while loop, in which the loop-controlling Boolean expression is the first statement in the loop

» A for loop, which is usually used as a concise format in which to execute loops

» A do...while loop, in which the loop-controlling Boolean expression is the last statement in the loop

»TWO TRUTHS AND A LIE: LEARNING ABOUT THE LOOP STRUCTURE

1. A loop is a structure that allows repeated execution of a block of statements as long as a tested expression is true.

2. If a loop's tested Boolean expression is true, a block of statements called the loop body executes before the Boolean expression is evaluated again.

3. When the Boolean evaluation tested in a loop becomes false, the loop body executes one last time.

The false statement is #3. When the Boolean evaluation tested in a loop is false, the loop ends.

USING A while LOOP TO CREATE A DEFINITE LOOP

You can use a **while loop** to execute a body of statements continually as long as the Boolean expression that controls entry into the loop continues to be `true`. In Java, a `while` loop consists of the keyword `while` followed by a Boolean expression within parentheses, followed by the body of the loop, which can be a single statement or a block of statements surrounded by curly braces.

You can use a `while` loop when you need to perform a task a predetermined number of times. A loop that executes a specific number of times is a **definite loop** or a counted loop. To write a definite loop, you initialize a **loop control variable**, a variable whose value determines whether loop execution continues. While the Boolean value that results from comparing the loop control variable and another value is `true`, the body of the `while` loop continues to execute. In the body of the loop, you must include a statement that alters the loop control variable. For example, the program segment shown in Figure 6-2 prints the series of integers 1 through 10. The variable `val` is the loop control variable—it starts the loop holding a value of 1, and while the value remains under 11, the `val` continues to print and be increased.

```
int val;
final int LIMIT = 11;

val = 1;
while(val < LIMIT)
{
    System.out.println(val);
    val = val + 1;
}
```

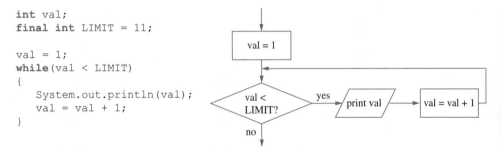

> **NOTE**
> To an algebra student, a statement such as `val = val + 1;` looks wrong—a value can never be one more than itself. In algebra, the equal sign means equivalency. In Java, however, the equal sign assigns a value to the variable on the left. Therefore, `val = val + 1;` takes the value of `val`, adds 1 to it, and then assigns the new value back into `val`.

Figure 6-2 A `while` loop that prints the integers 1 through 10

When you write applications containing loops, it is easy to make mistakes. For example, executing the code shown in Figure 6-3 causes the message "Hello" to display (theoretically) forever because there is no code to end the loop. A loop that never ends is called an **infinite loop**.

```
while(4 > 2)
{
    System.out.println("Hello");
}
```

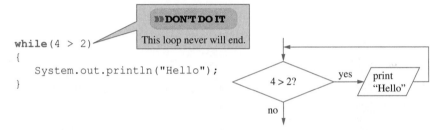

> **DON'T DO IT**
> This loop never will end.

Figure 6-3 A loop that displays "Hello" infinitely

» NOTE
As an inside joke to programmers, the address of Apple Computer, Inc. is One Infinite Loop, Cupertino, California.

» NOTE An infinite loop might not actually execute infinitely. Depending on the tasks the loop performs, eventually the computer memory might be exhausted (literally and figuratively) and execution might stop. Also, it's possible that the processor has a time-out feature that forces the loop to end. Either way, and depending on your system, quite a bit of time could pass before the loop stops running.

In Figure 6-3, the expression 4 > 2 evaluates to true. You obviously never need to make such an evaluation, but if you do so in this while loop, the body of the loop is entered and "Hello" displays. Next, the expression is evaluated again. The expression 4 > 2 is still true, so the body is entered again. "Hello" displays repeatedly; the loop never finishes because 4 > 2 is never false.

» NOTE
On many keyboards, the Break key is also the Pause key.

It is a bad idea to intentionally write an infinite loop. However, even experienced programmers write them by accident. So, before you start writing loops, it is good to know how to exit from an infinite loop in the event you find yourself in the midst of one. You might suspect an infinite loop if the same output is displayed repeatedly or if the screen simply remains idle for an extended period of time without displaying the expected output. If you think your application is in an infinite loop, you can press and hold Ctrl, and then press C or Break; the looping program should terminate.

To prevent a while loop from executing infinitely, three separate actions must occur:

» A named loop control variable is initialized to a starting value.

» The loop control variable is tested in the while statement.

» If the test expression is true, the body of the while statement must take some action that alters the value of the loop control variable; the test of the while statement must eventually evaluate to false so that the loop can end.

All of these conditions are met by the example in Figure 6-4. First, a loop control variable loopCount is named and set to a value of 1. Second, the statement while(loopCount < 3) is tested. Third, the loop body is executed because the loop control variable loopCount is less than 3. Note that the loop body shown in Figure 6-4 consists of two statements made into a block by their surrounding curly braces. The first statement prints "Hello" and then the second statement adds 1 to loopCount. The next time loopCount is evaluated, it is 2. It is still less than 3, so the loop body executes again. "Hello" prints a second time, and loopCount becomes 3. Finally, because the expression loopCount < 3 now evaluates to false, the loop ends. Program execution then continues with any subsequent statements.

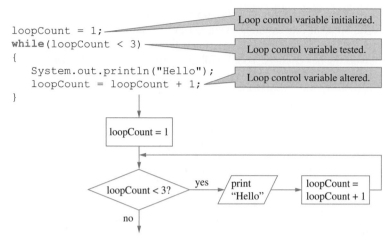

```
loopCount = 1;
while(loopCount < 3)
{
    System.out.println("Hello");
    loopCount = loopCount + 1;
}
```

Loop control variable initialized.

Loop control variable tested.

Loop control variable altered.

Figure 6-4 A `while` loop that prints "Hello" twice

It is important that the loop control variable be altered within the body of the loop. Figure 6-5 shows the same code as in Figure 6-4, but the curly braces have been eliminated. In this case, the `while` loop body ends at the semicolon that appears at the end of the "Hello" statement. Adding 1 to the `loopCount` is no longer part of a block that contains the loop, so the value of `loopCount` never changes and an infinite loop is created.

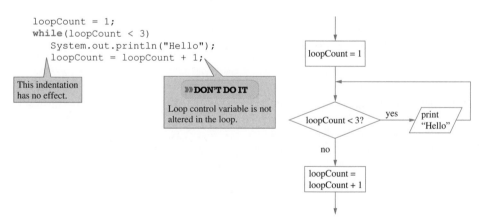

```
loopCount = 1;
while(loopCount < 3)
    System.out.println("Hello");
    loopCount = loopCount + 1;
```

This indentation has no effect.

▶▶ **DON'T DO IT**

Loop control variable is not altered in the loop.

Figure 6-5 A `while` loop that prints "Hello" infinitely because `loopCount` is not altered in the loop body

As with the decision making `if` statement that you learned about in Chapter 5, placement of the statement ending semicolon is important when you work with the `while` statement. If a semicolon is mistakenly placed at the end of the partial statement `while (loopCount < 3);`, as shown in Figure 6-6, the loop is also infinite. This loop has an **empty body**, or a body with no statements in it. So, the Boolean expression is evaluated, and because it is true, the loop body is entered. Because the loop body is empty, no action is taken, and the Boolean expression is evaluated again. Nothing has changed, so it is still true, the empty body is entered, and the infinite loop continues.

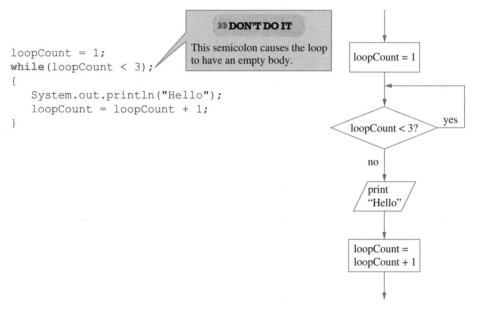

```
loopCount = 1;
while(loopCount < 3);
{
    System.out.println("Hello");
    loopCount = loopCount + 1;
}
```

>> **DON'T DO IT**

This semicolon causes the loop to have an empty body.

Figure 6-6 A while loop that loops infinitely with no output because the loop body is empty

It is very common to alter the value of a loop control variable by adding 1 to it, or **incrementing** the variable. However, not all loops are controlled by adding 1. The loop shown in Figure 6-7 prints "Hello" twice, just as the loop in Figure 6-4 does, but its loop is controlled by subtracting 1 from a loop control variable, or **decrementing** it.

```
loopCount = 3;
while(loopCount > 1)
{
    System.out.println("Hello");
    loopCount = loopCount - 1;
}
```

Figure 6-7 A while loop that prints "Hello" twice, decrementing the loopCount variable in the loop body

In the program segment shown in Figure 6-7, the variable loopCount begins with a value of 3. The loopCount is greater than 1, so the loop body prints "Hello" and decrements loopCount to 2. The Boolean expression in the while loop is tested again. Because 2 is more than 1, "Hello" prints again and loopCount becomes 1. Now loopCount is not greater than 1, so the loop ends. There are many ways to execute a loop two times. For example, you can initialize a loop control variable to 10 and continue to print while the value is greater than 8, decreasing the value by 1 each time you pass through the loop. Similarly, you can initialize the loop control variable to 12, continue while it is greater than 2, and decrease the value by 5 each time. In general, you should not use such unusual methods to count repetitions because they simply make a program confusing. To execute a loop a specific number of times, the clearest and best method is to start the loop control variable at 0 or 1, stop when the loop control variable reaches the appropriate limit, and increment by 1 each time through the loop.

> **»NOTE** When you first start programming, it seems reasonable to initialize counter values to 1, and that is a workable approach. However, many seasoned programmers start counter values at 0 because they are used to doing so when working with arrays. When you study arrays in Chapter 8, you will learn that their elements are numbered beginning with 0.

»TWO TRUTHS AND A LIE: USING A while **LOOP TO CREATE A DEFINITE LOOP**

1. A finite loop executes a specific number of times; an indefinite loop is one that never ends.
2. A well-written `while` loop contains an initialized loop control variable that is tested in the `while` expression and then altered in the loop body.
3. When a variable is incremented, 1 is added to it; when it is decremented, 1 is subtracted from it.

The false statement is #1. A loop that executes a specific number of times is a definite loop or a counted loop; a loop that never ends is an infinite loop.

USING A while LOOP TO CREATE AN INDEFINITE LOOP

Within a loop, you are not required to alter the loop control variable by adding to it or subtracting from it. Often, the value of a loop control variable is not altered by arithmetic, but instead is altered by user input. For example, perhaps you want to continue performing some task as long as the user indicates a desire to continue. In this case, while you are writing the program, you do not know whether the loop eventually will be executed two times, 200 times, or at all. Unlike a loop that you program to execute a fixed number of times, a loop controlled by the user is a type of **indefinite loop** because you don't know how many times it will eventually loop.

> **»NOTE**
> A definite loop is a **counter-controlled loop**. An indefinite loop is an **event-controlled loop**; that is, an event occurs that determines whether the loop continues.

Consider an application in which you ask the user for a bank balance and then ask whether the user wants to see the balance after interest has accumulated for each year. Each time the user chooses to continue, an increased balance appears, reflecting one more year of accumulated interest. When the user finally chooses to exit, the program ends. The program appears in Figure 6-8.

```java
import java.util.Scanner;
public class BankBalance
{
    public static void main(String[] args)
    {
        double balance;
        String response;
        char responseChar;
        int tempBalance;
        int year = 1;
        final double INT_RATE = 0.03;
        Scanner keyboard = new Scanner(System.in);
        System.out.print("Enter initial bank balance > ");
        balance = keyboard.nextDouble();
        keyboard.nextLine();
        System.out.println("Do you want to see next year's balance?");
        System.out.print("Enter y or n > ");
        response = keyboard.nextLine();
        responseChar = response.charAt(0);
        while(responseChar == 'y')
        {
            balance = balance + balance * INT_RATE;
            tempBalance = (int)(balance * 100);
            balance = tempBalance / 100.0;
            System.out.println("After year " + year + " at " +  INT_RATE +
                " interest rate, balance is $" + balance);
            year = year + 1;
            System.out.print("Do you want to see the balance " +
                "\nat the end of another year? y or n? >");
            response = keyboard.nextLine();
            responseChar = response.charAt(0);
        }
    }
}
```

In Chapter 2, you learned to call nextLine() after numeric input so that the Enter key is consumed before using the next call to nextLine().

The call to charAt(0) retrieves the first character from response.

These two statements round the balance to two decimal places.

Figure 6-8 The BankBalance application

The program shown in Figure 6-8 declares needed variables and a constant for a 3% interest rate, and then asks the user for a balance. The application accepts a user's answer from the keyboard as a String, and then uses the first character of the String to determine whether the loop should continue. As long as the user wants to continue, the application continues to display increasing bank balances.

The loop in the application in Figure 6-8 begins with the line that contains:

```
while(responseChar == 'y')
```

If the user enters any value other than 'y', the loop body never executes; instead, the program ends. However, if the user enters 'y', all the statements within the loop body execute. The application increases the balance by the interest rate value. Then, the balance times 100 is cast to an integer (for example, a calculated balance of 10.635 becomes 1063), and the result is divided by 100 (for example, 1063 becomes 10.63). The net effect of these two statements is to limit the number of decimal places in the balance to two. After these calculations, the application displays the new balance and asks whether the user wants another balance. The `year` variable increases and the loop body ends with a closing curly brace. After the loop body executes, control returns to the top of the loop, where the Boolean expression in the `while` loop is tested again. If the user enters 'y' to continue, the loop is entered and the process begins again. Figure 6-9 shows the output of the `BankBalance` application after the user enters a $575.00 starting balance and responds with 'y' five times to the prompt for increased interest payments.

>>NOTE
You first learned about type casting in Chapter 2.

```
C:\Java>java BankBalance
Enter initial bank balance > 575.00
Do you want to see next year's balance?
Enter y or n > y
After year 1 at 0.03 interest rate, balance is $592.25
Do you want to see the balance
at the end of another year? y or n? >y
After year 2 at 0.03 interest rate, balance is $610.01
Do you want to see the balance
at the end of another year? y or n? >y
After year 3 at 0.03 interest rate, balance is $628.31
Do you want to see the balance
at the end of another year? y or n? >y
After year 4 at 0.03 interest rate, balance is $647.15
Do you want to see the balance
at the end of another year? y or n? >y
After year 5 at 0.03 interest rate, balance is $666.56
Do you want to see the balance
at the end of another year? y or n? >n

C:\Java>
```

Figure 6-9 Typical execution of the `BankBalance` application

Programmers commonly use indefinite loops when validating input data. **Validating data** is the process of ensuring that a value falls within a specified range. For example, suppose you require a user to enter a value no greater than 3. Figure 6-10 shows an application that does not progress past the data entry loop until the user enters a correct value. If the user enters 3 or less at the first prompt, the shaded loop never executes. However, if the user enters a number greater than 3, the shaded loop executes, providing the user with another chance to enter a correct value. While the user continues to enter incorrect data, the loop repeats. Figure 6-11 shows a typical execution.

```java
import java.util.Scanner;
public class EnterSmallValue
{
   public static void main(String[] args)
   {
      int userEntry;
      final int LIMIT = 3;
      Scanner input = new Scanner(System.in);
      System.out.print("Please enter an integer no higher than " +
         LIMIT + " > ");
      userEntry = input.nextInt();
      while(userEntry > LIMIT)
      {
         System.out.println("The number you entered was too high");
         System.out.print("Please enter an integer no higher than " +
            LIMIT + " > ");
         userEntry = input.nextInt();
      }
      System.out.println("You correctly entered " + userEntry);
   }
}
```

Figure 6-10 The EnterSmallValue application

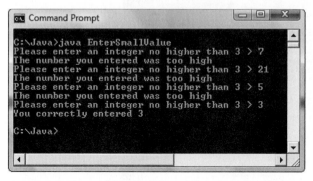

Figure 6-11 Typical execution of the EnterSmallValue program

>> **NOTE** Figure 6-10 illustrates an excellent method for validating input. Before the loop is entered, the first input is retrieved. This first input might be a value that prevents any executions of the loop. This first input statement prior to the loop is called a **priming read** or **priming input**. Within the loop, the last statement retrieves subsequent input values for the same variable that will be checked at the entrance to the loop.

Novice programmers often make the mistake of checking for invalid data using a decision instead of a loop. That is, they ask whether the data is invalid using an if statement; if the data is invalid, they reprompt the user. However, they forget that a user might enter incorrect data multiple times. Usually, a loop is the best structure to use when validating input data.

»TWO TRUTHS AND A LIE: USING A while LOOP TO CREATE AN INDEFINITE LOOP

1. To avoid creating an infinite loop, you must alter the loop control variable arithmetically within the loop body.
2. In an indefinite loop, you don't know how many times the loop will occur.
3. Validating data is the process of ensuring that a value falls within a specified range.

The false statement is #1. Within a loop, you are not required to alter the loop control variable by adding to it or subtracting from it. Often, the value of a loop control variable is not altered by arithmetic, but instead is altered by user input.

USING SHORTCUT ARITHMETIC OPERATORS

Programmers commonly need to increase the value of a variable in a program. As you saw in the previous section, many loops are controlled by continually adding 1 to some variable, as in count = count + 1;. Incrementing a variable in a loop to keep track of the number of occurrences of some event is also known as **counting**. Similarly, in the looping bank balance program shown in Figure 6-8, the program not only incremented the year variable by adding 1, but also increased a bank balance by an interest amount with the statement balance = balance + balance * INT_RATE;. In other words, the bank balance became its old value *plus* a new interest amount; the process of repeatedly increasing a value by some amount is known as **accumulating**.

Because increasing a variable is so common, Java provides you with several shortcuts for incrementing and accumulating. The statement count += 1; is identical in meaning to count = count + 1. The += is the **add and assign operator**; it adds and assigns in one operation. Similarly, balance += balance * INT_RATE; increases a balance by the INT_RATE percentage. Besides using the shortcut operator +=, you can use the **subtract and assign operator** (-=), the **multiply and assign operator** (*=), the **divide and assign operator** (/=), and the **remainder and assign operator** (%=). Each of these operators is used to perform the operation and assign the result in one step. For example, balanceDue -= payment subtracts payment from balanceDue and assigns the result to balanceDue.

When you want to increase a variable's value by exactly 1, you can use two other shortcut operators—the **prefix ++**, also known as the **prefix increment operator**, and the **postfix ++**, also known as the **postfix increment operator**. To use a prefix ++, you type two plus signs before the variable name. The statement someValue = 6; followed by ++someValue; results in someValue holding 7—one more than it held before you applied the ++. To use a postfix ++, you type two plus signs just after a variable name. The statements anotherValue = 56; anotherValue++; result in anotherValue containing 57. Figure 6-12 shows four ways you can increase a value by 1; each method produces the same result. You are never required to use shortcut operators; they are merely a convenience.

```
int value;
value = 24;
++value;   // Result: value is 25
value = 24;
value++;   // Result: value is 25
value = 24;
value = value + 1;    // Result: value is  25
value = 24;
value += 1;   // Result: value is 25
```

Figure 6-12 Four ways to add 1 to a value

>> **NOTE** You can use the prefix ++ and postfix ++ with variables, but not with constants. An expression such as ++84; is illegal because an 84 must always remain an 84. However, you can create a variable as int val = 84 and then write ++val; or val++; to increase the variable's value.

>> **NOTE** The prefix and postfix increment operators are unary operators because you use them with one value. As you learned in Chapter 2, most arithmetic operators, such as those used for addition and multiplication, are binary operators—they operate on two values. Other examples of unary operators include the cast operator, as well as + and – when used to indicate positive and negative values.

When you simply want to increase a variable's value by 1, there is no difference between using the prefix and postfix increment operators. For example, when value is set to 24 in Figure 6-12, both ++value and value++ result in value becoming 25; each operator results in increasing the variable by 1. However, these operators do function differently in terms of *when* the increment operation occurs. When you use the prefix ++, the result is calculated and stored, and then the variable is used. For example, if b = 4 and c = ++b, the result is that both b and c hold the value 5. When you use the postfix ++, the variable is used, and then the result is calculated and stored. For example, if b = 4 and c = b++, 4 is assigned to c, and then after the assignment, b is increased and takes the value 5. In other words, if b = 4, the value of b++ is also 4, but after the statement is completed, the value of b is 5. If d = 8 and e = 8, both ++d == 9 and e++ == 8 are true expressions.

Figure 6-13 shows an application that illustrates the difference between how the prefix and postfix increment operators work. Notice from the output in Figure 6-14 that when the prefix increment operator is used on myNumber, the value of myNumber increases from 17 to 18, and the result is stored in answer, which also becomes 18. After the value is reset to 17, the postfix increment operator is used; 17 is assigned to answer, and myNumber is incremented to 18.

```
public class IncrementDemo
{
   public static void main(String[] args)
   {
      int myNumber, answer;
      myNumber = 17;
      System.out.println("Before incrementing, myNumber is " +
         myNumber);
      answer = ++myNumber;
      System.out.println("After prefix increment, myNumber is " +
         myNumber);
      System.out.println("  and answer is " + answer);
         myNumber = 17;
      System.out.println("Before incrementing, myNumber is " +
         myNumber);
      answer = myNumber++;
      System.out.println("After postfix increment, myNumber is " +
         myNumber);
      System.out.println("  and answer is " + answer);
   }
}
```

Figure 6-13 The IncrementDemo application

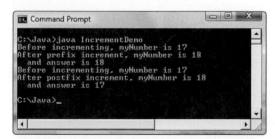

Figure 6-14 Output of the IncrementDemo application

Similar logic can be applied when you use the **prefix and postfix decrement operators**. For example, if b = 4 and c = b--, 4 is assigned to c, and then after the assignment, b is decreased and takes the value 3. If b = 4 and c = --b, b is decreased to 3 and 3 is assigned to c.

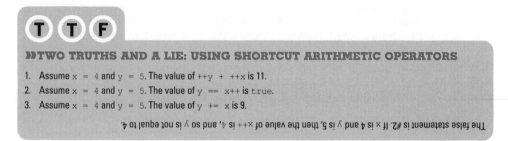

»TWO TRUTHS AND A LIE: USING SHORTCUT ARITHMETIC OPERATORS

1. Assume x = 4 and y = 5. The value of ++y + ++x is 11.
2. Assume x = 4 and y = 5. The value of y == x++ is true.
3. Assume x = 4 and y = 5. The value of y += x is 9.

The false statement is #2. If x is 4 and y is 5, then the value of x++ is 4, and so y is not equal to 4.

USING A for LOOP

»NOTE
A for loop provides a convenient way to create a counter-controlled loop.

A **for loop** is a special loop that is used when a definite number of loop iterations is required. Although a while loop can also be used to meet this requirement, the for loop provides you with a shorthand notation for this type of loop. When you use a for loop, you can indicate the starting value for the loop control variable, the test condition that controls loop entry, and the expression that alters the loop control variable—all in one convenient place.

You begin a for loop with the keyword for followed by a set of parentheses. Within the parentheses are three sections separated by exactly two semicolons. The three sections are usually used for the following:

- » Initializing the loop control variable
- » Testing the loop control variable
- » Updating the loop control variable

The body of the for statement follows the parentheses. As with an if statement or a while loop, you can use a single statement as the body of a for loop, or you can use a block of statements enclosed in curly braces. The for statement shown in Figure 6-15 produces the same output as the while statement shown below it—both print the integers 1 through 10.

```
for(int val = 1; val < 11; ++val)
   System.out.println(val);

int val = 1;
while(val < 11)
{
   System.out.println(val);
   ++val;
}
```

Figure 6-15 A for loop and a while loop that print the integers 1 through 10

»NOTE
If you declare a variable within a for statement, the variable can only be used in the block that depends on the for statement; when the block ends, the variable goes out of scope.

»NOTE The variable val did not have to be declared within the for statement. If val was declared earlier in the program block as int val;, the for statement would be for(val = 1; val < 11; ++val). In other words, the for statement does not need to declare a variable; it can simply give a starting value to a previously declared variable. However, programmers frequently declare a variable within a for statement just for use within that loop.

Within the parentheses of the for statement shown in Figure 6-15, the first section prior to the first semicolon declares a variable named val and initializes it to 1. The program executes this statement once, no matter how many times the body of the for loop executes.

After initialization, program control passes to the middle, or test section, of the for statement. If the Boolean expression found there evaluates to true, the body of the for loop is entered. In the program segment shown in Figure 6-15, val is set to 1, so when val < 11 is tested, it evaluates to true. The loop body prints the val. In this example, the loop body is a single statement, so no curly braces are needed. If you want multiple statements to execute within the loop, they have to be blocked within a pair of curly braces. This is the same technique you use to execute multiple statements that depend on an if or a while.

After the loop body executes, the final one-third of the for loop executes, and val is increased to 2. Following the third section in the for statement, program control returns to the second section, where val is compared to 11 a second time. Because val is still less than 11, the body executes: val (now 2) prints, and then the third altering portion of the for loop executes again. The variable val increases to 3 and the for loop continues.

Eventually, when val is not less than 11 (after 1 through 10 have printed), the for loop ends, and the program continues with any statements that follow the for loop. Although the three sections of the for loop are most commonly used for initializing, testing, and incrementing, you can also perform the following tasks:

» Initialization of more than one variable by placing commas between the separate statements, as in the following:

```
for(g = 0, h = 1; g < 6; ++g)
```

» Performance of more than one test using AND or OR operators, as in the following:

```
for(g = 0; g < 3 && h > 1; ++g)
```

» Decrementation or performance of some other task, as in the following:

```
for(g = 5; g >= 1; --g)
```

» Altering more than one value, as in the following:

```
for(g = 0; g < 10; ++g, ++h, sum += g)
```

» You can leave one or more portions of a for loop empty, although the two semicolons are still required as placeholders. For example, if x has been initialized in a previous program statement, you might write the following:

```
for(; x < 10; ++x)
```

Usually, you should use the for loop for its intended purpose—a shorthand way of programming a definite loop. Occasionally, you will encounter a for loop that contains no body, such as the following:

```
for(x = 0; x < 100000; ++x);
```

This kind of loop exists simply to use time—that is, to occupy the central processing unit for thousands of processing cycles—when a brief pause is desired during program execution, for example. As with if and while statements, usually you do not want to place a semicolon at the end of the for statement before the body of the loop.

»TWO TRUTHS AND A LIE: USING A for LOOP

1. A for loop must always contain two semicolons within its parentheses.
2. The body of a for loop might never execute.
3. Within the parentheses of a for loop, the last section must alter the loop control variable.

The false statement is #3. Frequently, the third section of a for loop is used to alter the loop control variable, but it is not required.

LEARNING HOW AND WHEN TO USE A `do...while` LOOP

With all the loops you have written so far, the loop body might execute many times, but it is also possible that the loop will not execute at all. For example, recall the bank balance program that displays compound interest, part of which is shown in Figure 6-16.

```
System.out.println("Do you want to see next year's balance?");
System.out.print("Enter y or n > ");
response = keyboard.nextLine();
responseChar = response.charAt(0);
while(responseChar == 'y')
{
   balance = balance + balance * INT_RATE;
   tempBalance = (int)(balance * 100);
   balance = tempBalance / 100.0;
   System.out.println("After year " + year + " at " + INT_RATE +
       " interest rate, balance is $" + balance);
   year = year + 1;
   System.out.print("Do you want to see the balance " +
       "\nat the end of another year? y or n? >");
   response = keyboard.nextLine();
   responseChar = response.charAt(0);
}
```

Figure 6-16 A loop from the `BankBalance` application

The program segment begins by showing the prompts "Do you want to see next year's balance?" and "Enter y or n > ". If the user enters anything other than a line that starts with 'y', the loop body never executes. The `while` loop checks a value at the "top" of the loop before the body has a chance to execute. Sometimes, you might need to ensure that a loop body executes at least one time. If so, you want to write a loop that checks at the "bottom" of the loop after the first iteration. The **`do...while` loop** checks the value of the loop control variable at the bottom of the loop after one repetition has occurred.

Figure 6-17 shows the general structure of a `do...while` loop. Notice that the loop body executes before the loop-controlling question is asked even one time. Figure 6-18 shows a `do...while` loop that could be used in the `BankBalance` application. The loop starts with the keyword `do`. The body of the loop follows and is contained within curly braces. The first year's balance is output before the user has any option of responding. At the end of the loop, the user is prompted,

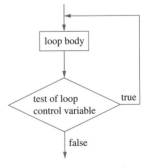

Figure 6-17 General structure of a `do...while` loop

"Do you want to see the balance at the end of another year?" Now the user has the option of seeing more balances, but the first display was unavoidable. The user's response is checked at the bottom of the loop; if it is 'y' for Yes, the loop repeats.

```
do
{
    balance = balance + balance * INT_RATE;
    tempBalance = (int)(balance * 100);
    balance = tempBalance / 100.0;
    System.out.println("After year " + year + " at " + INT_RATE +
        " interest rate, balance is $" + balance);
    year = year + 1;
    System.out.print("Do you want to see the balance " +
        "\nat the end of another year? y or n? >");
    response = keyboard.nextLine();
    responseChar = response.charAt(0);
} while(response == 'y');
```

Figure 6-18 A `do...while` loop for the `BankBalance` application

In any situation in which you want to loop, you are never required to use a `do...while` loop. Within the bank balance example, you could achieve the same results as the logic shown in Figure 6-18 by unconditionally displaying the first year's bank balance once before starting the loop, prompting the user, and then starting a `while` loop that might not be entered. However, when you know you want to perform some task at least one time, the `do...while` loop is convenient.

When the body of a `do...while` loop contains a single statement, you do not need to use curly braces to block the statement. For example, the following loop correctly adds `numberValue` to `total` while `total` remains less than 200:

```
do
    total += numberValue;
while(total < 200);
```

Even though curly braces are not required in this case, many programmers recommend using them. Doing so prevents the third line of code from looking like it should begin a new `while` loop. Therefore, even though the result is the same, the following is less likely to be misunderstood by a reader:

```
do
{
    total += numberValue;
} while(total < 200);
```

**»TWO TRUTHS AND A LIE: LEARNING HOW AND WHEN TO USE
A do...while LOOP**

1. The do...while loop checks the value of the loop control variable at the top of the loop prior to loop execution.
2. When the statements in a loop body must execute at least one time, it is convenient to use a do...while loop.
3. When the body of a do...while loop contains a single statement, you do not need to use curly braces to block the statement.

The false statement is #1. The do...while loop checks the value of the loop control variable at the bottom of the loop after one repetition has occurred.

LEARNING ABOUT NESTED LOOPS

Just as if statements can be nested, so can loops. You can place a while loop within a while loop, a for loop within a for loop, a while loop within a for loop, or any other combination. When loops are nested, each pair contains an **inner loop** and an **outer loop**. The inner loop must be entirely contained within the outer loop; loops can never overlap. Figure 6-19 shows a diagram in which the shaded loop is nested within another loop; the shaded area is the inner loop as well as the body of the outer loop.

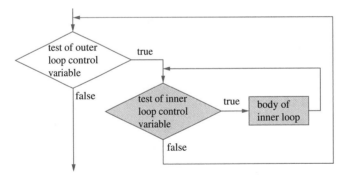

Figure 6-19 Nested loops

Suppose you want to display future bank balances for any number of years, but also for a variety of interest rates. Figure 6-20 shows an application that contains an indefinite outer loop controlled by the user's response to a question about viewing the next year's balance. Each time the user responds 'y' (for Yes) when asked to see next year's balance, the outer loop body is entered. Within this outer loop, an inner definite loop displays balance values calculated with every interest rate from 2% to 5%. Only after the user has viewed each of the four interest rate calculations for a year (finishing the shaded inner loop) does the program prompt the user about viewing a new year's values (starting another repetition of the outer loop). Figure 6-21 shows a typical execution.

```
import java.util.Scanner;
public class BankBalanceVaryingInterest
{
    public static void main(String[] args)
    {
        double balance;
        String response;
        char responseChar;
        int tempBalance;
        int year = 1;
        double interest;
        final double LOW = 0.02;
        final double HIGH = 0.05;
        final double INCREMENT = 0.01;
        Scanner keyboard = new Scanner(System.in);
        System.out.print("Enter initial bank balance > ");
        balance = keyboard.nextDouble();
        keyboard.nextLine();
        System.out.println("Do you want to see next year's balance?");
        System.out.print("Enter y or n > ");
        response = keyboard.nextLine();
        responseChar = response.charAt(0);
        while(responseChar == 'y')
        {
            for(interest = LOW; interest <= HIGH; interest += INCREMENT)
            {
                balance = balance + balance * interest;
                tempBalance = (int)(balance * 100);
                balance = tempBalance / 100.0;
                System.out.println("After year " + year + " at " +
                    interest + " interest rate, balance is $" + balance);
            }
            year = year + 1;
            System.out.print("Do you want to see the balance " +
                "\nat the end of another year? y or n? >");
            response = keyboard.nextLine();
            responseChar = response.charAt(0);
        }
    }
}
```

Figure 6-20 The `BankBalanceVaryingInterest` class containing nested loops

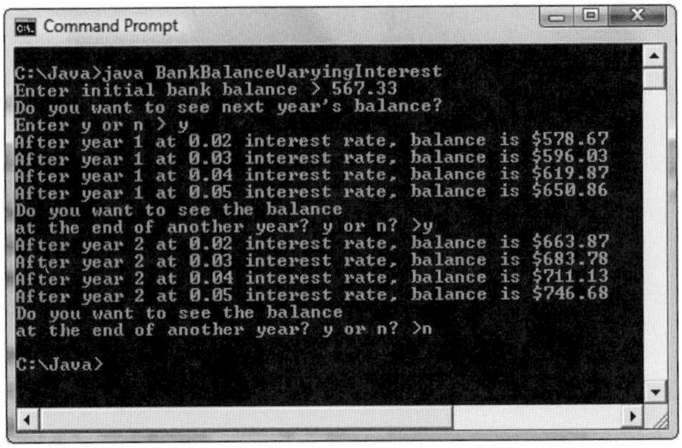

Figure 6-21 Typical execution of the BankBalanceVaryingInterest program

»NOTE
You can use virtually any number of nested loops; however, at some point, your machine will no longer be able to store all the necessary looping information.

When you use a loop within a loop, you should always think of the outer loop as the all-encompassing loop. When you describe the task at hand, you often use the word "each" when referring to the inner loop. For example, if you want to print three mailing labels each for 20 customers, the label variable would control the inner loop, as shown in the following code:

```
for(customer = 1; customer <= 20; ++customer)
   for(label = 1; label <= 3; ++label)
      printLabelMethod();
```

T T F

»TWO TRUTHS AND A LIE: LEARNING ABOUT NESTED LOOPS

1. You can place a while loop within a while loop or a for loop within a for loop, but you cannot mix loop types.

2. An inner nested loop must be entirely contained within its outer loop.

3. The body of the following loop executes 20 times:
   ```
   for(int x = 0; x < 4; ++x)
      for(int y = 0; y < 5; ++y)
         System.out.println("Hi");
   ```

The false statement is #1. You can place a while loop within a while loop, a for loop within a for loop, a while loop within a for loop, or any other combination.

IMPROVING LOOP PERFORMANCE

Whether you decide to use a while, for, or do...while loop in an application, you can improve loop performance by doing the following:

» Making sure the loop does not include unnecessary operations or statements
» Considering the order of evaluation for short-circuit operators
» Making a comparison to 0
» Employing loop fusion

AVOIDING UNNECESSARY OPERATIONS

You can make loops more efficient by not using unnecessary operations or statements, either within a loop's tested expression or within the loop body. For example, suppose a loop should execute while x is less than the sum of two integers, a and b. The loop could be written as:

```
while (x < a + b)
    // loop body
```

»DON'T DO IT

It might be inefficient to recalculate a + b for every loop iteration.

If this loop executes 1000 times, then the expression a + b is calculated 1000 times. Instead, if you use the following code, the results are the same, but the arithmetic is performed only once:

```
int sum = a + b;
while(x < sum)
    // loop body
```

Of course, if a or b is altered in the loop body, then a new sum must be calculated with every loop iteration. However, if the sum of a and b is fixed prior to the start of the loop, then writing the code the second way is far more efficient.

Similarly, try to avoid a function call within a loop if possible. For example, if the method getNumberOfEmployees() always returns the same value during a program's execution, then a loop that begins as follows might unnecessarily call the function many times:

```
while(count < getNumberOfEmployees ())...
```

It is more efficient to call the method once, store the result in a variable, and use the variable in the repeated evaluations.

CONSIDERING THE ORDER OF EVALUATION OF SHORT-CIRCUIT OPERATORS

In Chapter 5 you learned that the expressions in each part of an AND or an OR expression are evaluated only as much as necessary to determine whether the entire expression is true or false. This feature is called short-circuit evaluation. When a loop might execute many times, it becomes increasingly important to consider the number of evaluations that take place.

For example, suppose a user can request any number of printed copies of a report from 0 to 15, and you want to validate the user's input before proceeding. If you believe that users are far more likely to enter a value that is too high than to enter a negative one, then you want to start a loop that reprompts the user with the following expression:

```
while(requestedNum > LIMIT || requestedNum < 0)...
```

Because you believe that the first Boolean expression is more likely to be true than the second one, you can eliminate testing the second one on more occasions. The order of the expressions is not very important in a single loop, but if this loop is nested within another loop, then the difference in the number of tests increases. Similarly, the order of the evaluations in if statements is more important when the if statements are nested within a loop.

COMPARING TO ZERO

Making a comparison to 0 is faster than making a comparison to any other value. Therefore, if your application makes a comparison to 0 feasible, you can improve loop performance by structuring your loops to compare the loop control variable to 0 instead of some other value. For example, a loop that performs based on a variable that varies from 0 up to 100,000 executes the same number of times as a loop based on a variable that varies from 100,000 down to 0. However, the second loop performs slightly faster.

Figure 6-22 contains a program that tests the execution times of two nested do-nothing loops. (A **do-nothing loop** is one that performs no actions other than looping.) Before each loop, the System method currentTimeMillis() is called to retrieve the current time represented in milliseconds. After each nested loop repeats 100,000 times, the current time is retrieved again. Subtracting the two times computes the interval. As the execution in Figure 6-23 shows, there is a small difference in execution time between the two loops—about 1/100 of a second. The difference would become more pronounced with additional repetitions or further nesting levels. If the loops used the loop control variable, for example, to display a count to the user, then they might need to increment the variable. However, if the purposes of the loops are just to count iterations, you might consider making the loop comparison use 0.

```java
public class CompareLoops
{
   public static void main(String[] args)
   {
      long startTime1, startTime2, endTime1, endTime2;
      final int REPEAT = 100000;
      startTime1 = System.currentTimeMillis();
      for(int x = 0; x <= REPEAT; ++x)
         for(int y = 0; y <= REPEAT; ++y);
      endTime1 = System.currentTimeMillis();
      System.out.println("Time for loops starting from 0: " +
         (endTime1 - startTime1)+ " milliseconds");
      startTime2 = System.currentTimeMillis();
      for(int x = REPEAT; x >= 0; --x)
         for(int y = REPEAT; y >= 0; --y);
      endTime2 = System.currentTimeMillis();
      System.out.println("Time for loops ending at 0: " +
         (endTime2 - startTime2)+ " milliseconds");
   }
}
```

Figure 6-22 The CompareLoops application

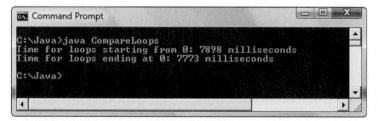

Figure 6-23 Execution of the `CompareLoops` application

»NOTE
Depending on your processor speed, the time intervals on your computer might be different from those shown in Figure 6-23.

EMPLOYING LOOP FUSION

Loop fusion is the technique of combining two loops into one. For example, suppose you want to call two methods 100 times each. You can set a constant to 100 and use the following code:

```
for(int x = 0; x < TIMES; ++x)
    method1();
for(int x = 0; x < TIMES; ++x)
    method2();
```

However, you can also use the following code:

```
for(int x = 0; x < TIMES; ++x)
{
    method1();
    method2();
}
```

Fusing loops will not work in every situation; sometimes all the activities for `method1()` must be finished before those in `method2()` can begin. However, if the two methods do not depend on each other, fusing the loops can improve performance.

As you become an experienced programmer, you will discover other ways to enhance the operation of the programs you write. You should always be on the lookout for ways to improve program performance. However, if saving a few milliseconds ends up making your code harder to understand, you should almost always err in favor of slower but more readable programs.

»TWO TRUTHS AND A LIE: IMPROVING LOOP PERFORMANCE

1. You can improve the performance of a loop by making sure the loop does not include unnecessary operations in the tested expression.
2. You can improve loop performance by making sure the loop does not include unnecessary operations in the body of the loop.
3. You can improve loop performance when two conditions must both be true by testing for the most likely occurrence first.

The false statement is #3. You can improve loop performance when two conditions must both be true by testing for the least likely occurrence first. That way, the second test will need to be performed less frequently.

YOU DO IT

WRITING A LOOP TO VALIDATE DATA ENTRIES

In Chapter 5, you created a `ChooseManager` application. The application allowed the user to enter a 1 or 2 to select a private or corporate event to be held by Event Handlers Incorporated. The output was the name of the manager in charge of the event type. Next, you will improve the `ChooseManager` program so the user cannot make an invalid choice for the type of event—if the user does not enter a 1 or 2, the user will continue to be prompted until a valid selection is entered.

To improve the `ChooseManager` program to prevent invalid data entry:

1. Enter the first lines of the `ChooseManagerWithValidation` class. Except for the class name, these statements are identical to those in the `ChooseManager` class you created in Chapter 5, so you can save time if you want by copying these lines of code from that file. The statements create a `ChooseManagerWithValidation` class and start a `main()` method that contains constants for the managers' codes and names. The user is prompted to enter a 1 or 2, representing a private or corporate event:

```java
import java.util.Scanner;
public class ChooseManagerWithValidation
{
   public static void main(String[] args)
   {
      int eventType;
      String chosenManager;
      final int PRIVATE_CODE = 1;
      final int CORPORATE_CODE = 2;
      final String PRIV_MANAGER = "Dustin Britt";
      final String CORP_MANAGER = "Carmen Lindsey";
      Scanner input = new Scanner(System.in);
      System.out.println
         ("What type of event are you scheduling?");
      System.out.print("Enter " + PRIVATE_CODE +
         " for private, " + CORPORATE_CODE +
         " for corporate... ");
      eventType = input.nextInt();
```

2. Type the `while` loop that will continue to execute while the user's entry is not one of the two allowed event types. When the user's entry is not a 1 or a 2, the user is informed of the error and is allowed to type a new choice:

```java
while(eventType != PRIVATE_CODE && eventType != CORPORATE_CODE)
{
   System.out.println("You made an invalid selection");
   System.out.println("You entered " + eventType);
   System.out.print("Please enter " + PRIVATE_CODE +
      " for private, " + CORPORATE_CODE + " for corporate... ");
   eventType = input.nextInt();
}
```

3. On a new line, type the decision structure that sets the `chosenManager` variable. If the `eventType` is not 1, then it must be 2, or the program would still be executing the loop waiting for a 1 or 2 from the user:

```
if(eventType == PRIVATE_CODE)
    chosenManager = PRIV_MANAGER;
else
    chosenManager = CORP_MANAGER;
```

4. Display the manager for the chosen event type:

```
System.out.println("You entered " + eventType);
System.out.println("Manager for this event will be " +
    chosenManager);
```

5. Add the closing curly brace for the `main()` method and the closing curly brace for the class. Save the file as **ChooseManagerWithValidation.java**.

6. Compile and execute the application. No matter how many invalid entries you make, the program continues to prompt you until you enter a 1 or 2 for the event type. Figure 6-24 shows a typical execution.

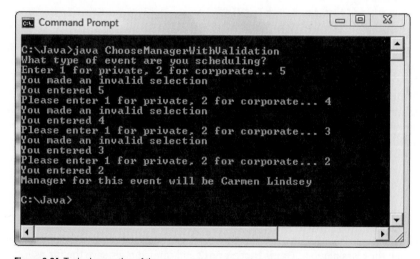

Figure 6-24 Typical execution of the `ChooseManagerWithValidation` program

WORKING WITH PREFIX AND POSTFIX INCREMENT OPERATORS

Next, you will write an application that demonstrates how prefix and postfix operators are used in incrementation and how incrementing affects the expressions that contain these operators.

To demonstrate the effect of the prefix and postfix increment operators:

1. Open a new text file and begin a demonstration class named DemoIncrement by typing:

```
public class DemoIncrement
{
    public static void main(String[] args)
    {
```

2. On a new line, add a variable v and assign it a value of 4. Then declare a variable named plusPlusV and assign it a value of ++v by typing:

```
int v = 4;
int plusPlusV = ++v;
```

3. The last statement, int plusPlusV = ++v;, will increase v to 5, so before declaring a vPlusPlus variable to which you assign v++, reset v to 4 by typing:

```
v = 4;
int vPlusPlus = v++;
```

4. Add the following statements to print the three values:

```
System.out.println("v is " + v);
System.out.println("++v is " + plusPlusV);
System.out.println("v++ is " + vPlusPlus);
```

5. Add the closing curly brace for the main() method and the closing curly brace for the DemoIncrement class. Save the file as **DemoIncrement.java**, then compile and execute the program. Your output should look like Figure 6-25.

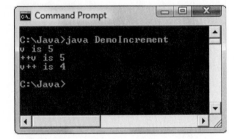

Figure 6-25 Output of the DemoIncrement class

6. To illustrate how comparisons are made, add a few more variables to the DemoIncrement program. Change the class name to **DemoIncrement2** and immediately save the file as **DemoIncrement2.java**.

7. After the last println() statement, add three new integer variables and two new Boolean variables. The first Boolean variable compares ++w to y; the second Boolean variable compares x++ to y:

```
int w = 17, x = 17, y = 18;
boolean compare1 = (++w == y);
boolean compare2 = (x++ == y);
```

8. Add the following statements to display the values stored in the `compare` variables:

```
System.out.println("First compare is " + compare1);
System.out.println("Second compare is " + compare2);
```

9. Save, compile, and run the program. The output appears in Figure 6-26. Make certain you understand why each statement displays the values it does. Experiment by changing the values of the variables and see if you can predict the output before recompiling and rerunning the program.

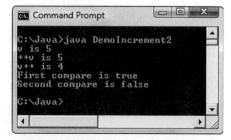

Figure 6-26 Output of the `DemoIncrement2` application

WORKING WITH DEFINITE LOOPS

Suppose you want to find all the numbers that divide evenly into 100. You want to write a definite loop—one that executes exactly 100 times. You can write a `for` loop that sets a variable to 1 and increments it to 100. Each of the 100 times through the loop, if 100 is evenly divisible by the variable, the application prints the number.

To write an application that finds the values that divide evenly into 100:

1. Open a new text file. Begin the application named `DivideEvenly` by typing the following code. Use a named constant for the 100 value and a variable named `var` that will hold, in turn, every value from 1 to 100:

```
public class DivideEvenly
{
 public static void main(String[] args)
 {
    final int LIMIT = 100;
    int var;
```

2. Type a statement that explains the purpose of the program:

```
System.out.print(LIMIT + " is evenly divisible by ");
```

3. Write the `for` loop that varies `var` from 1 to 100. With each iteration of the loop, test whether 100 % `var` is 0. If you divide 100 by a number and there is no remainder, the number goes into 100 evenly:

```
for(var = 1; var <= LIMIT; ++var)
   if(LIMIT % var == 0)
      System.out.print(var + " ");
      // Print the number and two spaces
```

4. Add an empty `println()` statement to advance the insertion point to the next line by typing the following:

```
System.out.println();
```

5. Type the closing curly braces for the `main()` method and the `DivideEvenly` class.

6. Save the program as **DivideEvenly.java**. Compile and run the program. Figure 6-27 shows the output.

Figure 6-27 Output of the `DivideEvenly` application

WORKING WITH NESTED LOOPS

>>**NOTE**
If you want to print divisors for each number from 1 to 100, the loop that varies the number to be divided is the outside loop. You need to perform 100 mathematical calculations on each number, so that constitutes the "smaller" or inside loop.

Suppose you want to know not just what numbers go evenly into 100, but also what numbers go evenly into every positive number, up to and including 100. You can write 99 more loops— one that shows the numbers that divide evenly into 1, another that shows the numbers that divide evenly into 2, and so on—or you can place the current loop inside a different, outer loop, as you will do next.

To create a nested loop to print even divisors for every number up to 100:

1. If necessary, open the file **DivideEvenly.java** in your text editor, change the class name to **DivideEvenly2**, and then save the class as **DivideEvenly2.java**.

2. Add a new variable declaration:

```
int number;
```

3. Replace the existing `for` loop with the following nested loop. The outer loop varies `number` from 1 to 100. For each number in the outer loop, the inner loop uses each positive integer from 1 up to the number, and tests whether it divides evenly into the number:

```
for(number = 1; number <= LIMIT; ++number)
{
    System.out.print(number + " is evenly divisible by ");
    for(var = 1; var <= number; ++var)
        if(number % var == 0)
            System.out.print(var + " ");
            // Print the number and two spaces
    System.out.println();
}
```

4. Make sure that the file ends with three curly braces—one for the `for` outer loop that varies `number`, one for the `main()` method, and one for the class. The inner loop does not need curly braces because it contains a single output statement.

5. Save the file as **DivideEvenly2.java**, compile, and execute the application. When the output stops scrolling, it should look similar to Figure 6-28.

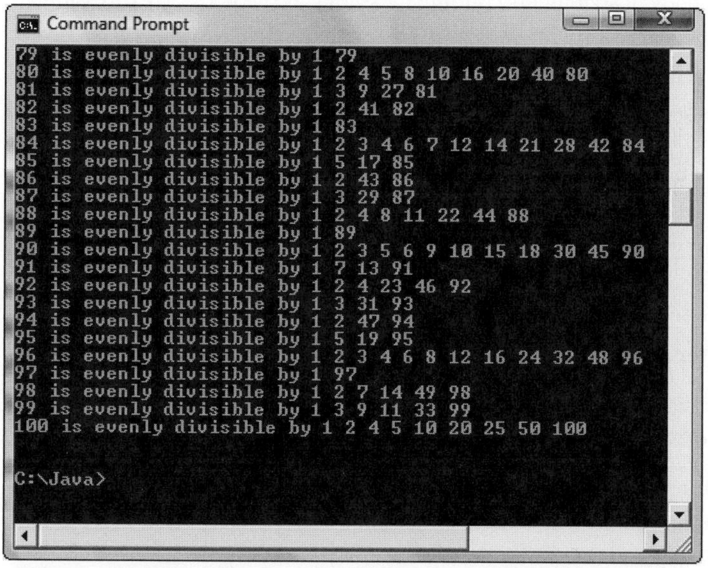

Figure 6-28 Output of the `DivideEvenly2` application when scrolling stops

DON'T DO IT

» Don't insert a semicolon at the end of a `while` clause before the loop body; doing so creates an empty loop body.

» Don't forget to block multiple statements that should execute in a loop.

» Don't make the mistake of checking for invalid data using a decision instead of a loop. Users might enter incorrect data multiple times, so a loop is the superior choice for input validation.

» Don't ignore subtleties in the boundaries used to stop loop performance. For example, looping while interest rates are less than 8% is different from looping while interest rates are no more than 8%.

» Don't repeat steps within a loop that could just as well be placed outside the loop; your program performance will improve.

KEY TERMS

A **loop** is a structure that allows repeated execution of a block of statements.

A **loop body** is the block of statements that executes when the Boolean expression that controls the loop is `true`.

An **iteration** is one loop execution.

A `while` **loop** executes a body of statements continually as long as the Boolean expression that controls entry into the loop continues to be `true`.

A loop that executes a specific number of times is a **definite loop** or a counted loop.

A **loop control variable** is a variable whose value determines whether loop execution continues.

A loop that never ends is called an **infinite loop**.

An **empty body** is a block with no statements in it.

Incrementing a variable adds 1 to its value.

Decrementing a variable reduces its value by 1.

A definite loop is a **counter-controlled loop**.

An indefinite loop is an **event-controlled loop**.

An **indefinite loop** is one in which the final number of loops is unknown.

Validating data is the process of ensuring that a value falls within a specified range.

A **priming read** or **priming input** is the first input statement prior to a loop that will execute subsequent input statements for the same variable.

Counting is the process of continually incrementing a variable to keep track of the number of occurrences of some event.

Accumulating is the process of repeatedly increasing a value by some amount to produce a total.

The **add and assign operator** (+=) alters the value of the operand on the left by adding the operand on the right to it.

The **subtract and assign operator** (-=) alters the value of the operand on the left by subtracting the operand on the right from it.

The **multiply and assign operator** (*=) alters the value of the operand on the left by multiplying the operand on the right by it.

The **divide and assign operator** (/=) alters the value of the operand on the left by dividing the operand on the right into it.

The **remainder and assign operator** (%=) alters the value of the operand on the left by assigning the remainder when the left operand is divided by the right operand.

The **prefix** ++, also known as the **prefix increment operator**, adds 1 to a variable, then evaluates it.

The **postfix ++**, also known as the **postfix increment operator**, evaluates a variable, then adds 1 to it.

The **prefix and postfix decrement operators** subtract 1 from a variable. For example, if `b = 4;` and `c = b--;`, 4 is assigned to `c`, and then after the assignment, `b` is decreased and takes the value 3. If `b = 4;` and `c = --b;`, `b` is decreased to 3, and 3 is assigned to `c`.

A **for loop** is a special loop that can be used when a definite number of loop iterations is required.

A **pretest loop** is one in which the loop control variable is tested before the loop body executes.

A **posttest loop** is one in which the loop control variable is tested after the loop body executes.

The **do...while loop** executes a loop body at least one time; it checks the loop control variable at the bottom of the loop after one repetition has occurred.

An **inner loop** is contained entirely within another loop.

An **outer loop** contains another loop.

A **do-nothing loop** is one that performs no actions other than looping.

Loop fusion is the technique of combining two loops into one.

CHAPTER SUMMARY

» A loop is a structure that allows repeated execution of a block of statements. Within a looping structure, a Boolean expression is evaluated, and if it is `true`, a block of statements called the loop body executes; then the Boolean expression is evaluated again.

» You can use a `while` loop to execute a body of statements continually while some condition continues to be `true`. To execute a `while` loop, you initialize a loop control variable, test it in a `while` statement, and then alter the loop control variable in the body of the `while` structure.

» The add and assign operator (+=) adds and assigns in one operation. Similar versions are available for subtraction, multiplication, and division. The prefix ++ and the postfix ++ increase a variable's value by 1. The prefix -- and postfix -- decrement operators reduce a variable's value by 1. When you use the prefix ++, the result is calculated and stored, and then the variable is used. When you use the postfix ++, the variable is used, and then the result is calculated and stored.

» A `for` loop initializes, tests, and increments in one statement. There are three sections within the parentheses of a `for` loop that are separated by exactly two semicolons.

» The `do...while` loop tests a Boolean expression after one repetition has taken place, at the bottom of the loop.

» Loops can be nested.

» You can improve loop performance by making sure that the loop does not include unnecessary operations or statements.

REVIEW QUESTIONS

1. A structure that allows repeated execution of a block of statements is a _____ .

   a. cycle

   b. loop

   c. ring

   d. band

2. A loop that never ends is a(n) _____ loop.

   a. iterative

   b. infinite

   c. structured

   d. illegal

3. To construct a loop that works correctly, you should initialize a loop control _____ .

   a. variable

   b. constant

   c. structure

   d. condition

4. What is the output of the following code?

```
b = 1;
while (b < 4)
    System.out.print(b + " ");
```

   a. 1

   b. 1 2 3

   c. 1 2 3 4

   d. 1 1 1 1 1 1 ...

5. What is the output of the following code?

```
b = 1;
while (b < 4)
{
    System.out.print(b + " ");
    b = b + 1;
}
```

   a. 1

   b. 1 2 3

   c. 1 2 3 4

   d. 1 1 1 1 1 ...

6. What is the output of the following code?

```
e = 1;
while (e < 4);
    System.out.print(e + " ");
```

   a. nothing

   b. 1 1 1 1 1 1 ...

   c. 1 2 3 4

   d. 4 4 4 4 4 4 ...

7. If `total = 100` and `amt = 200`, then after the statement `total += amt`, _____.

    a. `total` is equal to 200   c. `amt` is equal to 100

    b. `total` is equal to 300   d. `amt` is equal to 300

8. The modulus operator % is a _____ operator.

    a. unary   c. tertiary

    b. binary   d. postfix

9. The prefix ++ is a _____ operator.

    a. unary   c. tertiary

    b. binary   d. postfix

10. If `g = 5`, then after `h = ++g`, the value of h is _____.

    a. 4   c. 6

    b. 5   d. 7

11. If `m = 9`, then after `n = m++`, the value of n is _____.

    a. 8   c. 10

    b. 9   d. 11

12. If `j = 5` and `k = 6`, then the value of `j++ == k` is _____.

    a. 5   c. `true`

    b. 6   d. `false`

13. You must always include _____ in a `for` loop's parentheses.

    a. two semicolons   c. two commas

    b. three semicolons   d. three commas

14. What does the following statement print?
    ```
    for(a = 0; a < 5; ++a)
        System.out.print(a + " ");
    ```
    a. 0 0 0 0 0   c. 0 1 2 3 4 5

    b. 0 1 2 3 4   d. nothing

15. What does the following statement print?
    ```
    for(b = 1; b > 3; ++b)
        System.out.print(b + " ");
    ```
    a. 1 1 1   c. 1 2 3 4

    b. 1 2 3   d. nothing

16. What does the following statement print?

    ```
    for(f = 1, g = 4; f < g; ++f, --g)
       System.out.print(f + " " + g + " ");
    ```

    a. 1 4 2 5 3 6 4 7...   c. 1 4 2 3

    b. 1 4 2 3 3 2   d. nothing

17. The loop that performs its conditional check at the bottom of the loop is a _____ loop.

    a. while   c. for

    b. do...while   d. for...while

18. What does the following program segment print?

    ```
    d = 0;
    do
    {
        System.out.print(d + " ");
        d++;
    } while (d < 2);
    ```

    a. 0   c. 0 1 2

    b. 0 1   d. nothing

19. What does the following program segment print?

    ```
    for(f = 0; f < 3; ++f)
       for(g = 0; g < 2; ++g)
          System.out.print(f + " " + g + " ");
    ```

    a. 0 0 0 1 1 0 1 1 2 0 2 1   c. 0 1 0 2 1 1 1 2

    b. 0 1 0 2 0 3 1 1 1 2 1 3   d. 0 0 0 1 0 2 1 0 1 1 1 2 2 0 2 1 2 2

20. What does the following program segment print?

    ```
    for(m = 0; m < 4; ++m);
       for(n = 0; n < 2; ++n);
          System.out.print(m + " " + n + " ");
    ```

    a. 0 0 0 1 1 0 1 1 2 0 2 1 3 0 3 1   c. 4 2

    b. 0 1 0 2 1 1 1 2 2 1 2 2   d. 3 1

EXERCISES

1. Write an application that prints all even numbers from 2 to 100 inclusive, and that starts a new line after every multiple of 20 (20, 40, 60, and 80). Save the file as **EvenNums.java**.

2. Write an application that asks a user to type 1, 2, 3, or 4. When the user types 4, the program ends. When the user types 1, 2, or 3, the program displays the message "Good job!" and then asks for another input. When the user types anything else, the application issues an error message and then asks for another input. Save the file as **Input123.java**.

3. Write an application that prints every integer value from 1 to 20 along with the squared value of each integer. Save the file as **TableOfSquares.java**.

4. Write an application that sums the integers from 1 to 50 (that is, 1 + 2 + 3 ... + 50). Save the file as **Sum50.java**.

5. Write an application that shows the sum of 1 to n for every n from 1 to 50. That is, the program prints 1 (the sum of 1 alone), 3 (the sum of 1 and 2), 6 (the sum of 1, 2, and 3), 10 (the sum of 1, 2, 3, and 4), and so on. Save the file as **EverySum.java**.

6. Write an application that prints every perfect number from 1 to 1000. A perfect number is one that equals the sum of all the numbers that divide evenly into it. For example, 6 is perfect because 1, 2, and 3 divide evenly into it, and their sum is 6; however, 12 is not a perfect number because 1, 2, 3, 4, and 6 divide evenly into it, and their sum is greater than 12. Save the file as **Perfect.java**.

7. a. Write an application that calculates the amount of money earned on an investment, based on an 8% annual return. Prompt the user to enter an investment amount and the number of years for the investment. Display an error message if the user enters 0 for either value; otherwise, display the total amount (balance) for each year of the investment. Save the file as **Investment.java**.

   b. Modify the `Investment` application in Exercise 7a so the user also enters the interest rate. In addition to the error message that displays when the investment or term is 0, display an error message if the interest rate is 0. Save the file as **Investment2.java**.

8. Write an application that displays a series of at least four survey questions; the survey can be on any social or political topic you want, and each question should have at least three possible numeric-choice answers. At the end of the survey, use a dialog box to ask whether the user wants to (1) enter another set of responses to the same set of questions, or (2) quit. Continue to accept sets of responses until the user chooses to quit, and then display the results of the survey—for each question indicate how many users chose the first option, second option, and so on. Save the file as **Survey.java**.

9. a. Write an application that displays the results of a series of 10 coin tosses. Use the `Math.random()` function explained in Appendix D to generate a number between 0 and 1; you will use a statement similar to:

```
result = Math.random();
```

After each coin toss, display whether the toss represents "heads" or "tails." If the `result` is 0.5 or less, the result represents "heads"; otherwise, it represents "tails." After the 10 tosses are complete, display the percentages of heads and tails. Run the application several times until you are confident that the coin tosses occur randomly. Save the file as **FlipCoin.java**.

b. Modify the application in Exercise 9a so that you generate 1000 coin tosses and keep track of the heads and tails. Do not display the coin toss result with each flip, but instead display percentages of the heads and tails after the 1000 coin tosses are complete. Save the file as **FlipCoin2.java**.

10. a. Create a class named `Purchase`. Each `Purchase` contains an invoice number, amount of sale, and amount of sales tax. Include set methods for the invoice number and sale amount. Within the `set()` method for the sale amount, calculate the sales tax as 5% of the sale amount. Also include a display method that displays a purchase's details. Save the file as **Purchase.java**.

b. Create an application that declares a `Purchase` object and prompts the user for purchase details. When you prompt for an invoice number, do not let the user proceed until a number between 1000 and 8000 has been entered. When you prompt for a sale amount, do not proceed until the user has entered a nonnegative value. After a valid `Purchase` object has been created, display the object's invoice number, sale amount, and sales tax. Save the file as **CreatePurchase.java**.

11. Create a `Delivery` class for a delivery service. The class contains fields to hold the following:

  » A delivery number that contains eight digits. The first four digits represent the year, and the last four digits represent the delivery number. For example, the 76th delivery in 2011 has a complete delivery number of 20110076.

  » A code representing the delivery area. A local delivery is code 1, and a long-distance delivery is code 2.

  » A weight, in pounds, of the item to be delivered.

  » The fee for the delivery, as follows:

Distance	Weight	Fee ($)
1	Under 5 pounds	12.00
1	5–20 pounds	16.50
1	Over 20 pounds	22.00
2	Under 5 pounds	35.00
2	5 pounds or more	47.95

Create a constructor for the `Delivery` class that accepts arguments for the year, delivery number within the year, delivery distance code, and weight of the package. The constructor determines the eight-digit delivery number and delivery fee. Also include a method that displays every `Delivery` object field. Save the file as **Delivery.java**.

Next, create an application that prompts the user for data for a delivery. Keep prompting the user for each of the following values until they are valid:

» A four-digit year between 2001 and 2025 inclusive

» A delivery number for the year between 1 and 9999 inclusive

» A package weight between 0.10 pound and 100 pounds inclusive

» A delivery distance code that is either 1 or 2

When all the data entries are valid, construct a `Delivery` object, and then display its values. Save the file as **CreateDelivery.java**.

DEBUGGING EXERCISES

Each of the following files in the Chapter.06 folder on your Student Disk has syntax and/or logic errors. In each case, determine the problem and fix the program. After you correct the errors, save each file using the same filename preceded with Fix. For example, save DebugSix1.java as FixDebugSix1.java.

a. DebugSix1.java   c. DebugSix3.java

b. DebugSix2.java   d. DebugSix4.java

GAME ZONE

1. a. Write an application that creates a quiz. The quiz contains at least five questions about a hobby, popular music, astronomy, or any other personal interest. Each question should be a multiple-choice question with at least four options. When the user answers the question correctly, display a congratulatory message. If the user responds to a question incorrectly, display an appropriate message as well as the correct answer. At the end of the quiz, display the number of correct and incorrect answers, and the percentage of correct answers. Save the file as **Quiz.java**.

    b. Modify the `Quiz` application so that the user is presented with each question continually until it is answered correctly. Remove the calculation for percentage of correct answers—all users will have 100% correct by the time they complete the application. Save the file as **Quiz2.java**.

2. In Chapter 1, you created a class called `RandomGuess`. In this game, players guess a number, the application generates a random number, and players determine whether they were correct. In Chapter 5, you improved the application to display a message indicating whether the player's guess was correct, too high, or too low. Now, add a loop that continuously prompts the user for the number, indicating whether the guess is high or low, until the user enters the correct value. After the user correctly guesses the number, display a count of the number of attempts it took. Save the file as **RandomGuess3.java**.

3. In Chapter 4, you created a `Die` class from which you could instantiate an object containing a random value from 1 to 6. Now use the class to create a simple dice game in

which the user chooses a number between 2 (the lowest total possible from two dice) and 12 (the highest total possible). The user "rolls" two dice up to three times. If the number chosen by the user comes up, the user wins and the game ends. If the number does not come up within three rolls, the computer wins. Save the application as **TwoDice3.java**.

4. a. Using the `Die` class you created in Chapter 4, create a version of the dice game Pig that a user can play against the computer. The object of the game is to be the first to score 100 points. The user and computer take turns rolling a pair of dice following these rules:

   » On a turn, each player "rolls" two dice. If no 1 appears, the dice values are added to a running total, and the player can choose whether to roll again or pass the turn to the other player.

   » If a 1 appears on one of the dice, nothing more is added to the player's total and it becomes the other player's turn.

   » If a 1 appears on both of the dice, not only is the player's turn over, but the player's entire accumulated score is reset to 0.

   » In this version of the game, when the computer does not roll a 1 and can choose whether to roll again, generate a random value between 0 and 1. Have the computer continue to roll the dice when the value is 0.5 or more, and have the computer quit and pass the turn to the player when the value is not 0.5 or more.

   Save the game as **PigDiceGame.java**.

   b. Modify the `PigDiceGame` application so that if a player rolls a 1, not only does the player's turn end, but all the player's earned points during that round are eliminated. (Points from earlier rounds are not affected.) Save the game as **PigDiceGame2.java**.

TOUGH QUESTIONS

1. Suppose that the multiplication operator did not exist. Write a method that would accept two integers and return their product.

2. Suppose that the division operator did not exist. Write a method that would accept two integers and produce the result when the first integer is divided by the second.

3. If you need a variable inside a loop, should it be declared before the loop, or inside it? For example, which of the following is better?

```
double money;
for(int x = 0; x < LIMIT; ++x)
{
    money = input.nextDouble();
    System.out.println("You entered " + money);
}

for(int x = 0; x < LIMIT; ++x)
{
    double money = input.nextDouble();
    System.out.println("You entered " + money);
}
```

The variable money is declared outside the loop.

The variable money is declared inside the loop.

4. What is the output of the following? Why?

```
final int STOP = Integer.MAX_VALUE;
final int START = STOP - 10;
int count = 0;
for(int x = START; x < STOP; ++x)
{
    ++count;
    System.out.println(count);
}
count = 0;
for(int x = START; x <= STOP; ++x)
{
    ++count;
    System.out.println(count);
}
```

5. What is the output of the following? Why?

```
int total = 0;
for(int x = 0; x < 100; ++x)
    total = total++;
System.out.println("Total is " + total);
```

UP FOR DISCUSSION

1. Suppose you wrote a program that you suspect is in an infinite loop because it keeps running for several minutes with no output and without ending. What would you add to your program to help you discover the origin of the problem?

2. Suppose that every employee in your organization has a seven-digit logon ID number that they can use to retrieve their own personal information, some of which might be sensitive in nature. For example, each employee has access to his own salary data and insurance claim information, but not to the information of others. Writing a loop would be useful to guess every combination of seven digits in an ID. Are there any circumstances in which you should try to guess another employee's ID number?

3. So far, you have created extremely simple games that rely on random number generation, but as you proceed through the chapters in this book, the games are becoming more complex. People can consume many hours playing computer games. Is there a point at which gaming interferes with family obligations or other parts of life? How many hours per week is too much? Do game developers have any obligation to make games less addictive?

7

CHARACTERS, STRINGS, AND THE STRINGBUILDER

In this chapter, you will:

Identify problems that can occur when you manipulate string data

Manipulate characters

Declare a String object

Compare String values

Use other String methods

Convert Strings to numbers

Learn about the StringBuilder and StringBuffer classes

IDENTIFYING PROBLEMS THAT CAN OCCUR WHEN YOU MANIPULATE STRING DATA

Manipulating characters and groups of characters provides some challenges for the beginning Java programmer. For example, consider the `TryToCompareStrings` application shown in Figure 7-1. The `main()` method declares a `String` named `aName` and assigns "Carmen" to it. The user is then prompted to enter a name. The application compares the two names using the equivalency operator (==) and displays one of two messages indicating whether the strings are equivalent. Figure 7-2 shows the execution of the application. When the user types "Carmen" as the value for `anotherName`, the application concludes that the two names are not equal.

```
import java.util.Scanner;
public class TryToCompareStrings
{
   public static void main(String[] args)
   {
      String aName = "Carmen";
      String anotherName;
      Scanner input = new Scanner(System.in);
      System.out.print("Enter your name > ");
      anotherName = input.nextLine();
      if(aName == anotherName)
         System.out.println(aName + " equals " + anotherName);
      else
         System.out.println(aName + " does not equal " + anotherName);
   }
```

>> **DON'T DO IT**

Do not use == to compare Strings' contents.

The `TryToCompareStrings` application

Figure 7-2 Execution of the `TryToCompareStrings` application

The application in Figure 7-1 seems to produce incorrect results. The problem stems from the fact that in Java, `String` is a class and each created `String` is a class object. As an object, a `String` variable name is not a simple data type—it is a **reference**; that is, a variable that holds a memory address. Therefore, when you compare two `Strings` using the == operator, you are not comparing their values, but their computer memory locations.

Programmers want to compare the contents of memory locations (the values stored there) more frequently than they want to compare the locations themselves (the addresses). Fortunately, the creators of Java have provided three classes that you can use when working with character data; these classes provide you with many methods that make working with characters and strings easier:

» **Character**—A class whose instances can hold a single character value. This class also defines methods that can manipulate or inspect single-character data.

» **String**—A class for working with fixed-string data—that is, unchanging data composed of multiple characters.

» **StringBuilder** and **StringBuffer**—Classes for storing and manipulating changeable data composed of multiple characters.

»TWO TRUTHS AND A LIE: IDENTIFYING PROBLEMS THAT CAN OCCUR WHEN YOU MANIPULATE STRING DATA

1. A `String` is a simple data type that can hold text data.

2. Programmers want to compare the values of `Strings` more frequently than they want to compare their memory addresses.

3. `Character`, `String`, and `StringBuilder` are useful built-in classes for working with text data.

The false statement is #1. A `String` variable name is a reference; that is, it holds a memory address.

MANIPULATING CHARACTERS

You learned in Chapter 2 that the `char` data type is used to hold any single character—for example, letters, digits, and punctuation marks. In addition to the primitive data type `char`, Java offers a `Character` class. The `Character` class contains standard methods for testing the values of characters. Table 7-1 describes many of the `Character` class methods. The methods that begin with "is", such as `isUpperCase()`, return a Boolean value that can be used in comparison statements; the methods that begin with "to", such as `toUpperCase()`, return a character that has been converted to the stated format.

» NOTE
The `Character` class is defined in `java.lang` and is automatically imported into every program you write. The `Character` class inherits from `java.lang.Object`. You will learn more about the `Object` class when you study inheritance concepts in Chapter 10.

Method	Description
`isUpperCase()`	Tests if character is uppercase
`toUpperCase()`	Returns the uppercase equivalent of the argument
`isLowerCase()`	Tests if character is lowercase
`toLowerCase()`	Returns the lowercase equivalent of the argument
`isDigit()`	Returns `true` if the argument is a digit (0–9) and `false` otherwise
`isLetter()`	Returns `true` if the argument is a letter and `false` otherwise
`isLetterOrDigit()`	Returns `true` if the argument is a letter or digit and `false` otherwise
`isWhitespace()`	Returns `true` if the argument is whitespace and `false` otherwise; this includes the space, tab, newline, carriage return, and form feed

Table 7-1 Commonly used methods of the `Character` class

Figure 7-3 contains an application that uses many of the methods shown in Table 7-1. The application asks a user to enter a character. A `String` is accepted and the `charAt()` method is used to extract the first character in the user-entered `String`. The application determines the attributes of the character and displays information about it.

```
import java.util.Scanner;
public class TestCharacter
{
    public static void main(String[] args)
    {
        char aChar;
        String aString;
        Scanner keyboard = new Scanner(System.in);
        System.out.print("Enter a character... ");
        aString = keyboard.nextLine();
        aChar = aString.charAt(0);
        System.out.println("The character is " + aChar);
        if(Character.isUpperCase(aChar))
            System.out.println(aChar + " is uppercase");
        else
            System.out.println(aChar + " is not uppercase");
        if(Character.isLowerCase(aChar))
            System.out.println(aChar + " is lowercase");
        else
            System.out.println(aChar + " is not lowercase");
        aChar = Character.toLowerCase(aChar);
        System.out.println("After toLowerCase(), aChar is " + aChar);
        aChar = Character.toUpperCase(aChar);
        System.out.println("After toUpperCase(), aChar is " + aChar);
        if(Character.isLetterOrDigit(aChar))
            System.out.println(aChar + " is a letter or digit");
        else
            System.out.println(aChar +
                " is neither a letter nor a digit");
        if(Character.isWhitespace(aChar))
            System.out.println(aChar + " is whitespace");
        else
            System.out.println(aChar + " is not whitespace");
    }
}
```

Figure 7-3 The TestCharacter application

>> **NOTE** You can tell that each of the Character class methods used in the TestCharacter application in Figure 7-3 is a static method because the method name is used without an object reference—you only use the class name, a dot, and the method name. You learned about the difference between static and instance methods in Chapter 3.

The output of three typical executions of the `TestCharacter` application is shown in Figure 7-4. For example, notice in Figure 7-4 that when the character "C" is tested, you can see the following:

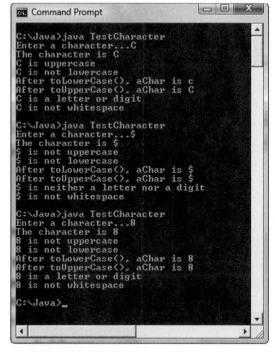

» The value returned by the `isUpperCase()` method is `true`.

» The value returned by the `isLowerCase()` method is `false`.

» The value returned by the `toLowerCase()` method is "c".

» The value returned by the `toUpperCase()` method is "C".

» The value returned by the `isLetterOrDigit()` method is `true`.

» The value returned by the `isWhitespace()` method is `false`.

Figure 7-4 Three typical executions of the `TestCharacter` application

»TWO TRUTHS AND A LIE: MANIPULATING CHARACTERS

1. `Character` is a class, but `char` is a simple data type.

2. The `Character` class method `isLowerCase()` returns the lowercase version of any uppercase character.

3. If a `char` variable holds the Unicode value for the Tab key, `isWhitespace()` would be `true` and `isLetterOrDigit()` would be `false`.

The false statement is #2. The `Character` class method `isLowerCase()` returns `true` or `false`, as do all the `Character` class methods whose names use the "is" prefix.

DECLARING A `String` OBJECT

You learned in Chapter 1 that a sequence of characters enclosed within double quotation marks is a literal string. You have used many literal strings, such as "First Java application", and you have assigned values to `String` objects and used them within methods, such as `println()` and `showMessageDialog()`. A literal string is an unnamed object, or **anonymous object**, of the `String` class, and a **String variable** is simply a named object of the same class. The class `String` is defined in `java.lang.String`, which is automatically imported into every program you write.

When you declare a `String` object, the `String` itself—that is, the series of characters contained in the `String`—is distinct from the identifier you use to refer to it. You can create a `String` object by using the keyword `new` and the `String` constructor, just as you would create an object of any other type. For example, the following statement defines an object named `aGreeting`, declares it to be of type `String`, and assigns an initial value of "Hello" to the `String`:

```
String aGreeting = new String("Hello");
```

The variable `aGreeting` stores a reference to a `String` object—it keeps track of where the `String` object is stored in memory. When you declare and initialize `aGreeting`, it links to the initializing `String` value. Alternatively, you can declare a `String` containing "Hello" with the following:

```
String aGreeting = "Hello";
```

Unlike other classes, the `String` class is special because you can create a `String` object without using the keyword `new` or explicitly calling the class constructor.

>>**TWO TRUTHS AND A LIE: DECLARING A `String` OBJECT**

1. An unnamed literal string is an anonymous object of the `String` class, and a `String` variable is simply a named object of the same class.
2. The class `String` is defined in `java.lang.String`, which is automatically imported into every program you write.
3. To create a `String` object, you must use the keyword `new` and explicitly call the class constructor.

The false statement is #3. You can create a `String` object by using the keyword `new` and explicitly calling the `String` constructor, just as you would create an object of any other type. However, you can also create `String` objects without using the keyword `new` or explicitly calling the constructor.

COMPARING `String` VALUES

In Java, `String` is a class, and each created `String` is a class object. A `String` variable name is a reference; that is, a `String` variable name refers to a location in memory, rather than to a particular value.

The distinction is subtle, but when you declare a variable of a basic, primitive type, such as `int x = 10;`, the memory address where `x` is located holds the value 10. If you later assign a new value to `x`, the new value replaces the old one at the assigned memory address. For example, if you code `x = 45;`, then 45 replaces 10 at the address of `x`. In contrast, when you declare a `String`, such as `String aGreeting = "Hello";`, `aGreeting` does not hold the characters "Hello"; instead it holds a memory address where the characters are stored.

The left side of Figure 7-5 shows a diagram of computer memory if `aGreeting` happens to be stored at memory address 10876 and the `String` "Hello" happens to be stored at memory address 26040. When you refer to `aGreeting`, you actually are accessing the address of the characters you want to use. (In the example in Figure 7-5, the memory location beginning at address 32564 has not yet been used and holds garbage values.)

If you subsequently assign a new value to `aGreeting`, such as `aGreeting = "Bonjour";`, the address held by `aGreeting` is altered; now, `aGreeting` holds a new address where the characters "Bonjour" are stored. As shown on the right side of Figure 7-5, "Bonjour" is an entirely new object created with its own location. The "Hello" `String` is still in memory, but `aGreeting` no longer holds its address. Eventually, a part of the Java system called the garbage collector discards the "Hello" characters. `Strings`, therefore, are never actually changed; instead, new `Strings` are created and `String` references hold the new addresses. `Strings` and other objects that can't be changed are **immutable**.

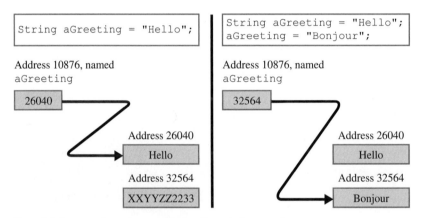

Figure 7-5 Contents of `aGreeting` at declaration and after an assignment

Because `String` references hold memory addresses, making simple comparisons between them often produces misleading results. For example, recall the `TryToCompareStrings` application in Figure 7-1. In this example, Java evaluates the `String` variables `aName` and `anotherName` as not equal because even though the variables contain the same series of characters, one set is assigned directly and the other is entered from the keyboard and stored in a different area of memory. When you compare `Strings` with the `==` operator, you are comparing their memory addresses, not their values. Furthermore, when you try to compare `Strings` using the `<` or `>` operator, the program will not even compile.

Fortunately, the `String` class provides you with a number of useful methods. The `String` class **equals() method** evaluates the contents of two `String` objects to determine if they are equivalent. The method returns `true` if the objects have identical contents. For example, Figure 7-6 shows a `CompareStrings` application, which is identical to the `TryToCompareStrings` application in Figure 7-1 except for the shaded comparison.

```
import java.util.Scanner;
public class CompareStrings
{
   public static void main(String[] args)
   {
      String aName = "Carmen";
      String anotherName;
      Scanner input = new Scanner(System.in);
      System.out.print("Enter your name > ");
      anotherName = input.nextLine();
      if(aName.equals(anotherName))
         System.out.println(aName + " equals " + anotherName);
      else
         System.out.println(aName + " does not equal " + anotherName);
   }
}
```

Figure 7-6 The CompareStrings application

When a user runs the CompareStrings application and enters "Carmen" for the name, the output appears as shown in Figure 7-7; the contents of the Strings are equal.

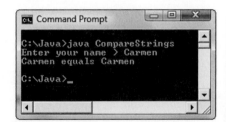

Figure 7-7 Output of the CompareStrings application

> **» NOTE**
> The String class equals() method returns true only if two Strings are identical in content. Thus, a String that refers to "Roger " (with a space after the "r") is not equivalent to a String that refers to "Roger" (with no space after the "r").

Each String declared in Figure 7-6 (aName and anotherName) is an object of type String, so each String has access to the String class equals() method. If you analyze how the equals() method is used in the application in Figure 7-6, you can tell quite a bit about how the method was written by Java's creators:

» Because you use the equals() method with a String object and the method uses the unique contents of that object to make a comparison, you can tell that it is not a static method.

» Because the call to the equals() method can be used in an if statement, you can tell that it returns a Boolean value.

» Because you see a String used between the parentheses in the method call, you can tell that the equals() method takes a String argument.

So, the method header of the equals() method within the String class must be similar to the following:

```
public boolean equals(String s)
```

The only thing you do not know about the method header is the local name used for the String argument—it might be s, or it might be any other legal Java identifier. When you use a prewritten method such as equals(), you do not know how the code looks inside it. For example, you do not know whether the equals() method compares the characters in the Strings from left to right or from right to left. All you know is that the method returns true if the two Strings are completely equivalent and false if they are not.

Because both aName and anotherName are Strings in the application in Figure 7-6, the aName object can call equals() with aName.equals(anotherName) as shown, or the anotherName object could call equals() with anotherName.equals(aName). The equals() method can take either a variable String object or a literal string as its argument. The String class **equalsIgnoreCase() method** is similar to the equals() method. As its name implies, this method ignores case when determining if two Strings are equivalent. Thus, if you declare a String as String aName = "Roger";, then aName.equals("roGER") is false, but aName.equalsIgnoreCase("roGER") is true. This method is useful when users type responses to prompts in your programs. You cannot predict when a user might use the Shift key or the Caps Lock key during data entry. The equalsIgnoreCase() method allows you to test entered data without regard to capitalization.

» NOTE
Technically, the equals() method does not perform an alphabetical comparison with Strings; it performs a **lexicographical comparison**—a comparison based on the integer Unicode values of the characters.

When the String class **compareTo() method** is used to compare two Strings, it provides additional information to the user in the form of an integer value. When you use compareTo() to compare two String objects, the method returns zero only if the two Strings refer to the same value. If there is any difference between the Strings, a negative number is returned if the calling object is "less than" the argument, and a positive number is returned if the calling object is "more than" the argument. Strings are considered "less than" or "more than" each other based on their Unicode values; thus, "a" is less than "b", and "b" is less than "c". For example, if aName refers to "Roger", then aName.compareTo("Robert"); returns a 5. The number is positive, indicating that "Roger" is more than "Robert". This does not mean that "Roger" has more characters than "Robert"; it means that "Roger" is alphabetically "more" than "Robert". The comparison proceeds as follows:

» The R in "Roger" and the R in "Robert" are compared, and found to be equal.

» The o in "Roger" and the o in "Robert" are compared, and found to be equal.

» The g in "Roger" and the b in "Robert" are compared; they are different. The numeric value of g minus the numeric value of b is 5 (because g is five letters after b in the alphabet), so the compareTo() method returns the value 5.

Often, you won't care what the specific return value of compareTo() is; you simply want to determine if it is positive or negative. For example, you can use a test such as if(aWord.compareTo(anotherWord) < 0)... to determine whether aWord is alphabetically less than anotherWord. If aWord is a String variable that refers to the value "hamster", and anotherWord is a String variable that refers to the value "iguana", the comparison if(aWord.compareTo(anotherWord) < 0) yields true.

USING OTHER String METHODS

A wide variety of additional String methods are available with the String class. The **toUpperCase() method** and **toLowerCase() method** convert any String to its uppercase or lowercase equivalent, respectively. For example, if you declare a String as String aWord = "something";, then the string "something" is created in memory and its address is assigned to aWord. The statement aWord = aWord.toUpperCase() creates "SOMETHING" in memory and assigns its address to aWord. Because aWord now refers to "SOMETHING," aWord = aWord.toLowerCase() alters aWord to refer to "something".

The **length() method** returns the length of a String. For example, the following statements result in the variable len that holds the value 5.

```
String greeting = "Hello";
int len = greeting.length();
```

> **» NOTE**
> Methods that return information about an object are called **accessor methods**. The length() method is an example of an accessor method.

The **indexOf() method** determines whether a specific character occurs within a String. If it does, the method returns the position of the character; the first position of a String begins with zero. The return value is –1 if the character does not exist in the String. For example, in String myName = "Stacy";, the value of myName.indexOf('a') is 2, and the value of myName.indexOf('q') is –1.

The **charAt() method** requires an integer argument that indicates the position of the character that the method returns. For example, if myName is a String that refers to "Stacy", the value of myName.charAt(0) is 'S' and the value of myName.charAt(1) is 't'.

> **» NOTE**
> When you must determine whether a String is empty, it is more efficient to compare its length to 0 than it is to use the equals() method.

The **endsWith() method** and the **startsWith() method** each take a String argument and return true or false if a String object does or does not end or start with the specified argument. For example, if String myName = "Stacy";, then myName.startsWith("Sta") is true, and myName.endsWith("z") is false.

The **replace() method** allows you to replace all occurrences of some character within a String. For example, if String yourName = "Annette";, then String goofyName = yourName.replace('n', 'X'); assigns "AXXette" to goofyName.

Although not part of the String class, the **toString() method** is useful when working with String objects. It converts any object to a String. In particular, it is useful when you want to convert primitive data types to Strings. So, if you declare theString and someInt = 4;, as follows, then after the following statements, theString refers to "4":

```
String theString;
int someInt = 4;
theString = Integer.toString(someInt);
```

If you declare another String and a double as follows, then after the following statements, aString refers to "8.25":

```
String aString;
double someDouble = 8.25;
aString = Double.toString(someDouble);
```

>> NOTE
In Chapter 10, you will learn more about the toString() method and how to construct your own versions for classes you create.

You can also use **concatenation** to convert any primitive type to a String. You can join a simple variable to a String, creating a longer String using the + operator. For example, if you declare a variable as int myAge = 25;, the following statement results in aString that refers to "My age is 25":

```
String aString = "My age is " + myAge;
```

Similarly, if you write the following, then anotherString refers to "12.34".

```
String anotherString;
float someFloat = 12.34f;
anotherString = "" + someFloat;
```

The Java interpreter first converts the float 12.34f to a String "12.34" and adds it to the null String "".

> >> NOTE   The toString() method does not originate in the String class; it is a method included in Java that you can use with any type of object (including a String). In Chapter 10, you will learn that toString() resides in the Object class. You have been using toString() throughout this book without knowing it. When you use print() and println(), their arguments are automatically converted to Strings if necessary. You don't need import statements to use toString() because it is part of java.lang, which is imported automatically. Because the toString() method you use with println() takes arguments of any primitive type, including int, char, double, and so on, it is a working example of polymorphism.

You already know that you can concatenate Strings with other Strings or values by using a plus sign (+); you have used this approach in methods such as println() and showMessageDialog() since Chapter 1. For example, you can print a firstName, a space, and a lastName with the following statement:

```
System.out.println(firstName + " " + lastName);
```

In addition, you can extract part of a String with the **substring() method**, and use it alone or concatenate it with another String. The substring() method takes two integer arguments—a start position and an end position—that are both based on the fact that a String's first position is position zero. The length of the extracted substring is the difference between the second integer and the first integer; if you write the method without a second integer, the substring extends to the end of the original string.

For example, the application in Figure 7-8 prompts the user for a customer's first and last names. The application then extracts these names so that a friendly business letter can be constructed. After the application prompts the user to enter a name, a loop control variable is initialized to 0. While the variable remains less than the length of the entered name, each character is compared to the space character. When a space is found, two new strings are created. The first, firstName, is the substring of the original entry from position 0 to the location where the space was found. The second, familyName, is the substring of the original entry from the position after the space to the end of the string. Once the first and last names have been created, the loop control variable is set to the length of the original string so that the loop will exit and proceed to the display of the friendly business letter. Figure 7-9 shows the data entry screen as well as the output letter created.

```
import javax.swing.*;
public class BusinessLetter
{
    public static void main(String[] args)
    {
        String name;
        String firstName = "";
        String familyName = "";
        int x;
        char c;
        name = JOptionPane.showInputDialog(null,
            "Please enter customer's first and last name");
        x = 0;
        while(x < name.length())
        {
            if(name.charAt(x) == ' ')
            {
                firstName = name.substring(0, x);
                familyName = name.substring(x + 1, name.length());
                x = name.length();
            }
            ++x;
        }
        JOptionPane.showMessageDialog(null,
            "Dear " + firstName +
            ",\nI am so glad we are on a first name basis" +
            "\nbecause I would like the opportunity to" +
            "\ntalk to you about an affordable insurance" +
            "\nprotection plan for the entire " + familyName +
            "\nfamily. Call A-One Family Insurance today" +
            "\nat 1-800-555-9287.");
    }
}
```

Figure 7-8 The BusinessLetter application

>>**NOTE** To keep the example simple, the `BusinessLetter` application in Figure 7-8 displays a letter for just one customer. An actual business application would most likely allow a clerk to enter dozens or even hundreds of customer names and store them in a data file for future use. You will learn to store data permanently in files in Chapter 12. For now, just concentrate on the string-handling capabilities of the application.

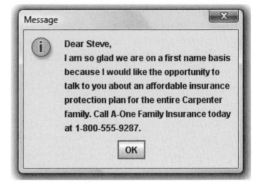

Figure 7-9 Typical execution of the `BusinessLetter` application

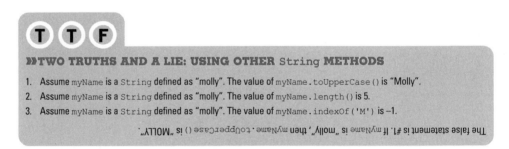

>>**TWO TRUTHS AND A LIE: USING OTHER** `String` **METHODS**

1. Assume `myName` is a `String` defined as "molly". The value of `myName.toUpperCase()` is "Molly".
2. Assume `myName` is a `String` defined as "molly". The value of `myName.length()` is 5.
3. Assume `myName` is a `String` defined as "molly". The value of `myName.indexOf('M')` is –1.

The false statement is #1. If `myName` is "molly", then `myName.toUpperCase()` is "MOLLY".

CONVERTING Strings TO NUMBERS

If a `String` contains all numbers, as in "649," you can convert it from a `String` to a number so you can use it for arithmetic, or use it like any other number. For example, suppose you ask a user to enter a salary in an input dialog box. When you accept input using `showInputDialog()`, the accepted value is always a `String`. To be able to use the value in arithmetic statements, you must convert the `String` to a number.

>>**NOTE** When you use any of the methods described in this section to attempt to convert a `String` to a number, but the `String` does not represent a valid number (for example, if it contains letters), or the `String` represents the wrong kind of number (for example, it contains a decimal point, but is being converted to an integer), an error called a `NumberFormatException` occurs. You will learn about exceptions in Chapter 11.

To convert a `String` to an integer, you use the **Integer class**, which is part of `java.lang` and is automatically imported into programs you write. The `Integer` class is an example of a wrapper. A **wrapper** is a class or object that is "wrapped around" a simpler element;

the Integer wrapper class contains a simple integer and useful methods to manipulate it. You have already used the **parseInt() method**, which is part of the Integer class; it takes a String argument and returns its integer value. For example, int anInt = Integer.parseInt("649"); stores the numeric value 649 in the variable anInt. You can then use the integer value just as you would any other integer.

Alternatively, you can use the Integer class valueOf() method to convert a String to an Integer class object, and then use the Integer class intValue() method to extract the simple integer from its wrapper class. The ConvertStringToInteger application in Figure 7-10 shows how you can accomplish the conversion. When the user enters a String in the showInputDialog() method, the String is stored in stringHours. The application then uses the valueOf() method to convert the String to an Integer object, and uses the intValue() method to extract the integer. When the user enters "37" as the String, it is converted to a number that can be used in a mathematical statement, and the output appears as expected; this output is shown in Figure 7-11.

> **》NOTE**
> The word "parse" in English means "to resolve into component parts," as when you parse a sentence. In Java, to parse a String means to break down its separate characters into a numeric format.

> **》NOTE**
> You can tell parseInt() is a static method because you use it with the class name and not with an object.

```java
import javax.swing.JOptionPane;
public class ConvertStringToInteger
{
    public static void main(String[] args)
    {
        String stringHours;
        int hours;
        Integer integerHours;
        final double PAY_RATE = 12.25;
        stringHours = JOptionPane.showInputDialog(null,
          "How many hours did you work this week?");
        integerHours = Integer.valueOf(stringHours);
        hours = integerHours.intValue();
        JOptionPane.showMessageDialog(null, "You worked " +
            hours + " hours at $" + PAY_RATE + " per hour" +
            "\nThat's $" + (hours * PAY_RATE));
    }
}
```

Figure 7-10 The ConvertStringToInteger application

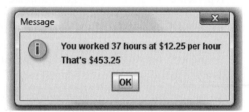

Figure 7-11 Typical execution of the ConvertStringToInteger application

It is also easy to convert a `String` object to a `double` value. You must use the **Double class**, which, like the `Integer` class, is a wrapper class and is imported into your programs automatically. A method of the `Double` class is the **parseDouble() method**, which takes a `String` argument and returns its `double` value. For example, `double doubleValue = Double.parseDouble("147.82");` stores the numeric value 147.82 in the variable `doubleValue`.

»NOTE

The methods `parseInt()` and `parseDouble()` are newer than the `valueOf()` methods, and many programmers prefer to use them when writing new applications.

To convert a `String` containing "147.82" to a `double`, you also can use the following code:

```
String stringValue = new String("147.82");
Double tempValue = Double.valueOf(stringValue);
double value = tempValue.doubleValue();
```

The `stringValue` is passed to the `Double.valueOf()` method, which returns a `Double` object. The `doubleValue()` method is used with the `tempValue` object; this method returns a simple `double` that is stored in `value`.

»NOTE

Besides `Double` and `Integer`, other wrapper classes such as `Float` and `Long` also provide `valueOf()` methods that convert `Strings` to the wrapper types. Additionally, the classes provide `parseFloat()` and `parseLong()` methods, respectively.

»TWO TRUTHS AND A LIE: CONVERTING Strings TO NUMBERS

1. The `Integer` and `Double` classes are wrapper classes.
2. The value of `Integer.parseInt("22.22")` is 22.
3. The value of `Double.parseDouble("22.22")` is 22.22.

The false statement is #2. `Integer.parseInt("22.22")` does not work because the String argument to the `parseInt()` method cannot be converted to an integer.

LEARNING ABOUT THE StringBuilder AND StringBuffer CLASSES

In Java, the value of a `String` is fixed after the `String` is created; `Strings` are immutable, or unchangeable. When you write `someString = "Hello";` and follow it with `someString = "Goodbye";`, you have neither changed the contents of computer memory at the address represented by `someString` nor eliminated the characters "Hello". Instead, you have stored "Goodbye" at a new computer memory location and stored the new address in the `someString` variable. If you want to modify `someString` from "Goodbye" to "Goodbye Everybody", you cannot add a space and "Everybody" to the `someString` that contains "Goodbye". Instead, you must create an entirely new `String`, "Goodbye Everybody", and assign it to the `someString` address.

To circumvent these limitations, you can use either the `StringBuilder` or `StringBuffer` class. You use one of these classes, which are alternatives to the `String` class, when you know a String will be modified; usually, you can use a StringBuilder or StringBuffer object anywhere you would use a String. Like the String class, these two classes are part of the java.lang package and are automatically imported into every program. The classes are identical except for the following:

» StringBuilder is more efficient.
» StringBuffer is thread safe. This means that you should use it in applications that run multiple threads, which are paths of control taken during program execution. Because most programs you write (and all the programs you have written so far) contain a single thread, usually you should use StringBuilder.

The rest of this section discusses StringBuilder, but every statement is also true of StringBuffer.

You can create a StringBuilder object that contains a String with a statement such as the following:

```
StringBuilder eventString = new StringBuilder("Hello there");
```

When you create a String, you have the option of omitting the keyword new, but when you initialize a StringBuilder object you must use the keyword new, the constructor name, and an initializing value between the constructor's parentheses. You can create an empty StringBuilder variable using a statement such as the following:

```
StringBuilder uninitializedString = null;
```

The variable does not refer to anything until you initialize it with a defined StringBuilder object. Generally, when you create a String object, sufficient memory is allocated to accommodate the number of Unicode characters in the string. A StringBuilder object, however, contains a memory block called a **buffer**, which might or might not contain a string. Even if it does contain a string, the string might not occupy the entire buffer. In other words, the length of a string can be different from the length of the buffer. The actual length of the buffer is the **capacity** of the StringBuilder object.

You can change the length of a string in a StringBuilder object with the **setLength()** **method**. The **length property** is an attribute of the StringBuilder class that identifies the number of characters in the String contained in the StringBuilder. When you increase a StringBuilder object's length to be longer than the String it holds, the extra characters contain '\u0000'. If you use the setLength() method to specify a length shorter than its String, the string is truncated.

To find the capacity of a StringBuilder object, you use the **capacity() method**. For example, the StringBuilderDemo application in Figure 7-12 demonstrates the StringBuilder capacity() method. The application creates a nameString object containing the seven characters "Barbara". The capacity of the StringBuilder object is obtained and stored in an integer variable named nameStringCapacity and then it is printed.

```
import javax.swing.JOptionPane;
public class StringBuilderDemo
{
   public static void main(String[] args)
   {
      StringBuilder nameString = new StringBuilder("Barbara");
      int nameStringCapacity = nameString.capacity();
      System.out.println("Capacity of nameString is " +
         nameStringCapacity);
      StringBuilder addressString = null;
      addressString = new
         StringBuilder("6311 Hickory Nut Grove Road");
      int addStringCapacity = addressString.capacity();
      System.out.println("Capacity of addressString is " +
         addStringCapacity);
      nameString.setLength(20);
      System.out.println("The name is " + nameString + "end");
      addressString.setLength(20);
      System.out.println("The address is " + addressString);
   }
}
```

Figure 7-12 The `StringBuilderDemo` application

Figure 7-13 shows the `StringBuilder` capacity is 23, which is 16 characters more than the length of the string "Barbara". When you create a `StringBuilder` object, its capacity is the length of the `String` contained in `StringBuilder`, plus 16. The "extra" 16 positions allow for reasonable modification of the `StringBuilder` object after creation without allocating any new memory locations.

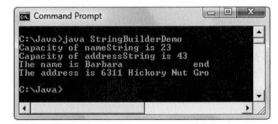

Figure 7-13 Output of the `StringBuilderDemo` application

In the application in Figure 7-12, the `addressString` variable is created as `StringBuilder addressString = null;`. The variable does not refer to anything until it is initialized with the defined `StringBuilder` object in the following statement:

```
addressString = new StringBuilder("6311 Hickory Nut Grove Road");
```

The capacity of this new `StringBuilder` object is shown in Figure 7-13 as the length of the string plus 16, or 43.

In the application shown in Figure 7-12, the length of each of the `Strings` is changed to 20 using the `setLength()` method. The application prints the expanded `nameString` and "end", so you can see in the output that there are 13 extra spaces at the end of the `String`. The application also prints the truncated `addressString` so that you can see the effect of reducing its length to 20.

Using `StringBuilder` objects provides improved computer performance over `String` objects because you can insert or append new contents into a `StringBuilder`. In other words, unlike immutable `Strings`, the ability of `StringBuilders` to be modified makes them more efficient when you know string contents will change.

> **»NOTE** Although the `equals()` method compares `String` object contents, when you use it with `StringBuilder` objects, it compares references. You can compare the contents of two `StringBuilder` objects with an expression such as the following:
>
>   obj1.toString().equals(obj2.toString())
>
> The `toString()` method converts each `StringBuilder` object to its `String` equivalent so that the `Strings` can be compared.

The `StringBuilder` class provides you with four constructors. Three of them are introduced in the following list:

» `public StringBuilder()` constructs a `StringBuilder` with no characters and a default size of 16 characters.

» `public StringBuilder(int capacity)` constructs a `StringBuilder` with no characters and a capacity specified by the parameter.

» `public StringBuilder(String s)` contains the same characters as those stored in the `String` object s. (The capacity of the `StringBuilder` is the length of the `String` argument you provide, plus 16 additional characters.)

The **append() method** lets you add characters to the end of a `StringBuilder` object. For example, if a `StringBuilder` object is declared as `StringBuilder someBuilder = new StringBuilder("Happy");`, the statement `someBuilder.append(" birthday")` alters `someBuilder` to refer to "Happy birthday".

The **insert() method** lets you add characters at a specific location within a `StringBuilder` object. For example, if `someBuilder` refers to "Happy birthday", then `someBuilder.insert(6, "30th ");` alters the `StringBuilder` to contain "Happy 30th birthday". The first character in the `StringBuilder` object occupies position zero. To alter just one character in a `StringBuilder`, you can use the **setCharAt() method**, which allows you to change a character at a specified position within a `StringBuilder` object. This method requires two arguments: an integer position and a character. If `someBuilder` refers to "Happy 30th birthday", then `someBuilder.setCharAt(6, '4');` changes the `someBuilder` value into a 40th birthday greeting.

One way you can extract a character from a `StringBuilder` object is to use the `charAt()` method. The **charAt() method** accepts an argument that is the offset of the character position from the beginning of a `String` and returns the character at that position. If you declare the following, then `text.charAt(5)` refers to the character "P";

    StringBuilder text = new StringBuilder("Java Programming");

> **»NOTE** The fourth `StringBuilder` constructor uses an argument of `CharSequence`. `CharSequence` is another Java class; it is an interface that holds a sequence of `char` values. You will learn to create interfaces in Chapter 10.

> **»NOTE** If you try to use an index that is less than 0 or greater than the index of the last position in the `StringBuilder` object, you cause an error known as an exception and your program terminates.

When you can approximate the eventual size needed for a `StringBuilder` object, assigning sufficient capacity can improve program performance. For example, the program in Figure 7-14 compares the time needed to append "Java" 20,000 times to two `StringBuilder` objects—one that has the initial default size of 16 characters and another that has an initial size of 80,000 characters. Figure 7-15 shows the execution. The extra time needed for the loop that uses the shorter `StringBuilder` is the result of repeatedly assigning new memory as the object grows in size.

```java
public class CompareConcatenationTimes
{
    public static void main(String[] args)
    {
        long startTime1, startTime2,
            endTime1, endTime2;
        final int TIMES = 20000;
        StringBuilder string1 = new StringBuilder("");
        StringBuilder string2 = new StringBuilder(TIMES * 4);
        startTime1 = System.currentTimeMillis();
        for(int x = 0; x < TIMES; ++x)
            string1.append("Java");
        endTime1 = System.currentTimeMillis();
        System.out.println("Time for empty StringBuilder : "
            + (endTime1 - startTime1)+ " milliseconds");
        startTime2 = System.currentTimeMillis();
        for(int x = 0; x < TIMES; ++x)
            string2.append("Java");
        endTime2 = System.currentTimeMillis();
        System.out.println("Time for large StringBuilder : "
            + (endTime2 - startTime2)+ " milliseconds");
    }
}
```

Figure 7-14 The `CompareConcatenationTimes` application

▶▶NOTE
Many additional `String` and `StringBuilder` methods exist. Visit the Java Web site at *http://java.sun.com.* Select API Specifications and the version of Java you are using, then select any class from the list to learn about its methods.

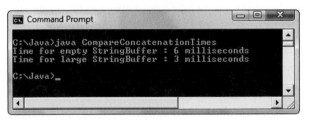

Figure 7-15 Output of the `CompareConcatenationTimes` program

▶▶NOTE You saw a demonstration of the `currentTimeMillis()` method in Chapter 6.

»TWO TRUTHS AND A LIE: LEARNING ABOUT THE StringBuilder
AND StringBuffer **CLASSES**

1. When you create a String, you have the option of omitting the keyword new, but when you initialize a StringBuilder object, you must use the keyword new, the constructor name, and an initializing value between the constructor's parentheses.

2. When you create a StringBuilder object with an initial value of "Juan", its capacity is 16.

3. If a StringBuilder named myAddress contains "817 ", then myAddress.append("Maple Lane"); alters myAddress to contain "817 Maple Lane".

The false statement is #2. When you create a StringBuilder object with an initial value of "Juan", its capacity is the length of the String contained in StringBuilder, 4, plus 16 more, for a total of 20.

YOU DO IT

USING String CLASS METHODS

To demonstrate the use of the String methods, you will create an application that asks a user for a name and then "fixes" the name so that the first letter of each new word is uppercase, whether the user entered the name that way or not.

To create the name-repairing application:

1. Open a new text file in your text editor. Enter the following first few lines of a RepairName program. The program declares several variables, including two strings that will refer to a name: one will be "repaired" with correct capitalization; the other will be saved as the user entered it so it can be displayed in its original form at the end of the program. After declaring the variables, prompt the user for a name:

```
import javax.swing.*;
public class RepairName
{
    public static void main(String[] args)
    {
        String name, saveOriginalName;
        int stringLength;
        int i;
        char c;
        name = JOptionPane.showInputDialog(null,
            "Please enter your first and last name");
```

2. Store the name entered in the saveOriginalName variable. Next, calculate the length of the name the user entered, then begin a loop that will examine every character in the name. The first character of a name is always capitalized, so when the loop control variable i is 0, the character in that position in the name string is extracted and converted to its uppercase equivalent. Then the name is replaced with the uppercase character appended to the remainder of the existing name.

```
saveOriginalName = name;
stringLength = name.length();
for(i=0; i < stringLength; i++)
{
    c = name.charAt(i);
    if(i == 0)
    {
        c = Character.toUpperCase(c);
        name = c + name.substring(1, stringLength);
    }
```

3. After the first character in the name is converted, the program looks through the rest of the name, testing for spaces and capitalizing every character that follows a space. When a space is found at position i, i is increased, the next character is extracted from the name, the character is converted to its uppercase version, and a new name string is created using the old string up to the current position, the newly capitalized letter, and the remainder of the name string. The if...else ends and the for loop ends.

```
    else
        if(name.charAt(i) == ' ')
        {
            ++i;
            c = name.charAt(i);
            c = Character.toUpperCase(c);
            name = name.substring(0, i) + c +
                name.substring(i + 1, stringLength);
        }
}
```

4. After every character has been examined, display the original and repaired names, and add closing braces for the main() method and the class:

```
    JOptionPane.showMessageDialog(null, "Original name was " +
        saveOriginalName + "\nRepaired name is " + name);
    }
}
```

5. Save the application as **RepairName.java**, and then compile and run the program. Figure 7-16 shows a typical program execution. Make certain you understand how all the String methods contribute to the success of this program.

Figure 7-16 Typical execution of the RepairName application

CONVERTING A String TO AN INTEGER

When planning an event, Event Handlers Incorporated must know how many guests to expect. Next, you will prompt the user for the number of guests, read characters from the keyboard, store the characters in a String, and then convert the String to an integer.

To create a program that accepts integer input:

1. Open a new text file in your text editor. Type the first few lines of a NumberInput class that will accept String input:

```
import javax.swing.*;
public class NumberInput
{
    public static void main(String[] args)
    {
```

2. Declare the following variables for the input String and the resulting integer:

```
String inputString;
int inputNumber;
```

3. Declare a constant that holds the maximum number of guests. If a party has more guests than the maximum, an extra charge is incurred:

```
final int MAX_GUESTS = 100;
```

4. Enter the following input dialog box statement that stores the user keyboard input in the String variable inputString:

```
inputString = JOptionPane.showInputDialog(null,
    "Enter the number of guests at your event");
```

5. Use the following Integer.parseInt() method to convert the input String to an integer. Then use the integer in a numeric decision that displays a message dialog box when the number of guests entered is greater than 100:

```
inputNumber = Integer.parseInt(inputString);
if(inputNumber > MAX_GUESTS)
    JOptionPane.showMessageDialog(null,
        "A surcharge will apply!");
```

6. Add the final two closing curly braces for the program, then save the program as **NumberInput.java** and compile and test the program. Figure 7-17 shows a typical execution. Even though the user enters a String, it can be compared successfully to a numeric value because it was converted using the parseInt() method.

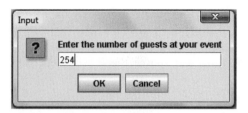

Figure 7-17 Typical execution of NumberInput program

USING StringBuilder METHODS
To use StringBuilder methods:

1. Open a new text file and type the following first lines of a DemoStringBuilder class:

```
public class DemoStringBuilder
{
    public static void main(String[] args)
    {
```

2. Use the following code to create a StringBuilder variable, and then call a print() method (that you will create in Step 7) to print the StringBuilder:

```
StringBuilder str = new StringBuilder("singing");
print(str);
```

3. Enter the following append() method to add characters to the existing StringBuilder and print it again:

```
str.append(" in the dead of ");
print(str);
```

4. Enter the following insert() method to insert characters, print, insert additional characters, and print the StringBuilder again:

```
str.insert(0, "Black");
print(str);
str.insert(5, "bird ");
print(str);
```

5. Add one more append() and print() combination:

```
str.append("night");
print(str);
```

6. Add a closing curly brace for the main() method.

7. Enter the following print() method that prints StringBuilder objects:

```
public static void print(StringBuilder s)
{
    System.out.println(s);
}
```

8. Type the closing curly brace for the class, and then save the file as **DemoStringBuilder.java**. Compile and execute, and then compare your output to Figure 7-18.

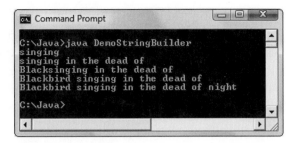

Figure 7-18 Output of the `DemoStringBuilder` application

DON'T DO IT

» Don't attempt to compare `String`s using the standard comparison operators. The == operator will only compare the addresses of `String`s, and the < and > operators will not work.

» Don't forget to use the `new` operator and the constructor when declaring initialized `StringBuilder` objects.

KEY TERMS

A **reference** is a variable that holds a memory address.

The **`Character`** class is one whose instances can hold a single character value. This class also defines methods that can manipulate or inspect single-character data.

The **`String`** class is for working with fixed-string data—that is, unchanging data composed of multiple characters.

The **`StringBuilder`** and **`StringBuffer`** classes are for storing and manipulating change-able data composed of multiple characters. It is an alternative to the `String` class when you know a `String` will be modified.

An **anonymous object** is an unnamed object.

A **`String` variable** is a named object of the `String` class.

Immutable objects cannot be changed.

The `String` class **`equals()` method** evaluates the contents of two `String` objects to determine if they are equivalent.

The `String` class **`equalsIgnoreCase()` method** is similar to the `equals()` method. As its name implies, it ignores case when determining if two `String`s are equivalent.

The `String` class **`compareTo()` method** is used to compare two `String`s; the method returns zero only if the two `String`s refer to the same value. If there is any difference between the `String`s, a negative number is returned if the calling object is "less than" the argument, and a positive number is returned if the calling object is "more than" the argument.

A **lexicographical comparison** is based on the integer Unicode values of characters.

The `String` class **toUpperCase() method** converts any `String` to its uppercase equivalent.

The `String` class **toLowerCase() method** converts any `String` to its lowercase equivalent.

The `String` class **length() method** returns the length of a `String`.

Accessor methods return information about an object.

The `String` class **indexOf() method** determines whether a specific character occurs within a `String`. If it does, the method returns the position of the character; the first position of a `String` begins with zero. The return value is –1 if the character does not exist in the `String`.

The `String` class **charAt() method** requires an integer argument that indicates the position of the character that the method returns.

The `String` class **endsWith() method** takes a `String` argument and returns `true` or `false` if a `String` object does or does not end with the specified argument.

The `String` class **startsWith() method** takes a `String` argument and returns `true` or `false` if a `String` object does or does not start with the specified argument.

The `String` class **replace() method** allows you to replace all occurrences of some character within a `String`.

The **toString() method** converts any object to a `String`.

Concatenation is the process of joining a variable to a string to create a longer string.

The **substring() method** allows you to extract part of a `String`.

The **Integer class** is a wrapper class that contains a simple integer and useful methods to manipulate it.

A **wrapper** is a class or object that is "wrapped around" a simpler element.

The `Integer` class **parseInt() method** takes a `String` argument and returns its integer value.

The **Double class** is a wrapper class that contains a simple `double` and useful methods to manipulate it.

The `Double` class **parseDouble() method** takes a `String` argument and returns its `double` value.

A **buffer** is a block of memory.

The **capacity** of a `StringBuilder` object is the actual length of the buffer, as opposed to that of the string contained in the buffer.

The `StringBuilder` class **setLength() method** changes the length of the characters in the `String` in a `StringBuilder` object.

The **length property** is an attribute of the `StringBuilder` class that identifies the number of characters in the `String` contained in the `StringBuilder`.

The `StringBuilder` class **capacity() method** returns the actual length, or capacity, of the `StringBuilder` object.

The `StringBuilder` class **append() method** lets you add characters to the end of a `StringBuilder` object.

The `StringBuilder` class **insert() method** lets you add characters at a specific location within a `StringBuilder` object.

The `StringBuilder` class **setCharAt() method** allows you to change a character at a specified position within a `StringBuilder` object.

The `StringBuilder` class **charAt() method** accepts an argument that is the offset of the character position from the beginning of a `String` and returns the character at that position.

CHAPTER SUMMARY

» `String` variables are references.

» The `Character` class is one whose instances can hold a single character value. This class also defines methods that can manipulate or inspect single-character data.

» A sequence of characters enclosed within double quotation marks is a literal string. You can create a `String` object by using the keyword `new` and the `String` constructor. Unlike other classes, you also can create a `String` object without using the keyword `new` or explicitly calling the class constructor.

» Each `String` is a class object. `Strings` are never changed; they are immutable. Useful `String` class methods include the `equals()` method. The `compareTo()`, `toUpperCase()`, `toLowerCase()`, `indexOf()`, `endsWith()`, and `startsWith()` methods provide useful `String` information and manipulation.

» The `toString()` method converts any object to a `String`. You can join `Strings` with other `Strings` or values by using a plus sign (+); this process is called concatenation. You can extract part of a `String` with the `substring()` method, which takes two arguments— a start and end position—both of which are based on the fact that a `String`'s first position is position zero.

» If a `String` contains appropriate characters, you can convert it to a number. The `Integer.parseInt()` method takes a `String` argument and returns its integer value. The `Integer.valueOf()` method converts a `String` to an `Integer` object; the `intValue()` method converts an `Integer` object to an `int` variable. The `Double.parseDouble()` method takes a `String` argument and returns its `double` value. The `Double.valueOf()` method converts a `String` to a `Double` object; the `doubleValue()` method converts a `Double` object to a `double` variable.

» You can use the `StringBuilder` or `StringBuffer` class to improve performance when a string's contents must change. You can insert or append new contents into a `StringBuilder`.

REVIEW QUESTIONS

1. A sequence of characters enclosed within double quotation marks is a _____ .

   a. symbolic string

   b. literal string

   c. prompt

   d. command

2. To create a `String` object, you can use the keyword _____ before the constructor call, but you are not required to use this format.

   a. `object`

   b. `create`

   c. `char`

   d. `new`

3. A `String` variable name is a _____ .

   a. reference

   b. value

   c. constant

   d. literal

4. The term that programmers use to describe objects that cannot be changed is _____ .

   a. irrevocable

   b. nonvolatile

   c. immutable

   d. stable

5. Suppose you declare two `String` objects as:

   ```
   String word1 = new String("happy");
   String word2;
   ```

   When you ask a user to enter a value for `word2`, if the user types "happy", the value of `word1 == word2` is _____ .

   a. `true`

   b. `false`

   c. illegal

   d. unknown

6. If you declare two `String` objects as:

   ```
   String word1 = new String("happy");
   String word2 = new String("happy");
   ```

   the value of `word1.equals(word2)` is _____ .

   a. `true`

   b. `false`

   c. illegal

   d. unknown

7. The method that determines whether two `String` objects are equivalent, regardless of case, is _____ .

   a. `equalsNoCase()`

   b. `toUpperCase()`

   c. `equalsIgnoreCase()`

   d. `equals()`

8. If a `String` is declared as:

   ```
   String aStr = new String("lima bean");
   ```
   then `aStr.equals("Lima Bean")` is _____.

   a. `true`   c. illegal

   b. `false`   d. unknown

9. If you create two `String` objects:

   ```
   String name1 = new String("Jordan");
   String name2 = new String("Jore");
   ```
   then `name1.compareTo(name2)` has a value of _____.

   a. `true`   c. –1

   b. `false`   d. 1

10. If `String myFriend = new String("Ginny");`, which of the following has the value 1?

    a. `myFriend.compareTo("Gabby");`   c. `myFriend.compareTo("Ghazala");`

    b. `myFriend.compareTo("Gabriella");`   d. `myFriend.compareTo("Hammie");`

11. If `String movie = new String("West Side Story");`, the value of `movie.indexOf('s')` is _____.

    a. `true`   c. 2

    b. `false`   d. 3

12. The `String` class `replace()` method replaces _____.

    a. a `String` with a character

    b. one `String` with another `String`

    c. one character in a `String` with another character

    d. every occurrence of a character in a `String` with another character

13. The `toString()` method converts a(n) _____ to a `String`.

    a. `char`   c. `float`

    b. `int`   d. all of the above

14. Joining `String`s with a '+' is called _____.

    a. chaining   c. linking

    b. parsing   d. concatenation

15. The first position in a `String` _____.

    a. must be alphabetic   c. is position zero

    b. must be uppercase   d. is ignored by the `compareTo()` method

16. The method that extracts a string from within another string is _____ .

    a. `extract()`   c. `substring()`

    b. `parseString()`   d. `append()`

17. The method `parseInt()` converts a(n) _____ .

    a. integer to a `String`   c. `Double` to a `String`

    b. integer to a `Double`   d. `String` to an integer

18. The difference between `int` and `Integer` is _____ .

    a. `int` is a primitive type; `Integer` is a class   c. nonexistent; both are primitive types

    b. `int` is a class; `Integer` is a primitive type   d. nonexistent; both are classes

19. For an alternative to the `String` class, and so that you can change a `String`'s contents, you can use _____ .

    a. `char`   c. `StringBuilder`

    b. `StringHolder`   d. `StringMerger`

20. Unlike when you create a `String`, when you create a `StringBuilder`, you must use the keyword _____ .

    a. `buffer`   c. `null`

    b. `new`   d. `class`

EXERCISES

1. Write an application that concatenates the following three `Strings`: "Event Handlers is dedicated ", "to making your event ", and "a most memorable one". Print each `String` and the concatenated `String`. Save the file as **JoinStrings.java**.

2. a. Write an application that counts the total number of vowels contained in the `String` "Event Handlers is dedicated to making your event a most memorable one". Save the file as **CountVowels.java**.

    b. Write an application that counts the total number of vowels contained in a `String` entered by the user. Save the file as **CountVowels2.java**.

3. a. Write an application that counts the total number of letters contained in the `String` "Event Handlers Incorporated, 8900 U.S. Highway 14, Crystal Lake, IL 60014". Save the file as **CountLetters.java**.

    b. Write an application that counts the total number of letters contained in a `String` entered by the user. Save the file as **CountLetters2.java**.

4. a. Write an application that counts the total number of whitespaces contained in a stored `String`. Save the file as **CountWhitespaces.java**.

   b. Write an application that counts the total number of whitespaces contained in a `String` entered by the user. Save the file as **CountWhitespaces2.java**.

5. Write an application that demonstrates that when two identical names are compared and the case differs, the `equals()` method returns `false`, but the `equalsIgnoreCase()` method returns `true`. Save the file as **ComparisonCase.java**.

6. Write an application that demonstrates conditions under which the `compareTo()` method returns a positive number, a negative number, and a zero when used to compare two `Strings`. Save the file as **CompareStringValues.java**.

7. Write an application that demonstrates each of the following methods, based on the statement `String dedicate = "Dedicated to making your event a most memorable one";`.

   » `indexOf('D')`
   » `charAt(15)`
   » `endsWith(one)`
   » `replace('a', 'A')`

   Save the file as **Demonstrate.java**.

8. Three-letter acronyms are common in the business world. For example, in Java you use the IDE (Integrated Development Environment) in the JDK (Java Development Kit) to write programs used by the JVM (Java Virtual Machine) that you might send over a LAN (Local Area Network). Write a program that allows a user to enter three words, and display the appropriate three-letter acronym in all uppercase letters. If the user enters more than three words, ignore the extra words. Figure 7-19 shows a typical execution. Save the file as **ThreeLetterAcronym.java**.

» **NOTE**
TLA is a three-letter acronym for "three-letter acronym."

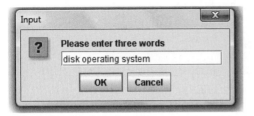

Figure 7-19 Typical execution of `ThreeLetterAcronym` program

9. Create a class that holds three initialized `StringBuilder` objects: your first name, middle name, and last name. Create three new `StringBuilder` objects as follows:

   » An object named `entireName` that refers to your three names, separated by spaces

   » An object named `lastFirst` that refers to your last name, a comma, a space, and your first name, in that order

   » An object named `signature` that refers to your first name, a space, your middle initial (not the entire name), a period, a space, and your last name

   Display all three objects. Save the file as **Builder.java**.

10. Write an application that determines whether a phrase entered by the user is a palindrome. A palindrome is a phrase that reads the same backward and forward without regarding capitalization or punctuation. For example, "Dot saw I was Tod", "Was it a car or a cat I saw?", and "Madam, I'm Adam" are palindromes. Save the file as **Palindrome.java**.

11. Write an application that prompts a user for a full name and street address and constructs an ID from the user's initials and numeric part of the address. For example, the user William Henry Harrison who lives at 34 Elm would have an ID of WHH34, whereas user Addison Mitchell who lives at 1778 Monroe would have an ID of AM1778. Save the file as **ConstructID.java**.

12. Write an application that accepts a user's password from the keyboard. When the entered password is less than six characters, more than 10 characters, or does not contain at least one letter and one digit, prompt the user again. When the user's entry meets all the password requirements, prompt the user to reenter the password, and do not let the user continue until the second password matches the first one. Save the file as **Password.java**.

13. Create a `TaxReturn` class with fields that hold a taxpayer's Social Security number, last name, first name, street address, city, state, zip code, annual income, marital status, and tax liability. Include a constructor that requires arguments that provide values for all the fields other than the tax liability. The constructor calculates the tax liability based on annual income and the percentages in the following table.

Income ($)	Marital status	
	Single	Married
0–20,000	15%	15%
20,001–50,000	22%	20%
50,001 and over	30%	28%

In the `TaxReturn` class, also include a display method that displays all the `TaxReturn` data. Save the file as **TaxReturn.java**.

Create an application that prompts a user for the data needed to create a `TaxReturn`. Continue to prompt the user for data as long as any of the following are true:

» The Social Security number is not in the correct format, with digits and dashes in the appropriate positions; for example, 999-99-9999.

» The zip code is not five digits.

» The marital status does not begin with one of the following: "S", "s", "M", or "m".

» The annual income is negative.

After all the input data is correct, create a `TaxReturn` object and then display its values. Save the file as **PrepareTax.java**.

DEBUGGING EXERCISES

Each of the following files in the Chapter.07 folder on your Student Disk has syntax and/or logic errors. In each case, determine the problem and fix the program. After you correct the errors, save each file using the same filename preceded with Fix. For example, DebugSeven1.java will become FixDebugSeven1.java.

a. DebugSeven1.java   c. DebugSeven3.java

b. DebugSeven2.java   d. DebugSeven4.java

GAME ZONE

1. a. In Chapter 3, you designed a `Card` class. The class holds fields that contain a `Card`'s value and suit. Currently, the suit is represented by a single character (s, h, d, or c). Modify the class so that the suit is a string ("Spades", "Hearts", "Diamonds", or "Clubs"). Also, add a new field to the class to hold the string representation of a `Card`'s rank based on its value. Within the `Card` class `setValue()` method, besides setting the numeric value, also set the string rank value as follows.

Numeric value	String value for rank
1	"Ace"
2–10	"2" through "10"
11	"Jack"
12	"Queen"
13	"King"

b. In Chapter 5, you created a War `Card` game that randomly selects two cards (one for the player and one for the computer) and declares a winner (or a tie). Modify the game to set each `Card`'s suit as the appropriate string, then execute the game using the newly modified `Card` class. Figure 7-20 shows four typical executions. Save the game as **War2.java**.

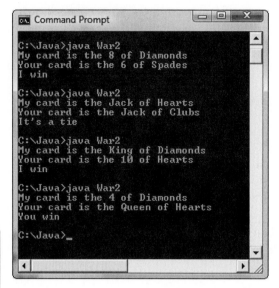

Figure 7-20 Four typical executions of the War2 game

》NOTE
Recall that in this version of War, you assume that the Ace is the lowest-valued card.

2. In Chapter 5, you created a Rock Paper Scissors game. In the game, a player entered a number to represent one of the three choices. Make the following improvements to the game:

   » Allow the user to enter a string ("rock", "paper", or "scissors") instead of a digit.

   » Make sure the game works correctly whether the player enters a choice in uppercase or lowercase letters or a combination of the two.

   » To allow for player misspellings, accept the player's entry as long as the first two letters are correct. (In other words, if a player types "scixxrs", you will accept it as "scissors" because at least the first two letters are correct.)

   » When the player does not type at least the first two letters of the choice correctly, reprompt the player and continue to do so until the player's entry contains at least the first two letters of one of the options.

   » Allow 10 complete rounds of the game. At the end, display counts of the number of times the player won, the number of times the computer won, and the number of tie games.

   Save the file as **RockPaperScissors2.java**.

3. Create a simple guessing game, similar to Hangman, in which the user guesses letters and then attempts to guess a partially hidden phrase. Display a phrase in which some of the letters are replaced by asterisks; for example, "G* T***" (for "Go Team"). Each time the user guesses a letter, either place the letter in the correct spot (or spots) in the phrase and display it again, or tell the user that the guessed letter is not in the phrase. Display a congratulatory message when the entire correct phrase has been deduced. Save the game

as **SecretPhrase.java**. In Chapter 8, you will modify this program so that instead of presenting the user with the same phrase every time the game is played, the program will randomly select the phrase from a list of phrases.

4. Eliza is a famous 1966 computer program written by Joseph Weizenbaum. It imitates a psychologist (more specifically, a Rogerian therapist) by rephrasing many of a patient's statements as questions and posing them to the patient. This type of therapy (sometimes called nondirectional) is often parodied in movies and television shows, in which the therapist does not even have to listen to the patient, but gives "canned" responses that lead the patient from statement to statement. For example, when the patient says, "I am having trouble with my brother," the therapist might say, "Tell me more about your brother." If the patient says, "I dislike school," the therapist might say, "Why do you say you dislike school?" Eliza became a milestone in the history of computers because it was the first time a computer programmer attempted to create the illusion of human-to-human interaction.

Create a simple version of Eliza by allowing the user to enter statements continually until the user quits by typing "Goodbye". After each statement, have the computer make one of the following responses:

» If the user entered the word "my" (for example, "I am having trouble with my brother"), respond with "Tell me more about your" and insert the noun in question—for example, "Tell me more about your brother".

» If the user entered a strong word, such as "love" or "hate", respond with, "You seem to have strong feelings about that".

» Add a few other appropriate responses of your choosing.

» In the absence of any of the preceding inputs, respond with a random phrase from the following: "Please go on", "Tell me more", or "Continue".

Save the file as **Eliza.java**.

> **»» NOTE**
> When you search for a word in the user's entry, make sure it is truly the word and not just letters hidden within another word. For example, when searching for "my", make sure it is not hidden in "dummy".

TOUGH QUESTIONS

1. What is the output of the following code? Why?

```
StringBuilder firstBuilder = new StringBuilder("Hello");
StringBuilder secondBuilder = new StringBuilder("Hello");
System.out.println(firstBuilder == secondBuilder);
System.out.println(firstBuilder.equals(secondBuilder));
```

2. What is the output of the following? Why?

```
System.out.print("A" + "B");
System.out.print('A' + 'B');
```

3. Assume there is no equalsIgnoreCase() method built into the String class. How could you accomplish the same result?

UP FOR DISCUSSION

1. Read the description of the Eliza program in the preceding Game Zone exercise. Is it ethical to make people think they are talking to another person when they are not? Does it make a difference if they find the program to be helpful? Would you mind if a Help facility for some software you were using was a machine instead of a person? Have you ever been embarrassed when you thought you were talking to a person but later found out you were not? (For example, have you ever started to respond on the phone only to realize you were listening to an answering machine?)

2. Read the description of the Eliza program in the preceding Game Zone exercise. Robots can be programmed to respond to people in very "natural" ways. A famous author, Isaac Asimov, proposed three laws of robotics, and later added a "zeroth" law. What are these four laws? Do you agree with them? Would you add more?

3. If you are completing all the programming exercises at the ends of the chapters in this book, you are getting a sense of the considerable amount of work that goes into a full-blown professional program. How would you feel if someone copied your work without compensating you? Investigate the magnitude of software piracy in our society. What are the penalties for illegally copying software? Are there circumstances under which it is acceptable to copy a program? If a friend asked you to make a copy of a program for him, would you? What should be done about the problem of software piracy, if anything?

8

ARRAYS

In this chapter, you will:

Declare and initialize an array
Use subscripts with an array
Declare an array of objects
Search an array for an exact match
Search an array for a range match
Pass arrays to and return arrays from methods
Manipulate arrays of `String`s
Sort array elements
Use two-dimensional and multidimensional arrays
Use the `Arrays` class
Use the `ArrayList` class

JAVA ON THE JOB, SCENE 8

"I've learned how to create objects and how to use decisions and loops to perform a variety of tasks with the objects," you explain to Lynn Greenbrier at Event Handlers Incorporated. "Still, it seems as though I'm doing a lot of work. If I need to check a variable's value against 20 possibilities, it takes me 20 `if` statements or a long `switch` statement to get the job done. I thought computers were supposed to make things easier!"

"I think what you're looking for," Lynn says, "is how to use the power of arrays."

DECLARING AND INITIALIZING AN ARRAY

While completing the first five chapters in this book, you stored values in variables. In those early chapters, you simply stored a value and used it, usually only once, but never more than a few times. In Chapter 6, you created loops that allow you to "recycle" variables and use them many times; that is, after creating a variable, you can assign a value, use the value, and then, in successive cycles through the loop, reuse the variable as it holds different values.

At times, however, you might encounter situations in which storing just one value at a time in memory does not meet your needs. For example, a sales manager who supervises 20 employees might want to determine whether each employee has produced sales above or below the average amount. When you enter the first employee's sales figure into an application, you can't determine whether it is above or below average because you don't know the average until you have all 20 figures. Unfortunately, if you attempt to assign 20 sales figures to the same variable, when you assign the figure for the second employee, it replaces the figure for the first employee.

A possible solution is to create 20 separate employee sales variables, each with a unique name, so you can store all the sales until you can determine an average. A drawback to this method is that if you have 20 different variable names to be assigned values, you need 20 separate assignment statements. For 20 different variable names, the statement that calculates total sales will be unwieldy, such as:

```
total = firstAmt + secondAmt + thirdAmt + ...
```

This method might work for 20 salespeople, but what if you have 10,000 salespeople?

The best solution is to create an array. An **array** is a named list of data items that all have the same type. You declare an array variable in the same way you declare any simple variable, but you insert a pair of square brackets after the type. For example, to declare an array of `double` values to hold sales figures for salespeople, you can write the following:

```
double[] salesFigure;
```

Similarly, to create an array of integers to hold student ID numbers, you can write the following:

```
int[] idNum;
```

>> **NOTE** You can also declare an array variable by placing the square brackets after the array name, as in `double salesFigure[];`. This format is familiar to C and C++ programmers, but the preferred format among Java programmers is to place the brackets following the variable type and before the variable name, as in `double[] salesFigure;`. This format emphasizes that the data type of `salesFigure` is an array of `double`s and not simply a `double`.

After you create an array variable, you still need to reserve memory space. You use the same procedure to create an array that you use to create an object. Recall that when you create a class named `Employee`, you can declare an `Employee` object with a declaration such as:

```
Employee oneWorker;
```

However, that declaration does not actually create the `oneWorker` object. You create the `oneWorker` object when you use the keyword `new` and the constructor method, as in:

```
oneWorker = new Employee();
```

Similarly, declaring an array and reserving memory space for it are two distinct processes. To reserve memory locations for 20 `salesFigure` objects, you declare the array variable with:

```
double[] salesFigure;
```

Then you create the array with:

```
salesFigure = new double[20];
```

Just as with objects, you can declare and create an array in one statement with the following:

```
double[] salesFigure = new double[20];
```

The statement `double[] salesFigure = new double[20];` reserves 20 memory locations for 20 `salesFigure` values. You can distinguish each `salesFigure` from the others with a subscript. A **subscript** is an integer contained within square brackets that indicates one of an array's variables, or **elements**. In Java, any array's elements are numbered beginning with zero, so you can legally use any subscript from 0 to 19 when working with an array that has 20 elements. In other words, the first `salesFigure` array element is `salesFigure[0]` and the last `salesFigure` element is `salesFigure[19]`. Figure 8-1 shows how the array of 20 sales figures appears in computer memory.

>> **NOTE**
In Java, the size of an array is never declared in brackets following the array name, as in `double salesFigure[20]`. That syntax is used in C++, but it causes a compiler error in Java.

>> **NOTE**
Other languages, such as Visual Basic, BASIC, and COBOL, use parentheses rather than brackets to refer to individual array elements. By using brackets, the creators of Java made it easier for you to distinguish array names from methods.

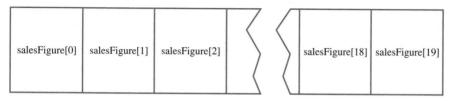

Figure 8-1 An array of 20 `salesFigure` items in memory

It is common to forget that the first element in an array is element 0, especially if you know another programming language in which the first array element is element 1. Making this mistake means you will be "off by one" in your use of any array. It is also common to forget that the last element's subscript is one less than the array's size, and not the array's size. For example, the highest allowed subscript for a 100-element array is 99.

When you work with any individual array element, you treat it no differently than you would treat a single variable of the same type. For example, to assign a value to the first salesFigure in an array, you use a simple assignment statement, such as the following:

```
salesFigure[0] = 2100.00;
```

To print the last salesFigure in an array of 20, you write:

```
System.out.println(salesFigure[19]);
```

When you declare an array, you can use any expression to represent the size, as long as the expression is an integer. For example, to declare a double array named money, you might use any of the following:

» A literal integer constant; for example:
```
double[] money = new double[10];
```

» A named integer constant; for example:
```
double[] money = new double[NUMBER_ELS];
```

» An integer variable; for example:
```
double[] money = new double[num];
```

In this example, the variable num must have been assigned a value before the array is declared. The value might come from an assignment, a calculation, or user input.

» A calculation; for example:
```
double[] money = new double[x + y * z];
```

» A method's return value; for example:
```
double[] money = new double[getElements()];
```

In this example, the method getElements() must return an integer.

INITIALIZING AN ARRAY

A variable that has a primitive type, such as int, holds a value. A variable with a reference type, such as an array, holds a memory address where a value is stored.

Array names represent computer memory addresses; that is, array names contain references, as do all Java objects. When you declare an array name, no computer memory address is assigned to it. Instead, the array variable name has the special value null, or Unicode value "\u0000". When you declare int[] someNums;, the variable someNums has a value of null.

When you use the keyword new to define an array, the array name acquires an actual memory address value. For example, when you define someNums in the following statement, a memory address is assigned:

```
int[] someNums = new int[10];
```

When you declare int[] someNums = new int[10];, each element of someNums has a value of 0 because someNums is a numeric array. (Each element in a double or float array is assigned 0.0.) By default, `char` array elements are assigned "\u0000" and `boolean` array elements automatically are assigned the value `false`.

You already know how to assign a different value to a single element of an array, as in:

```
someNums[0] = 46;
```

You can also assign nondefault values to array elements upon creation. To initialize an array, you use a list of values separated by commas and enclosed within curly braces. For example, if you want to create an array named `tenMult` and store the first six multiples of 10 within the array, you can declare `tenMult` as follows:

```
int[] tenMult = {10, 20, 30, 40, 50, 60};
```

> **» NOTE**
> Providing values for all the elements in an array is called **populating the array**.

When you initialize an array by giving it values upon creation, you do not give the array a size—the size is assigned based on the number of values you place in the initializing list. For example, the `tenMult` array just defined has a size of 6. Also, when you initialize an array, you do not need to use the keyword `new`; instead, new memory is assigned based on the length of the list of provided values.

> **» NOTE**
> In Java, you cannot directly initialize part of an array. For example, you cannot create an array of 10 elements and initialize only five; you either must initialize every element or none of them.

> **» NOTE** In Java, you do not usually use a semicolon after a closing curly brace, such as at the end of a method body. However, every statement in Java requires a semicolon, and an array initialization is a statement. Remember to type the semicolon after the closing brace at the end of an array's initialization list.

» TWO TRUTHS AND A LIE: DECLARING AND INITIALIZING AN ARRAY

1. The statement `int[] idNum = new int[35];` reserves enough memory for exactly 34 integers.
2. The first element in any array has a subscript of 0 no matter what data type is stored.
3. When you declare `int[] idNum = new int[35];`, each element of the array has a value of 0 because it is a numeric array.

The false statement is #1. The statement `int[] idNum = new int[35];` reserves enough memory for exactly 35 integers numbered 0–34.

USING SUBSCRIPTS WITH AN ARRAY

If you treat each array element as an individual entity, there isn't much of an advantage to declaring an array over declaring individual **scalar** (primitive) variables, such as `int`, `double`, or `char`. The power of arrays becomes apparent when you begin to use subscripts that are variables, rather than subscripts that are constant values.

For example, suppose you declare an array of five integers that holds quiz scores, such as the following:

```
int[] scoreArray = {2, 14, 35, 67, 85};
```

You might want to perform the same operation on each array element, such as increasing each score by a constant amount. To increase each `scoreArray` element by three points, for example, you can write the following:

```
final int INCREASE = 3;
scoreArray[0] += INCREASE;
scoreArray[1] += INCREASE;
scoreArray[2] += INCREASE;
scoreArray[3] += INCREASE;
scoreArray[4] += INCREASE;
```

With five `scoreArray` elements, this task is manageable, requiring only five statements. However, you can reduce the amount of program code needed by using a variable as the subscript. Then, you can use a loop to perform arithmetic on each array element, as in the following example:

```
final int INCREASE = 3;
for(sub = 0; sub < 5; ++sub)
    scoreArray[sub] += INCREASE;
```

The variable `sub` is set to 0, and then it is compared to 5. Because the value of `sub` is less than 5, the loop executes and 3 is added to `scoreArray[0]`. Then, the variable `sub` is incremented and it becomes 1, which is still less than 5, so when the loop executes again, `scoreArray[1]` is increased by 3, and so on. A process that took five statements now takes only one. In addition, if the array had 100 elements, the first method of increasing the array values by 3 in separate statements would result in 95 additional statements. The only changes required using the second method would be to change the array size to 100 by inserting additional initial values for the scores, and to change the middle portion of the `for` statement to compare `sub` to 100 instead of to 5. The loop to increase 100 separate scores by 3 each is:

```
for(sub = 0; sub < 100; ++sub)
    scoreArray[sub] += INCREASE;
```

When an application contains an array and you want to use every element of the array in some task, it is common to perform loops that vary the loop control variable from 0 to one less than the size of the array. For example, if you get input values for the elements in the array, alter every value in the array, sum all the values in the array, or display every element in the array, you need to perform a loop that executes the same number of times as there are elements. When there are 10 array elements, the subscript varies from 0 to 9; when there are 800 elements, the subscript varies from 0 to 799. Therefore, in an application that includes an array, it is convenient to declare a symbolic constant equal to the size of the array and use the symbolic constant as a limiting value in every loop that processes the array. That way, if the array size changes in the future, you need to modify only the value stored in the symbolic constant, and you do not need to search for and modify the limiting value in every loop that processes the array.

For example, if you declare a symbolic constant as:

```
final int NUMBER_OF_SCORES = 5;
```

the following two loops are identical:

```
for(sub = 0;  sub < 5;  ++sub)
    scoreArray[sub] += INCREASE;
for(sub = 0;  sub < NUMBER_OF_SCORES;  ++sub)
    scoreArray[sub] += INCREASE;
```

The second format has two advantages. First, by using the symbolic constant, NUMBER_OF_SCORES, the reader understands that you are processing every array element for the size of the entire array. If you use the number 5, the reader must look back to the array declaration to confirm that 5 represents the full size of the array. Second, if the array size changes because you remove or add scores, you change the symbolic constant value only once, and all loops that use the constant are automatically altered to perform the correct number of repetitions.

As another option, you can use a field (instance variable) that is automatically assigned a value for every array you create; the **length field** contains the number of elements in the array. For example, when you declare the following, the field scoreArray.length is assigned the value 5:

```
int[] scoreArray = new int[5];
```

Therefore, you can use the following loop to add 3 to every array element:

```
for(sub = 0;  sub < scoreArray.length;  ++sub)
    scoreArray[sub] += INCREASE;
```

Later, if you modify the size of the array and recompile the program, the value in the length field of the array changes appropriately. When you work with array elements, it is always better to use a symbolic constant or the length field when writing a loop that manipulates an array.

In Chapter 6, you learned to use the for loop. Java 5 and 6 also support an **enhanced for loop**. This loop allows you to cycle through an array without specifying the starting and ending points for the loop control variable. For example, you can use either of the following statements to display every element in an array named scoreArray:

```
for(int sub = 0;  sub < scoreArray.length;  ++sub)
    System.out.println(scoreArray[sub]);
for(int val : scoreArray)
    System.out.println(val);
```

In the second code line, val is defined to be the same type as the array named following the colon. Within the loop, val takes on, in turn, each value in the array.

> **»NOTE**
> A frequent programmer error is to attempt to use length as an array method, referring to scoreArray.length(). However, length is not an array method; it is a field.

> **»NOTE**
> An instance variable or object field such as length is also called a **property** of the object.

> **»NOTE**
> You can also use the enhanced for loop with more complicated Java objects. For details, go to http://java.sun.com.

»TWO TRUTHS AND A LIE: USING SUBSCRIPTS WITH AN ARRAY

1. When an application contains an array, it is common to perform loops that vary the loop control variable from 0 to one less than the size of the array.
2. An array's length field contains the highest value that can be used as the array's subscript.
3. The enhanced for loop allows you to cycle through an array without specifying the starting and ending points for the loop control variable.

The false statement is #2. An array's length field contains the number of elements in the array.

DECLARING AN ARRAY OF OBJECTS

Just as you can declare arrays of integers or doubles, you can declare arrays that hold elements of any type, including objects. For example, assume you create the Employee class shown in Figure 8-2. This class has two data fields (empNum and empSal), a constructor, and a get method for each field.

```
public class Employee
{
    private int empNum;
    private double empSal;
    Employee(int e, double s)
    {
        empNum = e;
        empSal = s;
    }
    public int getEmpNum()
    {
        return empNum;
    }
    public double getSalary()
    {
        return empSal;
    }
}
```

Figure 8-2 The Employee class

You can create separate Employee objects with unique names, such as either of the following:

```
Employee painter, electrician, plumber;
Employee firstEmployee, secondEmployee, thirdEmployee;
```

However, in many programs it is far more convenient to create an array of Employee objects. An array named emp that holds seven Employee objects is defined as:

```
Employee[] emp = new Employee[7];
```

Alternatively, if you have declared a symbolic constant such as final int NUM_EMPLOYEES = 7;, you can write the following:

```
Employee[] emp = new Employee[NUM_EMPLOYEES];
```

These statements reserve enough computer memory for seven Employee objects named emp[0] through emp[6]. However, the statements do not actually construct those Employee objects; instead, you must call the seven individual constructors. According to the class definition shown in Figure 8-2, the Employee constructor requires two arguments: an employee number and a salary. If you want to number your Employees 101, 102, 103, and so on, and start each Employee at a salary of $6.35, the loop that constructs seven Employee objects is as follows:

```
final int START_NUM = 101;
final double PAYRATE = 6.35;
for(int x = 0; x < NUM_EMPLOYEES; ++x)
    emp[x] = new Employee(START_NUM + x, PAYRATE);
```

As x varies from 0 to 6, each of the seven `emp` objects is constructed with an employee number that is 101 more than x, and each of the seven `emp` objects holds the same salary of $6.35, as assigned in the constant `PAYRATE`.

Unlike the `Employee` class in Figure 8-2, which contains a constructor that requires arguments, some classes only contain the automatically supplied default constructor and others contain an explicitly written default constructor that requires no arguments. In either of these cases, if a class only has a default constructor, you must still call the constructor using the keyword `new` for each declared array element. For example, suppose you have created a class named `InventoryItem` but have not written a constructor. To create an array of 1000 `InventoryItem` objects, you would write the following:

```
final int NUM_ITEMS = 1000;
InventoryItem[] items = new InventoryItem[NUM_ITEMS];
for(int x = 0; x < NUM_ITEMS; ++x)
   items[x] = new InventoryItem();
```

To use a method that belongs to an object that is part of an array, you insert the appropriate subscript notation after the array name and before the dot that precedes the method name. For example, to print data for seven `Employees` stored in the `emp` array, you can write the following:

```
for(int x = 0; x < NUM_EMPLOYEES; ++x)
   System.out.println (emp[x].getEmpNum() + " " + emp[x].getSalary());
```

Pay attention to the syntax of the `Employee` objects' method calls, such as `emp[x].getEmpNum()`. Although you might be tempted to place the subscript at the end of the expression after the method name—as in `emp.getEmpNum[x]` or `emp.getEmpNum()[x]`—you cannot; the values in x (0–6) refer to a particular `emp`, each of which has access to a single `getEmpNum()` method. Placement of the bracketed subscript so it follows `emp` means the method "belongs" to a particular `emp`.

»TWO TRUTHS AND A LIE: DECLARING AN ARRAY OF OBJECTS

1. The following statement declares an array named `students` that holds 10 `Student` objects:
`Student[] students = new Student[10];`

2. When a class has a default constructor and you create an array of objects from the class, you do not need to call the constructor explicitly.

3. To use a method that belongs to an object that is part of an array, you insert the appropriate subscript notation after the array name and before the dot that precedes the method name.

The false statement is #2. Whether a class has a default constructor or not, when you create an array of objects from the class, you must call the constructor using the keyword `new` for each declared array element.

SEARCHING AN ARRAY FOR AN EXACT MATCH

When you want to determine whether a variable holds one of many valid values, one option is to use a series of `if` statements to compare the variable to a series of valid values. Suppose that a company manufactures 10 items. When a customer places an order for an item, you need to determine whether the item number on the order form is valid. If valid item numbers are sequential, such as 101–110, the following simple `if` statement that uses a logical AND can verify the order number and set a Boolean field to `true`:

```
final int LOW = 101;
final int HIGH = 110;
boolean validItem = false;
if(itemOrdered >= LOW && itemOrdered <= HIGH)
    validItem = true;
```

If the valid item numbers are nonsequential—for example, 101, 108, 201, 213, 266, 304, and so on—you can code the following deeply nested `if` statement or a lengthy OR comparison to determine the validity of an item number:

```
if(itemOrdered == 101)
    validItem = true;
else if(itemOrdered == 108)
    validItem = true;
else if(itemOrdered == 201)
    validItem = true;
// and so on
```

NOTE
From earlier in this chapter, recall that when you initialize an array with 10 values using this technique, exactly 10 array elements are created in memory, and their subscripts are 0–9.

Instead of a long series of `if` statements, a more elegant solution is to compare the `itemOrdered` variable to a list of values in an array, a process called **searching an array**. You can initialize the array with the valid values with the following statement:

```
int[] validValues = {101, 108, 201, 213, 266,
    304, 311, 409, 411, 412};
```

After the list of valid values is set up, you can use a `for` statement to loop through the array, and set a Boolean variable to `true` when a match is found:

```
for(int x = 0; x < validValues.length; ++x)
{
    if(itemOrdered == validValues[x])
        validItem = true;
}
```

This simple `for` loop replaces the long series of `if` statements; it checks the `itemOrdered` value against each of the 10 array values in turn. Also, if a company carries 1000 items instead of 10, nothing changes in the `for` statement—the value of `validValues.length` is updated automatically.

As an added bonus, if you set up another parallel array with the same number of elements and corresponding data, you can use the same subscript to access additional information.

A **parallel array** is one with the same number of elements as another, and for which the values in corresponding elements are related. For example, if the 10 items your company carries have 10 different prices, you can set up an array to hold those prices as follows:

```
double[] prices = {0.29, 1.23, 3.50, 0.69...};
```

The prices must appear in the same order as their corresponding item numbers in the validValues array. Now, the same for loop that finds the valid item number also finds the price, as shown in the application in Figure 8-3. In the shaded portion of the code, notice that when the ordered item's number is found in the validValues array, the itemPrice value is "pulled" from the prices array. In other words, if the item number is found in the second position in the validValues array, you can find the correct price in the second position in the prices array. Figure 8-4 shows a typical execution of the program, in which a user requests item 409.

```java
import javax.swing.*;
public class FindPrice
{
    public static void main(String[] args)
    {
        final int NUMBER_OF_ITEMS = 10;
        int[] validValues = {101,  108,  201,  213,  266,
            304,  311,  409,  411,  412};
        double[] prices = {0.29,  1.23,  3.50,  0.69,  6.79,
            3.19,  0.99,  0.89,  1.26,  8.00};
        String strItem;
        int itemOrdered;
        double itemPrice = 0.0;
        boolean validItem = false;
        strItem = JOptionPane.showInputDialog(null,
            "Enter the item number you want to order");
        itemOrdered = Integer.parseInt(strItem);
        for(int x = 0; x < NUMBER_OF_ITEMS; ++x)
        {
            if(itemOrdered == validValues[x])
            {
                validItem = true;
                itemPrice = prices[x];
            }
        }
        if(validItem)
            JOptionPane.showMessageDialog(null, "The price for item " +
                itemOrdered + " is $" + itemPrice);
        else
            JOptionPane.showMessageDialog(null,
                "Sorry - invalid item entered");
    }
}
```

Figure 8-3 The FindPrice application that accesses information in parallel arrays

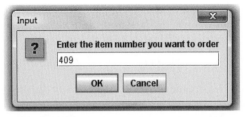

Figure 8-4 Typical execution of the `FindPrice` application

Within the code shown in Figure 8-3, you compare every `itemOrdered` with each of the 10 `validValues`. Even when an `itemOrdered` is equivalent to the first value in the `validValues` array (101), you always make nine additional cycles through the array. On each of these nine additional cycles, the comparison between `itemOrdered` and `validValues[x]` is always `false`. As soon as a match for an `itemOrdered` is found, it is most efficient to break out of the `for` loop early. An easy way to accomplish this is to set `x` to a high value within the block of statements executed when there is a match. Then, after a match, the `for` loop does not execute again because the limiting comparison (`x < NUMBER_OF_ITEMS`) is surpassed. Figure 8-5 shows this loop.

```
for(int x = 0; x < NUMBER_OF_ITEMS; ++x)
{
    if(itemOrdered == validValues[x])
    {
        validItem = true;
        itemPrice = prices[x];
        x = NUMBER_OF_ITEMS;
    }
}
```

Figure 8-5 A `for` loop with an early exit

» NOTE In Figure 8-5, instead of the statement that sets `x` to 10 (the value of `NUMBER_OF_ITEMS`) when a match is found, in its place within the `for` loop you could insert a `break` statement. However, many programmers feel that breaking out of a `for` loop early, whether you do it by setting a variable's value or by using a `break` statement, disrupts the loop flow and makes the code harder to understand. If you (or your instructor) agree with this philosophy, consider using a method that employs a `while` loop, as described next.

You can choose to forgo the `for` loop entirely, and as an alternative use a `while` loop to search for a match. Using this approach, you set a subscript to zero, and while the `itemOrdered` is not equal to a value in the array, you increase the subscript and keep looking. You search only while the subscript remains lower than the number of elements in the array. If the subscript increases to 10, you never found a match in the 10-element array. If the loop ends before the subscript reaches 10, you found a match and the correct price can be assigned to the `itemPrice` variable. Figure 8-6 shows a loop that uses this programming approach.

```
x = 0;
while(x < NUMBER_OF_ITEMS && itemOrdered != validValues[x])
    ++x;
if(x != NUMBER_OF_ITEMS)
{
    validItem = true;
    itemPrice = prices[x];
}
```

Figure 8-6 A while loop with an early exit

》TWO TRUTHS AND A LIE: SEARCHING AN ARRAY FOR AN EXACT MATCH

1. Searching an array for a match involves making a series of comparisons with each element until a match is found.
2. A parallel array is one with the same number of elements as another, and for which the values in corresponding elements are related.
3. When searching an array, it is usually the best programming practice to compare the searched-for item with every array element.

The false statement is #3. When searching an array, it is most efficient to break out of the searching loop as soon as a match is found.

SEARCHING AN ARRAY FOR A RANGE MATCH

Searching an array for an exact match is not always practical. Suppose your company gives customer discounts based on the quantity of items ordered. Perhaps no discount is given for any order of fewer than a dozen items, but there are increasing discounts available for orders of increasing quantities, as shown in Table 8-1.

Total Quantity Ordered	Discount
1–12	None
13–49	10%
50–99	14%
100–199	18%
200 or more	20%

Table 8-1 Discount table

One awkward programming option is to create a single array to store the discount rates. You could use a variable named numOfItems as a subscript to the array, but the array would need hundreds of entries, as in the following example:

```
double[] discount = {0, 0, 0, 0, 0, 0, 0, 0,
    0, 0, 0, 0, 0, 0.10, 0.10, 0.10 ...};
```

When `numOfItems` is 3, for example, `discount[numOfItems]`, or `discount[3]`, is 0. When `numOfItems` is 14, `discount[numOfItems]`, or `discount[14]`, is 0.10. Because a customer might order thousands of items, the `discount` array would need to be ridiculously large to hold an exact value for each possible order.

A better option is to create two corresponding arrays and perform a **range match**, in which you compare a value to the endpoints of numerical ranges to find the category in which a value belongs. For example, one array can hold the five discount rates, and the other array can hold five discount range limits. The Total Quantity Ordered column in Table 8-1 shows five ranges. If you only use the first figure in each range, you can create an array that holds five low limits:

```
int[] discountRangeLimit= {1, 13, 50, 100, 200};
```

A parallel array can hold the five discount rates:

```
double[] discountRate = {0, 0.10, 0.14, 0.18, 0.20};
```

Then, starting at the last `discountRangeLimit` array element, for any `numOfItems` greater than or equal to `discountRangeLimit[4]`, the appropriate discount is `discount[4]`. In other words, for any `numOrdered` less than `discountRangeLimit[4]`, you should decrement the subscript and look in a lower range. Figure 8-7 shows an application that uses the parallel arrays, and Figure 8-8 shows a typical execution of the program, in which a user enters an order for 54 items.

```java
import javax.swing.*;
public class FindDiscount
{
    public static void main(String[] args)
    {
        final int NUM_RANGES = 5;
        int[] discountRangeLimit = {    1,    13,    50,   100,   200};
        double[] discountRate =      {0.00,  0.10,  0.14, 0.18,  0.20};
        double customerDiscount;
        String strNumOrdered;
        int numOrdered;
        int sub = NUM_RANGES - 1;
        strNumOrdered = JOptionPane.showInputDialog(null,
            "How many items are ordered?");
        numOrdered = Integer.parseInt(strNumOrdered);
        while(sub >= 0 && numOrdered < discountRangeLimit[sub])
            --sub;
        customerDiscount = discountRate[sub];
        JOptionPane.showMessageDialog(null, "Discount rate for " +
            numOrdered + " items is " + customerDiscount);
    }
}
```

Figure 8-7 The `FindDiscount` class

Figure 8-8 Typical execution of the `FindDiscount` class

NOTE In the `while` loop in the application in Figure 8-7, `sub` is required to be greater than or equal to 0 before the second half of the statement that compares `numOrdered` to `discountRangeLimit[sub]` executes. It is a good programming practice to ensure that a subscript to an array does not fall below zero, causing a run-time error. This would happen if a user entered a value of less than 1 for `numOrdered`.

T T F

»TWO TRUTHS AND A LIE: SEARCHING AN ARRAY FOR A RANGE MATCH

1. In a range match, you commonly compare a value to the low endpoint of each of a series of numerical ranges.
2. In a range match, you commonly compare a value to the midpoint of each of a series of numerical ranges.
3. In a range match, you commonly compare a value to the high endpoint of each of a series of numerical ranges.

The false statement is #2. In a range match, you commonly compare a value to the low or high endpoint of each of a series of numerical ranges, but not to the midpoint.

PASSING ARRAYS TO AND RETURNING ARRAYS FROM METHODS

You have already seen that you can use any individual array element in the same manner as you use any single variable of the same type. That is, if you declare an integer array as `int[] someNums = new int[12];`, you can subsequently print `someNums[0]`, or increment `someNums[1]`, or work with any element just as you do for any integer. Similarly, you can pass a single-array element to a method in exactly the same manner as you pass a variable.

Examine the `PassArrayElement` application shown in Figure 8-9 and the output shown in Figure 8-10. The application creates an array of four integers and prints them. Then, the application calls the `methodGetsOneInt()` method four times, passing each element in turn. The method prints the number, changes the number to 999, and then prints the number again. Finally, back in the `main()` method, the four numbers are printed again.

```
public class PassArrayElement
{
   public static void main(String[] args)
   {
      final int NUM_ELEMENTS = 4;
      int[] someNums = {5, 10, 15, 20};
      int x;
      System.out.print("At start of main: ");
      for(x = 0; x < NUM_ELEMENTS; ++x)
         System.out.print(" " + someNums[x] );
      System.out.println();
      for(x = 0; x < NUM_ELEMENTS; ++x)
         methodGetsOneInt(someNums[x]);
      System.out.print("At end of main: ");
      for(x = 0; x < NUM_ELEMENTS; ++x)
         System.out.print(" " + someNums[x]);
      System.out.println();
   }
   public static void methodGetsOneInt(int one)
   {
      System.out.print("At start of method one is: " + one);
      one = 999;
      System.out.println(" and at end of method one is: " + one);
   }
}
```

Figure 8-9 The `PassArrayElement` class

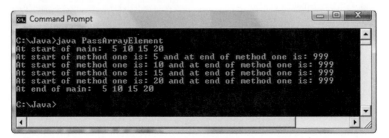

Figure 8-10 Output of the `PassArrayElement` application

As you can see in Figure 8-10, the four numbers that were changed in the `methodGetsOneInt()` method remain unchanged back in `main()` after the method executes. The variable named `one` is local to the `methodGetsOneInt()` method, and any changes to variables passed into the method are not permanent and are not reflected in the array in the `main()` program. Each variable named `one` in the `methodGetsOneInt()` method holds only a copy of the array element passed into the method. The individual array elements are **passed by value**; that is, a copy of the value is made and used within the receiving method. When any primitive type (`boolean`, `char`, `byte`, `short`, `int`, `long`, `float`, or `double`) is passed to a method, the value is passed.

The outcome is quite different when you pass an array (that is, pass its name) to a method. Arrays, like all nonprimitive objects, are **reference types**; this means that the object actually holds a memory address where the values are stored and the receiving method gets a copy of the array's actual memory address. Therefore, the receiving method has access to, and the ability to alter, the original values in the array elements in the calling method. The class shown in Figure 8-11 creates an array of four integers. After the integers print, the array name (its address) is passed to a method named `methodGetsArray()`. Within the method, the numbers print, which shows that they retain their values from `main()`, but then the value 888 is assigned to each number. Even though the `methodGetsArray()` method is a `void` method—meaning nothing is returned to the `main()` method—when the program prints the array for the second time within `main()`, all of the values have been changed to 888, as you can see in the output in Figure 8-12. Because the method receives a reference to the array, the `methodGetsArray()` method "knows" the address of the array declared in `main()` and makes its changes directly to the original array that was declared in the `main()` method.

>> **NOTE**
In some languages, arrays are **passed by reference**, meaning that a receiving method gets the memory address. It is a subtle distinction, but in Java, the receiving method gets a copy of the original address. In other words, a reference to the object is passed by value.

```java
public class PassArray
{
   public static void main(String[] args)
   {
      final int NUM_ELEMENTS = 4;
      int[] someNums = {5, 10, 15, 20};
      int x;
      System.out.print("At start of main: ");
      for(x = 0; x < NUM_ELEMENTS; ++x)
         System.out.print(" " + someNums[x] );
      System.out.println();
      methodGetsArray(someNums);
      System.out.print("At end of main: ");
      for(x = 0; x < NUM_ELEMENTS; ++x)
         System.out.print(" " + someNums[x]);
      System.out.println();
   }
   public static void methodGetsArray(int arr[])
   {
      int x;
      System.out.print("At start of method arr holds: ");
      for(x = 0; x < arr.length; ++x)
         System.out.print(" " + arr[x] );
      System.out.println();
      for(x = 0; x < arr.length; ++x)
         arr[x] = 888;
      System.out.print(" and at end of method arr holds: ");
      for(x = 0; x < arr.length; ++x)
         System.out.print(" " + arr[x] );
      System.out.println();
   }
}
```

Figure 8-11 The `PassArray` class

>> **NOTE**
Notice that in the first shaded statement in Figure 8-11, the array name is passed to the method and no brackets are used. In the method header, brackets are used to show that the parameter is a reference and not a simple `int`.

Figure 8-12 Output of the `PassArray` application

RETURNING AN ARRAY FROM A METHOD

A method can return an array reference. When a method returns an array reference, you include square brackets with the return type in the method header. For example, Figure 8-13 shows a `getArray()` method that returns a locally declared array of `ints`. Square brackets are used as part of the return type; the `return` statement returns the array name without any brackets.

```java
public static int[] getArray()
{
    int[] scores = {90, 80, 70, 60};
    return scores;
}
```

Figure 8-13 The `getArray()` method

»TWO TRUTHS AND A LIE: PASSING ARRAYS TO AND RETURNING ARRAYS FROM METHODS

1. You pass a single-array element to a method using its name, and the method must be prepared to receive the appropriate data type.
2. You pass an array to a method using its name followed by a pair of brackets; arrays are passed by value.
3. When a method returns an array reference, you include square brackets with the return type in the method header.

The false statement is #2. You pass an array to a method using its name; a copy of the array's address is passed to the method.

MANIPULATING ARRAYS OF Strings

As with any other object, you can create an array of `Strings`. For example, you can store three company department names as follows:

```java
String[] deptName = {"Accounting", "Human Resources", "Sales"};
```

You can access these department names like any other array object. For example, you can use the following code to print the list of `Strings` stored in the `deptName` array:

```java
for(int a = 0; a < deptName.length; ++a)
    System.out.println(deptName[a]);
```

>> **NOTE** Notice that `deptName.length;` refers to the length of the array `deptName` (three elements) and not to the length of any `String` objects stored in the `deptName` array. Arrays use a `length` field (no parentheses follow). Each `String` object has access to a `length()` method that returns the length of a `String`. For example, if `deptName[0]` is "Accounting", `deptName[0].length()` is 10 because "Accounting" contains 10 characters.

In Chapter 7, you learned about methods for comparing characters and comparing strings. You determined whether they were the same and, if they were different, which one was considered larger. With arrays, you often want to know whether a certain character or string can be found within the elements of the array. For example, does the letter 'z' appear in an array of characters, or does the name "John" appear in the array of first names? The idea is to search the array to see if you can find an exact match. The `SearchList` application in Figure 8-14 shows an example of such a search. The user enters a department name, and the application provides a message indicating whether the `String` was found. Figure 8-15 shows a typical execution.

```java
import javax.swing.*;
public class SearchList
{
    public static void main(String[] args)
    {
        String[] deptName = {"Accounting", "Human Resources", "Sales"};
        String dept;
        int x;
        boolean deptWasFound = false;
        dept = JOptionPane.showInputDialog(null,
            "Enter a department name");
        for(x = 0; x < deptName.length; ++x)
            if(dept.equals(deptName[x]))
                deptWasFound = true;
        if(deptWasFound)
            JOptionPane.showMessageDialog(null, dept +
                " was found in the list");
        else
            JOptionPane.showMessageDialog(null, dept +
                " was not found in the list");
    }
}
```

Figure 8-14 The `SearchList` class

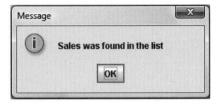

Figure 8-15 Typical execution of the `SearchList` application

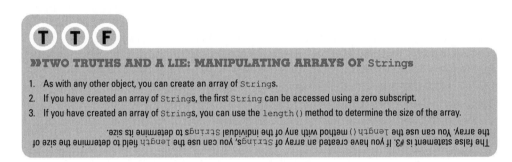

»TWO TRUTHS AND A LIE: MANIPULATING ARRAYS OF Strings

1. As with any other object, you can create an array of Strings.
2. If you have created an array of Strings, the first String can be accessed using a zero subscript.
3. If you have created an array of Strings, you can use the length() method to determine the size of the array.

The false statement is #3. If you have created an array of Strings, you can use the length field to determine the size of the array. You can use the length() method with any of the individual Strings to determine its size.

SORTING ARRAY ELEMENTS

Sorting is the process of arranging a series of objects in some logical order. When you place objects in order, beginning with the object that has the lowest value, you are sorting in **ascending** order; conversely, when you start with the object that has the largest value, you are sorting in **descending** order.

The simplest possible sort involves two values that are out of order. To place the values in order, you must swap the two values. Suppose that you have two variables—valA and valB— and further suppose that valA = 16 and valB = 2. To exchange the values of the two variables, you cannot simply use the following code:

```
valA = valB; // 2 goes to valA
valB = valA; // 2 goes to valB
```

If valB is 2, after you execute valA = valB;, both variables hold the value 2. The value 16 that was held in valA is lost. When you execute the second assignment statement, valB = valA;, each variable still holds the value 2.

The solution that allows you to retain both values is to employ a variable to hold valA's value temporarily during the swap:

```
temp = valA; // 16 goes to temp
valA = valB; // 2 goes to valA
valB = temp; // 16 goes to valB
```

Using this technique, valA's value (16) is assigned to the temp variable. The value of valB (2) is then assigned to valA, so valA and valB are equivalent. Then, the temp value (16) is assigned to valB, so the values of the two variables are finally swapped.

If you want to sort any two values, `valA` and `valB`, in ascending order so that `valA` is always the lower value, you use the following `if` statement to make the decision whether to swap. If `valA` is more than `valB`, you want to swap the values. If `valA` is not more than `valB`, you do not want to swap the values.

```
if(valA > valB)
{
    temp = valA;
    valA = valB;
    valB = temp;
}
```

Sorting two values is a fairly simple task; sorting more values (`valC`, `valD`, `valE`, and so on) is more complicated. Without the use of an array, sorting a series of numbers is a daunting task; the task becomes manageable when you know how to use an array.

As an example, you might have a list of five numbers that you want to place in ascending numerical order. One approach is to use a method popularly known as a bubble sort. In a **bubble sort**, you continue to compare pairs of items, swapping them if they are out of order, so that the smallest items "bubble" to the top of the list, eventually creating a sorted list.

To use a bubble sort, you place the original, unsorted values in an array, such as the following:

```
int[] someNums = {88, 33, 99, 22, 54};
```

You compare the first two numbers; if they are not in ascending order, you swap them. You compare the second and third numbers; if they are not in ascending order, you swap them. You continue down the list. Generically, for any `someNums[x]`, if the value of `someNums[x]` is larger than `someNums[x + 1]`, you want to swap the two values.

With the numbers 88, 33, 99, 22, and 54, the process proceeds as follows:

» Compare 88 and 33. They are out of order. Swap them. The list becomes 33, 88, 99, 22, and 54.

» Compare the second and third numbers in the list—88 and 99. They are in order. Do nothing.

» Compare the third and fourth numbers in the list—99 and 22. They are out of order. Swap them. The list becomes 33, 88, 22, 99, and 54.

» Compare the fourth and fifth numbers—99 and 54. They are out of order. Swap them. The list becomes 33, 88, 22, 54, and 99.

When you reach the bottom of the list, the numbers are not in ascending order, but the largest number, 99, has moved to the bottom of the list. This feature gives the bubble sort its name— the "heaviest" value has sunk to the bottom of the list as the "lighter" values have bubbled to the top.

Assuming b and temp both have been declared as integer variables, the code so far is as follows:

```
for(b = 0; b < someNums.length - 1; ++b)
   if(someNums[b] > someNums[b + 1])
   {
      temp = someNums[b];
      someNums[b] = someNums[b + 1];
      someNums[b + 1] = temp;
   }
```

> **» NOTE** Instead of comparing b to someNums.length - 1 on every pass through the loop, it would be more efficient to declare a variable to which you assign someNums.length -1 and use that variable in the comparison. That way, the arithmetic is performed just once. That step is omitted here to reduce the number of steps in the example.

Notice that the for statement tests every value of b from 0 to 3. The array someNums contains five integers. The subscripts in the array range in value from 0 to 4. Within the for loop, each someNums[b] is compared to someNums[b + 1], so the highest legal value for b is 3 when array element b is compared to array element b + 1. For a sort on any size array, the value of b must remain less than the array's length minus 1.

The list of numbers that began as 88, 33, 99, 22, and 54 is currently 33, 88, 22, 54, and 99. To continue to sort the list, you must perform the entire comparison-swap procedure again.

» Compare the first two values—33 and 88. They are in order; do nothing.

» Compare the second and third values—88 and 22. They are out of order. Swap them so the list becomes 33, 22, 88, 54, and 99.

» Compare the third and fourth values—88 and 54. They are out of order. Swap them so the list becomes 33, 22, 54, 88, and 99.

» Compare the fourth and fifth values—88 and 99. They are in order; do nothing.

After this second pass through the list, the numbers are 33, 22, 54, 88, and 99—close to ascending order, but not quite. You can see that with one more pass through the list, the values 22 and 33 will swap, and the list is finally placed in order. To fully sort the worst-case list, one in which the original numbers are descending (as out-of-ascending order as they could possibly be), you need to go through the list four times, making comparisons and swaps. At most, you always need to pass through the list as many times as its length minus one. Figure 8-16 shows the entire procedure.

```
for(a = 0; a < someNums.length - 1; ++a)
   for(b = 0; b < someNums.length - 1; ++b)
      if(someNums[b] > someNums[b + 1])
      {
          temp = someNums[b];
          someNums[b] = someNums[b + 1];
          someNums[b + 1] = temp;
      }
```

Figure 8-16 Ascending bubble sort of the someNums array elements

>>**NOTE** To place the list in descending order, you need to make only one change in the code in Figure 8-16: You change the greater-than sign (>) in if(someNums[b] > someNums[b + 1]) to a less-than sign (<).

When you use a bubble sort to sort any array into ascending order, the largest value "falls" to the bottom of the array after you have compared each pair of values in the array one time. The second time you go through the array making comparisons, there is no need to check the last pair of values. The largest value is guaranteed to already be at the bottom of the array. You can make the sort process even more efficient by using a new variable for the inner for loop and reducing the value by one on each cycle through the array. Figure 8-17 shows how you can use a new variable named comparisonsToMake to control how many comparisons are made in the inner loop during each pass through the list of values to be sorted. In the shaded statement, the comparisonsToMake value is decremented by 1 on each pass through the list.

```
int comparisonsToMake = someNums.length - 1;
for(a = 0; a < someNums.length - 1; ++a)
{
   for(b = 0; b < comparisonsToMake; ++b)
   {
      if(someNums[b] > someNums[b + 1])
      {
          temp = someNums[b];
          someNums[b] = someNums[b + 1];
          someNums[b + 1] = temp;
      }
   }
   --comparisonsToMake;
}
```

Figure 8-17 More efficient ascending bubble sort of the someNums array elements

SORTING ARRAYS OF OBJECTS

You can sort arrays of objects in much the same way that you sort arrays of primitive types. The major difference occurs when you make the comparison that determines whether you want to swap two array elements. When you construct an array of the primitive element type, you compare the two array elements to determine whether they are out of order. When array elements are objects, you usually want to sort based on a particular object field.

Assume you have created a simple `Employee` class, as shown in Figure 8-18. (Figure 8-2 showed a different, briefer `Employee` class. The class shown in the following figure contains more fields and methods.) The class holds four data fields, a constructor, and get and set methods for the fields.

```java
public class Employee
{
    private int empNum;
    private String lastName;
    private String firstName;
    private double salary;
    public int getEmpNum()
    {
        return empNum;
    }
    public void setEmpNum(int emp)
    {
        empNum = emp;
    }
    public String getLastName()
    {
        return lastName;
    }
    public void setLastName(String name)
    {
        lastName = name;
    }
    public String getFirstName()
    {
        return firstName;
    }
    public void setFirstName(String name)
    {
        firstName = name;
    }
    public double getSalary()
    {
        return salary;
    }
    public void setSalary(double sal)
    {
        salary = sal;
    }
}
```

Figure 8-18 An expanded `Employee` class

You can write a program that contains an array of `Employee` objects using the following statement:

```java
Employee[] someEmps = new Employee[5];
```

Assume that after you assign employee numbers and salaries to the Employee objects, you want to sort the Employees in salary order. You can pass the array to a bubbleSort() method that is prepared to receive Employee objects. Figure 8-19 shows the method.

```
public static void bubbleSort(Employee[] array)
{
   int a, b;
   Employee temp;
   int highSubscript = array.length - 1;
   for(a = 0; a < highSubscript; ++a)
    for(b = 0; b < highSubscript; ++b)
      if(array[b].getSalary() > array[b + 1].getSalary())
      {
         temp = array[b];
         array[b] = array[b + 1];
         array[b + 1] = temp;
      }
}
```

Figure 8-19 The bubbleSort() method that sorts Employee objects by their salaries

Examine Figure 8-19 carefully and notice that the bubbleSort() method is very similar to the bubbleSort() method you use for an array of any primitive type, but there are three major differences:

» The bubbleSort() method header shows that it receives an array of type Employee.

» The temp variable created for swapping is type Employee. The temp variable will hold an Employee object, not just one number or one field.

» The comparison for determining whether a swap should occur uses method calls to the getSalary() method to compare the returned salary for each Employee object in the array with the salary of the adjacent Employee object.

»TWO TRUTHS AND A LIE: SORTING ARRAY ELEMENTS

1. In an ascending bubble sort, you compare pairs of items, swapping them if they are out of order, so that the largest items "bubble" to the top of the list, eventually creating a sorted list.

2. When you sort objects, you usually want to sort based on a particular object field.

3. When you make a swap while sorting an array of objects, you typically swap entire objects and not just the field on which the comparison is made.

The false statement is #1. In an ascending bubble sort, you compare pairs of items, swapping them if they are out of order, so that the smallest items "bubble" to the top of the list, eventually creating a sorted list.

USING TWO-DIMENSIONAL AND MULTIDIMENSIONAL ARRAYS

When you declare an array such as int[] someNumbers = new int[3];, you can envision the three declared integers as a column of numbers in memory, as shown in Figure 8-20. In other words, you can picture the three declared numbers stacked one on top of the next. An array that you can picture as a column of values, and whose elements you can access using a single subscript, is a **one-dimensional** or **single-dimensional array**.

someNumbers[0]
someNumbers[1]
someNumbers[2]

Figure 8-20 View of a single-dimensional array in memory

Java also supports two-dimensional arrays. **Two-dimensional arrays** have two or more columns of values, as shown in Figure 8-21. It is easiest to picture two-dimensional arrays as having both rows and columns. You must use two subscripts when you access an element in a two-dimensional array. When mathematicians use a two-dimensional array, they often call it a **matrix** or a **table**; you might have used a two-dimensional array called a spreadsheet.

someNumbers[0][0]	someNumbers[0][1]	someNumbers[0][2]	someNumbers[0][3]
someNumbers[1][0]	someNumbers[1][1]	someNumbers[1][2]	someNumbers[1][3]
someNumbers[2][0]	someNumbers[2][1]	someNumbers[2][2]	someNumbers[2][3]

Figure 8-21 View of a two-dimensional array in memory

When you declare a one-dimensional array, you type a set of square brackets after the array type. To declare a two-dimensional array, you type two sets of brackets after the array type. For example, the array in Figure 8-21 can be declared as the following, creating an array named someNumbers that holds three rows and four columns:

```
int[][] someNumbers = new int[3][4];
```

Just as with a one-dimensional array, if you do not provide values for the elements in a two-dimensional numerical array, the values default to zero. You can assign other values to the array elements later. For example, someNumbers[0][0] = 14; assigns the value 14 to the element of the someNumbers array that is in the first column of the first row. Alternatively, you can initialize a two-dimensional array with values when it is created. For example, the following code assigns values to someNumbers when it is created:

```
int[][] someNumbers = {{8, 9, 10, 11},
                       {1, 3, 12, 15},
                       {5, 9, 44, 99} };
```

The someNumbers array contains three rows and four columns. You contain the entire set of values within a pair of curly braces. The first row of the array holds the four integers 8, 9, 10, and 11. Notice that these four integers are placed within their own set of curly braces to indicate that they constitute one row, or the first row, which is row 0. Similarly, 1, 3, 12, and 15 make up the second row (row 1), which you reference with the subscript 1. Next, 5, 9, 44, and 99 are the values in the third row (row 2), which you reference with the subscript 2. The value of someNumbers[0][0] is 8. The value of someNumbers[0][1] is 9. The value of someNumbers[2][3] is 99. The value within the first set of brackets following the array name always refers to the row; the value within the second brackets refers to the column.

As an example of how useful two-dimensional arrays can be, assume you own an apartment building with four floors—a basement, which you refer to as floor zero, and three other floors numbered one, two, and three. In addition, each of the floors has studio (with no bedroom) and one- and two-bedroom apartments. The monthly rent for each type of apartment is different—the higher the floor, the higher the rent (the view is better), and the rent is higher for apartments with more bedrooms. Table 8-2 shows the rental amounts.

Floor	Zero Bedrooms	One Bedroom	Two Bedrooms
0	400	450	510
1	500	560	630
2	625	676	740
3	1000	1250	1600

Table 8-2 Rents charged (in dollars)

To determine a tenant's rent, you need to know two pieces of information: the floor on which the tenant rents an apartment and the number of bedrooms in the apartment. Within a Java program, you can declare an array of rents using the following code:

```
int[][] rents = { {400, 450, 510},
                  {500, 560, 630},
                  {625, 676, 740},
                  {1000, 1250, 1600} };
```

Assume you declare two integers to hold the floor number and bedroom count, as in the following statement:

```
int floor, bedrooms;
```

Then any tenant's rent can be referred to as rents[floor][bedrooms].

When you pass a two-dimensional array to a method, you include the appropriate number of bracket pairs in the method header. For example, the following method headers accept two-dimensional arrays of ints, doubles, and Employees, respectively:

```
public static void displayScores(int[][]scoresArray)
public static boolean areAllPricesHigh(double[][] prices)
public static double computePayrollForAllEmployees(Employee[][] staff)
```

In each case, notice that the brackets indicating the array in the method header are empty. There is no need to insert numbers into the brackets because each passed array name is a starting memory address. The way you manipulate subscripts within the method determines how rows and columns are accessed.

USING THE `length` FIELD WITH A TWO-DIMENSIONAL ARRAY

A one-dimensional array has a `length` field that holds the number of elements in the array. With a two-dimensional array, the `length` field holds the number of rows in the array. Each row, in turn, has a `length` field that holds the number of columns in the row. For example, suppose you declare a `rents` array as follows:

```
int[][] rents = { {400, 450, 510},
                  {500, 560, 630},
                  {625, 676, 740},
                  {1000, 1250, 1600} };
```

The value of `rent.length` is 4 because there are four rows in the array. The value of `rents[0].length` is 3 because there are three columns in the first row of the `rents` array. Similarly, the value of `rents[1].length` is also 3 because there are three columns in the second row.

UNDERSTANDING RAGGED ARRAYS

In a two-dimensional array, each row is an array. In Java, you can declare each row to have a different length. When a two-dimensional array has rows of different lengths, it is a **ragged array** because you can picture the ends of each row as uneven. You create a ragged array by defining the number of rows for a two-dimensional array, but not defining the number of columns in the rows. For example, suppose you have four sales representatives, each of whom covers a different number of states as their sales territory. Further suppose you want an array to store total sales for each state for each sales representative. You would define the array as follows:

```
double[][] sales = new double[4][];
```

This statement declares an array with four rows, but the rows are not yet created. Then, you can declare the individual rows, based on the number of states covered by each salesperson as follows:

```
sales[0] = new double[12];
sales[1] = new double[18];
sales[2] = new double[9];
sales[3] = new double[11];
```

USING MULTIDIMENSIONAL ARRAYS

Besides one- and two-dimensional arrays, Java also supports **multidimensional arrays** with more than two dimensions. For example, if you own an apartment building with a number of floors and different numbers of bedrooms available in apartments on each floor, you can use a two-dimensional array to store the rental fees. If you own several apartment buildings, you might want to employ a third dimension to store the building number. An expression such as `rents[building][floor][bedrooms]` refers to a specific rent figure for a building whose building number is stored in the `building` variable and whose floor and bedroom numbers are stored in the `floor` and `bedrooms` variables. Specifically, `rents[5][1][2]` refers to a two-bedroom apartment on the first floor of building 5. When you are programming in Java, you can use four, five, or more dimensions in an array. As long as you can keep track of the order of the variables needed as subscripts, and as long as you don't exhaust your computer's memory, Java lets you create arrays of any size.

》》TWO TRUTHS AND A LIE: USING TWO-DIMENSIONAL AND MULTIDIMENSIONAL ARRAYS

1. Two-dimensional arrays have both rows and columns, so you must use two subscripts when you access an element in a two-dimensional array.

2. The following array contains two columns and three rows:
```
int[][] myArray = {{12, 14, 19},
                   {33, 45, 88}};
```

3. With a two-dimensional array, the `length` field holds the number of rows in the array; each row has a `length` field that holds the number of columns in the row.

The false statement is #2. The array shown has two rows and three columns.

USING THE Arrays CLASS

When you fully understand the power of arrays, you will want to use them to store all kinds of objects. Frequently, you will want to perform similar tasks with different arrays—for example, filling them with values and sorting their elements. Java provides an **Arrays class**, which contains many useful methods for manipulating arrays. Table 8-3 shows some of the useful methods of the Arrays class. For each method listed in the left column of the table, `type` stands for a data type; an overloaded version of each method exists for each appropriate data type. For example, there is a version of the `sort()` method to sort `int`, `double`, `char`, `byte`, `float`, `long`, `short`, and `Object` arrays.

》》NOTE
You will learn about the Object class in Chapter 10.

Method	Purpose
`static int binarySearch(type [] a, type key)`	Searches the specified array for the specified key value using the binary search algorithm
`static boolean equals(type[] a, type[] a2)`	Returns `true` if the two specified arrays of the same type are equal to one another
`static void fill (type[] a, type val)`	Assigns the specified value to each element of the specified array
`static void sort (type[] a)`	Sorts the specified array into ascending numerical order
`static void sort(type[] a, int fromIndex, int toIndex)`	Sorts the specified range of the specified array into ascending numerical order

Table 8-3 Useful methods of the Arrays class

The methods in the Arrays class are static methods, which means you use them with the class name without instantiating an Arrays object. The ArraysDemo application in Figure 8-22 provides a demonstration of how some of the methods in the Arrays class can be used. In the ArraysDemo class, the myScores array is created to hold five integers. Then, a message and the array reference are passed to a display() method. The first line of the output in Figure 8-23 shows that the original array is filled with 0s at creation. After the first display, the Arrays.fill() method is called in the first shaded statement in Figure 8-22. Because the arguments are the name of the array and the number 8, when the array is displayed a second time the output is all 8s. In the application, two of the array elements are changed to 6 and 3, and the array is displayed again. Finally, in the second shaded statement, the Arrays.sort() method is called. The output in Figure 8-23 shows that when the display() method executes the fourth time, the array elements have been sorted in ascending order.

>> NOTE
The Arrays class is located in the java.util package, so you can use the statement import java.util.*; to access it.

```java
import java.util.*;
public class ArraysDemo
{
    public static void main(String[] args)
    {
        int[] myScores = new int[5];
        display("Original array:                 ", myScores);
        Arrays.fill(myScores, 8);
        display("After filling with 8s:          ", myScores);
        myScores[2] = 6;
        myScores[4] = 3;
        display("After changing two values:      ", myScores);
        Arrays.sort(myScores);
        display("After sorting:                  ", myScores);
    }

    public static void display(String message, int array[])
    {
        int sz = array.length;
        System.out.print(message);
        for(int x = 0; x < sz; ++x)
            System.out.print(array[x] + " ");
        System.out.println();
    }
}
```

Figure 8-22 The ArraysDemo application

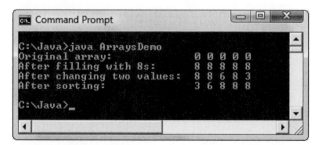

Figure 8-23 Output of the `ArraysDemo` application

The `Arrays` class `binarySearch()` methods provide convenient ways to search through sorted lists of values of various data types. It is important that the list be in order before you use it in a call to `binarySearch()`; otherwise, the results are unpredictable. You do not have to understand how a binary search works to use the `binarySearch()` method, but basically the operation takes place as follows:

» You have a sorted array and an item for which you are searching within the array. Based on the array size, you determine the middle position. (In an array with an even number of elements, this can be either of the two middle positions.)

» You compare the item you are looking for with the element in the middle position of the array and decide whether your item is above that point in the array—that is, whether your item's value is less than the middle-point value.

» If it is above that point in the array, you next find the middle position of the top half of the array; if it is not above that point, you find the middle position of the bottom half. Either way, you compare your item with that of the new middle position and divide the search area in half again.

» Ultimately, you find the element or determine that it is not in the array.

Figure 8-24 contains an `ArraysDemo2` application that verifies a letter grade entered by the user. The array `grades` holds five values in ascending order. The user enters a grade that is extracted from the first `String` position using the `String` class `charAt()` method. Next, the array of valid characters and the user-entered character are passed to the `Arrays.binarySearch()` method. If the character is found in the array, its position is returned. If the character is not found in the array, a negative integer is returned and the application displays an error message. Figure 8-25 shows the program's execution when the user enters an 'A'; the character is found in position 0 in the array.

>> **NOTE**
Programmers often refer to a binary search as a "divide and conquer" procedure. If you have ever played a game in which you tried to guess what number someone was thinking, you might have used a similar technique.

>> **NOTE** The negative integer returned by the `binarySearch()` method when the value is not found is the negative equivalent of the array size. In most applications, you do not care about the exact value returned when there is no match, but only whether it is negative.

```
import java.util.*;
import javax.swing.*;
public class ArraysDemo2
{
   public static void main(String[] args)
   {
      char[] grades = {'A', 'B', 'C', 'D', 'F'};
      String entry;
      char myGrade;
      int position;
      entry = JOptionPane.showInputDialog(null,
         "Enter student grade");
      myGrade = entry.charAt(0);
      position = Arrays.binarySearch(grades, myGrade);
      if(position >= 0)
         JOptionPane.showMessageDialog(null, "Position of " +
            myGrade + " is " + position);
      else
         JOptionPane.showMessageDialog(null, "Invalid grade");
   }
}
```

Figure 8-24 The `ArraysDemo2` application

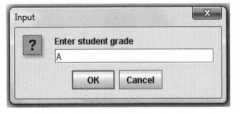

Figure 8-25 Typical execution of the `ArraysDemo2` application

≫NOTE
The `sort()` and `binarySearch()` methods in the `Arrays` class are very useful and allow you to achieve results by writing many fewer instructions than if you had to write the methods yourself. This does not mean you wasted your time reading about sorting and searching methods earlier in this chapter. The more completely you understand how arrays can be manipulated, the more useful, efficient, and creative your future applications will be.

≫TWO TRUTHS AND A LIE: USING THE Arrays **CLASS**

1. The `Arrays` class contains methods for manipulating arrays, such as `binarySearch()`, `fill()`, and `sort()`.

2. You can use the `Arrays` class `binarySearch()` method successfully on any array as soon as you have assigned values to the array elements.

3. The `binarySearch()` method works by continuously deciding whether the element sought is above or below the halfway point in sublists of the original list.

The false statement is #2. Before you can use the `Arrays` class `binarySearch()` method successfully, the array elements must be in order.

USING THE ArrayList CLASS

In addition to the Arrays class, Java provides an **ArrayList class** which can be used to create containers that store lists of objects. The ArrayList class provides some advantages over the Arrays class. Specifically, an ArrayList is **dynamically resizable**, meaning that its size can change during program execution. This means that:

» You can add an item at any point in an ArrayList container and the array size expands automatically to accommodate the new item.

» You can remove an item at any point in an ArrayList container and the array size contracts automatically.

To use the ArrayList class, you must use the following import statement:

```
import java.util.ArrayList;
```

Then, to declare an ArrayList, you can use the default constructor, as in the following example:

```
ArrayList names = new ArrayList();
```

The default constructor creates an ArrayList with a capacity of 10 items. An ArrayList's **capacity** is the number of items it can hold without having to increase its size. You can also specify a capacity if you like. For example, the following statement declares an ArrayList that can hold 20 names:

```
ArrayList names = new ArrayList(20);
```

If you know you will need more than 10 items at the outset, it is more efficient to create an ArrayList with a larger capacity.

Table 8-4 summarizes some useful ArrayList methods.

> **NOTE**
> As an alternative to importing java.util.ArrayList specifically, you can import the entire util package with the statement import java.util.*;.

> **NOTE**
> By definition, an ArrayList's capacity is greater than or equal to its size.

> **NOTE**
> In Chapter 10, you will learn that the Object class is the most generic Java class.

Method	Purpose
public void add(Object) public void add(int, Object)	Adds an item to an ArrayList. The default version adds an item at the next available location; an overloaded version allows you to specify a position at which to add the item
public void remove(int)	Removes an item from an ArrayList at a specified location
public void set(int, Object)	Alters an item at a specified ArrayList location
Object get(int)	Retrieves an item from a specified location in an ArrayList
public int size()	Returns the current ArrayList size

Table 8-4 Useful methods of the ArrayList class

To add an item to the end of an `ArrayList`, you can use the `add()` method. For example, to add the name "Abigail" to an `ArrayList` named `names`, you can make the following statement:

```
names.add("Abigail");
```

NOTE
With each of the methods described in this section, you receive an error message if the position number is invalid for the `ArrayList`.

You can insert an item into a specific position in an `ArrayList` by using an overloaded version of the `add()` method that includes the position. For example, to insert the name "Bob" in the first position of the `names` `ArrayList`, you use the following statement:

```
names.add(0, "Bob");
```

As you can see from Table 8-4, you also can alter and remove items from an `ArrayList`. The `ArrayList` class contains a `size()` method that returns the current size of the `ArrayList`. Figure 8-26 contains a program that demonstrates each of these methods.

NOTE
When you compile the `ArrayListDemo` program, you receive a compiler warning indicating that the program uses unchecked or unsafe operations. You will learn how to eliminate this message in the next section.

```java
import java.util.ArrayList;
public class ArrayListDemo
{
   public static void main(String[] args)
   {
      ArrayList names = new ArrayList();
      names.add("Abigail");
      display(names);
      names.add("Brian");
      display(names);
      names.add("Zachary");
      display(names);
      names.add(2, "Christy");
      display(names);
      names.remove(1);
      display(names);
      names.set(0, "Annette");
      display(names);
   }
   public static void display(ArrayList names)
   {
      System.out.println("\nThe size of the list is " + names.size());
      for(int x = 0; x < names.size(); ++x)
         System.out.println("position " + x + " Name: " +
            names.get(x));
   }
}
```

Figure 8-26 The `ArrayListDemo` program

In the application in Figure 8-26, an `ArrayList` is created and "Abigail" is added to the list. The `ArrayList` is passed to a `display()` method that displays the current list size and all the names in the list. You can see from the output in Figure 8-27 that at this point, the `ArrayList` size is 1 and there is just one name in the array. Examine the program in Figure 8-26 along with the output in Figure 8-27 so that you understand how the `ArrayList` is altered as names are added, removed, and replaced.

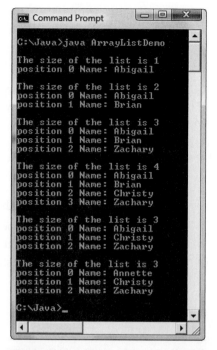

Figure 8-27 Output of the `ArrayListDemo` program

> **NOTE** You can display the contents of an `ArrayList` of `String`s without looping through the values; the contents are displayed between square brackets. For example, if an `ArrayList` named `names` has been populated with the `String`s "Annette", "Christy", and "Zachary", then the statement `System.out.println("The names are " + names);` produces the following output:
>
> The names are [Annette, Christy, Zachary]
>
> You can display the name for `ArrayList`s of any class type. In Chapter 7, you learned that every class contains a `toString()` method that converts its objects to `String`s; this method is used when you display an `ArrayList`'s name. However, unless you have overridden the `toString()` method within a class, the `String` that is returned by `toString()` is not very useful. You will learn more about writing this method in Chapter 10.

UNDERSTANDING THE LIMITATIONS OF THE `ArrayList` CLASS

An `ArrayList` can be used to store any type of object reference. In fact, one `ArrayList` can store multiple types. However, this creates two drawbacks:

» You cannot use an `ArrayList` to store primitive types such as `int`, `double`, or `char` because those types are not references. If you want to work with primitive types, you can create an array or use the `Arrays` class, but you cannot use the `ArrayList` class.

» When you want to store `ArrayList` elements, you must cast them to the appropriate reference type before you can do so, or you must declare a reference type in the `ArrayList` declaration.

For example, if you want to declare a `String` to hold the first name in the `names` `ArrayList`, you must make statements such as the following:

```
String firstName;
firstName = (String)names.get(0);
```

The cast operator (`String`) converts the generic returned object from the `get()` method to a `String`. If you do not perform this cast, you receive an error message indicating that you are using incompatible types.

You can eliminate the need to perform a cast with `ArrayList` objects by specifying the type that an `ArrayList` can hold. For example, you can declare an `ArrayList` of names as follows:

```
ArrayList<String> names = new ArrayList<String>;
```

Creating an `ArrayList` declaration with a specified type provides several advantages:

» You no longer have to use the cast operator when retrieving an item from the `ArrayList`.

» Java checks to make sure that only items of the appropriate type are added to the list.

» The compiler warning that indicates your program uses an unchecked or unsafe operation is eliminated.

»TWO TRUTHS AND A LIE: USING THE `ArrayList` CLASS

1. An advantage of the `ArrayList` class over the `Arrays` class is that an `ArrayList` is dynamically resizable.
2. An advantage of the `ArrayList` class over the `Arrays` class is that it can hold multiple object types.
3. An advantage of the `ArrayList` class over the `Arrays` class is that it can hold primitive data types such as `int` and `double`.

The false statement is #3. A disadvantage of the `ArrayList` class is that it cannot hold primitive types.

YOU DO IT

CREATING AND POPULATING AN ARRAY

In this section, you will create a small array to see how arrays are used. The array will hold salaries for four categories of employees.

To create a program that uses an array:

1. Open a new text file in your text editor.

2. Begin the class that demonstrates how arrays are used by typing the following class and `main()` headers and their corresponding opening curly braces:

```
public class DemoArray
{
    public static void main(String[] args)
    {
```

3. On a new line, declare and create an array that can hold four `double` values by typing the following:

```
double[] salary = new double[4];
```

4. One by one, assign four values to the four salary array elements by typing the following:

```
salary[0] = 6.25;
salary[1] = 6.55;
salary[2] = 10.25;
salary[3] = 16.85;
```

5. To confirm that the four values have been assigned, print the salaries, one by one, using the following code:

```
System.out.println("Salaries one by one are:");
System.out.println(salary[0]);
System.out.println(salary[1]);
System.out.println(salary[2]);
System.out.println(salary[3]);
```

6. Add the two closing curly braces that end the `main()` method and the `DemoArray` class.

7. Save the program as **DemoArray.java**. Compile and run the program. The program's output appears in Figure 8-28.

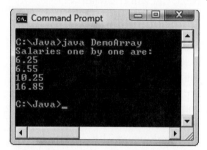

Figure 8-28 Output of the `DemoArray` application

INITIALIZING AN ARRAY

Next, you will alter your `DemoArray` program to initialize the array of `doubles`, rather than declaring the array and assigning values later.

To initialize an array of `doubles`:

1. Open the **DemoArray.java** file in your text editor. Immediately save the file as **DemoArray2.java**. Change the class name to **DemoArray2**. Delete the statement that declares the array of four `doubles` named `salary`, and then replace it with the following initialization statement:

```
double[] salary = {6.25, 6.55, 10.25, 16.85};
```

2. Delete the following four statements that individually assign the values to the array:

```
salary[0] = 6.25; salary[1] = 6.55; salary[2] = 10.25;
   salary[3] = 16.85;
```

3. Save the file (as **DemoArray2.java**), compile, and test the application. The values that are output are the same as those shown for the `DemoArray` application in Figure 8-28.

USING A `for` LOOP TO ACCESS ARRAY ELEMENTS

Next, you will modify the `DemoArray2` program to use a `for` loop with the array.

To use a `for` loop with the array:

1. Open the **DemoArray2.java** file in your text editor. Immediately save the file as **DemoArray3.java**. Change the class name to **DemoArray3**. Delete the four `println()` statements that print the four array values, and then replace them with the following `for` loop:

```
for(int x = 0; x < salary.length; ++x)
   System.out.println(salary[x]);
```

2. Save the program (as **DemoArray3.java**), compile, and run the program. Again, the output is the same as that shown in Figure 8-28.

CREATING PARALLEL ARRAYS TO ELIMINATE NESTED `if` STATEMENTS

Next, you will create an `Event` class for Event Handlers Incorporated. The class contains three data fields: an integer representing the type of event, a `double` representing the rate that is charged for the event, and a `String` that holds the event manager's name. The class also contains methods to get and set the field values. You will create a constructor that bases field values on data stored in parallel arrays.

To create the `Event` class:

1. Open a new file in your text editor and create the `Event` class, as shown in Figure 8-29. Save the file as **Event.java**. Alternatively, you can use the **Event.java** class file you created in Chapter 5.

```java
public class Event
{
   private int typeOfEvent;
   private double rate;
   private String manager;
   public int getType()
   {
      return typeOfEvent;
   }
   public double getRate()
   {
      return rate;
   }
   public String getManager()
   {
      return manager;
   }
   public void setType(int eventType)
   {
      typeOfEvent = eventType;
   }
   public void setRate(double eventRate)
   {
      rate = eventRate;
   }
   public void setManager(String managerName)
   {
      manager = managerName;
   }
}
```

Figure 8-29 The `Event` class

2. Add a constructor to the `Event` class. The constructor requires an argument for the event type; the constructor uses it to determine the rate charged and the manager's name for the event. Table 8-5 shows the appropriate values based on the event type. Although with only three event types it would be possible to make assignments using nested `if` statements, the constructor will use arrays to hold the possible field values. That way, when event types are added in the future, the only necessary change will be to add the data that corresponds to the new type of event. Also notice two features when you examine the constructor code:

» The event types are 1, 2, and 3, but arrays begin with element 0, so the 0 position of the `rateSchedule` and `managerList` arrays is reserved for error codes—a rate of 0 and a manager name of "X".

» Then, if the event code passed to the constructor is too high, it is forced to 0 before the arrays are accessed to assign rates and manager names.

Event Type Code	Event Type	Manager	Rate ($)
1	Private	Dustin Britt	47.99
2	Corporate	Carmen Lindsey	75.99
3	Nonprofit	Robin Armanetti	40.99

Table 8-5 Events, managers, and rates charged per person

```java
public Event(int eType)
{
   double[] rateSchedule = {0.0, 47.99, 75.99, 40.99};
   String[] managerList = {"X", "Dustin Britt",
      "Carmen Lindsey", "Robin Armanetti"};
   typeOfEvent = eType;
   if(eType > rateSchedule.length)
      eType = 0;
   rate = rateSchedule[eType];
   manager = managerList[eType];
}
```

3. Save the file (as **Event.java**) and compile it.

CREATING AN APPLICATION WITH AN ARRAY OF OBJECTS

Next, you will create an application that can hold an array of `Event` class objects.

To create an application that holds an array of objects:

1. Open a new text file in your text editor to create an `EventArray` application.

2. Type the following class header, the `main()` method header, and their opening curly braces:

```java
public class EventArray
{
   public static void main(String[] args)
   {
```

3. Declare an array of five `Event` objects using the following code. You also declare an integer that can be used as a subscript:

```
Event[] someEvents = new Event[5];
int x;
```

4. Enter the following `for` loop that calls the `Event` constructor five times, making each `Event` type 1:

```
for(x = 0; x < someEvents.length; ++x)
    someEvents[x] = new Event(1);
```

5. To confirm that the `Event` objects have been created, print their values by typing the following:

```
for(x = 0; x < someEvents.length; ++x)
    System.out.println(someEvents[x].getType() +
        " " + someEvents[x].getRate() +
        " " + someEvents[x].getManager());
```

6. Add the two curly braces that end the `main()` method and the class definition.

7. Save the program as **EventArray.java**. Compile and run the application. Figure 8-30 shows the program's output, in which five type-1 `Events` are displayed.

Figure 8-30 Output of the `EventArray` application

CREATING AN INTERACTIVE APPLICATION THAT CREATES AN ARRAY OF OBJECTS

An array of five `Event` objects—each of which has the same event type and fee—is not very interesting or useful. Next, you will create an `EventArray2` application that creates the events interactively so that each event possesses unique properties.

To create an interactive `EventArray2` program:

1. Open a new file in your text editor and enter the following code to begin the class. The `main()` method contains an array of `Strings` describing the event types and two more `Strings`; the first of these `Strings` is used to construct a `choicesString` prompt, and the second is used to accept the user's response from the keyboard. In addition, you include an integer to hold the selected event number, an array of five `Event` objects, and an integer to be used as a subscript when accessing arrays:

```
import javax.swing.*;
public class EventArray2
{
    public static void main(String[] args)
    {
        String[] eventTypes = {"", "Private", "Corporate",
            "Non-profit"};
        String choicesString = "";
        String strSelectedEvent;
        int selectedEvent;
        Event[] someEvents = new Event[5];
        int x;
```

2. Add a for loop that builds the String to be used as part of the prompt for the user, listing the available choices for event types. Instead of this loop, you could declare a String as "1 Private\n2 Corporate\n3 Non-profit" and the results would be identical. However, by creating the String in a loop, you avoid being required to change this prompt if the event-type codes and names are altered in the future. Also notice that this loop begins with x = 1 because you do not want to display the 0 option:

```
for(x = 1; x < eventTypes.length; ++x)
    choicesString = choicesString + "\n" + x + " " +
        eventTypes[x];
```

3. The next for loop executes one time for each Event object that is instantiated. It prompts the user, converts the user's choice to an integer, forces the choice to 0 if it is invalid, and finally creates the object:

```
for(x = 0; x < someEvents.length; ++x)
{
    strSelectedEvent = JOptionPane.showInputDialog(null,
        "Event #" + (x + 1) +
        "Enter the number for the type of event you want" +
        choicesString);
    selectedEvent = Integer.parseInt(strSelectedEvent);
    if(selectedEvent < 1 || selectedEvent > 3)
        selectedEvent = 0;
    someEvents[x] = new Event(selectedEvent);
}
```

4. The last for loop lists the details of each created Event:

```
for(x = 0; x < someEvents.length; ++x)
    System.out.println(someEvents[x].getType() +
        " " + eventTypes[someEvents[x].getType()] +
        " " + someEvents[x].getRate() +
        " " + someEvents[x].getManager());
```

5. Add the two closing curly braces—one for the main() method and the other for the class.

6. Save the file as **EventArray2.java**. Compile and execute the application. Provide an event number at each prompt and confirm that the correct objects are created. For example, Figure 8-31 shows the output when the user enters 0, 1, 2, 3, and 4 in that order for the event types. Notice that the last event type has been forced to 0 because an invalid entry (4) was made.

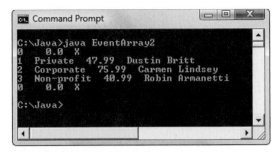

Figure 8-31 Output of the EventArray2 application

PASSING AN ARRAY TO A METHOD

Next, you will add a new method to the EventArray2 application that increases the rate for each Event. This application demonstrates that changes made to a passed array within a method permanently affect values in the array.

To add a new method to the EventArray2 class:

1. In your text editor, open the **EventArray2.java** file if it is not already open. Immediately save the file as **EventArray3.java**. Change the class name to match the filename.

2. Just before the closing curly brace for the class, add the following method that accepts two arguments—an array of Event objects and an amount by which each Event rate should be increased. Within the method, each array element is processed in a for loop that executes as many times as there are elements in the array. With each element, you use the getRate() method of the Event class to retrieve the Event current rate, add a fixed amount to it, and return the sum to the class field using the Event class setRate() method:

```
public static void increaseFees(Event[] e, double increaseAmt)
{
    int x;
    for(x = 0; x < e.length; ++x)
        e[x].setRate(e[x].getRate() + increaseAmt);
}
```

3. After the final for loop in the existing class, add the following statement, which calls the increaseFees() method, passing the array of Event objects and a flat $100.00 per event increase:

```
increaseFees(someEvents, 100.00);
```

> **NOTE**
> If you do not want to type this last println() statement, you can simply use your text editor's copy function to copy the identical statement that already exists within the program.

4. On the next lines, add a statement that heads the list of Events after the increases have taken place, and then displays all the Event details in a loop:

```
System.out.println("After increases: ");
for(x = 0; x < someEvents.length; ++x)
    System.out.println(someEvents[x].getType() +
        " " + eventTypes[someEvents[x].getType()] +
        " " + someEvents[x].getRate() +
        " " + someEvents[x].getManager());
```

5. Save the file (as **EventArray3.java**) and compile and execute the program. The output appears as shown in Figure 8-32 after the user enters 1, 2, 3, 2, and 1 as Event choices. Notice that the changes you made to each Event in the method persist when the Event array is displayed in the main() method.

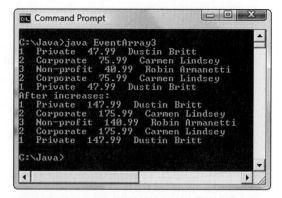

Figure 8-32 Typical output of the EventArray3 application

USING Arrays CLASS METHODS

Next, you will create an application for Event Handlers Incorporated that demonstrates several Arrays class methods. The application will allow the user to enter the menu of entrees that are available for the day. Then, it will present the menu to the user, allow a request, and indicate whether the requested item is on the menu.

To write an application that uses Arrays class methods:

1. Open a new file in your text editor and type the import statements you need to create an application that will use the JOptionPane and the Arrays classes:

```
import java.util.*;
import javax.swing.*;
```

2. Add the first few lines of the MenuSearch application class:

```
public class MenuSearch
{
    public static void main(String[] args)
    {
```

3. Declare an array to hold the day's menu choices; the user is allowed to enter up to 10 entrees. Also declare two Strings—one to hold the user's current entry and the other to accumulate the entire menu list as it is entered. The two String variables are initialized to empty Strings using quotation marks; if you do not initialize these Strings, you receive a compiler error because you might attempt to display them without having entered a legitimate value. Also, declare an integer to use as a subscript for the array, another to hold the number of menu items entered, and a third to hold the highest allowable subscript, which is 1 less than the array size:

```
String[] menuChoices = new String[10];
String entry= "", menuString = "";
int x = 0;
int numEntered;
int highestSub = menuChoices.length - 1;
```

» NOTE
Lowercase zs were purposely chosen as the array fill characters because they have a higher value than any other letter. Therefore, when the user's entries are sorted, the "zzzzzzz" entries will be at the bottom of the list.

4. Use the `Arrays.fill()` method to fill the menu array with "z" characters, as shown in the following line of code. You use this method so that when you perform a search later, actual values will be stored in any unused menu positions. If you ignore this step and fill less than half the array, your search method might generate an error.

```
Arrays.fill(menuChoices, "zzzzzzz");
```

5. Display an input dialog box into which the user can enter a menu item. Allow the user to quit before entering 10 items by typing "zzz". (Using a value such as "zzz" is a common programming technique to check for the user's desire to stop entering data. If the data items are numeric instead of text, you might use a value such as 999. Values the user enters that are not "real" data, but just signals to stop, are often called **dummy values**.) After the user enters the first menu item, the application enters a loop that continues to add the entered item to the menu list, increases the subscript, and prompts for a new menu item. The loop continues while the user has not entered "zzz" and the subscript has not exceeded the allowable limit. When the loop ends, save the number of menu items entered:

```
menuChoices[x] = JOptionPane.showInputDialog(null,
    "Enter an item for today's menu, or zzz to quit:");
while(!menuChoices[x].equals("zzz") && x < highestSub)
{
    menuString = menuString + menuChoices[x] + "\n";
    ++x;
    if(x < highestSub)
        menuChoices[x] = JOptionPane.showInputDialog(null,
            "Enter an item for today's menu, or zzz to quit");
}
numEntered = x;
```

6. When the menu is complete, display it for the user and allow the user to make a request:

```
entry = JOptionPane.showInputDialog(null,
    "Today's menu is:\n" + menuString + "Please make a selection:");
```

7. Sort the array from index position 0 to `numEntered` so that it is in ascending order prior to using the `binarySearch()` method. If you do not sort the array, the result of the `binarySearch()` method is unpredictable. You could sort the entire array, but it is more efficient to sort only the elements that hold actual menu items:

```
Arrays.sort(menuChoices, 0, numEntered);
```

8. Use the `Arrays.binarySearch()` method to search for the requested entry in the previously sorted array. If the method returns a nonnegative value that is less than the `numEntered` value, display the message "Excellent choice"; otherwise, display an error message:

```
x = Arrays.binarySearch(menuChoices, entry);
if(x >= 0 && x < numEntered)
    JOptionPane.showMessageDialog(null, "Excellent choice");
else
    JOptionPane.showMessageDialog(null,
        "Sorry - that item is not on tonight's menu");
```

9. Add the closing curly braces for the `main()` method and the class, and save the file as **MenuSearch.java**. Compile and execute the application. When prompted, enter as many menu choices as you want, and enter "zzz" when you want to quit data entry. When prompted again, enter a menu choice and observe the results. (A choice you enter must match the spelling in the menu exactly.) Figure 8-33 shows a typical menu as it is presented to the user, and the results after the user makes a valid choice.

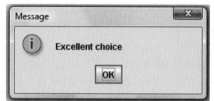

Figure 8-33 Typical execution of the `MenuSearch` application

DON'T DO IT

» Don't forget that the lowest array subscript is 0.

» Don't forget that the highest array subscript is one less than the length.

» Don't forget that `length` is an array property and not a method. Conversely, `length()` is a `String` method, and not a property.

» Don't place a subscript after an object's field or method name when accessing an array of objects. Instead, the subscript for an object follows the object and comes before the dot and the field or method name.

» Don't forget that array names are references. Therefore, you cannot assign one array to another using the = operator, nor can you compare arrays using the == operator.

» Don't use brackets with an array name when you pass it to a method. Instead, use brackets in the method header that accepts the array.

» Don't assume that an array of characters is a string. Although an array of characters can be treated like a string in languages like C++, you can't do this in Java. For example, if you display the name of a character array, you will see its address, not its contents.

» Don't forget that the first subscript used with a two-dimensional array represents the row, and that the second subscript represents the column.

KEY TERMS

An **array** is a named list of data items that all have the same type.

A **subscript** is an integer contained within square brackets that indicates one of an array's variables, or elements.

An **element** is one variable or object in an array.

Providing values for all the elements in an array is called **populating the array**.

Scalar variables are simple, primitive variables, such as `int`, `double`, or `char`.

The `length` **field** contains the number of elements in an array.

The **enhanced `for` loop** allows you to cycle through an array without specifying the starting and ending points for the loop control variable.

An object's instance variable or field is also called a **property** of the object.

Searching an array is the process of comparing a value to a list of values in an array, looking for a match.

A **parallel array** is one with the same number of elements as another, and for which the values in corresponding elements are related.

A **range match** is the process of comparing a value to the endpoints of numerical ranges to find a category in which the value belongs.

When a variable is **passed by value** to a method, a copy is made in the receiving method.

Arrays are **reference types**, meaning that the object actually holds a memory address where the values are stored.

When a value is **passed by reference** to a method, the address is passed to the method.

Sorting is the process of arranging a series of objects in some logical order.

When you place objects in order, beginning with the object that has the lowest value, you are sorting in **ascending** order.

When you place objects in order, beginning with the object that has the highest value, you are sorting in **descending** order.

A **bubble sort** is a type of sort in which you continue to compare pairs of items, swapping them if they are out of order, so that the smallest items "bubble" to the top of the list, eventually creating a sorted list.

A **one-dimensional** or **single-dimensional array** contains one column of values; you access its elements using a single subscript.

Two-dimensional arrays have two or more columns of values, and you must use two subscripts to access an element.

When mathematicians use a two-dimensional array, they often call it a **matrix** or a **table**.

A **ragged array** is a two-dimensional array that has rows of different lengths.

Multidimensional arrays contain two or more dimensions.

The Java **Arrays class** is a built-in class that contains many useful methods for manipulating arrays, such as methods to search, fill, compare, and sort arrays.

The **ArrayList class** provides a dynamically resizable container that stores lists of objects.

Dynamically resizable describes an object whose size can change during program execution.

An ArrayList's **capacity** is the number of items it can hold without having to increase its size.

Dummy values are values the user enters that are not "real" data, but just signals to stop data entry.

CHAPTER SUMMARY

» An array is a named list of data items that all have the same type. You declare an array variable in the same way you declare any simple variable, but you insert a pair of square brackets after the type. To reserve memory space for an array, you use the keyword new. You use a subscript contained within square brackets to refer to one of an array's variables, or elements. In Java, any array's elements are numbered beginning with zero.

» Array names represent computer memory addresses. When you declare an array name, no computer memory address is assigned to it. Instead, the array variable name has the special value null, or Unicode value "\u0000". When you use the keyword new, as in int[] someNums = new int[10];, then someNums has an actual memory address value. The default value for elements of a numeric array is 0, char array elements are assigned "\u0000" by default, and boolean array elements are automatically assigned false. To initialize an array to nondefault values, you use a list separated by commas and enclosed within curly braces.

» You can shorten many array-based tasks by using a variable as a subscript. When an application contains an array, it is common to perform loops that execute from 0 to one less than the size of the array. The length field is an automatically created field that is assigned to every array; it contains the number of elements in the array.

» Just as you can declare arrays of integers or doubles, you can declare arrays that hold elements of any type, including objects. To use a method that belongs to an object that is part of an array, you insert the appropriate subscript notation after the array name and before the dot that precedes the method name.

» By looping through an array and making comparisons, you can search an array to find a match to a value. You can use a parallel array with the same number of elements to hold related elements.

» You perform a range match by placing end values of a numeric range in an array and making greater-than or less-than comparisons.

» You can pass a single-array element to a method in exactly the same manner as you would pass a simple variable, and the array receives a copy of the passed value. However, arrays, like all objects, are reference types; this means that when an array name is passed to a method, the method receives a copy of the array's actual memory address and has access to the values in the original array.

» As with any other object, you can create an array of `Strings`.

» Sorting is the process of arranging a series of objects in some logical order. When you place objects in order, beginning with the object that has the lowest value, you are sorting in ascending order; conversely, when you start with the object that has the largest value, you are sorting in descending order. A bubble sort is a type of sort in which you continue to compare pairs of items, swapping them if they are out of order, so that the smallest items "bubble" to the top of the list, eventually creating a sorted list.

» You can sort arrays of objects in much the same way that you sort arrays of primitive types. The major difference occurs when you make the comparison that determines whether you want to swap two array elements. When array elements are objects, you usually want to sort based on a particular object field.

» An array that you can picture as a column of values, and whose elements you can access using a single subscript, is a one-dimensional or single-dimensional array. Two-dimensional arrays have both rows and columns. You must use two subscripts when you access an element in a two-dimensional array. When you declare a one-dimensional array, you type a set of square brackets after the array type. To declare a two-dimensional array, you type two sets of brackets after the array type.

» The Java `Arrays` class contains many useful methods for manipulating arrays. These methods provide ways to easily search, compare, fill, and sort arrays.

» The Java `ArrayList` class contains useful methods for manipulating dynamically sized arrays. You can add objects to, remove objects from, and replace objects in `ArrayList` containers.

REVIEW QUESTIONS

1. An array is a list of data items that _____ .

   a. all have the same type   c. are all integers

   b. all have different names   d. are all `null`

2. When you declare an array, _____ .

   a. you always reserve memory for it in the same statement

   b. you might reserve memory for it in the same statement

   c. you cannot reserve memory for it in the same statement

   d. the ability to reserve memory for it in the same statement depends on the type of the array

3. You reserve memory locations for an array when you _____ .

   a. declare the array name   c. use the keyword `mem`

   b. use the keyword `new`   d. explicitly store values within the array elements

4. For how many integers does the following statement reserve room?

```
int[] value = new int[34];
```

a. 0   c. 34

b. 33   d. 35

5. A(n) _____ contained within square brackets is used to indicate one of an array's elements.

a. character   c. int

b. double   d. String

6. If you declare an array as follows, how do you indicate the final element of the array?

```
int[] num = new int[6];
```

a. num[0]   c. num[5]

b. num[1]   d. impossible to tell

7. If you declare an integer array as follows, what is contained in the element num[2]?

```
int[] num = {101, 202, 303, 404, 505, 606};
```

a. 101   c. 303

b. 202   d. impossible to tell

8. Array names represent _____.

a. values   c. references

b. functions   d. allusions

9. Unicode value "\u0000" is also known as _____.

a. nil   c. nada

b. void   d. null

10. When you initialize an array by giving it values upon creation, you _____.

a. do not explicitly give the array a size

b. also must give the array a size

c. must make all the values zero, blank, or false

d. must make certain each value is different from the others

11. Assume an array is declared as follows. Which of the following statements correctly assigns the value 100 to each of the four array elements?

    ```
    int[] num = new int[4];
    ```
    a. `for (x = 0; x < 3; ++x) num[x] = 100;`

    b. `for (x = 0; x < 4; ++x) num[x] = 100;`

    c. `for (x = 1; x < 4; ++x) num[x] = 100;`

    d. `for (x = 1; x < 5; ++x) num[x] = 100;`

12. If a class named `Student` contains a method `setID()` that takes an `int` argument and you write an application in which you create an array of 20 `Student` objects named `scholar`, which of the following statements correctly assigns an ID number to the first `Student scholar`?

    a. `Student[0].setID(1234);`   c. `Student.setID[0](1234);`

    b. `scholar[0].setID(1234);`   d. `scholar.setID[0](1234);`

13. In which of the following situations would setting up parallel arrays be most useful?

    a. You need to look up an employee's ID number to find the employee's last name.

    b. You need to calculate interest earned on a savings account balance.

    c. You need to store a list of 20 commonly misspelled words.

    d. You need to determine the shortest distance between two points on a map.

14. When you pass an array element to a method, the method receives _____.

    a. a copy of the array   c. a copy of the value in the element

    b. the address of the array   d. the address of the element

15. When you pass an array to a method, the method receives _____.

    a. a copy of the array   c. the address of the array

    b. a copy of the first element in the array d. nothing

16. When you place objects in order beginning with the object with the highest value, you are sorting in _____ order.

    a. acquiescing   c. demeaning

    b. ascending   d. descending

17. Using a bubble sort involves _____ .

    a. comparing parallel arrays

    b. comparing each array element to the average

    c. comparing each array element to the adjacent array element

    d. swapping every array element with its adjacent element

18. Which array types cannot be sorted?

    a. arrays of characters   c. arrays of objects

    b. arrays of Strings   d. You can sort all of these array types.

19. When array elements are objects, you usually want to sort based on a particular _____ of the object.

    a. field   c. name

    b. method   d. type

20. The following defines a _____ array:

    ```
    int[][]nums={{1, 2}, {3, 4}, {5, 6}};
    ```

    a. one-dimensional   c. three-dimensional

    b. two-dimensional   d. six-dimensional

EXERCISES

1. Write an application that can hold five integers in an array. Display the integers from first to last, and then display the integers from last to first. Save the file as **IntArray.java**.

2. Write an application that prompts the user to make a choice for a pizza size—S, M, L, or X—and then displays the price as $6.99, $8.99, $12.50, or $15.00, accordingly. Display an error message if the user enters an invalid pizza size. Save the file as **PizzaChoice.java**.

3. a. Create a class named Taxpayer. Data fields for Taxpayer include yearly gross income and Social Security number (use an int for the type, and do not use dashes within the Social Security number). Methods include a constructor that requires values for both data fields, and two methods that each return one of the data field values. Write an application named UseTaxpayer that declares an array of 10 Taxpayer objects. Set each Social Security number to 999999999 and each gross income to zero. Display the 10 Taxpayer objects. Save the files as **Taxpayer.java** and **UseTaxpayer.java**.

   b. Modify your UseTaxpayer application so that each Taxpayer has a successive Social Security number from 1 to 10 and a gross income that ranges from $10,000 to $100,000, increasing by $10,000 for each successive Taxpayer. Save the file as **UseTaxpayer2.java**.

4. Create an application containing an array that stores 20 prices, such as $2.34, $7.89, $1.34, and so on. The application should (1) display the sum of all the prices, (2) display all values less than $5.00, (3) calculate the average of the prices, and (4) display all values that are higher than the calculated average value. Save the file as **Prices.java**.

5. a. Create a `CollegeCourse` class. The class contains fields for the course ID (for example, "CIS 210"), credit hours (for example, 3), and a letter grade (for example, 'A'). Include `get()` and `set()` methods for each field. Create a `Student` class containing an ID number and an array of five `CollegeCourse` objects. Create a `get()` and `set()` method for the `Student` ID number. Also create a `get()` method that returns one of the `Student`'s `CollegeCourses`; the method takes an integer argument and returns the `CollegeCourse` in that position (0–4). Next, create a `set()` method that sets the value of one of the `Student`'s `CollegeCourses`; the method takes two arguments—a `CollegeCourse` and an integer representing the `CollegeCourse`'s position (0–4). Save the files as **CollegeCourse.java** and **Student.java**.

   b. Write an application that prompts a professor to enter grades for five different courses each for 10 students. Prompt the professor to enter data for one student at a time, including student ID and course data for five courses. Use prompts containing the number of the student whose data is being entered and the course number—for example, "Enter ID for student #s", where s is an integer from 1 to 10, indicating the student, and "Enter course ID #n", where n is an integer from 1 to 5, indicating the course number. Verify that the professor enters only A, B, C, D, or F for the grade value for each course. Save the file as **InputGrades.java**.

6. Write an application in which the user can enter a date using digits and slashes (for example, "2/4/2010"), and receive output that displays the date with the month shown as a word (such as "February 4, 2010"). Allow for the fact that the user might or might not precede a month or day number with a zero (for example, the user might type "02/04/2010" or "2/4/2010"). Do not allow the user to enter an invalid date, defined as one for which the month is less than 1 or more than 12, or one for which the day number is less than 1 or greater than the number of days in the specified month. Also display the date's ordinal position in the year; for example, 2/4 is the 35th day. In this application, use your knowledge of arrays to store the month names, as well as values for the number of days in each month so that you can calculate the number of days that have passed. Figure 8-34 shows the output when the user has entered 2/4/2010. Save the application as **ConvertDate.java**.

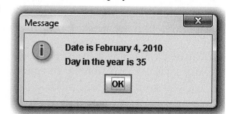

Figure 8-34 Typical execution of `ConvertDate` application

>> **NOTE** When determining whether a date is valid and when calculating the number of days that have passed, remember that some years are leap years. In a leap year, February 29th is added to the calendar. A leap year is any year that is evenly divisible by 4, unless the year is also evenly divisible by 100. So 1908 and 2008 were both leap years, but 1900 was not a leap year. Another exception occurs when a year is evenly divisible by 400—the year is a leap year. Therefore, 2000 was a leap year, but 2100 will not be one.

7. a. Write an application that stores vowels (a, e, i, o, and u) in an array. Ask the user to enter a character. Then, the program should indicate whether the entered character is a lowercase vowel. Save the file as **VowelArray.java**.

   b. Modify the `VowelArray` application so that uppercase vowels are also recognized as vowels. Save the file as **VowelArray2.java**.

8. Write an application that allows a user to enter the names and phone numbers of up to 20 friends. Continue to prompt the user for names and phone numbers until the user enters "zzz" or has entered 20 names, whichever comes first. When the user is finished entering names, produce a count of how many names were entered, but make certain not to count the application-ending dummy "zzz" entry. Then display the names. Ask the user to type one of the names and display the corresponding phone number. Save the application as **PhoneBook.java**.

9. Store 20 employee ID numbers in an integer array and 20 corresponding employee last names in a `String` array. Use dialog boxes to accept an ID number, and display the appropriate last name. Save the application as **EmployeeIDArray.java**.

10. Create an array of `String`s, each containing one of the top 10 reasons that you like Java. Prompt a user to enter a number from 1 to 10, convert the number to an integer, and then use the integer to display one of the reasons. Save the application as **JavaArray.java**.

11. Create an array of five `String`s containing the first names of people in your family. Write a program that counts and displays the total number of vowels (both uppercase and lowercase) in all five `String`s that you entered. Save the file as **Vowels.java**.

12. Write an application containing three parallel arrays that hold 10 elements each. The first array holds four-digit student ID numbers, the second holds first names, and the third holds the students' grade point averages. Use dialog boxes to accept a student ID number and display the student's first name and grade point average. If a match is not found, display an appropriate error message that contains the erroneous ID number, and allow the user to search for a new ID number. Save the file as **StudentIDArray.java**.

13. A personal phone directory contains room for first names and phone numbers for 30 people. Assign names and phone numbers for the first 10 people. Prompt the user for a name, and if the name is found in the list, display the corresponding phone number. If the name is not found in the list, prompt the user for a phone number, and add the new name and phone number to the list. Continue to prompt the user for names until the user enters "quit". After the arrays are full (containing 30 names), do not allow the user to add new entries. Save the file as **PhoneNumbers.java**.

14. a. Write an application containing an array of 15 `double` values. Include a method to sort and display the values in ascending order. Compile, run, and check the results. Save the file as **SortDoubles.java**.

    b. Modify the `SortDoubles` application to prompt the user whether to view the list in ascending or descending order. Save the file as **SortDoublesWithOption.java**.

15. a. Create a class named `LibraryBook` that contains fields to hold methods for setting and getting a `LibraryBook`'s title, author, and page count. Save the file as **LibraryBook.java**.

    b. Write an application that instantiates five `LibraryBook` objects and prompts the user for values for the data fields. Then prompt the user to enter which field the `LibraryBook`s should be sorted by—title, author, or page count. Perform the requested sort procedure and display the `LibraryBook` objects. Save the file as **LibraryBookSort.java**.

16. Write an application that stores at least four different course names and meeting days and times in a two-dimensional array. Allow the user to enter a course name (such as "CIS 110") and display the day of the week and time that the course is held (such as "Th 3:30"). If the course does not exist, display an error message. Save the file as **Schedule.java**.

17. a. Table 8-6 shows the various services offered by a hair salon, including its prices and times required:

Service Description	Price ($)	Time (Minutes)
Cut	8.00	15
Shampoo	4.00	10
Manicure	18.00	30
Style	48.00	55
Permanent	18.00	35
Trim	6.00	5

Table 8-6 Salon services, prices, and times

Create a class that holds the service description, price, and the number of minutes it takes to perform the service. Include a constructor that requires arguments for all three data fields and three get methods that each return one of the data field's values. Save the class as **Service.java**.

    b. Write an application named `SalonReport` that contains an array to hold six `Service` objects and fill it with the data from Table 8-6. Include methods to sort the array in ascending order by each of the data fields. Prompt the user for the preferred sort order, and display the list of services in the requested order. Save the program as **SalonReport.java**.

DEBUGGING EXERCISES

Each of the following files in the Chapter.08 folder on your Student Disk has syntax and/ or logic errors. In each case, determine the problem and fix the program. After you correct the errors, save each file using the same filename preceded with Fix. For example, DebugEight1.java will become FixDebugEight1.java.

a. DebugEight1.java   c. DebugEight3.java

b. DebugEight2.java   d. DebugEight4.java

GAME ZONE

1. Write an application that contains an array of 10 multiple-choice quiz questions related to your favorite hobby. Each question contains three answer choices. Also create an array that holds the correct answer to each question—A, B, or C. Display each question and verify that the user enters only A, B, or C as the answer—if not, keep prompting the user until a valid response is entered. If the user responds to a question correctly, display "Correct!"; otherwise, display "The correct answer is" and the letter of the correct answer. After the user answers all the questions, display the number of correct and incorrect answers. Save the file as **Quiz.java**.

2. a. In Chapter 4, you created a Die application that randomly "throws" five dice for the computer and five dice for the player. The application displays the values. Modify the application to decide the winner based on the following hierarchy of Die values. Any higher combination beats a lower one; for example, five of a kind beats four of a kind.

    » Five of a kind

    » Four of a kind

    » Three of a kind

    » A pair

    For this game, the dice values do not count; for example, if both players have three of a kind, it's a tie, no matter what the values are of the three dice. Additionally, the game does not recognize a full house (three of a kind plus two of a kind). Figure 8-35 shows a sample execution. Save the application as **FiveDice2.java**.

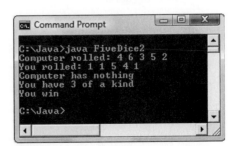

Figure 8-35 Typical execution of FiveDice2 application

b. Improve the `FiveDice2` game so that when both players have the same combination of dice, the higher value wins. For example, two 6s beats two 5s. Figure 8-36 shows an example execution. Save the application as **FiveDice3.java**.

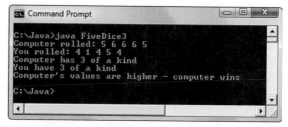

Figure 8-36 Typical execution of `FiveDice3` application

3. a. In Chapter 7, you modified a previously created `Card` class so that each `Card` would hold the name of a suit ("Spades", "Hearts", "Diamonds", or "Clubs") as well as a value ("Ace", "King", "Queen", "Jack", or a number value). Now, create an array of 52 `Card` objects, assigning a different value to each `Card`, and display each `Card`. Save the application as **FullDeck.java**.

b. In Chapter 7, you created a `War2` card game that randomly selects two `Card` objects (one for the player and one for the computer) and declares a winner or a tie based on the card values. Now create a game that plays 26 rounds of War, dealing a full deck with no repeated cards. Some hints:

» Start by creating an array of all 52 playing cards, as in Exercise 3a.

» Select a random number for the deck position of the player's first card and assign the card at that array position to the player.

» Move every higher-positioned card in the deck "down" one to fill in the gap. In other words, if the player's first random number is 49, select the card at position 49, move the card that was in position 50 to position 49, and move the card that was in position 51 to position 50. Only 51 cards remain in the deck after the player's first card is dealt, so the available-card array is smaller by one.

» In the same way, randomly select a card for the computer and "remove" the card from the deck.

» Display the values of the player's and computer's cards, compare their values, and determine the winner.

» When all the cards in the deck are exhausted, display a count of the number of times the player wins, the number of times the computer wins, and the number of ties.

Save the game as **War3.java**.

4. In Chapter 7, you created a Secret Phrase game similar to Hangman, in which the user guesses letters in a partially hidden phrase in an attempt to determine the complete phrase. Modify the program so that:

» The phrase to be guessed is selected randomly from a list of at least 10 phrases.

» The clue is presented to the user with asterisks replacing letters to be guessed, but with spaces in the appropriate locations. For example, if the phrase to be guessed is "No man is an island," then the user sees the following as a first clue:

** *** ** ** ******

The spaces provide valuable clues as to where individual words start and end.

» Make sure that when a user makes a correct guess, all the matching letters are filled in, regardless of case.

Save the game as **SecretPhrase2.java**.

5. Create a guessing game called "Does It Have Legs?", in which you think of an animal and the computer tries to guess what it is. The game continually becomes "smarter" as you play because you teach it how to become more specific with its questions. For example, a typical game session might proceed as follows:

Computer: Does the animal you are thinking of have legs?

Player: Yes.

Computer: Is it a dog?

Player: Yes.

Computer: Yay! I win. Do you want to play again?

Player: Yes.

Computer: Does the animal you are thinking of have legs?

Player: Yes.

Computer: Is it a dog?

Player: No.

Computer: I give up. What was your animal?

Player: Horse.

Computer: Type a question for which the answer is Yes for Dog but No for Horse.

Player: Does it live in the house?

Computer: Do you want to play again?

Player: Yes.

Computer: Does the animal you are thinking of have legs?

Player: Yes.

Computer: Does it live in the house?

Player: No.

Computer: Is it a Horse?

Player: No.

Computer: I give up. What was your animal?

Player: Cow.

Computer: Type a question for which the answer is Yes for Horse but No for Cow.

Player: Do people ride it?

Computer: Do you want to play again?

Player: Yes.

Computer: Does the animal you are thinking of have legs?

Player: Yes.

Computer: Does it live in the house?

Player: No.

Computer: Do people ride it?

Player: No.

Computer: Is it a Cow?

Player: Yes.

Computer: Yay! I win. Do you want to play again?

Player: No.

(Hint: You might want to look up "binary trees" on the Internet as a method to organize this application.)

Save the application as **DoesItHaveLegs.java**.

6. a. Create a Tic Tac Toe game. In this game, two players alternate placing Xs and Os into a grid until one player has three matching symbols in a row, either horizontally, vertically, or diagonally. Create a game in which the user is presented with a three-by-three grid containing the digits 1–9, similar to the first window shown in Figure 8-37. When the user chooses a position by typing a number, place an X in the appropriate spot. For example, after the user chooses 3, the screen looks like the second window in Figure 8-37. Generate a random number for the position where the computer will place an O. Do not allow the player or the computer to place a symbol where one has already been placed. When either the player or computer has three symbols in a row, declare a winner; if all positions have been exhausted and no one has three symbols in a row, declare a tie. Save the game as **TicTacToe.java**.

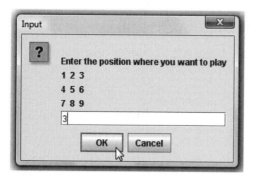 

Figure 8-37 Typical execution of TicTacToe

   b. In the `TicTacToe` application in Exercise 6a, the computer's selection is chosen randomly. Improve the `TicTacToe` game so that when the computer has two Os in any row, column, or diagonal, it selects the winning position for its next move rather than selecting a position randomly. Save the improved game as **TicTacToe2.java**.

TOUGH QUESTIONS

1. Logically speaking, why must all elements in an array have the same data type?

2. Write a method that reverses all the elements in an array of `doubles`, no matter how many elements are in the array.

3. Write a method that returns `true` or `false` to indicate whether a passed integer array contains any duplicates.

4. Write a method that displays the majority value in an integer array, if there is one. A majority value is one that resides in half or more of the elements of an array.

UP FOR DISCUSSION

1. A train schedule is an everyday, real-life example of an array. Think of at least four more.

2. In the "You Do It" section, an array is used to hold a restaurant menu. Where else do you use menus?

3. This chapter discusses sorting data. Suppose you are hired by a large hospital to write a program that displays lists of potential organ recipients. The hospital's doctors will consult this list if they have an organ that can be transplanted. You are instructed to sort potential recipients by last name and display them sequentially in alphabetical order. If more than 10 patients are waiting for a particular organ, the first 10 patients are displayed; the user can either select one of these or move on to view the next set of 10 patients. You worry that this system gives an unfair advantage to patients with last names that start with A, B, C, and D. Should you write and install the program? If you do not, many transplant opportunities will be missed while the hospital searches for another programmer to write the program.

4. This chapter discusses sorting data. Suppose your supervisor asks you to create a report that lists all employees sorted by salary. Suppose you also know that your employer will use this report to lay off the highest-paid employee in each department. Would you agree to write the program? Instead, what if the report's purpose was to list the worst performer in each department in terms of sales? What if the report grouped employees by gender? What if the report grouped employees by race? Suppose your supervisor asks you to sort employees by the dollar value of medical insurance claims they have in a year, and you fear the employer will use the report to eliminate workers who are driving up the organization's medical insurance costs. Do you agree to write the program even if you know that the purpose of the report is to eliminate workers?

9

INTRODUCTION TO INHERITANCE

In this chapter, you will:

Learn about the concept of inheritance
Extend classes
Override superclass methods
Understand how constructors are called
   during inheritance
Use superclass constructors that require arguments
Access superclass methods
Learn about information hiding
Learn which methods you cannot override

JAVA ON THE JOB, SCENE 9

"You look exhausted," Lynn Greenbrier says one Friday afternoon.

"I am," you reply. "Now that I know some Java, I am writing programs for several departments in the company. It's fun, but it's a lot of work, and the worst thing is that I seem to do the same work over and over."

"What do you mean?" Lynn asks.

"Well, the Event Planning Department asked me to develop several classes that will hold information for every event type handled by Event Handlers. There are weekday and weekend events, events with or without dinners, and events with or without guest speakers. Sure, these various types of events have differences, but all events have many things in common, such as an event number and a number of guests."

"I see," Lynn says. "So you'd like to create a class based on an existing class, just by adding the specific new components needed by the new class. You want to avoid rewriting components that you already created."

"Exactly," you say. "But, because I can't do that, I'll have to get back to work."

"Go home and relax," Lynn says. "On Monday morning, I'll teach you how to use inheritance to solve these problems."

LEARNING ABOUT THE CONCEPT OF INHERITANCE

»NOTE
In Chapter 3, you first learned about inheritance, in which a class object can inherit all the attributes of an existing class. You can create a functional new class simply by indicating how it is different from the class from which it is derived.

In Java and all object-oriented languages, **inheritance** is a mechanism that enables one class to inherit, or assume, both the behavior and the attributes of another class. Inheritance is the principle that allows you to apply your knowledge of a general category to more specific objects. You are familiar with the concept of inheritance from all sorts of nonprogramming situations.

When you use the term *inheritance*, you might think of genetic inheritance. You know from biology that your blood type and eye color are the product of inherited genes; you can say that many facts about you—your attributes, or "data fields"—are inherited. Similarly, you can often credit your behavior to inheritance. For example, your attitude toward saving money might be the same as your grandma's, and the odd way that you pull on your ear when you are tired might match what your Uncle Steve does—thus, your methods are inherited, too.

You also might choose plants and animals based on inheritance. You plant impatiens next to your house because of your shady street location; you adopt a Doberman pinscher because you need a watchdog. Every individual plant and pet has slightly different characteristics, but within a species, you can count on many consistent inherited attributes and behaviors. Similarly, the classes you create in object-oriented programming languages can inherit data and methods from existing classes. When you create a class by making it inherit from another class, you are provided with data fields and methods automatically.

Beginning with the first chapter of this book, you have been creating classes and instantiating objects that are members of those classes. Programmers and analysts sometimes use a graphical language to describe classes and object-oriented processes; this **Unified Modeling Language** (**UML**) consists of many types of diagrams.

For example, consider the simple `Employee` class shown in Figure 9-1. The class contains two data fields, `empNum` and `empSal`, and four methods, a get and set method for each field. Figure 9-2 shows a UML class diagram for the `Employee` class. A **class diagram** is a visual tool that provides you with an overview of a class. It consists of a rectangle divided into three sections—the top section contains the name of the class, the middle section contains the names and data types of the attributes, and the bottom section contains the methods. Only the method return type, name, and arguments are provided in the diagram—the instructions that make up the method body are omitted.

>> **NOTE**
By convention, a class diagram contains the data type following each attribute or method, as shown in Figure 9-2. A minus sign (–) is inserted in front of each private field or method, and a plus sign (+) is inserted in front of each public field or method.

```java
public class Employee
{
    private int empNum;
    private double empSal;
    public int getEmpNum()
    {
        return empNum;
    }
    public double getEmpSal()
    {
        return empSal;
    }
    public void setEmpNum(int num)
    {
        empNum = num;
    }
    public void setEmpSal(double sal)
    {
        empSal = sal;
    }
}
```

Figure 9-1 The `Employee` class

Employee
-empNum : **int**
-empSal : **double**
+getEmpNum : **int**
+getEmpSal : **double**
+setEmpNum(**int** num) : **void**
+setEmpSal(**double** sal) : **void**

Figure 9-2 The `Employee` class diagram

>> **NOTE**   Commonly, UML diagram creators refrain from using Java terminology such as `int` in a class diagram. Instead, they might use a more general term, such as integer. The `Employee` class is designed in natural language (English) and might be implemented in any programming language, and languages other than Java might use a different keyword to designate integer variables. Because you are studying Java, this book uses the Java keywords in diagrams. For more information on UML, you can go to the Object Management Group's Web site at *www.omg.org*. OMG is an international, nonprofit computer industry consortium.

After you create the Employee class, you can create specific Employee objects, such as the following:

```
Employee receptionist = new Employee();
Employee deliveryPerson = new Employee();
```

These Employee objects can eventually possess different numbers and salaries, but because they are Employee objects, you know that each Employee has *some* number and salary.

Suppose you hire a new type of Employee named serviceRep, and that a serviceRep object requires not only an employee number and a salary, but also a data field to indicate territory served. You can create a class with a name such as EmployeeWithTerritory, and provide the class three fields (empNum, empSal, and empTerritory) and six methods (get and set methods for each of the three fields). However, when you do this, you are duplicating much of the work that you have already done for the Employee class. The wise, efficient alternative is to create the class EmployeeWithTerritory so it inherits all the attributes and methods of Employee. Then, you can add just the one field and two methods that are new within EmployeeWithTerritory objects. Figure 9-3 shows a class diagram of this relationship; the arrow that extends from the EmployeeWithTerritory class and points to the Employee class shows the inheritance relationship.

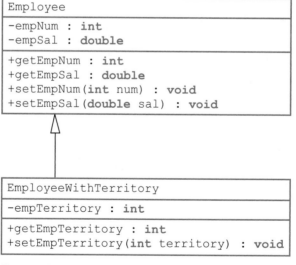

Figure 9-3 Class diagram showing the relationship between Employee and EmployeeWithTerritory

When you use inheritance to create the EmployeeWithTerritory class, you:

» Save time because the Employee fields and methods already exist

» Reduce errors because the Employee methods have already been used and tested

» Reduce the amount of new learning required to use the new class, because you have used the Employee methods on simpler objects and already understand how they work

The ability to use inheritance in Java makes programs easier to write, less error-prone, and more quickly understood. Besides creating `EmployeeWithTerritory`, you can also create several other specific `Employee` classes (perhaps `EmployeeEarningCommission`, including a commission rate, or `DismissedEmployee`, including a reason for dismissal). By using inheritance, you can develop each new class correctly and more quickly.

>> **NOTE** In Chapter 4, you learned about the `GregorianCalendar` class. It descends from a more general class named `Calendar`.

A class that is used as a basis for inheritance, such as `Employee`, is a **base class**. When you create a class that inherits from a base class (such as `EmployeeWithTerritory`), it is a **derived class**. When considering two classes that inherit from each other, you can tell which is the base class and which is the derived class by using the two classes in a sentence with the phrase "is a(n)." A derived class always "is a" case or example of the more general base class. For example, a `Tree` class can be a base class to an `Evergreen` class. An `Evergreen` "is a" `Tree`, so `Tree` is the base class; however, it is not true for all `Tree`s that "a `Tree` is an `Evergreen`." Similarly, an `EmployeeWithTerritory` "is an" `Employee`—but not the other way around—so `Employee` is the base class.

>> **NOTE** Do not confuse "is a" situations with "has a" situations. For example, you might create a `Business` class that contains an array of `Department` objects; in turn, each `Department` object might contain an array of `Employee` objects. You would not say "A department is a business," but that "a business has departments." Therefore, this relationship is not inheritance; it is **composition**—the relationship in which a class contains one or more members of another class, when those members would not continue to exist without the object that contains them. (For example, if a `Business` closes, its `Department`s do too.) Similarly, you would not say "an employee is a department," but that "a department has employees." This relationship is not inheritance either; it is a specific type of composition known as **aggregation**—the relationship in which a class contains one or more members of another class, when those members would continue to exist without the object that contains them. (For example, if a business or department closed, the employees would continue to exist.)

You can use the terms **superclass** and **subclass** as synonyms for base class and derived class, respectively. Thus, `Evergreen` can be called a subclass of the `Tree` superclass. You can also use the terms **parent class** and **child class**. An `EmployeeWithTerritory` is a child to the `Employee` parent. Use the pair of terms with which you are most comfortable; all of these terms are used interchangeably throughout this book.

As an alternative way to discover which of two classes is the base class or subclass, you can try saying the two class names together. When people say their names together, they state the more specific name before the all-encompassing family name, as in "Ginny Kroening." Similarly, with classes, the order that "makes more sense" is the child-parent order. "Evergreen Tree" makes more sense than "Tree Evergreen," so `Evergreen` is the child class.

Finally, you can usually distinguish superclasses from their subclasses by size. Although it is not required, in general a subclass is larger than a superclass because it usually has additional fields and methods. A subclass description might look small, but any subclass contains all the fields and methods of its superclass, as well as the new, more specific fields and methods you add to that subclass.

>> **NOTE**
The concept of inheritance is useful because it makes class code reusable. Each method already written and tested in the original class becomes part of the new class that inherits it.

>> **NOTE**
Because a derived class object "is an" instance of the base class, too, you can assign a derived class object's reference to a base class reference. Similarly, if a method accepts a base class object reference, it will also accept references to its derived classes.

EXTENDING CLASSES

You use the keyword **extends** to achieve inheritance in Java. For example, the following class header creates a superclass-subclass relationship between Employee and EmployeeWithTerritory:

```
public class EmployeeWithTerritory extends Employee
```

Each EmployeeWithTerritory automatically receives the data fields and methods of the superclass Employee; you then add new fields and methods to the newly created subclass. Figure 9-4 shows an EmployeeWithTerritory class.

```
public class EmployeeWithTerritory extends Employee
{
    private int empTerritory;
    public int getEmpTerritory()
    {
        return empTerritory;
    }
    public void setEmpTerritory(int num)
    {
        empTerritory = num;
    }
}
```

Figure 9-4 The EmployeeWithTerritory class

You can write a statement that instantiates an object, such as the following:

```
EmployeeWithTerritory northernRep = new EmployeeWithTerritory();
```

Then you can use any of the next statements to get field values for the northernRep object:

```
northernRep.getEmpNum();
northernRep.getEmpSal();
northernRep.getEmpTerritory();
```

The northernRep object has access to all three get methods—two methods that it inherits from Employee and one method that belongs to EmployeeWithTerritory.

Similarly, after the northernRep object is declared, any of the following statements are legal:

```
northernRep.setEmpNum(915);
northernRep.setEmpSal(210.00);
northernRep.setEmpTerritory(5);
```

The northernRep object has access to all the parent Employee class set methods, as well as its own class's new set method.

Inheritance is a one-way proposition; a child inherits from a parent, not the other way around. When you instantiate an Employee object, as in Employee aClerk = new Employee();, the Employee object does not have access to the EmployeeWithTerritory methods. Employee is the parent class, and aClerk is an object of the parent class. It makes sense that a parent class object does not have access to its child's data and methods. When you create the parent class, you do not know how many future subclasses it might have or what their data or methods might look like.

In addition, subclasses are more specific than the superclass they extend. An Orthodontist class and Periodontist class are children of the Dentist parent class. You do not expect all members of the general parent class Dentist to have the Orthodontist's applyBraces() method or the Periodontist's deepClean() method. However, Orthodontist objects and Periodontist objects have access to the more general Dentist methods conductExam() and billPatients().

Within a program, you can use the **instanceof operator** to determine whether an object is a member or descendant of a class. For example, if northernRep is an EmployeeWithTerritory object, then the value of each of the following expressions is true:

```
northernRep instanceof EmployeeWithTerritory
northernRep instanceof Employee
```

If aClerk is an Employee object, then the following is true:

```
aClerk instanceof Employee
```

However, the following is false:

```
aClerk instanceof EmployeeWithTerritory
```

> **»NOTE**
> Programmers say that instanceof yields true if the operand on the left can be **upcast** to the operand on the right.

»TWO TRUTHS AND A LIE: EXTENDING CLASSES

1. You use the keyword inherits to achieve inheritance in Java.
2. A derived class has access to all its parents' nonprivate methods.
3. Subclasses are more specific than the superclass they extend.

The false statement is #1. You use the keyword extends to achieve inheritance in Java.

OVERRIDING SUPERCLASS METHODS

When you create a subclass by extending an existing class, the new subclass contains data and methods that were defined in the original superclass. In other words, any child class object has all the attributes of its parent. Sometimes, however, the superclass data fields and methods are not entirely appropriate for the subclass objects; in these cases, you want to override the parent class members.

» NOTE
You first learned the term *polymorphism* in Chapter 1. Polymorphism is one of the basic principles of object-oriented programming. If a programming language does not support polymorphism, the language is not considered object-oriented.

When you use the English language, you often use the same method name to indicate diverse meanings. For example, if you think of `MusicalInstrument` as a class, you can think of `play()` as a method of that class. If you think of various subclasses such as `Guitar` and `Drum`, you know that you carry out the `play()` method quite differently for each subclass. Using the same method name to indicate different implementations is called **polymorphism**, a term that means "many forms"—many different forms of action take place, even though you use the same word to describe the action. In other words, many forms of the same word exist, depending on the object associated with the word.

For example, suppose you create an `Employee` superclass containing data fields such as `firstName`, `lastName`, `socialSecurityNumber`, `dateOfHire`, `rateOfPay`, and so on, and the methods contained in the `Employee` class include the usual collection of get and set methods. If your usual time period for payment to each `Employee` object is weekly, your `printRateOfPay()` method might include a statement such as:

```
System.out.println("Pay is " + rateOfPay + " per week");
```

Imagine your company has a few `Employees` who are not paid weekly. Maybe some are paid by the hour, and others are `Employees` whose work is contracted on a job-to-job basis. Because each `Employee` type requires different paycheck-calculating procedures, you might want to create subclasses of `Employee`, such as `HourlyEmployee` and `ContractEmployee`.

When you call the `printRateOfPay()` method for an `HourlyEmployee` object, you want the display to include the phrase "per hour", as in "Pay is $8.75 per hour". When you call the `printRateOfPay()` method for a `ContractEmployee`, you want to include "per contract", as in "Pay is $2000 per contract". Each class—the `Employee` superclass and the two subclasses—requires its own `printRateOfPay()` method. Fortunately, if you create separate `printRateOfPay()` methods for each class, the objects of each class use the appropriate method for that class. When you create a method in a child class that has the same name and parameter list as a method in its parent class, you **override the method** in the parent class. When you use the method name with a child object, the child's version of the method is used.

» NOTE
You first saw the term *override* in Chapter 4, when you learned that a variable declared within a block overrides another variable with the same name declared outside the block.

» NOTE It is important to note that each subclass method overrides any method in the parent class that has both the same name and parameter list. If the parent class method has the same name but a different parameter list, the subclass method does not override the parent class version; instead, the subclass method overloads the parent class method and any subclass object has access to both versions. You learned about overloading methods in Chapter 4.

If you could not override superclass methods, you could always create a unique name for each subclass method, such as `printRateOfPayForHourly()`, but the classes you create are easier to write and understand if you use one reasonable name for methods that do essentially the same thing. Because you are attempting to print the rate of pay for each object, `printRateOfPay()` is an excellent method name for all the object types.

Object-oriented programmers use the term *polymorphism* when discussing any operation that has multiple meanings. For example, the plus sign (+) is polymorphic because you can use it to add integers or `doubles`, to concatenate strings, or to indicate a positive value. As another example, methods with the same name but different argument lists are polymorphic because the method call operates differently depending on the arguments. When Java developers refer to polymorphism, they most often mean **subtype polymorphism**—the ability of one method name to work appropriately for different subclass objects of the same parent class.

»NOTE
A child class object can use an overridden parent's method by using the keyword `super`. You will learn about this word later in this chapter.

»TWO TRUTHS AND A LIE: OVERRIDING SUPERCLASS METHODS

1. Any child class object has all the attributes of its parent, but all of those attributes might not be directly accessible.

2. You override a parent class method by creating a child class method with the same identifier but a different parameter list or return type.

3. When a child class method overrides a parent class method, and you use the method name with a child class object, the child class method version executes.

The false statement is #2. You override a parent class method by creating a child class method with the same identifier and parameter list. The return type is not a factor in overloading.

UNDERSTANDING HOW CONSTRUCTORS ARE CALLED DURING INHERITANCE

When you create any object, as in the following statement, you are calling a class constructor that has the same name as the class itself:

```
SomeClass anObject = new SomeClass();
```

When you instantiate an object that is a member of a subclass, you are actually calling at least two constructors: the constructor for the base class and the constructor for the extended, derived class. When you create any subclass object, the superclass constructor must execute first, and *then* the subclass constructor executes.

When a superclass contains a default constructor and you instantiate a subclass object, the execution of the superclass constructor is often transparent—that is, nothing calls attention to the fact that the superclass constructor is executing. However, you should realize that when you create an object such as the following (where `HourlyEmployee` is a subclass of `Employee`), *both* the `Employee()` and `HourlyEmployee()` constructors execute:

```
HourlyEmployee clerk = new HourlyEmployee();
```

»NOTE
In Chapter 10, you will learn that every Java object automatically is a child of a class named `Object`. So, when you instantiate any object, you call its constructor and `Object`'s constructor, and when you create parent and child classes of your own, the child classes use three constructors.

For example, Figure 9-5 shows three classes. The class named ASuperClass has a constructor that displays a message. The class named ASubClass descends from ASuperClass, and its constructor displays a different message. The DemoConstructors class contains just one statement that instantiates one object of type ASubClass.

```java
public class ASuperClass
{
   public ASuperClass()
   {
      System.out.println("In superclass constructor");
   }
}
public class ASubClass extends ASuperClass
{
   public ASubClass()
   {
      System.out.println("In subclass constructor");
   }
}
public class DemoConstructors
{
   public static void main(String[] args)
   {
      ASubClass child = new ASubClass();
   }
}
```

Figure 9-5 Three classes that demonstrate constructor calling when a subclass object is instantiated

Figure 9-6 shows the output when DemoConstructors executes. You can see that when DemoConstructors instantiates the ASubClass object, the parent class constructor executes first, displaying its message, and then the child class constructor executes. Even though only one object is created, two constructors execute.

Figure 9-6 Output of the DemoConstructors application

Of course, most constructors perform many more tasks than printing a message to inform you that they exist. When constructors initialize variables, you usually want the superclass constructor to take care of initializing the data fields that originate in the superclass. Usually, the subclass constructor only needs to initialize the data fields that are specific to the subclass.

USING SUPERCLASS CONSTRUCTORS THAT REQUIRE ARGUMENTS

When you create a class and do not provide a constructor, Java automatically supplies you with a default constructor—one that never requires arguments. When you write your own constructor, you replace the automatically supplied version. Depending on your needs, a constructor you create for a class might be a default constructor or might require arguments. When you use a class as a superclass and the class has only constructors that require arguments, you must be certain that any subclasses provide the superclass constructor with the arguments it needs.

When a superclass has a default constructor, you can create a subclass with or without its own constructor. This is true whether the default constructor is the automatically supplied one or one you have written. However, when a superclass contains only constructors that require arguments, you must include at least one constructor for each subclass you create. Your subclass constructors can contain any number of statements, but if all superclass constructors require arguments, then the first statement within each subclass constructor must call the superclass constructor. When a superclass requires arguments upon object instantiation, even if you have no other reason to create a subclass constructor, you must write the subclass constructor so it can call its superclass's constructor.

The format of the statement that calls a superclass constructor is:

```
super(list of arguments);
```

The keyword **super** always refers to the superclass of the class in which you use it. If a superclass contains only constructors that require arguments, you must create a subclass constructor, but the subclass constructor does not necessarily have to have parameters of its own. For example, suppose that you create an `Employee` class with a constructor that requires three arguments—a character, a `double`, and an integer—and you create an

» NOTE
Except for any comments, the super() statement must be the first statement in any subclass constructor that uses it. Not even data field definitions can precede it.

HourlyEmployee class that is a subclass of Employee. The following code shows a valid constructor for HourlyEmployee:

```
public HourlyEmployee()
{
    super('P', 12.35, 40);
    // Other statements can go here
}
```

This version of the HourlyEmployee constructor requires no arguments, but it passes three constant arguments to its superclass constructor. A different, overloaded version of the HourlyEmployee constructor can require arguments. It could then pass the appropriate arguments to the superclass constructor. For example:

» NOTE
Although it seems that you should be able to use the superclass constructor name to call the superclass constructor—for example, Employee()—Java does not allow this. You must use the keyword super.

```
public HourlyEmployee(char dept, double rate, int hours)
{
    super(dept, rate, hours);
    // Other statements can go here
}
```

» NOTE In Chapter 4, you learned that you can call one constructor from another using this(). In this chapter, you learned that you can call a base class constructor from a derived class using super(). However, you cannot use both this() and super() in the same constructor because each is required to be the first statement in any constructor in which it appears.

»TWO TRUTHS AND A LIE: USING SUPERCLASS CONSTRUCTORS THAT REQUIRE ARGUMENTS

1. When a superclass has a default constructor, you can create a subclass with or without its own constructor.
2. When a superclass contains only nondefault constructors, you must include at least one constructor for each subclass you create.
3. The first statement within any subclass constructor must include the keyword super.

The false statement is #3. If a superclass contains only nondefault constructors, then the first statement within any subclass constructor must include the keyword super.

ACCESSING SUPERCLASS METHODS

Earlier in this chapter, you learned that a subclass could contain a method with the same name and arguments (the same signature) as a method in its parent class. When this happens, using the subclass method overrides the superclass method. However, you might want to use the superclass method within a subclass that contains an overriding method. If so, you can use the keyword super to access the parent class method.

For example, examine the Customer class in Figure 9-7 and the PreferredCustomer class in Figure 9-8. A Customer has an idNumber and balanceOwed. In addition to these fields, a

PreferredCustomer receives a discountRate. In the PreferredCustomer display() method, you want to display all three fields—idNumber, balanceOwed, and discountRate. Because two-thirds of the code to accomplish the display has already been written for the Customer class, it is convenient to have the PreferredCustomer display() method use its parent's version of the display() method before printing its own discount rate. Figure 9-9 shows a brief application that displays one object of each class, and Figure 9-10 shows the output.

```java
public class Customer
{
    private int idNumber;
    private double balanceOwed;
    public Customer(int id, double bal)
    {
        idNumber = id;
        balanceOwed = bal;
    }
    public void display()
    {
        System.out.println("Customer #" + idNumber +
          " Balance $" + balanceOwed);
    }
}
```

Figure 9-7 The Customer class

```java
public class PreferredCustomer extends Customer
{
    double discountRate;
    public PreferredCustomer(int id, double bal, double rate)
    {
        super(id, bal);
        discountRate = rate;
    }
    public void display()
    {
        super.display();
        System.out.println("Discount rate is " + discountRate);
    }
}
```

Figure 9-8 The PreferredCustomer class

> **» NOTE**
> Unlike when you call a superclass constructor from a subclass constructor, when you call an ordinary superclass method within a subclass method, the call is not required to be the first statement in the method.

```
public class TestCustomers
{
    public static void main(String[] args)
    {
        Customer oneCust = new Customer(124, 123.45);
        PreferredCustomer onePCust = new
            PreferredCustomer(125, 3456.78, 0.15);
        oneCust.display();
        onePCust.display();
    }
}
```

Figure 9-9 The TestCustomers application

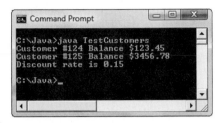

Figure 9-10 Output of the TestCustomers application

COMPARING this AND super

Within a subclass, you can think of the keyword this as the opposite of super.

For example, if a subclass has overridden a superclass method named someMethod(), then within the subclass, super.someMethod() refers to the superclass version of the method, and both someMethod() and this.someMethod() refer to the subclass version.

On the other hand, when a parent class contains a method that is not overridden within its child, the child can use the method name with super (because the method is a member of the superclass), with this (because the method is a member of the subclass by virtue of inheritance), or alone (again, because the method is a member of the subclass).

»TWO TRUTHS AND A LIE: ACCESSING SUPERCLASS METHODS

1. You can use the keyword this from within a derived class method to access an overridden base class method.
2. You can use the keyword super from within a derived class method to access an overridden base class method.
3. You can use the keyword super from within a derived class method to access a base class method that has not been overridden.

The false statement is #1. You can use the keyword super from within a derived class method to access an overridden base class method; if you use the keyword this, then you will access the overriding subclass method.

LEARNING ABOUT INFORMATION HIDING

The Student class shown in Figure 9-11 is an example of a typical Java class. Within the Student class, as with most Java classes, the keyword private precedes each data field, and the keyword public precedes each method. In fact, the four get and set methods are public within the Student class specifically because the data fields are private. Without the public get and set methods, there would be no way to access the private data fields.

```
public class Student
{
    private int idNum;
    private double gpa;
    public int getIdNum()
    {
        return idNum;
    }
    public double getGpa()
    {
        return gpa;
    }
    public void setIdNum(int num)
    {
        idNum = num;
    }
    public void setGpa(double gradePoint)
    {
        gpa = gradePoint;
    }
}
```

Figure 9-11 The Student class

When an application is a client of the Student class (that is, it instantiates a Student object), the client cannot directly alter the data in any private field. For example, when you write a main() method that creates a Student as:

```
Student someStudent = new Student();
```

you cannot change the Student's idNum with a statement such as:

```
someStudent.idNum = 812;
```

> **DON'T DO IT**
> You cannot access a private data member of an object.

The idNum of the someStudent object is not accessible in the main() method that uses the Student object because idNum is private. Only methods that are part of the Student class itself are allowed to alter private Student data. To alter a Student's idNum, you must use a public method, as in the following:

```
someStudent.setIdNum(812);
```

The concept of keeping data private is known as **information hiding**. When you employ information hiding, your data can be altered only by the methods you choose and only in ways that you can control. For example, you might want the setIdNum() method to check to make certain the idNum is within a specific range of values. If a class other than the Student class could alter idNum, idNum could be assigned a value that the Student class couldn't control.

> **NOTE**
> You first learned about information hiding and using the public and private keywords in Chapter 3. You might want to review these concepts.

»NOTE
If the members of a base class don't have an explicit modifier, their access modifier is package by default. Such base class members cannot be accessed within a child class unless the two classes are in the same package. You will learn about packages in Chapter 10.

When a class serves as a superclass to other classes you create, your subclasses inherit all the data and methods of the superclass. The methods in a subclass can use all of the data fields and methods that belong to its parent, with one exception: private members of the parent class are not accessible within a child class's methods. If you could use private data outside its class, you would lose the advantages of information hiding. For example, if you want the Student class data field idNum to be private, you don't want any outside classes using the field. If a new class could simply extend your Student class and get to its data fields without going through the proper channels, information hiding would not be operating.

Sometimes, you want to access parent class data from within a subclass. For example, suppose you create two child classes—PartTimeStudent and FullTimeStudent—that extend the Student class. If you want the subclass methods to be able to directly access idNum and gpa, these data fields cannot be private. However, if you don't want other, nonchild classes to access these data fields, they cannot be public. To solve this problem, you can create the fields using the modifier protected. Using the keyword **protected** provides you with an intermediate level of security between public and private access. If you create a protected data field or method, it can be used within its own class or in any classes extended from that class, but it cannot be used by "outside" classes. In other words, protected members are those that can be used by a class and its descendants.

»NOTE
Classes that depend on field names from parent classes are said to be **fragile** because they are prone to errors—that is, they are easy to "break."

You are seldom required to make parent class fields protected. A child class can access its parent's private data fields by using public methods defined in the parent class, just as any other class can. You only need to make parent class fields protected if you want child classes to be able to access private data directly. (For example, perhaps you do not want a parent class to have a get method for a field, but you do want a child class to be able to access the field.) Using the protected access modifier for a field can be convenient, and it also improves program performance because a child class can use an inherited field directly instead of "going through" methods to access the data. However, protected data members should be used sparingly. Whenever possible, the principle of information hiding should be observed, so even child classes should have to go through public methods to "get to" their parent's private data. When child classes are allowed direct access to a parent's fields, the likelihood of future errors increases.

»TWO TRUTHS AND A LIE: LEARNING ABOUT INFORMATION HIDING

1. Information hiding describes the concept of keeping data private.
2. A subclass inherits all the data and methods of its superclass, except the private ones.
3. If a data field is defined as protected, then a method in a child class can use it directly.

The false statement is #2. A subclass inherits all the data and methods of its superclass, but it cannot access the private ones directly.

METHODS YOU CANNOT OVERRIDE

Sometimes when you create a class, you might choose not to allow subclasses to override some of the superclass methods. For example, an `Employee` class might contain a method that calculates each `Employee`'s ID number based on specific `Employee` attributes, and you might not want any derived classes to be able to alter this method. As another example, perhaps a class contains a statement that displays legal restrictions to using the class. You might decide that no derived class should be able to alter the statement that is displayed.

The three types of methods that you cannot override in a subclass are:

- » `static` methods
- » `final` methods
- » Methods within `final` classes

A SUBCLASS CANNOT OVERRIDE `static` METHODS IN ITS SUPERCLASS

A subclass cannot override methods that are declared `static` in the superclass. In other words, a subclass cannot override a class method—a method you use without instantiating an object. A subclass can *hide* a `static` method in the superclass by declaring a `static` method in the subclass with the same signature as the `static` method in the superclass; then, you can call the new `static` method from within the subclass or in another class by using a subclass object. However, this `static` method that hides the superclass `static` method cannot access the parent method using the `super` object.

Figure 9-12 shows a `BaseballPlayer` class that contains a single `static` method named `printOrigins()`. Figure 9-13 shows a `ProfessionalBaseballPlayer` class that extends the `BaseballPlayer` class to provide a salary. Within the `ProfessionalBaseballPlayer` class, an attempt is made to override the `printOrigins()` method to display the general Abner Doubleday message about baseball as well as the more specific message about professional baseball. However, the compiler returns the error message shown in Figure 9-14—you cannot override a `static` method with a nonstatic method.

```
public class BaseballPlayer
{
    private int jerseyNumber;
    private double battingAvg;
    public static void printOrigins()
    {
        System.out.println("Abner Doubleday is often " +
            "credited with inventing baseball");
    }
}
```

Figure 9-12 The `BaseballPlayer` class

```
public class ProfessionalBaseballPlayer extends BaseballPlayer
{
    double salary;
    public void printOrigins()
    {
        super.printOrigins();
        System.out.println("The first professional " +
            "major league baseball game was played in 1871");
    }
}
```

>> DON'T DO IT
You cannot override a static member of a parent class.

Figure 9-13 The `ProfessionalBaseballPlayer` class attempting to override the parent's `static` method

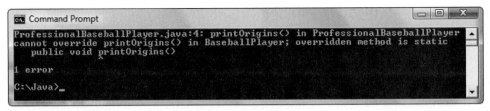

Figure 9-14 Error message when compiling the `ProfessionalBaseballPlayer` class in Figure 9-13

Figure 9-15 shows a second version of the `ProfessionalBaseballPlayer` class. In this version, the `printOrigins()` method has been changed to `static`. Figure 9-16 shows the error message that displays, proving that the parent class method is not overridden.

```
public class ProfessionalBaseballPlayer extends BaseballPlayer
{
    double salary;
    public static void printOrigins()
    {
        super.printOrigins();
        System.out.println("The first professional " +
            "major league baseball game was played in 1871");
    }
}
```

>> DON'T DO IT
You cannot override a static member of a parent class.

Figure 9-15 The `ProfessionalBaseballPlayer` class attempting to reference `super`

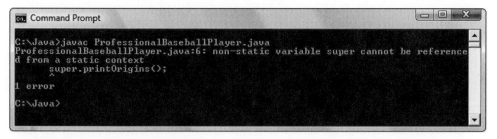

Figure 9-16 Error message when compiling the `ProfessionalBaseballPlayer` class in Figure 9-15

Finally, Figure 9-17 shows a `ProfessionalBaseballPlayer` class that compiles without error. Its `printOrigins()` method is `static`. Because this method has the same name as the parent class method, when you use the name with a child class object, this method hides the original. However, it does not override the original, or the `super` call in the version of the method in Figure 9-15 would have compiled without error. If you want the `ProfessionalBaseballPlayer` class to display information about baseball in general as well as professional baseball in particular, you can do either of the following:

» You can display both messages from within a child class method with `println()` statements.

» You can use the parent class name, a dot, and the method name. Although a child class cannot inherit its parent's `static` methods, it can access its parent's `static` methods the same way any other class can.

```java
public class ProfessionalBaseballPlayer extends BaseballPlayer
{
   double salary;
   public static void printOrigins()
   {
      BaseballPlayer.printOrigins();
      System.out.println("The first professional " +
         "major league baseball game was played in 1871");
   }
}
```

Figure 9-17 The `ProfessionalBaseballPlayer` class

Figure 9-18 shows a class that creates a `ProfessionalBaseballPlayer` and tests the method; Figure 9-19 shows the output.

```
public class TestProPlayer
{
    public static void main(String[] args)
    {
        ProfessionalBaseballPlayer aYankee =
            new ProfessionalBaseballPlayer();
        aYankee.printOrigins();
    }
}
```

Figure 9-18 The `TestProPlayer` class

Figure 9-19 Output of the `TestProPlayer` application

A SUBCLASS CANNOT OVERRIDE final METHODS IN ITS SUPERCLASS

A subclass cannot override methods that are declared `final` in the superclass. For example, consider the `BasketballPlayer` and `ProfessionalBasketballPlayer` classes in Figures 9-20 and 9-21, respectively. When you attempt to compile the `ProfessionalBasketballPlayer` class, you receive the error message in Figure 9-22, because the class cannot override the `final printMessage()` method in the parent class.

```
public class BasketballPlayer
{
    private int jerseyNumber;
    public final void printMessage()
    {
        System.out.println("Michael Jordan is the " +
            "greatest basketball player - and that is final");
    }
}
```

Figure 9-20 The `BasketballPlayer` class

```
public class ProfessionalBasketballPlayer extends BasketballPlayer
{
    double salary;
    public void printMessage()

    {
        System.out.println("I have nothing to say");
    }
}
```

»DON'T DO IT

A child class method cannot override a final parent class method.

Figure 9-21 The `ProfessionalBasketballPlayer` class that attempts to override a `final` method

Figure 9-22 Error message when compiling the `ProfessionalBasketballPlayer` class in Figure 9-21

»NOTE If you make the `printMessage()` method `final` in the `ProfessionalBasketballPlayer` class in Figure 9-21, you receive the same compiler error message shown in Figure 9-22. If you make the `printMessage()` method `static` in the `ProfessionalBasketballPlayer` class, the class does not compile, but you do receive an additional error message.

In Chapter 2, you learned that you can use the keyword `final` when you want to create a constant, as in `final double TAXRATE = 0.065;`. You can also use the `final` modifier with methods when you don't want the method to be overridden—that is, when you want every child class to use the original parent class version of a method.

In Java, all instance method calls are **virtual method calls** by default—that is, the method used is determined when the program runs because the type of the object used might not be known until the method executes. For example, with the following method you can pass in a `BasketballPlayer` object, or any object that is a child of `BasketballPlayer`, so the "actual" type of the argument `bbplayer`, and which version of `printMessage()` to use, is not known until the method executes.

```
public void display(BasketballPlayer bbplayer)
{
    bbplayer.printMessage();
}
```

In other words, the version of `printMessage()` that is called is not determined when the program is compiled; it is determined when the method call is made. An advantage to making a method `final` is that the compiler knows there will be only one version of the method—the parent class version. Therefore, the compiler *does* know which method version will be used—the only version.

Because a `final` method's definition can never change—that is, can never be overridden with a modified version—the compiler can optimize a program's performance by removing the calls to `final` methods and replacing them with the expanded code of their definitions at each method call location. This process is called **inlining** the code. You are never aware that inlining is taking place; the compiler chooses to use this procedure to save the overhead of calling a method, and this makes the program run faster. The compiler chooses to inline a `final` method only if it is a small method that contains just one or two lines of code.

A SUBCLASS CANNOT OVERRIDE METHODS IN A `final` SUPERCLASS

You can declare a class to be `final`. When you do, all of its methods are `final`, regardless of which access modifier precedes the method name. A `final` class cannot be a parent. Figure 9-23 shows two classes: a `HideAndGoSeekPlayer` class that is a `final` class because of the word `final` in the class header, and a `ProfessionalHideAndGoSeekPlayer` class that attempts to extend the `final` class, adding a salary field. Figure 9-24 shows the error message generated when you try to compile the `ProfessionalHideAndGoSeekPlayer` class.

»NOTE
Java's `Math` class, which you learned about in Chapter 4, is an example of a `final` class.

```
public final class HideAndGoSeekPlayer
{
    private int count;
    public void printRules()
    {
        System.out.println("You have to count to " + count +
            " before you start looking for hiders");
    }
}
public final class ProfessionalHideAndGoSeekPlayer
    extends HideAndGoSeekPlayer
{
    private double salary;
}
```

»DON'T DO IT
You cannot extend a `final` class.

Figure 9-23 The `HideAndGoSeekPlayer` and `ProfessionalHideAndGoSeekPlayer` classes

»NOTE
A subclass cannot override a method in a `final` class. Conversely, a subclass *is required* to override methods that are declared `abstract` in the superclass (or the subclass itself must be `abstract`). You will learn about `abstract` classes and methods in Chapter 10.

Figure 9-24 Error message when compiling the `ProfessionalHideAndGoSeekPlayer` class in Figure 9-23

»TWO TRUTHS AND A LIE: METHODS YOU CANNOT OVERRIDE

1. A subclass cannot override methods that are declared `static` in the superclass.
2. A subclass cannot override methods that are declared `final` in the superclass.
3. A subclass cannot override methods that are declared `private` in the superclass.

The false statement is #3. A subclass can override `private` methods as well as `public` or `protected` ones.

YOU DO IT

In this section, you create a working example of inheritance. To see the effects of inheritance, you create this example in four stages:

» First, you create a general `Event` class for Event Handlers Incorporated. This `Event` class is small—it holds just one data field and two methods.

» After you create the general `Event` class, you write an application to demonstrate its use.

» Then, you create a more specific `DinnerEvent` subclass that inherits the attributes of the `Event` class.

» Finally, you modify the demonstration application to add an example using the `DinnerEvent` class.

CREATING A SUPERCLASS
AND AN APPLICATION TO USE IT

To create the general `Event` class:

1. Open a new file in your text editor, and enter the following first few lines for a simple `Event` class. The class hosts one integer data field—the number of guests expected at the event:

```
import javax.swing.*;
public class Event
{
    private int eventGuests;
```

2. To the `Event` class, add the following method that displays the number of eventGuests:

```
public void displayEventGuests()
{
    JOptionPane.showMessageDialog(null, "Event guests: " +
        eventGuests);
}
```

3. Add a second method that prompts the user for the number of guests, temporarily stores the response in the `guestsString` field, and then uses the `parseInt()` method to convert the number to an integer to be stored in the class `eventGuests` field:

```
public void inputEventGuests()
{
    char inChar;
    String guestsString = new String("");
    guestsString = JOptionPane.showInputDialog(null,
        "Enter the number of guests at your event ");
    eventGuests = Integer.parseInt(guestsString);
}
```

4. Add the closing curly brace for the class, then save the file as **Event.java**. At the command prompt, compile the class using the javac **Event.java** command. If necessary, correct any errors and compile again.

Now that you have created a class, you can use it in an application. A very simple application creates an `Event` object, calls the method to set a value for the data field, and displays the results.

To write a simple application that uses the `Event` class:

1. Open a new file in your text editor.

2. Write a `UseSimpleEvent` application that has one method—a `main()` method. Enter the following `main()` method, which declares an `Event` object, supplies it with a value, and then displays the value:

```
public class UseSimpleEvent
{
    public static void main(String[] args)
    {
        Event anEvent = new Event();
        anEvent.inputEventGuests();
        anEvent.displayEventGuests();
    }
}
```

3. Save the file as **UseSimpleEvent.java**, then compile the class using the **javac UseSimpleEvent.java** command. After the class compiles without errors, run the application by typing **java UseSimpleEvent**. When the program prompts you, enter an integer. Figure 9-25 shows a typical execution. Click **OK** to dismiss the dialog box.

Figure 9-25 Execution of the `UseSimpleEvent` application

CREATING A SUBCLASS AND AN APPLICATION TO USE IT

Next, you create a class named `DinnerEvent`. A `DinnerEvent` "is a" type of `Event` at which dinner is served, so `DinnerEvent` is a child class of `Event`.

To create a `DinnerEvent` class that extends `Event`:

1. Open a new file in your text editor, and type the first few lines for the `DinnerEvent` class:

```
import javax.swing.*;
public class DinnerEvent extends Event
{
```

2. A `DinnerEvent` contains a number of guests, but you do not have to define the variable here. The variable is already defined in `Event`, which is the superclass of this class. You only need to add any variables that are particular to a `DinnerEvent`. Enter the following code to add an integer to hold the dinner menu choices, which are 1 or 2 for beef or chicken, respectively:

```
private int dinnerChoice;
```

3. Then add constants that represent the dinner choices:

```
final int BEEF_CHOICE = 1;
final int CHICKEN_CHOICE = 2;
```

4. The `Event` class already contains methods to input and display the number of guests, so `DinnerEvent` only needs methods to input and display the `dinnerChoice` variable. To keep this example simple, you do not validate the input character to ensure that it is 1 or 2; you can add this improvement to the method later. The `displayDinnerChoice()` method assumes that if the choice is not beef, it must be chicken. Type the `displayDinnerChoice()` method as follows:

```
public void displayDinnerChoice()
{
   if(dinnerChoice == BEEF_CHOICE)
      JOptionPane.showMessageDialog(null,
         "Dinner choice is beef");
   else
      JOptionPane.showMessageDialog(null,
         "Dinner choice is chicken");
}
```

5. Enter the following `inputDinnerChoice()` method, which prompts the user for the choice of entrees at the event. Then add a closing curly brace for the class:

```
public void inputDinnerChoice()
{
   String choice;
   choice = JOptionPane.showInputDialog(null,
   "Enter dinner choice\n" + BEEF_CHOICE + " for beef, " +
   CHICKEN_CHOICE + " for chicken");
   dinnerChoice = Integer.parseInt(choice);
}
}
```

6. Save the file as **DinnerEvent.java**, and then compile it.

Now, you can modify the `UseSimpleEvent` application so that it creates a `DinnerEvent` as well as a plain `Event`.

To modify the `UseSimpleEvent` application:

1. Open the **UseSimpleEvent.java** file in your text editor. Change the class name from `UseSimpleEvent` to **UseDinnerEvent**.

2. The application uses dialog boxes, so add an `import` line as follows:

```
import javax.swing.*;
```

3. After the statement that constructs `anEvent`, type the following statement so that when you run the application, you know that you are using the `Event` class to create the event:

```
JOptionPane.showMessageDialog(null, "Creating an event");
```

4. After the line that displays the event guests (just before the closing brace of the program), add the following two new statements—one constructs a `DinnerEvent`, and the other displays a message so that when you run the application you understand you are creating a `DinnerEvent`:

```
DinnerEvent aDinnerEvent = new DinnerEvent();
JOptionPane.showMessageDialog(null,
   "Creating an event with dinner");
```

5. Add the following method calls to set the number of guests and dinner choice for the `DinnerEvent` object. Even though the `DinnerEvent` class does not contain an `inputEventGuests()` method, its parent class (`Event`) does, so `aDinnerEvent` can use the `inputEventGuests()` method.

```
aDinnerEvent.inputEventGuests();
aDinnerEvent.inputDinnerChoice();
```

6. Enter the following code to call the methods that display the entered data:

```
aDinnerEvent.displayEventGuests();
aDinnerEvent.displayDinnerChoice();
```

7. Save the file as **UseDinnerEvent.java**. Compile the class and run it using values of your choice. Figure 9-26 shows a typical execution. The DinnerEvent object successfully uses the data field and methods of its superclass, as well as its own data field and methods.

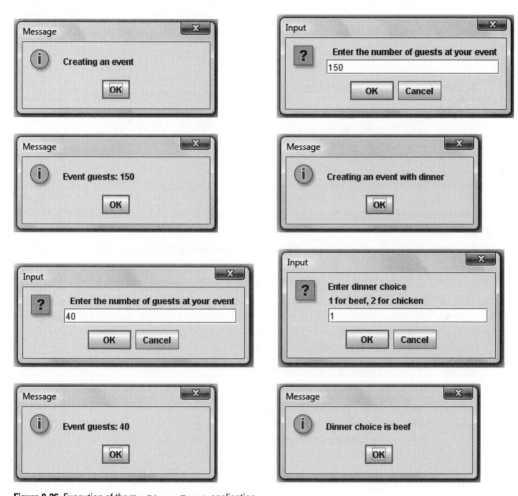

Figure 9-26 Execution of the UseDinnerEvent application

CREATING A SUBCLASS METHOD THAT OVERRIDES A SUPERCLASS METHOD

Next, you create two methods with the same name, displayPricingInfo(), with one version in the Event superclass and another in the DinnerEvent subclass. When you call the displayPricingInfo() method, the correct version executes based on the object you use.

To add a `displayPricingInfo()` method to the `Event` class:

1. In your text editor, open the **Event.java** file. Change the class name from `Event` to `EventWithInfo` because this new class contains a method that allows you to display pricing information for an event. Save the file as **EventWithInfo.java**. In addition to providing a descriptive name, changing the class name serves another purpose. By giving the class a new name, you retain the original class on your disk so you can study the differences later.

2. After the closing curly brace for the `inputEventGuests()` method, add the following `displayPricingInfo()` method:

```
public void displayPricingInfo()
{
    JOptionPane.showMessageDialog(null,
        "Events cost $100 per hour\n" +
        "There is a three-hour minimum");
}
```

3. Save the file and then compile it.

To demonstrate that a subclass method overrides a superclass method with the same signature:

1. Open the **DinnerEvent.java** file. Change the class name from `DinnerEvent` to `DinnerEventWithInfo`, and change the class from which it extends—`Event`—to `EventWithInfo`. Save the file as **DinnerEventWithInfo.java**.

2. Because dinner events have a different pricing schedule than "ordinary" events, you override the parent class `displayPricingInfo()` method within the child class. After the closing curly brace for the `inputDinnerChoice()` method, add the following `displayPricingInfo()` method to this class:

```
public void displayPricingInfo()
{
    JOptionPane.showMessageDialog(null,
        "Dinner events cost $85 per hour\n" +
        "Plus the cost of the meals\n" +
        "There is a four-hour minimum");
}
```

3. Save the file and then compile it.

You just created an `EventWithInfo` class that contains a `displayPricingInfo()` method. Then, you extended the class by creating a `DinnerEventWithInfo` subclass containing a method with the same name. Now, you will write an application demonstrating that the correct method executes, depending on the object.

To create an application demonstrating that the correct `displayPricingInfo()` method executes, depending on the object:

1. Open a new file in your text editor, and then enter the first few lines of a `UseEventWithInfo` class:

```
import javax.swing.*;
public class UseEventWithInfo
{
    public static void main(String[] args)
    {
```

2. Enter the following code to create two objects—an EventWithInfo and a DinnerEventWithInfo:

```
EventWithInfo anEvent = new EventWithInfo();
DinnerEventWithInfo aDinnerEvent = new DinnerEventWithInfo();
```

3. Enter the code to call the displayPricingInfo() method with each object type, then add the closing curly braces for the main() method and the class:

```
anEvent.displayPricingInfo();
aDinnerEvent.displayPricingInfo();
    }
}
```

4. Save the file as **UseEventWithInfo.java**. Compile and run the application. The output looks like Figure 9-27. Each type of object uses the method appropriate for that type; the child class method has successfully overridden the parent class method.

Figure 9-27 Execution of the UseEventWithInfo application

UNDERSTANDING THE ROLE OF CONSTRUCTORS IN INHERITANCE

Next, you add a constructor to the EventWithInfo class that you created for Event Handlers Incorporated. When you instantiate a subclass object, the superclass constructor executes before the subclass constructor executes.

To demonstrate that instantiating a subclass object calls the superclass constructor:

1. Open the **EventWithInfo.java** file in your text editor and save it as **EventWithConstructor.java**. Be certain to change the class name from EventWithInfo to EventWithConstructor.

2. Following the statement that declares the `eventGuests` data field, type a constructor for the `EventWithConstructor` class that does nothing other than display a message indicating it is working:

```
public EventWithConstructor()
{
    System.out.println("Creating an Event");
}
```

3. Save the file and compile it.

4. In your text editor, open the **DinnerEventWithInfo.java** file, and change the class header so that both the class name and the parent class name read as follows:

```
public class DinnerEventWithConstructor extends EventWithConstructor
```

5. Save the file as **DinnerEventWithConstructor.java**, and then compile it.

6. In your text editor, open a new file so you can write an application to demonstrate the use of the base class constructor with an extended class object. This application only creates one child class object:

```
public class UseEventWithConstructor
{
    public static void main(String[] args)
    {
        DinnerEventWithConstructor aDinnerEvent =
            new DinnerEventWithConstructor();
    }
}
```

7. Save the application as **UseEventWithConstructor.java**, then compile and run it. The output is shown in Figure 9-28. Even though the application only creates one subclass object (and no superclass objects) and the subclass contains no constructor of its own, the superclass constructor executes.

Figure 9-28 Output of the `UseEventWithConstructor` application

INHERITANCE WHEN THE SUPERCLASS REQUIRES CONSTRUCTOR ARGUMENTS

Next, you modify the `EventWithConstructor` class so that its constructor requires an argument. Then, you will observe that a subclass without a constructor cannot compile.

To demonstrate how inheritance works when a superclass constructor requires an argument:

1. Open the **EventWithConstructor.java** file in your text editor, and then change the class name to **EventWithConstructorArg**.

2. Replace the existing constructor with a new version that requires an argument, which it uses to set the number of guests who will attend an event:

```
public EventWithConstructorArg(int numGuests)
{
    eventGuests = numGuests;
}
```

3. Save the file as **EventWithConstructorArg.java**, and then compile it.

Next, you modify the `DinnerEventWithConstructor` class so it inherits from `EventWithConstructorArg`.

To create the child class:

1. Open the **DinnerEventWithConstructor.java** file in your text editor.

2. Change the class header as follows so that the name of the class is `DinnerEventWithConstructorArg`, and thus inherits from `EventWithConstructorArg`:

```
public class DinnerEventWithConstructorArg extends
    EventWithConstructorArg
```

3. Save the file as **DinnerEventWithConstructorArg.java**, and then compile it. An error message appears, as shown in Figure 9-29. When you attempt to compile the subclass, a call is made to the superclass constructor, but because this constructor requires a passed parameter, the compile fails.

Figure 9-29 Error message generated when compiling the `DinnerEventWithConstructorArg` class

To correct the error:

1. Open the **DinnerEventWithConstructorArg.java** file in your text editor, if it is not still open.

2. Following the declaration of the `dinnerChoice` field, insert a constructor for the class as follows:

```
public DinnerEventWithConstructorArg(int numGuests)
{
    super(numGuests);
}
```

3. Save the file and compile it. This time, the compile is successful because the subclass calls its parent's constructor, passing along an integer value. Note that the `DinnerEventWithConstructorArg` subclass constructor is not required to receive an integer argument, although in this example it does. For example, it would be acceptable to create a subclass constructor that required no arguments but passed a constant (for example, 0) to its parent. Similarly, the subclass constructor could require several arguments and pass one of them to its parent. The requirement is not that the subclass constructor must have the same number or types of parameters as its parent; the only requirement is that the subclass constructor calls `super()` and passes to the parent what it needs to execute.

Now, you can create an application to demonstrate creating parent and child class objects when the parent constructor needs an argument.

To create the application:

1. Open a new file in your text editor, and then enter the following first few lines of an application that demonstrates creating superclass and subclass objects using the classes you just created:

```
public class UseEventsWithConstructorArg
{
    public static void main(String[] args)
    {
```

2. Enter the following code to create two objects: an `EventWithConstructorArg` object with 45 guests and a `DinnerEventWithConstructorArg` object with 65 guests.

```
EventWithConstructorArg anEvent = new EventWithConstructorArg(45);
DinnerEventWithConstructorArg aDinnerEvent = new
   DinnerEventWithConstructorArg(65);
```

3. Add the following statements to display guest values for each object, and add closing curly braces for the method and the class:

```
        anEvent.displayEventGuests();
        aDinnerEvent.displayEventGuests();
    }
}
```

4. Save the file as **UseEventsWithConstructorArg.java**, and then compile and execute the application. The output appears in Figure 9-30. Each object is initialized correctly because the superclass constructor was called correctly in each case.

Figure 9-30 Output of the `UseEventsWithConstructorArg` application

ACCESSING AN OVERRIDDEN SUPERCLASS METHOD FROM WITHIN A SUBCLASS

When a subclass contains a method with the same signature as a method in the parent class, and you then use the method name with a subclass object, the subclass version of the method executes. If you want to access the superclass version of the method instead, you must use the keyword `super`. To demonstrate, you will create a simple subclass that has a method with the same name and argument list as a method that is part of its superclass.

To create an application that demonstrates accessing a superclass method from within a subclass:

1. Open a new file in your text editor, and then create the following parent class with a single method:

```
public class AParentClass
{
    private int aVal;
    public void displayClassName()
    {
        System.out.println("AParentClass");
    }
}
```

2. Save the file as **AParentClass.java**, and then compile it.

3. Open a new text file and create the following child class that inherits from the parent. The child class has one method. The method has the same signature as the parent's method, but the child class can call the parent's method without conflict by using the keyword `super`.

```
public class AChildClass extends AParentClass
{
    public void displayClassName()
    {
        System.out.println("I am AChildClass");
        System.out.print("My parent is ");
        super.displayClassName();
    }
}
```

4. Save the file as **AChildClass.java**, and then compile it.

5. Finally, open a new text file and enter the following demonstration application to show that the child class can call its parent's method:

```
public class DemoSuper
{
    public static void main(String[] args)
    {
        AChildClass child = new AChildClass();
        child.displayClassName();
    }
}
```

6. Save the file as **DemoSuper.java**, and then compile and execute the application. As the output in Figure 9-31 shows, even though the child and parent classes have methods with the same name, the child class can use the parent class method correctly by employing the keyword super.

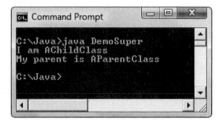

Figure 9-31 Output of the DemoSuper application

> **》》NOTE** If you omit the keyword super within the displayClassName() method in AChildClass, you cause an infinite loop because the displayClassName() method calls itself. In other words, each time displayClassName() executes, it starts executing again when it gets to the third statement. The method executes repeatedly until an error message is finally generated.

DON'T DO IT

» Don't capitalize the "o" in the instanceof operator. Although the second word in an identifier frequently is capitalized in Java, instanceof is an exception.

» Don't try to directly access private superclass members from a subclass.

» Don't forget to call a superclass constructor from within a subclass constructor if the superclass does not contain a default constructor.

KEY TERMS

In Java, **inheritance** is a mechanism that enables one class to inherit, or assume, both the behavior and the attributes of another class.

The **Unified Modeling Language** (**UML**) is a graphical language used by programmers and analysts to describe classes and object-oriented processes.

A **class diagram** is a visual tool that provides you with an overview of a class. It consists of a rectangle divided into three sections—the top section contains the name of the class, the middle section contains the names and data types of the attributes, and the bottom section contains the methods.

A **base class** is a class that is used as a basis for inheritance.

A **derived class** is a class that inherits from a base class.

Composition is the relationship in which one class contains one or more members of another class that would not continue to exist without the object that contains them.

Aggregation is a type of composition in which a class contains one or more members of another class that would continue to exist without the object that contains them.

Superclass and **subclass** are synonyms for base class and derived class.

Parent class and **child class** are synonyms for base class and derived class.

You use the keyword **extends** to achieve inheritance in Java.

The **instanceof operator** determines whether an object that is the operand on the left is a member or descendant of the class that is the operand on the right.

To **upcast** an object is to change it to an object of a class higher in the object's inheritance hierarchy.

Using the same method name to indicate different implementations is called **polymorphism**.

You **override the method** in a parent class when you create a method in a child class that has the same name and argument list as a method in its parent class.

Subtype polymorphism is the ability of one method name to work appropriately for different subclasses of a parent class.

The keyword **super** always refers to the superclass of the class in which you use it.

Information hiding is the concept of keeping data private.

Using the keyword **protected** provides you with an intermediate level of security between `public` and `private` access. `Protected` members are those that can be used by a class and its descendants.

Fragile classes are those that are prone to errors.

Virtual method calls are those in which the method used is determined when the program runs, because the type of the object used might not be known until the method executes. In Java, all instance method calls are virtual calls by default.

Inlining the code is an automatic process that optimizes performance. Because a `final` method's definition can never be overridden, the compiler can optimize a program's performance by removing the calls to `final` methods and replacing them with the expanded code of their definitions at each method call location.

CHAPTER SUMMARY

» In Java, inheritance is a mechanism that enables one class to inherit both the behavior and the attributes of another class. Using inheritance saves time because the original fields and methods already exist, have been tested, and are familiar to users. A class that is used as a basis for inheritance is a base class. A class you create that inherits from a base class is called a derived class. You can use the terms *superclass* and *subclass* as synonyms for base class and derived class; you can also use the terms *parent class* and *child class*.

» You use the keyword `extends` to achieve inheritance in Java. A parent class object does not have access to its child's data and methods, but when you create a subclass by extending an existing class, the new subclass contains data and methods that were defined in the original superclass.

» Sometimes, superclass data fields and methods are not entirely appropriate for the subclass objects. Polymorphism is the act of using the same method name to indicate different implementations. You use polymorphism when you override a superclass method in a subclass by creating a method with the same name and argument list.

» When you instantiate an object that is a member of a subclass, you are actually calling at least two constructors: the constructor for the base class and the constructor for the extended, derived class. When you create any subclass object, the superclass constructor must execute first, and *then* the subclass constructor executes. When a superclass contains a default constructor, the execution of the superclass constructor when a subclass object is instantiated is often transparent.

» When a superclass contains only constructors that require arguments, you must include at least one constructor for each subclass you create. Your subclass constructors can contain any number of statements, but the first statement within each constructor must call the superclass constructor. When a superclass requires parameters upon instantiation, even if you have no other reason to create a subclass constructor, you must write the subclass constructor so it can call its superclass's constructor. The format of the statement that calls a superclass constructor is `super(list of arguments);`.

» If you want to use a superclass method within a subclass, you can use the keyword `super` to access the parent class method.

» When a class serves as a superclass to other classes you create, the subclasses inherit all the data and methods of the superclass. The methods in a subclass can use all of the data fields and methods that belong to its parent, but `private` members of the parent class are not accessible with a child class's methods. Using the keyword `protected` provides you with an intermediate level of security between `public` and `private` access. If you create a `protected` data field or method, it can be used within its own class or in any classes extended from that class, but it cannot be used by "outside" classes. A subclass cannot override methods that are declared `static` in the superclass. A subclass can *hide* a `static` method in the superclass by declaring a `static` method in the subclass with the same signature as the `static` method in the superclass. A subclass cannot override methods that are declared `final` in the superclass or methods declared within a `final` class.

REVIEW QUESTIONS

1. As an alternative way to discover which of two classes is the base class or subclass, _____ .

   a. look at the class size   c. use polymorphism

   b. try saying the two class names together   d. Both a and b are correct.

2. Employing inheritance reduces errors because _____ .

   a. the new classes have access to fewer data fields

   b. the new classes have access to fewer methods

   c. you can copy methods that you already created

   d. many of the methods you need have already been used and tested

3. A base class can also be called a _____ .

   a. child class   c. derived class

   b. subclass   d. superclass

4. Which of the following choices is the best example of a parent class/child class relationship?

   a. `Rose/Flower`   c. `Dog/Poodle`

   b. `Present/Gift`   d. `Sparrow/Bird`

5. The Java keyword that creates inheritance is _____ .

   a. `static`   c. `extends`

   b. `enlarge`   d. `inherits`

6. A class named `Building` has a `public`, nonstatic method named `getFloors()`. If `School` is a child class of `Building`, and `modelHigh` is an object of type `School`, which of the following statements is valid?

   a. `Building.getFloors();`   c. `modelHigh.getFloors();`

   b. `School.getFloors();`   d. All of the previous statements are valid.

7. Which of the following statements is false?

   a. A child class inherits from a parent class.   c. Both of the preceding statements are false.

   b. A parent class inherits from a child class.   d. Neither a nor b is false.

8. When a subclass method has the same name and argument types as a superclass method, the subclass method can _____ the superclass method.

   a. override   c. overload

   b. overuse   d. overcompensate

9. When you instantiate an object that is a member of a subclass, the _____ constructor executes first.

   a. subclass   c. extended class

   b. child class   d. parent class

10. The keyword `super` always refers to the _____ of the class in which you use it.

   a. child class   c. subclass

   b. derived class   d. parent class

11. If a superclass constructor requires arguments, its subclass _____ .

   a. must contain a constructor

   b. must not contain a constructor

   c. must contain a constructor that requires arguments

   d. must not contain a constructor that requires arguments

12. If a superclass constructor requires arguments, any constructor of its subclasses must call the superclass constructor _____ .

   a. as the first statement
   c. at some time

   b. as the last statement
   d. multiple times if multiple arguments are involved

13. A child class `Motorcycle` extends a parent class `Vehicle`. Each class constructor requires one `String` argument. The `Motorcycle` class constructor can call the `Vehicle` class constructor with the statement _____ .

   a. `Vehicle("Honda");`
   c. `super("Suzuki");`

   b. `Motorcycle("Harley");`
   d. none of the above

14. In Java, the concept of keeping data private is known as _____ .

   a. polymorphism
   c. data deception

   b. information hiding
   d. concealing fields

15. If you create a data field or method that is _____ , it can be used within its own class or in any classes extended from that class.

   a. `public`
   c. `private`

   b. `protected`
   d. both a and b

16. Within a subclass, you cannot override _____ methods.

   a. `public`
   c. `static`

   b. `private`
   d. constructor

17. You call a `static` method using _____ .

   a. the name of its class, a dot, and the method name

   b. the name of the class's superclass, a dot, and the method name

   c. the name of an object in the same class, a dot, and the method name

   d. either a or b

18. You use a _____ method access modifier when you create methods for which you want to prevent overriding in extended classes.

   a. `public`
   c. `final`

   b. `protected`
   d. subclass

19. A compiler can decide to _____ a `final` method—that is, determine the code of the method call when the program is compiled.

   a. duplicate
   c. redline

   b. inline
   d. beeline

20. When a parent class contains a `static` method, child classes _____ override it.

a. frequently   c. must

b. seldom   d. cannot

EXERCISES

1. Create a class named `Book` that contains data fields for the title and number of pages. Include get and set methods for these fields. Next, create a subclass named `Textbook`, which contains an additional field that holds a grade level for the `Textbook` and additional methods to get and set the grade level field. Write an application that demonstrates using objects of each class. Save the files as **Book.java**, **Textbook.java**, and **DemoBook.java**.

2. Create a class named `Square` that contains data fields for `height`, `width`, and `surfaceArea`, and a method named `computeSurfaceArea()`. Create a child class named `Cube`. `Cube` contains an additional data field named `depth`, and a `computeSurfaceArea()` method that overrides the parent method. Write an application that instantiates a `Square` object and a `Cube` object and displays the surface areas of the objects. Save the files as **Cube.java**, **Square.java**, and **DemoSquare.java**.

3. Create a class named `Order` that performs order processing of a single item. The class has five fields: customer name, customer number, quantity ordered, unit price, and total price. Include set and get methods for each field except the total price field. The set methods prompt the user for values for each field. This class also needs a method to compute the total price (quantity times unit price) and a method to display the field values. Create a subclass named `ShippedOrder` that overrides `computePrice()` by adding a shipping and handling charge of $4.00. Write an application named `UseOrder` that instantiates an object of each of these classes. Prompt the user for data for the `Order` object, and display the results; then prompt the user for data for the `ShippedOrder` object, and display the results. Save the files as **Order.java**, **ShippedOrder.java**, and **UseOrder.java**.

4. a. Create a class named `Year` that contains a data field that holds the number of days in a year. Include a get method that displays the number of days and a constructor that sets the number of days to 365. Create a subclass named `LeapYear`. `LeapYear`'s constructor overrides `Year`'s constructor and sets the number of days to 366. Write an application named `UseYear` that instantiates one object of each class and displays their data. Save the files as **Year.java**, **LeapYear.java**, and **UseYear.java**.

   b. Add a method named `daysElapsed()` to the `Year` class you created in Exercise 4a. The `daysElapsed()` method accepts two arguments representing a month and a day; it returns an integer indicating the number of days that have elapsed since January 1 of that year. For example, on March 3 in nonleap years, 61 days have elapsed (31 in January, 28 in February, and 2 in March). Create a `daysElapsed()` method for the `LeapYear` class that overrides the method in the `Year` class. For example, on March 3 in a LeapYear, 62 days have elapsed (31 in January, 29 in February, and 2 in March). Write an application named UseYear2 that prompts the user for a month and day, and calculates the days elapsed in a Year and in a LeapYear. Save the files as **Year2.java**, **LeapYear2.java**, and **UseYear2.java**.

5. Create a class named HotelRoom that includes an integer field for the room number and a double field for the nightly rental rate. Include get methods for these fields and a constructor that requires an integer argument representing the room number. The constructor sets the room rate based on the room number; rooms numbered 299 and below are $69.95 per night, and others are $89.95 per night. Create an extended class named Suite whose constructor requires a room number and adds a $40 surcharge to the regular hotel room rate, which again is based on the room number. Write an application named UseHotelRoom that creates an object of each class, and demonstrate that all the methods work correctly. Save the files as **HotelRoom.java**, **Suite.java**, and **UseHotelRoom.java**.

6. Create a class named Package with data fields for weight in ounces, shipping method, and shipping cost. The shipping method is a character: 'A' for air, 'T' for truck, or 'M' for mail. The Package class contains a constructor that requires arguments for weight and shipping method. The constructor calls a calculateCost() method that determines the shipping cost, based on the following table:

Weight (oz.)	Air ($)	Truck ($)	Mail ($)
1–8	2.00	1.50	.50
9–16	3.00	2.35	1.50
17 and over	4.50	3.25	2.15

The Package class also contains a display() method that displays the values in all four fields. Create a subclass named InsuredPackage that adds an insurance cost to the shipping cost, based on the following table:

Shipping Cost Before Insurance ($)	Additional Cost ($)
0–1.00	2.45
1.01–3.00	3.95
3.01 and over	5.55

Write an application named UsePackage that instantiates at least three objects of each type (Package and InsuredPackage) using a variety of weights and shipping method codes. Display the results for each Package and InsuredPackage. Save the files as **Package.java**, **InsuredPackage.java**, and **UsePackage.java**.

7. Create a class named CarRental that contains fields that hold a renter's name, zip code, size of the car rented, daily rental fee, length of rental in days, and total rental fee. The

class contains a constructor that requires all the rental data except the daily rate and total fee, which are calculated based on the size of the car: economy at $29.99 per day, midsize at $38.99 per day, or full size at $43.50 per day. The class also includes a `display()` method that displays all the rental data. Create a subclass named `LuxuryCarRental`. This class sets the rental fee at $79.99 per day and prompts the user to respond to the option of including a chauffeur at $200 more per day. Override the parent class `display()` method to include chauffeur fee information. Write an application named `UseCarRental` that prompts the user for the data needed for a rental and creates an object of the correct type. Display the total rental fee. Save the files as **CarRental.java**, **LuxuryCarRental.java**, and **UseCarRental.java**.

8. Create a class named `CollegeCourse` that includes data fields that hold the department (for example, "ENG"), the course number (for example, 101), the credits (for example, 3), and the fee for the course (for example, $360). All of the fields are required as arguments to the constructor, except for the fee, which is calculated at $120 per credit hour. Include a `display()` method that displays the course data. Create a subclass named `LabCourse` that adds $50 to the course fee. Override the parent class `display()` method to indicate that the course is a lab course and to display all the data. Write an application named `UseCourse` that prompts the user for course information. If the user enters a class in any of the following departments, create a `LabCourse`: BIO, CHM, CIS, or PHY. If the user enters any other department, create a `CollegeCourse` that does not include the lab fee. Then display the course data. Save the files as **CollegeCourse.java**, **LabCourse.java**, and **UseCourse.java**.

9. Create a class named `Vehicle` that acts as a superclass for vehicle types. The `Vehicle` class contains private variables for the number of wheels and the average number of miles per gallon. The `Vehicle` class also contains a constructor with integer arguments for the number of wheels and average miles per gallon, and a `toString()` method that returns a `String` containing these values. Create two subclasses, `Car` and `MotorCycle`, that extend the `Vehicle` class. Each subclass contains a constructor that accepts the miles-per-gallon value as an argument and forces the number of wheels to the appropriate value—2 for a `MotorCycle` and 4 for a `Car`. Write a `UseVehicle` class to instantiate the two `Vehicle` objects and print the objects' values. Save the files as **Vehicle.java**, **Car.java**, **MotorCycle.java**, and **UseVehicle.java**.

10. Develop a set of classes for a college to use in various student service and personnel applications. Classes you need to design include the following:

   » `Person`—A `Person` contains a first name, last name, street address, zip code, and phone number. The class also includes a method that sets each data field, using a series of dialog boxes and a display method that displays all of a `Person`'s information on a single line at the command line on the screen.

   » `CollegeEmployee`—`CollegeEmployee` descends from `Person`. A `CollegeEmployee` also includes a Social Security number, an annual salary, and a department name, as well as methods that override the `Person` methods to accept and display all `CollegeEmployee` data.

» Faculty—Faculty descends from CollegeEmployee. This class also includes a Boolean field that indicates whether the Faculty member is tenured, as well as methods that override the CollegeEmployee methods to accept and display this additional piece of information.

» Student—Student descends from Person. In addition to the fields available in Person, a Student contains a major field of study and a grade point average as well as methods that override the Person methods to accept and display these additional facts.

Write an application named CollegeList that declares an array of four "regular" CollegeEmployees, three Faculty, and seven Students. Prompt the user to specify which type of person's data will be entered ("C", "F", or "S"), or allow the user to quit ("Q"). While the user chooses to continue (that is, does not quit), accept data entry for the appropriate type of Person. If the user attempts to enter data for more than four CollegeEmployees, three Faculty, or seven Students, display an error message. When the user quits, display a report on the screen listing each group of Persons under the appropriate heading "College Employees," "Faculty," or "Students." If the user has not entered data for one or more types of Persons during a session, display an appropriate message under the appropriate heading.

Save the files as **Person.java**, **CollegeEmployee.java**, **Faculty.java**, **Student.java**, and **CollegeList.java**.

DEBUGGING EXERCISES

Each of the following files in the Chapter.09 folder on your Student Disk has syntax and/or logic errors. In each case, determine the problem and fix the program. After you correct the errors, save each file using the same filename preceded with Fix. For example, DebugNine1.java will become FixDebugNine1.java.

a. DebugNine1.java

b. DebugNine2.java

c. DebugNine3.java

d. DebugNine4.java

e. Eight other Debug files in the Chapter.09 folder; these files are used by the DebugNine exercises

GAME ZONE

 1. a. Create an Alien class. Include at least three protected data members of your choice, such as the number of eyes the Alien has. Include a constructor that requires a value for each data field and a toString() method that returns a String containing a complete description of the Alien. Save the file as **Alien.java**.

b. Create two classes—Martian and Jupiterian—that descend from Alien. Supply each with a constructor that sets the Alien data fields with values you choose. For example, you can decide that a Martian has four eyes but a Jupiterian has only two. Save the files as **Martian.java** and **Jupiterian.java**.

c. Create an application that instantiates one Martian and one Jupiterian. Call the toString() method with each object and display the results. Save the application as **CreateAliens.java**.

2. a. In Chapter 4, you created a Die class that you can use to instantiate objects that hold one of six randomly selected values. Modify this class so that its value field is protected instead of private. This will allow a child class to access the value. Save the file as **Die.java**.

b. Create a LoadedDie class that can be used to give a player a slight advantage over the computer. A LoadedDie never rolls a 1; it only rolls values 2–6. Save the file as **LoadedDie.java**.

c. Create a program that rolls two Die objects against each other 1,000 times and count the number of times the first Die has a higher value than the other Die. Then roll a Die object against a LoadedDie object 1,000 times, and count the number of times the Die wins. Display the results. Save the application as **TestLoadedDie.java**. Figure 9-32 shows two typical executions.

Figure 9-32 Typical execution of the TestLoadedDie application

TOUGH QUESTIONS

1. Describe the difference between overloading and overriding in an inheritance situation.

2. Suppose a base class contains a default constructor. Can you call it explicitly from within a derived class constructor?

3. Within a child class you can call a parent class method using the keyword super, a dot, and the method name. Can you also call a parent method using the parent class name, a dot, and the method name? Why or why not?

UP FOR DISCUSSION

1. In this chapter, you learned the difference between `public`, `private`, and `protected` class members. Some programmers are opposed to classifying class members as `protected`. Why do they feel that way? Do you agree with them?

2. Some programmers argue that, in general, superclasses are larger than subclasses. Others argue that, in general, subclasses are larger. How can both be correct?

3. Playing computer games has been shown to increase the level of dopamine in the human brain. High levels of this substance are associated with addiction to drugs. Suppose you work for a game manufacturer that decides to research how its games can produce more dopamine in the brains of players. Would you support the company's decision?

4. In one of the exercises at the end of this chapter, you store an employee's Social Security number. Besides using it for tax purposes, many organizations also use this number as an identification number. Is this a good idea? Is a Social Security number unique?

10

ADVANCED INHERITANCE CONCEPTS

In this chapter, you will:

Create and use abstract classes
Use dynamic method binding
Create arrays of subclass objects
Use the Object class and its methods
Use inheritance to achieve good software design
Create and use interfaces
Create and use packages

JAVA ON THE JOB, SCENE 10

"Inheritance sure makes my programming job easier," you tell Lynn Greenbrier over a frosty lemonade at the Event Handlers Incorporated company picnic.

"So, everything is going well, I take it?" asks Lynn.

"It is," you say, "but I'm ready to learn more. What else can you tell me about inheritance?"

"Enjoy the picnic for today," Lynn says. "On Monday morning, I'll teach you about superclass arrays that can use subclass methods, interfaces, and packages. Then you will be an inheritance pro."

CREATING AND USING ABSTRACT CLASSES

>> NOTE Recall from Chapter 9 that the terms *base class*, *superclass*, and *parent* are equivalent. Similarly, the terms *derived class*, *subclass*, and *child* are equivalent.

Developing new classes is easier after you understand the concept of inheritance. When you use a class as a basis from which to create extended child classes, the child classes are more specific than their parent. When you create a child class, it inherits all the general attributes you need; thus, you must create only the new, more specific attributes. For example, a `SalariedEmployee` and an `HourlyEmployee` are more specific than an `Employee`. They can inherit general `Employee` attributes, such as an employee number, but they add specific attributes, such as pay-calculating methods.

>> NOTE Nonabstract classes from which objects can be instantiated are called **concrete classes**. Before this chapter, all the classes you created were concrete.

Notice that a superclass contains the features that are shared by its subclasses. For example, the attributes of the `Dog` class are shared by every `Poodle` and `Spaniel`. The subclasses are more specific examples of the superclass type; they add more features to the shared, general features. Conversely, when you examine a subclass, you see that its parent is more general and less specific; for example, `Animal` is more general than `Dog`.

>> NOTE Recall from Chapter 9 that a child class contains all the members of its parent, whether those members are `public`, `protected`, or `private`. However, a child object cannot directly access a `private` member inherited from a parent.

>> NOTE In Chapter 9, you learned to create class diagrams. By convention, when you show abstract classes and methods in class diagrams, their names appear in italics.

Sometimes, a parent class is so general that you never intend to create any specific instances of the class. For example, you might never create an object that is "just" an `Employee`; each `Employee` is more specifically a `SalariedEmployee`, `HourlyEmployee`, or `ContractEmployee`. A class such as `Employee` that you create only to extend from is an abstract class. An **abstract class** is one from which you cannot create any concrete objects, but from which you can inherit. Abstract classes usually have one or more empty abstract methods. You use the keyword `abstract` when you declare an abstract class.

>> NOTE In other programming languages, such as C++, abstract classes are known as **virtual classes**.

>> NOTE In Chapter 4, you worked with the `GregorianCalendar` class. `GregorianCalendar` is a concrete class that extends the abstract class `Calendar`. In other words, there are no "plain" `Calendar` objects.

>> NOTE In Chapter 9, you learned that you can create `final` classes if you do not want other classes to be able to extend them. Classes that you declare to be `abstract` are the opposite; your only purpose in creating them is to enable other classes to extend them.

You cannot create instances of abstract classes by using the `new` operator; you create abstract classes simply to provide a superclass from which other objects can inherit. Abstract classes are like regular classes because they have data and methods, but they are different in that they usually contain at least one abstract method. An **abstract method** has no body—no curly braces and no method statements. When you create an abstract method, you provide the keyword `abstract` and the rest of the header, including the method type, name, and arguments. However, the declaration ends there: you do not provide curly braces or any statements within the method—just a semicolon at the end of the declaration. When you create a subclass that inherits an abstract method from a parent, you write a method with the same signature. Either the new method must itself be abstract, or you must provide the actions, or implementation, for the inherited method. It's important to understand that you are required to code a subclass method to override the empty superclass method that is inherited.

》》NOTE Programmers of an abstract class can include two method types: (1) nonabstract methods such as those you create in any class, which are implemented in the abstract class and are simply inherited by its children; and (2) methods that are abstract and must be implemented by its children.

》》NOTE If you attempt to instantiate an object from an abstract class, you receive an error message from the compiler that you have committed an `InstantiationError`.

》》NOTE If you provide an empty method within an abstract class, the method is an abstract method even if you do not explicitly use the keyword `abstract` when defining the method.

Suppose you want to create classes to represent different animals, such as `Dog` and `Cow`. You can create a generic abstract class named `Animal` so you can provide generic data fields, such as the animal's name, only once. An `Animal` is generic, but all specific `Animal`s make a sound; the actual sound differs from `Animal` to `Animal`. If you code an empty `speak()` method in the abstract `Animal` class, you require all future `Animal` subclasses to code a `speak()`

```
public abstract class Animal
{
    private String name;
    public abstract void speak();
    public String getName()
    {
        return name;
    }
    public void setName(String animalName)
    {
        name = animalName;
    }
}
```

Figure 10-1 The abstract `Animal` class

method that is specific to the subclass. Figure 10-1 shows an abstract `Animal` class containing a data field for the name, `getName()` and `setName()` methods, and an abstract `speak()` method.

NOTE
If you declare any
method to be an
abstract method,
you must also
declare its class
to be abstract.

The `Animal` class in Figure 10-1 is declared as `abstract`. You cannot place a statement such as `Animal myPet = new Animal("Murphy");` within another class, because a class that attempts to instantiate an `Animal` object does not compile. `Animal` is an abstract class, so no `Animal` objects can exist.

You create an abstract class such as `Animal` only so you can extend it. For example, because a dog is an animal, you can create a `Dog` class as a child class of `Animal`. Figure 10-2 shows a `Dog` class that extends `Animal`.

```
public class Dog extends Animal
{
    public void speak()
    {
        System.out.println("Woof!");
    }
}
```

Figure 10-2 The `Dog` class

The `speak()` method within the `Dog` class is required because the abstract, parent `Animal` class contains an abstract `speak()` method. You can code any statements you want within the `Dog speak()` method, but the `speak()` method must exist. Remember, you cannot instantiate an `Animal` object; however, instantiating a `Dog` object is perfectly legal because `Dog` is not an abstract class. When you code `Dog myPet = new Dog("Murphy");`, you create a `Dog` object. Then, when you code `myPet.speak();`, the correct `Dog speak()` method executes.

NOTE If you do not provide a subclass method to override a superclass abstract method, you cannot instantiate any subclass objects. In this case, you also must declare the subclass itself to be abstract. Then, you can extend the subclass into sub-subclasses in which you write code for the method.

The classes in Figures 10-3 and 10-4 also inherit from the `Animal` class. Figure 10-5 contains a `UseAnimals` application.

```
public class Cow extends Animal
{
    public void speak()
    {
        System.out.println("Moo!");
    }
}
```

Figure 10-3 The `Cow` class

```
public class Snake extends Animal
{
    public void speak()
    {
        System.out.println("Ssss!");
    }
}
```

Figure 10-4 The `Snake` class

```
public class UseAnimals
{
   public static void main(String[] args)
   {
      Dog myDog = new Dog();
      Cow myCow = new Cow();
      Snake mySnake = new Snake();
      myDog.setName("My dog Murphy");
      myCow.setName("My cow Elsie");
      mySnake.setName("My snake Sammy");
      System.out.print(myDog.getName() + " says ");
      myDog.speak();
      System.out.print(myCow.getName() + " says ");
      myCow.speak();
      System.out.print(mySnake.getName() + " says ");
      mySnake.speak();
   }
}
```

Figure 10-5 The `UseAnimals` application

The output in Figure 10-6 shows that when you create Dog, Cow, and Snake objects, each is an Animal with access to the Animal class getName() and setName() methods, and each uses its own speak() method appropriately. In Figure 10-6, notice how the myDog.getName() and myDog.speak() method calls produce different output from when the same method names are used with myCow and mySnake.

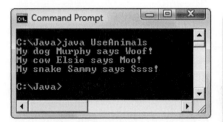

Figure 10-6 Output of the `UseAnimals` application

> **»NOTE**
> In Chapter 9, you learned that using the same method name to indicate different implementations is called polymorphism. Using polymorphism, one method name causes different actions for different types of objects.

»TWO TRUTHS AND A LIE: CREATING AND USING ABSTRACT CLASSES

1. An abstract class is one from which you cannot inherit, but from which you can create concrete objects.
2. Abstract classes usually have one or more empty abstract methods.
3. An abstract method has no body, curly braces, or statements.

The false statement is #1. An abstract class is one from which you cannot create any concrete objects, but from which you can inherit.

USING DYNAMIC METHOD BINDING

When you create a superclass and one or more subclasses, each object of each subclass "is a" superclass object. Every SalariedEmployee "is an" Employee; every Dog "is an" Animal. (The opposite is not true. Superclass objects are not members of any of their subclasses. An Employee is not a SalariedEmployee. An Animal is not a Dog.) Because every subclass object "is a" superclass member, you can convert subclass objects to superclass objects.

As you are aware, when a superclass is abstract, you cannot instantiate objects of the superclass; however, you can indirectly create a reference to a superclass abstract object. A reference is not an object, but it points to a memory address. When you create a reference, you do not use the keyword new to create a concrete object; instead, you create a variable name in which you can hold the memory address of a concrete object. So, although a reference to an abstract superclass object is not concrete, you can store a concrete subclass object reference there.

> **≫NOTE** You learned how to create a reference in Chapter 4. When you code SomeClass someObject;, you are creating a reference. If you later code the following statement, including the keyword new and the constructor name, then you actually set aside memory for someObject:
>
> ```
> someObject = new SomeClass();
> ```

> **≫NOTE**
> Recall from Chapter 2 that when you assign a variable or constant of one type to a variable of another type, the behavior is called *promotion* or *implicit casting*. In Chapter 9, you also learned that such promotion is called *upcasting*.

For example, if you create an Animal class, as shown previously in Figure 10-1, and various subclasses, such as Dog, Cow, and Snake, as shown in Figures 10-2 through 10-4, you can create an application containing a generic Animal reference variable into which you can assign any of the concrete Animal child objects. Figure 10-7 shows an AnimalReference application, and Figure 10-8 shows its output. The variable ref is a type of Animal. No superclass Animal object is created (none can be); instead, Dog and Cow objects are created using the new keyword. When the Cow object is assigned to the Animal reference, the ref.speak() method call results in "Moo!"; when the Dog object is assigned to the Animal reference, the method call results in "Woof!"

```
public class AnimalReference
{
    public static void main(String[] args)
    {
        Animal ref;
        ref = new Cow();
        ref.speak();
        ref = new Dog();
        ref.speak();
    }
}
```

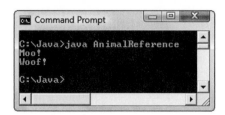

Figure 10-7 The AnimalReference application

Figure 10-8 Output of the AnimalReference application

NOTE The application in Figure 10-7 shows that using a reference polymorphically allows you to extend a base class and use extended objects when a base class type is expected. For example, you could pass a Dog or a Cow to a method that expects an Animal. This means that all methods written to accept a superclass argument can also be used with its children—a feature that saves child-class creators a lot of work.

NOTE Recall from Chapter 9 that you can use the instanceof keyword to determine whether an object is an instance of any class in its hierarchy. For example, both of the following expressions are true if myPoodle is a Dog object:

```
myPoodle instanceof Animal
myPoodle instanceof Dog
```

The application in Figure 10-7 demonstrates polymorphic behavior. The same statement, ref.speak();, repeats after ref is set to each new animal type. Each call to the speak() method results in different output. Each reference "chooses" the correct speak() method, based on the type of animal referenced. This flexible behavior is most useful when you pass references to methods; you will learn more about this in the next section. In Chapter 9, you learned that in Java all instance method calls are virtual method calls by default—the method that is used is determined when the program runs, because the type of the object used might not be known until the method executes. An application's ability to select the correct subclass method is known as **dynamic method binding**. When the application executes, the correct method is attached (or bound) to the application based on the current, changing context (dynamically).

NOTE
Dynamic method binding is also called **late binding**. The opposite of dynamic method binding is **static (fixed) method binding**. Dynamic method binding makes programs flexible; however, static method binding operates more quickly.

NOTE In the example in this section, the objects using speak() happen to be related (Cow and Dog are both Animals). Be aware that polymorphic behavior can apply to nonrelated classes as well. For example, a DebateStudent and a VentriloquistsDummy might also speak().

USING A SUPERCLASS AS A METHOD PARAMETER TYPE

Dynamic method binding is most useful when you want to create a method that has one or more parameters that might be one of several types. For example, the shaded header for the talkingAnimal() method in Figure 10-9 accepts any type of Animal argument. The method can be used in programs that contain Dog objects, Cow objects, or objects of any other class that descends from Animal. The application in Figure 10-9 passes first a Dog and then a Cow to the method. The output in Figure 10-10 shows that the method works correctly no matter which type of Animal descendant it receives.

```
public class TalkingAnimalDemo
{
   public static void main(String[] args)
   {
      Dog dog = new Dog();
      Cow cow = new Cow();
      dog.setName("Ginger");
      cow.setName("Molly");
      talkingAnimal(dog);
      talkingAnimal(cow);
   }
   public static void talkingAnimal(Animal animal)
   {
      System.out.println("Come one. Come all.");
      System.out.println
         ("See the amazing talking animal!");
      System.out.println(animal.getName() +
         " says");
      animal.speak();
      System.out.println("***************");
   }
}
```

Figure 10-9 The `TalkingAnimalDemo` class

Figure 10-10 Output of the `TalkingAnimalDemo` application

»TWO TRUTHS AND A LIE: USING DYNAMIC METHOD BINDING

1. If `Parent` is a parent class and `Child` is its child, then you can assign a `Child` object to a `Parent` reference.
2. If `Parent` is a parent class and `Child` is its child, then you can assign a `Parent` object to a `Child` reference.
3. Dynamic method binding refers to a program's ability to select the correct subclass method for a superclass reference while a program is running.

The false statement is #2. If `Parent` is a parent class and `Child` is its child, then you cannot assign a `Parent` object to a `Child` reference; you can only assign a `Child` object to a `Child` reference. However, you can assign a `Parent` object or a `Child` object to a `Parent` reference.

CREATING ARRAYS OF SUBCLASS OBJECTS

»NOTE
In Chapter 8, you learned that all elements in a single array must be of the same type.

One reason you might want to create a superclass reference and treat subclass objects as superclass objects is to create an array of different objects that share the same ancestry. For example, even though `Employee` is an abstract class, and every `Employee` object is either a `SalariedEmployee` or an `HourlyEmployee` subclass object, it can be convenient to create an array of generic `Employee` references. Likewise, an `Animal` array might contain individual elements that are `Dog`, `Cow`, or `Snake` objects. As long as every `Employee` subclass has access to a `calculatePay()` method, or every `Animal` subclass has access to a `speak()` method, you can manipulate an array of superclass objects by invoking the appropriate method for each subclass member.

The following statement creates an array of three `Animal` references:

```
Animal[] ref = new Animal[3];
```

The statement reserves enough computer memory for three `Animal` objects named `ref[0]`, `ref[1]`, and `ref[2]`. The statement does not actually instantiate `Animals`; `Animals` are abstract and cannot be instantiated. The statement simply reserves memory for three `Animal` object references. If you instantiate three `Animal` subclass objects, you can place references to those objects in the `Animal` array, as Figure 10-11 illustrates. Figure 10-12 shows the output of the `AnimalArrayDemo` application. The array of three references is used to access each appropriate `speak()` method.

```
public class AnimalArrayDemo
{
    public static void main(String[] args)
    {
        Animal[] ref = new Animal[3];
        ref[0] = new Dog();
        ref[1] = new Cow();
        ref[2] = new Snake();
        for(int x = 0; x < 3; ++x)
            ref[x].speak();
    }
}
```

Figure 10-11 The `AnimalArrayDemo` application

Figure 10-12 Output of the `AnimalArrayDemo` application

In the `AnimalArrayDemo` application in Figure 10-11, a new instance of the `Dog` class is assigned to the first `Animal` reference, and then new instances of `Cow` and `Snake` are assigned to the second and third array elements. After the objects are in the array, you can manipulate them like any other array objects. For example, you can use a `for` loop and a subscript to get each individual reference to `speak()`.

>>NOTE
When you create an array of any type of objects, concrete or abstract, you are not actually constructing those objects. Instead, you are creating space for references to objects that are not yet instantiated. In other words, although it is convenient to refer to "an array of objects," every array of objects is really an array of object references.

>>TWO TRUTHS AND A LIE: CREATING ARRAYS OF SUBCLASS OBJECTS

1. You can manipulate an array of superclass objects by invoking the appropriate method for each subclass member.
2. The following statement creates an array of 10 `Table` objects:
   `Table[] table = new Table[10];`
3. You can assign subclass objects to an array that is their superclass type.

The false statement is #2. The statement creates an array of 10 references, not concrete objects.

USING THE Object CLASS AND ITS METHODS

Every class in Java is actually a subclass, except one. When you define a class, if you do not explicitly extend another class, your class is an extension of the Object class. The **Object class** is defined in the java.lang package, which is automatically imported every time you write a program; in other words, the following two class declarations have identical outcomes:

```
public class Animal
{
}
public class Animal extends Object
{
}
```

When you declare a class that does not extend any other class, you are always extending the Object class. The Object class includes methods that descendant classes can use or override as you see fit. Table 10-1 describes the methods built into the Object class; every Object you create has access to these methods.

Method	Description
Object clone()	Creates and returns a copy of this object.
boolean equals(Object obj)	Indicates whether some object is equal to the parameter object. This method is described in detail below.
void finalize()	Called by the garbage collector on an object when there are no more references to the object.
Class<?> getClass()	Returns the class to which this object belongs at run time.
int hashCode()	Returns a hash code value for the object. This method is described briefly below.
void notify()	Wakes up a single thread that is waiting on this object's monitor.
void notifyAll()	Wakes up all threads that are waiting on this object's monitor.
String toString()	Returns a string representation of the object. This method is described in detail below.
void wait(long timeout)	Causes the current thread to wait until either another thread invokes the notify() method or the notifyAll() method for this object, or a specified amount of time has elapsed.
void wait(long timeout, int nanos)	Causes the current thread to wait until another thread invokes the notify() or notifyAll() method for this object, or some other thread interrupts the current thread, or a certain amount of real time has elapsed.

Table 10-1 Object class methods

USING THE toString() METHOD

The Object class **toString()** **method** converts an Object into a String that contains information about the Object. Within a class, if you do not create a toString() method that overrides the version in the Object class, you can use the superclass version of the toString() method. For example, examine the Dog class originally shown in Figure 10-2 and repeated in Figure 10-13. Notice that it does not contain a toString() method and that it extends the Animal class.

```java
public abstract class Animal
{
    private String name;
    public abstract void speak();
    public String getName()
    {
        return name;
    }
    public void setName(String animalName)
    {
        name = animalName;
    }
}

public class Dog extends Animal
{
    public void speak()
    {
        System.out.println("Woof!");
    }
}

public class DisplayDog
{
    public static void main(String[] args)
    {
        Dog myDog = new Dog();
        String dogString = myDog.toString();
        System.out.println(dogString);
    }
}
```

Figure 10-13 The Animal and Dog classes and the DisplayDog application

Examine the Animal parent class originally shown in Figure 10-1 and repeated in Figure 10-13. Notice that it does not define a toString() method. Yet, when you write the DisplayDog application in Figure 10-13, it uses a toString() method with a Dog object in the shaded statement. The class compiles correctly, converts the Dog object to a String, and produces the output shown in Figure 10-14 because Dog inherits toString() from Object.

Figure 10-14 Output of the DisplayDog application

The output of the `DisplayDog` application in Figure 10-14 is not very useful. It consists of the class name of which the object is an instance (`Dog`), the at sign (@), and a hexadecimal (base 16) number that represents a unique identifier for every object in the current application.

> **»NOTE** The hexadecimal number that is part of the `String` returned by the `toString()` method is an example of a **hash code**—a calculated number used to identify an object. Later in this chapter, you will learn about the `equals()` method. Java uses the same hash code when you call the built-in version of this method.

Instead of using the automatic `toString()` method with your classes, it is usually more useful to write your own overloaded version of the `toString()` method that displays some or all of the data field values for the object with which you use it. A good `toString()` method can be very useful in debugging a program. If you do not understand why a class is behaving as it is, you can display the `toString()` value and examine its contents. For example, Figure 10-15 shows a `BankAccount` class that contains a mistake in the shaded line—the `BankAccount` balance value is set to the account number instead of the balance amount. Of course, if you made such a mistake within one of your own classes, there would be no shading or comment to help you find the mistake. In addition, a useful `BankAccount` class would be much larger, so the mistake would be more difficult to locate. However, when you ran programs containing `BankAccount` objects, you would notice that the balances of your `BankAccounts` were incorrect. To help you discover why, you could create a short application like the `TestBankAccount` class in Figure 10-16. This application uses the `BankAccount` class `toString()` method to display the relevant details of a `BankAccount` object. The output of the `TestBankAccount` application appears in Figure 10-17.

```
public class BankAccount
{
    private int acctNum;
    private double balance;
    public BankAccount(int num, double bal)
    {
        acctNum = num;
        balance = num;                    »DON'T DO IT
    }                                      The bal parameter should be
    public String toString()              assigned to balance, not
    {                                      the num parameter.
        String info = "BankAccount acctNum = " + acctNum +
            "   Balance = $" + balance;
        return info;
    }
}
```

Figure 10-15 The `BankAccount` class

```
public class TestBankAccount
{
    public static void main(String[] args)
    {
        BankAccount myAccount = new BankAccount(123, 4567.89);
        System.out.println(myAccount.toString());
    }
}
```

Figure 10-16 The `TestBankAccount` application

Figure 10-17 Output of the `TestBankAccount` application

From the output in Figure 10-17, you can see that the account number and balance have the same value, and this knowledge might help you to pin down the location of the incorrect statement in the `BankAccount` class. Of course, you do not have to use a method named `toString()` to discover a `BankAccount`'s attributes. If the class had methods such as `getAcctNum()` and `getBalance()`, you could use them to create a similar application. The advantage of creating a `toString()` method for your classes is that `toString()` is Java's conventional name for a method that converts an object's relevant details into `String` format. Because `toString()` originates in the `Object` class, you can be assured that `toString()` compiles with any object whose details you want to see, even if the method has not been rewritten for the subclass in question. In addition, as you write your own applications and use classes written by others, you can hope that those programmers have overridden `toString()` to provide useful information. You don't have to search documentation to discover a useful method—instead you can rely on the likely usefulness of `toString()`.

> **»NOTE**
> In Chapter 7, you learned that you can use the `toString()` method to convert any object to a `String`. Now you understand why this works.

USING THE `equals()` METHOD

The `Object` class also contains an **equals() method** that takes a single argument, which must be the same type as the type of the invoking object, as in the following example:

```
if(someObject.equals(someOtherObjectOfTheSameType))
    System.out.println("The objects are equal");
```

The `Object` class `equals()` method returns a `boolean` value indicating whether the objects are equal. This `equals()` method considers two objects of the same class to be equal only if they have the same hash code; in other words, they are equal only if one is a reference to the other. For example, two `BankAccount` objects named `myAccount` and `yourAccount` are not automatically equal, even if they have the same account numbers and balances; they are equal only if they have the same memory address. If you want to consider two objects to be equal only when one is a reference to the other, you can use the built-in `Object` class `equals()`

> **»NOTE**
> Other classes, such as the `String` class, also have their own `equals()` methods that overload the `Object` class method. You first used the `equals()` method to compare `String` objects in Chapter 7. Two `String` objects are considered equal only if their `String` contents are identical.

method. However, if you want to consider objects to be equal based on their contents, you must write your own `equals()` method for your classes.

> **NOTE** When you want to compare the contents of two objects, you do not have to overload the `Object` class `equals()` method. Instead, you can write a method with a unique name, such as `areTheyEqual()` or `areContentsSame()`. However, users of your classes will appreciate that you use the expected, usual, and conventional identifiers for your methods.

> **NOTE** Java's `Object` class contains a `public` method named `hashCode()` that returns an integer representing the hash code. (Discovering this number is of little use to you. The default hash code is the internal JVM memory address of the object.) However, whenever you override the `equals()` method in a professional class, you generally want to override the `hashCode()` method as well, because equal objects should have equal hash codes, particularly if the objects will be used in hash-based methods. See the documentation at *http://java.sun.com* for more details.

The application shown in Figure 10-18 instantiates two `BankAccount` objects, using the `BankAccount` class in Figure 10-15. The `BankAccount` class does not include its own `equals()` method, so it does not override the `Object equals()` method. Thus, the application in Figure 10-18 produces the output in Figure 10-19. Even though the two `BankAccount` objects have the same account numbers and balances, the `BankAccounts` are not considered equal because they do not have the same memory address.

```java
public class CompareAccounts
{
    public static void main(String[] args)
    {
        BankAccount acct1 = new BankAccount(1234, 500.00);
        BankAccount acct2 = new BankAccount(1234, 500.00);
        if(acct1.equals(acct2))
            System.out.println("Accounts are equal");
        else
            System.out.println("Accounts are not equal");
    }
}
```

Figure 10-18 The `CompareAccounts` application

Figure 10-19 Output of the `CompareAccounts` application

If your intention is that within applications, two `BankAccount` objects with the same account number and balance are equal, and you want to use the `equals()` method to make the comparison, you must write your own `equals()` method within the `BankAccount` class.

For example, Figure 10-20 shows a new version of the BankAccount class containing a shaded equals() method. When you reexecute the CompareAccounts application in Figure 10-18, the result appears as in Figure 10-21. The two BankAccount objects are equal because their account numbers and balances match. Because the equals() method in Figure 10-20 is part of the BankAccount class, within the method, the object that calls the method is held by the this reference. That is, in the application in Figure 10-18, acct1 becomes the this reference in the equals() method, so the fields acctNum and balance refer to acct1 object values. In the CompareAccounts application, acct2 is the parameter to the equals() method. That is, within the equals() method, acct2 becomes secondAcct, and the secondAcct.acctNum and secondAcct.balance refer to acct2's values.

```java
public class BankAccount
{
    private int acctNum;
    private double balance;
    public BankAccount(int num, double bal)
    {
        acctNum = num;
        balance = bal;
    }
    public String toString()
    {
        String info = "BankAccount acctNum = " + acctNum +
        "    Balance = $" + balance;
        return info;
    }
    public boolean equals(BankAccount secondAcct)
    {
        boolean result;
        if(acctNum == secondAcct.acctNum &&
            balance == secondAcct.balance)
            result = true;
        else
            result = false;
        return result;
    }
}
```

Figure 10-20 The BankAccount class containing its own equals() method

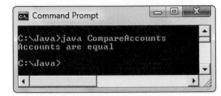

```
C:\Java>java CompareAccounts
Accounts are equal

C:\Java>
```

Figure 10-21 Output of the CompareAccounts application after adding an overloaded equals() method to the BankAccount class

>> **NOTE** If you change a class (such as changing `BankAccount` by adding a new method), not only must you recompile the class, you must also recompile any client applications (such as `CompareAccounts`) so the newly updated class can be relinked to the application and so the clients include the new features of the altered class. If you execute the `CompareAccounts` application but do not recompile `BankAccount`, the application continues to use the previously compiled version of the class.

>> **TWO TRUTHS AND A LIE: USING THE** `Object` **CLASS AND ITS METHODS**

1. When you define a class, if you do not explicitly extend another class, your class is an extension of the `Object` class.
2. The `Object` class is defined in the `java.lang` package, which is imported automatically every time you write a program.
3. The `Object` class `toString()` and `equals()` methods are abstract.

The false statement is #3. The `toString()` and `equals()` methods are not abstract—you are not required to override them in a subclass.

USING INHERITANCE TO ACHIEVE GOOD SOFTWARE DESIGN

When an automobile company designs a new car model, the company does not build every component of the new car from scratch. The company might design a new feature completely from scratch; for example, at some point someone designed the first air bag. However, many of a new car's features are simply modifications of existing features. The manufacturer might create a larger gas tank or more comfortable seats, but even these new features still possess many properties of their predecessors in the older models. Most features of new car models are not even modified; instead, existing components, such as air filters and windshield wipers, are included on the new model without any changes.

Similarly, you can create powerful computer programs more easily if many of their components are used either "as is" or with slight modifications. Inheritance does not give you the ability to write programs that you could not write if inheritance did not exist. If Java did not allow you to extend classes, you *could* create every part of a program from scratch. Inheritance simply makes your job easier. Professional programmers constantly create new class libraries for use with Java programs. Having these classes available makes programming large systems more manageable.

You have already used many "as is" classes, such as `System` and `String`. In these cases, your programs were easier to write than if you had to write these classes yourself. Now that you have learned about inheritance, you have gained the ability to modify existing classes. When you create a useful, extendable superclass, you and other future programmers gain several advantages:

>> Subclass creators save development time because much of the code needed for the class has already been written.

>> Subclass creators save testing time because the superclass code has already been tested and probably used in a variety of situations. In other words, the superclass code is reliable.

» Programmers who create or use new subclasses already understand how the superclass works, so the time it takes to learn the new class features is reduced.

» When you create a new subclass in Java, neither the superclass source code nor the superclass bytecode is changed. The superclass maintains its integrity.

When you consider classes, you must think about the commonalities between them; then you can create superclasses from which to inherit. You might be rewarded professionally when you see your own superclasses extended by others in the future.

»TWO TRUTHS AND A LIE: USING INHERITANCE TO ACHIEVE GOOD SOFTWARE DESIGN

1. If object-oriented programs did not support inheritance, programs could still be written, but they would be harder to write.
2. When you create a useful, extendable superclass, you save development and testing time.
3. When you create a new subclass in Java, you must remember to revise and recompile the superclass code.

The false statement is #3. When you create a new subclass in Java, neither the superclass source code nor the superclass bytecode is changed.

CREATING AND USING INTERFACES

Some object-oriented programming languages, such as C++, allow a subclass to inherit from more than one parent class. For example, you might create an `InsuredItem` class that contains data fields pertaining to each possession for which you have insurance. Data fields might include the name of the item, its value, the insurance policy type, and so on. You might also create an `Automobile` class that contains data fields such as vehicle identification number, make, model, and year. When you create an `InsuredAutomobile` class for a car rental agency, you might want to include `InsuredItem` information and methods, as well as `Automobile` information and methods. It would be convenient to inherit from both the `InsuredItem` and `Automobile` classes. The capability to inherit from more than one class is called **multiple inheritance**.

Many programmers consider multiple inheritance to be a difficult concept, and when inexperienced programmers use it they encounter many problems. Programmers have to deal with the possibility that variables and methods in the parent classes might have identical names, which creates conflict when the child class uses one of the names. Also, you have already learned that a child class constructor must call its parent class constructor. When there are two or more parents, this task becomes more complicated—to which class should `super()` refer when a child class has multiple parents? For all of these reasons, multiple inheritance is prohibited in Java.

Java, however, does provide an alternative to multiple inheritance—an interface. An **interface** looks much like a class, except that all of its methods (if any) are implicitly `public` and `abstract`, and all of its data items (if any) are implicitly `public`, `static`, and `final`.

»NOTE
In Java, a class can inherit from a superclass that has inherited from another superclass—this represents single inheritance with multiple generations. What Java does not allow is for a class to inherit directly from two or more parents.

An interface is a description of what a class does, but not how it is done; it declares method headers, but not the instructions within those methods. When you create a class that uses an interface, you include the keyword `implements` and the interface name in the class header. This notation requires class objects to include code for every method in the interface that has been implemented. Whereas using `extends` allows a subclass to use nonprivate, nonoverridden members of its parent's class, `implements` requires the subclass to implement its own version of each method.

> **»NOTE** In English, an interface is a device or a system that unrelated entities use to interact. Within Java, an interface provides a way for unrelated objects to interact with each other. An interface is analogous to a protocol, which is an agreed-on behavior. In some respects, an `Automobile` can behave like an `InsuredItem`, and so can a `House`, a `TelevisionSet`, and a `JewelryPiece`.

As an example, recall the `Animal` and `Dog` classes from earlier in this chapter. Figure 10-22 shows these classes, with `Dog` inheriting from `Animal`.

```
public abstract class Animal
{
    private String name;
    public abstract void speak();
    public String getName()
    {
        return name;
    }
    public void setName(String animalName)
    {
        name = animalName;
    }
}
public class Dog extends Animal
{
    public void speak()
    {
        System.out.println("Woof!");
    }
}
```

Figure 10-22 The `Animal` and `Dog` classes

You can create a `Worker` interface, as shown in Figure 10-23. For simplicity, this example gives the `Worker` interface a single method named `work()`. When any class implements `Worker`, it must also include a `work()` method.

```
public interface Worker
{
    public void work();
}
```

Figure 10-23 The `Worker` interface

The WorkingDog class in Figure 10-24 extends Dog and implements Worker. A WorkingDog contains a data field that a "regular" Dog does not—an integer that holds hours of training received. The WorkingDog class also contains get and set methods for this field. Because the WorkingDog class implements the Worker interface, it also must contain a work() method that calls the Dog speak() method, and then produces two more lines of output—a statement about working and the number of training hours.

```java
public class WorkingDog extends Dog implements Worker
{
    private int hoursOfTraining;
    public void setHoursOfTraining(int hrs)
    {
        hoursOfTraining = hrs;
    }
    public int getHoursOfTraining()
    {
        return hoursOfTraining;
    }
    public void work()
    {
        speak();
        System.out.println("I am a dog who works");
        System.out.println("I have " + hoursOfTraining +
            " hours of professional training!");
    }
}
```

Figure 10-24 The WorkingDog class

>>**NOTE** As you know from many classes you have seen in this chapter and in Chapter 9, a class can extend another without implementing any interfaces. A class can also implement an interface even though it does not extend any other class. When a class both extends and implements, like the WorkingDog class, by convention the implements clause follows the extends clause in the class header.

The DemoWorkingDogs application in Figure 10-25 instantiates two WorkingDog objects. Each object can use the following methods:

» The setName() and getName() methods that WorkingDog inherits from the Animal class
» The speak() method that WorkingDog inherits from the Dog class
» The setHoursOfTraining() and getHoursOfTraining() methods contained within the WorkingDog class
» The work() method that the WorkingDog class was required to contain when it used the phrase implements Worker; the work() method also calls the speak() method contained in the Dog class

```
public class DemoWorkingDogs
{
   public static void main(String[] args)
   {
      WorkingDog aSheepHerder = new WorkingDog();
      WorkingDog aSeeingEyeDog = new WorkingDog();
      aSheepHerder.setName("Simon, the Border Collie");
      aSeeingEyeDog.setName("Sophie, the German Shepherd");
      aSheepHerder.setHoursOfTraining(40);
      aSeeingEyeDog.setHoursOfTraining(300);

      System.out.println(aSheepHerder.getName() + " says ");
      aSheepHerder.speak();
      aSheepHerder.work();
      System.out.println(); // prints a blank line for readability

      System.out.println(aSeeingEyeDog.getName() + " says ");
      aSeeingEyeDog.speak();
      aSeeingEyeDog.work();
   }
}
```

Figure 10-25 The DemoWorkingDogs application

Figure 10-26 shows the output when the DemoWorkingDogs application executes. Each Animal knows how to "work"—that is, each can execute the work() method contained in the implemented interface. Of course, the WorkingDog class was not required to implement the Worker interface; instead, it could have just contained a work() method that all WorkingDog objects could use. If WorkingDog was the only class that would ever use work(), such an approach would

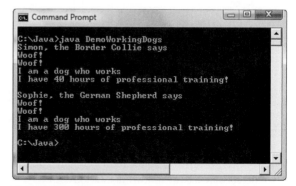

Figure 10-26 Output of the DemoWorkingDogs application

probably be the best course of action. However, if many classes will be Workers—that is, require a work() method—they can all implement work(). If you are already familiar with the Worker interface and its method, when you glance at a class definition for a WorkingHorse, WorkingBird, or Employee and see that it implements Worker, you do not have to guess at the name of the method that shows the work the class objects perform.

>>NOTE   Notice that when a class implements an interface, it represents a situation similar to inheritance. Just as a `WorkingDog` "is a" `Dog` and "is an" `Animal`, so too it "is a" `Worker`. When a class implements an interface, it is promising to "take care of" all the methods listed in the interface class. Either the class must implement all the methods declared in the interface (and any interfaces that the interface itself inherits from), or the class must be declared abstract so that other classes that inherit from it can implement the methods.

You can compare abstract classes and interfaces as follows:

» Abstract classes and interfaces are similar in that you cannot instantiate concrete objects from either one.

» Abstract classes differ from interfaces because abstract classes can contain nonabstract methods, but all methods within an interface must be abstract.

» A class can inherit from only one abstract superclass, but it can implement any number of interfaces.

Beginning programmers sometimes find it difficult to decide when to create an abstract superclass and when to create an interface. Remember, you create an abstract class when you want to provide data or methods that subclasses can inherit, but at the same time these subclasses maintain the ability to override the inherited methods.

Suppose you create a `CardGame` class to use as a base class for different card games. It contains four methods named `shuffle()`, `deal()`, `displayRules()`, and `keepScore()`. The `shuffle()` method works the same way for every `CardGame`, so you write the statements for `shuffle()` within the superclass, and any `CardGame` objects you create later inherit `shuffle()`. The methods `deal()`, `displayRules()`, and `keepScore()` operate differently for every subclass, so you force `CardGame` children to contain instructions for those methods by leaving them empty in the superclass. The `CardGame` class, therefore, should be an abstract superclass. When you write classes named `Hearts`, `Solitaire`, and `Poker`, you extend the `CardGame` parent class, inherit the `shuffle()` method, and write code within the `deal()`, `displayRules()`, and `keepScore()` methods for each specific child.

You create an interface when you know what actions you want to include, but you also want every user to separately define the behavior that must occur when the method executes. Suppose you create a `MusicalInstrument` class to use as a base for different musical instrument object classes such as `Piano`, `Violin`, and `Drum`. The parent `MusicalInstrument` class contains methods such as `playNote()` and `outputSound()` that apply to every instrument, but you want to implement these methods differently for each type of instrument. By making `MusicalInstrument` an interface, you require every subclass to code all the methods.

You also create an interface when you want a class to implement behavior from more than one parent. For example, suppose that you want to create an interactive `NameThatInstrument` card game in which you play an instrument sound from the computer speaker, and ask players to identify the instrument they hear by clicking one of several cards that display instrument images. This game class could not extend from two classes, but it could extend from `CardGame` and implement `MusicalInstrument`.

>>NOTE
An interface specifies only the messages to which an object can respond; an abstract class can include methods that contain the actual behavior the object performs when those messages are received.

>> NOTE When you create a class and use the implements clause to implement an interface, but fail to code one of the interface's methods, the compiler error generated indicates that you must declare your class to be abstract. If you want your class to be used only for extending, you can make it abstract. However, if your intention is to create a class from which you can instantiate objects, do not make it abstract. Instead, find out which methods from the interface you have failed to implement within your class and code those methods.

CREATING INTERFACES TO STORE RELATED CONSTANTS

Interfaces can contain data fields, but they must be public, static, and final. It makes sense that interface data must not be private because interface methods cannot contain method bodies; and without method bodies, you have no way to retrieve private data. It also makes sense that the data fields in an interface are static because you cannot create interface objects. Finally, it makes sense that interface data fields are final because, without methods containing bodies, you have no way, other than at declaration, to set the data fields' values, and you have no way to change them.

Your purpose in creating an interface containing constants is to provide a set of data that a number of classes can use without having to redeclare the values. For example, the interface class in Figure 10-27 provides a number of constants for a pizzeria. Any class written for the pizzeria can implement this interface and use the permanent values. Figure 10-28 shows an example of one application that uses each value, and Figure 10-29 shows the output. The application in Figure 10-28 only needs a declaration for the current special price; all the constants, such as the name of the pizzeria, are retrieved from the interface.

```java
public interface PizzaConstants
{
    public static final int SMALL_DIAMETER = 12;
    public static final int LARGE_DIAMETER = 16;
    public static final double TAX_RATE = 0.07;
    public static final String COMPANY = "Antonio's Pizzeria";
}
```

Figure 10-27 The PizzaConstants interface

```java
public class PizzaDemo implements PizzaConstants
{
    public static void main(String[] args)
    {
        double specialPrice = 11.25;
        System.out.println("Welcome to " + COMPANY);
        System.out.println("We are having a special offer:\na " +
            SMALL_DIAMETER + " inch pizza with four ingredients\nor a " +
            LARGE_DIAMETER +
            " inch pizza with one ingredient\nfor only $" + specialPrice);
        System.out.println("With tax, that is only $" +
            (specialPrice + specialPrice * TAX_RATE));
    }
}
```

Figure 10-28 The PizzaDemo application

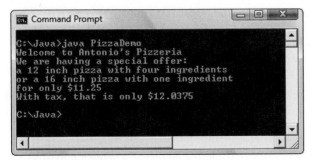

Figure 10-29 Output of the `PizzaDemo` application

»TWO TRUTHS AND A LIE: CREATING AND USING INTERFACES

1. Java's capability to inherit from more than one class is called multiple inheritance.

2. All of the methods in an interface are implicitly `public` and `abstract`, and all of its data items (if any) are implicitly `public`, `static`, and `final`.

3. When a class inherits from another, the child class can use the nonprivate, nonoverridden members of its parent's class, but when a class uses an interface, it must implement its own version of each method.

The false statement is #1. The ability to inherit from more than one class is called multiple inheritance, but Java does not have that ability.

CREATING AND USING PACKAGES

Throughout most of this book, you have imported packages into your programs. You learned in Chapter 4 that the `java.lang` package is automatically imported into every program you write. You have explicitly imported packages such as `java.util` and `javax.swing`. A **package** is a named collection of classes; when you create your own classes, you can place them in packages so that you or other programmers can easily import related classes into new programs. Placing classes in packages for other programmers increases the classes' reusability. When you create a number of classes that inherit from each other, as well as multiple interfaces that you want to implement with these classes, you often will find it convenient to place these related classes in a package.

>**»NOTE** A package is often called a **class library** or a **library of classes**.

>**»NOTE** Creating packages encourages others to reuse software because it makes it convenient to import many related classes at once. In Chapter 3, you learned that if you do not use one of the three access modifiers `public`, `private`, or `protected` for a class, then it has default access, which means that the unmodified class is accessible to any other class in the same package.

>**»NOTE** In the Java programming language, a package or class library is often delivered to users as a **Java ARchive (JAR) file**. JAR files compress the data they store, which reduces the size of archived class files. The JAR format is based on the popular Zip file format.

When you create classes for others to use, you often do not want to provide the users with your source code in the files with .java extensions. You expend significant effort developing workable code for your programs, and you do not want other programmers to be able to copy your programs, make minor changes, and market the new product themselves. Rather, you

»NOTE
When a file contains a `package` declaration, it must be the first statement in the file (excluding comments). If there are `import` declarations, they follow the package declaration.

»NOTE
The `package` statement, `import` statements, and comments are the only statements that appear outside class definitions in Java program files.

»NOTE
If you do not specify a package for a class, it is placed in an unnamed **default package**.

»NOTE
The dot (period) in the compiler command indicates that the path shown in the package statement in the file should be created within the current directory.

»NOTE
You cannot import more than one package in one statement; for example, if multiple packages are stored in a folder named com, you cannot import them with the statement `import com.*`. The `import` statement only imports files from one folder at a time.

want to provide users with the compiled files with the .class extensions. These are the files the user needs to run the program you have developed. Likewise, when other programmers use the classes you have developed, they need only the completed compiled code to import into their programs. The .class files are the files you place in a package so other programmers can import them.

A class that will be placed in a package for others to use must be `public`. If a class is not `public`, it can be used only by other classes within the same package. To place a class in a package, you include a package declaration at the beginning of the source code file. The `package` statement indicates the folder into which the compiled code will be placed. For example, when it appears at the beginning of a class file, the following statement indicates that the compiled file should be placed in a folder named com.course.animals:

```
package com.course.animals;
```

That is, the compiled file should be stored in the animals subfolder inside the course subfolder inside the com subfolder (or com\course\animals). The pathname can contain as many levels as you want. Within the file, the `package` statement must appear outside the class definition.

When you compile a file that you want to place in a package, you must use a compiler option with the `javac` command. The `-d` option indicates that you want to place the generated .class file in a folder. For example, the following command indicates that the compiled Animal.java file should be placed in the directory indicated by the `import` statement within the Animal.java file:

```
javac -d . Animal.java
```

»NOTE The d in the `-d` compiler option stands for *directory*, which is another name for folder. If you do not use the `-d` compiler option, then you must move the compiled .class file to the correct package directory.

If the `Animal` class file contains the statement `package com.course.animals;`, the Animal.class file is placed in C:\com\course\animals. If any of these subfolders do not exist, Java creates them. Similarly, if you package the compiled files for Dog.java, Cow.java, and so on, future programs need only use the following statement to be able to use all the related classes:

```
import com.course.animals.*;
```

The wildcard format is known as a **type-import-on-demand declaration**. Alternatively, you can list each class separately, as in the following two statements:

```
import com.course.Dog;
import com.course.Cow;
```

Usually, if you want to use only one or two classes in a package, you use separate `import` statements for each class. Using the fully qualified name is the most precise method and provides documentation by explicitly listing all imported classes at the top of the source code file. However, if you want to use many classes in a package, it takes less typing to import the entire package; you should use this more efficient method even if you will not use some of the classes.

Because Java is used extensively on the Internet, it is important to give every package a unique name. Sun Microsystems, the creator of Java, has defined a package-naming convention in which you use your Internet domain name in reverse order. For example, if your domain name is course.com, you begin all of your package names with com.course. Subsequently, you organize your packages into reasonable subfolders. Using this convention ensures that your package names do not conflict with those of any other Java code providers. For example, if programmers at another organization with the domain abcdefg.org create an `Animal` class, it will be distributed as org.abcdefg.Animal and its name will not conflict with yours.

>> **NOTE** Creating packages also helps avoid naming conflicts—different programmers might create classes with the same name, but they are contained in different packages. Class-naming conflicts are sometimes called **collisions**. Because of packages, you can create a class without worrying that its name already exists in Java. For example, you can create a class named `Font` and place it in a package named com.course.display. To use each class, you can use the complete name, or **fully qualified name**. The fully qualified name of your `Font` class is `com.course.display.Font`, and the fully qualified name of the built-in `Font` class is `java.awt.Font`.

>> **TWO TRUTHS AND A LIE: CREATING AND USING PACKAGES**

1. Typically, you place .class files in a package so other programmers can import them into their programs.
2. A class that will be placed in a package for others to use must be `protected` so that others cannot read your source code.
3. Java's creators have defined a package-naming convention in which you use your Internet domain name in reverse order.

The false statement is #2. A class that will be placed in a package for others to use must be `public`. If a class is not `public`, it can be used only by other classes within the same package. To prevent others from viewing your source code, you place compiled .class files in distributed packages.

YOU DO IT
CREATING AN ABSTRACT CLASS

In this section, you will create an abstract `Entertainment` class for Event Handlers Incorporated. The `Entertainment` class holds data about entertainment acts that customers can hire to perform at their events. The class includes fields for the name of the act and for the fee charged for providing the act. `Entertainment` is an abstract class; there will never be a "plain" `Entertainment` object. You will create two subclasses, `MusicalEntertainment` and `OtherEntertainment`; these more specific classes include different methods for calculating the entertainment act's fee (musical acts are paid by the performance; other acts are paid by the hour), as well as different methods for displaying data.

To create an abstract `Entertainment` class:

1. Open a new file in your text editor and enter the following first few lines to begin creating an abstract `Entertainment` class:

```
import javax.swing.*;
public abstract class Entertainment
{
```

2. Define the two data fields that hold the entertainer's name and fee as `protected` rather than `private`, because you want child classes to be able to access the fields when the fee is set and when the fields are shown on the screen. Define the fields as follows:

```
protected String entertainer;
protected int fee;
```

3. The `Entertainment` constructor calls two methods. The first method accepts the entertainer's name from the keyboard. The second method sets the entertainer's fee.

```
public Entertainment()
{
    setEntertainerName();
    setEntertainmentFee();
}
```

4. Include the following two `get` methods that return the values for the entertainer's name and the act's fee:

```
public String getEntertainerName()
{
    return entertainer;
}
public double getEntertainmentFee()
{
    return fee;
}
```

5. Enter the following `setEntertainerName()` method, which is a data-entry method that prompts the user for the name of an entertainment act and assigns the entered `String` to the `entertainer` field.

```
public void setEntertainerName()
{
    entertainer = JOptionPane.showInputDialog
        (null, "Enter name of entertainer ");
}
```

6. The `setEntertainmentFee()` method is an abstract method. Each subclass you eventually create that represents different entertainment types will have a different fee schedule. Type the abstract method definition and the closing curly brace for the class:

```
    public abstract void setEntertainmentFee();
}
```

7. Save the file as **Entertainment.java**. At the command prompt, compile the file using the **javac** command.

EXTENDING AN ABSTRACT CLASS

You just created an abstract class, but you cannot instantiate any objects from this class. Rather, you must extend this class to be able to create any `Entertainment`-related objects. Next, you will create a `MusicalEntertainment` class that extends the `Entertainment` class. This new class is concrete; that is, you can create actual `MusicalEntertainment` class objects.

To create the `MusicalEntertainment` class:

1. Open a new file in your text editor, and then type the following, including a header for a `MusicalEntertainment` class that is a child of the `Entertainment` class:

```
import javax.swing.*;
public class MusicalEntertainment extends Entertainment
{
```

2. Add the definition of a music type field that is specific to musical entertainment by typing the following code:

```
private String typeOfMusic;
```

3. The `MusicalEntertainment` constructor must call its parent's constructor. It also uses the following method that sets the music type in which the entertainer specializes:

```
public MusicalEntertainment()
{
    super();
    setTypeOfMusic();
}
```

4. Enter the following `setTypeOfMusic()` method, which asks for user input:

```
public void setTypeOfMusic()
{
    typeOfMusic = JOptionPane.showInputDialog
        (null, "What kind of music does this act play? ");
}
```

5. Event Handlers Incorporated charges a flat rate of $600 per event for musical entertainment. Add the following `setEntertainmentFee()` method to your program:

```
public void setEntertainmentFee()
{
    fee = 600;
}
```

6. Add the following `toString()` method that you can use when you want to convert the details of a `MusicalEntertainment` object into a `String`, so you can easily and efficiently display the contents of the object. Add the closing curly brace for the class.

```
public String toString()
{
    return(entertainer + " features " + typeOfMusic +
        " music; the fee is $ " + fee + " per event.");
}
}
```

> **NOTE**
> In Chapter 7, you first used the automatically included `toString()` method that converts objects to `String`s. Now, you are overriding that method for this class by writing your own version.

7. Save the file as **MusicalEntertainment.java**, and then compile the file.

EXTENDING AN ABSTRACT CLASS WITH A SECOND SUBCLASS

Event Handlers Incorporated classifies all nonmusical entertainment acts, such as clowns, jugglers, and stand-up comics, as `OtherEntertainment`. The `OtherEntertainment` class inherits from `Entertainment`, just as the `MusicalEntertainment` class does. Whereas the `MusicalEntertainment` class requires a data field to hold the type of music played by the act, the `OtherEntertainment` class requires a field for the type of act. Other differences lie in the content of the prompt within the `setTypeOfAct()` method and in the handling of fees. Event Handlers Incorporated charges $50 per hour for nonmusical acts, so both the `setEntertainmentFee()` and `toString()` methods differ from those in the `MusicalEntertainment` class.

Next, you will create an `OtherEntertainment` class to implement the abstract method `setEntertainmentFee()`.

To create the `OtherEntertainment` class file:

1. Open a new file in your text editor, and then type the following first lines of the `OtherEntertainment` class:

```
import javax.swing.*;
public class OtherEntertainment extends Entertainment
{
```

2. Create the following `String` variable to hold the type of entertainment act (such as comedian):

```
private String typeOfAct;
```

3. Enter the following code so the `OtherEntertainment` class constructor calls the parent constructor, and then calls its own method to set the act type:

```
public OtherEntertainment()
{
    super();
    setTypeOfAct();
}
```

4. Enter the following `setTypeOfAct()` method:

```
public void setTypeOfAct()
{
    typeOfAct = JOptionPane.showInputDialog
        (null, "What type of act is this? ");
}
```

5. The fee for nonmusical acts is $50 per hour, so add the following `setEntertainmentFee()` method:

```
public void setEntertainmentFee()
{
    fee = 50;
}
```

6. Enter the following toString() method and add the closing curly brace for the class:

```
public String toString()
{
    return(entertainer + " is a " + typeOfAct +
        "; the fee is $ " + fee + " per hour.");
}
}
```

7. Save the file as **OtherEntertainment.java**, and then compile the class.

INSTANTIATING OBJECTS FROM SUBCLASSES

Next, you will create a program that instantiates concrete objects from each of the two child classes you just created.

To create an application that demonstrates using the MusicalEntertainment and OtherEntertainment classes:

1. Open a new file in your text editor, and then enter the DemoEntertainment class header, opening curly brace, main() method header, and its opening curly brace as follows:

```
import javax.swing.*;
public class DemoEntertainment
{
    public static void main(String[] args)
    {
```

2. Enter the following statement that prompts the user to enter a musical act description. Then instantiate a MusicalEntertainment object.

```
JOptionPane.showMessageDialog (null,
    "You will be asked to enter a musical act description");
    MusicalEntertainment anAct = new MusicalEntertainment();
```

3. Enter the following similar statements for a nonmusical act:

```
JOptionPane.showMessageDialog (null,
    "You will be asked to enter a nonmusical act description");
    OtherEntertainment anotherAct = new OtherEntertainment();
```

4. Enter the following lines to display the contents of the two objects and exit. Add the closing curly brace for the main() method and for the class:

```
        JOptionPane.showMessageDialog(null,
            "\nDescription of entertainment acts:\n" +
            anAct.toString() + "\n" + anotherAct.toString());
    }
}
```

5. Save the file as **DemoEntertainment.java**, and then compile it. After you compile the class with no errors, run this application using the **java DemoEntertainment** command. When the application prompts you, enter the name of a musical act, a type of music, the name of a nonmusical act, and the type of act. Figure 10-30 shows a sample execution.

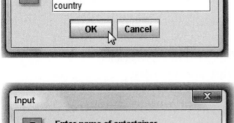

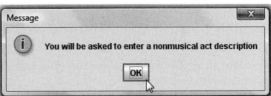

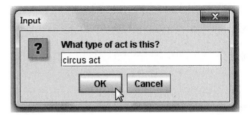

Figure 10-30 Typical execution of the `DemoEntertainment` application

USING OBJECT REFERENCES

Next, you will write an application for Event Handlers Incorporated in which you create an array of `Entertainment` references. Within the application, you assign `MusicalEntertainment` objects and `OtherEntertainment` objects to the same array. Then, because the different object types are stored in the same array, you can easily manipulate them by using a `for` loop.

To write an application that uses an `Entertainment` array:

1. Open a new file in your text editor, and then enter the following first few lines of the `EntertainmentDatabase` program:

```
import javax.swing.*;
public class EntertainmentDatabase
{
    public static void main(String[] args)
    {
```

2. Create the following array of six `Entertainment` references and an integer subscript to use with the array:

```
Entertainment[] actArray = new Entertainment[6];
int x;
```

3. Enter the following `for` loop that prompts you to select whether to enter a musical or nonmusical entertainment act. Based on user input, instantiate either a `MusicalEntertainment` or an `OtherEntertainment` object.

```
for(x = 0; x < actArray.length; ++x)
{
    String userEntry;
    int actType;
    userEntry = JOptionPane.showInputDialog(null,
        "Please select the type of\n " +
        "act you want to enter: \n1 - Musical act\n" +
        " 2 - Any other type of act");
    actType = Integer.parseInt(userEntry);
    if(actType == 1)
        actArray[x] = new MusicalEntertainment();
    else
        actArray[x] = new OtherEntertainment();
}
```

4. After entering the information for all the acts, display the array contents by typing the following code. First create a `StringBuffer` to hold the list of acts. Then, in a `for` loop, build an output `String` by repeatedly adding a newline character and an act from the array to the `StringBuffer` object. Display the constructed `StringBuffer` in a dialog box. Then type the closing curly braces for the `main()` method and for the class:

```
StringBuffer actsString = new StringBuffer();
for(x = 0; x < actArray.length; ++x)
{
    actsString.append("\n");
    actsString.append(actArray[x].toString());
}
JOptionPane.showMessageDialog(null,
    "Our available entertainment selections include:\n" +
    actsString);
}
}
```

5. Save the file as **EntertainmentDatabase.java**, and then compile it. Run the application, entering several acts of your choice. Figure 10-31 shows typical output after the user has entered data.

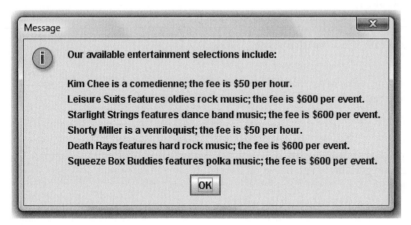

Figure 10-31 Output of the `EntertainmentDatabase` application

OVERRIDING THE `Object` CLASS `equals()` METHOD

Next, you will add an `equals()` method to the Event Handlers Incorporated `Entertainment` class. The built-in `equals()` method determines that two acts are equal only if they had the same hash code; the new, overriding version of the method will consider two `Entertainment` acts equal when they have the same act name. You will use the `equals()` method in the `EntertainmentDatabase` program to compare each new `Entertainment` act to every act residing in the database. Your improved application will not allow two acts to have the same name.

To add an `equals()` method to the `Entertainment` class:

1. Open the **Entertainment.java** file in your text editor, and change the constructor and the class name to **Entertainment2**.

2. Add the `equals()` method as follows:

```
public boolean equals(Entertainment2 act)
{
   boolean result;
   if(entertainer.equals(act.entertainer))
      result = true;
   else
      result = false;
   return result;
}
```

3. Save the file as **Entertainment2.java**, and then compile.

ELIMINATING DUPLICATE USER ENTRIES

Next, you will modify the `EntertainmentDatabase` program so the user cannot enter `Entertainment` objects with the same entertainer names.

To modify the `EntertainmentDatabase` class:

1. Open the **EntertainmentDatabase.java** file in your text editor, and then save it as **EntertainmentNoDuplicates.java**. Change the class name in the file from `EntertainmentDatabase` to **EntertainmentNoDuplicates**.

2. Change the statement that declares `actArray` to the following, because you just updated the `Entertainment` class to an `Entertainment2` class containing an `equals()` method:

```
Entertainment2[] actArray = new Entertainment2[6];
```

3. In the `if` statement that tests the selected act, change `actArray[x] = new MusicalEntertainment();` and `actArray[x] = new OtherEntertainment();` to the following two statements, respectively, and then save the file:

```
actArray[x] = new MusicalEntertainment2();
actArray[x] = new OtherEntertainment2();
```

4. Open the **MusicalEntertainment** file and change the names of both the class and the constructor to **MusicalEntertainment2**. Change the class that this class extends to **Entertainment2**. Save the file as **MusicalEntertainment2.java**, and then compile it.

5. Open the **OtherEntertainment** file and change the names of both the class and the constructor to **OtherEntertainment2**. Change the class that this class extends to **Entertainment2**. Save the file as **OtherEntertainment2.java**, and then compile it.

6. Open the **EntertainmentNoDuplicates** file. Just before the closing curly brace for the `for` loop that controls data entry, add the following additional `for` loop that compares the most recently entered `actArray` element with all previously entered `actArray` elements. If the new element equals any previously entered `Entertainment` act, issue an error

message and reduce the subscript by one. Reducing the subscript ensures that the next act you enter overwrites the duplicate act.

```
for(int y = 0; y < x; ++y)
    if(actArray[x].equals(actArray[y]))
    {
        JOptionPane.showMessageDialog(null,
            "Sorry, you entered a duplicate act");
        --x;
    }
```

7. Save the file, compile it, and then execute the application. When you see the prompts, enter any appropriate data. Be certain that you repeat an entertainer's name for several of the prompts. Each time you repeat a name, you see an error message and get another opportunity to enter an act. The application does not end until you enter six acts with unique names.

CREATING A PACKAGE

Next, you will place some of the Event Handlers Incorporated classes into a package. Because Event Handlers Incorporated sponsors a Web site at *eventhandlers.com*, you will use the com.eventhandlers package. First, you must create a folder named EntertainmentPackage in which to store your project. You can use any technique that is familiar to you. For example, in Windows Vista, you can double-click Computer, navigate to the device or folder where you want to store the package, right-click, click New, click Folder, replace "New Folder" with the new folder name (EntertainmentPackage), and press Enter. Alternatively, from the command prompt, you can navigate to the drive and folder where you want the new folder to reside by using the following commands:

» If the command prompt does not indicate the storage device you want, type the name of the drive and a colon to change the command prompt to a different device. For example, to change the command prompt to the F drive on your system, type `F:`.

» If the directory is not the one you want, type `cd\` to navigate to the root directory. The `cd` command stands for "change directory," and the backslash indicates the root directory. Then type `cd` followed by the name of the subdirectory you want. You can repeat this command as many times as necessary to get to the correct subdirectory if it resides many levels down the directory hierarchy.

Next, you will place three classes into a package.

To place three of your classes for Event Handlers Incorporated into a package:

1. Open the **Entertainment.java** file in your text editor.

2. As the first line in the file, insert the following statement:

```
package com.eventhandlers.entertainment;
```

3. Save the file as **Entertainment.java** in the **EntertainmentPackage** folder.

4. At the command line, at the prompt for the EntertainmentPackage folder, compile the file using the following command:

```
javac -d . Entertainment.java
```

Be certain that you type a space between each element in the command, including surrounding the dot. Java creates a folder named com\eventhandlers\entertainment within the directory from which you compiled the program, and the compiled **Entertainment.class** file is placed in this folder.

> **»NOTE** The development tool GRASP generates software visualizations to make programs easier to understand. A copy of this tool is included with your Student Disk. If you are using jGRASP to compile your Java programs, you can also use it to set compiler options. To set a compiler option to −d, do the following:
>
> » Open a jGRASP project workspace. Click the **Settings** menu, point to **Compiler Settings**, and then click **Workspace**. The Settings for the workspace dialog box appears.
> » Under the FLAGS or ARGS section of the dialog box, click the dot inside the square next to the Compile option and enter the compiler option (**-d**). Then click the **Apply** button.
> » Click the **OK** button to close the dialog box, and then compile your program as usual.

» **NOTE** If you see a list of compile options when you try to compile the file, you did not type the spaces within the command correctly. Repeat Step 4 to compile again.

5. Examine the folders on your storage device, using any operating system program with which you are familiar. For example, if you are compiling at the DOS command line, type **dir** at the command-line prompt to view the folders stored in the current directory. You can see that Java created a folder named com. (If you have too many files and folders stored, it might be difficult to locate the com folder. If so, type **dir com*.*** to see all files and folders in the current folder that begin with "com".) Figure 10-32 shows the command to compile in the EntertainmentPackage directory that has been stored within the Java directory on the C: drive. Then it shows the results of the dir command.

```
C:\Java\EntertainmentPackage>javac -d . Entertainment.java

C:\Java\EntertainmentPackage>dir
 Volume in drive C is OS
 Volume Serial Number is 9277-CEAD

 Directory of C:\Java\EntertainmentPackage

05/01/2010  06:55 AM    <DIR>          .
05/01/2010  06:55 AM    <DIR>          ..
05/01/2010  06:55 AM    <DIR>          com
05/01/2010  06:54 AM               606 Entertainment.java
               1 File(s)            606 bytes
               3 Dir(s)  96,688,934,912 bytes free

C:\Java\EntertainmentPackage>
```

Figure 10-32 Compiling the Entertainment.java file in a package and viewing the results

Alternatively, to view the created folders in a Windows operating system, you can double-click **Computer**, double-click the appropriate storage device, and locate the com folder. Within the com folder is an eventhandlers folder, and within eventhandlers is an entertainment folder. The **Entertainment.class** file is within the entertainment subfolder, and not in the same folder as the .java source file where it ordinarily would be placed.

» **NOTE** If you cannot find the com folder on your storage device, you probably are not looking in the same folder where you compiled the class. Repeat Steps 4 and 5, but be certain that you first change to the command prompt for the directory where your source code file resides.

》NOTE
If you don't want to delete the **Entertainment.java** file from the folder where you compiled the class, and you do not have another copy, you can move it to another location.

6. You could now delete the copy of the **Entertainment.java** file from the EntertainmentPackage folder (although you most likely want to retain a copy elsewhere). There is no further need for this source file in the folder you will distribute to users because the compiled .class file is stored in the com\eventhandlers\entertainment folder. Don't delete the copy of your code from its original storage location; you might want to retain a copy of the code for modification later.

7. Open the **MusicalEntertainment.java** file in your text editor. For the first line in the file, insert the following statement:

   ```
   package com.eventhandlers.entertainment;
   ```

8. Save the file in the same directory as you saved Entertainment.java. At the command line, compile the file using the following command:

   ```
   javac -d . MusicalEntertainment.java
   ```

   Then you can delete the **MusicalEntertainment.java** source file from the EntertainmentPackage folder (not from its original location—you want to retain a copy of your original code).

9. Repeat Steps 7 and 8 to perform the same operations using the **OtherEntertainment.java** file.

10. Open the **EntertainmentDatabase.java** file in your text editor. For the first line in the file, insert the following statements:

    ```
    import com.eventhandlers.entertainment.Entertainment;
    import com.eventhandlers.entertainment.MusicalEntertainment;
    import com.eventhandlers.entertainment.OtherEntertainment;
    ```

11. Save the file as **C:\EntertainmentPackage\EntertainmentDatabase.java**. Compile the file, and then run the program at the EntertainmentPackage prompt using the **java EntertainmentDatabase** command. The program's output should be the same as it was before you added the import statements.

12. Examine the contents of the EntertainmentPackage folder. The only .class file in that directory is the EntertainmentDatabase.class file. Because this file imports the class files from the com.eventhandlers.entertainment package, your program recognizes the `Entertainment`, `MusicalEntertainment`, and `OtherEntertainment` classes, even though neither their .java files nor their .class files are in the same folder with the `EntertainmentDatabase`.

Placing the `Entertainment`-related class files in a folder is not required for the `EntertainmentDatabase` program to execute correctly; you ran it in exactly the same manner before you learned about creating packages. The first time you executed the `EntertainmentDatabase`, all the files you used (source files as well as .class compiled files) were in the same folder on your Student Disk. If you distribute that folder to clients, they have access to all the code you have written.

After placing the class files in a package, you could import the package into the `EntertainmentDatabase` program and run the program from a separate folder.

The folder with the three .class files is the only folder you would want to distribute to programmers who use your `Entertainment` classes to write programs similar to `EntertainmentDatabase`. Placing classes in packages gives you the ability to more easily isolate and distribute files.

DON'T DO IT

» Don't write a body for an abstract method.

» Don't forget to end an abstract method header with a semicolon.

» Don't forget to override any abstract methods in any subclasses you derive.

» Don't mistakenly overload an abstract method instead of overriding it; the subclass method must have the same parameter list as the parent's abstract method.

» Don't try to instantiate an abstract class object.

» Don't forget to override all the methods in an interface that you implement.

KEY TERMS

Concrete classes are nonabstract classes from which objects can be instantiated.

An **abstract class** is one from which you cannot create any concrete objects, but from which you can inherit. Abstract classes usually have one or more empty abstract methods.

Virtual classes is the name given to abstract classes in other programming languages, such as C++.

An **abstract method** is declared with the keyword `abstract`. It is a method with no body—no curly braces and no method statements—just a return type, a method name, an optional argument list, and a semicolon. You are required to code a subclass method to override the empty superclass method that is inherited.

Dynamic method binding is the ability of an application to select the correct subclass method when the program executes.

Late binding is another term for dynamic method binding.

Static or **fixed method binding** is the opposite of dynamic method binding; it occurs when a subclass method is selected when the program compiles rather than while it is running.

The **Object class** is defined in the `java.lang` package, which is imported automatically every time you write a program; it includes methods that you can use or override. When you define a class, if you do not explicitly extend another class, your class is an extension of the `Object` class.

The `Object` class **toString() method** converts an `Object` into a `String` that contains information about the `Object`.

A **hash code** is a calculated number used to identify an object.

The `Object` class **equals() method** takes a single argument, which must be the same type as the type of the invoking object, and returns a `boolean` value indicating whether two object references are equal.

Multiple inheritance is the capability to inherit from more than one class.

An **interface** looks much like a class, except that all of its methods must be abstract and all of its data (if any) must be `static final`; it declares method headers, but not the instructions within those methods.

A **package** is a named collection of classes.

A package is often called a **class library** or a **library of classes**.

A **Java ARchive (JAR) file** compresses the stored data.

A **default package** is the unnamed one in which a class is placed if you do not specify a package for the class.

A **type-import-on-demand declaration** is an import statement that uses the wildcard format to import a package in an application.

Collision is a term that describes a class naming conflict.

A **fully qualified name** includes the entire hierarchy in which a class is stored.

CHAPTER SUMMARY

» A class that you create only to extend from, but not to instantiate from, is an abstract class. Usually, abstract classes contain abstract methods—methods with no method statements. You must code a subclass method to override any inherited abstract superclass method.

» When you create a superclass and one or more subclasses, each object of the subclass "is a" superclass object. Because every subclass object "is a" superclass member, you can convert subclass objects to superclass objects. The ability of a program to select the correct subclass method is known as dynamic method binding.

» Dynamic method binding is most useful when you want to create a method that has one or more parameters that might be one of several types. You also can create an array of superclass object references but store subclass instances in it.

» Every class in Java is an extension of the `Object` class, whether or not you explicitly extend it. Every class inherits several methods from `Object`, including `toString()`, which converts an `Object` into a `String`, and `equals()`, which returns a `boolean` value indicating whether one object is a reference to another. You can override these methods to make them more useful for your classes.

» When you create a useful, extendable superclass, you save development time because much of the code needed for the class has already been written. In addition, you save testing time and, because the superclass code is reliable, you reduce the time it takes to learn the new class features. You also maintain superclass integrity.

» An interface is similar to a class, but all of its methods are implicitly `public` and `abstract`, and all of its data (if any) is implicitly `public`, `static`, and `final`. When you create a class that uses an interface, you include the keyword `implements` and the interface name in the class header. This notation serves to require class objects to include code for all the methods in the interface.

» Abstract classes and interfaces are similar in that you cannot instantiate concrete objects from either. Abstract classes differ from interfaces because abstract classes can contain nonabstract methods, but all methods within an interface must be abstract. A class can inherit from only one abstract superclass, but it can implement any number of interfaces.

» You can place classes in packages so you or other programmers can easily import related classes into new classes. The convention for naming packages uses Internet domain names in reverse order to ensure that your package names do not conflict with those of any other Internet users.

REVIEW QUESTIONS

1. Parent classes are _____ than their child classes.

   a. less specific   c. easier to understand

   b. more specific   d. more cryptic

2. Abstract classes differ from other classes in that you _____ .

   a. must not code any methods within them   c. cannot instantiate objects from them

   b. must instantiate objects from them   d. cannot have data fields within them

3. Abstract classes can contain _____ .

   a. abstract methods   c. both of the above

   b. nonabstract methods   d. none of the above

4. An abstract class `Product` has two subclasses, `Perishable` and `NonPerishable`. None of the constructors for these classes requires any arguments. Which of the following statements is legal?

   a. `Product myProduct = new Product();`

   b. `Perishable myProduct = new Product();`

   c. `NonPerishable myProduct = new NonPerishable();`

   d. none of the above

5. An abstract class `Employee` has two subclasses, `Permanent` and `Temporary`. The `Employee` class contains an abstract method named `setType()`. Before you can instantiate `Permanent` and `Temporary` objects, which of the following statements must be true?

   a. You must code statements for the `setType()` method within the `Permanent` class.

   b. You must code statements for the `setType()` method within both the `Permanent` and `Temporary` classes.

   c. You must not code statements for the `setType()` method within either the `Permanent` or `Temporary` class.

   d. You can code statements for the `setType()` method within the `Permanent` class or the `Temporary` class, but not both.

6. When you create a superclass and one or more subclasses, each object of the subclass _____ superclass object.

   a. overrides the   c. "is not a"

   b. "is a"   d. is a new

7. Which of the following statements is true?

   a. Superclass objects are members of their subclass.

   b. Superclasses can contain abstract methods.

   c. You can create an abstract class object using the `new` operator.

   d. An abstract class cannot contain an abstract method.

8. When you create a _____ in Java, you create a variable name in which you can hold the memory address of an object.

   a. field   c. recommendation

   b. pointer   d. reference

9. An application's ability to select the correct subclass method to execute is known as _____ method binding.

   a. polymorphic   c. early

   b. dynamic   d. intelligent

10. Which statement creates an array of five reference objects of an abstract class named `Currency`?

    a. `Currency[] = new Currency[5];`

    b. `Currency[] currencyref = new Currency[5];`

    c. `Currency[5] currencyref = new Currency[5];`

    d. `Currency[5] = new Currency[5];`

11. You _____ override the `toString()` method in any class you create.

    a. cannot   c. must

    b. can   d. must implement `StringListener` to

12. The `Object` class `equals()` method takes _____ .

    a. no arguments   c. two arguments

    b. one argument   d. as many arguments as you need

13. Assume the following statement appears in a working Java program:

    ```
    if(thing.equals(anotherThing))  x = 1;
    ```

    You know that _____ .

    a. `thing` is an object of the `Object` class   c. Both of the above are correct.

    b. `anotherThing` is the same type as `thing`   d. None of the above are correct.

14. The `Object` class `equals()` method considers two object references to be equal if they have the same _____ .

    a. value in all data fields   c. data type

    b. value in any data field   d. memory address

15. Java subclasses have the ability to inherit from _____ parent class(es).

    a. one   c. multiple

    b. two   d. no

16. The alternative to multiple inheritance in Java is known as a(n) _____ .

    a. superobject   c. interface

    b. abstract class   d. none of the above

17. When you create a class that uses an interface, you include the keyword _____ and the interface's name in the class header.

    a. `interface`   c. `accouterments`

    b. `implements`   d. `listener`

18. You can instantiate concrete objects from a(n) _____ .

    a. abstract class   c. either a or b

    b. interface   d. neither a nor b

19. In Java, a class can _____ .

    a. inherit from one abstract superclass at most   c. both a and b

    b. implement one interface at most   d. neither a nor b

20. When you want to provide some data or methods that subclasses can inherit, but you want the subclasses to override some specific methods, you should write a(n) _____ .

    a. abstract class   c. final superclass

    b. interface   d. concrete object

EXERCISES

1. a. Create an abstract class named `Book`. Include a `String` field for the book's title and a `double` field for the book's price. Within the class, include a constructor that requires the book title and add two get methods—one that returns the title and one that returns the price. Include an abstract method named `setPrice()`. Create two child classes of `Book`: `Fiction` and `NonFiction`. Each must include a `setPrice()` method that sets the price for all `Fiction Books` to $24.99 and for all `NonFiction Books` to $37.99. Write a constructor for each subclass, and include a call to `setPrice()` within each. Write an application demonstrating that you can create both a `Fiction` and a `NonFiction Book`, and display their fields. Save the files as **Book.java**, **Fiction.java**, **NonFiction.java**, and **UseBook.java**.

   b. Write an application named `BookArray` in which you create an array that holds 10 `Books`, some `Fiction` and some `NonFiction`. Using a `for` loop, display details about all 10 books. Save the file as **BookArray.java**.

2. a. Create an abstract class named `Account` for a bank. Include an integer field for the account number and a `double` field for the account balance. Also include a constructor that requires an account number and that sets the balance to 0.0. Include a set method for the balance. Also include two abstract get methods—one for each field. Create two child classes of `Account`: `Checking` and `Savings`. Within the `Checking` class, the get method displays the `String` "Checking Account Information", the account number, and the balance. Within the `Savings` class, add a field to hold the interest rate, and require the `Savings` constructor to accept an argument for the value of the interest rate. The `Savings` get method displays the `String` "Savings Account Information", the account number, the balance, and the interest rate. Write an application that demonstrates you can instantiate and display both `Checking` and `Savings` objects. Save the files as **Account.java**, **Checking.java**, **Savings.java**, and **DemoAccounts.java**.

   b. Write an application named `AccountArray` in which you enter data for a mix of 10 `Checking` and `Savings` accounts. Use a `for` loop to display the data. Save the file as **AccountArray.java**.

3. Create an abstract `Auto` class with fields for the car make and price. Include get and set methods for these fields; the `setPrice()` method is abstract. Create two subclasses for individual automobile makers (for example, Ford or Chevy), and include appropriate `setPrice()` methods in each subclass (for example, $20,000 or $22,000). Finally, write an application that uses the `Auto` class and subclasses to display information about different cars. Save the files as **Auto.java**, **Ford.java**, **Chevy.java**, and **UseAuto.java**.

4. Create an abstract `Division` class with fields for a company's division name and account number, and an abstract `display()` method. Use a constructor in the superclass that requires values for both fields. Create two subclasses named `InternationalDivision` and `DomesticDivision`. The `InternationalDivision` includes a field for the country in which the division is located and a field for the language spoken; its constructor requires both. The `DomesticDivision` includes a field for the state in which the division

is located; a value for this field is required by the constructor. Write an application named `UseDivision` that creates `InternationalDivision` and `DomesticDivision` objects for two different companies and displays information about them. Save the files as **Division.java**, **InternationalDivision.java**, **DomesticDivision.java**, and **UseDivision.java**.

5. Write an application named `UseChildren` that creates and displays at least two `Child` objects—one `Male` and one `Female`. `Child` is an abstract class and `Male` and `Female` are subclasses. The `Child` class contains fields that hold the name, gender, and age of a child. The `Child` class constructor requires a name and a gender. The `Child` class also contains two abstract methods named `setAge()` and `display()`. The `Male` and `Female` subclass constructors require only a name; they pass the name and appropriate gender to the `Child`. The subclass constructors also prompt the user for an age using the `setAge()` method, and display the `Child`'s data using the `display()` method. Save the files as **Child.java**, **Male.java**, **Female.java**, and **UseChildren.java**.

6. Create a class named `NewspaperSubscriber` with fields for a subscriber's street address and the subscription rate. Include get and set methods for the subscriber's street address, and include get and set methods for the subscription rate. The set method for the rate is abstract. Include an `equals()` method that indicates two `Subscribers` are equal if they have the same street address. Create child classes named `SevenDaySubscriber`, `WeekdaySubscriber`, and `WeekendSubscriber`. Each child class constructor sets the rate as follows: `SevenDaySubscribers` pay $4.50 per week, `WeekdaySubscribers` pay $3.50 per week, and `WeekendSubscribers` pay $2.00 per week. Each child class should include a `toString()` method that returns the street address, rate, and service type. Write an application named `Subscribers` that prompts the user for the subscriber's street address and requested service, and then creates the appropriate object based on the service type. Do not let the user enter more than one subscription type for any given street address. Save the files as **NewspaperSubscriber.java**, **WeekdaySubscriber.java**, **WeekendSubscriber.java**, **SevenDaySubscriber.java**, and **Subscribers.java**.

7. a. Create an interface named `Turner`, with a single method named `turn()`. Create a class named `Leaf` that implements `turn()` to print "Changing colors". Create a class named `Page` that implements `turn()` to print "Going to the next page". Create a class named `Pancake` that implements `turn()` to print "Flipping". Write an application named `DemoTurners` that creates one object of each of these class types and demonstrates the `turn()` method for each class. Save the files as **Turner.java**, **Leaf.java**, **Page.java**, **Pancake.java**, and **DemoTurners.java**.

   b. Think of two more objects that use `turn()`, create classes for them, and then add objects to the `DemoTurners` application, renaming it **DemoTurners2.java**. Save the files, using the names of new objects that use `turn()`.

8. Write an application named `UseInsurance` that uses an abstract `Insurance` class and `Health` and `Life` subclasses to display different types of insurance policies and the cost per month. The `Insurance` class contains a `String` representing the type of insurance and a `double` that holds the monthly price. The `Insurance` class constructor requires

a `String` argument indicating the type of insurance, but the `Life` and `Health` class constructors require no arguments. The `Insurance` class contains a get method for each field; it also contains two abstract methods named `setCost()` and `display()`. The `Life` class `setCost()` method sets the monthly fee to $36, and the `Health` class sets the monthly fee to $196. Write an application named `UseInsurance` that prompts the user for the type of insurance to be displayed, and then create the appropriate object. Save the files as **Life.java**, **Health.java**, **Insurance.java**, and **UseInsurance.java**.

9. Write an application named `UseLoan` that uses an abstract class named `PersonalLoan` and subclasses to display two different types of loans—home and car—and the cost per month for each. Each of the subclasses contains a constructor that sets the cost per month based on the loan type, after prompting the user for at least one data-entry item that is used in the cost-determining decision. (For example, with a car loan, you might ask the age of the car, or whether it is a sports car.) Include an abstract `toString()` method in the `PersonalLoan` class that constructs a `String` containing all the relevant data. Prompt the user for the type of insurance, and then create and display the appropriate object. Save the files as **PersonalLoan.java**, **CarLoan.java**, **HomeLoan.java**, and **UseLoan.java**.

10. Create an abstract class called `GeometricFigure`. Each figure includes a height, a width, a figure type, and an area. Include an abstract method to determine the area of the figure. Create two subclasses called `Square` and `Triangle`. Create an application that demonstrates creating objects of both subclasses, and store them in an array. Save the files as **GeometricFigure.java**, **Square.java**, **Triangle.java**, and **UseGeometric.java**.

11. Modify Exercise 10, adding an interface called `SidedObject` that contains a method called `printSides()`; this method displays the number of sides the object possesses. Modify the `GeometricFigure` subclasses to include the use of the interface to print the number of sides of the figure. Create an application that demonstrates the use of both subclasses. Save the files as **GeometricFigure2.java**, **Square2.java**, **Triangle2.java**, **SidedObject.java**, and **UseGeometric2.java**.

12. Create an interface called `Player`. The interface has an abstract method called `play()` that displays a message describing the meaning of "play" to the class. Create classes called `Child`, `Musician`, and `Actor` that all implement `Player`. Create an application that demonstrates the use of the classes. Save the files as **Player.java**, **Child.java**, **Actor.java**, **Musician.java**, and **UsePlayer.java**.

13. Create an abstract class called `Student`. The `Student` class includes a name and a `boolean` value representing full-time status. Include an abstract method to determine the tuition, with full-time students paying a flat fee of $2000 and part-time students paying $200 per credit hour. Create two subclasses called `FullTime` and `PartTime`. Create an application that demonstrates how to create objects of both subclasses. Save the files as **Student.java**, **FullTime.java**, **PartTime.java**, and **UseStudent.java**.

14. Create a `Building` class and two subclasses, `House` and `School`. The `Building` class contains fields for square footage and stories. The `House` class contains additional fields for number of bedrooms and baths. The `School` class contains additional fields for

number of classrooms and grade level (for example, elementary or junior high). All the classes contain appropriate get and set methods. Place the `Building`, `House`, and `School` classes in a package named com.course.buildings. Create an application that declares objects of each type and uses the package. Save the necessary files as **Building.java**, **House.java**, **School.java**, and **CreateBuildings.java**.

15. Sanchez Construction Loan Co. makes loans of up to $100,000 for construction projects. There are two categories of `Loans`—those to businesses and those to individual applicants.

    Write an application that tracks all new construction loans. The application must also calculate the total amount owed at the due date (original loan amount + loan fee). The application should include the following classes:

    » `Loan`—A public abstract class that implements the `LoanConstants` interface. A `Loan` includes a loan number, customer last name, amount of loan, interest rate, and term. The constructor requires data for each of the fields except interest rate. Do not allow loan amounts over $100,000. Force any loan term that is not one of the three defined in the `LoanConstants` class to a short-term, one-year loan. Create a `toString()` method that displays all the loan data.

    » `LoanConstants`—A public interface class. `LoanConstants` includes constant values for short-term (one year), medium-term (three years), and long-term (five years) loans. It also contains constants for the company name and the maximum loan amount.

    » `BusinessLoan`—A public class that extends `Loan`. The `BusinessLoan` constructor sets the interest rate to 1% over the current prime interest rate.

    » `PersonalLoan`—A public class that extends `Loan`. The `PersonalLoan` constructor sets the interest rate to 2% over the current prime interest rate.

    » `CreateLoans`—An application that creates an array of five `Loans`. Prompt the user for the current prime interest rate. Then, in a loop, prompt the user for a loan type and all relevant information for that loan. Store the created `Loan` objects in the array. When data entry is complete, display all the loans.

    Save the files as **Loan.java**, **LoanConstants.java**, **BusinessLoan.java**, **PersonalLoan.java**, and **CreateLoans.java**.

DEBUGGING EXERCISES

Each of the following files in the Chapter.10 folder on your Student Disk has syntax and/or logic errors. In each case, determine the problem and fix the program. After you correct the errors, save each file using the same filename preceded with Fix. For example, DebugTen1.java will become FixDebugTen1.java.

a. DebugTen1.java

b. DebugTen2.java

c. DebugTen3.java

d. DebugTen4.java

e. Three other Debug files in the Chapter.10 folder

GAME ZONE

1. In Chapter 9, you created an `Alien` class as well as two descendant classes, `Martian` and `Jupiterian`. Because you never create any "plain" `Alien` objects, alter the `Alien` class so it is abstract. Verify that the `Martian` and `Jupiterian` classes can still inherit from `Alien` and that the `CreateAliens` program still works correctly. Save the altered `Alien` file as **Alien.java**.

2. a. Create an abstract `CardGame` class similar to the one described in this chapter. The class contains a "deck" of 52 playing cards that uses a `Card` class that holds a suit and value for each `Card` object. It also contains an integer field that holds the number of cards dealt to a player in a particular game. The class contains a constructor that initializes the deck of cards with appropriate values (e.g., "King of Hearts"), and a `shuffle()` method that randomly arranges the positions of the `Card`s in the array. The class also contains two abstract methods: `displayDescription()`, which displays a brief description of the game in child classes, and `deal()`, which deals the appropriate number of `Card` objects to one player of a game. Save the file as **CardGame.java**.

   b. Create two child classes that extend `CardGame`. You can choose any games you prefer. For example, you might create a `Poker` class or a `Bridge` class. Create a constructor for each child class that initializes the field that holds the number of cards dealt to the correct value. (For example, in standard poker, a player receives five cards, but in bridge, a player receives 13.) Create an appropriate `displayDescription()` and `deal()` method for each child class. Save each file using an appropriate name—for example, **Poker.java** or **Bridge.java**.

   c. Create an application that instantiates one object of each game type and demonstrates that the methods work correctly. Save the application as **PlayCardGames.java**.

TOUGH QUESTIONS

1. Describe the signature of the `Object` class constructor and explain how you know your answer is correct.

2. Can an `abstract` class have a `final` method? Why or why not?

3. Write the `Object` class `equals()` method to match as closely as possible the original version written by Java's creators.

UP FOR DISCUSSION

1. Programming sometimes can be done from a remote location. For example, as a professional programmer, you might be able to work from home. Does this appeal to you? What are the advantages and disadvantages? If you have other programmers working for you, would you allow them to work from home? Would you require any "face time"—that is, time in the office with you or other workers?

2. Programming sometimes can be done from a remote location. For example, your organization might contract programmers who live in another country, where wages are considerably lower than in the United States. Do you have any objections to employers using these workers? If not, what objections do you think others might have?

3. Suppose your organization hires programmers to work in another country. Suppose you also discover that working conditions there are not the same as in your country. For example, the buildings in which the workers do their jobs might not be subject to the same standards for ventilation and fire codes as the building where you work. Is your company under any obligation to change the working conditions?

11

EXCEPTION HANDLING

In this chapter, you will:

Learn about exceptions
Try code and catch `Exceptions`
Throw and catch multiple `Exceptions`
Use the `finally` block
Understand the advantages of exception handling
Specify the `Exceptions` a method can throw
Trace `Exceptions` through the call stack
Create your own `Exceptions`
Use an assertion

JAVA ON THE JOB, SCENE 11

You're muttering to yourself at your desk at Event Handlers Incorporated.

"Anything wrong?" Lynn Greenbrier asks as she passes by.

"It's these errors!" you complain.

"Aren't you going overboard?" Lynn asks. "Everyone makes errors when they code programs."

"Oh, I expect typos and compiler errors while I'm developing my programs," you say, "but no matter how well I write my code, the user can still mess everything up by inputting bad data. The Event Planning Department told me that it has events planned for the 32nd day of the month and for negative five attendees. Even if my code is perfect, the user can enter mistakes."

"Then your code isn't perfect yet," Lynn says. "Besides writing programs that can handle ordinary situations, you must enable your programs to handle exceptions."

LEARNING ABOUT EXCEPTIONS

An **exception** is an unexpected or error condition. The programs you write can generate many types of potential exceptions, such as when you do the following:

» You issue a command to read a file from a disk, but the file does not exist there.

» You attempt to write data to a disk, but the disk is full or unformatted.

» Your program asks for user input, but the user enters invalid data.

» The program attempts to divide a value by 0, access an array with a subscript that is too large, or calculate a value that is too large for the answer's variable type.

> **NOTE**
> Providing for exceptions involves an oxymoron; you must expect the unexpected.

These errors are called exceptions because, presumably, they are not usual occurrences; they are "exceptional." The object-oriented techniques to manage such errors comprise the group of methods known as **exception handling**.

> **NOTE**
> Unplanned exceptions that occur during a program's execution are also called **runtime exceptions**.

Like all other classes in Java, exceptions are `Objects`. Java has two basic classes of errors: `Error` and `Exception`. Both of these classes descend from the `Throwable` class, as shown in Figure 11-1.

```
java.lang.Object
|
+--java.lang.Throwable
   |
   +--java.lang.Exception
   |  |
   |  +--java.io.IOException
   |  |
   |  +--java.lang.RuntimeException
   |  |  |
   |  |  +--java.lang.ArithmeticException
   |  |  |
   |  |  +-- java.lang.IndexOutOfBoundsException
   |  |  |  |
   |  |  |  +—java.lang.ArrayIndexOutOfBoundsException
   |  |  |
   |  |  +-- java.util.NoSuchElementException
   |  |  |   |
   |  |  |   +--java.util.InputMismatchException
   |  |  |
   |  |  +--Others..
   |  |
   |  +--Others..
   |  |
   |  +--java.lang.Error
   |     |
   |     +-- java.lang.VirtualMachineError
   |         |
   |         +--java.lang.OutOfMemoryError
   |         |
   |         +--java.lang.InternalError
   |         |
   |         +--Others...
```

Figure 11-1 The Exception and Error class inheritance hierarchy

>> **NOTE** With Java SE 6 (Java Standard Edition version 6.0), Java acknowledges more than 75 categories of Exceptions with unusual names such as ActivationException, AlreadyBoundException, AWTException, CloneNotSupportedException, PropertyVetoException, and UnsupportedFlavorException. See *http://java.sun.com* for more details about these and other Exceptions.

The **Error class** represents more serious errors from which your program usually cannot recover. Usually, you do not use or implement Error objects in your programs. A program cannot recover from Error conditions on its own.

NOTE
In this chapter, when you see the word "error" with a lowercase "e," think of a general mistake-generating condition. When you see "Error" with an uppercase "E," think of the Error class.

The **Exception class** comprises less serious errors that represent unusual conditions that arise while a program is running and from which the program *can* recover. Some examples of Exception class errors include using an invalid array subscript or performing certain illegal arithmetic operations.

Java displays an Exception message when the program code could have prevented an error. For example, Figure 11-2 shows a class named Division that contains a single, small main() method. The method declares three integers, prompts the user for values for two of them, and calculates the value of the third integer by dividing the first two values.

```java
import java.util.Scanner;
public class Division
{
    public static void main(String[] args)
    {
        Scanner input = new Scanner(System.in);
        int numerator, denominator, result;
        System.out.print("Enter numerator >> ");
        numerator = input.nextInt();
        System.out.print("Enter denominator >> ");
        denominator = input.nextInt();
        result = numerator / denominator;
        System.out.println(numerator + " / " + denominator +
            " = " + result);
    }
}
```

Figure 11-2 The Division class

Figure 11-3 shows two typical executions of the Division program. In the first execution, the user enters two usable values and the program executes normally. In the second execution, the user enters 0 as the value for the denominator and an Exception message is displayed.

NOTE
Java does not allow integer division by 0, but floating-point division by 0 is allowed— the result displays as Infinity.

Figure 11-3 Two typical executions of the Division application

464

In Figure 11-3, the Exception is a java.lang.ArithmeticException. An ArithmeticException is one of the many subclasses of Exception. You also get some information about the error ("/ by zero"), the method that generated the error (Division.main), and the file and line number for the error (Division.java, line 12).

NOTE
You learned about subclasses and inheritance in Chapters 9 and 10.

Figure 11-4 shows two more executions of the Division class. In each execution, the user has entered noninteger data for the denominator—first a string of characters, and second, a floating-point value. In each case, a different type of Exception occurs. You can see from either set of error messages that the Exception is an InputMismatchException. The last line of the messages indicates that the problem occurred in line 11 of the Division program, and the second-to-last error message shows that the problem occurred within the call to nextInt(). Because the user did not enter an integer, the nextInt() method failed. The second-to-last message also shows that the error occurred in line 2050 of the nextInt() method, but clearly you do not want to alter the nextInt() method that resides in the Scanner class—you either want to rerun the program and enter an integer, or alter the program so that these errors cannot occur in subsequent executions.

```
Command Prompt

C:\Java>java Division
Enter numerator >> 13
Enter denominator >> five
Exception in thread "main" java.util.InputMismatchException
        at java.util.Scanner.throwFor(Scanner.java:840)
        at java.util.Scanner.next(Scanner.java:1461)
        at java.util.Scanner.nextInt(Scanner.java:2091)
        at java.util.Scanner.nextInt(Scanner.java:2050)
        at Division.main(Division.java:11)

C:\Java>java Division
Enter numerator >> 13
Enter denominator >> 5.5
Exception in thread "main" java.util.InputMismatchException
        at java.util.Scanner.throwFor(Scanner.java:840)
        at java.util.Scanner.next(Scanner.java:1461)
        at java.util.Scanner.nextInt(Scanner.java:2091)
        at java.util.Scanner.nextInt(Scanner.java:2050)
        at Division.main(Division.java:11)

C:\Java>_
```

Figure 11-4 Two executions of the Division application in which the user enters noninteger values

NOTE The list of error messages after each attempted execution in Figure 11-4 is called a **stack trace history list**, or more simply, a **stack trace**. (You might also hear the terms *stack backtrace* or *stack traceback*.) The list shows each method that was called as the program ran. You will learn more about tracing the stack later in this chapter.

Just because an Exception occurs, you don't necessarily have to deal with it. In the Division class, you can simply let the offending program terminate. However, the program termination is abrupt and unforgiving. When a program divides two numbers (or performs a less trivial task such as balancing a checkbook), the user might be annoyed if the program ends abruptly. However, if the program is used for a more critical task such as air-traffic control or to monitor a patient's vital statistics during surgery, an abrupt conclusion could be disastrous. Object-oriented error-handling techniques provide more elegant (and safer) solutions.

Of course, you can write programs without using exception-handling techniques—you have already written many such programs as you have worked through this book. Programmers had to deal with error conditions long before object-oriented methods were conceived. Probably the most common error-handling solution has been to use a decision to avoid an error. For example, you can change the main() method of the Division class to avoid dividing by 0 by adding the decision shown in the shaded portion of Figure 11-5.

```java
import java.util.Scanner;
public class Division2
{
    public static void main(String[] args)
    {
        Scanner input = new Scanner(System.in);
        int numerator, denominator, result;
        System.out.print("Enter numerator >> ");
        numerator = input.nextInt();
        System.out.print("Enter denominator >> ");
        denominator = input.nextInt();
        if(denominator == 0)
            System.out.println("Cannot divide by 0");
        else
        {
            result = numerator / denominator;
            System.out.println(numerator + " / " + denominator +
                " = " + result);
        }
    }
}
```

Figure 11-5 A Division2 application using a traditional error-handling technique

The application in Figure 11-5 displays a message to the user when 0 is entered for a denominator value, but it is not able to recover when noninteger data is entered. Exception handling provides a more elegant solution for handling error conditions. In object-oriented terminology, you "try" a procedure that might cause an error. A method that detects an error condition or Exception "throws an exception," and the block of code that processes the error "catches the exception."

»NOTE
Even if you choose never to use exception-handling techniques in your own programs, you must understand them because built-in Java methods will throw exceptions to your programs.

»NOTE Programs that can handle exceptions appropriately are said to be more fault-tolerant and robust. **Fault-tolerant** applications are designed so that they continue to operate, possibly at a reduced level, when some part of the system fails. **Robustness** represents the degree to which a system is resilient to stress, maintaining correct functioning.

TRYING CODE AND CATCHING Exceptions

When you create a segment of code in which something might go wrong, you place the code in a **try block**, which is a block of code you attempt to execute while acknowledging that an exception might occur. A `try` block consists of the following elements:

» The keyword `try`
» An opening curly brace
» Executable statements, including some that might cause exceptions
» A closing curly brace

You usually code at least one `catch` block immediately following a `try` block. A **catch block** is a segment of code that can handle an exception that might be thrown by the `try` block that precedes it. The exception might be thrown automatically, or you might explicitly write a `throw` statement. A **throw statement** is one that sends an `Exception` out of a block or a method so it can be handled elsewhere. A thrown `Exception` can be caught by a `catch` block. Each `catch` block can "catch" one type of exception—that is, one object that is an object of type `Exception` or one of its child classes. You create a `catch` block by typing the following elements:

» The keyword `catch`
» An opening parenthesis
» An `Exception` type
» A name for an instance of the `Exception` type
» A closing parenthesis
» An opening curly brace
» The statements that take the action you want to use to handle the error condition
» A closing curly brace

Figure 11-6 shows the general format of a method that includes a shaded `try...catch` pair.

»NOTE
If you do not include a `catch` block immediately after a `try` block, then you must code a `finally` block. You will learn about `finally` blocks later in this chapter.

```
returnType methodName(optional arguments)
{
    // optional statements prior to code that is tried
    try
    {
        // statement or statements that might generate an exception
    }
    catch(Exception someException)
    {
        // actions to take if exception occurs
    }
    // optional statements that occur after try,
    // whether catch block executes or not
}
```

Figure 11-6 Format of `try...catch` pair

In Figure 11-6, `someException` represents an object of the `Exception` class or any of its subclasses. If an `Exception` occurs during the execution of the `try` block, the statements in the `catch` block execute. If no `Exception` occurs within the `try` block, the `catch` block does not execute. Either way, the statements following the `catch` block execute normally.

Figure 11-7 shows an application named `DivisionMistakeCaught` that improves on the `Division` class. The `main()` method in the class contains a `try` block with code that attempts division. When illegal integer division is attempted, an `ArithmeticException` is automatically created and the `catch` block executes, displaying the output shown in Figure 11-8.

```java
import java.util.Scanner;
public class DivisionMistakeCaught
{
    public static void main(String[] args)
    {
        Scanner input = new Scanner(System.in);
        int numerator, denominator, result;
        System.out.print("Enter numerator >> ");
        numerator = input.nextInt();
        System.out.print("Enter denominator >> ");
        denominator = input.nextInt();
        try
        {
            result = numerator / denominator;
            System.out.println(numerator + " / " + denominator +
                " = " + result);
        }
        catch(ArithmeticException mistake)
        {
            System.out.println("Attempt to divide by zero");
        }
    }
}
```

Figure 11-7 The `DivisionMistakeCaught` application

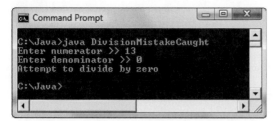

Figure 11-8 Output of the DivisionMistakeCaught application

When the DivisionMistakeCaught application displays the error message ("Attempt to divide by zero"), you cannot confirm that division by 0 was the source of the error. In reality, *any* ArithmeticException generated within the try block in the program would be caught by the catch block in the method. Instead of writing your own message, you can use the getMessage() method that ArithmeticException inherits from the Throwable class. To retrieve Java's message about any ThrowableException named someException, you code someException.getMessage().

For example, Figure 11-9 shows a DivisionMistakeCaught2 class that uses the getMessage() method (see the shaded statement) to generate the message that "comes with" the caught ArithmeticException argument to the catch block. Figure 11-10 shows the output; the message is "/ by zero".

```
import java.util.Scanner;
public class DivisionMistakeCaught2
{
    public static void main(String[] args)
    {
        Scanner input = new Scanner(System.in);
        int numerator, denominator, result;
        System.out.print("Enter numerator >> ");
        numerator = input.nextInt();
        System.out.print("Enter denominator >> ");
        denominator = input.nextInt();
        try
        {
            result = numerator / denominator;
            System.out.println(numerator + " / " + denominator +
                " = " + result);
        }
        catch(ArithmeticException mistake)
        {
            System.out.println(mistake.getMessage());
        }
    }
}
```

Figure 11-9 The `DivisionMistakeCaught2` application

Figure 11-10 Output of the `DivisionMistakeCaught2` application

Of course, you might want to do more in a `catch` block than print an error message; after all, Java did that for you without requiring you to write the code to catch any `Exceptions`. You also might want to add code to correct the error; for example, such code could force the arithmetic to divide by 1 rather than by 0. Figure 11-11 shows `try...catch` code in which the `catch` block computes the result by dividing by 1 instead of by the `denominator` value. After the `catch` block, the application could continue with a guarantee that `result` holds a valid value—either the division worked in the `try` block and the `catch` block did not execute, or the `catch` block remedied the error.

```
try
{
    result = numerator / denominator;
}
catch(ArithmeticException mistake)
{
    result = numerator / 1;
}
// program continues here; result is guaranteed to have a valid value
```

Figure 11-11 A `try...catch` block in which the `catch` block corrects the error

》NOTE In the code in Figure 11-11, you can achieve the same result in the `catch` block by coding `result = numerator;` instead of `result = numerator / 1;`. Explicitly dividing by 1 simply makes the code's intention clearer. As an alternative, you could make the program more efficient by omitting the division by 1 and adding clarity with a comment.

》TWO TRUTHS AND A LIE: TRYING CODE AND CATCHING Exceptions

1. A `try` block is a block of code you attempt to execute while acknowledging that an exception might occur.
2. You usually code at least one `catch` block immediately following a `try` block to handle an exception that might be thrown by the `try` block.
3. A `throw` statement is one that sends an `Exception` to a `try` block so it can be handled.

The false statement is #3. A `throw` statement sends an `Exception` to a `catch` block.

THROWING AND CATCHING MULTIPLE Exceptions

You can place as many statements as you need within a `try` block, and you can catch as many Exceptions as you want. If you try more than one statement, only the first error-generating statement throws an Exception. As soon as the Exception occurs, the logic transfers to the `catch` block, which leaves the rest of the statements in the `try` block unexecuted.

When a program contains multiple `catch` blocks, they are examined in sequence until a match is found for the type of Exception that occurred. Then, the matching `catch` block executes and each remaining `catch` block is bypassed.

For example, consider the application in Figure 11-12. The `main()` method in the `DivisionMistakeCaught3` class throws two types of Exceptions: an `ArithmeticException` and an `InputMismatchException`. The `try` block in the application surrounds all the statements in which the exceptions might occur.

```
import java.util.*;
public class DivisionMistakeCaught3
{
   public static void main(String[] args)
   {
      Scanner input = new Scanner(System.in);
      int numerator, denominator, result;
      try
      {
         System.out.print("Enter numerator >> ");
         numerator = input.nextInt();
         System.out.print("Enter denominator >> ");
         denominator = input.nextInt();
         result = numerator / denominator;
         System.out.println(numerator + " / " + denominator +
            " = " + result);
      }
      catch(ArithmeticException mistake)
      {
          System.out.println(mistake.getMessage());
      }
      catch(InputMismatchException mistake)
      {
          System.out.println("Wrong data type");
      }
   }
}
```

Figure 11-12 The `DivisionMistakeCaught3` class

>> **NOTE** The program in Figure 11-12 must import the `java.util.InputMismatchException` class to be able to use an `InputMismatchException` object. The `java.util` package is also needed for the `Scanner` class, so it's easiest to import the whole package.

>> **NOTE** If you use the `getMessage()` method with the `InputMismatchException` object, you see that the message is `null`, because `null` is the default message value for an `InputMismatchException` object.

In the `main()` method of the program in Figure 11-12, the `try` block executes. Several outcomes are possible:

» If the user enters two usable integers, `result` is calculated and normal output is displayed.

» If the user enters an invalid (noninteger) value at either the first or second shaded statement, an `InputMismatchException` object is created and thrown. When the program encounters the first `catch` block (that catches an `ArithmeticException`), the block is bypassed because the `Exception` types do not match. When the program encounters the second `catch` block, the types match, and the "Wrong data type" message is displayed.

» If the user enters 0 for `denominator`, the division statement throws an `ArithmeticException` and the `try` block is abandoned. When the program encounters the first `catch` block, the `Exception` types match, the value of the `getMessage()` method is displayed, and then the second `catch` block is bypassed.

Figure 11-13 shows the output of four typical program executions.

Figure 11-13 Four executions of the `DivisionMistakeCaught3` application

Sometimes, you want to execute the same code no matter which `Exception` type occurs. For example, within the `DivisionMistakeCaught3` application in Figure 11-12, each of the two `catch` blocks prints a unique message. Instead, you might want both `catch` blocks to display the same message. Because `ArithmeticExceptions` and `InputMismatchExceptions` are both subclasses of `Exception`, you can rewrite the program as shown in Figure 11-14, using a single generic `catch` block (shaded) that can catch any type of `Exception`.

```
import java.util.*;
public class DivisionMistakeCaught4
{
    public static void main(String[] args)
    {
        Scanner input = new Scanner(System.in);
        int numerator, denominator, result;
        try
        {
            System.out.print("Enter numerator >> ");
            numerator = input.nextInt();
            System.out.print("Enter denominator >> ");
            denominator = input.nextInt();
            result = numerator / denominator;
            System.out.println(numerator + " / " + denominator +
                " = " + result);
        }
        catch(Exception mistake)
        {
            System.out.println("Operation unsuccessful");
        }
    }
}
```

Figure 11-14 The `DivisionMistakeCaught4` application

The `catch` block in Figure 11-14 accepts a more generic `Exception` argument type than that thrown by either of the potentially error-causing `try` statements, so the generic `catch` block can act as a "catch-all" block. When either an arithmetic error or incorrect input type error occurs, the thrown exception is "promoted" to an `Exception` error in the `catch` block. Through inheritance, `ArithmeticExceptions` and `InputMismatchExceptions` are `Exceptions`, and one `catch` block can catch both. Figure 11-15 shows several executions of the `DivisionMistakeCaught4` application. Notice that no matter

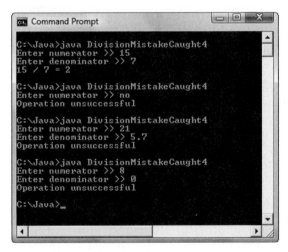

Figure 11-15 Four executions of the `DivisionMistakeCaught4` application

which type of mistake occurs during execution, the general "Operation unsuccessful" message is displayed from the generic `catch` block.

When you list multiple `catch` blocks following a `try` block, you must be careful that some `catch` blocks don't become unreachable. Unreachable statements are program statements that can never execute under any circumstances. For example, if two successive `catch` blocks catch an `ArithmeticException` and an ordinary `Exception`, respectively, the `ArithmeticException` errors cause the first `catch` to execute and other `Exceptions` "fall through" to the more general `Exception` catch block. However, if you reverse the sequence of the `catch` blocks so that the one that catches general `Exception` objects is first, even `ArithmeticExceptions` are caught by the `Exception` catch. The `ArithmeticException` catch block is unreachable because the `Exception` catch block is in its way and the class does not compile.

> **NOTE** You first learned about unreachable statements in Chapter 3. Statements that follow a method's `return` statement are unreachable. Creating an unreachable `catch` block causes a compiler error that generates a message indicating that the exception "has already been caught."

Although a method can throw any number of `Exception` types, many developers believe that it is poor style for a method to throw more than three or four types. If it does, one of the following conditions might be true:

» Perhaps the method is trying to accomplish too many diverse tasks and should be broken up into smaller methods.

» Perhaps the `Exception` types thrown are too specific and should be generalized, as they are in the `DivisionMistakeCaught4` application in Figure 11-14. As another example, both `EOFExceptions` (which occur when the end of a file is reached) and `FileNotFoundExceptions` (which occur when a method attempts to open a file that it cannot find) are children of the `IOException` class (which, in turn, is a child of the `Exception` class). If a method throws both subclass `Exception` types, using the one superclass type might be sufficient.

> **NOTE** Chapter 12 describes `EOFExceptions` and `FileNotFoundExceptions` and uses both types in sample programs.

»TWO TRUTHS AND A LIE: THROWING AND CATCHING MULTIPLE Exceptions

1. When multiple `try` block statements throw `Exceptions`, multiple `catch` blocks might execute.

2. As soon as an `Exception` occurs, the `try` block that contains it is abandoned and the rest of its statements are unexecuted.

3. When a program contains multiple `catch` blocks, the first one that matches the thrown `Exception` type is the one that executes.

The false statement is #1. If you try more than one statement, only the first error-generating statement throws an Exception. Then the rest of the try block is abandoned.

USING THE `finally` BLOCK

When you have actions you must perform at the end of a `try...catch` sequence, you can use a **finally block**. The code within a `finally` block executes regardless of whether the preceding `try` block identifies an `Exception`. Usually, you use a `finally` block to perform cleanup tasks that must happen whether or not any `Exceptions` occurred, and whether or not any `Exceptions` that occurred were caught. Figure 11-16 shows the format of a `try...catch` sequence that uses a `finally` block.

```
try
{
   // statements to try
}
catch(Exception e)
{
   // actions that occur if exception was thrown
}
finally
{
   // actions that occur whether catch block executed or not
}
```

Figure 11-16 Format of `try...catch...finally` sequence

Compare Figure 11-16 to Figure 11-6 shown earlier in this chapter. When the `try` code works without error in Figure 11-6, control passes to the statements at the end of the method. Also, when the `try` code fails and throws an `Exception`, and the `Exception` is caught, the `catch` block executes and control again passes to the statements at the end of the method. At first glance, it seems as though the statements at the end of the method always execute. However, the final set of statements might never execute for at least two reasons:

» An unplanned `Exception` might occur.
» The `try` or `catch` block might contain a `System.exit();` statement.

Any `try` block might throw an `Exception` for which you did not provide a `catch` block. After all, `Exceptions` occur all the time without your handling them, as one did in the first `Division` application in Figure 11-2 earlier in this chapter. In the case of an unhandled `Exception`, program execution stops immediately, the `Exception` is sent to the operating system for handling, and the current method is abandoned. Likewise, if the `try` block contains an `exit()` statement, execution stops immediately.

When you include a `finally` block, you are assured that the `finally` statements will execute before the method is abandoned, even if the method concludes prematurely. For example, programmers often use a `finally` block when the program uses data files that must be closed. You will learn more about writing to and reading from data files in Chapter 12. For now, however, consider the format shown in Figure 11-17, which represents part of the logic for a typical file-handling program.

```
try
{
    // Open the file
    // Read the file
    // Place the file data in an array
    // Calculate an average from the data
    // Display the average
}
catch(IOException e)
{
    // Issue an error message
    // System exit
}
finally
{
    // If the file is open, close it
}
```

Figure 11-17 Pseudocode that tries reading a file and handles an `IOException`

>> **NOTE** You can avoid using a `finally` block, but you would need repetitious code. For example, instead of using the `finally` block in the pseudocode in Figure 11-17, you could insert the statement "If the file is open, close it" as both the last statement in the `try` block and the second-to-last statement in the `catch` block, just before `System exit`. However, writing code just once in a `finally` block is clearer and less prone to error.

The pseudocode in Figure 11-17 represents an application that opens a file; in Java, if a file does not exist when you open it, an input/output exception, or `IOException`, is thrown and the `catch` block handles the error. However, because the application uses an array (see the statement "Place the file data in an array"), it is possible that, even though the file opened successfully, an uncaught `IndexOutOfBoundsException` might occur. (An `IndexOutOfBoundsException` occurs, as its name implies, when a subscript is not in the range of valid subscripts for an array.) The `IndexOutOfBoundsException` would not be caught by the existing `catch` block. Also, because the application calculates an average, it might divide by 0 and an `ArithmeticException` might occur; it also would not be caught. In any of these events, you might want to close the file before proceeding. By using the `finally` block, you ensure that the file is closed because the code in the `finally` block executes before control returns to the operating system. The code in the `finally` block executes no matter which of the following outcomes of the `try` block occurs:

» The `try` ends normally.

» The `catch` executes.

» An uncaught `Exception` causes the method to abandon prematurely. An uncaught `Exception` does not allow the `try` block to finish, nor does it cause the `catch` block to execute.

>> **NOTE** If an application might throw several types of exceptions, you can try some code, catch the possible exception, try some more code, catch the possible exception, and so on. Usually, however, the superior approach is to try all the statements that might throw exceptions, then include all the needed `catch` blocks and an optional `finally` block. This is the approach shown in Figure 11-17, and it usually results in logic that is easier to follow.

>> **NOTE** If a `try` block calls the `System.exit()` method and the `finally` block calls the same method, the `exit()` method in the `finally` block executes. The `try` block's `exit()` method call is abandoned.

>> **NOTE** C++ programmers are familiar with `try` and `catch` blocks, but C++ does not provide a `finally` block. C# and Visual Basic contain the keywords `try`, `catch`, and `finally`.

UNDERSTANDING THE ADVANTAGES OF EXCEPTION HANDLING

Before the inception of object-oriented programming languages, potential program errors were handled using somewhat confusing, error-prone methods. For example, a traditional, non-object-oriented, procedural program might perform three methods that depend on each other using code that provides error checking similar to the pseudocode in Figure 11-18.

```
call methodA()
if methodA() worked
{
    call methodB()
    if methodB() worked
    {
        call methodC()
        if methodC() worked
            everything's okay, so print finalResult
        else
            set errorCode to 'C'
    }
    else
        set errorCode to 'B'
}
else
    set errorCode to 'A'
```

Figure 11-18 Pseudocode representing traditional error checking

The pseudocode in Figure 11-18 represents an application in which the logic must pass three tests before a final result can be displayed. It performs methodA(); it then performs methodB() only if methodA() is successful. Similarly, methodC() executes only when methodA() and methodB() are both successful. When any method fails, the program sets an appropriate errorCode to 'A', 'B', or 'C'. (Presumably, the errorCode is used later in the application.) The logic is difficult to follow, and the application's purpose and intended outcome—to print the finalResult—is lost in the maze of if statements. Also, you can easily make coding mistakes within such a program because of the complicated nesting, indenting, and opening and closing of curly braces.

Compare the same program logic using Java's object-oriented, error-handling technique shown in Figure 11-19. Using the try...catch object-oriented technique provides the same results as the traditional method, but the statements of the program that do the "real" work (calling methods A, B, and C and printing finalResult) are placed together, where their logic is easy to follow. The try steps should usually work without generating errors; after all, the errors are "exceptions." It is convenient to see these business-as-usual steps in one location. The unusual, exceptional events are grouped and moved out of the way of the primary action.

```
try
{
    call methodA() and maybe throw an exception
    call methodB() and maybe throw an exception
    call methodC() and maybe throw an exception
    everything's okay, so display finalResult
}
catch(methodA()'s error)
{
    set errorCode to "A"
}
catch(methodB()'s error)
{
    set errorCode to "B"
}
catch(methodC()'s error)
{
    set errorCode to "C"
}
```

Figure 11-19 Pseudocode representing object-oriented exception handling

Besides clarity, an advantage to object-oriented exception handling is the flexibility it allows in the handling of error situations. When a method you write throws an Exception, the same method can catch the Exception, although it is not required to do so, and in most object-oriented programs it does not. Often, you don't want a method to handle its own Exception. In many cases, you want the method to check for errors, but you do not want to require a method to handle an error if it finds one. Another advantage to object-oriented exception handling is that you gain the ability to appropriately deal with Exceptions as you decide how to handle them. When you write a method, it can call another, catch a thrown Exception, and you can decide what you want to do. Just as a police officer can deal with a speeding driver differently depending on circumstances, you can react to Exceptions specifically for your current purposes.

Methods are flexible partly because they are reusable—that is, a well-written method might be used by any number of applications. Each calling application might need to handle a thrown error differently, depending on its purpose. For example, an application that uses a method that divides values might need to terminate if division by 0 occurs. A different program simply might want the user to reenter the data to be used, and a third program might want to force division by 1. The method that contains the division statement can throw the error, but each calling program can assume responsibility for handling the error detected by the method in an appropriate way.

»TWO TRUTHS AND A LIE: UNDERSTANDING THE ADVANTAGES OF EXCEPTION HANDLING

1. An advantage to using object-oriented error-handling techniques is that programs are clearer and more flexible.
2. An advantage to using object-oriented error-handling techniques is that when a method throws an exception, it will always be handled in the same, consistent way.
3. In many cases, you want a method to check for errors, but you do not want to require the method to handle an error if it finds one.

The false statement is #2. A well-written method might be used by any number of applications. An advantage of object-oriented exception-handling techniques is that each calling application can handle thrown errors differently, depending on its purpose.

SPECIFYING THE Exceptions A METHOD CAN THROW

If a method throws an Exception that it will not catch but that will be caught by a different method, you must use the keyword throws followed by an Exception type in the method header. This practice is known as **exception specification**.

For example, Figure 11-20 shows a PriceList class used by a company to hold a list of prices for items it sells. For simplicity, there are only four prices and a single method that displays the price of a single item. The displayPrice() method accepts an argument to use as the array subscript, but because the subscript could be out of bounds, the method contains a shaded throws clause, acknowledging it could throw an exception.

```
public class PriceList
{
    private static final double[] price = {15.99, 27.88, 34.56, 45.89};
    public static void displayPrice(int item) throws IndexOutOfBoundsException
    {
        System.out.println("The price is $" + price[item]);
    }
}
```

Figure 11-20 The PriceList class

Figures 11-21 and 11-22 show two applications in which programmers have chosen to handle the exception differently. In the first class, PriceListApplication1, the programmer has chosen to handle the exception in the shaded catch block by displaying a price of $0. In the second class, PriceListApplication2, the programmer has chosen to handle the exception by using the highest price in the array. Figure 11-23 shows several executions of each program. Other programmers writing other applications that use the PriceList class could choose still different actions, but they all can use the flexible displayPrice() method from the class because it throws an exception but doesn't limit the calling method's choice of recourse.

```
import java.util.*;
public class PriceListApplication1
{
    public static void main(String[] args)
    {
        int item;
        Scanner input = new Scanner(System.in);
        System.out.print("Enter item number >> ");
        item = input.nextInt();
        try
        {
            PriceList.displayPrice(item);
        }
        catch(IndexOutOfBoundsException e)
        {
            System.out.println("Price is $0");
        }
    }
}
```

Figure 11-21 The PriceListApplication1 class

```
import java.util.*;
public class PriceListApplication2
{
    public static void main(String[] args)
    {
        int item;
        Scanner input = new Scanner(System.in);
        final int MAXITEM = 3;
        System.out.print("Enter item number >> ");
        item = input.nextInt();
        try
        {
            PriceList.displayPrice(item);
        }
        catch(IndexOutOfBoundsException e)
        {
            PriceList.displayPrice(MAXITEM);
        }
    }
}
```

Figure 11-22 The `PriceListApplication2` class

Figure 11-23 Several executions of `PriceListApplication1` and `PriceListApplication2`

When you write a method that might throw an `Exception`, such as the `displayPrice()` method in the `PriceList` class in Figure 11-20, you can type the clause `throws <name>Exception` after the method header to indicate the type of `Exception` that might be thrown. Every Java method you write has the potential to throw an `Exception`. Some `Exceptions`, such as an `InternalErrorException`, can occur anywhere at any time. However, for most Java methods that you write, you do not use a `throws` clause. For example, you have not needed to use a `throws` clause in any of the many programs you have written while working through this book; however, in those methods, if you divided by 0 or went beyond an array's bounds, an `Exception` was thrown nevertheless. Most of the time, you let Java handle any `Exception` by shutting down the program. Imagine how unwieldy your programs would become if you were required to provide instructions for handling every possible error, including equipment failures and memory problems. Most exceptions never have to be explicitly thrown or caught, nor do you have to include a `throws` clause in the headers of methods that automatically throw these `Exceptions`.

Java's exceptions can be categorized into two types:

>> Checked exceptions
>> Unchecked exceptions

Unchecked exceptions come in two types:

>> Errors
>> Runtime exceptions

Unchecked exceptions inherit from the `Error` class or the `RuntimeException` class. Many programmers feel that you should not handle these exceptions in your programs because they represent the type of errors from which programs cannot reasonably be expected to recover while the program is running. **Checked exceptions** are the type that programmers should anticipate and from which programs should be able to recover. All Java exceptions are checked exceptions except those of the `Error` and `RuntimeException` classes and their subclasses.

Java programmers say that checked exceptions are subject to the **catch or specify requirement**, which means they require catching or declaration. This requirement is optional for unchecked exceptions. Code that uses a checked exception will not compile if the catch or specify rule is not followed.

For example, suppose a program prompts a user for the name of a data file to open. If the file can't be found, you might want to provide the user with additional opportunities to provide the correct filename. Such an error should be a checked exception. In contrast, programmers usually cannot do anything about errors or runtime exceptions. Errors are mistakes that are external to the program—for example, hardware failures. Runtime exceptions are internal to the program—for example, logic errors. Although an application could catch either type of error, it usually makes sense for a technician to fix external problems or for a programmer to fix internal problems. On the other hand, a program can handle checked exceptions while it is executing.

All exceptions that you explicitly throw that descend from the `Exception` class are checked exceptions. The compiler checks that these exceptions are either caught or specified to be thrown in the method header. If you throw a checked exception from a method, you must do one of the following:

>> Catch it within the method.
>> Declare the exception in your method header's `throws` clause.

If you write a method with a `throws` clause in the header, then any method that uses your method must do one of the following:

» Catch and handle the possible exception.
» Declare the exception in its `throws` clause. The called method can then rethrow the exception to yet another method that might either catch it or throw it yet again.

In other words, when an exception is a checked exception, client programmers are forced to deal with the possibility that an exception will be thrown.

> **»NOTE** Some programmers feel that using checked exceptions is an example of "syntactic salt." **Syntactic sugar** is a term coined by Peter J. Landin to describe aspects of a computer language that make it "sweeter," or easier, for programmers to use. For example, you learned in Chapter 1 that you do not have to write `import java.lang;` at the top of every Java program file because the package is automatically imported for you. The metaphor has been extended by the term **syntactic salt**, which is a language feature designed to make it harder to write bad code.

`Errors` and `RuntimeExceptions` are unchecked exceptions. You never have to throw these exceptions explicitly. Most of the errors you received earlier in this book when you made mistakes in your Java programs are runtime exceptions—members of the `RuntimeException` class that represent unplanned exceptions that occur during a program's execution. Runtime exceptions can occur anywhere in a program and can be numerous in a typical program. Most Java programmers feel that the cost of checking for many runtime exceptions exceeds the benefit of catching or specifying them. Those that represent logical errors should be fixed in the code.

> **»NOTE** An `IOException` is a checked exception, so you do not have to explicitly use a `throws IOException` clause in a method header. For example, you will learn in Chapter 12 that you must include a `throws` clause in the header of methods that use file input (or catch the potential exception within the method), even though you might not use the keyword `throws` within the method. `InterruptedException` is another example of an `Exception` you must catch or specify in a `throws` clause when you work with threads. A **thread** is the flow of execution of one set of program statements; programs containing multiple threads accomplish a variety of tasks concurrently. For more information on threads, visit the Java Web site at *http://java.sun.com*.

> **»NOTE** A method that overrides another cannot throw an exception unless it throws the same type as its parent or a subclass of its parent's thrown type. These rules do not apply to overloaded methods. Any exceptions may (or may not) be thrown from one version of an overloaded method without considering what exceptions are thrown by other versions of an overloaded method.

If you write a method that explicitly throws a checked `Exception` that is not caught within the method, Java requires that you use the `throws` clause in the header of the method. Using the `throws` clause does not mean that the method *will* throw an `Exception`—everything might go smoothly. Instead, it means the method *might* throw an `Exception`. You include the `throws` clause in the method header so applications that use your methods are notified of the potential for an `Exception`.

> **»NOTE** In Chapter 3, you learned that a method's signature is the combination of the method name and the number, types, and order of arguments. Some programmers argue that any `throws` clause is also part of the signature, but most authorities disagree. You cannot create a class that contains multiple methods that differ only in their `return` types; such methods are not overloaded. The same is true for methods with the same signatures that differ only in their `throws` clauses; the compiler considers the methods to have an identical signature.

To be able to use a method to its full potential, you must know the method's name and three additional pieces of information:

» The method's `return` type
» The type and number of arguments the method requires
» The type and number of `Exception`s the method throws

To use a method, you must first know what types of arguments are required. You can call a method without knowing its `return` type, but if you do, you can't benefit from any value that the method returns. (Also, if you use a method without knowing its return type, you probably don't understand the purpose of the method.) Likewise, you can't make sound decisions about what to do in case of an error if you don't know what types of `Exception`s a method might throw.

When a method might throw more than one `Exception` type, you can specify a list of potential `Exception`s in the method header by separating them with commas. As an alternative, you could specify that the methods might throw an object of a more general `Exception` parent class to cover all specific instances. For example, if your method might throw either an `ArithmeticException` or an `ArrayIndexOutOfBoundsException`, you can just specify that your method throws a `RuntimeException`. One advantage to this technique is that when your method is modified to include more specific `RuntimeException`s in the future, the method signature will not change. This saves time and money for users of your methods, who will not have to modify their own methods to accommodate new `RuntimeException` types.

An extreme alternative is simply to specify that your method throws a general `Exception`, so that all exceptions are included in one clause. Doing this simplifies the exception specification you write. However, using this technique disguises information about the specific types of exceptions that might occur, and such information is usually of great value to the users of your methods.

> **»NOTE** Usually, you declare only checked exceptions. Remember that runtime exceptions can occur anywhere in a program, and can be numerous. Programs would be less clear if you had to account for runtime exceptions in every method declaration. Therefore, the Java compiler does not require that you catch or specify runtime exceptions.

»TWO TRUTHS AND A LIE: SPECIFYING THE Exceptions
A METHOD CAN THROW

1. Exception specification is the practice of listing possible `Exception`s in a `throws` clause in a method header.
2. Many exceptions never have to be explicitly thrown or caught, nor do you have to include a `throws` clause in the headers of methods that automatically throw these `Exception`s.
3. If you write a method with a `throws` clause for a checked exception in the header, then any method that uses your method must catch and handle the possible exception.

The false statement is #3. If you write a method with a `throws` clause for a checked exception in the header, then any method that uses your method must catch and handle the possible exception *or* declare the exception in its `throws` clause so that the exception can be rethrown.

TRACING Exceptions THROUGH THE CALL STACK

When one method calls another, the computer's operating system must keep track of where the method call came from, and program control must return to the calling method when the called method is completed. For example, if methodA() calls methodB(), the operating system has to "remember" to return to methodA() when methodB() ends. Likewise, if methodB() calls methodC(), the computer must "remember" while methodC() executes to return to methodB() and eventually to methodA(). The memory location known as the **call stack** is where the computer stores the list of method locations to which the system must return.

When a method throws an Exception and the method does not catch it, the Exception is thrown to the next method up the call stack, or in other words, to the method that called the offending method. Figure 11-24 shows how the call stack works. If methodA() calls methodB(), and methodB() calls methodC(), and methodC() throws an Exception, Java first looks for a catch block in methodC(). If none exists, Java looks for the same thing in methodB(). If methodB() does not have a catch block, Java looks to methodA(). If methodA() cannot catch the Exception, it is thrown to the Java Virtual Machine, which displays a message at the command prompt.

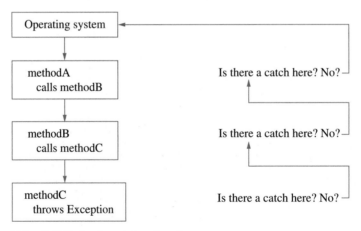

Figure 11-24 Cycling through the call stack

For example, examine the application in Figure 11-25. The main() method of the application calls methodA(), which displays a message and calls methodB(). Within methodB(), another message displays and methodC() is called. In methodC(), yet another message displays. Then, a three-integer array is declared, and the program attempts to display the fourth element in the array. This program compiles correctly—no error is detected until methodC() attempts to access the out-of-range array element. Figure 11-26 shows the output when the application executes.

```
public class DemoStackTrace
{
   public static void main(String[] args)
   {
      methodA();   // line 5
   }
   public static void methodA()
   {
      System.out.println("In methodA()");
      methodB();   // line 10
   }
   public static void methodB()
   {
      System.out.println("In methodB()");
      methodC();   // line 15
   }
   public static void methodC()
   {
      System.out.println("In methodC()");
      int [] array = {0, 1, 2};
      System.out.println(array[3]);   // line 21
   }
}
```

》DON'T DO IT

You would never purposely use an out-of-range subscript in a professional program.

Figure 11-25 The DemoStackTrace class

Figure 11-26 Error messages generated by the DemoStackTrace application

》NOTE
In Figure 11-25, the comments indicating line numbers were added so you could more easily follow the sequence of generated error messages. You probably would not add such comments to a working application.

As you can see in Figure 11-26, three messages display, indicating that methodA(), methodB(), and methodC() were called in order. However, when methodC() attempts to access the out-of-range element in the array, an ArrayIndexOutOfBoundsException is automatically thrown. The error message generated, as shown in Figure 11-26, shows that the exception occurred at line 21 of the file in methodC(), which was called in line 15 of the file by methodB(), which was called in line 10 of the file by methodA(), which was called by the main() method in line 5 of the file. Using this list of error messages, you could track down the location where the error was generated. Of course, in a larger application that contains thousands of lines of code, the stack trace history list would be even more useful.

The technique of cycling through the methods in the stack has great advantages because it allows methods to handle Exceptions wherever the programmer has decided it is most appropriate—including allowing the operating system to handle the error. However, when a program uses several classes, the disadvantage is that the programmer finds it difficult to locate the original source of an Exception.

You have already used the Throwable method getMessage() to obtain information about an Exception. Another useful Exception method is the printStackTrace() method. When you catch an Exception, you can call printStackTrace() to display a list of methods in the call stack so that you can determine the location of the Exception.

For example, Figure 11-27 shows a DemoStackTrace2 application in which the printStackTrace() method produces a trace of the trail taken by a thrown exception. The differences in the executable statements from the DemoStackTrace application are shaded. The call to methodB() has been placed in a try block so that the exception can be caught. Instead of throwing the exception to the operating system, this application catches the exception, displays a stack trace history list, and continues to execute. The output of the list of methods in Figure 11-28 is similar to the one shown in Figure 11-26, but the application does not end abruptly.

```java
public class DemoStackTrace2
{
    public static void main(String[] args)
    {
        methodA();   // line 5
    }
    public static void methodA()
    {
        System.out.println("In methodA()");
        try
        {
            methodB();    // line 12
        }
        catch(ArrayIndexOutOfBoundsException error)
        {
            System.out.println("In methodA() - The stack trace:");
            error.printStackTrace();
        }
        System.out.println("methodA() ends normally.");
        System.out.println("Application could continue " +
            "from this point.");
    }
```

Figure 11-27 The DemoStackTrace2 class (*continued*)

```
    public static void methodB()
    {
        System.out.println("In methodB()");
        methodC();   // line 25
    }
    public static void methodC()
    {
        System.out.println("In methodC()");
        int[] array = {0, 1, 2};
        System.out.println(array[3]);   // line 31
    }
}
```

Figure 11-27 (*continued*)

Figure 11-28 Output of the `DemoStackTrace2` application

Usually, you do not want to place a `printStackTrace()` method call in a finished program. The typical application user has no interest in the cryptic messages that display. However, while you are developing an application, `printStackTrace()` can be a useful tool for diagnosing your class's problems.

»TWO TRUTHS AND A LIE: TRACING Exceptions **THROUGH THE CALL STACK**

1. The memory location known as the call stack is where the computer stores the list of locations to which the system must return after each method call.

2. When a method throws an `Exception` and the method does not catch it, the `Exception` is thrown to the next method down the call stack, or in other words, to the next method that the offending method calls.

3. When you catch an `Exception`, you can call `printStackTrace()` to display a list of methods in the call stack so that you can determine the location of the `Exception`; however, usually you do not want to place a `printStackTrace()` method call in a finished program.

The false statement is #2. When a method throws an `Exception` and the method does not catch it, the `Exception` is thrown to the next method up the call stack, or in other words, to the method that called the offending method.

CREATING YOUR OWN Exceptions

Java provides over 40 categories of Exceptions that you can use in your programs. However, Java's creators could not predict every condition that might be an Exception in your applications. For example, you might want to declare an Exception when your bank balance is negative or when an outside party attempts to access your e-mail account. Most organizations have specific rules for exceptional data; for example, an employee number must not exceed three digits, or an hourly salary must not be less than the legal minimum wage. Of course, you can handle these potential error situations with if statements, but Java also allows you to create your own Exceptions.

NOTE When you create an Exception subclass, it's conventional to end its name with Exception.

To create your own throwable Exception, you must extend a subclass of Throwable. Recall from Figure 11-1 that Throwable has two subclasses, Exception and Error, which are used to distinguish between recoverable and nonrecoverable errors. Because you always want to create your own Exceptions for recoverable errors, you should extend your Exceptions from the Exception class. You can extend any existing Exception subclass, such as ArithmeticException or NullPointerException, but usually you want to inherit directly from Exception.

The Exception class contains four constructors. You can provide no arguments, include a String that contains the message that can be returned by the getMessage() method, include a Throwable object that is the cause of the exception, or include both. The constructors are:

- Exception()—Constructs a new exception with null as its detail message
- Exception(String message)—Constructs a new exception with the specified detail message
- Exception(String message, Throwable cause)—Constructs a new exception with the specified detail message and cause
- Exception(Throwable cause)—Constructs a new exception with the specified cause and a detail message of cause.toString(), which typically contains the class and the detail message of cause, or null if the cause argument is null

For example, Figure 11-29 shows a HighBalanceException class. Its constructor contains a single statement that passes a description of an error to the parent Exception constructor. This String would be retrieved if you called the getMessage() method with a HighBalanceException object.

```
public class HighBalanceException extends Exception
{
   public HighBalanceException()
   {
      super("Customer balance is high");
   }
}
```

Figure 11-29 The HighBalanceException class

Figure 11-30 shows a `CustomerAccount` class that uses a `HighBalanceException`. The `CustomerAccount` constructor header indicates that it might throw a `HighBalanceException` (see the first shaded statement); if the balance used as an argument to the constructor exceeds a set limit, a new, unnamed instance of the `HighBalanceException` class is thrown (see the second shaded statement).

```
public class CustomerAccount
{
   private int acctNum;
   private double balance;
   public static double HIGH_CREDIT_LIMIT = 20000.00;
   public CustomerAccount(int num, double bal) throws HighBalanceException
   {
      acctNum = num;
      balance = bal;
      if(balance > HIGH_CREDIT_LIMIT)
         throw(new HighBalanceException());
   }
}
```

Figure 11-30 The `CustomerAccount` class

>> **NOTE** In the `CustomerAccount` class in Figure 11-30, you could choose to instantiate a named `HighBalanceException` and throw it when the balance exceeds the credit limit. By waiting and instantiating an unnamed object only when it is needed, you improve program performance.

>> **NOTE** When a constructor throws an exception, no object is constructed; its intended reference variable value will be `null`.

Figure 11-31 shows an application that instantiates a `CustomerAccount`. In this application, a user is prompted for an account number and balance. After the values are entered, an attempt is made to construct a `CustomerAccount` in a `try` block (as shown in the first shaded section). If the attempt is successful—that is, if the `CustomerAccount` constructor does not throw an `Exception`—the `CustomerAccount` information is displayed in a dialog box. However, if the `CustomerAccount` constructor does throw a `HighBalanceException`, the `catch` block receives it (as shown in the second shaded section) and displays a message. A different application could take any number of different actions; for example, it could display the return value of the `getMessage()` method, construct a `CustomerAccount` object with a lower balance, or construct a different type of object—perhaps a child of `CustomerAccount` called `PreferredCustomerAccount` that allows a higher balance. Figure 11-32 shows a typical execution of the application in which a customer's balance is too high.

```
import javax.swing.*;
public class UseCustomerAccount
{
    public static void main(String[] args)
    {
        int num;
        double balance;
        String input;
        input = JOptionPane.showInputDialog(null,
            "Enter account number");
        num = Integer.parseInt(input);
        input = JOptionPane.showInputDialog(null, "Enter balance due");
        balance = Double.parseDouble(input);
        try
        {
            CustomerAccount ca = new CustomerAccount(num, balance);
            JOptionPane.showMessageDialog(null, "Customer #" +
                num + " has a balance of $" + balance);
        }
        catch( HighBalanceException hbe)
        {
            JOptionPane.showMessageDialog(null, "Customer #" +
                num + " has a balance higher than the credit limit");
        }
    }
}
```

Figure 11-31 The `UseCustomerAccount` class

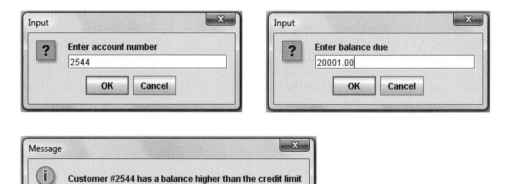

Figure 11-32 Typical execution of `UseCustomerAccount` application

Instead of hard coding error messages into your exception classes, as shown in Figure 11-31, you might consider creating a catalog of possible messages to use. This approach provides several advantages:

»NOTE
In Exercises 10 and 11 at the end of this chapter, you will create catalogs of error messages for applications to use.

» All the messages are stored in one location instead of being scattered throughout the program, making them easier to see and modify.

» The list of possible errors serves as a source of documentation, listing potential problems when running the application.

» Other applications might want to use the same catalog of messages.

» If your application will be used internationally, you can provide messages in multiple languages and other programmers can use the version that is appropriate for their country.

> **»NOTE** You can throw any type of `Exception` at any time, not just `Exception`s of your own creation. For example, within any program you can code `throw(new RuntimeException());`. Of course, you would want to do so only with good reason because Java handles `RuntimeException`s for you by stopping the program. Because you cannot anticipate every possible error, Java's automatic response is often the best course of action.

You should not create an excessive number of special `Exception` types for your classes, especially if the Java development environment already contains an `Exception` that will catch the error. Extra `Exception` types add complexity for other programmers who use your classes. However, when appropriate, specialized `Exception` classes provide an elegant way for you to handle error situations. They enable you to separate your error code from the usual, nonexceptional sequence of events; they allow errors to be passed up the stack and traced; and they allow clients of your classes to handle exceptional situations in the manner most suitable for their application.

»TWO TRUTHS AND A LIE: CREATING YOUR OWN Exceptions

1. You must create your own `Exception` classes for your programs to be considered truly object-oriented.

2. To create your own throwable `Exception`, you should extend your `Exception`s from the `Exception` class.

3. The `Exception` class contains four constructors, including a default constructor and one that requires a `String` that contains the message that can be returned by the `getMessage()` method.

The false statement is #1. You are not required to throw exceptions in object-oriented programs. However, Java does provide many built-in categories of `Exception`s that you can use, and you also can create your own `Exception` classes.

USING ASSERTIONS

In Chapter 1, you learned that you might inadvertently create syntax or logical errors when you write a program. Syntax errors are mistakes using the Java language; they are compile-time errors that prevent a program from compiling and creating an executable file with a .class extension.

In Chapter 1, you also learned that a program might contain logical errors even though it is free of syntax errors. Some logical errors cause runtime errors, or errors that cause a program to terminate. In this chapter, you learned how to use `Exception`s to handle many of these kinds of errors.

Some logical errors do not cause a program to terminate, but nevertheless produce incorrect results. For example, if a payroll program should determine gross pay by multiplying hours worked by hourly pay rate, but you inadvertently divide the numbers, no runtime error occurs and no Exception is thrown, but the output is wrong. An **assertion** is a Java language feature that can help you detect such logic errors and debug a program. You use an **assert statement** to create an assertion; when you use an assert statement, you state a condition that should be true, and Java throws an AssertionError when it is not.

The syntax of an assert statement is:

```
assert booleanExpression : optionalErrorMessage
```

The Boolean expression in the assert statement should always be true if the program is working correctly. The optionalErrorMessage is displayed if the booleanExpression is false.

Figure 11-33 contains an application that prompts a user for an hourly pay rate and is intended to calculate the user's new weekly pay after all the following steps have occurred: a raise has been applied to the hourly rate, the weekly gross pay has been calculated assuming a 40-hour work week, and withholding tax and insurance have been deducted. The application in Figure 11-33 is free from syntax errors; it compiles and executes. However, when the user enters a current pay rate of 12.00, the output (which should be a positive amount of more than $355) is negative $140. The result does not make sense—a user's weekly pay after a raise should not be less than the hourly pay before the raise, and certainly should not be negative (see Figure 11-34).

```java
import javax.swing.*;
class PayRaise
{
   public static void main(String[] args)
   {
      double oldPay = 0;
      double newPay = 0;
      final double INCREASE = 0.04;
      final double TAXRATE = 0.28;
      final double HRSPERWEEK = 40;
      final double INSURANCE = 140.00;
      String entry;
      entry = JOptionPane.showInputDialog(null,
         "Enter old pay per hour");
      oldPay = Double.parseDouble(entry);
      oldPay = oldPay + oldPay * INCREASE;
      newPay = (newPay * HRSPERWEEK) -
         (newPay * TAXRATE) - INSURANCE;
      JOptionPane.showMessageDialog(null,
         "New net pay is $" + newPay + " per week");
   }
}
```

Figure 11-33 The flawed PayRaise application without any assertion

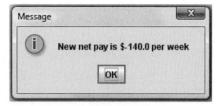

Figure 11-34 Input and incorrect output produced by `PayRaise` application in Figure 11-33

If you carefully examine the code in Figure 11-33, you might be able to find the logical error that is the source of the incorrect output. However, in a more complicated program, you might prefer to use an assertion to help you debug the application. Figure 11-35 contains the same `PayRaise` application to which the shaded `assert` statement has been added. The statement asserts that `oldPay` is less than `newPay`—a condition that should always be true after a pay raise has been applied. If the expression is not true, a message is created using the values of both `oldPay` and `newPay`.

```java
import javax.swing.*;
class PayRaise
{
    public static void main(String[] args)
    {
        double oldPay = 0;
        double newPay = 0;
        final double INCREASE = 0.04;
        final double TAXRATE = 0.28;
        final double HRSPERWEEK = 40;
        final double INSURANCE = 140.00;
        String entry;
        entry = JOptionPane.showInputDialog(null,
            "Enter old pay per hour");
        oldPay = Double.parseDouble(entry);
        oldPay = oldPay + oldPay * INCREASE;
        newPay = (newPay * HRSPERWEEK) -
            (newPay * TAXRATE) - INSURANCE;
        assert oldPay < newPay:
            "Old Pay is " + oldPay +
            "\nNew pay is $" + newPay +
            "\nNew pay should be more than old pay";
        JOptionPane.showMessageDialog(null,
            "New net pay is $" + newPay + " per week");
    }
}
```

Figure 11-35 The flawed `PayRaise` application that contains an assertion

》》NOTE

If you are not using Java version 6 (version 6 is the product version; 1.6 is used by developers), you should use the appropriate number with the −source compiler option. The assertion option was not available in its present form in versions earlier than 1.4.

If you execute the application in Figure 11-35 in the usual way, you get the same incorrect output as in Figure 11-34. To enable the assertion, you must use the −ea option when you execute the program; *ea* stands for *enable assertion*. Figure 11-36 shows the command prompt where the program executes.

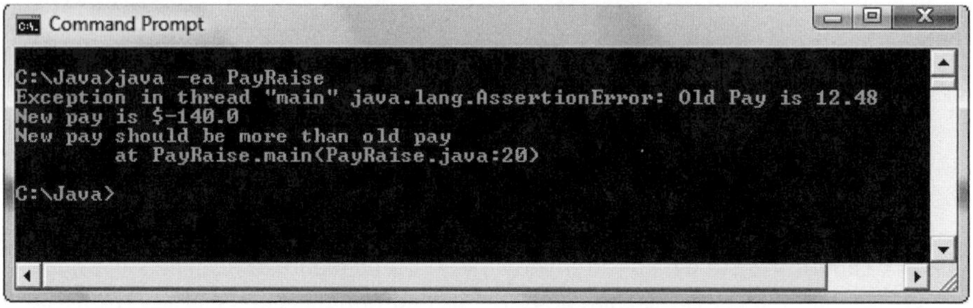

Figure 11-36 Executing an application using the enable assertion option

When the PayRaise program executes and the user enters 12.00, the program displays the messages in Figure 11-36 instead of displaying incorrect output. You can see from the message that an AssertionError was thrown and that both the oldPay value (which is 12.48 but should be only 12.00) and the newPay value are incorrect.

When the programmer sees that the oldPay value is not what was entered, the reasonable course of action is to return to the source code and examine all the changes that are applied to the oldPay variable. The programmer can see that oldPay is correctly declared as a double in the first statement in the main() method. The next two statements that alter oldPay are:

```
oldPay = Double.parseDouble(entry);
oldPay = oldPay + oldPay * INCREASE;
```

In the first of these statements, the user's entry is correctly converted to a double and stored in oldPay. In the second statement, oldPay is increased by a percentage of itself. This is an incorrect statement; newPay should be a factor of oldPay. The programmer should make the shaded change shown in Figure 11-37. When this new version is compiled and executed using a $12.00 starting pay, the output appears as in Figure 11-38.

```
import javax.swing.*;
class PayRaise
{
    public static void main(String[] args)
    {
        double oldPay = 0;
        double newPay = 0;
        final double INCREASE = 0.04;
        final double TAXRATE = 0.28;
        final double HRSPERWEEK = 40;
        final double INSURANCE = 140.00;
        String entry;
        entry = JOptionPane.showInputDialog(null,
            "Enter old pay per hour");
        oldPay = Double.parseDouble(entry);
        newPay = oldPay + oldPay * INCREASE;
        newPay = (newPay * HRSPERWEEK) -
            (newPay * TAXRATE) - INSURANCE;
        assert oldPay < newPay:
            "Old Pay is " + oldPay +
            "\nNew pay is $" + newPay +
            "\nNew pay should be more than old pay";
        JOptionPane.showMessageDialog(null,
            "New net pay is $" + newPay + " per week");
    }
}
```

Figure 11-37 The correct `PayRaise` application

>> **NOTE**
The output in Figure 11-38 looks awkward because of the number of decimal places shown. Appendix C shows you how to format numeric output to a specific number of decimal places.

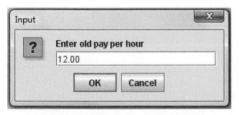
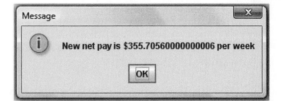

Figure 11-38 Execution of `PayRaise` application

>> **NOTE**
When you run the `PayRaise` program that contains an assertion, you do not need to use the –ea option; you can use it only if you modify the program in the future and want to test the `oldPay` and `newPay` values again.

An experienced programmer could have found the error in the original `PayRaise` application without using an assertion. For example, the programmer might have found the error simply by examining the code carefully. Alternatively, the programmer could have inserted print statements to display variable values at strategic points in the program. However, after the mistake is found and fixed, any extra print statements should be removed when the final product is ready for distribution to users. In contrast, any `assert` statements can be left in place, and if the user does not use the –ea option when running the program, the user will see no evidence that the `assert` statements exist. Placing `assert` statements in key program locations can reduce development and debugging time.

>>NOTE You do not want to use assertions to check for every type of error that could occur in a program. For example, if you want to ensure that a user enters numeric data, you should use exception-handling techniques that provide the means for your program to recover from the mistake. If you want to ensure that the data falls within a specific range, you should use a decision or a loop. Assertions are meant to be helpful in the development stage of a program, not when it is in production and in the hands of users.

>>TWO TRUTHS AND A LIE: USING ASSERTIONS

1. All logical errors cause a program to terminate, and they should be handled by throwing and catching `Exception`s.
2. The Boolean expression in an `assert` statement should always be `true` if the program is working correctly.
3. To enable an assertion, you must use the `-ea` option when you execute the program.

The false statement is #1. Many logical errors do not cause program termination—they simply produce incorrect results.

YOU DO IT

CATCHING AN Exception AND USING getMessage()

In this section, you will create an application that catches an `ArithmeticException` if you attempt to divide by 0, and you will use the `getMessage()` method to display the automatically generated message for the exception.

To write an application that catches an `ArithmeticException`:

1. Open a new file in your text editor and type the first few lines of an interactive application named `PerformDivision`.

```java
import javax.swing.*;
public class PerformDivision
{
   public static void main(String[] args)
   {
```

2. Declare three integers—two to be input by the user and a third to hold the result after dividing the first two. Also declare an input `String` to hold the return value of the `JOptionPane showInputDialog()` method.

```java
int num1, num2, result;
String inputString;
```

3. Add code to prompt the user for two values, and convert each entered `String` to an integer.

```java
inputString = JOptionPane.showInputDialog(null,
   "Enter a number to be divided");
num1 = Integer.parseInt(inputString);
   inputString = JOptionPane.showInputDialog(null,
      "Enter a number to divide into the first number");
num2 = Integer.parseInt(inputString);
```

4. Place the division operation in a `try` block. Follow the block with a `catch` clause that catches an `ArithmeticException` if an attempt is made to divide by 0. If the `try` is successful, it holds the result of the division. If the `try` fails, the `catch` block displays the `String` returned by the `getMessage()` method message and sets the result to 0.

```
try
{
    result = num1 / num2;
}
catch(ArithmeticException exception)
{
    JOptionPane.showMessageDialog(null,
        exception.getMessage());
    result = 0;
}
```

5. Whether the `try` block succeeds or not, display the result (which might have been set to 0). Include closing curly braces for the `main()` method and for the class.

```
        JOptionPane.showMessageDialog(null, num1 +
            " / " + num2 + "\nResult is " + result);
    }
}
```

6. Save the file as **PerformDivision.java**, then compile and execute the application. Enter two nonzero values. For example, Figure 11-39 shows the output when the user enters 12 and 3 as the two input values.

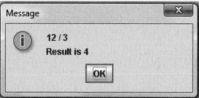

Figure 11-39 Output of the `PerformDivision` application when the user enters 12 and 3

7. Close the application. Execute it again using 0 as the second input value. For example, when the user enters 12 and 0, the first output looks like the dialog box on the left in Figure 11-40. Click **OK**, and the next dialog box looks like the one on the right in Figure 11-40. The output shows that the `Exception` was caught successfully, setting the result to 0.

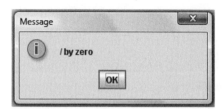 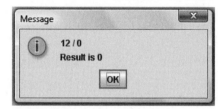

Figure 11-40 Output of the `PerformDivision` application when the user enters 12 and 0

8. Close the application.

GENERATING A NumberFormatException

The `PerformDivision` application works, dividing numbers it can and handling any attempt to divide by 0. However, the application is not forgiving if you do not enter integers when prompted. Next, you will test the `PerformDivision` application using noninteger input, and then you will remedy the error caused by the unhandled exception.

To test the `PerformDivision` application with noninteger input:

1. Run the `PerformDivision` application again. When prompted for the first value, enter some text instead of a number. For example, when the user enters "a", the screen looks like Figure 11-41. The automatically generated error messages indicate that a `NumberFormatException` has been thrown for the input string "a".

```
Command Prompt                                                    [_][□][X]

C:\Java>java PerformDivision
Exception in thread "main" java.lang.NumberFormatException: For input string: "a
"
        at java.lang.NumberFormatException.forInputString(NumberFormatException.
java:48)
        at java.lang.Integer.parseInt(Integer.java:447)
        at java.lang.Integer.parseInt(Integer.java:497)
        at PerformDivision.main(PerformDivision.java:10)

C:\Java>_
```

Figure 11-41 Messages generated when the user types a letter as input for the `PerformDivision` application

ADDING NumberFormatException HANDLING CAPABILITIES TO AN APPLICATION

Next, you will modify the `PerformDivision` application so that the statements that convert the input strings to integers are within `try` blocks; in this way, any thrown `Exception` can be handled.

To handle the `NumberFormatException` in the `PerformDivision` application:

1. If it is not still open, open the **PerformDivision.java** file in your text editor. Change the class name to **PerformDivision2** and save the file as **PerformDivision2.java**.

2. Provide initial values for the num1 and num2 variables, changing the integer declaration statement to the following:

```
int num1 = 0, num2 = 0, result;
```

This step is necessary because you will place the statements that provide values for num1 and num2 in a `try` block. The compiler understands that a `try` block might not complete; that is, it might throw an `Exception` before it is through. Therefore, when the application reaches the point where num1 and num2 are displayed following the `try` and `catch` blocks, it might attempt to display invalid, or "garbage," values. In other words, the compiler does not allow you to display num1 and num2 at the end of the application if it is not certain that these variables were provided with legitimate values beforehand.

3. Cut the two lines that contain `try` and its opening curly brace from their current position just before the division operation, and insert them immediately after the statement that declares the `inputString`. In other words, now all the input statements and their conversion to integers are within the `try` block, along with the division operation.

4. After the closing curly brace of the `catch` block that catches the `ArithmeticException`, add a second `catch` block to handle potential `NumberFormatExceptions` by displaying a message, setting `num1` and `num2` to 999, and forcing the `result` to 1.

```
catch(NumberFormatException exception)
{
    JOptionPane.showMessageDialog(null,
        "This application accepts digits only!");
    num1 = 999;
    num2 = 999;
    result = 1;
}
```

5. Save the application, then compile and execute it. This time, if you type some letters instead of a number, the program does not end abruptly—instead, the dialog boxes in Figure 11-42 appear. Click **OK** to dismiss each dialog box.

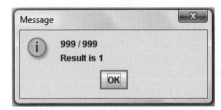

Figure 11-42 Output of the `PerformDivision2` application when the user types letters for an input value

CREATING A CLASS THAT AUTOMATICALLY THROWS Exceptions

Next, you will create a class that contains two methods that throw `Exceptions` but don't catch them. The `PickMenu` class allows Event Handlers Incorporated customers to choose a dinner menu selection as part of their event planning. Before you create `PickMenu`, you will create the `Menu` class, which lists dinner choices for customers and allows them to make a selection.

To create the Menu class:

1. Open a new file in your text editor, and then enter the following import statement, class header, and opening curly brace for the `Menu` class:

```
import javax.swing.*;
public class Menu
{
```

2. Type the following `String` array for three entree choices. Also include a `String` to build the menu that you will display and an integer to hold the numeric equivalent of the selection.

```
private String[] entreeChoice = {"Rosemary Chicken",
   "Beef Wellington", "Maine Lobster"};
private String menu = "";
private int choice;
```

3. Add the `displayMenu()` method, which lists each entree option with a corresponding number the customer can type to make a selection. Even though the allowable `entreeChoice` array subscripts are 0, 1, and 2, most users would expect to type 1, 2, or 3. So, you code `x + 1` rather than `x` as the number in the prompt. After the user enters a selection, convert it to an integer. Return the `String` that corresponds to the user's menu selection—the one with the subscript that is 1 less than the entered value. After the closing curly brace for the `displayMenu()` method, add the closing curly brace for the class.

```
public String displayMenu()
{
    for(int x = 0; x < entreeChoice.length; ++x)
    {
        menu = menu + "\n" + (x + 1) + " for " +
            entreeChoice[x];
    }
    String input = JOptionPane.showInputDialog(null,
        "Type your selection, then press Enter." + menu);
    choice = Integer.parseInt(input);
    return(entreeChoice[choice - 1]);
}
}
```

> **» NOTE**
> The curly braces are not necessary in the `for` loop of the `displayMenu()` method because the loop contains only one statement. However, in a later exercise, you will add another statement within this block.

4. Examine the code within the `displayMenu()` method. Consider the exceptions that might occur. The user might not type an integer, so the `parseInt()` method can fail, and even if the user does type an integer, it might not be in the range allowed to access the `entreeChoice` array. Therefore, the `displayMenu()` method, like most methods in which you rely on the user to enter data, might throw exceptions that you can anticipate. (Of course, any method might throw an unanticipated exception.)

5. Save the file as **Menu.java**, and compile the class using the **javac** command.

CREATING A CLASS THAT PASSES ON AN `Exception`

Next, you will create the `PickMenu` class, which lets a customer choose from the available dinner entree options. The `PickMenu` class declares a `Menu` and a `String` named `guestChoice` that holds the name of the entree the customer selects.

To enable the `PickMenu` class to operate with different kinds of `Menu`s in the future, you will pass a `Menu` to `PickMenu`'s constructor. This technique provides two advantages: First, when the menu options change, you can alter the contents of the Menu.java file without changing any of the code in programs that use `Menu`. Second, you can extend `Menu`, perhaps to `VegetarianMenu`, `LowSaltMenu`, or `KosherMenu`, and still use the existing `PickMenu` class. When you pass any `Menu` or `Menu` subclass into the `PickMenu` constructor, the correct customer options appear.

The `PickMenu` class is unlikely to directly generate any exceptions because it does not request user input. (Keep in mind that any class might generate an exception for such uncontrollable events as the system not having enough memory available.) However, `PickMenu` declares a `Menu` object; the `Menu` class, because it relies on user input, is likely to generate an `Exception`.

To create the `PickMenu` class:

1. Open a new file in your text editor, and then add the following first few lines of the `PickMenu` class with its data fields (a `Menu` and a `String` that reflect the customer's choice):

```
import javax.swing.*;
public class PickMenu
{
    private Menu briefMenu;
    private String guestChoice = new String();
```

2. Enter the following `PickMenu` constructor, which receives an argument representing a `Menu`. The constructor assigns the `Menu` that is the argument to the local `Menu`, and then calls the `setGuestChoice()` method, which prompts the user to select from the available menu. The `PickMenu()` constructor might throw an `Exception` because it calls `setGuestChoice()`, which calls `displayMenu()`, a method that uses keyboard input and might throw an `Exception`.

```
public PickMenu(Menu theMenu)
{
    briefMenu = theMenu;
    setGuestChoice();
}
```

3. The following `setGuestChoice()` method displays the menu and reads keyboard data entry (so that the method throws an `Exception`). It also displays instructions and then retrieves the user's selection.

```
public void setGuestChoice()
{
    JOptionPane.showMessageDialog(null,
        "Choose from the following menu:");
    guestChoice = briefMenu.displayMenu();
}
```

4. Add the following `getGuestChoice()` method that returns a guest's `String` selection from the `PickMenu` class. Also, add a closing curly brace for the class.

```
public String getGuestChoice()
{
    return(guestChoice);
}
}
```

5. Save the file as **PickMenu.java**, and compile it using the **javac** command.

CREATING AN APPLICATION THAT CAN CATCH Exceptions

You have created a Menu class that simply holds a list of food items, displays itself, and allows the user to make a selection. You also created a PickMenu class with fields that hold a user's specific selection from a given menu and methods to get and set values for those fields. The PickMenu class might throw Exceptions, but it contains no methods that catch those Exceptions. Next, you will write an application that uses the PickMenu class. This application can catch Exceptions that PickMenu throws.

To write the PlanMenu class:

1. Open a new file in your text editor, and start entering the following PlanMenu class, which has just one method—a main() method:

    ```
    import javax.swing.*;
    public class PlanMenu
    {
        public static void main(String[] args)
        {
    ```

2. Construct the following Menu named briefMenu, and declare a PickMenu object that you name entree. You do not want to construct a PickMenu object yet because you want to be able to catch the Exception that the PickMenu constructor might throw. Therefore, you want to wait and construct the PickMenu object within a try block. For now, you just declare entree and assign it null. Also, you declare a String that holds the customer's menu selection.

    ```
    Menu briefMenu = new Menu();
    PickMenu entree = null;
    String guestChoice = new String();
    ```

3. Write the following try block that constructs a PickMenu item. If the construction is successful, the next statement assigns a selection to the entree object. Because entree is a PickMenu object, it has access to the getGuestChoice() method in the PickMenu class, and you can assign the method's returned value to the guestChoice String.

    ```
    try
    {
        PickMenu selection = new PickMenu(briefMenu);
        entree = selection;
        guestChoice = entree.getGuestChoice();
    }
    ```

4. The catch block must immediately follow the try block. When the try block fails, guestChoice will not have a valid value, so recover from the Exception by assigning a value to guestChoice within the following catch block:

    ```
    catch(Exception error)
    {
        guestChoice = "an invalid selection";
    }
    ```

5. After the `catch` block, the application continues. Use the following code to display the customer's choice at the end of the `PlanMenu` application, and then add closing curly braces for the `main()` method and the class:

```
JOptionPane.showMessageDialog(null,
    "You chose " + guestChoice);
    }
}
```

6. Save the file as **PlanMenu.java**, and then compile and execute it. Read the instructions, click **OK**, choose an entree by typing its number from the menu, and click **OK** again. Confirm that the menu selection displayed is the one you chose, and click **OK** to dismiss the last dialog box. Figure 11-43 shows the first dialog box of instructions, the menu that displays, and the output when the user selects option 2.

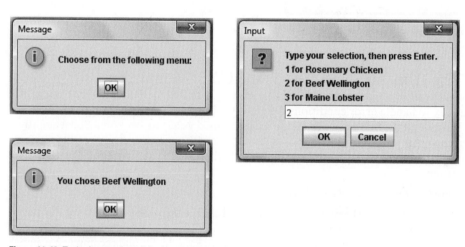

Figure 11-43 Typical execution of the `PlanMenu` application

7. The `PlanMenu` application works well when you enter a valid menu selection. One way that you can force an `Exception` is to enter an invalid menu selection at the prompt. Run the `PlanMenu` application again, and type **4**, **A**, or any invalid value at the prompt. Entering "4" produces an `ArrayIndexOutOfBoundsException`, and entering "A" produces a `NumberFormatException`. If the program lacked the `try...catch` pair, either entry would halt the program. However, because the `setGuestChoice()` method in the `PickMenu` class throws the `Exception` and the `PlanMenu` application catches it, `guestChoice` takes on the value "an invalid selection" and the application ends smoothly, as shown in Figure 11-44.

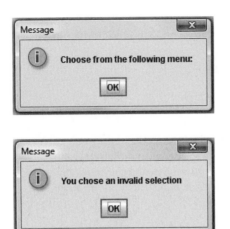

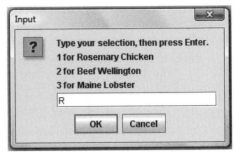

Figure 11-44 Exceptional execution of the PlanMenu application

EXTENDING A CLASS THAT THROWS Exceptions

An advantage to using object-oriented Exception handling techniques is that you gain the ability to handle error conditions differently within each program you write. Next, you will extend the Menu class to create a class named VegetarianMenu. Subsequently, when you write an application that uses PickMenu with a VegetarianMenu object, you can deal with any thrown Exception differently than when you wrote the PlanMenu application.

To create the VegetarianMenu class:

1. Open the **Menu.java** file in your text editor and change the access specifier for the entreeChoice array from private to protected. That way, when you extend the class, the derived class will have access to the array. Save the file and recompile it using the **javac** command.

2. Open a new file in your text editor, and then type the following class header for the VegetarianMenu class that extends Menu:

```
public class VegetarianMenu extends Menu
{
```

3. Provide new menu choices for the VegetarianMenu as follows:

```
String[] vegEntreeChoice = {"Spinach Lasagna",
    "Cheese Enchiladas", "Fruit Plate"};
```

4. Add the following constructor that calls the superclass constructor and assigns each vegetarian selection to the Menu superclass entreeChoice array, and then add the closing curly brace for the class:

```
public VegetarianMenu()
{
    super();
    for(int x = 0; x < vegEntreeChoice.length; ++x)
        entreeChoice[x] = vegEntreeChoice[x];
}
}
```

5. Save the class as **VegetarianMenu.java**, and then compile it.

6. Now write an application that uses VegetarianMenu. You could write any program, but for demonstration purposes, you can simply modify PlanMenu.java. Open the **PlanMenu.java** file in your text editor, then immediately save it as **PlanVegetarianMenu.java**.

7. Change the class name in the header to **PlanVegetarianMenu**.

8. Change the first statement within the main() method as follows so it declares a VegetarianMenu instead of a Menu:

```
VegetarianMenu briefMenu = new VegetarianMenu();
```

9. Change the guestChoice assignment statement in the catch block as follows so it is specific to the program that uses the VegetarianMenu:

```
guestChoice = "an invalid vegetarian selection";
```

10. Save the file, compile it, and run the application. When you see the vegetarian menu, enter a valid selection and confirm that the program works correctly. Run the application again and enter an invalid selection. The error message shown in Figure 11-45 identifies your invalid entry as "an invalid vegetarian selection". Remember that you did not change the PickMenu class. Your new PlanVegetarianMenu application uses the PickMenu class that you wrote and compiled before a VegetarianMenu ever existed. However, because PickMenu throws uncaught Exceptions, you can handle those Exceptions as you see fit in any new applications in which you catch them. Click **OK** to end the application.

Figure 11-45 Output of the PlanVegetarianMenu application when the user makes an invalid selection

USING THE printStackTrace() METHOD

The printStackTrace() method can help you locate the origin of a thrown Exception. In this section, you will add a call to printStackTrace() in the catch block in the PlanMenu class.

To use the printStackTrace() method:

1. Open the **PlanMenu.java** file in your text editor and save it as **PlanMenuWithStackTrace.java**.

2. Change the class header to **PlanMenuWithStackTrace**.

3. Within the `catch` block, after the statement `guestChoice = "an invalid selection";`, type the following two new statements to identify and print the stack trace:

```
System.out.println("StackTrace");
error.printStackTrace();
```

4. Save the file, then compile and execute it. After the menu appears, enter an invalid selection. If you enter "4", your command screen looks like Figure 11-46. If you read the list that follows the Stack Trace heading, you see that an `ArrayIndexOutOfBoundsException` occurred in the method `Menu.displayMenu()`, and that the value that caused the `Exception` was 3 (the 4 you entered, minus 1). That method was called by the `PickMenu.setGuestChoice()` method, which in turn was initiated by the `PickMenu` constructor. The `PickMenu` constructor was called from the `PlanMenuWithStackTrace.main()` method. You see the line number as additional information within each method in which the `Exception` occurred. (Your line numbers might be different if you added comments to your classes or changed the layout of your lines from that shown in this book.) If you did not understand why entering 4 caused an error, you would use the stack trace information to first examine the `Menu.displayMenu()` method as the original source of the error. Using `printStackTrace()` can be a helpful debugging tool.

Figure 11-46 Messages generated by `printStackTrace()` after the user enters 4

5. Close the application by clicking **OK** in the dialog box or by pressing **Ctrl+C**. Run the **PlanMenuWithStackTrace** application again, and enter **A** for the user selection. You can see from the stack trace that this time the `Exception` does not originate directly in the `Menu.displayMenu()` method. This execution of the application generates a `NumberFormatException` at the `parseInt()` method within the `displayMenu()` method before the application attempts to access the array (see Figure 11-47).

```
Command Prompt - java PlanMenuWithStackTrace

C:\Java>java PlanMenuWithStackTrace
StackTrace
java.lang.NumberFormatException: For input string: "A"
        at java.lang.NumberFormatException.forInputString(NumberFormatException.
java:48)
        at java.lang.Integer.parseInt(Integer.java:447)
        at java.lang.Integer.parseInt(Integer.java:497)
        at Menu.displayMenu(Menu.java:17)
        at PickMenu.setGuestChoice(PickMenu.java:15)
        at PickMenu.<init>(PickMenu.java:9)
        at PlanMenuWithStackTrace.main(PlanMenuWithStackTrace.java:11)
```

Figure 11-47 Messages generated by `printStackTrace()` after the user enters A

6. Close the application by clicking **OK** in the dialog box or by pressing **Ctrl+C** when the command prompt window is the active window.

CREATING AN Exception CLASS

Besides using the built-in Exceptions such as NumberFormatException and IndexOutOfBoundsException, you can create your own Exception classes. For example, suppose that although you have asked a user to type a number representing a menu selection, you realize that some users might mistakenly type the initial letter of an option, such as "R" for "Rosemary Chicken". Although the user has made an error, you want to treat this type of error more leniently than other errors, such as typing a letter that has no discernable connection to the presented menu. In the next section, you will create a MenuException class that you can use with the Menu class you created earlier to represent a specific type of error.

To create the MenuException class:

1. Open a new file in your text editor and enter the MenuException class. The class extends Exception. Its constructor requires a String argument, which is passed to the parent class to be used as a return value for the getMessage() method.

```
public class MenuException extends Exception
{
    public MenuException(String choice)
    {
        super(choice);
    }
}
```

2. Save the file as **MenuException.java** and compile it.

USING AN Exception YOU CREATED

Next, you will modify the Menu, PickMenu, and PlanMenu classes to demonstrate how to use a MenuException object.

To modify the Menu class to throw a MenuException object:

1. Open the **Menu** class in your text editor, and immediately save the file as **Menu2.java**.

2. Change the class name to **Menu2**.

3. At the end of the list of class data fields, add an array of characters that can hold the first letter of each of the entrees in the menu.

```
protected char initial[] = new char[entreeChoice.length];
```

4. At the end of the method header for the displayMenu() class, add the following clause:

```
throws MenuException
```

You add this clause because you are going to add code that throws such an exception.

5. Within the displayMenu() method, just before the closing curly brace of the for loop that builds the menu String, add a statement that takes the first character of each

entreeChoice and stores it in a corresponding element of the initial array. At the end of the for loop, the initial array holds the first character of each available entree.

```
initial[x] = entreeChoice[x].charAt(0);
```

6. After displaying the JOptionPane dialog box that displays the menu and receives the user's input, add a loop that compares the first letter of the user's choice to each of the initials of valid menu options. If a match is found, throw a new instance of the MenuException class that uses the corresponding entree as its String argument. In other words, when this thrown Exception is caught by another method, the assumed entree is the String returned by the getMessage() method. By placing this test before the call to parseInt(), you cause entries of "R", "B", or "M" to throw a MenuException before they can cause a NumberFormatException.

```
for(int y = 0; y < entreeChoice.length; ++ y)
    if(input.charAt(0) == initial[y])
        throw (new MenuException(entreeChoice[y]));
```

7. Compare your new class with Figure 11-48, in which all of the changes to the Menu class are shaded.

```java
import javax.swing.*;
public class Menu2
{
    protected String[] entreeChoice = {"Rosemary Chicken",
        "Beef Wellington", "Maine Lobster"};
    private String menu = "";
    private int choice;
    protected char initial[] = new char[entreeChoice.length];
    public String displayMenu() throws MenuException
    {
        for(int x = 0; x < entreeChoice.length; ++x)
        {
            menu = menu + "\n" + (x + 1) + " for " +
                entreeChoice[x];
            initial[x] = entreeChoice[x].charAt(0);
        }
        String input = JOptionPane.showInputDialog(null,
            "Type your selection, then press Enter." + menu);
        for(int y = 0; y < entreeChoice.length; ++y)
            if(input.charAt(0) == initial[y])
                throw(new MenuException(entreeChoice[y]));
        choice = Integer.parseInt(input);
        return(entreeChoice[choice - 1]);
    }
}
```

Figure 11-48 The Menu2 class

8. Save the class and compile it.

To modify the `PickMenu` class to throw a `MenuException` object:

1. Open the **PickMenu** file in your text editor and immediately save it as **PickMenu2.java**.

2. Change the class name to **PickMenu2** and change the declaration of the `Menu` object to a **Menu2** object. Change the constructor name to **PickMenu2** and its argument to type **Menu2**. Also add a `throws` clause to the `PickMenu2` constructor header so that it throws a `MenuException`. This constructor does not throw an `Exception` directly, but it calls the `setGuestChoice()` method, which calls the `displayMenu()` method, which throws a `MenuException`.

3. Add the following `throws` clause to the `setGuestChoice()` method header:

   `throws MenuException`

4. Compare your modifications to the `PickMenu2` class in Figure 11-49, in which the changes from the `PickMenu` class are shaded. Save your file and compile it.

```
import javax.swing.*;
public class PickMenu2
{
    private Menu2 briefMenu;
    private String guestChoice = new String();
    public PickMenu2(Menu2 theMenu) throws MenuException
    {
        briefMenu = theMenu;
        setGuestChoice();
    }
    public void setGuestChoice() throws MenuException
    {
        String inputString = new String();
        JOptionPane.showMessageDialog(null,
            "Choose from the following menu:");
        guestChoice = briefMenu.displayMenu();
    }
    public String getGuestChoice()
    {
        return(guestChoice);
    }
}
```

Figure 11-49 The `PickMenu2` class

To modify the `PlanMenu` class to handle a `MenuException` object:

1. Open the **PlanMenu.java** file in your text editor and immediately save it as **PlanMenu2.java**.

2. Change the class name to **PlanMenu2**. Within the `main()` method, declare a **Menu2** object and a **PickMenu2** reference instead of the current `Menu` object and `PickMenu` reference.

3. Within the `try` block, change both references of `PickMenu` to **PickMenu2**.

Using Figure 11-50 as a reference, add a `catch` block after the `try` block and before the existing `catch` block. This `catch` block will catch any thrown `MenuExceptions` and display their messages. The message will be the name of a menu item, based on the initial the user entered. All other `Exceptions`, including `NumberFormatExceptions` and `IndexOutOfBoundsExceptions`, will fall through to the second `catch` block and be handled as before.

```java
import javax.swing.*;
public class PlanMenu2
{
    public static void main(String[] args)
    {
        Menu2 briefMenu = new Menu2();
        PickMenu2 entree = null;
        String guestChoice = new String();
        try
        {
            PickMenu2 selection = new PickMenu2(briefMenu);
            entree = selection;
            guestChoice = entree.getGuestChoice();
        }
        catch(MenuException error)
        {
            guestChoice = error.getMessage();
        }
        catch(Exception error)
        {
            guestChoice = "an invalid selection";
        }
        JOptionPane.showMessageDialog(null,
            "You chose " + guestChoice);
    }
}
```

Figure 11-50 The `PlanMenu2` class

4. Save the file, then compile and execute it several times. When you are asked to make a selection, try entering a valid number, an invalid number, an initial letter that is part of the menu, and a letter that is not one of the initial menu letters, and observe the results each time. Whether you enter a valid number or not, the application works as expected. Entering an invalid number still results in an error message. When you enter a letter or a string of letters, the application assumes your selection is valid if you enter the same initial letter, using the same case, as one of the menu options.

DON'T DO IT

» Don't forget that all the statements in a `try` block might not execute. If an exception is thrown, no statements after that point in the `try` block will execute.

» Don't forget to place a more general `Exception catch` block after `catch` blocks that handle more specific `Exception`s.

» Don't forget to write a `throws` clause for a method that throws an `exception` but does not handle it.

» Don't forget to handle any checked exception thrown to your method either by writing a `catch` block or by listing it in your method's `throws` clause.

KEY TERMS

An **exception** is an unexpected or error condition.

Exception handling is an object-oriented technique for managing errors.

Runtime exceptions are unplanned exceptions that occur during a program's execution. The term is also used more specifically to describe members of the `RuntimeException` class.

The **Error class** represents more serious errors than the `Exception` class—those from which your program usually cannot recover.

The **Exception class** comprises less serious errors than those from the `Error` class; the `Exception` class represents unusual conditions that arise while a program is running, and from which the program can recover.

A **stack trace history list**, or more simply a **stack trace**, displays all the methods that were called during program execution.

Fault-tolerant applications are designed so that they continue to operate, possibly at a reduced level, when some part of the system fails.

Robustness represents the degree to which a system is resilient to stress, maintaining correct functioning.

When you create a segment of code in which something might go wrong, you place the code in a **try block**, which is a block of code you attempt to execute while acknowledging that an exception might occur.

A **catch block** is a segment of code that can handle an exception that might be thrown by the `try` block that precedes it.

A **throw statement** is one that sends an `Exception` out of a block or a method so it can be handled elsewhere.

When you have actions you must perform at the end of a `try...catch` sequence, you can use a **finally block**.

Exception specification is the practice of using the keyword `throws` followed by an `Exception` type in the method header. If a method throws a checked `Exception` that it will not catch but that will be caught by a different method, you must use an exception specification.

The term **mission critical** refers to any process that is crucial to an organization.

Unchecked exceptions are those that cannot reasonably be expected to be recovered from while a program is executing.

Checked exceptions are those that a programmer should plan for and from which a program should be able to recover. They are not `RuntimeExceptions`; the compiler checks that these exceptions are caught or specified.

The **catch or specify requirement** is the Java rule that checked exceptions require catching or declaration.

Syntactic sugar is a term to describe aspects of a computer language that make it "sweeter," or easier, for programmers to use.

Syntactic salt describes a language feature designed to make it harder to write bad code.

A **thread** is the flow of execution of one set of program statements.

The memory location known as the **call stack** is where the computer stores the list of method locations to which the system must return.

An **assertion** is a Java language feature that can help you detect logic errors and debug a program.

You use an **assert statement** to create an assertion.

CHAPTER SUMMARY

» An exception is an unexpected or error condition. The object-oriented techniques to manage such errors comprise the group of methods known as exception handling. In Java, the two basic classes of errors are `Error` and `Exception`; both descend from the `Throwable` class. In object-oriented terminology, you "try" a procedure that might cause an error. A method that detects an error condition or `Exception` "throws an exception," and the block of code that processes the error "catches the exception."

» A `try` block is a block of code you attempt to execute while acknowledging that an exception might occur. You must code at least one `catch` block immediately following a `try` block (or else you must code a `finally` block). A `catch` block is a segment of code that can handle an exception that might be thrown by the `try` block that precedes it.

» You can place as many statements as you need within a `try` block, and you can catch as many `Exceptions` as you want. If you try more than one statement, only the first error-generating statement throws an `Exception`. As soon as the `Exception` occurs, the logic transfers to the `catch` block, which leaves the rest of the statements in the `try` block unexecuted. When a program contains multiple `catch` blocks, they are examined in sequence until a match is found for the type of `Exception` that occurred. Then, the matching `catch` block executes and each remaining `catch` block is bypassed.

» When you have actions you must perform at the end of a `try...catch` sequence, you can use a `finally` block. The code within a `finally` block executes regardless of whether the preceding `try` block identifies an `Exception`. Usually, you use a `finally` block to perform cleanup tasks that must happen whether or not any `Exceptions` occurred, and whether or not any `Exceptions` that occurred were caught.

» Besides clarity, an advantage to object-oriented exception handling is the flexibility it allows in the handling of error situations. Each calling application might need to handle the same error differently, depending on its purpose.

» When you write a method that might throw a checked `Exception` that is not caught within the method, you must type the clause `throws <name>Exception` after the method header to indicate the type of `Exception` that might be thrown. Methods in which you explicitly throw a checked exception require a catch or a declaration.

» The memory location known as the call stack is where the computer stores the list of method locations to which the system must return. When you catch an `Exception`, you can call `printStackTrace()` to display a list of methods in the call stack so you can determine the location of the `Exception`.

» Java provides over 40 categories of `Exceptions` that you can use in your programs. However, Java's creators could not predict every condition that might be an `Exception` in your applications, so Java also allows you to create your own `Exceptions`. To create your own throwable `Exception`, you must extend a subclass of `Throwable`.

» An assertion is a Java language feature that can help you detect logic errors and debug a program. When you use an assertion, you state a condition that should be true, and Java throws an `AssertionError` when it is not.

REVIEW QUESTIONS

1. In object-oriented programming terminology, an unexpected or error condition is a(n) _____ .

   a. anomaly   c. deviation

   b. aberration   d. exception

2. All Java `Exceptions` are _____ .

   a. `Errors`   c. `Throwables`

   b. `RuntimeExceptions`   d. `Omissions`

3. Which of the following statements is true?

   a. `Exceptions` are more serious than `Errors`.

   b. `Errors` are more serious than `Exceptions`.

   c. `Errors` and `Exceptions` are equally serious.

   d. `Exceptions` and `Errors` are the same thing.

4. The method that ends the current application and returns control to the operating system is _____ .

   a. `System.end()`   c. `System.exit()`

   b. `System.done()`   d. `System.abort()`

5. In object-oriented terminology, you _____ a procedure that might not complete correctly.

    a. try

    b. catch

    c. handle

    d. encapsulate

6. A method that detects an error condition or `Exception` _____ an `Exception`.

    a. throws

    b. catches

    c. handles

    d. encapsulates

7. A `try` block includes all of the following elements except _____ .

    a. the keyword `try`

    b. the keyword `catch`

    c. curly braces

    d. statements that might cause `Exceptions`

8. The segment of code that handles or takes appropriate action following an exception is a _____ block.

    a. `try`

    b. `catch`

    c. `throws`

    d. `handles`

9. You _____ within a `try` block.

    a. must place only a single statement

    b. can place any number of statements

    c. must place at least two statements

    d. must place a `catch` block

10. If you include three statements in a `try` block and follow the block with three `catch` blocks, and the second statement in the `try` block throws an `Exception`, then _____ .

    a. the first `catch` block executes

    b. the first two `catch` blocks execute

    c. only the second `catch` block executes

    d. the first matching `catch` block executes

11. When a `try` block does not generate an `Exception` and you have included multiple `catch` blocks, _____ .

    a. they all execute

    b. only the first one executes

    c. only the first matching one executes

    d. no `catch` blocks execute

12. The `catch` block that begins `catch (Exception e)` can catch `Exceptions` of type _____ .

    a. `IOException`

    b. `ArithmeticException`

    c. both of the above

    d. none of the above

13. The code within a `finally` block executes when the `try` block _____ .

    a. identifies one or more `Exception`s   c. either a or b

    b. does not identify any `Exception`s   d. neither a nor b

14. An advantage to using a `try...catch` block is that exceptional events are _____ .

    a. eliminated   c. integrated with regular events

    b. reduced   d. isolated from regular events

15. Which methods can throw an `Exception`?

    a. methods with a `throws` clause   c. methods with both a `throws` clause and a `catch` block

    b. methods with a `catch` block   d. any method

16. A method can _____ .

    a. check for errors but not handle them   c. either of the above

    b. handle errors but not check for them   d. neither of the above

17. Which of the following is least important to know if you want to be able to use a method to its full potential?

    a. the method's return type

    b. the type of arguments the method requires

    c. the number of statements within the method

    d. the type of `Exception`s the method throws

18. The memory location where the computer stores the list of method locations to which the system must return is known as the _____ .

    a. registry   c. chronicle

    b. call stack   d. archive

19. You can get a list of the methods through which an `Exception` has traveled by using the _____ method.

    a. `getMessage()`   c. `getPath()`

    b. `callStack()`   d. `printStackTrace()`

20. A(n) _____ is a statement used in testing programs that should be true; if it is not true, an `Exception` is thrown.

    a. assertion   c. verification

    b. throwable   d. declaration

EXERCISES

1. Write an application named `GoTooFar` in which you declare an array of five integers and store five values in the array. Write a `try` block in which you loop to display each successive element of the array, increasing a subscript by 1 on each pass through the loop. Create a `catch` block that catches the eventual `ArrayIndexOutOfBoundsException` and displays the message, "Now you've gone too far". Save the file as **GoTooFar.java**.

2. The `Integer.parseInt()` method requires a `String` argument, but fails if the `String` cannot be converted to an integer. Write an application in which you try to parse a `String` that does not represent an integer value. Catch the `NumberFormatException` that is thrown, and then display an appropriate error message. Save the file as **TryToParseString.java**.

3. Write an application that prompts the user to enter a number to use as an array size, and then attempt to declare an array using the entered size. If the array is created successfully, display an appropriate message. Java generates a `NegativeArraySizeException` if you attempt to create an array with a negative size, and a `NumberFormatException` if you attempt to create an array using a nonnumeric value for the size. Use a `catch` block that executes if the array size is nonnumeric or negative, displaying a message that indicates the array was not created. Save the file as **NegativeArray.java**.

4. Write an application that throws and catches an `ArithmeticException` when you attempt to take the square root of a negative value. Prompt the user for an input value and try the `Math.sqrt()` method on it. The application either displays the square root or catches the thrown `Exception` and displays an appropriate message. Save the file as **SqrtException.java**.

5. Create an `EmployeeException` class whose constructor receives a `String` that consists of an employee's ID and pay rate. Save the file as **EmployeeException.java**. Create an `Employee` class with two fields: `idNum` and `hourlyWage`. The `Employee` constructor requires values for both fields. Upon construction, throw an `EmployeeException` if the `hourlyWage` is less than $6.00 or over $50.00. Save the class as **Employee.java**. Write an application that establishes at least three `Employees` with `hourlyWages` that are above, below, and within the allowed range. Display an appropriate message when an `Employee` is successfully created and when one is not. Save the file as **ThrowEmployee.java**.

6. a. Create an `IceCreamConeException` class whose constructor receives a `String` that consists of an ice cream cone's flavor and an integer representing the number of scoops in the `IceCreamCone`. Pass this `String` to the `IceCreamConeException`'s parent so it can be used in a `getMessage()` call. Save the class as **IceCreamConeException.java**. Create an `IceCreamCone` class with two fields—`flavor` and `scoops`. The `IceCreamCone` constructor calls two data-entry methods—`setFlavor()` and `setScoops()`. The `setScoops()` method throws an `IceCreamConeException` when the scoop quantity exceeds three. Save the class as **IceCreamCone.java**. Write an application that establishes several `IceCreamCone` objects and handles the `Exceptions`. Save the file as **ThrowIceCream.java**.

b. Create an `IceCreamCone2` class in which you modify the `IceCreamCone setFlavor()` method to ensure that the user enters a valid flavor. Allow at least four flavors of your choice. If the user's entry does not match a valid flavor, throw an `IceCreamConeException`. Write an application that establishes several `IceCreamCone` objects and demonstrates the handling of the new `Exception`. Save the new class file as **IceCreamCone2.java** and save the new application file as **ThrowIceCream2.java**.

7. Write an application that displays a series of at least five student ID numbers (that you have stored in an array) and asks the user to enter a numeric test score for the student. Create a `ScoreException` class, and throw a `ScoreException` for the class if the user does not enter a valid score (less than or equal to 100). Catch the `ScoreException` and then display an appropriate message. In addition, store a 0 for the student's score. At the end of the application, display all the student IDs and scores. Save the files as **ScoreException.java** and **TestScore.java**.

8. Write an application that displays a series of at least 10 student ID numbers (that you have stored in an array) and asks the user to enter a test letter grade for the student. Create an `Exception` class named `GradeException` that contains a `static public` array of valid grade letters ('A', 'B', 'C', 'D', 'F', and 'I'), which you can use to determine whether a grade entered from the application is valid. In your application, throw a `GradeException` if the user does not enter a valid letter grade. Catch the `GradeException` and then display an appropriate message. In addition, store an 'I' (for Incomplete) for any student for whom an exception is caught. At the end of the application, display all the student IDs and grades. Save the files as **GradeException.java** and **TestGrade.java**.

9. Create a `DataEntryException` class whose `getMessage()` method returns information about invalid integer data. Write a program named `GetIDAndAge` that continually prompts the user for an ID number and an age until a terminal 0 is entered for both. Throw a `DataEntryException` if the ID is not in the range of valid ID numbers (0–999), or if the age is not in the range of valid ages (0–119). Catch any `DataEntryException` or `InputMismatchException` that is thrown and display an appropriate message. Save the files as **DataEntryException.java** and **GetIDAndAge.java**.

10. A company accepts user orders by part numbers interactively. Users might make the following errors as they enter data:
   » The part number is not numeric.
   » The quantity is not numeric.
   » The part number is too low (less than 0).
   » The part number is too high (more than 999).
   » The quantity ordered is too low (less than 1).
   » The quantity ordered is too high (more than 5000).

   Create a class that stores an array of usable error messages; save the file as **DataMessages.java**. Create a `DataException` class for which each object stores one of the messages; save the file as **DataException.java**. Create an application that prompts the user for a part number and quantity. Allow for the possibility of nonnumeric entries as well as out-of-range entries, and display the appropriate message when an error occurs. If no error occurs, display the message "Valid entry". Save the program as **PartAndQuantityEntry.java**.

11. A company accepts user orders for its products interactively. Users might make the following errors as they enter data:

    » The item number ordered is not numeric.

    » The quantity is not numeric.

    » The item number is too low (less than 0).

    » The item number is too high (more than 9999).

    » The quantity ordered is too low (less than 1).

    » The quantity ordered is too high (more than 12).

    » The item number is not a currently valid item.

    Although the company might expand in the future, its current inventory consists of the following items:

Item Number	Price ($)
111	0.89
222	1.47
333	2.43
444	5.99

    Create a class that stores an array of usable error messages; save the file as **OrderMessages.java**. Create an `OrderException` class that stores one of the messages; save the file as **OrderException.java**. Create an application that contains prompts for an item number and quantity. Allow for the possibility of nonnumeric entries as well as out-of-range entries and entries that do not match any of the currently available item numbers. The program should display an appropriate message if an error has occurred. If no errors exist in the entered data, compute the user's total amount due (quantity times price each) and display it. Save the program as **PlaceAnOrder.java**.

12. a. Gadgets by Mail sells many interesting items through its catalogs. Write an application that prompts the user for order details, including item numbers and quantity of each item ordered, based on the available items shown in Table 11-1.

Item #	Description	Price ($)
101	Electric hand warmer	12.99
124	Battery-operated plant waterer	7.55
256	Gerbil trimmer	9.99
512	Talking bookmark	6.89

Table 11-1 Items offered by Gadgets by Mail

The shipping and handling fee for an order is based on the total order price, as shown in Table 11-2.

Price of Order ($)	Shipping and Handling ($)
0–24.99	5.55
25.00–49.99	8.55
50.00 or more	11.55

Table 11-2 Shipping and handling fees charged by Gadgets by Mail

Create the following classes:

» Gadget, which contains an item number, description, and price for a gadget; a constructor that sets all the fields; and get methods to retrieve the field values.

» Order, which contains an order number, customer name, and address (assume you need just a street address, not city, state, and zip code); a list of item numbers ordered (up to four); the total price of all items ordered; and a shipping and handling fee for the order. Include a constructor to set the field values and get methods to retrieve the field values.

» GadgetOrderTaker, which is an interactive application that takes four customer orders. The class contains an array of the four Gadget objects offered (from Table 11-1). The application prompts each user for a name and street address and assigns a unique order number to each customer, starting with 101. The application asks each user to enter an item number and quantity wanted. When the user enters 999 for the item number, the order is complete, and the next customer can enter data. Each customer can order up to four item numbers. When a customer's order is complete (the customer has entered 999 for an item number, or has ordered four different items), calculate the shipping and handling charges. After all four customers have placed Orders, display each Order's data, including the order number, the name and address of the customer, and the list of items ordered, including the item number, description, and price of each Order, the total price for the order, and the shipping and handling charge. The GadgetOrderTaker class handles all thrown Exceptions by displaying an explanatory message and ending the application.

» `OrderException`, which is an `Exception` that is created and thrown under any of the following conditions:

» A customer attempts to order more than four different items.

» A customer orders more than 100 of any item.

» A customer enters an invalid item number.

» Also, catch the `Exception` generated by either of these conditions:

» A customer enters a nonnumeric character as the item number.

» A customer enters a nonnumeric character as the quantity.

Save the files as **Gadget.java**, **Order.java**, **GadgetOrderTaker.java**, and **OrderException.java**.

b. The `GadgetOrderTaker` class handles all thrown `Exceptions` by displaying an explanatory message and ending the application. Create a new application that handles all `Exceptions` by requiring the user to reenter the offending data. Save the file as **GadgetOrderTaker2.java**.

DEBUGGING EXERCISES

Each of the following files in the Chapter.11 folder on your Student Disk has syntax and/ or logic errors. In each case, determine the problem and fix the program. After you correct the errors, save each file using the same filename preceded with Fix. For example, DebugEleven1.java will become FixDebugEleven1.java. You will also use a file named DebugEmployeeIDException.java with the DebugEleven4.java file.

a. DebugEleven1.java

b. DebugEleven2.java

c. DebugEleven3.java

d. DebugEleven4.java

GAME ZONE

1. In Chapter 1, you created a class called `RandomGuess`. In this game, the application generates a random number for a player to guess. In Chapter 5, you improved the application to display a message indicating whether the player's guess was correct, too high, or too low. In Chapter 6, you further improved the game by adding a loop that continually prompts the user to enter the correct value, if necessary. As written, the game should work as long as the player enters numeric guesses. However, if the player enters a letter or other nonnumeric character, the game throws an exception. Discover the type of `Exception` thrown, then improve the game by handling the exception so that the user is informed of the error and allowed to attempt to correct the data entry again. Save the file as **RandomGuess4.java**.

2. In Chapter 8, you created a `Quiz` class that contains an array of 10 multiple-choice quiz questions to which the user was required to respond with an A, B, or C. At the time, you knew how to handle the user's response if an invalid character was entered. Rerun the program now to determine whether an exception is thrown if the user enters nothing—that is, the user just presses the Enter key without making an entry. If so, improve the program by catching the exception, displaying an appropriate error message, and presenting the same question to the user again. Save the file as **QuizWithExceptionsCaught.java**.

TOUGH QUESTIONS

1. Many Java `Exception` classes are located in the package java.lang. Why is the `InputMismatchException` class located in java.util?

2. Under what circumstances will a `finally` block not execute or not execute completely?

3. What is output by the following method?
```java
public class Test
{
    public static void main(String[] args)
    {
        System.out.println(method());
    }
    public static boolean method()
    {
        try
        {
            return true;
        }
        finally
        {
            return false;
        }
    }
}
```

4. Write a loop that assigns the number 15 to every element in an array without using any comparison operators such as <, ==, >, or !=.

UP FOR DISCUSSION

1. The terms *syntactic sugar* and *syntactic salt* were described in this chapter. There are no hard and fast rules to assigning these terms to language features; it is somewhat a matter of opinion. From your knowledge of the Java programming language, list as many syntactic sugar and salt features as you can.

2. In the programming community, there is controversy over whether Java's requirement of specifying checked exceptions is a good policy. Investigate the controversy and explain your opinion.

3. Have you ever been victimized by a computer error? For example, were you ever incorrectly denied credit, billed for something you did not purchase, or assigned an incorrect grade in a course? How did you resolve the problem? On the Web, find the most outrageous story you can involving a computer error.

4. Search the Web for information about educational video games in which historical simulations are presented in an effort to teach students about history. For example, Civilization III is a game in which players control a society as it progresses through time. Do you believe such games are useful to history students? Does the knowledge gained warrant the hours it takes to master the games? Do the makers of the games have any obligations to present history factually? Do they have a right to penalize players who choose options of which the game writers disapprove (such as using nuclear weapons or allowing slavery)? Do game creators have the right to create characters who possess negative stereotypical traits—for example, a person of a specific nationality portrayed as being stupid, weak, or evil? Would you like to take a history course that uses similar games?

12

FILE INPUT AND OUTPUT

In this chapter, you will:

Understand computer files
Use the `File` class
Understand data file organization and streams
Use streams
Write to and read from a file
Write formatted file data
Read formatted file data
Use a variable filename
Create and use random access files
Write records to a random access file
Read records from a random access file
Read and write objects to and from files

UNDERSTANDING COMPUTER FILES

When data items are stored in a computer system, they can be stored for varying periods of time—temporarily or permanently.

» Temporary storage is usually called computer memory or **random access memory** (RAM). When you write a Java program that stores a value in a variable, you are using temporary storage; the value you store is lost when the program ends or the computer loses power. This type of storage is **volatile**.

» Permanent storage, on the other hand, is not lost when a computer loses power; it is **nonvolatile**. When you write a Java program and save it to a disk, you are using permanent storage.

>>**NOTE** When discussing computer storage, "temporary" and "permanent" refer to volatility, not length of time. For example, a "temporary" variable might exist for several hours in a large program or one that the user forgets to close, but a "permanent" piece of data might be saved and then deleted within a few seconds.

A **computer file** is a collection of information stored on a nonvolatile device in a computer system. Files exist on **permanent storage devices**, such as hard disks, Zip disks, USB drives, reels or cassettes of magnetic tape, and compact discs. Some files are **data files** that contain facts and figures, such as a payroll file that contains employee numbers, names, and salaries; some files are **program files** or **application files** that store software instructions. (You have created many such files throughout this book.) Other files can store graphics, text, or operating system instructions (such as the compiled files with a .class extension that your compiler has created for every .java class that you compile). Although their contents vary, files have many common characteristics—each file occupies space on a section of disk (or other storage device) and has a name and a specific time of creation.

Computer files are the electronic equivalent of paper files often stored in file cabinets in offices. When you store a permanent file, you can place it in the main or **root directory** of your storage device. If you picture computer storage as similar to a file cabinet drawer, this is equivalent to tossing a loose document into the drawer. However, for better organization, most office clerks place documents in folders, and most computer users also organize their files into **folders** or **directories**. Users also can place folders within folders to form a hierarchy. A complete list of the disk drive plus the hierarchy of directories in which a file resides is its **path**. For example, in the Windows operating system, the complete path for a file named Data.txt on the C drive in a folder named Chapter.12 in a folder named Java is:

```
C:\Java\Chapter.12\Data.txt
```

When you work with stored files in an application, you typically perform all or some of the following tasks:

» Determining whether and where a file exists
» Opening a file
» Reading data from a file
» Writing information to a file
» Closing a file

Java provides built-in classes that contain methods to help you with all these tasks.

»TWO TRUTHS AND A LIE: UNDERSTANDING COMPUTER FILES

1. An advantage of modern computer systems is that both internal computer memory and disk storage are nonvolatile.
2. Data files contain facts and figures; program files store software instructions that might use data files.
3. A complete list of the disk drive plus the hierarchy of directories in which a file resides is the file's path.

The false statement is #1. Internal computer memory (RAM) is volatile; disk storage is nonvolatile.

USING THE File CLASS

You can use Java's **File class** to gather file information, such as its size, its most recent modification date, and whether the file even exists. You must include the following statement to use the File class:

```
import java.io.File;
```

The java.io package contains all the classes you use in file processing, so it is usually easiest to import the entire package using the wildcard * character, as follows:

```
import java.io.*;
```

The File class is a direct descendant of the Object class. You can create a File object using a constructor that includes a filename as its argument; for example, you make the following statement when Data.txt is a file on the default disk drive:

```
File someData = new File("Data.txt");
```

You can also specify a path for the file; for example, the following argument to the constructor contains a disk drive and path:

```
File someData = new File("C:\\Java\\Chapter.12\\Data.txt");
```

> **»NOTE**
> The *io* in java.io stands for *input/output*. The io package contains 50 classes, a dozen interfaces, and 15 specific Exceptions.

》》NOTE In a file path, the backslash character (\) separates folders and files. On a Windows computer, the backslash is the separator character, but on a UNIX computer the forward slash (/) is the separator character. Java processes both characters identically when they are used in a path. However, if you use the backslash, you must recall that it is also used as part of an escape sequence in Java. (For example, '\n' represents a newline character.) You must type two backslashes to indicate a single backslash to the operating system. You learned about escape sequences in Chapter 2. Instead of explicitly using "\\" or "/" as part of a string representing a path, you also can use the `File` class `String` field `File.separator`. This field holds the correct separator for the current operating system.

Table 12-1 lists some useful `File` class methods.

Method Signature	Purpose
`boolean canRead()`	Returns `true` if a file is readable
`boolean canWrite()`	Returns `true` if a file is writable
`boolean exists()`	Returns `true` if a file exists
`String getName()`	Returns the file's name
`String getPath()`	Returns the file's path
`String getParent()`	Returns the name of the folder in which the file can be found
`long length()`	Returns the file's size
`long lastModified()`	Returns the time the file was last modified; this time is system dependent and should be used only for comparison with other files' times, not as an absolute time

Table 12-1 Selected `File` class methods

Figure 12-1 contains an application that demonstrates some of the `File` class methods. In the `main()` method, a `File` object named `myFile` is declared. The `String` passed to the constructor is "SomeData.txt", which is the stored file's system name. In other words, although SomeData.txt might be the name of a stored file when the operating system refers to it, the file is known as `myFile` within the application. The idea of a file having one name when referenced by the operating system and a different name within an application is similar to the concept of how a method can contain a variable with one name, but a method that uses the value can refer to the same value using a different name. In both cases, a specific item has an "outside" name and an "inside" name, just as a student known as "Arthur" in school might be "Junior" at home. To use this application with a different file, you would change only the `String` passed to the `File` constructor.

```
import java.io.*;
public class FileDemo
{
   public static void main(String[] args)
   {
      File myFile = new File("SomeData.txt");
      if(myFile.exists())
      {
         System.out.println(myFile.getName() + " exists");
         System.out.println("The file is " +
            myFile.length () + " bytes long");
         if(myFile.canRead())
            System.out.println(" ok to read");
         else
            System.out.println(" not ok to read");
         if(myFile.canWrite())
            System.out.println(" ok to write");
         else
            System.out.println(" not ok to write");
      }
      else
         System.out.println("File does not exist");
   }
}
```

Figure 12-1 The FileDemo class

In the main() method of the FileDemo class, an if statement tests for the existence of the file. If the file exists, its name, length, and reading and writing capabilities display; otherwise, a message indicates "File does not exist". Figure 12-2 shows the output when the application executes and no such file is stored in the same folder as the application, and then again after such a file has been created.

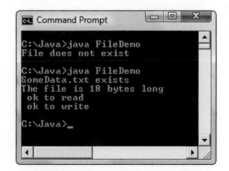

Figure 12-2 Output of the FileDemo application when run before and after creation of the SomeData.txt file

In the second execution of the FileDemo application shown in Figure 12-2, the application found the file named SomeData.txt because the file was physically located in the current directory—that is, the directory in which the application was stored and from which it was executed. You can check the status of files in other directories by using a File constructor with two String arguments. The first String represents a path to the filename, and the second `String` represents the filename. For example, the following statement refers to the SomeData.txt file located in the EventHandlers folder within the com folder on the current drive:

```
File someFile = new File("\\com\\EventHandlers", "SomeData.txt");
```

You can also refer to files on other storage devices. For example, the following statement refers to the SomeOtherData.txt file in the Temp folder on the A drive:

```
File someOtherFile = new File("A:\\Temp", "SomeOtherData.txt");
```

»TWO TRUTHS AND A LIE: USING THE File CLASS

1. You can use Java's `File` class to gather file information, such as its size, its most recent modification date, and whether the file even exists.
2. You must be careful to use the same name that the operating system uses when referencing a file within an application.
3. The current directory is the directory in which an application is stored and from which it was executed.

The false statement is #2. A file can have one name when referenced by the operating system and a different name within an application.

UNDERSTANDING DATA FILE ORGANIZATION AND STREAMS

Most businesses generate and use large quantities of data every day. You can store data in variables within a program, but this type of storage is temporary. When the application ends, the variables no longer exist and the data is lost. Variables are stored in the computer's main or primary memory (RAM). When you need to retain data for any significant amount of time, you must save the data on a permanent, secondary storage device, such as a floppy disk, hard drive, or compact disc (CD).

»NOTE Because you can erase data from files, some programmers prefer the term "persistent storage" to permanent storage. In other words, you can remove data from a file stored on a device such as a disk drive, so it is not technically permanent. However, the data remains in the file even when the computer loses power, so, unlike RAM, the data persists, or perseveres.

»NOTE
Java uses Unicode to represent its characters. You first learned about Unicode in Chapter 1, and more information is contained in Appendix B.

Businesses store data in a hierarchy, as shown in Figure 12-3. The smallest useful piece of data to most people is the character. A character can be any one of the letters, numbers, or other special symbols, such as punctuation marks, that comprise data. Characters are made up of bits (the zeros and ones that represent computer circuitry), but people who use data are not concerned with whether the internal representation for an 'A' is 01000001 or 10111110; rather, they are concerned with the meaning of 'A'—for example, it might represent a grade in a course, a person's initial, or a company code.

»NOTE In computer terminology, a character can be any group of bits, and it does not necessarily represent a letter or number. Some of these do not correspond to characters in natural language; for example, some "characters" produce a sound or control display. You have also used escape sequences in which characters are constructed from multiple keystrokes; for example, the '\n' character starts a new line.

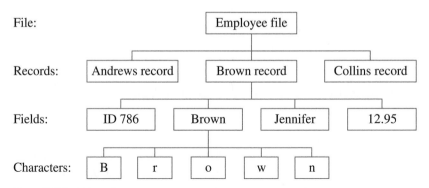

File: Employee file

Records: Andrews record | Brown record | Collins record

Fields: ID 786 | Brown | Jennifer | 12.95

Characters: B | r | o | w | n

Figure 12-3 Data hierarchy

» NOTE
Sometimes, you can think of a character as a unit of information instead of data with a particular appearance. For example, the mathematical character pi (π) and the Greek letter pi look the same, but have two different Unicode values.

When businesses use data, they group characters into fields. A **field** is a group of characters that has some meaning. For example, the characters *T*, *o*, and *m* might represent your first name. Other data fields might represent items such as last name, Social Security number, zip code, and salary.

Fields are grouped together to form records. A **record** is a collection of fields that contain data about an entity. For example, a person's first and last names, Social Security number, zip code, and salary represent that person's record. When programming in Java, you have created many classes, such as an `Employee` class or a `Student` class. You can think of the data typically stored in each of these classes as a record. These classes contain individual variables that represent data fields. A business's data records usually represent a person, item, sales transaction, or some other concrete object or event.

Records are grouped to create files. Data files consist of related records, such as a company's personnel file that contains one record for each company employee. Some files have only a few records; perhaps your professor maintains a file for your class with 25 records—one record for each student. Other files contain thousands or even millions of records. For example, a large insurance company maintains a file of policyholders, and a mail-order catalog company maintains a file of available items. A data file is used as a **sequential access file** when each record is stored in order based on the value in some field; for example, employees might be stored in Social Security number order, or inventory items might be stored in item number order.

» NOTE
When records are not used in sequence, the file is used as a random access file. You will learn more about random access files later in this chapter.

Before an application can use a data file, it must open the file. A Java application **opens a file** by creating an object and associating a stream of bytes with that object. Similarly, when you finish using a file, the program should **close the file**—that is, make it no longer available to your application. If you fail to close an input file—that is, a file from which you are reading data—there usually are no serious consequences; the data still exists in the file. However, if you fail to close an output file—a file to which you are writing data—the data might become inaccessible. You should always close every file you open, and usually you should close the file as soon as you no longer need it. When you leave a file open for no reason, you use computer resources and your computer's performance suffers. Also, particularly within a network, another program might be waiting to use the file.

Whereas people view files as a series of records, with each record containing data fields, Java views files as a series of bytes. When you perform an input operation in an application, you can picture bytes flowing into your program from an input device through a **stream**, which functions as a pipeline or channel. When you perform output,

Figure 12-4 File streams

some bytes flow out of your application through another stream to an output device, as shown in Figure 12-4. A stream is an object, and like all objects, streams have data and methods. The methods allow you to perform actions such as opening, closing, and flushing (clearing) the stream.

»NOTE
Random access files use streams that flow in two directions. You will use a random access file later in this chapter.

Most streams flow in only one direction; each stream is either an input or output stream. You might open several streams at once within an application. For example, an application that reads a data disk and separates valid records from invalid ones might require three streams. The data arrives via an input stream, and as the program checks the data for invalid values, one output stream writes some records to a file of valid records, and another output stream writes other records to a file of invalid records.

»TWO TRUTHS AND A LIE: UNDERSTANDING DATA FILE ORGANIZATION AND STREAMS

1. A field is a group of characters that has some meaning; a record is a collection of fields.
2. A data file is used as a sequential access file when the first field for each record is stored first in a file, the second fields are stored next, and so on.
3. Java views files as a series of bytes that flow into and out of your applications through a stream.

The false statement is #2. A data file is used as a sequential access file when each record is stored in order based on the value in some field.

USING STREAMS

»NOTE
You first learned about abstract classes in Chapter 10.

Figure 12-5 shows a partial hierarchical relationship of Java's Stream classes; it shows that InputStream and OutputStream are subclasses of the Object class. **InputStream** and **OutputStream** are abstract classes that contain methods for performing input and output, respectively. As abstract classes, these classes contain methods that must be overridden in their child classes. The capabilities of the most commonly used classes that provide input and output are summarized in Table 12-2.

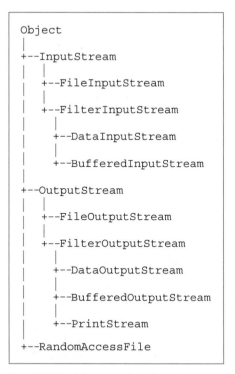

```
Object
 |
+--InputStream
 |  |
 |  +--FileInputStream
 |  |
 |  +--FilterInputStream
 |     |
 |     +--DataInputStream
 |     |
 |     +--BufferedInputStream
 |
+--OutputStream
 |  |
 |  +--FileOutputStream
 |  |
 |  +--FilterOutputStream
 |     |
 |     +--DataOutputStream
 |     |
 |     +--BufferedOutputStream
 |     |
 |     +--PrintStream
 |
+--RandomAccessFile
```

Figure 12-5 Partial Stream class hierarchy

Class	Description
InputStream	Abstract class containing methods for performing input
OutputStream	Abstract class containing methods for performing output
FileInputStream	Child of InputStream that provides the capability to read from disk files
FileOutputStream	Child of OutputStream that provides the capability to write to disk files
PrintStream	Child of FilterOutputStream, which is a child of OutputStream; PrintStream handles output to a system's standard (or default) output device, usually the monitor
BufferedInputStream	Child of FilterInputStream, which is a child of InputStream; BufferedInputStream handles input from a system's standard (or default) input device, usually the keyboard

Table 12-2 Description of selected classes used for input and output

Java's `System` class instantiates a `PrintStream` object. This object is `System.out`, which you have used extensively in this book with its `print()` and `println()` methods. Besides `System.out`, the `System` class defines an additional `PrintStream` object named `System.err`. The output from `System.err` and `System.out` can go to the same device; in fact, `System.err` and `System.out` by default are both directed to the command line on the monitor. The difference is that `System.err` is usually reserved for error messages, and `System.out` is reserved for valid output. You can direct either `System.err` or `System.out` to a new location, such as a disk file or printer. For example, you might want to keep a hard-copy (printed) log of the error messages generated by a program, but direct the standard output to a disk file.

Java also contains a `FileWriter` class, which is a convenience class for writing character files. A **convenience class** is one that has been designed to make the programmer's job easier.

Figure 12-5 shows that the `InputStream` class is the parent to `FilterInputStream`, which is the parent to `BufferedInputStream`. The object `System.in` is a `BufferedInputStream` object. The `System.in` object captures keyboard input. A **buffer** is a memory location that you use to hold data temporarily. The `BufferedInputStream` class allows keyboard data to be entered at the command line and held until the user presses Enter. That way, the user can backspace over typed characters to change the data before the application stores it. This allows the operating system—instead of your program—to handle the complicated tasks of deleting characters as the user backspaces, and then replacing the deleted characters with new ones.

>> **NOTE** Using a buffer to hold input or output before the actual IO command is issued improves program performance. Input and output operations are relatively slow compared to computer processor speeds. Holding input or output until there is a "batch" makes programs run faster.

>> **NOTE** You can create your own `InputStream` and `OutputStream` objects and assign `System.in` and `System.out` to them, respectively. Then, you can use the `InputStream`'s `read()` method to read one character at a time from the location you choose. The `read()` method returns an integer that represents the Unicode value of the typed character; it returns a value of –1 when it encounters an end-of-file condition, known as **EOF**. Whenever you use the `read()` or `close()` methods, there is a possibility that they might throw an `IOException`. Therefore, any method that contains these statements might throw `Exception`s and must either catch the `Exception`s or pass them through to another method that catches them. You learned about `Exception` objects in Chapter 11. You can also identify `EOF` by throwing an `EOFException`; you will use this technique later in this chapter.

>> **NOTE**
Ctrl+Z represents `EOF` in Windows. You can create an `EOF` character on a UNIX keyboard by using Ctrl+D.

Figure 12-6 contains a demonstration application named `ReadAndWrite`. In the application's `main()` method, `InputStream` and `OutputStream` objects are declared and `System.in` and `System.out` are assigned to them. After the prompt "Type some characters", a `try` block holds the shaded `while` statement. The `while` statement continues to read while it does not return –1, the `EOF` value. In the case of keyboard input, –1 is returned when you press Ctrl+Z. Until you enter `EOF`, the `while` statement displays the input character and retrieves another.

```java
import java.io.*;
public class ReadAndWrite
{
    public static void main(String[] args)
    {
        InputStream istream;
        OutputStream ostream;
        int c;
        final int EOF = -1;
        istream = System.in;
        ostream = System.out;
        System.out.println("Type some characters ");
        try
        {
            while((c = istream.read()) != EOF)
                ostream.write(c);
        }
        catch(IOException e)
        {
            System.out.println("Error: " + e.getMessage());
        }
        finally
        {
            try
            {
                istream.close();
                ostream.close();
            }
            catch (IOException e)
            {
                System.out.println("File did not close");
            }
        }
    }
}
```

Figure 12-6 The ReadAndWrite class

>> NOTE Before you knew about input and output streams, you wrote applications that read data from the keyboard and displayed it on the screen, so the application in Figure 12-6 initially might seem to contain a lot of unnecessary work. However, you soon will see that the InputStream and OutputStream objects can be assigned other input and output devices, allowing your applications to save and retrieve data using storage devices.

>> NOTE The while loop in the ReadAndWrite application continues until the read() method returns –1. However, you cannot end the program by typing –1. Typing a minus sign (–) and a one (1) causes two additional characters to be sent to the buffer, and neither character represents –1. Instead, you must press Ctrl+Z, which forces the read() method to return –1, and which the operating system recognizes as the end of the file.

Figure 12-7 shows a sample run of the application. To create this output, the user types "abcdefg". After each input character, a character is written to the OutputStream but held until the user presses Enter. Next, the user types "the quick brown fox" followed by Enter, and the output appears again. Finally, the user presses Ctrl+Z and Enter at the beginning of a line, indicating EOF, so the logic continues with the finally block, where the files are closed in their own try block. Notice that the keystroke combination Ctrl+Z appears on the screen as ^Z.

Figure 12-7 Sample execution of the ReadAndWrite application

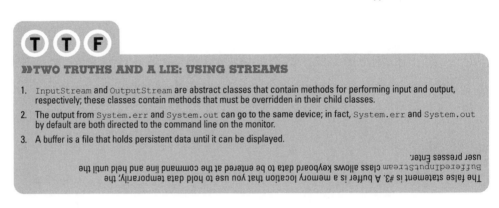

»TWO TRUTHS AND A LIE: USING STREAMS

1. InputStream and OutputStream are abstract classes that contain methods for performing input and output, respectively; these classes contain methods that must be overridden in their child classes.

2. The output from System.err and System.out can go to the same device; in fact, System.err and System.out by default are both directed to the command line on the monitor.

3. A buffer is a file that holds persistent data until it can be displayed.

The false statement is #3. A buffer is a memory location that you use to hold data temporarily; the BufferedInputStream class allows keyboard data to be entered at the command line and held until the user presses Enter.

WRITING TO AND READING FROM A FILE

Instead of assigning files to the standard input and output devices, you can also assign a file to the InputStream or OutputStream. For example, you can read data items from the keyboard and store them permanently on a disk. To accomplish this, you can construct a FileOutputStream object and assign it to the OutputStream. If you want to change an application's output device, you don't have to make any other changes to the application other than assigning a new object to the OutputStream; the rest of the logic remains the same. Java lets you assign a file to a Stream object so that screen output and file output work in exactly the same manner.

You can associate a File object with the output stream in one of two ways:

» You can pass the filename to the constructor of the FileOutputStream class.

» You can create a File object by passing the filename to the File constructor. Then, you can pass the File object to the constructor of the FileOutputStream class.

The second method has some benefits: if you create a File object, you can use the File class methods, such as exists() and lastModified(), to retrieve file information. Figure 12-8 shows a ReadAndWriteToAFile application that is similar to the ReadAndWrite application, but it writes output to a file rather than to the screen. In Figure 12-8, the first shaded statement declares a File object named outputFile that creates a file named MyData.dat in the current folder. (The filename and the extension are the programmer's choice; in this case, .dat is used to stand for "data," but any extension that is acceptable to the current operating system could be used.)

```java
import java.io.*;
public class ReadAndWriteToAFile
{
    public static void main(String[] args)
    {
        InputStream istream;
        OutputStream ostream;
        File outputFile = new File("MyData.dat");
        int c;
        final int EOF = -1;
        istream = System.in;
        try
        {
            ostream = new FileOutputStream(outputFile);
            System.out.println("Type some characters ");
            try
            {
                while((c = istream.read()) != EOF)
                    ostream.write(c);
            }
            catch(IOException e)
            {
                System.out.println("Error: " + e.getMessage());
            }
            finally
            {
                try
                {
                    istream.close();
                    ostream.close();
                }
                catch(IOException e)
                {
                    System.out.println("File did not close");
                }
            }
        }
        catch(FileNotFoundException e)
        {
            System.exit(1);
        }
    }
}
```

Figure 12-8 The ReadAndWriteToAFile class

When you call the FileOutputStream constructor, it might throw a FileNotFoundException, so the creation of the assignment to the ostream object is placed in a try block (shaded). Near the end of the code in Figure 12-8, a shaded catch block catches any thrown FileNotFoundException. In this case, the application ends with a System.exit() call, but the programmer could choose to display a message or take any other action. As an alternative, the programmer could add the clause throws Exception to the end of the main() method header and remove all the try and catch clauses from the application. Then, any thrown Exceptions would simply be thrown to the operating system, and error messages would display at the command line.

Other than the shaded changes, the ReadAndWriteToAFile class in Figure 12-8 is the same as the ReadAndWrite class in Figure 12-6. However, the outcome when you execute the application is different; although the user still types input at the keyboard and presses Ctrl+Z when done, the output is sent to a file instead of to the screen. Figure 12-9 shows the execution of the application along with the file output displayed in a text editor.

 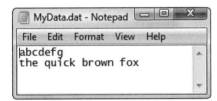

Figure 12-9 Execution of the ReadAndWriteToAFile application and the file contents after the file is opened in a text editor

READING FROM A FILE

The process you use to read data from a file is similar to the one you use to write data to a file. You can create a File object and assign it to the input stream, as shown in the shaded statements in the ReadFromAFileAndWrite application in Figure 12-10. The only other differences between this application and the ReadAndWriteToAFile class in Figure 12-8 are that the OutputStream has been reassigned to the screen (the screen object is System.out), and the prompt to enter characters has been removed because a storage device does not need a prompt the way a human user does. If the MyFile.dat file exists and opens successfully, its contents display on the screen. For example, Figure 12-11 shows the output produced from the MyData.dat file created in Figure 12-9.

```java
import java.io.*;
public class ReadFromAFileAndWrite
{
    public static void main(String[] args)
    {
        InputStream istream;
        OutputStream ostream;
        File inputFile = new File("MyData.dat");
        int c;
        final int EOF = -1;
        ostream = System.out;
        try
        {
            istream = new FileInputStream(inputFile);
            try
            {
                while((c = istream.read()) != EOF)
                    ostream.write(c);
            }
            catch(IOException e)
            {
                System.out.println("Error: " + e.getMessage());
            }
            finally
            {
                try
                {
                    istream.close();
                    ostream.close();
                }
                catch(IOException e)
                {
                    System.out.println("File did not close");
                }
            }
        }
        catch(FileNotFoundException e)
        {
            System.exit(1);
        }
    }
}
```

Figure 12-10 The `ReadFromAFileAndWrite` class

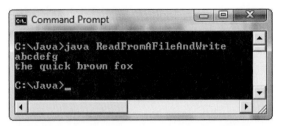

Figure 12-11 Output of the `ReadFromAFileAndWrite` class, using the data file created in the execution of `ReadAndWriteToAFile` in Figure 12-9

»TWO TRUTHS AND A LIE: WRITING TO AND READING FROM A FILE

1. You can associate a file with an output stream only by using a set method to set the name of a `FileOutputStream` object.

2. When you call the `FileOutputStream` constructor, it might throw a `FileNotFoundException`.

3. When you read data from a file, you do not include prompts like you do when you read data from the keyboard.

The false statement is #1. You can pass a filename to the constructor of the `FileOutputStream` class to associate the file with an output stream or you can create a `File` object and pass it to the constructor of the `FileOutputStream` class. (There is no set method to set a `FileOutputStream`'s file.)

WRITING FORMATTED FILE DATA

Frequently, it is inconvenient to read a data file as a series of characters. For example, you might have a data file that contains personnel records that include an `int` employee ID number, a `String` name, and `double` pay rate for each employee in your organization. Rather than reading a series of bytes, it is more useful to be able to read such a file in groups of bytes that constitute a record containing an `int`, a `String`, and a `double`. You can use the `DataInputStream` and `DataOutputStream` classes to accomplish formatted input and output.

`DataOutputStream` objects enable you to write binary data to an `OutputStream`. Much of the data that you write with `DataOutputStream` objects is not readable in a text editor because it is not stored as characters. Instead, the data is formatted correctly for its type. For example, a `double` with the value 123.45 is not stored as six separate readable characters that can correctly display in a text editor. Instead, numeric values are stored in a more compact form that you can read later with a `DataInputStream` object.

The `DataOutput` interface is implemented by `DataOutputStream`. The `DataOutput` interface includes methods such as `writeBoolean()`, `writeChar()`, `writeDouble()`, `writeFloat()`, and `writeInt()`. Each method writes data in the correct format for the data type indicated by its name. You can use the method `writeUTF()` to write Unicode format strings.

When you create a `DataOutputStream`, you can assign a `FileOutputStream` object to it so that your data is stored in a file. Using `DataOutputStream` with a `FileOutputStream` allows you to use the write method that is appropriate for your data. When you use a `DataOutputStream` connected to `FileOutputStream`, the approach is known as

chaining the stream objects. That is, if you define a DataOutputStream object with a statement such as DataOutputStream out;, and then call the DataOutputStream constructor, you pass a FileOutputStream object to it. For example:

```
out = new DataOutputStream(new FileOutputStream ("someFile"));
```

Figure 12-12 contains a class named CreateEmployeeFile, which demonstrates an application that writes formatted data to a file. The class prompts the user for and accepts data that is written to a file. When the user indicates that data entry is complete by typing 999 for an employee's ID number, the output stream is closed.

```java
import java.io.*;
import java.util.*;
public class CreateEmployeeFile
{
    public static void main(String[] args)
    {
        DataOutputStream ostream;
        Scanner input = new Scanner(System.in);
        final int DONE = 999;
        int id;
        String lastName;
        double pay;
        try
        {
            ostream = new DataOutputStream
                (new FileOutputStream("EmpData.dat"));
            System.out.print("Enter ID number or " + DONE +
                " to quit >> ");
            id = input.nextInt();
            while(id != DONE)
            {
                input.nextLine();
                System.out.print("Enter last name            >> ");
                lastName = input.nextLine();
                System.out.print("Enter hourly pay rate       >> ");
                pay = input.nextDouble();
                ostream.writeInt(id);
                ostream.writeUTF(lastName);
                ostream.writeDouble(pay);
                System.out.print("Enter ID number or " + DONE +
                    " to quit >> ");
                id = input.nextInt();
            }
            ostream.close();
        }
    }
```

Figure 12-12 The CreateEmployeeFile class (*continued*)

```
     catch(IOException e)
     {
        System.err.println("Error opening file");
     }
     catch(InputMismatchException e)
     {
        System.err.println("Invalid data entry");
     }
  }
}
```

Figure 12-12 (*continued*)

> **» NOTE** In the `CreateEmployeeFile` program, the extra call to `nextLine()` after the ID number is retrieved is to consume the Enter key remaining in the buffer. This allows the data entry for the last name to work correctly.

In the class in Figure 12-12, a `try...catch` pair contains the attempt to create a new output file and the statements that continuously read input data of the appropriate types. The file creation code is written within the `try` block because creating a `File` object might throw an `Exception`. For example, if the default storage device is full or write-protected, no file can be created. If that happens, the thrown `Exception` is caught by the `catch` block that accepts an `IOException`, the application displays a message, and the program ends. Likewise, the input statements are in the `try...catch` block because the user might enter invalid data. If that happens, the thrown `Exception` is caught by the `catch` block that accepts an `InputMismatchException`, a different message is displayed, and the program ends.

In the data entry loop in the program, when no exception is thrown, the `writeInt()` method writes the integer that represents the employee's ID number to the output file, the `writeUTF()` method writes the employee's last name, and the `writeDouble()` method writes the employee's pay rate. Then, the user is prompted for the next employee ID. Figure 12-13 shows a typical execution of the program.

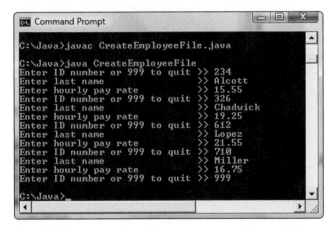

Figure 12-13 Typical execution of the `CreateEmployeeFile` application

After you execute the `CreateEmployeeFile` application, you can examine its contents in a text editor. For example, Figure 12-14 shows the output file after a user has entered data for four employees. Some of the data, for example, the `String` names, is readable. However, the numbers that represent the pay rates of each employee are not understandable. Data written with `writeInt()` and `writeDouble()` is stored in a condensed format that you cannot easily interpret; the same would be true for data written with any of the other `DataOutput` interface write methods. Although it is interesting to view the file data in an editor, data written to a file is never intended for human consumption; file data is simply stored for later use. For example, you might want to write an application that reads stored file data and sends it to a printer or to a monitor.

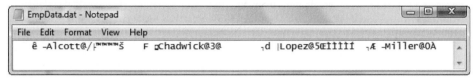

Figure 12-14 The EmpData.dat file in a text editor after the user enters data for four employees

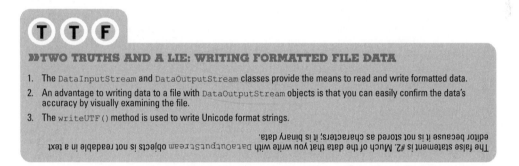

»TWO TRUTHS AND A LIE: WRITING FORMATTED FILE DATA

1. The `DataInputStream` and `DataOutputStream` classes provide the means to read and write formatted data.
2. An advantage to writing data to a file with `DataOutputStream` objects is that you can easily confirm the data's accuracy by visually examining the file.
3. The `writeUTF()` method is used to write Unicode format strings.

The false statement is #2. Much of the data that you write with `DataOutputStream` objects is not readable in a text editor because it is not stored as characters; it is binary data.

READING FORMATTED FILE DATA

`DataInputStream` objects enable you to read binary data from an `InputStream`. The `DataInput` interface is implemented by the `DataInputStream`. The `DataInput` interface includes methods such as `readByte()`, `readChar()`, `readDouble()`, `readFloat()`, `readInt()`, and `readUTF()`. In the same way that the different write methods of `DataOutput` correctly format data you write to a file, each `DataInput` read method correctly reads the type of data indicated by its name.

When you want to create a `DataInputStream` object that reads from a file, you use the same chaining technique you used for output files. In other words, if you define a `DataInputStream` object as `DataInputStream in;`, you can associate it with a file when you call its constructor, as in the following:

```
in = new DataInputStream(new FileInputStream("someFile"));
```

When you read data from a file, you need to determine when the end of the file has been reached. Earlier in this chapter, you learned that you can determine EOF by checking for a return value of –1 from the `read()` method. Alternatively, if you attempt each file `read()` from within a `try` block, you can catch an `EOFException`. When you catch an `EOFException`, it means you have reached the end of the file and you should take appropriate action, such as closing the file.

>> **NOTE** Most Exceptions represent error conditions. An EOFException is more truly an "exception" in that most read() method calls do not result in EOF. For example, when a file contains 999 records, only the 1000th, or last, read() for a file causes an EOFException.

Figure 12-15 contains a ReadEmployeeFile application that reads an EmpData.dat file created by the CreateEmployeeFile application. The ReadEmployeeFile application opens a DataInputStream, reads data from the file using readInt(), readUTF(), and readDouble(), and displays each record, one at a time. When the EOFException is caught, the message "Processing complete" is displayed.

```java
import java.io.*;
import java.util.*;
public class ReadEmployeeFile
{
    public static void main(String[] args) throws IOException
    {
        DataInputStream istream;
        final int EOF = -1;
        int id;
        String lastName;
        double pay;
        try
        {
            istream = new DataInputStream
                (new FileInputStream("EmpData.dat"));
            while((id = istream.readInt()) != EOF)
            {
                lastName = istream.readUTF();
                pay = istream.readDouble();
                System.out.println("Employee # " + id + ": " + lastName +
                    " Pay rate $" + pay);
            }
        }
        catch(EOFException e)
        {
            System.out.println("Processing complete");
        }
    }
}
```

Figure 12-15 The ReadEmployeeFile class

>> **NOTE** The main() method in the ReadEmployeeFile program contains a throws clause in the header because the method does not catch the Exception that will be thrown if the input file is not found. Instead, the Exception will be thrown to the operating system, ending the program.

Figure 12-16 shows the output when the file created in Figure 12-13 is used as input. Notice that although the employees' ID numbers and pay rates are not decipherable when the data file is displayed in the text editor in Figure 12-14, the readInt() and readDouble() methods read them correctly in the application, so they can be displayed legibly in Figure 12-16.

Figure 12-16 Output of the ReadEmployeeFile application, using the EmpData.dat data file

»TWO TRUTHS AND A LIE: READING FORMATTED FILE DATA

1. DataInputStream objects enable you to read binary data using methods such as readDouble(), readInt(), and readUTF().

2. When you want to create a DataInputStream object that reads from a file, you can define a DataInputStream object and associate it with a file when you call its constructor.

3. When you read data from a file, you must be careful to stop processing before an EOFException is thrown.

The false statement is #3. When you read data from a file, you can determine when the end of the file has been reached by catching an EOFException.

USING A VARIABLE FILENAME

A program that reads a data file and displays its contents for you is useful. A program that can read any data file, regardless of what you name it, is even more useful. For example, suppose data files for employees exist for several branches of an organization, or suppose inventory files exist for each month of the year. Instead of hard-coding a filename to be written or read, it is more flexible to use a variable filename; then, the same application can process different data sets.

One approach to using a variable filename is to pass the name to the method that opens the file. For example, in the ReadEmployeeFile application in Figure 12-15, you could alter the FileInputStream constructor call to include a String argument that you use as the filename. Figure 12-17 shows the new program; the shaded sections show the changes from the original ReadEmployeeFile application. Figure 12-18 shows an execution when an incorrect filename is used. The displayed message is the one retrieved using the getMessage() object with the automatically thrown FileNotFoundException object.

```
import java.io.*;
import java.util.*;
public class ReadEmployeeFile2
{
    public static void main(String[] args) throws IOException
    {
        DataInputStream istream;
        final int EOF = -1;
        int id;
        String lastName;
        double pay;
        Scanner input = new Scanner(System.in);
        String fileName = "";
        try
        {
            System.out.print("Enter file name to use >> ");
            fileName = input.nextLine();
            istream = new DataInputStream
                (new FileInputStream(fileName));
            while((id = istream.readInt()) != EOF)
            {
                lastName = istream.readUTF();
                pay = istream.readDouble();
                System.out.println("Employee # " + id + ": " + lastName +
                    " Pay rate $" + pay);
            }
        }
        catch(EOFException e)
        {
            System.out.println("Processing complete");
        }
        catch(FileNotFoundException e)
        {
            System.out.println(e.getMessage());
        }
    }
}
```

»NOTE
You might want to rewrite the program in Figure 12-17 so that the requested filename uses a full path.

Figure 12-17 The ReadEmployeeFile2 program

Figure 12-18 Execution of ReadEmployeeFile2 program when user types an invalid filename

Figure 12-19 presents an alternative. In this `main()` method, the first element of the `args` array that is passed to the `main()` method becomes the filename. When you execute the application with this approach, instead of the command `java ReadEmployeeFile3`, you provide a list of arguments with the command by typing a statement similar to the following:

```
java ReadEmployeeFile3 EmpData.dat
```

This command not only executes the application but the `String` following the application name becomes the zero-element argument in the `args` array. When a user wants to run the `ReadEmployeeFile3` application, the user simply types the correct current data filename at the end of the command to execute it.

»NOTE
You can use `args[1]`, `args[2]`, and so on as `String`s passed to the `main()` method of any application by listing as many `String`s as you need, separated by spaces, after the application name when you use the `java` command.

```java
import java.io.*;
import java.util.*;
public class ReadEmployeeFile3
{
   public static void main(String[] args) throws IOException
   {
      DataInputStream istream;
      final int EOF = -1;
      int id;
      String lastName;
      double pay;
      try
      {
         istream = new DataInputStream
            (new FileInputStream(args[0]));
         while((id = istream.readInt()) != EOF)
         {
            lastName = istream.readUTF();
            pay = istream.readDouble();
            System.out.println("Employee # " + id + ": " + lastName +
               " Pay rate $" + pay);
         }
      }
      catch(EOFException e)
      {
         System.out.println("Processing complete");
      }
      catch(FileNotFoundException e)
      {
         System.out.println(e.getMessage());
      }
   }
}
```

Figure 12-19 A program that uses the first element of the `main()` method `args` array as the filename

CREATING AND USING RANDOM ACCESS FILES

The examples of files that have been written to and read from in this chapter are sequential access files, which means that you access the records in sequential order from beginning to end. For example, if you wrote an employee record with an ID number 234, and then you created a second record with an ID number 326, you would see when you retrieved the records that they remain in the original data-entry order. Businesses store data in sequential order when they use the records for **batch processing**, or processing that involves performing the same tasks with many records, one after the other. For example, when a company produces paychecks, the records for the pay period are gathered in a batch and the checks are calculated and printed in sequence. It really doesn't matter whose check is produced first because none are distributed to employees until all have been printed.

For many applications, sequential access is inefficient. These applications, known as **real-time** applications, require that a record be accessed immediately while a client is waiting. A program in which the user makes direct requests is an **interactive program**. For example, if a customer telephones a department store with a question about a monthly bill, the customer service representative does not need or want to access every customer account in sequence. With tens of thousands of account records to read, it would take too long to access the customer's record. Instead, customer service representatives require **random access files**, files in which records can be located in any order. Files in which records must be accessed immediately are also called **instant access files**. Because they enable you to locate a particular record directly (without reading all of the preceding records), random access files are also called **direct access files**. You can use Java's `RandomAccessFile` class to create your own random access files.

The RandomAccessFile class contains the same read(), write(), and close() method names as InputStream and OutputStream, but it also contains a seek() method that lets you select a beginning position within a file before you read or write data, and places a file pointer at the selected location. A **file pointer**, or **file position pointer**, is an automatically created variable that holds the byte number of the next file position to be used. For example, if you declare a RandomAccessFile object named myFile, the following statement selects the 200th position within the file:

```
myFile.seek(200);
```

The 200th position represents the 201st byte because, as with Java arrays, the numbering of file positions begins at zero. The next read() or write() method operates from the newly selected starting point.

When you declare a RandomAccessFile object, you include a filename as you do with other file objects. You also include "r" or "rw" as a String within double quotation marks as a second argument, which indicates that the file is open for reading only ("r") or for both reading and writing ("rw"). For example, the following statement opens the SomeData.dat file so that either the read() or write() method can be used on the file:

```
RandomAccessFile myFile = new
    RandomAccessFile("C:\\Temp\\SomeData.dat","rw");
```

This feature is particularly useful in random access processing. Consider a business with 20,000 customer accounts. When the customer who has the 14,607th record in the file acquires a new telephone number, it is convenient to directly access the 14,607th record. The read() method confirms that the record represents the correct customer, and then the write() method writes the new telephone number to the file in the location in which the old number was previously stored.

Figure 12-20 shows an application named AccessACharacter that creates a RandomAccessFile object using a file named AQuote.txt, the contents of which are shown in Figure 12-21. An integer named pos is declared and assigned the value 34. In the first shaded statement, the seek() method is used with the input file object to access position 34 in the file; in the second shaded statement, the file is read. Position 34 holds a "W", which is the character that is displayed as output in Figure 12-22.

```
import java.io.*;
public class AccessACharacter
{
    public static void main(String[] args) throws IOException
    {
        OutputStream ostream;
        int c;
        RandomAccessFile inFile = new RandomAccessFile("AQuote.txt","r");
        ostream = System.out;
        int pos = 34;
        try
        {
            inFile.seek(pos);
            c = inFile.read();
            System.out.print("The character in position " + pos + " is ");
            ostream.write(c);
        }
        catch(IOException e)
        {
            System.out.println("Error: " + e.getMessage());
        }
        finally
        {
            System.out.println();
            inFile.close();
            ostream.close();
        }
    }
}
```

Figure 12-20 The AccessACharacter class

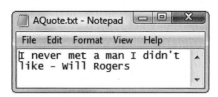

Figure 12-21 The AQuote.txt file used as input to the AccessACharacter application

Figure 12-22 Output of the AccessACharacter application

In the AccessACharacter application, only one read() command was issued, yet the application accessed a byte 34 positions into the file. When you access a file randomly, you do not read all the data that precedes the data you are seeking. Accessing data randomly is one of the major features that makes large data systems maintainable.

WRITING RECORDS TO A RANDOM ACCESS FILE

Accessing one character in a text file is of limited value. When you store records in a file, it is often more useful to be able to access the 34th record, rather than the 34th byte. In this case, you multiply each record's size by the position you want to access. For example, if you store records that are 50 bytes long, you can access the *n*th record using the following statement:

```
myFile.seek((n-1) * 50);
```

One approach to writing a random access file is to place records into the file based on a key field. A **key field** is the field in a record that makes the record unique from all others. For example, in a file of students, many records might have the same last name, first name, or grade point average, but each record has a key field, such as a student ID number or Social Security number.

Figure 12-23 contains an example that asks a user to enter student data and writes a random access data file using the student's ID number as a key field. So that the example can be brief and concentrate on the random access file writing, this application makes several assumptions:

»NOTE
Although the Social Security Administration (SSA) intended that Social Security numbers be unique, occasionally the same number has been given to multiple people. If you completed the Up for Discussion questions at the end of Chapter 9, you have researched this topic.

» A student record contains only an ID number and a grade point average. In a real application, each student would require many more data fields, such as name, address, phone number, and so on.

» Each student ID number is three digits or fewer. In a real application, ID numbers would be longer to ensure unique values. (Three-digit numbers provide only 1000 unique combinations.)

» The user will enter a valid ID number. In a real application, this would be a foolhardy assumption. However, to streamline the code and concentrate on the writing of a random access file, error checking for valid ID numbers is eliminated from this example.

» The user will not duplicate student ID numbers. In a real application, a key field should be checked against all existing key fields to ensure that a record is unique before adding it to a file.

» Each student's record will be placed in the random access file position that is one less than the student's ID number. In many real applications, the mathematical computations performed on a key field to determine file placement are more complicated.

» The user will enter a valid grade point average. Again, this assumption is seldom reasonable in a professional application, but it is made here to streamline the code.

```java
import java.util.*;
import java.io.*;
public class WriteRandomStudentFile
{
    public static void main(String[] args) throws IOException
    {
        int pos;
        RandomAccessFile stuFile =
            new RandomAccessFile("StudentData.dat", "rw");
        Scanner input = new Scanner(System.in);
        int id;
        double gpa;
        final int RECORDSIZE = 12;
        final int NUMRECORDS = 1000;
        final int STOP = 999;
        try
        {
            for(int x = 0; x < NUMRECORDS; ++x)
            {
                stuFile.writeInt(0);
                stuFile.writeDouble(0.0);
            }
        }

        catch(IOException e)
        {
            System.out.println("Error: " + e.getMessage());
        }
        finally
        {
            stuFile.close();
        }
        stuFile =
            new RandomAccessFile("StudentData.dat","rw");
        try
        {
            System.out.print("Enter student ID number or " +
                STOP + " to quit ");
            id = input.nextInt();
```

Figure 12-23 The WriteRandomStudentFile class (*continued*)

```
        while(id != STOP)
        {
            System.out.print("Enter grade point average ");
            gpa = input.nextDouble();
            pos = id - 1;
            stuFile.seek(pos * RECORDSIZE);
            stuFile.writeInt(id);
            stuFile.writeDouble(gpa);
            System.out.print("Enter student ID number or " +
                STOP + " to quit ");
            id = input.nextInt();
        }
    }
    catch(IOException e)
    {
        System.out.println("Error: " + e.getMessage());
    }
    finally
    {
        stuFile.close();
    }
}
}
```

Figure 12-23 (*continued*)

At the start of the `WriteRandomStudentFile` application in Figure 12-23, an integer is declared to hold a calculated file position. A `RandomAccessFile` named StudentData.dat is opened, and variables are declared to hold the `int` ID number and `double` grade point average data. Three constants are declared; one of them, `RECORDSIZE`, is set to 12 because each student record consists of a four-byte `int` ID number plus an eight-byte `double` grade point average. Table 12-3 shows the byte sizes of the standard data types in Java.

Type	Size in Bytes
byte	1
short	2
int	4
float	4
long	8
double	8

Table 12-3 Sizes of data types

>> **NOTE**
You first learned about the sizes of data types, as well as the minimum and maximum values they can hold, in Chapter 2.

The application in Figure 12-23 also declares a constant for the number of records the file can hold. For this application, assume there can be no more than 1000 students stored. For convenience, also assume that each student's ID number is at least 1 but no more than 998. Because you begin numbering the disk storage locations with 0, each student's record is stored on the data disk at the location that corresponds to the student's ID number minus 1.

The first shaded section of the `WriteRandomStudentFile` application is a `try` block that executes preparation statements before the data-entry portion of the application begins. Within the `try` block, the application writes 1000 "empty" student records to the output file—that is, it writes 1000 records with an ID number of 0 and a grade point average of 0.0. When the user enters actual data later in the application, some of these records are replaced with "real" data. Writing the 1000 zero-filled records provides a blank slate that is 12,000 bytes long, into which actual records can later be inserted in the appropriate locations.

When the `try` block finishes writing 1000 records, the `finally` block executes. In the `finally` block, the open file is closed. Then, it is immediately reopened so the true work of the application can begin.

The user is prompted to enter an ID number or 999 to quit. The user enters a number, and while it is not 999, the user is prompted for a grade point average. Next, the file position for the record is calculated by subtracting one from the student's ID number.

The `seek()` method is used to locate a position on the disk. For example, if the student's ID number is 123, the position that is 122 times 12 bytes (or 1464 bytes) from the beginning of the disk file is accessed. At that location, the student's ID number and grade point average are written as an integer and `double`, respectively. Then, the user is prompted for the next student ID number.

Suppose that student data exists as shown in Figure 12-24.

Student ID	Grade Point Average
123	3.2
004	4.0
003	2.7
087	3.5
086	2.9

Figure 12-24 Sample student data

When a user executes the `WriteRandomStudentFile` application, assume that the user enters the data from the sample student data table in Figure 12-24. Figure 12-25 shows the execution of the program that produces the output file in Figure 12-26 when opened in a text editor. The data file appears mostly "blank," but if you examine the characters closely, you can see that some characters have been placed near the beginning of the file—these represent the data for student IDs 003 and 004. Several lines down, there is another "chunk" of data—these characters represent student records 086 and 087. The characters near the bottom of the viewing area for the file represent the data for student 123. As with the data you viewed in Figure 12-14 earlier in the chapter, this numeric data is not humanly readable; instead, it can be read by another Java application in which it can be interpreted for human consumption.

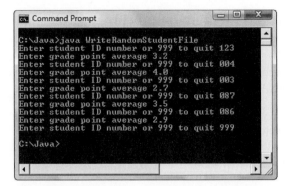

Figure 12-25 Typical execution of the `WriteRandomStudentFile` application

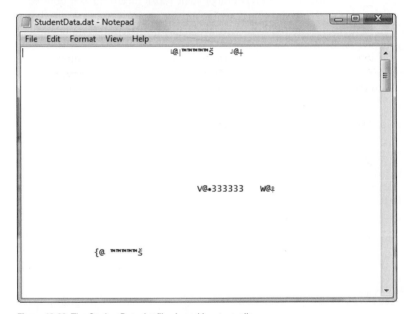

Figure 12-26 The StudentData.dat file viewed in a text editor

»TWO TRUTHS AND A LIE: WRITING RECORDS TO A RANDOM ACCESS FILE

1. A technique used to access a record directly is to multiply each record's size by the position you want to access.
2. A key field is the field in a record that holds the most crucial or most private information.
3. A useful technique to create a random access file involves first creating a file full of empty records, then placing records at locations within the file based on a key.

The false statement is #2. A key field is the field in a record that makes the record unique from all others.

READING RECORDS FROM A RANDOM ACCESS FILE

Just because a file is created as a random access file does not mean it has to be used as a random access file. You can process a random access file either sequentially or randomly.

ACCESSING A RANDOM ACCESS FILE SEQUENTIALLY

The StudentData.dat random access file created by the WriteRandomStudentFile application in Figure 12-23 contains 1000 records. However, only five of them contain valuable data; displaying every record would result in many irrelevant lines of data. It makes more sense to display only those records for which an ID number has been inserted. The ReadRandomStudentFile application in Figure 12-27 reads through the 1000-record StudentData.dat file sequentially in a for loop, reading int-double pairs. When an ID number value is 0, it means no user-entered record was stored at that point, so the application does not bother to print it. Figure 12-28 shows the application's output—a list of the entered records, conveniently in student ID number order, which reflects their relative positions within the file.

```java
import java.io.*;
public class ReadRandomStudentFile
{
    public static void main(String[] args) throws IOException
    {
        RandomAccessFile stuFile =
            new RandomAccessFile("StudentData.dat","rw");
        int id;
        double gpa;
        final int NUMRECORDS = 1000;
        try
        {
            for(int x = 0; x < NUMRECORDS; ++x)
            {
                id = stuFile.readInt();
                gpa = stuFile.readDouble();
                if(id != 0)
                    System.out.println("ID# " + id + "  GPA: " + gpa);
            }
        }
        catch(IOException e)
        {
            System.out.println("Error: " + e.getMessage());
        }
        finally
        {
            stuFile.close();
        }
    }
}
```

Figure 12-27 The ReadRandomStudentFile class

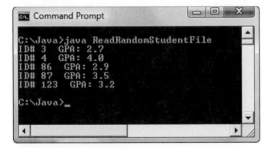

Figure 12-28 Output of the `ReadRandomStudentFile` application

> **» NOTE** In Figure 12-28, notice that the student ID numbers do not align because they display as integers—that is, without leading zeros even though they are assumed to be three-digit numbers. If you wanted the lower numbers to print with leading zeros, you could take several approaches, including using an `if` statement to decide to display extra zeros, storing the ID numbers as strings instead of integers, and using formatted output as discussed in Appendix C.

ACCESSING A RANDOM ACCESS FILE RANDOMLY

If you simply want to display records in order based on their key field, you do not need to create a random access file and waste so much unneeded storage. Instead, you could sort the records using one of the sorting techniques you learned about in Chapter 8. The true benefit of using a random access file is the ability to retrieve a specific record from a file directly, without reading through other records to locate the desired one.

The `ReadRandomStudentFile2` application in Figure 12-29 allows the user to enter a student's ID number. The application then calculates the student record's position in the data file (one less than the ID number) and positions the file pointer at the correct location to begin reading. In the application, a dialog box prompts the user for an ID number, which is converted to an integer with the `parseInt()` method. (To keep this example brief, the application does not check for a valid ID number, so the `parseInt()` method might throw an exception to the operating system, ending the execution of the application.) Then, in the shaded portion of the application in Figure 12-29, while the user does not enter 999 to quit, the position of the sought-after record is calculated by subtracting one from the ID number, multiplying it by the record size, and positioning the file pointer at the desired location with the `seek()` method. (Again, to keep the example short, the ID number is not checked to ensure it is 999 or less.) The student record `int-double` pair is retrieved from the data file and displayed in a dialog box. Then, the user is prompted for the next desired student ID number. Figure 12-30 shows the output when the user requests student number 086.

```
import javax.swing.*;
import java.io.*;
public class ReadRandomStudentFile2
{
   public static void main(String[] args) throws IOException
   {
      int pos;
      RandomAccessFile stuFile =
         new RandomAccessFile("StudentData.dat","rw");
      String inputString;
      int id;
      double gpa;
      final int RECORDSIZE = 12;
      final int STOP = 999;
      inputString = JOptionPane.showInputDialog(null,
         "Enter student ID number or " + STOP + " to quit");
      id = Integer.parseInt(inputString);
      try
      {
         while(id != STOP)
         {
            pos = id - 1;
            stuFile.seek(pos * RECORDSIZE);
            id = stuFile.readInt();
            gpa = stuFile.readDouble();
            JOptionPane.showMessageDialog(null, "For ID # " + id +
               "  GPA is " + gpa);
            inputString = JOptionPane.showInputDialog(null,
               "Enter student ID number or " + STOP + " to quit");
            id = Integer.parseInt(inputString);
         }
      }
      catch(IOException e)
      {
         System.out.println("Error: " + e.getMessage());
      }
      finally
      {
         stuFile.close();
      }
   }
}
```

Figure 12-29 The ReadRandomStudentFile2 class

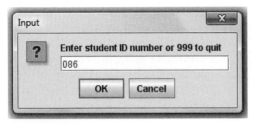
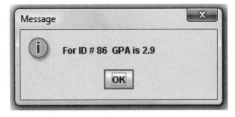

Figure 12-30 Output of the `ReadRandomStudentFile2` application when the user enters 086

>>**NOTE** In the application in Figure 12-29, you could eliminate the `readInt()` statement that retrieves the student's ID number; after all, the user has already entered the desired ID number. In this case, the seek statement would become:

```
stuFile.seek(pos * RECORDSIZE + 4);
```

You would add four bytes to the beginning of the desired record to access only the `double` grade point average of the appropriate student.

>>**TWO TRUTHS AND A LIE: READING RECORDS FROM A RANDOM ACCESS FILE**

1. When a file is created as a random access file, you must also read it randomly.

2. The benefit of using a random access file is the ability to retrieve a specific record from a file directly, without reading through other records to locate the desired one.

3. When you access a record from a random access file, you usually calculate its position based on a key.

The false statement is #1. Just because a file is created as a random access file does not mean it has to be used as a random access file. You can process a random access file either sequentially or randomly.

READING AND WRITING OBJECTS TO AND FROM FILES

Creating objects is a fundamental feature of Java and all other object-oriented languages. Throughout this book, you have created classes from which you can instantiate objects. Therefore, it makes sense that Java allows you to write entire objects to files, instead of separately writing individual fields.

»NOTE A full-blown `Employee` class might contain many more data fields and get and set methods for each field, but this class is purposely brief so you can more easily follow the program examples that use it.

»NOTE `Serializable` is an unusual class in that it has no methods or fields. Its purpose is only to identify the class as being serializable.

»NOTE Java developers say that when an object is serialized, it is *flattened* into bytes. They sometimes also say they are *deflating* the object.

Consider the `Employee` class in Figure 12-31. It is similar to many you have created throughout this book. It contains three data fields, a constructor, and a `display()` method. The only feature of this class that is new to you is the shaded clause in the class header: `implements Serializable`. **Serialization** is Java's built-in mechanism for manipulating objects as streams of bytes; the `Serializable` interface endows your class with the ability to be serialized.

```
import java.io.*;
public class Employee implements Serializable
{
   private int idNum;
   String name;
   private double payRate;
   public Employee(int num, String name, double rate)
   {
      idNum = num;
      this.name = name;
      payRate = rate;
   }
   public void display()
   {
     System.out.println("ID# " + idNum + " " +
        name + " Pay rate: $" + payRate);
   }
}
```

Figure 12-31 The `Employee` class

When you create an `Employee` object from the class in Figure 12-31, it will be a **serialized object**—one that is represented as a sequence of bytes and includes the object's data as well as information about the types of data stored in the object. After a serialized object has been written into a file, it can be read from the file and deserialized. **Deserialization** is the process of recreating an object in computer memory after it is retrieved from a file.

Figure 12-32 contains an application that creates `Employee` objects and saves them in a file. The `main()` method throws an `IOException` because opening and closing files might cause such an exception. Also, the statements that read data from the keyboard might encounter the wrong data type. In a full-blown application, you might choose to handle these exceptions within the application.

```java
import java.io.*;
import java.util.*;
public class CreateEmployeeObjectFile
{
   public static void main(String[] args) throws IOException
   {
      ObjectOutputStream output =
         new ObjectOutputStream
         (new FileOutputStream("Employees.dat"));
      Employee emp;
      int num = 0;
      final int QUIT = 999;
      String name;
      double rate;
      Scanner in = new Scanner(System.in);
      System.out.print("Enter employee number or " + QUIT +
         " to quit ");
      num = in.nextInt();
      while(num != QUIT)
      {
         System.out.print("Enter name ");
         name = in.next();
         System.out.print("Enter pay rate ");
         rate = in.nextDouble();
         emp = new Employee(num, name, rate);
         output.writeObject(emp);
         System.out.print("Enter employee number or " + QUIT +
            " to quit ");
         num = in.nextInt();
      }
      output.close();
   }
}
```

Figure 12-32 The CreateEmployeeObjectFile class

>>**NOTE** The input statements in the CreateEmployeeFile class are not placed in a try block to test for valid data types so that this example can remain short. In a professional program, you would want to try the data entry statements and catch and handle exceptions.

>>**NOTE**
In Chapter 2 you learned that a Scanner object is a text reader that can pull primitive types and strings from input data streams. The scanner works by dividing input into pieces called tokens, which are single, small elements of text.

In the CreateEmployeeObjectFile class, an ObjectOutputStream object is created using a FileOutputStream argument. The user is prompted for employee data, which is passed to the Employee class constructor in the first shaded statement. Then, in the second shaded statement, the Employee object is written to the output file. After a set of data has been entered and a record has been written, a new prompt is displayed and a new ID number is accepted so that the end-of-data condition can be tested at the top of the loop.

Figure 12-33 shows a typical execution of the `CreateEmployeeObjectFile` class.

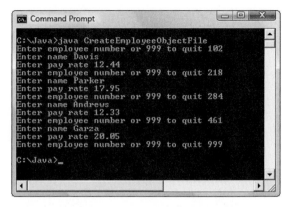

Figure 12-33 Typical execution of `CreateEmployeeObjectFile`

The `ReadEmployeeObjectFile` class in Figure 12-34 creates an `ObjectInputStream` object using the same filename as in the `CreateEmployeeFile` application. The shaded `readObject()` method returns an `Object` that is cast to an `Employee` before being stored in an `Employee` object. Then the `Employee` class `display()` method can be used. Figure 12-35 shows the output.

```java
import java.io.*;
public class ReadEmployeeObjectFile
{
   public static void main(String[] args)
      throws IOException, ClassNotFoundException
   {
      ObjectInputStream in = new
       ObjectInputStream
         (new FileInputStream("Employees.dat"));
      Employee emp;
      try
      {
         while(true)
         {
            emp = (Employee)in.readObject();
            emp.display();
         }
      }
      catch(EOFException e)
      {
         in.close();
      }
   }
}
```

Figure 12-34 The `ReadEmployeeObjectFile` application

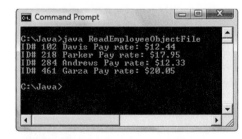

Figure 12-35 Execution of `ReadEmployeeObjectFile` application

>>**NOTE** When the cast is performed in the shaded line in the `ReadEmployeeObjectFile` program, it's possible that no appropriate class definition for `Employee` exists. Therefore, the `main()` method must either catch a `ClassNotFoundException` or list it as a potential `throw` in the header. A compiler error occurs if you don't accommodate this potential exception.

>>**NOTE** Many sophisticated file-handling techniques exist that are beyond the scope of this chapter. In particular, the package `java.nio` contains features for handling buffers, channels, and file locks that make input and output more efficient.

>>**NOTE** You cannot serialize a class that contains members that are not serializable. If you want to serialize a class and it contains fields that are objects of other classes, the contained classes must also implement `Serializable`.

>>**TWO TRUTHS AND A LIE: READING AND WRITING OBJECTS TO AND FROM FILES**

1. Serialization is Java's built-in mechanism for manipulating file data as objects.
2. The `Serializable` interface endows your class with the ability to be serialized.
3. Deserialization is the process of recreating an object in computer memory after it is retrieved from a file.

The false statement is #1. Serialization is Java's built-in mechanism for manipulating objects as streams of bytes.

YOU DO IT

USING THE `File` CLASS TO EXAMINE FILE STATUS

In this section, you will write a class that examines a file and prints appropriate messages concerning its status.

To create a class that examines a `File` object:

1. Open a new file in your text editor and type the following first few lines of a class that checks a file's status:

```
import java.io.*;
public class CheckFile
{
    public static void main(String[] args)
    {
```

2. Enter the following line to create a `File` object that represents a disk file named Data.txt. Although the filename on the disk is Data.txt, within the program the filename is `myFile`.

```
File myFile = new File("Data.txt");
```

3. Enter the following `if...else` statements to test for the file's existence. If the `File` object `myFile` exists, display its name and size, and then test whether the file can be read or written. Also display the date the file was last modified. The result is a long integer. If the file does not exist, simply print an appropriate message.

```
if(myFile.exists())
{
    System.out.println(myFile.getName() + " exists");
    System.out.println("It is " +
        myFile.length() + " bytes long");
    if(myFile.canRead())
        System.out.println("It can be read");
    if(myFile.canWrite())
        System.out.println("It can be written to");
    System.out.println("It was last modified " +
        myFile.lastModified());
}
else
    System.out.println("File does not exist");
```

4. Add a closing curly brace for the main() method and a closing curly brace for the class.

5. Save the file as **CheckFile.java** and compile the class.

6. Compile the application and execute it. Unless you have stored a file named Data.txt in the default folder, you see the message "File does not exist".

7. Open a new file in your text editor and type the company name:

Event Handlers Incorporated!

Save this file as **Data.txt** in the current directory (also called the current folder).

8. Run the CheckFile application again. Your output is similar to the output in Figure 12-36. The file exists and is 28 bytes long because each character you typed, including spaces and punctuation, consumes one byte of storage. The file has read and write capabilities. The date your file was last modified is represented by a long integer.

Figure 12-36 Output of the CheckFile application

COMPARING TWO FILE DATES

Next, you will create a second data file so that you can compare its size and time stamp with those of the Data.txt file.

To create a Data2.txt file and an application to compare two files' dates:

1. Open a new file in your text editor and type a shorter version of the company name:

Event Handlers

Save the file as **Data2.txt** in the current folder.

2. Open a new file in your text editor and type the following first few lines of the `CheckTwoFiles` application:

```
import java.io.*;
public class CheckTwoFiles
{
    public static void main(String[] args)
    {
```

3. Enter the following code to declare two file objects:

```
File f1 = new File("Data.txt");
File f2 = new File("Data2.txt");
```

4. Enter the following code to determine whether both files exist. If they do, comparing their creation times determines which file has the more recent time stamp, and comparing their lengths determines which file is longer.

```
if(f1.exists() && f2.exists())
{
    System.out.print("The more recent file is ");
    if(f1.lastModified() > f2.lastModified())
        System.out.println(f1.getName());
    else
        System.out.println(f2.getName());
    System.out.print("The longer file is ");
    if(f1.length() > f2.length())
        System.out.println(f1.getName());
    else if(f1.length() < f2.length())
        System.out.println(f2.getName());
    else System.out.println("neither one");
}
```

5. Add two more closing curly braces—one for the `main()` method and one for the class.

6. Save the file as **CheckTwoFiles.java** in the current folder, then compile and run the application. The output appears in Figure 12-37. Note that the Data2.txt file was created after the Data.txt file, so it is more recent, but it contains fewer characters.

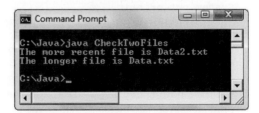

Figure 12-37 Output of the `CheckTwoFiles` application

USING InputStream AND OutputStream OBJECTS

Next, you will create `InputStream` and `OutputStream` objects so you can read from the keyboard and write to the screen. Of course, you have already written many programs that read from the keyboard and write to the screen without using these objects. By using them here with the default input/output devices, you can easily modify the `InputStream` and `OutputStream` objects later, and use whatever input and output devices you choose.

To create an application that reads from the keyboard and writes to the screen:

1. Open a new file in your text editor and type the following first few lines of a program that allows a user to enter data from the keyboard and then echo that data to the screen. The class name is `ReadKBWriteScreen`:

```
import java.io.*;
public class ReadKBWriteScreen
{
```

2. Add the following header and opening curly brace for the `main()` method. The `main()` method throws an `IOException` because you will perform input and output operations.

```
public static void main(String[] args) throws IOException
{
```

3. Enter the following code to declare `InputStream` and `OutputStream` objects, an integer to hold each character the user types, and a constant for the EOF value –1:

```
InputStream istream;
OutputStream ostream;
int c;
final int EOF = -1;
```

4. Enter the following code to assign the `System.in` object to `istream` and the `System.out` object to `ostream`. Then add a multiline prompt telling the user to enter some characters, and to press Ctrl+Z when the user is finished.

```
istream = System.in;
ostream = System.out;
System.out.println("Please enter some characters.");
System.out.println
    ("Press Enter after each group of characters");
System.out.println
    ("to see your input echoed to the screen.");
System.out.println("Press Ctrl + Z when you are done.");
```

5. Use the following `try` block to read from the file. If an `IOException` occurs, you can print an appropriate message. Within the `try` block, execute a loop that reads from the keyboard until the end-of-file condition occurs (when the `read()` method returns –1). While there is not an end-of-file condition, send the character to the `ostream` object.

```
try
{
    while((c = istream.read()) != EOF)
        ostream.write(c);
}
```

6. Use the following `catch` block to handle any `IOException`:

```
catch(IOException e)
{
    System.out.println("Error: " + e.getMessage());
}
```

7. Regardless of whether an `IOException` occurs, you want to close the streams. Use the following `finally` block to ensure that the streams are closed:

```
finally
{
    istream.close();
    ostream.close();
}
```

8. Add a closing curly brace for the `main()` method and another for the class.

9. Save the file as **ReadKBWriteScreen.java**, then compile and run the application. At the command line, type any series of characters and press **Enter**. As you type characters, the buffer holds them until you press Enter, at which time the stored characters echo to the screen. When you have entered a few lines of characters, press **Ctrl+Z**, then press **Enter** to end the application. Figure 12-38 shows a typical application execution. Notice that the keystroke combination Ctrl+Z appears on the screen as ^Z.

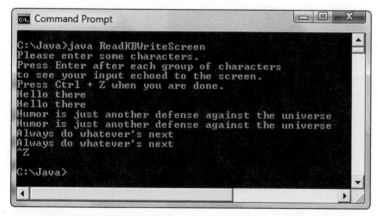

Figure 12-38 Typical execution of the `ReadKBWriteScreen` application

>> **NOTE** Do not press Ctrl+C to end the `ReadKBWriteScreen` application. Doing so breaks out of the program before its completion and does not properly close the files.

WRITING TO AN OUTPUT FILE

In the next set of steps, you will use a `FileOutputStream` to write keyboard-entered data to a file you create.

To create an application that writes keyboard data to a file:

1. Open the **ReadKBWriteScreen.java** file in your text editor and immediately save the file as **ReadKBWriteFile.java**.

2. Change the class header to **public class ReadKBWriteFile**.

3. Position your insertion point at the end of the line that defines the `ostream` object (`OutputStream ostream;`), then press **Enter** to start a new line. On the new line, define a `File` object as follows:

```
File outFile = new File("Datafile.dat");
```

4. Replace the statement that assigns `System.out` to the `ostream` object with the following statement:

```
ostream = new FileOutputStream(outFile);
```

5. Save the file, then compile and execute the application. At the command line, type **Event Handlers handles events of all sizes**, then press **Enter**. After you press Enter, the characters do not appear on the screen; instead, they are output to a file named Datafile.dat that is written in the default directory, the current directory from which you are working.

6. Press **Ctrl+Z**, then press **Enter** to stop the program.

7. In your text editor, open the **Datafile.dat** file. The characters are an exact copy of the ones you entered at the keyboard.

> **»NOTE** You could enter any number of characters to the output stream before ending the program, and they would be saved in the output file. If you run the `ReadKBWriteFile` program again, the program overwrites the existing Datafile.dat file with your new data.

READING DATA FROM A FILE

Next, you will read data from a file and write it to the screen.

To read data from a file:

1. In your text editor, open the **ReadKBWriteFile.java** file and immediately save it as **ReadFileWriteScreen.java**.

2. Change the class header to **public class ReadFileWriteScreen**.

3. In the `File` object declaration, change the object name to `inFile`; the object refers to the Datafile.dat file you created. Of course, the name `outFile` would also work, but it would

not be as descriptive because the file will be read into this application, not written from it. The statement becomes the following:

```
File inFile = new File("Datafile.dat");
```

4. Change the statement that assigns the `System.in` object to `istream` (`istream = System.in`) so that you can use the `File` object for input instead of the keyboard. Replace the statement with the following:

```
istream = new FileInputStream(inFile);
```

5. Change the `ostream` assignment to `System.out` so that output will display on the monitor:

```
ostream = System.out;
```

6. Remove the four statements that prompt the user for input; a disk file does not need a prompt.

7. Save the file, then compile and run the application. The data you stored in the Datafile.dat file ("Event Handlers handles events of all sizes") appears on the screen, and the application ends.

CREATING A CLASS TO USE IN A FILE OF OBJECTS

In the next sections, you will create an `Event` class that you can use to store `Event` objects in a file. Event Handlers Incorporated can then store event data, write a program that creates a file of `Event` objects, and write a program that allows a user to retrieve data based on requested criteria.

To create an `Event` class that can be used as the basis for a file of `Event` objects:

1. To begin, you have a choice. You can start with the `Event` class from the You Do It section in Chapter 8 and make the shaded changes shown in Figure 12-39, or you can create a new version of the class, as shown in Figure 12-39. The original class contains three `private` data fields, get and set methods for each field, and a constructor that determines the rate and manager for an event based on its type. If you use the class from Chapter 8, you will make the following shaded changes:

   » Implement `Serializable` so that `Event` objects can be manipulated as streams of bytes.
   » Add a field to hold an event number.
   » Add a new constructor parameter, which is the only way to set the event number field.
   » Include a method to return the event number.

2. Save the file as **Event.java**, compile it, and correct any errors.

```java
import java.io.*;
public class Event implements Serializable
{
    private int eventNum;
    private int typeOfEvent;
    private double rate;
    private String manager;
    public Event(int eNum, int eType)
    {
        double[] rateSchedule = {0.0, 47.99, 75.99, 40.99};
        String[] managerList = {"X", "Dustin Britt",
            "Carmen Lindsey", "Robin Armanetti"};
        eventNum = eNum;
        typeOfEvent = eType;
        if(eType > rateSchedule.length)
          eType = 0;
        rate = rateSchedule[eType];
        manager = managerList[eType];
    }
    public int getEventNum()
    {
        return eventNum;
    }
    public int getType()
    {
        return typeOfEvent;
    }
    public double getRate()
    {
        return rate;
    }
    public String getManager()
    {
        return manager;
    }
    public void setType(int eventType)
    {
        typeOfEvent = eventType;
    }
    public void setRate(double eventRate)
    {
        rate = eventRate;
    }
    public void setManager(String managerName)
    {
        manager = managerName;
    }
}
```

Figure 12-39 The Event class

CREATING A PROGRAM THAT WRITES Event OBJECTS TO A FILE

Next, you will write a program that accepts keyboard input and writes Event objects to an output file.

To write the CreateEventFile program:

1. Open a new file in your text editor. Type the first few lines of a class that will create a program that accepts keyboard data to create Event objects and saves them to a file.

```
import java.io.*;
import java.util.*;
public class CreateEventFile
{
```

2. Start the program's main() method by including a throws clause in the header. The program might throw an IOException because it works with a file. Then declare an ObjectOutputStream object so that Events can be written to a file.

```
public static void main(String[] args) throws IOException
{
    ObjectOutputStream output =
        new ObjectOutputStream
        (new FileOutputStream("Events.txt"));
```

3. Declare an Event object that will hold created Events that will be written to the output file. Also declare variables to accept event numbers and types from the user. Declare a constant that will end the data entry loop.

```
Event event;
int eventNum;
int eventType;
final int QUIT = 999;
```

4. Prompt the user for an event number, and while the user does not type the QUIT value, continue to prompt for an event type, construct an event in which the rate and a manager are assigned, and write the constructed object to the output file.

```
Scanner in = new Scanner(System.in);
System.out.print("Enter an event number or " +
    QUIT + " to quit ");
eventNum = in.nextInt();
while(eventNum != QUIT)
{
    System.out.print("Enter event type ");
    eventType = in.nextInt();
    event = new Event(eventNum, eventType);
    output.writeObject(event);
    System.out.print("Enter an event number or " +
        QUIT + " to quit ");
    eventNum = in.nextInt();
}
```

5. Close the data file and add curly braces to end the `main()` method and the class.

```
    output.close();
    }
}
```

6. Save the file as **CreateEventFile.java**. Compile it and then execute the program. Enter data for any number of event numbers and types. For example, Figure 12-40 shows a typical execution in which the user has entered eight events.

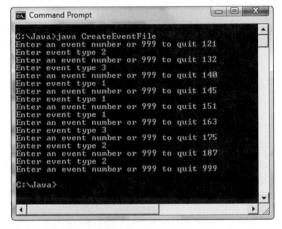

Figure 12-40 Typical execution of the `CreateEventFile` program

CREATING A PROGRAM THAT ACCESSES STORED Event OBJECT DATA

Next, you will write an application that uses the Events.txt data file created by the `CreateEventFile` program to produce requested information for the managers at Event Handlers Incorporated. The program will ask the user whether data should be displayed by event number or by event type, and appropriate information will be displayed.

To create a program that accesses stored Event data:

1. Open a new file in your text editor and type the first few lines for the program. The `main()` method will call methods that access files and convert them to `Event` objects, but to keep this example reasonably short, the program will not catch possibly thrown exceptions. Therefore, the `main()` method header includes a `throws` clause for the potential `IOException` and `ClassNotFoundException`.

```
import java.io.*;
import java.util.*;
public class CreateManagerReports
{
    public static void main(String[] args) throws
        IOException, ClassNotFoundException
    {
```

2. Two different types of reports are created by this application—by event type or event number—so declare a variable to hold the report type. Declare a constant to quit the program and constants for each report type. Then create a `Scanner` object for input, prompt the user for the type of report requested, and accept the user's response.

```
int reportType;
final int QUIT = 999;
final int BYTYPE = 1;
final int BYNUMBER = 2;
Scanner in = new Scanner(System.in);
System.out.println("Do you want to find events by type " +
    "or by number? ");
System.out.print("Enter " + BYTYPE + " for type, " + BYNUMBER +
    " for number, or " + QUIT + " to quit ");
reportType = in.nextInt();
```

3. In a loop that continues until the user decides to quit, call one of two methods—prepareReportByType() or prepareReportByNumber()—or display a message indicating the user's choice was not valid. Then prompt the user for and accept the next report choice. When you call the report methods, pass the `Scanner` input object because the methods will use keyboard input from the user to determine report options. Add a closing curly brace for the main() method.

```
while(reportType != QUIT)
{
    if(reportType == BYTYPE)
        prepareReportByType(in);
    else
        if(reportType == BYNUMBER)
            prepareReportByNumber(in);
        else
            System.out.println("****Invalid response");
    System.out.println("Do you want to find events by type " +
        "or by number? ");
    System.out.print("Enter " + BYTYPE + " for type, " +
        BYNUMBER + " for number, or " + QUIT + " to quit ");
    reportType = in.nextInt();
}
}
```

4. Next, start the prepareReportByType() method for the program. The method accepts a `Scanner` object to use with keyboard input. The method declares an ObjectInputStream object for the Events.txt file that holds event data. Declare variables for an Event, a type of event requested, and a count for how many events of the requested type reside in the data file.

```
public static void prepareReportByType (Scanner in)
    throws IOException, ClassNotFoundException
{
    ObjectInputStream input = new
        ObjectInputStream(new FileInputStream("Events.txt"));
    Event event;
    int eventType = 0;
    int count = 0;
```

5. In a `try` block, ask the user for an event type. Then, in a loop, read from the data file, comparing each event type for each record with the requested type. Each time they match, call a method to display the record, and add 1 to the count of matched records. When all the data records have been read, catch the `EOFException` that is thrown, display the final count of matches, and close the file. Add the method's closing brace.

```
    try
    {
        System.out.print("Enter event type to find ");
        eventType = in.nextInt();
        while(true)
        {
            event = (Event)input.readObject();
            if(eventType == event.getType())
            {
                display(event);
                ++count;
            }
        }
    }
    catch(EOFException e)
    {
        System.out.println("There are " + count +
            " events scheduled of type " + eventType);
        input.close();
    }
}
```

6. The method that displays requested data for a single event number is similar to the one that displays all the events for a type. The input file is set up and opened, the user is prompted for an event number, and the file is read until a matching event number is found, at which point a record is displayed and a `found` flag is set to `true`. When the end of the data file is reached and the `EOFException` is thrown, if the `found` flag has never been set to `true`, a message appears and reports that no record with the requested event number was located in the input file.

```
public static void prepareReportByNumber(Scanner in)
   throws IOException, ClassNotFoundException
   {
      ObjectInputStream input =
        new ObjectInputStream
        (new FileInputStream("Events.txt"));
      Event event;
      int eventNum = 0;
      boolean found = false;
      try
      {

         System.out.print("Enter event number to find ");
         eventNum = in.nextInt();
         while(true)
         {
            event = (Event)input.readObject();
            if(eventNum == event.getEventNum())
            {
                display(event);
                found = true;
            }
         }
      }
      catch(EOFException e)
      {
         if(!found)
            System.out.println("No such event as " + eventNum);
         input.close();
      }
   }
```

7. Add the `display()` method that is called by both report methods. It displays a line detailing a record's information. Add a closing curly brace for the class.

```
public static void display(Event e)
{
   System.out.println("Event # " + e.getEventNum() +
      "    Type is " + e.getType() + " Manager    " +
      e.getManager() + "   Rate: " + e.getRate());
}
}
```

8. Save the program as **CreateManagerReports.java**. Compile and execute the program. Figure 12-41 shows a typical execution in which the user requests different report types, and occasionally makes an invalid entry. Run the program several times until you are satisfied that each option works as expected.

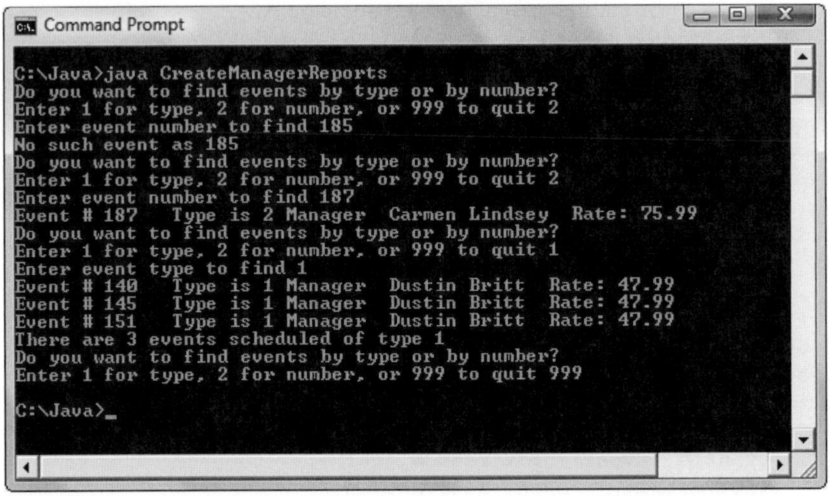

Figure 12-41 Typical execution of `CreateManagerReports` program

DON'T DO IT

» Don't forget to include a path with a file when the file is not stored in the same folder as the application that uses it.

» Don't forget that the backslash character starts the escape sequence in Java, so you must use two backslashes in a path.

» Don't serialize a class if it contains members that are not serializable. If a class contains fields that are objects themselves, and you want to serialize the class, the contained classes must also implement `Serializable`.

KEY TERMS

Random access memory (RAM) is temporary, volatile storage.

Volatile memory requires power to retain information.

Nonvolatile storage does not require power to retain information.

A **computer file** is a collection of stored information in a computer system.

Permanent storage devices retain data even when power is lost. Examples include hard disks, floppy disks, Zip disks, USB drives, reels or cassettes of magnetic tape, and compact discs.

Data files consist of related records that contain facts and figures, such as employee numbers, names, and salaries.

Program files or **application files** store software instructions.

The **root directory** of a storage device is its main directory, outside any folders.

Folders or **directories** provide a storage organization hierarchy.

A **path** is the complete list of the disk drive plus the hierarchy of directories in which a file resides.

Java's **File class** provides methods to gather file information.

A **field** is a group of characters that has some meaning.

A **record** is a collection of fields that contain data about an entity.

A data file is used as a **sequential access file** when each record is stored in order, based on the value in some field.

A Java application **opens a file** by creating an object and associating a stream of bytes with that object.

When an application **closes a file**, it is no longer available to an application.

A **stream** functions as a pipeline or channel through which bytes flow into and out of an application.

InputStream is an abstract class that contains methods for performing input.

OutputStream is an abstract class that contains methods for performing output.

A **convenience class** is one that has been designed to make the programmer's job easier.

A **buffer** is a memory location that you use to hold data temporarily.

EOF is the end-of-file condition.

Binary data is data stored in machine-readable code that must be read by an application before you can understand it.

When you use a `DataOutputStream` connected to `FileOutputStream`, the approach is known as **chaining the stream objects**.

Batch processing is processing that involves performing the same tasks with many records, one after the other.

Real-time applications require that a record be accessed immediately while a client is waiting.

An **interactive program** is one in which the user makes direct requests, as opposed to one in which input comes from a file.

Random access files are files in which records can be located in any order.

Files in which records must be accessed immediately are also called **instant access files**.

Random access files are also called **direct access files**.

A **file pointer**, or **file position pointer**, is an automatically created variable that holds the byte number of the next file position to be used.

A **key field** is the field in a record that makes the record unique from all others.

Serialization is Java's built-in mechanism for manipulating objects as streams of bytes.

A **serialized object** is represented as a sequence of bytes and includes the object's data as well as information about the types of data stored in the object.

Deserialization is the process of recreating an object in computer memory after it is retrieved from a file.

CHAPTER SUMMARY

» A computer file is a collection of information stored on a nonvolatile device in a computer system. A complete list of the disk drive plus the hierarchy of directories in which a file resides is its path.

» You can use Java's `File` class to gather file information, such as its size, its most recent modification date, and whether the file even exists.

» Businesses store data in a hierarchy of file, record, field, character. A data file is used as a sequential access file when each record is stored in order based on the value in some field. When you perform an input or output operation in an application, you can picture bytes flowing into your program from an input device through a stream.

» `InputStream` and `OutputStream` are abstract classes that contain methods for performing input and output. The `System` class defines the `PrintStream` objects `System.out` and `System.err`.

» Instead of assigning files to the standard input and output devices, you can also assign a file to the `InputStream` or `OutputStream`. For example, you can read data items from the keyboard and store them permanently on a disk. To accomplish this, you can construct a `FileOutputStream` object and assign it to the `OutputStream`.

» You can use the `DataInputStream` and `DataOutputStream` classes to accomplish formatted input and output. The `DataOutput` interface includes methods such as `writeBoolean()`, `writeChar()`, `writeDouble()`, `writeFloat()`, and `writeInt()`. Each method writes data in the correct format for the data type indicated by its name. You can use the method `writeUTF()` to write Unicode format strings.

» `DataInputStream` objects enable you to read binary data from an `InputStream`. The `DataInput` interface is implemented by `DataInputStream`. The `DataInput` interface includes methods such as `readByte()`, `readChar()`, `readDouble()`, `readFloat()`, `readInt()`, and `readUTF()`.

» Instead of hard-coding a filename to be written or read, it is more flexible to use a variable filename; then, the same application can process different data sets.

» Batch processing uses sequential files, but real-time, interactive applications use random access files. The `RandomAccessFile` class contains the same `read()`, `write()`, and `close()` method names as `InputStream` and `OutputStream`, but it also contains a `seek()` method that lets you select a beginning position within a file before you read or write data, and places a file pointer at the selected location.

» One approach to writing a random file is to place records into the file based on a key field—the field in a record that makes the record unique from all others.

» You can process a random access file either sequentially or randomly. The benefit of using a random access file is the ability to retrieve a specific record from a file directly, without reading through other records to locate the desired one.

» Serialization is Java's built-in mechanism for manipulating objects as streams of bytes; the `Serializable` interface endows your class with the ability to be serialized. Deserialization is the process of recreating an object in computer memory after it is retrieved from a file.

REVIEW QUESTIONS

1. Files always _____ .

   a. hold software instructions

   b. occupy a section of storage space

   c. remain open until the end of an application that uses them

   d. all of the above

2. The `File` class enables you to _____ .

   a. open a file   c. determine a file's size

   b. close a file   d. all of the above

3. The _____ package contains all the classes you use in file processing.

   a. `java.file`   c. `java.lang`

   b. `java.io`   d. `java.process`

4. The statement `File aFile = new File("myFile");` creates a file _____ .

   a. on the disk in drive A   c. in the Temp folder on the hard drive (drive C)

   b. on the hard drive (drive C)   d. on the default disk drive in the default directory

5. The `File` method `canWrite()` returns a(n) _____ value.

   a. `int`   c. `Object`

   b. `boolean`   d. `void`

6. Data used by businesses is stored in a data hierarchy that includes the following items, from largest to smallest:

   a. file, field, record, character   c. file, record, field, character

   b. record, file, field, character   d. record, field, file, character

7. A group of characters that has meaning is a _____ .

   a. file   c. field

   b. record   d. byte

8. Files consist of related _____ .

   a. records   c. data segments

   b. fields   d. archives

9. Before an application can read data from any file, the program must _____ the file.

    a. create   c. store

    b. open   d. close

10. When you perform an input operation in a Java application, you use a _____ .

    a. pipeline   c. moderator

    b. channel   d. stream

11. Most streams flow _____ .

    a. in   c. either in or out, but only in one direction

    b. out   d. both in and out concurrently

12. The output from `System.err` and `System.out` _____ go to the same device.

    a. must   c. might

    b. cannot   d. The answer depends on whether a mainframe or PC system is used.

13. A memory location that is used to temporarily hold data is a _____ .

    a. stream   c. bulwark

    b. buffer   d. channel

14. The `read()` method returns a value of –1 when it encounters a(n) _____ .

    a. input error   c. end-of-file condition

    b. integer   d. negative value

15. Much of the data that you write with `DataOutputStream` objects is not readable in a text editor because _____ .

    a. it does not exist in any physical sense

    b. it is stored in a noncharacter format

    c. you can read it only with a special piece of hardware called a Data Reader

    d. Java's security features prohibit it

16. You use a `DataOutputStream` connected to `FileOutputStream` by using a method known as _____ .

    a. sequencing   c. piggybacking

    b. iteration   d. chaining

17. When you catch an EOFException, it means you have _____ .

    a. failed to find the end of the file   c. forgotten to close a file

    b. forgotten to open a file   d. reached the end of a file

18. Which of the following applications is most likely to use random file processing?

    a. an application that schedules airline reservations

    b. a credit card company's end-of-month billing application

    c. a college's application that lists honor students at the end of each semester

    d. a manufacturing company's quarterly inventory reporting system

19. The method contained in the RandomAccessFile class, but which does not exist in the InputStream class, is _____ .

    a. read()   c. seek()

    b. close()   d. delete()

20. You can open a RandomAccessFile object for _____ .

    a. reading   c. both of the above

    b. writing   d. none of the above

EXERCISES

1. Create a file using any word-processing program or text editor. Write an application that displays the file's name, parent, size, and time of last modification. Save the file as **FileStatistics.java**.

2. Create two files using any word-processing program or text editor. Write an application that determines whether the two files are located in the same folder. Save the file as **SameFolder.java**.

3. Create a file that contains your favorite movie quote. Use a text editor such as Notepad and save the file as **quote.txt**. Copy the file contents and paste them into a word-processing program such as Word. Save the file as **quote.doc**. Write an application that displays the sizes of the two files as well as the ratio of their sizes to each other. Save the file as **FileStatistics2.java**.

4. Write an application that determines which, if any, of the following files are stored in the folder where you have been saving the exercises created in this chapter: autoexec.bat, SameFolder.java, FileStatistics.class, and Hello.java. Save the file as **FindSelectedFiles.java**.

5. a. Create a class named PhoneList that contains two Strings that hold a friend's name and phone number. Include appropriate methods and save the file as **PhoneList.java**.

Then create a program that allows the user to enter a series of friends' names and phone numbers and creates a file from the entered data. Save the file as **CreatePhoneList.java**.

b. Write an application that reads the file created by the CreatePhoneList application and displays the records. Save the file as **DisplaySavedPhoneList.java**.

c. Write an application that allows you to enter a friend's name and displays the corresponding phone number. Display an appropriate message if the friend's name cannot be found in the input file. The program should allow you to continue to request numbers until you want to quit. Save the file as **DisplayNumbers.java**.

6. a. Create a class named Order that holds an order number, item number ordered, quantity ordered, and total order price for a mail-order company. The constructor accepts an order number, item number, and quantity. The price is determined as follows:

Item Number	Price ($)
101	4.59
103	29.95
107	36.50
125	49.99

The total price is the quantity times the price per item. Include a display() method that displays a record's details and include get methods for each field. Save the class as **Order.java**. Write an application that allows you to enter any number of valid Order objects and save them to a file. If the user attempts to create an Order with an invalid item number, throw an exception and display an appropriate error message. Save the application as **MailOrderCreateFile.java**.

b. Write an application that reads the data file created by the MailOrderCreateFile application and displays the details contained in those records. Save the file as **MailOrderDisplayFile.java**.

c. Write an application that reads the data file created by the MailOrderCreateFile application. Allow the user to enter a specific item number. Display the number of orders for that item, the total quantity ordered, and the total price for all the items in all the orders. Display an appropriate error message if no orders were placed for the requested item. Allow the user to continue until an appropriate sentinel value is entered. Save the file as **MailOrderDisplayFile2.java**.

7. a. Write an application that allows a user to enter a filename and an integer representing a file position. Access the requested position within the file and display the character there. Save the file as **SeekPosition.java**.

b. Modify the SeekPosition application so that you display the next five characters after the requested position. Save the file as **SeekPosition2.java**.

    c. Modify the `SeekPosition2` application so that instead of displaying five characters, the user enters the number of characters to display, beginning with the requested position. Save the file as **SeekPosition3.java**.

8. Write an application that allows the user to type any number of characters and save them to a file. Then display the file contents backward. Save the file as **ReadBackwards.java**.

9. a. Create a `Student` class that holds an ID number, last and first names for a student, and number of credit hours completed. Include a constructor and a method that displays a record, and save the file as **Student.java**. Create an application that allows you to enter student data. Depending on the student's number of credit hours completed, write the data to either a lowerclassman student file (under 60 hours completed) or an upperclassman student file (60 hours or more completed). Save the file as **LowerAndUpper.java**.

    b. Create an application that, in turn, accesses each record in the lowerclassman file and then in the upperclassman file created in the `LowerAndUpper` application. Display an appropriate heading before each student. Save the file as **LowerAndUpperRead.java**.

10. a. The Rochester Bank maintains customer records in a random access file. Write an application that creates 10,000 blank records, and then allows the user to enter a balance and customer account information using an account number that is 9999 or less. Insert each new record into a data file at a location that is equal to the account number. Assume that the user will not enter invalid account numbers. Save the file as **CreateBankFile.java**.

    b. Create an application that uses the file created by the user in Exercise 10a and displays all existing accounts in account-number order. Save the file as **DisplayBankFileSequentially.java**.

    c. Create an application that uses the file created by the user in Exercise 10a and allows the user to enter an account number to view the account balance. Allow the user to view additional account balances until entering an application-terminating value. Save the file as **DisplayBankFileRandomly.java**.

    d. Create an `Exception` class for which you instantiate an object when a user attempts to create a bank account with an account number that has already been used. Save the file as **DuplicateAccountException.java**. Modify the `CreateBankFile` application created in Exercise 10a so that duplicate account numbers are not allowed and an appropriate error message is displayed. Save the file as **CreateBankFile2.java**. Make sure that the completed data file created by the new application still displays correctly with both `DisplayBankFileSequentially.java` and `DisplayBankFileRandomly.java`.

11. You first learned about the `GregorianCalendar` class in Chapter 4. `GregorianCalendar` implements `Serializable`. Write an application that prompts the user for a month, day, and year and creates `GregorianCalendar` objects that are saved to a file. Save the application as **CreateDateFile.java**. Create another application that reads the dates from the file and displays them formatted with slashes separating the month, day, and year. Save the second application as **ReadDateFile.java**.

DEBUGGING EXERCISES

Each of the following files in the Chapter.12 folder on your Student Disk has syntax and/or logic errors. In each case, determine the problem and fix the program. After you correct the errors, save each file using the same filename preceded with Fix. For example, DebugTwelve1.java will become FixDebugTwelve1.java.

a. DebugTwelve1.java

b. DebugTwelve2.java

c. DebugTwelve3.java

d. DebugTwelve4.java

GAME ZONE

1. In several Game Zone assignments earlier in this book, you have created games similar to Hangman in which the user guesses a secret phrase by selecting a series of letters. These versions had limited appeal because each contained only a few possible phrases to guess; after playing the games a few times, the user would have memorized all the possible phrases. Now create a version in which possible secret phrases can be saved to a file before the game is played. First create an application in which a user can enter any number of phrases to store. Save the application as **WritePhrases.java**. Then, create a guessing game that randomly selects a phrase from the file and allows the user to guess the phrase letter by letter. Save the game as **SecretPhraseUsingFile.java**.

> **»NOTE** In the SecretPhraseUsingFile game, the creator of the secret phrases and the player would most likely be different people. For example, a teacher might use the WritePhrases application to store famous quotes from history or scientific terms that correspond to the current lesson so that students could learn while playing the game.

2. In Chapter 8, you created a game named Quiz in which the user could respond to multiple-choice questions. Modify the game so that it stores the player's highest score from any previous game in a file and displays the previous score at the start of each new game. (The first time you play the game, the previous score should be 0.) Save the game as **QuizUsingFile.java**.

TOUGH QUESTIONS

1. Does the File class contain any methods for reading from or writing to files? Why?

2. Is there any reason why objects aren't serializable by default? In other words, why must you explicitly implement Serializable?

3. If a program must use a file several times, is it better to open and close it each time or keep it open for the duration of the program?

UP FOR DISCUSSION

1. In Exercise 3 earlier in this chapter, what did you discover about the size difference of files that held the same contents but were created using different software (such as Word and Notepad)? Why do you think the file sizes are so different, even though the files contain the same data?

2. Locate several .class files that resulted from compiling any Java programs you have written. (If you have deleted all your .class files, simply compile a few of your Java programs to recreate them.) Using a text editor, such as Notepad, open these files. Confirm that the first four characters (Ê p°¾) are the same in each of the compiled files. Find an online program that translates characters to their hexadecimal values and discover the translated value of this character set. What is the significance of the value? Why do all .class files start with the same set of characters?

3. Suppose your employer asks you to write a program that lists all the company's employees, their salaries, and their ages. You are provided with the personnel file to use as input. You decide to take the file home so you can create the report over the weekend. Is this acceptable? What if the file contained only employees' names and departments, but not more sensitive data such as salaries and ages?

13

INTRODUCTION TO SWING COMPONENTS

In this chapter, you will:

Understand Swing components

Use the JFrame class

Use the JLabel class

Use a layout manager

Extend the JFrame class

Add JTextFields, JButtons, and tool
   tips to a JFrame

Learn about event-driven programming

Understand Swing event listeners

Use the JCheckBox class

Use the ButtonGroup class

Use the JComboBox class

JAVA ON THE JOB, SCENE 13

"Learning about Java and object-oriented programming has been interesting," you say to Lynn Greenbrier, "but I am anxious to start making more interesting GUI programs that contain buttons, user lists, and other components I see in professional programs."

"You're ready to start," Lynn replies. "Everything you have learned about Java so far has prepared you to create GUI programs. For example, because you understand inheritance concepts, you will quickly grasp the relationships between all the little gadgets I will show you how to use, such as JFrames and JCheckBoxes. What's more important, if you have a thorough knowledge of how inheritance and components work in general, you can adapt your knowledge to other components."

"You won't show me how to use every component?" you ask worriedly.

"I don't have time to show you every component now," Lynn says, "but what you learn about some components will apply to the others. Besides, no matter what components you learn about now, you will need to learn about new ones soon—Java developers around the world are shaping new components right this minute."

"In other words, I can use the knowledge you give me about some components, and then I can extend that knowledge to other components. That's just like inheritance," you tell Lynn. "Please explain more."

> **NOTE**
> You have already used the JOptionPane component that is part of the Swing class.

> **NOTE**
> Swing components were named after a musical style that was popular in the 1940s.

> **NOTE**
> The Swing classes are part of a more general set of UI programming capabilities that are collectively called the **Java Foundation Classes**, or **JFC**. JFC includes Swing component classes and selected classes from the java.awt package.

UNDERSTANDING Swing COMPONENTS

Computer programs usually are more user-friendly (and more fun to use) when they contain user interface (UI) components. **UI components** are buttons, text fields, and other components with which the user can interact. Java's creators have packaged a number of prewritten components in the Swing package. **Swing components** are UI elements such as dialog boxes and buttons; you can usually recognize their names because they begin with J.

> **NOTE** In early versions of Java, components had simple names, such as Frame and Button. The components created from these original classes did not have a consistent appearance when used with different browsers and operating systems. When Java's creators designed new, improved classes, they needed new names for the classes, so they used a J in front of each new class name. Hence, Swing components have names like JFrame, JButton, JScrollbar, JOptionPane, and so on.

Each Swing component is a descendant of a JComponent, which in turn inherits from the java.awt.Container class. You insert the import statement import javax.swing.*; at the beginning of your Java program files so you can take advantage of the Swing UI components and their methods.

> **NOTE** When you import Swing classes, you use the javax.swing package instead of java.swing. The "x" originally stood for "extension," so named because the Swing classes were an extension of the original Java language specifications.

> **NOTE** Almost all Swing components are said to be **lightweight components** because they are written completely in Java and do not have to rely on the local operating system code. This means the components are not "weighed down" by having to interact with the operating system (for example, Windows or Macintosh) in which the application is running. Some Swing components, such as JFrames, are known as **heavyweight components** because they do require interaction with the local operating system.

> **NOTE** Components are also called controls or widgets.

When you use Swing components, you usually place them in containers. A **container** is a type of component that holds other components so you can treat a group of them as a single entity. Containers are defined in the Container class. Often, a container takes the form of a window that you can drag, resize, minimize, restore, and close.

As you know from reading about inheritance in Chapters 9 and 10, all Java classes are subclasses; they all descend from the Object class. The Component class is a child of the Object class, and the Container class is a child of the Component class. Therefore, every Container object "is a" Component, and every Component object (including every Container) "is an" Object. The Container class is also a parent class, and the Window class is a child of Container. However, Java programmers rarely use Window objects because the Window subclass Frame and its child, the Swing component **JFrame**, both allow you to create more useful objects. Window objects do not have title bars or borders, but JFrame objects do.

> **NOTE** A lightweight component reuses the native (original) window of its closest heavyweight ancestor; a heavyweight component has its own opaque native window.

»TWO TRUTHS AND A LIE: UNDERSTANDING Swing COMPONENTS

1. Swing components are elements such as buttons; you can usually recognize their names because they contain the word "Swing."
2. Each Swing component is a descendant of a JComponent, which in turn inherits from the java.awt.Container class.
3. You insert the import statement import javax.swing.*; at the beginning of your Java program files so you can use Swing components.

The false statement is #1. You can usually recognize Swing component names because they begin with J.

USING THE JFrame CLASS

You usually create a JFrame so that you can place other objects within it for display. Figure 13-1 shows the JFrame's inheritance tree.

```
java.lang.Object
   |--java.awt.Component
         |--java.awt.Container
               |--java.awt.Window
                     |--java.awt.Frame
                           |--javax.swing.JFrame
```

Figure 13-1 Relationship of the JFrame class to its ancestors

> **NOTE** Recall that the Object class is defined in the java.lang package, which is imported automatically every time you write a Java program. However, its descendants shown in Figure 13-1 are not automatically imported.

> **NOTE** The only heavyweight components used in Swing are swing.JFrame, swing.JDialog, swing.JWindow, swing.JApplet, awt.Component, awt.Container, and awt.JComponent.

The JFrame class has four constructors:

» JFrame() constructs a new frame that initially is invisible and has no title.

» JFrame(String title) creates a new, initially invisible JFrame with the specified title.

» JFrame(GraphicsConfiguration gc) creates a JFrame in the specified GraphicsConfiguration of a screen device with a blank title.

» JFrame(String title, GraphicsConfiguration gc) creates a JFrame with the specified title and the specified GraphicsConfiguration of a screen.

» NOTE You will learn about the GraphicsConfiguration class as you continue to study Java.

You can construct a JFrame as you do other objects, using the class name, an identifier, the assignment operator, the new operator, and a constructor call. For example, the following two statements construct two JFrames: one with the title "Hello" and another with no title:

```
JFrame firstFrame = new JFrame("Hello");
JFrame secondFrame = new JFrame();
```

After you create a JFrame object, you can use the now-familiar object-dot-method format you have used with other objects to call methods that manipulate a JFrame's features. Table 13-1 describes some useful JFrame class methods. For example, the following statements set the firstFrame object's size to 250 pixels horizontally by 100 pixels vertically and set the JFrame's title to display a String argument:

» NOTE
Pixels are the picture elements, or tiny dots of light, that make up the image on your computer monitor.

```
firstFrame.setSize(250, 100);

firstFrame.setTitle("My frame");
```

» NOTE When you set a JFrame's size, you do not have the full area available to use because part of the area is consumed by the JFrame's title bar and borders.

» NOTE The methods in Table 13-1 represent only a small portion of the available methods you can use with a JFrame. Each of the methods listed in Table 13-1 is inherited from either JFrame's Component or Frame parent class. These classes contain many useful methods in addition to the few listed here. You can read the documentation for all the methods at *http://java.sun.com*.

Method	Purpose
void setTitle(String)	Sets a JFrame's title using the String argument
void setSize(int, int)	Sets a JFrame's size in pixels with the width and height as arguments
void setSize(Dimension)	Sets a JFrame's size using a Dimension class object; the Dimension(int, int) constructor creates an object that represents both a width and a height
String getTitle()	Returns a JFrame's title
void setResizable(boolean)	Sets the JFrame to be resizable by passing true to the method, or sets the JFrame not to be resizable by passing false to the method
boolean isResizable()	Returns true or false to indicate whether the JFrame is resizable
void setVisible(boolean)	Sets a JFrame to be visible using the boolean argument true and invisible using the boolean argument false
void setBounds(int, int, int, int)	Overrides the default behavior for the JFrame to be positioned in the upper-left corner of the computer screen's desktop. The first two arguments are the horizontal and vertical positions of the JFrame's upper-left corner on the desktop. The final two arguments set the width and height.

Table 13-1 Useful methods inherited by the JFrame class

Figure 13-2 shows an application that creates a small, empty JFrame; the resulting JFrame shown in Figure 13-3 resembles frames that you have probably seen when using different UI programs you have downloaded or purchased. One reason to use similar frame objects in your own programs is that your program's user is already familiar with the frame environment. When users see frames on their computer screens, they expect to see a title bar at the top containing text information (such as "First frame"). Users also expect to see Minimize, Maximize or Restore, and Close buttons in the frame's upper-right corner. Most users assume that they can change a frame's size by dragging its border or reposition the frame on their screen by dragging the frame's title bar to a new location. The JFrame in Figure 13-3 has all of these capabilities.

```
import javax.swing.*;
public class JFrame1
{
    public static void main(String[] args)
    {
        JFrame aFrame = new JFrame("First frame");
        aFrame.setSize(250, 100);
        aFrame.setVisible(true);
    }
}
```

Figure 13-2 The `JFrame1` application

Figure 13-3 Output of the `JFrame1` application

» NOTE In the application in Figure 13-2, all three statements in the `main()` method are important. After you instantiate `aFrame`, if you do not use `setVisible(true)`, you do not see the `JFrame`, and if you do not set its size, you only see the title bar of the `JFrame` because the `JFrame` size is 0 × 0 by default.

» NOTE It might seem unusual that the default state for a `JFrame` is invisible. However, consider that you might want to construct a `JFrame` in the background while other actions are occurring and that you might want to make it visible later, when appropriate (for example, after the user has taken an action such as selecting an option). To make a frame visible, some Java programmers use the `show()` method instead of the `setVisible()` method.

When a user closes a `JFrame` by clicking the Close button in the upper-right corner, the default behavior is for the `JFrame` to become hidden and for the application to keep running. This makes sense when there are other tasks for the program to complete after the main frame is closed—for example, displaying additional frames, closing open data files, or printing an activity report. However, when a `JFrame` serves as a `Swing` application's main user interface (as happens frequently in interactive programs), you usually want the program to exit when the user clicks Close. To change this behavior, you can call a `JFrame`'s `setDefaultCloseOperation()` method and use one of the following four values as an argument:

» `JFrame.EXIT_ON_CLOSE` exits the program when the `JFrame` is closed. This value is used in Figure 13-7 and other examples later in this chapter.

» `WindowConstants.DISPOSE_ON_CLOSE` closes the frame, disposes of the `JFrame` object, and keeps running the application.

» `WindowConstants.DO_NOTHING_ON_CLOSE` keeps the `JFrame` and continues running. In other words, it disables the Close button.

» `WindowConstants.HIDE_ON_CLOSE` closes the `JFrame` and continues running; this is the default operation that you frequently want to override.

>> **NOTE** Each of the four usable setDefaultCloseOperation() arguments represents an integer; for example, the value of JFrame.EXIT_ON_CLOSE is 3. However, it is easier to remember the constant names than the numeric values they represent, and other programmers more easily understand your intentions if you use the named constant identifier.

CUSTOMIZING A JFrame's APPEARANCE

The appearance of the JFrame in Figure 13-3 is provided by the operating system in which the program is running (in this case, Windows). For example, the coffee-cup icon in the frame's title bar and the Minimize, Restore, and Close buttons look and act as they do in other Windows applications. The icon and buttons are known as **window decorations**; by default, window decorations are supplied by the operating system. However, you can request that Java's look and feel provide the decorations for a frame. A **look and feel** is the default appearance and behavior of any user interface.

Optionally, you can set a JFrame's look and feel using the setDefaultLookAndFeelDecorated() method. For example, Figure 13-4 shows an application in which this method is called. The program in Figure 13-4 differs from Figure 13-2 only in the shaded areas, which show the class name, the text in the title bar, and the look-and-feel statement. Figure 13-5 shows the output. If you compare the frame in Figure 13-5 with the one in Figure 13-3, you can see that Java's look and feel has similar features to that of Windows, but their appearance is different.

>> **NOTE** You might decide to use the setDefaultLookAndFeelDecorated() method call in all your applications that contain JFrames. To keep the examples simpler, this book usually omits the statement and uses the look and feel of the default operating system.

>> **NOTE**
You can provide a custom icon for a frame instead of using your operating system's default icon or the Java look-and-feel icon. For details, go to *http://java.sun.com* and search for "How to Make Frames."

```
import javax.swing.*;
public class JFrame2
{
    public static void main(String[] args)
    {
        JFrame.setDefaultLookAndFeelDecorated(true);
        JFrame aFrame = new JFrame("Second frame");
        aFrame.setSize(250, 100);
        aFrame.setVisible(true);
    }
}
```

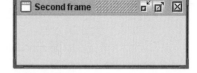

Figure 13-4 The JFrame2 class

Figure 13-5 Output of the JFrame2 application

>> **NOTE** Look and feel is a legal issue because some software companies claim that competitors are infringing on their copyright protection by copying the look and feel of their products. As of this writing, the courts have not made a definitive ruling on this matter.

>> **NOTE**
Java's look and feel is also known by the name "Metal."

1. The JFrame class contains overloaded constructors; for example, you can specify a title or not.
2. An advantage to using a JFrame is that it resembles traditional frames that people are accustomed to using.
3. When a user closes a JFrame by clicking the Close button in the upper-right corner, the default behavior is for the application to end.

The false statement is #3. When a user closes a JFrame by clicking the Close button in the upper-right corner, the default behavior is for the JFrame to become hidden and for the application to keep running.

USING A JLabel

One of the components you might want to place on a JFrame is a JLabel. **JLabel** is a built-in Java Swing class that holds text you can display. The inheritance hierarchy of the JLabel class is shown in Figure 13-6.

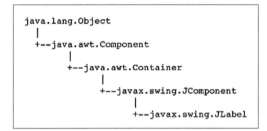

Figure 13-6 The JLabel class inheritance hierarchy

Available constructors for the JLabel class include the following:

» JLabel() creates a JLabel instance with no image and with an empty string for the title.

» JLabel(Icon image) creates a JLabel instance with the specified image.

» JLabel(Icon image, int horizontalAlignment) creates a JLabel instance with the specified image and horizontal alignment.

» JLabel(String text) creates a JLabel instance with the specified text.

» JLabel(String text, Icon icon, int horizontalAlignment) creates a JLabel instance with the specified text, image, and horizontal alignment.

» JLabel(String text, int horizontalAlignment) creates a JLabel instance with the specified text and horizontal alignment.

For example, you can create a JLabel named greeting that holds the words "Hello. Who are you?" by writing the following statement:

```
JLabel greeting = new JLabel("Hello. Who are you?");
```

You then can add the greeting object to the JFrame object named aFrame using the **add() method** as follows:

```
aFrame.add(greeting);
```

For example, Figure 13-7 shows an application in which a frame is created and its size, visibility, and close operation are set. Then a JLabel is created and added to the JFrame. Figure 13-8 shows the output.

```
import javax.swing.*;
public class JFrame3
{
    public static void main(String[] args)
    {
        final int FRAME_WIDTH = 250;
        final int FRAME_HEIGHT = 100;
        JFrame aFrame = new JFrame("Third frame");
        aFrame.setSize(FRAME_WIDTH, FRAME_HEIGHT);
        aFrame.setVisible(true);
        aFrame.setDefaultCloseOperation(JFrame.EXIT_ON_CLOSE);
        JLabel greeting = new JLabel("Hello");
        aFrame.add(greeting);
    }
}
```

Figure 13-7 The JFrame3 class

Figure 13-8 Output of the JFrame3 application

The counterpart to the add() method is the **remove() method**. The following statement removes greeting from aFrame:

```
aFrame.remove(greeting);
```

If you add or remove a component from a container after it has been made visible, you should also call the invalidate(), validate(), and repaint() methods, or else you will not see the results of your actions. Each performs slightly different functions, but all three together guarantee that the results of changes in your layout will take effect. The invalidate() and validate() methods are part of the Container class, and the repaint() method is part of the Component class.

NOTE
You will learn more about the repaint() method in Chapter 15.

You can change the text in a JLabel by using the **setText() method** with the JLabel object and passing a String to it. For example, the following code changes the value displayed in the greeting JLabel:

```
greeting.setText("Howdy");
```

» NOTE
Later in this chapter, you will see that setText() and getText() work with other Components as well.

You can retrieve the text in a JLabel by using the **getText() method**, which returns the String currently stored in the JLabel.

CHANGING A JLabel's FONT

If you use the Internet and a Web browser to visit Web sites, you probably are not very impressed with the simple application displayed in Figure 13-8. You might think that the string "Hello" is plain and lackluster. Fortunately, Java provides you with a **Font class** from which you can create an object that holds typeface and size information. The **setFont() method** requires a Font object argument. To construct a Font object, you need three arguments: typeface, style, and point size.

The **typeface argument** to the Font constructor is a String representing a font. Common fonts have names such as Arial, Century, Monospaced, and Times New Roman. The typeface argument in the Font constructor is only a request; the system on which your program runs might not have access to the requested font, and if necessary, it substitutes a default font. The **style argument** applies an attribute to displayed text and is one of three values: Font.PLAIN, Font.BOLD, or Font.ITALIC. The **point size argument** is an integer that represents about 1/72 of an inch. Printed text is commonly 12 points; a headline might be 30 points.

> **» NOTE** In printing, point size defines a measurement between lines of text in a single-spaced text document. The point size is based on typographic points, which are approximately 1/72 of an inch. Java adopts the convention that one point on a display is equivalent to one unit in user coordinates. For more information, see the Font documentation at http://java.sun.com.

To give a JLabel object a new font, you can create a Font object, as in the following:

```
Font headlineFont = new Font("Monospaced", Font.BOLD, 36);
```

The typeface name is a String, so you must enclose it in double quotation marks when you use it to declare the Font object. Then you use the setFont() method to assign the Font to a JLabel with a statement such as:

```
greeting.setFont(headlineFont);
```

Figure 13-9 shows a modified JFrame3 class named JFrame4. All the changes are shaded. This program contains a Font object named headlineFont that is applied to the greeting. Figure 13-10 shows the program execution.

```
import javax.swing.*;
import java.awt.*;
public class JFrame4
{
    public static void main(String[] args)
    {
        final int FRAME_WIDTH = 250;
        final int FRAME_HEIGHT = 100;
        Font headlineFont = new Font("Arial", Font.BOLD, 36);
        JFrame aFrame = new JFrame("Fourth frame");
        aFrame.setSize(FRAME_WIDTH, FRAME_HEIGHT);
        aFrame.setVisible(true);
        aFrame.setDefaultCloseOperation(JFrame.EXIT_ON_CLOSE);
        JLabel greeting = new JLabel("Hello");
        greeting.setFont(headlineFont);
        aFrame.add(greeting);
    }
}
```

Figure 13-9 The `JFrame4` program

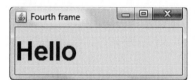

Figure 13-10 Output of the `JFrame4` program

»NOTE You are not required to provide a name for a `Font`. For example, you could omit the shaded statement that declares `headlineFont` in Figure 13-9 and set the `greeting` Font with the following statement that uses an anonymous `Font` object:

```
greeting.setFont(new Font("Arial", Font.BOLD, 36));
```

»TWO TRUTHS AND A LIE: USING A `JLabel`

1. `JLabel` is a built-in Java `Swing` class that holds text you can display.

2. You can change a `JLabel`'s text by using its `JFrame`'s name, a dot, and the `add()` method, and then using the desired text as the argument to the method.

3. If you add or remove a component from a container after it has been made visible, you should also call the `validate()` and `repaint()` methods, or else you will not see the results of your actions.

The false statement is #2. You change a JLabel's text using the setText() method, including the new text as the argument. You add a JLabel to a JFrame by using the JFrame's name, a dot, and the add() method, and then by using the JLabel's name as an argument to the method.

USING A LAYOUT MANAGER

When you want to add multiple components to a JFrame or other container, you usually need to provide instructions for the layout of the components. For example, Figure 13-11 shows an application in which two JLabels are created and added to a JFrame in the final shaded statements.

```
import javax.swing.*;
import java.awt.*;
public class JFrame5
{
   public static void main(String[] args)
   {
      final int FRAME_WIDTH = 250;
      final int FRAME_HEIGHT = 100;
      JFrame aFrame = new JFrame("Fifth frame");
      aFrame.setSize(FRAME_WIDTH, FRAME_HEIGHT);
      aFrame.setVisible(true);
      aFrame.setDefaultCloseOperation(JFrame.EXIT_ON_CLOSE);
      JLabel greeting = new JLabel("Hello");
      JLabel greeting2 = new JLabel("Who are you?");
      aFrame.add(greeting);
      aFrame.add(greeting2);
   }
}
```

Figure 13-11 The JFrame5 program

Figure 13-12 shows the output of the application in Figure 13-11. Although two JLabels are added to the frame, only the last one added is visible. The second JLabel has been placed on top of the first one, totally obscuring it. If you continued to add more JLabels to the program, only the last one added to the JFrame would be visible.

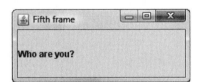

Figure 13-12 Output of the JFrame5 program

»NOTE
You will learn more about layout managers in Chapter 14.

To place multiple components at specified positions in a container so that they do not hide each other, you must explicitly use a **layout manager**—a class that controls component positioning. The normal (default) behavior of a JFrame is to use a layout format named BorderLayout. A **BorderLayout**, created by using the BorderLayout class, divides a container into regions. When you do not specify a region in which to place a component (as the JFrame5 program fails to do), all the components are placed in the same region, and they obscure each other.

When you use a FlowLayout instead of a BorderLayout, components do not lie on top of each other. Instead, the **flow layout manager** places components in a row, and when a row is filled, it automatically spills components into the next row. By default, the components in each row are centered.

» NOTE In the `FlowLayout` class, three constants are defined that specify how components are positioned in each row of their container. These constants are `FlowLayout.LEFT`, `FlowLayout.RIGHT`, and `FlowLayout.CENTER`. For example, to create a layout manager named `flow` that positions components to the right rather than in the center by default, you can use the following statement:

```
FlowLayout flow = new FlowLayout(FlowLayout.RIGHT);
```

Suppose you create a `FlowLayout` object named `flow` as follows:

```
FlowLayout flow = new FlowLayout();
```

Then the layout of a `JFrame` named `aFrame` can be set to the newly created `FlowLayout` using the statement:

```
aFrame.setLayout(flow);
```

A more compact syntax that uses an anonymous `FlowLayout` object is:

```
aFrame.setLayout(new FlowLayout());
```

Figure 13-13 shows an application in which the `JFrame`'s layout manager has been set so that multiple components are visible. Figure 13-14 shows the execution. The two `JLabel`s appear side by side. If there were more `JLabel`s or other components, they would continue to be placed side by side across the `JFrame` until there was no more room. Then, the additional components would be placed in a new row beneath the first row of components.

```java
import javax.swing.*;
import java.awt.*;
public class JFrame6
{
    public static void main(String[] args)
    {
        final int FRAME_WIDTH = 250;
        final int FRAME_HEIGHT = 100;
        JFrame aFrame = new JFrame("Sixth frame");
        aFrame.setSize(FRAME_WIDTH, FRAME_HEIGHT);
        aFrame.setVisible(true);
        aFrame.setDefaultCloseOperation(JFrame.EXIT_ON_CLOSE);
        JLabel greeting = new JLabel("Hello");
        JLabel greeting2 = new JLabel("Who are you?");
        aFrame.setLayout(new FlowLayout());
        aFrame.add(greeting);
        aFrame.add(greeting2);
    }
}
```

Figure 13-13 The `JFrame6` program

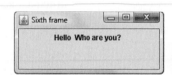

Figure 13-14 Output of the `JFrame6` program

»NOTE
The program that produces the output in Figure 13-15 can be found on your Student Disk. The program name is JFrame7.java. The changes from JFrame6 were very minor, so space is saved in this book by not showing the program here as a separate figure.

Figure 13-15 shows the output of a program in which the only changes made from the JFrame6 application are to the JFrame title and the value of FRAME_WIDTH, which has been reduced from 250 to 100. Instead of appearing side by side, the two components appear vertically because there is not enough room for both in the same row in the JFrame.

Figure 13-15 Output of the revised JFrame6 program

»TWO TRUTHS AND A LIE: USING A LAYOUT MANAGER

1. If you do not provide a layout manager for a JFrame, you cannot add multiple components to it.
2. The normal (default) behavior of a JFrame is to use a layout format named BorderLayout.
3. The flow layout manager places components in a row, and when a row is filled, it automatically spills components into the next row.

The false statement is #1. If you do not provide a layout manager for a JFrame, you can add multiple components to it, but only the most recently added one is visible.

»NOTE
Other layout managers exist that allow you to position components in a container more precisely. You will learn about these in Chapter 14. The examples in this chapter will use FlowLayout because it is the easiest of the layout managers to use.

EXTENDING THE JFrame CLASS

You can instantiate a simple JFrame object within an application's main() method or with any other method of any class you write. Alternatively, you can create your own class that descends from the JFrame class. The advantage to creating a child class of JFrame is that you can set the JFrame's properties within your object's constructor; then, when you create your JFrame child object, it is automatically endowed with the features you have specified, such as title, size, and default close operation.

»NOTE
Remember that when you use a call to super(), it must be the first statement within the child class constructor.

You already know that you create a child class by using the keyword extends in the class header, followed by the parent class name. You also know that you can call the parent class's constructor using the keyword super. For example, the JMyFrame class in Figure 13-16 extends JFrame. Within the JMyFrame constructor, the super() JFrame constructor is called; it accepts a String argument to use as the JFrame's title. (Alternatively, the setTitle() method could have been used.) The JMyFrame constructor also sets the size, visibility, and default close operation for every JMyFrame. Each of the methods—setSize(), setVisible(), and setDefaultCloseOperation()—appears in the constructor in Figure 13-16 without an object, because the object is the current JMyFrame being constructed. Each of the three methods could be preceded with a this reference with exactly the same meaning. That is, within the JMyFrame constructor, the following two statements have identical meanings:

```
setSize(WIDTH, HEIGHT);

this.setSize(WIDTH, HEIGHT);
```

Each statement sets the size of "this" current JMyFrame instance.

```
import javax.swing.*;
public class JMyFrame extends JFrame
{
    final int WIDTH = 400;
    final int HEIGHT = 120;
    public JMyFrame()
    {
        super("This is my frame");
        setSize(WIDTH, HEIGHT);
        setVisible(true);
        setDefaultCloseOperation(JFrame.EXIT_ON_CLOSE);
    }
}
```

Figure 13-16 The `JMyFrame` class

Figure 13-17 shows an application that declares two `JMyFrame` objects. Each has the same set of attributes, determined by the `JMyFrame` constructor. When you execute the application in Figure 13-17, the two `JMyFrame` objects display with the second one on top of, or obscuring, the first. Figure 13-18 shows the output of the `CreateTwoJMyFrameObjects` application after the top `JMyFrame` has been dragged to partially expose the bottom one.

```
public class CreateTwoJMyFrameObjects
{
    public static void main(String[] args)
    {
        JMyFrame myFrame = new JMyFrame();
        JMyFrame mySecondFrame = new JMyFrame();
    }
}
```

Figure 13-17 The `CreateTwoJMyFrameObjects` application

Figure 13-18 Output of the `CreateTwoJMyFrameObjects` application after dragging the top frame

»NOTE You could use the `setBounds()` method with one of the `JMyFrame` objects that produces the output in Figure 13-18 so that you don't have to move one `JMyFrame` object to view the other. See Table 13-1 for details. The `Object` class also includes a `setLocation()` method you can use with a `JFrame`. To use this method, you provide horizontal and vertical position values as method arguments. You will learn more about the `setLocation()` method in Chapter 15.

> **»NOTE** You exit the application when you click the Close button on either of the two JMyFrame objects shown in Figure 13-18. Each object has the same default close operation because each uses the same constructor that specifies this operation. To allow only one JMyFrame to control the program's exit, you could use the setDefaultCloseOperation() method with one or both of the objects in the application to change its close behavior. For example, you could use DISPOSE_ON_CLOSE to dismiss one of the frames but keep the application running.

When you extend a JFrame to create a new custom class, you must remember to make decisions as to which attributes you want to set within the class and which you want to leave to the applications that will use the class. For example, you can place the setVisible() statement within the JFrame child class constructor (using either an explicit or implied this reference), or you can allow the application to use a setVisible() statement (using the name of an instantiated object followed by a dot and the method name). Either one works, but if you fail to do either, the frame will not be visible.

»TWO TRUTHS AND A LIE: EXTENDING THE JFrame CLASS

1. The advantage to creating a child class of JFrame is that you can set the JFrame's properties within your object's constructor so that it is automatically endowed with the features that you have specified.

2. When a class descends from JFrame, you can use super() or setTitle() to set the title within any of the child's methods.

3. When you extend a JFrame to create a new custom class, you can decide which attributes you want to set within the class and which you want to leave to the applications that will use the class.

The false statement is #2. When a class descends from JFrame, you can use super() or setTitle() to set the title within the child's constructor. However, super() does not work in other methods.

ADDING JTextFields, JButtons, AND TOOL TIPS TO A JFrame

In addition to including JLabel objects, JFrames often contain other window features, such as JTextFields and JButtons. A **JTextField** is a component into which a user can type a single line of text data. (Text data comprises any characters you can enter from the keyboard, including numbers and punctuation.) Figure 13-19 shows the inheritance hierarchy of the JTextField class.

```
java.lang.Object
   |
   +--java.awt.Component
          |
          +--java.awt.Container
                 |
                 +--javax.swing.JComponent
                        |
                        +--javax.swing.text.JTextComponent
                               |
                               +--javax.swing.JTextField
```

Figure 13-19 The JTextField class inheritance hierarchy

Typically, a user types a line into a JTextField and then presses Enter on the keyboard or clicks a button with the mouse to enter the data. You can construct a JTextField object using one of several constructors:

» public JTextField() constructs a new JTextField.

» public JTextField(int columns) constructs a new, empty JTextField with a specified number of columns.

» public JTextField(String text) constructs a new JTextField initialized with the specified text.

» public JTextField(String text, int columns) constructs a new JTextField initialized with the specified text and columns.

For example, to provide a JTextField that allows enough room for a user to enter approximately 10 characters, you can code the following:

```
JTextField response = new JTextField(10);
```

To add the JTextField named response to a JFrame named frame, you write:

```
frame.add(response);
```

> **NOTE** Try to anticipate how many characters your users might enter when you create a JTextField. The user can enter more characters than those that display, but the extra characters scroll out of view. It can be disconcerting to try to enter data into a field that is not large enough. It is usually better to overestimate than underestimate the size of a text field.

Several other methods are available for use with JTextFields. The setText() method allows you to change the text in a JTextField (or other Component) that has already been created, as in the following:

```
response.setText("Thank you");
```

After a user has entered text in a JTextField, you can clear it out with a statement such as:

```
response.setText("");
```

The getText() method allows you to retrieve the String of text in a JTextField (or other Component), as in:

```
String whatDidUserSay = response.getText();
```

When a JTextField has the capability of accepting keystrokes, the JTextField is **editable**. If you do not want the user to be able to enter data in a JTextField, you can use the **setEditable() method** to change the editable status of a JTextField from its default value of true. For example, if you want to give a user only one chance to answer a question correctly, you can prevent the user from replacing or editing the characters in the JTextField by using the following statement:

```
response.setEditable(false);
```

If conditions change, and you want the user to be able to edit the JTextField, use the following statement:

```
response.setEditable(true);
```

> **NOTE**
> The number of characters a JTextField can display depends on the font being used and the actual characters typed. For example, in most fonts, 'w' is wider than 'i', so a JTextField of size 10 using the Arial font can display 24 'i' characters, but only eight 'w' characters.

ADDING JButtons

A **JButton** is a `Component` the user can click with a mouse to make a selection. A `JButton` is even easier to create than a `JTextField`. There are five `JButton` constructors:

» `public JButton()` creates a button with no set text.

» `public JButton(Icon icon)` creates a button with an icon of type `Icon` or `ImageIcon`.

» `public JButton(String text)` creates a button with text.

» `public JButton(String text, Icon icon)` creates a button with initial text and an icon of type `Icon` or `ImageIcon`.

» `public JButton(Action a)` creates a button in which properties are taken from the `Action` supplied. (`Action` is a Java class.)

The inheritance hierarchy of the `JButton` class is shown in Figure 13-20.

```
java.lang.Object
  |
  +--java.awt.Component
        |
        +--java.awt.Container
              |
              +--javax.swing.JComponent
                    |
                    +--javax.swing.AbstractButton
                          |
                          +--javax.swing.JButton
```

Figure 13-20 The `JButton` class inheritance hierarchy

To create a `JButton` with the label "Press when ready", you write the following:

```
JButton readyJButton = new JButton("Press when ready");
```

You can add a `JButton` to a `JFrame` (or other container) using the `add()` method. You can change a `JButton`'s label with the `setText()` method, as in:

```
readyJButton.setText("Don't press me again!");
```

You can get the `JButton` and assign it to a `String` object with the `getText()` method, as in:

```
String whatsOnJButton = readyJButton.getText();
```

> **》NOTE**
> Your programs are more user-friendly when the label on a JButton describes its function for the user.

Figure 13-21 shows a class that extends `JFrame` and holds several components. As the components (two `JLabels`, a `JTextField`, and a `JButton`) are added to the `JFrame`, they are placed from left to right in horizontal rows across the `JFrame`'s surface. Figure 13-22 shows the program that instantiates an instance of the `JFrame`, and Figure 13-23 shows the results when the program is executed.

```
import javax.swing.*;
import java.awt.*;
public class JFrameWithManyComponents extends JFrame
{
    final int FRAME_WIDTH = 300;
    final int FRAME_HEIGHT = 150;
    public JFrameWithManyComponents()
    {
        super("Demonstrating many components");
        setSize(FRAME_WIDTH, FRAME_HEIGHT);
        setDefaultCloseOperation(JFrame.EXIT_ON_CLOSE);
        JLabel heading = new JLabel("This frame has many components");
        heading.setFont(new Font("Arial", Font.BOLD, 16));
        JLabel namePrompt = new JLabel("Enter your name:");
        JTextField nameField = new JTextField(12);
        JButton button = new JButton("Click to continue");
        setLayout(new FlowLayout());
        add(heading);
        add(namePrompt);
        add(nameField);
        add(button);
        setVisible(true);
    }
}
```

Figure 13-21 The `JFrameWithManyComponents` class

>> **NOTE** The `JFrameWithManyComponents` class includes the statement `setVisible(true);` to make the `JFrame` visible. Many developers would prefer to remove this statement from the class and let client programs set the frame's visibility. For example, you might add the following statement to the client program in Figure 13-22:

```
frame.setVisible(true);
```

```
public class ComponentDemo
{
    public static void main(String[] args)
    {
        JFrameWithManyComponents frame =
            new JFrameWithManyComponents();
    }
}
```

Figure 13-22 A `ComponentDemo` application that instantiates a `JFrameWithManyComponents`

Figure 13-23 Execution of the `ComponentDemo` program

When you execute the ComponentDemo program, the JFrame that appears contains all the components that were added in the frame's constructor. A user can minimize or restore the frame and can alter its size by dragging the frame borders. The user can type characters in the JTextField and can click the JButton. When the button is clicked, it appears to be pressed just like buttons you have used in professional applications. However, when the user types characters or clicks the button, no resulting actions occur because code has not yet been written to handle those user-initiated events.

USING TOOL TIPS

Tool tips are popup windows that can help a user understand the purpose of components in an application; the tool tip appears when a user hovers the mouse pointer over the component. You define the text to be displayed in a tool tip by using the **setToolTipText() method** and passing an appropriate String to it. For example, in the JFrameWithManyComponents program in Figure 13-21, you can add a tool tip to the button component by using the following statement in the JFrame constructor:

```
button.setToolTipText("Click this button");
```

Figure 13-24 shows the result when the JFrame is displayed and the user's mouse pointer is placed over the button.

Figure 13-24 JFrameWithToolTip with added tool tip

>>NOTE The JFrameWithToolTip.java file on your Student Disk contains a revised version of JFrameWithManyComponents with the tool tip added. The ToolTipDemo.java file contains an application that instantiates a JFrameWithToolTip object.

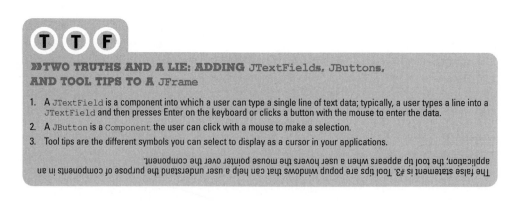

>>TWO TRUTHS AND A LIE: ADDING JTextFields, JButtons, AND TOOL TIPS TO A JFrame

1. A JTextField is a component into which a user can type a single line of text data; typically, a user types a line into a JTextField and then presses Enter on the keyboard or clicks a button with the mouse to enter the data.
2. A JButton is a Component the user can click with a mouse to make a selection.
3. Tool tips are the different symbols you can select to display as a cursor in your applications.

The false statement is #3. Tool tips are popup windows that can help a user understand the purpose of components in an application; the tool tip appears when a user hovers the mouse pointer over the component.

LEARNING ABOUT EVENT-DRIVEN PROGRAMMING

An **event** occurs when a user takes action on a component, such as clicking the mouse on a JButton object. In an **event-driven program**, the user might initiate any number of events in any order. For example, if you use a word-processing program, you have dozens of choices at your disposal at any moment in time. You can type words, select text with the mouse, click a button to change text to bold, click a button to change text to italic, choose a menu item, and so on. With each word-processing document you create, you choose options in any order that seems appropriate at the time. The word-processing program must be ready to respond to any event you initiate.

Within an event-driven program, a component on which an event is generated is the **source** of the event. A button that a user can click is an example of a source; a text field that a user can use to enter text is another source. An object that is interested in an event is a **listener**. Not all objects listen for all possible events—you probably have used programs in which clicking many areas of the screen has no effect. If you want an object to be a listener for an event, you must register the object as a listener for the source.

Newspapers around the world register with news services, such as the Associated Press or United Press International. The news services maintain a list of subscribers and send each one a story when important national or international events occur. Similarly, a Java component source object (such as a button) maintains a list of registered listeners and notifies all of them (such as a JFrame) when any event occurs, such as a mouse click. When the listener "receives the news," an event-handling method that is part of the listener object responds to the event.

> **NOTE**
> A source object and a listener object can be the same object. For example, you might program a JButton to change its own label when a user clicks it.

To respond to user events within any class you create, you must do the following:

» Prepare your class to accept event messages.
» Tell your class to expect events to happen.
» Tell your class how to respond to events.

PREPARING YOUR CLASS TO ACCEPT EVENT MESSAGES

You prepare your class to accept button-press events by importing the java.awt.event package into your program and adding the phrase implements ActionListener to the class header. The java.awt.event package includes event classes with names such as ActionEvent, ComponentEvent, and TextEvent. ActionListener is an interface—a class containing a set of specifications for methods that you can use. Implementing ActionListener provides you with standard event method specifications that allow your listener to work with ActionEvents, which are the types of events that occur when a user clicks a button.

> **NOTE** You can identify interfaces such as ActionListener because they use the keyword implements. In ordinary language, an item that is implemented is put into service, or used. Implementation has a similar meaning when applied to interfaces. In contrast, packages that are imported are brought into an application, and classes that are added onto are extended.

> **NOTE**
> You learned to create and implement interfaces in Chapter 10.

TELLING YOUR CLASS TO EXPECT EVENTS TO HAPPEN

You tell your class to expect `ActionEvent`s with the **addActionListener() method**. If you have declared a `JButton` named `aButton`, and you want to perform an action when a user clicks `aButton`, `aButton` is the source of a message, and you can think of your class as a target to which to send a message. You learned in Chapter 4 that the `this` reference means "this current object," so the code `aButton.addActionListener(this);` causes any `ActionEvent` messages (button clicks) that come from `aButton` to be sent to "this current object."

> **»NOTE** Not all `Event`s are `ActionEvent`s with an `addActionListener()` method. For example, `KeyListener`s have an `addKeyListener()` method, and `FocusListener`s have an `addFocusListener()` method. Additional event types and methods are covered in more detail in Chapter 14.

TELLING YOUR CLASS HOW TO RESPOND TO EVENTS

The `ActionListener` interface contains the **actionPerformed(ActionEvent e) method** specification. When a class, such as a `JFrame`, has registered as a listener with a `Component` such as a `JButton`, and a user clicks the `JButton`, the `actionPerformed()` method executes. You implement the `actionPerformed()` method, which contains a header and a body, like all methods. You use the following header, in which `e` represents any name you choose for the `Event` (the `JButton` click) that initiated the notification of the `ActionListener` (which is the `JFrame`):

```
public void actionPerformed (ActionEvent e)
```

The body of the method contains any statements that you want to execute when the action occurs. You might want to perform mathematical calculations, construct new objects, produce output, or execute any other operation. For example, Figure 13-25 shows a `JFrame` containing a `JLabel` that prompts the user for a name, a `JTextField` into which the user can type a response, a `JButton` to click, and a second `JLabel` that displays the name entered by the user. Within the `actionPerformed()` method that executes when the user clicks the `pressMe JButton`, the `String` that a user has typed into the `JTextField` is retrieved and stored in the `name` variable. The name is then used as part of a `String` that alters the second `JLabel` on the `JFrame`. Figure 13-26 shows an application that instantiates a `JHelloFrame` object. Figure 13-27 shows two versions of the `JFrame`: the first displays the frame after the user enters "Lindsey" into the `JTextField`, and the second shows the frame after the user clicks the button.

```
import javax.swing.*;
import java.awt.*;
import java.awt.event.*;
public class JHelloFrame extends JFrame implements ActionListener
{
   JLabel question = new JLabel("What is your name?");
   Font bigFont = new Font("Arial", Font.BOLD, 16);
   JTextField answer = new JTextField(10);
   JButton pressMe = new JButton("Press me");
   JLabel greeting = new JLabel("");
   final int WIDTH = 175;
   final int HEIGHT = 225;
   public JHelloFrame()
   {
      super("Hello Frame");
      setSize(WIDTH, HEIGHT);
      setLayout(new FlowLayout());
      question.setFont(bigFont);
      greeting.setFont(bigFont);
      add(question);
      add(answer);
      add(pressMe);
      add(greeting);
      setVisible(true);
      setDefaultCloseOperation(JFrame.EXIT_ON_CLOSE);
      pressMe.addActionListener(this);
   }
   public void actionPerformed(ActionEvent e)
   {
      String name = answer.getText();
      String greet = "Hello, " + name;
      greeting.setText(greet);
   }
}
```

Figure 13-25 The `JHelloFrame` class that produces output when the user clicks the `JButton`

```
public class JHelloDemo
{
   public static void main(String[] args)
   {
      JHelloFrame frame = new JHelloFrame();
   }
}
```

Figure 13-26 An application that instantiates a `JHelloFrame` object

Figure 13-27 Typical execution of the `JHelloDemo` program

When more than one component is added and registered to a `JFrame`, it might be necessary to determine which component was used. For example, in the `JHelloFrame` class in Figure 13-25, you might want the user to be able to either click the button or press Enter in the `JTextField` to view the displayed message. In that case, you would designate both the `pressMe` button and the `answer` text field to be message sources by using the `addActionListener()` method with each, as follows:

```
pressMe.addActionListener(this);
answer.addActionListener(this);
```

These two statements make the `JFrame` (`this`) the receiver of messages. The `JFrame` has only one `actionPerformed()` method, so it is the method that executes when either the `pressMe` button or the `answer` text field sends a message. If you want the same actions to occur whether the user clicks the button or presses Enter in the text field, then you code those actions in the `actionPerformed()` method.

If you want different actions to occur, you must determine the source of the event. Within the `actionPerformed()` method, you can use the `getSource()` method of the object sent to determine which component generated the event. For example, within a method with the header `public void actionPerformed(ActionEvent e)`, e is an `ActionEvent`. `ActionEvent` and other event classes are part of the `java.awt.event` package and are sub-classes of the `EventObject` class. To determine what object generated the `ActionEvent`, you can use the following statement:

```
Object source = e.getSource();
```

▶▶ NOTE
Every object is an `Object`; that is, every instance of a `JButton`, `JTextField`, or other object you create can be stored as an instance of the class named `Object`.

For example, if a `JFrame` contains two `JButtons` named `option1` and `option2`, you can use the following decision structure to take different courses of action based on the button that is clicked:

```
void actionPerformed(ActionEvent e)
{
    Object source = e.getSource();
    if (source == option1)
        //execute these statements when user clicks option1
    else
        //execute these statements when user clicks any other option
}
```

You can also use the `instanceof` keyword inside an event-handling method to determine the source of the event. The `instanceof` keyword is used when it is necessary to know only the component's type, rather than what component triggered the event. For example, if you want to take some action when a user enters data into any `JTextField`, you could use the following method format:

```
void actionPerformed(ActionEvent e)
{
    Object source = e.getSource();
    if(source instanceof JTextField)
    {
        // execute these statements when any JTextField
        // generates the event
    }
}
```

USING THE setEnabled() METHOD

You probably have used computer programs in which a component becomes disabled or unusable. For example, a JButton might become dim and unresponsive when the programmer no longer wants you to have access to the JButton's functionality. You can use the **setEnabled() method** to make a component unavailable and then make it available again in turn, perhaps after a specific series of actions has taken place. The setEnabled() method takes an argument of true if you want to enable a component or false if you want to disable a component. For example, Figure 13-28 shows a JFrame with two JButton objects. The one on top is enabled, but the one on the bottom has been disabled.

Figure 13-28 A JFrame with an enabled and a disabled JButton

»TWO TRUTHS AND A LIE: LEARNING ABOUT EVENT-DRIVEN PROGRAMMING

1. Within an event-driven program, a component on which an event is generated is a listener.
2. You prepare your class to accept button-press events by importing the java.awt.event package into your program and adding the phrase implements ActionListener to the class header.
3. A class that can react to ActionEvents includes an actionPerformed() method.

The false statement is #1. Within an event-driven program, a component on which an event is generated is the source of the event and an object that is interested in an event is a listener.

UNDERSTANDING Swing EVENT LISTENERS

When you need to perform actions based on user button clicks, you use the ActionListener interface. Many types of listeners exist in Java, and each of these listeners can handle a specific event type. A class can implement as many event listeners as it needs—for example, a class might need to respond to both a mouse button press and a keyboard key press, so you might implement ActionListener and KeyListener interfaces. Table 13-2 lists some event listeners and the types of events for which they are used.

Listener	Type of Events	Example
ActionListener	Action events	Button clicks
AdjustmentListener	Adjustment events	Scroll bar moves
ChangeListener	Change events	Slider is repositioned
FocusListener	Keyboard focus events	Text field gains or loses focus
ItemListener	Item events	Check box changes status
KeyListener	Keyboard events	Text is entered
MouseListener	Mouse events	Mouse clicks
MouseMotionListener	Mouse movement events	Mouse rolls
WindowListener	Window events	Window closes

Table 13-2 Alphabetical list of some event listeners

An event occurs every time a user types a character or clicks a mouse button. Any object can be notified of an event as long as it implements the appropriate interface and is registered as an event listener on the appropriate event source. You already know that you establish a relationship between a JButton and a JFrame that contains it by using the addActionListener() method. Similarly, you can create relationships between other Swing components and the classes that react to users' manipulations of them. In Table 13-3, each component listed on the left is associated with a method on the right. For example, when you want a JCheckBox to respond to a user's clicks, you can use the addItemListener() method to register the JCheckBox as the type of object that can create an ItemEvent. The argument you place within the parentheses of the call to the addItemListener() method is the object that should respond to the event—perhaps a JFrame that contains the JCheckBox that generates the event. The format is:

```
theSourceOfTheEvent.addListenerMethod (theClassThatShouldRespond);
```

Component(s)	Associated Listener-Registering Method(s)
JButton, JCheckBox, JComboBox, JTextField, and JRadioButton	addActionListener()
JScrollBar	addAdjustmentListener()
All Swing components	addFocusListener(), addKeyListener(), addMouseListener(), and addMouseMotionListener()
JButton, JCheckBox, JComboBox, and JRadioButton	addItemListener()
All JWindow and JFrame components	addWindowListener()
JSlider and JCheckBox	addChangeListener()

Table 13-3 Some Swing components and their associated listener-registering methods

The class of the object that responds to an event must contain a method that accepts the event object created by the user's action. In other words, when you register a component (such as a JFrame) to be a listener for events generated by another component (such as a JCheckBox), you must write a method that reacts to any generated event. You cannot choose your own name for the reacting methods—specific methods react to specific event types. Table 13-4 lists just some of the methods that react to events.

Listener	Method
ActionListener	actionPerformed(ActionEvent)
AdjustmentListener	adjustmentValueChanged(AdjustmentEvent)
FocusListener	focusGained(FocusEvent) and focusLost(FocusEvent)
ItemListener	itemStateChanged(ItemEvent)

Table 13-4 Selected methods that respond to events

Until you become familiar with the event-handling model, it can seem quite confusing. You will learn more about the event model in Chapter 14. For now, remember these points:

» When you declare a class that handles an event, you create the class to either implement a listener interface or extend a class that implements a listener interface. For example, if a JFrame named MyFrame needs to respond to a user's clicks on a JCheckBox, you would write the following class header:

```
public class MyFrame extends JFrame
    implements ItemListener
```

» If you then declare a class that extends MyFrame, you need not include implements ItemListener in its header. The new class will inherit the implementation.

» Register an instance of the event-handling class as a listener for one or more components. For example, if MyFrame contains a JCheckBox named myCheckBox, then within the JFrame class you would code:

```
myCheckBox.addItemListener(this);
```

» The this reference is to the class in which myCheckBox is declared—in this case, MyFrame. Write a method that accepts the generated event and reacts to it. A method that executes because it is called automatically when an appropriate event occurs is an **event handler**. For example:

```
public void itemStateChanged(ItemEvent event)
{
    // code that executes whenever the event occurs
}
```

TWO TRUTHS AND A LIE: UNDERSTANDING Swing EVENT LISTENERS

1. A class can implement as many event listeners as it needs.
2. Any object can be notified of a mouse click or keyboard press as long as it implements the appropriate interface and is registered as an event listener on the appropriate event source.
3. Every event-handling method accepts a parameter that represents the listener for the event.

The false statement is #3. Every event-handling method accepts a parameter that represents the generated event.

USING THE JCheckBox CLASS

A **JCheckBox** consists of a label positioned beside a square; you can click the square to display or remove a check mark. Usually, you use a JCheckBox to allow the user to turn an option on or off. For example, Figure 13-29 shows the code for an application that uses four JCheckBoxes, and Figure 13-30 shows the output.

```java
import java.awt.*;
import javax.swing.*;
import java.awt.event.*;
public class CheckBoxDemonstration extends JFrame implements ItemListener
{
    FlowLayout flow = new FlowLayout();
    JLabel label = new JLabel("What would you like to drink?");
    JCheckBox coffee = new JCheckBox("Coffee", false);
    JCheckBox cola = new JCheckBox("Cola", false);
    JCheckBox milk = new JCheckBox("Milk", false);
    JCheckBox water = new JCheckBox("Water", false);
    String output, insChosen;
    public CheckBoxDemonstration()
    {
        super("CheckBox Demonstration");
        setDefaultCloseOperation(JFrame.EXIT_ON_CLOSE);
        setLayout(new FlowLayout());
        label.setFont(new Font("Arial", Font.ITALIC, 22));
        coffee.addItemListener(this);
        cola.addItemListener(this);
        milk.addItemListener(this);
        water.addItemListener(this);
        add(label);
        add(coffee);
        add(cola);
        add(milk);
        add(water);
    }
```

Figure 13-29 The CheckBoxDemonstration class (*continued*)

```
    public void itemStateChanged(ItemEvent check)
    {
        // Actions based on choice go here
    }
    public static void main(String[] arguments)
    {
        final int FRAME_WIDTH = 350;
        final int FRAME_HEIGHT = 120;
        CheckBoxDemonstration frame =
            new CheckBoxDemonstration();
        frame.setSize(FRAME_WIDTH, FRAME_HEIGHT);
        frame.setVisible(true);
    }
}
```

Figure 13-29 (*continued*)

>> **NOTE** In the application in Figure 13-29, the CheckBoxDemonstration class and the main() method that instantiates an instance of it are part of the same class. You could also store the two parts in separate classes, as in previous examples.

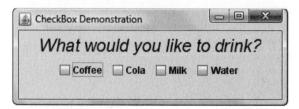

Figure 13-30 Output of the CheckBoxDemonstration class

The inheritance hierarchy of the JCheckBox class is shown in Figure 13-31; frequently used JCheckBox methods appear in Table 13-5.

```
java.lang.Object
   !--java.awt.Component
         !--java.awt.Container
               !--javax.swing.JComponent
                     !--javax.swing.AbstractButton
                           !--javax.swing.JToggleButton
                                 !--javax.swing.JCheckBox
```

Figure 13-31 The inheritance hierarchy of the JCheckBox class

Method	Purpose
`void setText(String)`	Sets the text for the `JCheckBox`
`String getText()`	Returns the `JCheckBox` text
`void setSelected(boolean)`	Sets the state of the `JCheckBox` to `true` for selected or `false` for unselected
`boolean isSelected()`	Gets the current state (checked or unchecked) of the `JCheckBox`

Table 13-5 Frequently used `JCheckBox` methods

Several constructors can be used with `JCheckBox`es. When you construct a `JCheckBox`, you can choose whether to assign it a label; you can also decide whether the `JCheckBox` appears selected (`JCheckBox`es start unselected by default). The following statements create four `JCheckBox` objects—one with no label and unselected, two with labels and unselected, and one with a label and selected.

» `JCheckBox box1 = new JCheckBox();`
    `// No label, unselected`
» `JCheckBox box2 = new JCheckBox("Check here");`
    `// Label, unselected`
» `JCheckBox box3 = new JCheckBox("Check here", false);`
    `// Label, unselected`
» `JCheckBox box4 = new JCheckBox("Check here", true);`
    `// Label, selected`

If you do not initialize a `JCheckBox` with a label and you want to assign one later, or if you want to change an existing label, you can use the `setText()` method, as in the following example:

```
box1.setText("Check this box now");
```

You can set the state of a `JCheckBox` with the `setSelected()` method; for example, you can use the following statement to ensure that `box1` is unchecked:

```
box1.setSelected(false);
```

The `isSelected()` method is most useful in Boolean expressions, as in the following example, which adds one to a `voteCount` variable if `box2` is currently checked:

```
if(box2.isSelected())
   ++voteCount;
```

When the status of a `JCheckBox` changes from unchecked to checked (or from checked to unchecked), an `ItemEvent` is generated, and the `itemStateChanged()` method executes.

You can use the getItem() method to determine which object generated the event and the getStateChange() method to determine whether the event was a selection or a deselection. The getStateChange() method returns an integer that is equal to one of two class variables—ItemEvent.SELECTED or ItemEvent.DESELECTED. For example, in Figure 13-32 the itemStateChanged() method calls the getItem() method, which returns the object named source. Then, the value of source is tested in an if statement to determine if it is equivalent to a JCheckBox object named checkBox. If the two references are to the same object, the code determines whether the checkBox was selected or deselected, and in each case appropriate actions are taken.

```java
public void itemStateChanged(ItemEvent e)
{
    Object source = e.getItem();
    if(source == checkBox)
    {
        int select = e.getStateChange();
        if(select == ItemEvent.SELECTED)
            // statements that execute when the box is checked
        else
            // statements that execute when the box is unchecked
    }
    else
    {
        // statements that execute when the source of the event is
        // some component other than the checkBox object
    }
}
```

Figure 13-32 Using the itemStateChanged() method

»TWO TRUTHS AND A LIE: USING THE JCheckBox CLASS

1. A JCheckBox consists of a label positioned beside a square; you can click the square to display or remove a check mark.
2. When you construct a JCheckBox, you must assign it a label; a new JCheckBox always appears selected.
3. When the status of a JCheckBox changes from unchecked to checked (or from checked to unchecked), an ItemEvent is generated, and the itemStateChanged() method executes.

The false statement is #2. When you construct a JCheckBox, you can choose whether to assign it a label; you can also decide whether the JCheckBox appears selected.

USING THE ButtonGroup CLASS

Sometimes, you want options to be mutually exclusive—that is, you want the user to be able to select only one of several choices. When you create a **ButtonGroup**, you can group several components, such as JCheckBoxes, so a user can select only one at a time. When you group JCheckBox objects, all of the other JCheckBoxes are automatically turned off when the user selects any one check box. The inheritance hierarchy for the ButtonGroup class is shown in Figure 13-33. You can see that ButtonGroup descends directly from the Object class.

```
java.lang.Object
 └--javax.swing.ButtonGroup
```

Figure 13-33 The inheritance hierarchy for the ButtonGroup class

>> **NOTE** Even though it does not begin with a "J", the ButtonGroup class is part of the javax.swing package.

>> **NOTE** A group of JCheckBoxes in which a user can select only one at a time also acts like a set of radio buttons (for example, those used to select preset radio stations on an automobile radio), which you can create using the JRadioButton class. The JRadioButton class is very similar to the JCheckBox class, and you might prefer to use it when you have a list of mutually exclusive user options. Each class is used to present a user with options that can be selected or not. It makes sense to use ButtonGroups with items that can be selected (that is, those that use an isSelected() method). You can find more information about the JRadioButton class at *http://java.sun.com*.

To create a ButtonGroup in a JFrame and then add a JCheckBox, you must perform four steps:

- » Create a ButtonGroup, such as ButtonGroup aGroup = new ButtonGroup();.
- » Create a JCheckBox, such as JCheckBox aBox = new JCheckBox();.
- » Add aBox to aGroup with aGroup.add(aBox);.
- » Add aBox to the JFrame with add(aBox);.

You can create a ButtonGroup and then create the individual JCheckBox objects, or you can create the JCheckBoxes and then create the ButtonGroup.

>> **NOTE** If you create a ButtonGroup but forget to add any JCheckBox objects to it, then the objects act as individual, nonexclusive check boxes.

A user can set one of the JCheckBoxes within a group to "on" by clicking it with the mouse, or the programmer can select a JCheckBox within a ButtonGroup with a statement such as the following:

```
aGroup.setSelected(aBox);
```

If you assign the selected state to multiple JCheckBoxes within a group, each new assignment negates the previous one because only one box can be selected within a group.

You can determine which, if any, of the JCheckBoxes in a ButtonGroup is selected using the isSelected() method.

>> **NOTE** Each individual JCheckBox object has access to every JCheckBox class method, regardless of whether the JCheckBox is part of a ButtonGroup.

After a JCheckBox in a ButtonGroup has been selected, one in the group will always be selected. In other words, you cannot "clear the slate" for all the items that are members of a ButtonGroup. You could cause all the JCheckBoxes in a ButtonGroup to initially *appear* unselected by adding one JCheckBox that is not visible (using the setVisible() method). Then, you could use the setSelected() method to select the invisible JCheckBox, and all the others would appear to be deselected.

1. When you create a ButtonGroup, you can group several components, such as JCheckBoxes, so a user can select multiple options simultaneously.

2. To create a ButtonGroup in a JFrame and then add a JCheckBox, you must add both the JCheckBox to the ButtonGroup and add the ButtonGroup to the JFrame.

3. You can create a ButtonGroup and then create the individual JCheckBox objects, or you can create the JCheckBoxes and then create the ButtonGroup.

The false statement is #1. When you create a ButtonGroup, you can group several components, such as JCheckBoxes, so a user can select only one at a time.

USING THE JComboBox CLASS

A **JComboBox** is a component that combines two features: a display area showing an option and a list box containing additional options. (A list box is also known as a combo box or a drop-down list.) The display area contains either a button that a user can click or an editable field into which the user can type. When a JComboBox appears on the screen, a default option displays. When the user clicks the JComboBox, a list of alternative items drops down; if the user selects one, it replaces the box's displayed item. Figure 13-34 shows a JComboBox as it looks when first displayed and as it looks after a user clicks it. The inheritance hierarchy of the JComboBox class is shown in Figure 13-35.

> **»NOTE**
> The code that produces the JComboBox in Figure 13-34 is contained in the file named JComboBoxDemonstration.java on your Student Disk.

```
java.lang.Object
    !--java.awt.Component
        !--java.awt.Container
            !--javax.swing.JComponent
                !--javax.swing.JComboBox
```

Figure 13-34 A JComboBox before and after the user clicks it

Figure 13-35 The inheritance hierarchy of the JComboBox class

You can build a JComboBox by using a constructor with no arguments and then adding items (for example, Strings) to the list with the addItem() method. The following statements create a JComboBox named majorChoice that contains three options from which a user can choose:

```
JComboBox majorChoice = new JComboBox();
majorChoice.addItem("English");
majorChoice.addItem("Math");
majorChoice.addItem("Sociology");
```

Alternatively, you can construct a JComboBox using an array of Objects as the constructor argument; the Objects in the array become the listed items within the JComboBox.

»NOTE
Users often
expect to view
JComboBox
options in alpha-
betical order. If it
makes sense for
your application,
consider displaying
your options this
way. Another rea-
sonable approach
is to place the most
frequently selected
options first.

For example, the following code creates the same `majorChoice` JComboBox as the preceding code:

```
String[] majorArray = {"English", "Math", "Sociology"};
JComboBox majorChoice = new JComboBox(majorArray);
```

Table 13-6 lists some methods you can use with a JComboBox object. For example, you can use the `setSelectedItem()` or `setSelectedIndex()` method to choose one of the items in a JComboBox to be the initially selected item. You also can use the `getSelectedItem()` or `getSelectedIndex()` method to discover which item is currently selected.

Method	Purpose
`void addItem(Object)`	Adds an item to the list
`void removeItem(Object)`	Removes an item from the list
`void removeAllItems()`	Removes all items from the list
`Object getItemAt(int)`	Returns the list item at the index position specified by the integer argument
`int getItemCount()`	Returns the number of items in the list
`int getMaximumRowCount()`	Returns the maximum number of items the combo box can display without a scroll bar
`int getSelectedIndex()`	Returns the position of the currently selected item
`Object getSelectedItem()`	Returns the currently selected item
`Object[] getSelectedObjects()`	Returns an array containing selected Objects
`void setEditable(boolean)`	Sets the field to be editable or not editable
`void setMaximumRowCount(int)`	Sets the number of rows in the combo box that can display at one time
`void setSelectedIndex(int)`	Selects the index at the position indicated by the argument
`void setSelectedItem(Object)`	Sets the selected item in the combo box display area to be the Object argument

Table 13-6 Some JComboBox class methods

You can treat the list of items in a JComboBox object as an array: the first item is at position 0, the second is at position 1, and so on. It is convenient to use the `getSelectedIndex()` method to determine the list position of the currently selected item; then you can use the index to access corresponding information stored in a parallel array. For example, if a JComboBox named `historyChoice` has been filled with a list of historical events, such as

"Declaration of Independence," "Pearl Harbor," and "Man walks on moon," you can code the following to retrieve the user's choice:

```
int positionOfSelection = historyChoice.getSelectedIndex();
```

The variable `positionOfSelection` now holds the position of the selected item, and you can use the variable to access an array of dates so that you can display the date that corresponds to the selected historical event. For example, if you declare the following, then `dates[positionOfSelection]` holds the year for the selected historical event:

```
int[] dates = {1776, 1941, 1969};
```

>> **NOTE** A `JComboBox` does not have to hold items declared as `Strings`; it can hold an array of `Object`s and display the results of the `toString()` method used with those objects. In other words, instead of using parallel arrays to store historical events and dates, you could design a `HistoricalEvent` class that encapsulates `String`s for the event and `int`s for the date.

In addition to `JComboBox`es for which users click items presented in a list, you can create `JComboBox`es into which users type text. To do this, you use the `setEditable()` method. A drawback to using an editable `JComboBox` is that the text a user types must exactly match an item in the list box. If the user misspells the selection or uses the wrong case, no valid value is returned from the `getSelectedIndex()` method. You can use an `if` statement to test the value returned from `getSelectedIndex()`; if it is negative, the selection did not match any items in the `JComboBox`, and you can issue an appropriate error message.

>>TWO TRUTHS AND A LIE: USING THE `JComboBox` CLASS

1. When a user clicks a `JComboBox`, a list of alternative items drops down; if the user selects one, it replaces the box's displayed item.
2. You must construct a `JComboBox` by using an array of initializers as the constructor argument.
3. You can treat the list of items in a `JComboBox` object as an array: the first item is at position 0, the second at position 1, and so on.

The false statement is #2. You can build a `JComboBox` by using a constructor with no arguments and then adding items (for example, `String`s) to the list, or you can use an array of initializers as the constructor argument.

YOU DO IT

CREATING A `JFrame`

In this section, you will create a `JFrame` object that appears on the screen.

To create a `JFrame` object:

1. Open a new file in your text editor.

2. Type the following statement to import the `javax.swing` classes:

```
import javax.swing.*;
```

3. On the next lines, type the following class header for the JDemoFrame class and its opening curly brace:

```
public class JDemoFrame
{
```

4. On the next lines, type the following main() method header and its opening curly brace:

```
public static void main(String[] args)
{
```

5. Within the body of the main() method, enter the following code to declare a JFrame with a title, set its size, and make it visible. If you neglect to set a JFrame's size, you see only the title bar of the JFrame (because the size is 0 × 0 by default); if you neglect to make the JFrame visible, you do not see anything. Add two closing curly braces—one for the main() method and one for the JDemoFrame class.

```
        JFrame aFrame = new JFrame("This is a frame");
        final int WIDTH = 250;
        final int HEIGHT = 250;
        aFrame.setSize(WIDTH, HEIGHT);
        aFrame.setVisible(true);
    }
}
```

6. Save the file as **JDemoFrame.java**. Compile and then run the program. The output looks like Figure 13-36—an empty JFrame with a title bar, a little taller than it is wide. The JFrame has all the properties of frames you have seen in applications you have used. For example, click the JFrame's **Minimize** button, and the JFrame minimizes to an icon on the Windows taskbar.

Figure 13-36 Output of the JDemoFrame application

7. Click the JFrame's **icon** on the taskbar. The JFrame returns to its previous size.

8. Click the JFrame's **Maximize** button. The JFrame fills the screen.

9. Click the JFrame's **Restore** button. The JFrame returns to its original size.

10. Position your mouse pointer on the JFrame's title bar and then drag the JFrame to a new position on your screen.

11. Click the JFrame's **Close** button. The JFrame disappears or hides. The default behavior of a JFrame is simply to hide when the user clicks the Close button—not to end the program.

12. To end the program and return control to the command line, click the Command Prompt window and then press **Ctrl+C**.

ENDING AN APPLICATION WHEN A JFrame CLOSES

Next, you will modify the JDemoFrame program so that the application ends when the user clicks the JDemoFrame Close button.

To modify the application so it ends when the user clicks the JDemoFrame Close button:

1. Within the JDemoFrame class file, change the class name to JDemoFrameThatCloses.

2. Add a new line of code as the final executable statement within the main() method, as follows:

```
aFrame.setDefaultCloseOperation(JFrame.EXIT_ON_CLOSE);
```

3. Save the file as **JDemoFrameThatCloses.java** and compile and execute the application.

4. When the JFrame appears on your screen, confirm that it still has Minimize, Maximize, and Restore capabilities. Then click the JFrame's **Close** button. The JFrame closes, and the command prompt returns as the program relinquishes control to the operating system.

ADDING COMPONENTS TO A JFrame

Next, you will create a Swing application that displays a JFrame that holds a JLabel, JTextField, and JButton.

To create a JFrame that displays three components:

1. Open a new file in your text editor, then type the following first few lines of an application. The import statements make the Swing and AWT components available, and the class header indicates that the class is a JFrame. The class contains several components: a label, field, and button.

```
import javax.swing.*;
import java.awt.*;
public class JFrameWithComponents extends JFrame
{
    JLabel label = new JLabel("Enter your name");
    JTextField field = new JTextField(12);
    JButton button = new JButton("OK");
```

2. In the JFrameWithComponents constructor, set the JFrame title to "Frame with Components" and the default close operation to exit the program when the JFrame is closed. Set the layout manager. Add the label, field, and button to the JFrame.

> **» NOTE**
> In Chapter 6, you learned to press Ctrl+C to stop a program that contains an infinite loop. This situation is similar—you want to stop a program that does not have a way to end automatically.

```java
public JFrameWithComponents()
{
    super("Frame with Components");
    setDefaultCloseOperation(JFrame.EXIT_ON_CLOSE);
    setLayout(new FlowLayout());
    add(label);
    add(field);
    add(button);
}
```

3. Add a closing curly brace for the class, and then save the file as **JFrameWithComponents.java.**

4. Compile the class and correct any errors.

5. Next, write an application that creates a new JFrameWithComponents named aFrame, sizes it using the setSize() method, and then sets its visible property to true.

```java
import javax.swing.*;
public class CreateJFrameWithComponents
{
    public static void main(String[] args)
    {
        JFrameWithComponents aFrame =
            new JFrameWithComponents();
        final int WIDTH = 350;
        final int HEIGHT = 100;
        aFrame.setSize(WIDTH, HEIGHT);
        aFrame.setVisible(true);
    }
}
```

6. Save the file as **CreateJFrameWithComponents.java**. Compile and then execute the application. The output is shown in Figure 13-37.

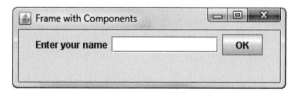

Figure 13-37 Output of the CreateJFrameWithComponents application

7. Click the JButton. It acts like a button should—that is, it appears to be pressed when you click it, but nothing happens because you have not yet written instructions for the button clicks to execute.

8. Close the application.

ADDING FUNCTIONALITY TO A JButton AND A JTextField

Next, you will add functionality to the JButton and JTextField that you created in the JFrameWithComponents class.

To create an application with a functional JButton:

1. Open the **JFrameWithComponents.java** file. Immediately save the file as **JAction.java**.

2. After the existing import statements at the top of the file, add the following import statement that will allow event handling:

```
import java.awt.event.*;
```

3. Change the class name to JAction to match the new filename. Also change the constructor header to match the new class name. Within the constructor, change the string argument to the super() method from "Frame with Components" to "Action".

4. After extends JFrame at the end of the JAction class header, add the following phrase so that the class can respond to ActionEvents:

```
implements ActionListener
```

5. Register the JAction class as a listener for events generated by either the button or the text field by adding the following statements at the end of, but within, the JAction() constructor:

```
button.addActionListener(this);
field.addActionListener(this);
```

6. Just prior to the closing curly brace for the class, add the following actionPerformed() method. The method changes the label's text to "Thank you" and the button's text to "Done" whenever the user clicks the button or presses Enter in the text field.

```
public void actionPerformed(ActionEvent e)
{
    label.setText("Thank you");
    button.setText("Done");
}
```

7. Just after the actionPerformed() method, and just before the closing curly brace for the class, add a main() method to the class so that you can instantiate a JAction object for demonstration purposes.

```
public static void main(String[] args)
{
    JAction aFrame = new JAction();
    final int WIDTH = 250;
    final int HEIGHT = 100;
    aFrame.setSize(WIDTH, HEIGHT);
    aFrame.setVisible(true);
}
```

8. Save the file, then compile and execute it. The output looks like the frame on the left side of Figure 13-38. Type a name in the text field and then click the **OK** button. Its text changes to "Done", and its size increases slightly because the label "Done" requires more space than the label "OK". The other label requires less space than it did because "Thank you" is a shorter message than "Enter your name". Therefore, all the components are redistributed because the FlowLayout manager places as many components as will fit horizontally in the top row before adding components to subsequent rows. The output looks like the right side of Figure 13-38.

Figure 13-38 Output of the JAction application after the user clicks the "OK" button

9. Close the application and then execute it again. This time, enter a name in the text field and press **Enter**. Again, the button text changes, showing that the actionPerformed() method reacts to actions that take place on either the button or the text field.

10. Close the application.

DISTINGUISHING EVENT SOURCES
Next, you will modify the actionPerformed() method of the JAction class so that different results occur depending on which action a user takes.

To determine the event source and take different actions:

1. Open the **JAction.java** file in your text editor if the file is not still open. Immediately save the file as **JAction2.java**.

2. Change the class name and the constructor name to match the new filename by adding **2** to each name.

3. In the main() method, change the statement that instantiates the JFrame object to the following:
```
JAction2 aFrame = new JAction2();
```

4. Within the actionPerformed() method, you can use the named ActionEvent argument and the getSource() method to determine the source of the event. Using an if statement, you can take different actions when the argument represents different sources. For example, you can change the label in the frame to indicate the event's source. Change the actionPerformed() method to:
```
public void actionPerformed(ActionEvent e)
{
   Object source = e.getSource();
   if(source == button)
      label.setText("You clicked the button");
   else
      label.setText("You pressed Enter");
}
```

5. Save the file (as **JAction2.java**), then compile and execute it. Type a name, press **Enter** or click the button, and notice the varying results in the frame's label. For example, Figure 13-39 shows the application after the user has typed a name and pressed Enter.

Figure 13-39 Typical execution of the JAction2 application

6. Close the application.

INCLUDING JCheckBoxes IN AN APPLICATION

Next, you will create an interactive program that Event Handlers Incorporated's clients can use to determine an event's price. The base price of an event is $300, and a user can choose from several options. Holding the event on a weekend adds $100 to the price, hosting over 200 guests adds $200, and including live entertainment adds $400. A guest can select none, some, or all of these premium additions. Each time the user changes the option package, the event price is recalculated.

To write a Swing application that includes three JCheckBox objects used to determine an event's price:

1. Open a new file in your text editor, then type the following first few lines of a Swing application that demonstrates the use of a JCheckBox. Note that the JCheckBoxEventPriceCalculator class implements the ItemListener interface.

```
import javax.swing.*;
import java.awt.*;
import java.awt.event.*;
public class JCheckBoxEventPriceCalculator extends
    JFrame implements ItemListener
{
```

2. Declare the named constants that hold the base price for an event and the premium amounts for holding the event on a weekend, having over 200 guests, and including live entertainment. Also include a variable that holds the total price of the event and initialize it to the value of the base price. Later, depending on the user's selections, premium fees might be added to totalPrice, making it more than BASE_PRICE.

```
final int BASE_PRICE = 300;
final int WEEKEND_PREMIUM = 100;
final int GUEST_PREMIUM = 200;
final int ENTERTAINMENT_PREMIUM = 400;
int totalPrice = BASE_PRICE;
```

3. Declare three JCheckBox objects. Each is labeled with a String that contains a description of the option and the cost of the option. Each JCheckBox starts unchecked or deselected.

```
JCheckBox weekendBox = new JCheckBox
   ("Weekend premium $" + WEEKEND_PREMIUM, false);
JCheckBox guestBox = new
   JCheckBox("Over 200 guests $" + GUEST_PREMIUM, false);
JCheckBox entertainBox = new JCheckBox
   ("Live entertainment $" + ENTERTAINMENT_PREMIUM, false);
```

4. Include JLabels to hold user instructions and information and a JTextField in which to display the total price:

```
JLabel eventHandlersLabel = new JLabel
   ("Event Handlers Incorporated");
JLabel ePrice = new JLabel("The price for your event is");
JTextField totPrice = new JTextField(10);
JLabel optionExplainLabel = new JLabel
   ("Base price for an event is $"
   + BASE_PRICE + ".");
JLabel optionExplainLabel2 = new JLabel
   ("Check the options you want.");
```

5. Begin the JCheckBoxEventPriceCalculator class constructor. Include instructions to set the title by passing it to the JFrame parent class constructor, to set the default close operation, and to set the layout manager. Then add all the necessary components to the JFrame.

```
public JCheckBoxEventPriceCalculator()
{
     super("Event Price Estimator");
     setDefaultCloseOperation(JFrame.EXIT_ON_CLOSE);
     setLayout(new FlowLayout());
     add(eventHandlersLabel);
     add(optionExplainLabel);
     add(optionExplainLabel2);
     add(weekendBox);
     add(guestBox);
     add(entertainBox);
     add(ePrice);
     add(totPrice);
```

6. Continue the constructor by setting the text of the totPrice JTextField to display a dollar sign and the totalPrice value. Register the class as a listener for events generated by each of the three JCheckBoxes. Finally, add a closing curly brace for the constructor.

```
     totPrice.setText("$" + totalPrice);
     weekendBox.addItemListener(this);
     guestBox.addItemListener(this);
     entertainBox.addItemListener(this);
}
```

7. Begin the `itemStateChanged()` method that executes when the user selects or deselects a JCheckBox. Use the appropriate methods to determine which JCheckBox is the source of the current ItemEvent and whether the event was generated by selecting a JCheckBox or by deselecting one.

```java
public void itemStateChanged(ItemEvent event)
{
   Object source = event.getSource();
   int select = event.getStateChange();
```

8. Write a nested if statement that tests whether the source is equivalent to the weekendBox, guestBox, or, by default, the entertainBox. In each case, depending on whether the event was a selection or deselection, add or subtract the corresponding premium fee from the totalPrice. Display the total price in the JTextField and add a closing curly brace for the method.

```java
   if(source == weekendBox)
      if(select == ItemEvent.SELECTED)
         totalPrice += WEEKEND_PREMIUM;
      else
         totalPrice -= WEEKEND_PREMIUM;
   else if(source == guestBox)
   {
      if(select == ItemEvent.SELECTED)
         totalPrice += GUEST_PREMIUM;
      else
         totalPrice -= GUEST_PREMIUM;
   }
   else     // if(source == entertainBox) by default
      if(select == ItemEvent.SELECTED)
         totalPrice += ENTERTAINMENT_PREMIUM;
      else
         totalPrice -= ENTERTAINMENT_PREMIUM;
      totPrice.setText("$" + totalPrice);
}
```

9. Add a main() method that creates an instance of the JFrame and sets its size and visibility. Then add a closing curly brace for the class.

```java
   public static void main(String[] args)
   {
      JCheckBoxEventPriceCalculator aFrame =
         new JCheckBoxEventPriceCalculator();
      final int WIDTH = 300;
      final int HEIGHT = 250;
      aFrame.setSize(WIDTH, HEIGHT);
      aFrame.setVisible(true);
   }
}
```

10. Save the file as **JCheckBoxEventPriceCalculator.java**. Compile and execute the application. The output appears in Figure 13-40 with the base price initially set to $300.

Figure 13-40 Initial output of the JCheckBoxEventPriceCalculator application

11. Select the **Weekend premium** JCheckBox and note the change in the total price of the event. Experiment with selecting and deselecting options to ensure that the price changes correctly. For example, Figure 13-41 shows the Event Price Estimator with the weekend and entertainment options selected, adding a total of $500 to the initial $300 base price.

12. Close the application.

Figure 13-41 Output of the JCheckBoxEventPriceCalculator application after the user has made selections

DON'T DO IT

» Don't forget the "x" in javax when you import Swing components into an application.
» Don't forget to use a JFrame's setVisible() method if you want the JFrame to be visible.
» Don't forget to use setLayout() when you add multiple components to a JFrame.
» Don't forget to call validate() and repaint() after you add or remove a component from a container that has been made visible.
» Don't forget that the ButtonGroup class does not begin with a "J".

KEY TERMS

UI components are user interface components, such as buttons and text fields, with which the user can interact.

Swing components are UI elements such as dialog boxes and buttons; you can usually recognize their names because they begin with J.

Java Foundation Classes, or **JFC**, include Swing component classes and selected classes from the java.awt package.

Lightweight components are written completely in Java and do not have to rely on the code written to run the local operating system.

Heavyweight components require interaction with the local operating system.

A **container** is a type of component that holds other components so that you can treat a group of them as a single entity. Often, a container takes the form of a window that you can drag, resize, minimize, restore, and close.

A **JFrame** is a container with a title bar and border.

Pixels are the picture elements, or tiny dots of light, that make up the image on your computer monitor.

Window decorations are the icons and buttons that are part of a window or frame.

A **look and feel** is the default appearance and behavior of any user interface.

JLabel is a built-in Java Swing class that holds text you can display.

The **add() method** adds components to a container.

The **remove() method** removes components from a container.

The **setText() method** allows you to change the text in a Component that has already been created.

The **getText() method** allows you to retrieve the String of text in a Component.

The **Font class** holds typeface and size information.

The **setFont() method** changes a JLabel's font.

The **typeface argument** to the Font constructor is a String representing a font. Common fonts have names such as Arial, Century, Monospaced, and Times New Roman.

The **style argument** to the Font constructor applies an attribute to displayed text and is one of three values: Font.PLAIN, Font.BOLD, or Font.ITALIC.

The **point size argument** to the Font constructor is an integer that represents about 1/72 of an inch.

A **layout manager** is a class that controls component positioning.

A **BorderLayout** is a layout manager that divides a container into regions.

The **flow layout manager** places components in a row, and when a row is filled, it automatically spills components into the next row. By default, the components in each row are centered.

A **JTextField** is a component into which a user can type a single line of text data.

Editable describes a component that can accept keystrokes.

The **setEditable() method** changes the editable status of a JTextField.

A **JButton** is a Component the user can click with a mouse to make a selection.

Tool tips are popup windows that can help a user understand the purpose of components in an application; a tool tip appears when a user hovers the mouse pointer over the component.

The **setToolTipText() method** defines the text to be displayed in a tool tip.

An **event** occurs when a user takes action on a component.

In an **event-driven program**, the user might initiate any number of events in any order.

The **source** of an event is the component on which an event is generated.

A **listener** is an object that is interested in an event.

You tell a class to expect ActionEvents with the **addActionListener() method**.

The **actionPerformed(ActionEvent e) method** specification defines the actions that occur in response to an event.

The **setEnabled() method** makes a component available or dimmed and unavailable.

An **event handler** is a method that executes because it is called automatically when an appropriate event occurs.

A **JCheckBox** consists of a label positioned beside a square; you can click the square to display or remove a check mark. Usually, you use a JCheckBox to allow the user to turn an option on or off.

A **ButtonGroup** groups several components, such as JCheckBoxes, so that a user can select only one at a time.

A **JComboBox** is a component that combines two features: a display area showing an option and a list box containing additional options. The display area contains either a button that a user can click or an editable field into which the user can type.

CHAPTER SUMMARY

» Swing components are UI elements such as dialog boxes and buttons. Each Swing component is a descendant of a JComponent, which in turn inherits from the java.awt.Container class. When you use Swing components, you usually place them in a container—a type of component that holds other components. Containers are defined in the Container class. Often, a container takes the form of a window that you can drag, resize, minimize, restore, and close.

» A JFrame holds and displays other objects. Useful methods include setSize(), setTitle(), setVisible(), setBounds(), and setDefaultCloseOperation(). JFrames include a title bar at the top containing text information, and Minimize, Maximize or Restore, and Close buttons in the frame's upper-right corner. When a user closes a JFrame by clicking the Close button in the upper-right corner, the default behavior is for the JFrame to become hidden and for the application to keep running.

» JLabel is a built-in Java Swing class that holds text you can display. You then can add a JLabel to a JFrame using the add() method. The setFont() method changes the font typeface, style, and point size.

» To place multiple components at specified positions in a container so that they do not hide each other, you must use a layout manager—a class that controls component positioning. The normal (default) behavior of a JFrame is to use a layout format named BorderLayout. When you use a FlowLayout instead of a BorderLayout, components do not lie on top of each other. Instead, components are placed in a row, and when a row is filled, components automatically spill into the next row.

» The advantage to creating a child class of JFrame is that you can set the JFrame's properties within your object's constructor; then, when you create your JFrame child object, it is automatically endowed with the features you have specified, such as title, size, and default close operation.

» A JTextField is a component into which a user can type a single line of text data.

» A JButton is a Component the user can click with a mouse to make a selection. Tool tips are popup windows that can help a user understand the purpose of components in an application; the tool tip appears when a user hovers the mouse pointer over the component.

» Within an event-driven program, a component on which an event is generated is the source of the event. An object that is interested in an event is a listener. You prepare your class to accept events by importing the java.awt.event package into your program and adding the phrase implements ActionListener to the class header. You tell your class to expect ActionEvents with the addActionListener() method. The ActionListener interface contains the actionPerformed(ActionEvent e) method specification. You implement this method with the actions that should occur in response to the event. Within the actionPerformed() method, you can use the getSource() method of the object sent to determine which component generated the event.

» A class can implement as many event listeners as it needs. Examples of event listeners are ActionListener, ItemListener, KeyListener, and MouseListener. Any object can be notified of an event as long as it implements the appropriate interface and is registered as an event listener on the appropriate event source. To add a listener method to a source, you must use the appropriate designated add method. Specific methods react to specific event types; they include actionPerformed() and itemStateChanged().

» A JCheckBox consists of a label positioned beside a square; you can click the square to display or remove a check mark. Usually, you use a JCheckBox to allow the user to turn an option on or off. When the status of a JCheckBox changes from unchecked to checked (or from checked to unchecked), an ItemEvent is generated and the itemStateChanged() method executes.

» A ButtonGroup groups components so that a user can select only one at a time. After a JCheckBox in a ButtonGroup has been selected, one in the group will always be selected.

» A JComboBox is a component that combines two features: a display area showing an option and a list box containing additional options. You can treat the list of items in a JComboBox object as an array and use the getSelectedIndex() method to determine the list position of the currently selected item.

REVIEW QUESTIONS

1. A JFrame is a descendant of each of the following classes except the _____ class.

   a. Component   c. Window

   b. Container   d. Jar

2. A programmer might prefer using a JFrame instead of a Window because, unlike a window, a JFrame _____ .

   a. can hold other objects   c. can have descendants

   b. can be made visible   d. has a title bar and border

3. The statement JFrame myFrame = new JFrame(); creates a JFrame that is _____ .

   a. invisible and has no title   c. visible and has no title

   b. invisible and has a title   d. visible and has a title

4. To create a JFrame named aFrame that is 300 pixels wide by 200 pixels tall, you can _____ .

   a. use the declaration JFrame aFrame = new JFrame(300, 200);

   b. declare a JFrame named aFrame and then code aFrame.setSize(300, 200);

   c. declare a JFrame named aFrame and then code aFrame.setBounds(300, 200);

   d. use any of the above

5. When a user closes a JFrame, the default behavior is for _____ .

   a. the JFrame to close and the application to keep running

   b. the JFrame to become hidden and the application to keep running

   c. the JFrame to close and the application to exit

   d. nothing to happen

6. An advantage of extending the JFrame class is _____ .

   a. you can set the child class properties within the class constructor

   b. there is no other way to cause an application to close when the user clicks a JFrame's Close button

   c. there is no other way to make a JFrame visible

   d. all of the above

7. Suppose you create an application in which you instantiate a JFrame named frame1 and a JLabel named label1. Which of the following statements within the application adds label1 to frame1?

    a. label1.add(frame1);   c. this.add(label1);

    b. frame1.add(label1);   d. two of the above

8. The arguments required by the Font constructor include all of the following except _____ .

    a. typeface   c. mode

    b. style   d. point size

9. A class that controls component positioning in a JFrame is a _____ .

    a. container   c. formatter

    b. layout manager   d. design supervisor

10. Which of the following is not true of a JTextField?

    a. A user can type text data into it.

    b. Its data can be set in the program instead of by the user.

    c. You can set its attributes so that a user cannot type in it.

    d. It is a type of Container.

11. _____ are popup windows that can help a user understand the purpose of components in an application and that appear when a user hovers the mouse pointer over the component.

    a. Navigation notes   c. Help icons

    b. Tool tips   d. Graphic suggestions

12. Within an event-driven program, a component on which an event is generated is the _____ .

    a. performer   c. source

    b. listener   d. handler

13. A class that will respond to button-press events must use which phrase in its header?

    a. import java.event   c. extends JFrame

    b. extends Action   d. implements ActionListener

14. A `JFrame` contains a `JButton` named `button1` that should execute an `actionPerformed()` method when clicked. Which statement is needed in the `JFrame` class?

    a. `addActionListener(this);`

    b. `addActionListener(button1);`

    c. `button1.addActionListener(this);`

    d. `this.addActionListener(button1);`

15. An application that must respond to button clicks must implement a(n) _____ .

    a. `ButtonListener`

    b. `ItemListener`

    c. `ClickListener`

    d. `ActionListener`

16. A class can implement _____ .

    a. one listener

    b. two listeners

    c. as many listeners as it needs

    d. any number of listeners as long as they are not conflicting listeners

17. When you write a method that reacts to `JCheckBox` changes, you name the method _____ .

    a. `itemStateChanged()`

    b. `actionPerformed()`

    c. `checkBoxChanged()`

    d. any legal identifier you choose

18. If a class contains two components that might each generate a specific event type, you can determine which component caused the event by using the _____ method.

    a. `addActionListener()`

    b. `getSource()`

    c. `whichOne()`

    d. `identifyOrigin()`

19. To group several components such as `JCheckBoxes` so that a user can select only one at a time, you create a _____ .

    a. `JCheckBoxGroup`

    b. `CheckBoxGroup`

    c. `JButtonGroup`

    d. `ButtonGroup`

20. Suppose you have declared a `ButtonGroup` named `threeOptions` and added three `JCheckBoxes` named `box1`, `box2`, and `box3` to it. If you code `threeOptions.setSelected(box1);`, then `threeOptions.setSelected(box2);`, and then `threeOptions.setSelected(box3);`, the selected box(es) are _____ .

    a. `box1`

    b. `box2`

    c. `box3`

    d. all of the above

EXERCISES

1. Write an application that displays a JFrame containing the words to any well-known nursery rhyme. Save the file as **JNurseryRhyme.java**.

2. a. Write an application that instantiates a JFrame that contains a JButton. Disable the JButton after the user clicks it. Save the file as **JFrameDisableButton.java**.

    b. Modify the JFrameDisableButton program so that the JButton is not disabled until the user has clicked at least eight times. At that point, display a JLabel that indicates "That's enough!". Save the file as **JFrameDisableButton2.java**.

3. Create an application with a JFrame that holds five labels describing reasons that a customer might not buy your product (for example, "Too expensive"). Every time the user clicks a JButton, remove one of the negative reasons. Save the file as **JDemoResistance.java**.

4. Write an application for a construction company to handle a customer's order to build a new home. Use separate ButtonGroups to allow the customer to select one of four models, the number of bedrooms, and a garage type. Assume that the models are the Aspen, $100,000; the Brittany, $120,000; the Colonial, $180,000; or the Dartmoor, $250,000. Assume that any model can have two, three, or four bedrooms and that each bedroom adds $10,500 to the base price. Assume that the garage type can be zero-, one-, two-, or three-car, and that each car adds $7,775 to the price. Save the file as **JMyNewHome.java**.

5. a. Write an application for a video store. Place the names of 10 of your favorite movies in a combo box. Let the user select a movie to rent. Charge $2.00 for most movies, $1.00 for two movies you don't like very much, and $3.00 for your favorite movie. Display the rental fee. Save the file as **JVideo.java**.

    b. Change the JVideo application to include an editable combo box. Allow the user to type the name of the movie to rent. Display an appropriate error message if the desired movie is not available. Save the file as **JVideo2.java**.

6. Design an application for a pizzeria. The user makes pizza order choices from list boxes, and the application displays the price. The user can choose a pizza size of small ($7), medium ($9), large ($11), or extra large ($14), and one of any number of toppings. There is no additional charge for cheese, but any other topping adds $1 to the base price. Offer at least five different topping choices. Save the file as **JPizza.java**.

7. Write an application that allows a user to select a favorite basketball team from a list box. Include at least five teams in the list, and display the chosen team in a text field after the user makes a selection. Save the file as **JBasketball.java**.

8. Write an application that allows the user to choose insurance options in JCheckBoxes. Use a ButtonGroup to allow the user to select only one of two insurance types—HMO

(health maintenance organization) or PPO (preferred provider organization). Use regular (single) JCheckBoxes for dental insurance and vision insurance options; the user can select one option, both options, or neither option. As the user selects each option, display its name and price in a text field; the HMO costs $200 per month, the PPO costs $600 per month, the dental coverage adds $75 per month, and the vision care adds $20 per month. When a user deselects an item, make the text field blank. Save the file as **JInsurance.java**.

9. a. Search the Java Web site at *http://java.sun.com* for information on how to use a JTextArea, its constructors, and its setText() and append() methods. Write an application that allows the user to select options for a dormitory room. Use JCheckBoxes for options such as private room, Internet connection, cable TV connection, microwave, refrigerator, and so on. When the application starts, use a text area to display a message listing the options that are not yet selected. As the user selects and deselects options, add appropriate messages to the common text area so that it accumulates a running list that reflects the user's choices. Save the file as **JDorm.java**.

    b. Modify the JDorm application so that instead of a running list of the user's choices, the application displays only the current choices. Save the file as **JDorm2.java**.

10. Create an application for Koch's Cottages, a weekend getaway resort that rents cottages and boats to use on the local lake. The application allows users to compute the price of their vacations. Include mutually exclusive check boxes to select a one-bedroom cottage at $600 per week or a two-bedroom cottage at $850 per week. The user can also choose a rowboat rental at $60 per week. Include labels as appropriate to explain the application's functionality. Save the file as **JCottageFrame.java**.

DEBUGGING EXERCISES

Each of the following files in the Chapter.13 folder on your Student Disk has syntax and/or logic errors. In each case, determine the problem and fix the program. After you correct the errors, save each file using the same filename preceded with Fix. For example, DebugThirteen1.java will become FixDebugThirteen1.java.

a. DebugThirteen1.java

b. DebugThirteen2.java

c. DebugThirteen3.java

d. DebugThirteen4.java

GAME ZONE

1. a. Create a quiz game that displays, in turn, five questions about any topic of your choice. All five questions should have the same three possible multiple-choice answers. For example, you might ask trivia questions about U.S. states for which the correct response is either California, Florida, or New York. After each question is displayed, allow the user to choose one, two, or all three answers by selecting `JCheckBoxes`. In other words, if the user is sure of an answer, he will select just one box, but if he is uncertain, he might select two or three boxes. When the user is ready to submit the answer(s), he clicks a button. If the user's answer to the question is correct and he has selected just one box, award 5 points. If the user is correct but has selected two boxes, award 2 points. If the user has selected all three boxes, award 1 point. If the user has selected fewer than three boxes but is incorrect, the user receives 0 points. A total of 25 points is possible. If the user has accumulated more than 21 points at the end of the quiz, display the message "Fantastic!". If the user has accumulated more than 15 points, display the message "Very good", and if the user has accumulated fewer points, display "OK". Save the file as **HedgeYourBet.java**.

    b. Modify the `HedgeYourBet` game so that it stores the player's score from the last game in a file and displays the previous score at the start of each new game. (The first time you play the game, the previous score should be 0.) Save the game as **HedgeYourBetUsingFile.java**.

    c. Modify the `HedgeYourBetUsingFile` game so that it records and displays the best previous score rather than the most immediate previous score. Save the game as **HedgeYourBetUsingFile2.java**.

2. In Chapter 5, you created a lottery game application. Create a similar game using check boxes. For this game, generate six random numbers, each between 0 and 30 inclusive. Allow the user to choose six check boxes to play the game. (Do not allow the user to choose more than six boxes.) After the player has chosen six numbers, display the randomly selected numbers, the player's numbers, and the amount of money the user has won, as follows:

Matching Numbers	Award ($)
Three matches	100
Four matches	10,000
Five matches	50,000
Six matches	1,000,000
Zero, one, or two matches	0

Save the file as **JLottery2.java**.

3. a. Create a game called Last Man Standing in which the objective is to select the last remaining JCheckBox. The game contains 10 JCheckBoxes. The player can choose one, two, or three boxes, and then click a JButton to indicate the turn is complete. The computer then randomly selects one, two, or three JCheckBox objects. When the last JCheckBox is selected, display a message indicating the winner. Save the game as **LastManStanding.java**.

b. In the current version of the Last Man Standing game, the computer might seem to make strategic mistakes because of its random selections. For example, when only two JCheckBox objects are left, the computer might randomly choose to check only one, allowing the player to check the last one and win. Modify the game to make it as smart as possible, using a random value for the number of the computer's selections only when there is no superior alternative. Save the improved game as **SmarterLastManStanding.java**.

TOUGH QUESTIONS

1. What happens when you use the following Font in a JLabel?

   ```
   Font newFont = new Font("Arial", 12, Font.BOLD);
   ```

2. The AWT provided for UI objects before Swing was invented. What are the advantages and disadvantages of using Swing components over those defined in the AWT?

UP FOR DISCUSSION

1. Suppose you are asked to create a Web application that allows users to play online gambling games in which they can win and lose real money after providing a credit card number. Would you want to work on such a site? Would you impose any restrictions on users' losses or the amount of time they can play in a day? If your supervisors asked you to create a Web site that would be so engaging that gamblers would not want to leave it, would you agree to write the application? If a family member of an addicted gambler contacted you (as the Webmaster of the site) and asked that their relative be barred from further gambling, would you block the user?

2. Would you ever use a computer dating site? Would you go on a date with someone you met over the Web? What precautions would you take before such a date?

3. At least one lawsuit has been filed by a Web user who claims a Web site discriminated against him on the basis of marital status. The Web site is a dating service that does not allow married participants. How do you feel about this case?

14

ADVANCED GUI TOPICS

In this chapter, you will:

Learn about content panes
Use color
Learn more about layout managers
Use `JPanel`s to increase layout options
Create `JScrollPane`s
Understand events and event handling more thoroughly
Use the `AWTEvent` class methods
Handle mouse events
Use menus

JAVA ON THE JOB, SCENE 14

You have been developing Java applications at Event Handlers Incorporated for several months now. "I love this job," you tell Lynn Greenbrier one day. "I've learned so much, yet there's so much more I don't know. Sometimes, I look at a program that I've created and think how far I've come; other times, I realize I barely have a start in Java."

"Go on," Lynn urges. "What do you need to know more about right now?"

"Well, I wish it were easier to place components accurately within `JFrame`s," you say. "I want to be able to create more complex applications, and one thing I'm really confused about is handling events. You've taught me about registering objects as listeners and about listening and handling, but I want to learn more about the big picture."

"Event handling is a complicated system," Lynn says. "Let's see if I can help you organize it in your mind. After all, we are the Event Handlers!"

UNDERSTANDING THE CONTENT PANE

The `JFrame` class is a **top-level container** `Swing` class. (The other two top-level container classes are `JDialog` and `JApplet`.) Every GUI component that appears on-screen must be part of a containment hierarchy. A **containment hierarchy** is a tree of components that has a top-level container as its root (that is, at its uppermost level). Every top-level container has a **content pane** that contains all the visible components in the container's user interface. The content pane can contain some components like `JButton`s directly, or it can hold other containers, like `JPanel`s, that in turn contain such components.

A top-level container can contain a menu bar. Conventionally, a **menu bar** is a horizontal strip that is placed at the top of a container and that contains user options. The menu bar, if there is one, is just above (and separate from) the content pane. A **glass pane** resides above the content pane.

> **»NOTE** The glass pane is a powerful container feature. Tool tips, which you learned about in Chapter 13, reside on the glass pane. You also can draw your own graphics on the glass pane "on top of" components on a `JFrame` or `JApplet`. (You will learn about drawing in Chapter 15, and about `JApplet`s in Chapter 16.) If you add a `MouseListener` to the glass pane, it prevents the mouse from triggering events on the components below the glass pane on the `JFrame`.

> **»NOTE**
> An additional layered pane exists above the root pane, but it is not often used explicitly by Java programmers. For more details, see *http://java.sun.com*.

Figure 14-1 shows the relationship between a `JFrame` and its root, content, and glass panes.

> **»NOTE**
> Later in this chapter, you will learn how to add menu bars to `JFrame`s.

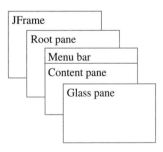

Figure 14-1 Parts of a `JFrame`

Whenever you create a JFrame (or other top-level container), you can get a reference to its content pane using the **getContentPane() method**. In Chapter 13, you added and removed components from JFrames and set their layout managers without understanding that you were using the content pane. You had this ability because Java automatically converts add(), remove(), and setLayoutManager() statements to more complete versions. For example, the following two statements are equivalent within a class that descends from JFrame:

```
add(aButton);

getContentPane().add(aButton);
```

Although you do not need to worry about the content pane if you only add components to, remove components from, or set the layout manager of a JFrame, you must refer to the content pane for all other actions, such as setting the background color.

When you write an application that adds multiple components to a content pane, it is more efficient to declare an object that represents the content pane than to keep calling the getContentPane() method. For example, consider the following code that adds three buttons to a JFrame:

```
getContentPane().add(button1);
getContentPane().add(button2);
getContentPane().add(button3);
```

You might prefer to write the following statements. The call to getContentPane() is made once, its reference is stored in a variable, and the reference name is used repeatedly with the call to the add() method:

```
Container con = getContentPane();
con.add(button1);
con.add(button2);
con.add(button3);
```

As an example, the class in Figure 14-2 creates a JFrame like the ones you created throughout Chapter 13. The getContentPane() method assigns a reference to a Container named con, and the Container reference is used later with the setLayout() and add() methods.

>> **NOTE** To keep the example simple in Figure 14-2, the default close operation was not set and the button was not assigned any tasks.

```
import java.awt.*;
import javax.swing.*;
public class JFrameWithExplicitContentPane extends JFrame
{
    private final int SIZE = 180;
    private Container con = getContentPane();
    private JButton button = new JButton("Press Me");
    public JFrameWithExplicitContentPane()
    {
        super("Frame");
        setSize(SIZE, SIZE);
        setVisible(true);
        con.setLayout(new FlowLayout());
        con.add(button);
    }
    public static void main(String[] args)
    {
        JFrameWithExplicitContentPane frame =
            new JFrameWithExplicitContentPane();
    }
}
```

Figure 14-2 The `JFrameWithExplicitContentPane` class

Figure 14-3 shows the result. The frame constructed from the class in Figure 14-2 is identical to the one that would be constructed if the shaded parts were omitted.

Figure 14-3 Output of the `JFrameWithExplicitContentPane` application

A problem arises when you want to use methods other than `add()`, `remove()`, or `setLayout()`. For example, Figure 14-4 shows a class in which `getContentPane()` is not called. The only changes from the class in Figure 14-2 are shaded—the class name is different, and a call is made to `setBackground()`. The intention is to set the background color of the frame to blue. (You will learn more about the `setBackground()` method in the next section.)

```
import java.awt.*;
import javax.swing.*;
public class JFrameWithoutExplicitContentPane extends JFrame
{
   private final int SIZE = 180;
   private JButton button = new JButton("Press Me");
   public JFrameWithoutExplicitContentPane()
   {
      super("Frame");
      setSize(SIZE, SIZE);
      setVisible(true);
      setLayout(new FlowLayout());
      add(button);
      setBackground(Color.BLUE);            ≫DON'T DO IT
   }                                        The setBackground()
                                            call has no effect.
   public static void main(String[] args)
   {
      JFrameWithoutExplicitContentPane frame =
         new JFrameWithoutExplicitContentPane();
   }
}
```

Figure 14-4 The `JFrameWithoutExplicitContentPane` class

Figure 14-5 shows the output when the class in Figure 14-4 is executed. The background color is not blue; it is the same as if there was no `setBackground()` call at all. That's because although the background of the `JFrame` has been set to blue, its content pane has not, and the content pane is what the viewer sees.

Figure 14-5 Execution of the `JFrameWithoutExplicitContentPane` application

Figure 14-6 shows the output when a `getContentPane()` call is added to a similar class in which `getContentPane()` is used. In this version, the content pane background is set to blue, and when the program executes, the color is visible. Figure 14-7 shows the results.

```
import java.awt.*;
import javax.swing.*;
public class JFrameWithExplicitContentPane2 extends JFrame
{
    private final int SIZE = 180;
    private Container con = getContentPane();
    private JButton button = new JButton("Press Me");
    public JFrameWithExplicitContentPane2()
    {
        super("Frame");
        setSize(SIZE, SIZE);
        setVisible(true);
        con.setLayout(new FlowLayout());
        con.add(button);
        con.setBackground(Color.BLUE);
    }
    public static void main(String[] args)
    {
        JFrameWithExplicitContentPane2 frame =
            new JFrameWithExplicitContentPane2();
    }
}
```

Figure 14-6 The `JFrameWithExplicitContentPane2` class

Figure 14-7 Output of the `JFrameWithExplicitContentPane2` application

»NOTE In the class in Figure 14-6, the reference to `con` could be omitted with no effect from the statements that set the layout manager and add the button. This book will follow the convention of using the content pane for `add()`, `remove()`, and `setLayout()` operations if it is required for other operations in the same class. By consistently referring to `con` explicitly, it is clearer to someone reading your program that the operations are taking place on the same level.

»TWO TRUTHS AND A LIE: UNDERSTANDING THE CONTENT PANE

1. Every Java component has a content pane that contains all the visible parts a user sees.

2. Whenever you create a `JFrame`, you can get a reference to its content pane using the `getContentPane()` method.

3. When you change the background color of a `JFrame`, you should change the content pane's color and not the `JFrame`'s color.

The false statement is #1. Every *top-level container* has a content pane that contains all the visible components in the container's user interface.

USING COLOR

In the application in Figure 14-6, you can see that Java contains a **Color class** that defines colors for you to use in your applications. The Color class can be used with the setBackground() and setForeground() methods of the Component class to make your applications more attractive and interesting. When you use the Color class, you include the statement import java.awt.*; at the top of your class file.

The Color class defines named constants that represent 13 colors, as shown in Table 14-1. Java constants are usually written in all uppercase letters, as you learned in Chapter 4. However, Java's creators declared two constants for every color in the Color class—an uppercase version, such as BLUE, and a lowercase version, such as blue. Earlier versions of Java contained only the lowercase Color constants. (The uppercase Color constants use an underscore in DARK_GRAY and LIGHT_GRAY; the lowercase versions are a single word: darkgray and lightgray.)

BLACK	GREEN	RED
BLUE	LIGHT_GRAY	WHITE
CYAN	MAGENTA	YELLOW
DARK_GRAY	ORANGE	
GRAY	PINK	

Table 14-1 Color class constants

You can also create your own Color object with the following statement:

```
Color someColor = new Color(r, g, b);
```

In this statement, r, g, and b are numbers representing the intensities of red, green, and blue you want in your color. The numbers can range from 0 to 255. For example, the following statement produces a dark purple color that has red and blue components, but no green:

```
Color darkPurple = new Color(100, 0, 100);
```

You can create more than 16 million custom colors using this approach.

You can discover the red, green, or blue components of any existing color with the methods getRed(), getGreen(), and getBlue(). Each of these methods returns an integer. For example, you can discover the amount of red in MAGENTA by printing the value of Color.MAGENTA.getRed();.

Figure 14-8 shows a short application that sets the background color of a JFrame's content pane and sets both the foreground and background colors of a JButton. Figure 14-9 shows the output.

>> **NOTE**
Some computers cannot display each of the 16 million possible colors. Each computer displays the color it can.

>> **NOTE**
The color black is created using r, g, and b values 0, 0, 0. White is created by 255, 255, 255.

```
import java.awt.*;
import javax.swing.*;
public class JFrameWithColor extends JFrame
{
    private final int SIZE = 180;
    private Container con = getContentPane();
    private JButton button = new JButton("Press Me");
    public JFrameWithColor()
    {
        super("Frame");
        setSize(SIZE, SIZE);
        setVisible(true);
        con.setLayout(new FlowLayout());
        con.add(button);
        con.setBackground(Color.YELLOW);
        button.setBackground(Color.RED);
        button.setForeground(Color.WHITE);
    }
    public static void main(String[] args)
    {
        JFrameWithColor frame =
            new JFrameWithColor();
    }
}
```

Figure 14-8 The `JFrameWithColor` class

Figure 14-9 Execution of the `JFrameWithColor` application

»TWO TRUTHS AND A LIE: USING COLOR

1. The `Color` class can be used with the `setBackground()` and `setForeground()` methods of the `Component` class to make your applications more attractive and interesting.

2. The `Color` class defines named constants that represent 256 colors.

3. You can create your own `Color` object using values that represent the intensities of red, green, and blue that you want in your color.

The false statement is #2. The `Color` class defines named constants that represent 13 colors.

LEARNING MORE ABOUT LAYOUT MANAGERS

A layout manager is an object that controls the size and position (that is, the layout) of components inside a `Container` object. The layout manager that you assign to the window determines how the components are sized and positioned within the window. For example, you have already learned that the `FlowLayout` layout manager positions components in rows from left to right across their container. Layout managers are interface classes that are part of the JDK; they align your components so the components neither crowd each other nor overlap. For example, one layout manager arranges components in equally spaced columns and rows; another layout manager centers components within their container. Each layout manager defines methods that arrange components within a `Container`; each component you place within a `Container` can also be a `Container` itself, so you can assign layout managers within layout managers. The Java platform supplies layout managers that range from the very simple (`FlowLayout` and `GridLayout`) to the special purpose (`BorderLayout` and `CardLayout`) to the very flexible (`GridBagLayout` and `BoxLayout`). Table 14-2 lists each layout manager and the situations in which each is commonly used.

Layout Manager	When to Use
BorderLayout	Use when you add components to a maximum of five sections arranged in north, south, east, west, and center positions.
FlowLayout	Use when you need to add components from left to right; FlowLayout automatically moves to the next row when needed, and each component takes its preferred size.
GridLayout	Use when you need to add components into a grid of rows and columns; each component is the same size.
CardLayout	Use when you need to add components that are displayed one at a time.
BoxLayout	Use when you need to add components into a single row or a single column.
GridBagLayout	Use when you need to set size, placement, and alignment constraints for every component that you add.

Table 14-2 Java layout managers

USING BorderLayout

The **BorderLayout manager** is the default manager class for all content panes. You can use the `BorderLayout` class with any container that has five or fewer components. (However, any of the components could be a container that holds even more components.) When you use the `BorderLayout` manager, the components fill the screen in five regions: north, south, east, west,

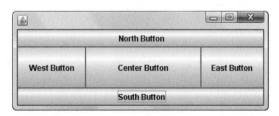

Figure 14-10 Output of the `JDemoBorderLayout` application

and center. Figure 14-10 shows a `JFrame` that contains five `JButton` objects that fill the five regions in a content pane that uses `BorderLayout`.

When you add a component to a container that uses BorderLayout, the add() method uses two arguments: the component and the region to which the component is added. The BorderLayout class provides five named constants for the regions—BorderLayout.NORTH, .SOUTH, .EAST, .WEST, and .CENTER—or you can use the Strings those constants represent: "North", "South", "East", "West", or "Center". Figure 14-11 shows the class that creates the output in Figure 14-10.

```java
import javax.swing.*;
import java.awt.*;
public class JDemoBorderLayout extends JFrame
{
    private JButton nb = new JButton("North Button");
    private JButton sb = new JButton("South Button");
    private JButton eb = new JButton("East Button");
    private JButton wb = new JButton("West Button");
    private JButton cb = new JButton("Center Button");
    public JDemoBorderLayout()
    {
        setLayout(new BorderLayout());
        add(nb, BorderLayout.NORTH);
        add(sb, BorderLayout.SOUTH);
        add(eb, BorderLayout.EAST);
        add(wb, BorderLayout.WEST);
        add(cb, BorderLayout.CENTER);
        setVisible(true);
        setSize(400, 150);
    }
    public static void main(String[] args)
    {
        JDemoBorderLayout frame = new JDemoBorderLayout();
    }
}
```

Figure 14-11 The JDemoBorderLayout class

> **NOTE** Figure 14-11 does not explicitly retrieve the content pane because it is not required by any operations in the class. You could alter the program to retrieve the content pane and then use it with each add() method call with no difference in the output.

> **NOTE** When using BorderLayout, you can use the constants PAGE_START, PAGE_END, LINE_START, LINE_END, and CENTER instead of NORTH, SOUTH, EAST, WEST, and CENTER. Rather than using geographical references, these constants correspond to positions as you might picture them on a printed page.

> **NOTE** In Java 5.0 and later you can use the static import feature, which allows you to use a static constant without the class name. For example, if you add the following import statement at the top of your file, you can simply refer to CENTER instead of BorderLayout.CENTER:
> ```java
> import static java.awt.BorderLayout.*;
> ```

When you place exactly five components in a container and use `BorderLayout`, each component fills one entire region, as illustrated in Figure 14-10. When the application runs, Java determines the exact size of each component based on the component's contents. When you resize a `Container` that uses `BorderLayout`, the regions also change in size. If you drag the `Container`'s border to make it wider, the north, south, and center regions become wider, but the east and west regions do not change. If you increase the `Container`'s height, the east, west, and center regions become taller, but the north and south regions do not change.

When you create a `Container` named con, you can set its layout manager to `BorderLayout` with the following statement:

```
con.setLayout(new BorderLayout());
```

Similarly, within a child class of `JFrame`, you can use either of the following statements to set the layout manager:

```
setLayout(new BorderLayout());

this.setLayout(new BorderLayout());
```

However, it's not necessary to use any of these statements to specify `BorderLayout` because it is the default layout manager for all content panes; that's why, in Chapter 13, you had to specify `FlowLayout` to acquire the easier-to-use manager.

When you use `BorderLayout`, you are not required to add components into each of the five regions. If you add fewer components, any empty component regions disappear, and the remaining components expand to fill the available space. If any or all of the north, south, east, or west areas are left out, the center area spreads into the missing area or areas. However, if the center area is left out, the north, south, east, or west areas do not change.

USING `FlowLayout`

Recall from Chapter 13 that you can use the **FlowLayout manager** class to arrange components in rows across the width of a `Container`—you used `FlowLayout` with the content panes of `JFrame`s in that chapter. With `FlowLayout`, each `Component` that you add is placed to the right of previously added components in a row; or, if the current row is filled, the `Component` is placed to start a new row.

When you use `BorderLayout`, the `Component`s you add fill their regions—that is, each `Component` expands or contracts based on its region's size. However, when you use `FlowLayout`, each `Component` retains its default size, or **preferred size**. For example, a `JButton`'s preferred size is the size that is large enough to hold the `JButton`'s text. When you use `BorderLayout` and then resize the window, the components change size accordingly because their regions change. When you use `FlowLayout` and then resize the window, each component retains its size, but it might become partially obscured or change position.

The `FlowLayout` class contains three constants you can use to align `Component`s with a `Container`:

» `FlowLayout.LEFT`
» `FlowLayout.CENTER`
» `FlowLayout.RIGHT`

»NOTE
A common mistake when using `BorderLayout` is to use `add(Component)` without naming the region. This can result in some of the components not being visible.

If you do not specify alignment, Components are center-aligned in a FlowLayout Container by default. Figure 14-12 shows an application that uses the FlowLayout.LEFT and FlowLayout.RIGHT constants to reposition JButtons. In this example, a FlowLayout object named layout is used to set the layout of the content pane. When the user clicks a button, the shaded code in the actionPerformed() method changes the alignment to left or right using the FlowLayout class setAlignment() method. Figure 14-13 shows the application when it starts, how the JButton Components are repositioned after the user clicks the "L" button, and how the Components are repositioned after the user clicks the "R" button.

```java
import javax.swing.*;
import java.awt.*;
import java.awt.event.*;
public class JDemoFlowLayout extends JFrame implements ActionListener
{
    private JButton lb = new JButton("L Button");
    private JButton rb = new JButton("R Button");
    private Container con = getContentPane();
    private FlowLayout layout = new FlowLayout();
    public JDemoFlowLayout()
    {
        con.setLayout(layout);
        con.add(lb);
        con.add(rb);
        lb.addActionListener(this);
        rb.addActionListener(this);
        setSize(500, 100);
        setVisible(true);
    }
    public void actionPerformed(ActionEvent event)
    {
        Object source = event.getSource();
        if(source == lb)
            layout.setAlignment(FlowLayout.LEFT);
        else
            layout.setAlignment(FlowLayout.RIGHT);
        con.invalidate();
        con.validate();
    }
    public static void main(String[] args)
    {
        JDemoFlowLayout frame = new JDemoFlowLayout();
    }
}
```

Figure 14-12 The JDemoFlowLayout application

>> **NOTE** The last statements in the `JDemoFlowLayout` class call `invalidate()` and `validate()`. The `invalidate()` call marks the container (and any of its parents) as needing to be laid out. The `validate()` call causes the components to be rearranged based on the newly assigned layout.

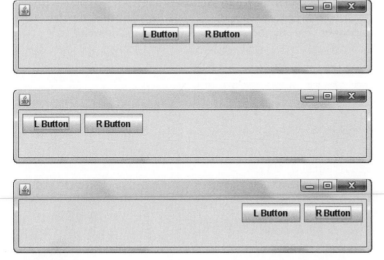

Figure 14-13 The `JDemoFlowLayout` application as it first appears on the screen, after the user chooses the "L" button, and after the user chooses the "R" button

>> **NOTE**
`FlowLayout` is the default layout manager for every `JPanel`. You will learn more about the `JPanel` class later in this chapter.

USING `GridLayout`

If you want to arrange components into equal rows and columns, you can use the **GridLayout manager** class. When you create a `GridLayout` object, you indicate the numbers of rows and columns you want, and then the container surface is divided into a grid, much like the screen you see when using a spreadsheet program. For example, the following statement establishes an anonymous `GridLayout` with four horizontal rows and five vertical columns in a `Container` named `con`:

```
con.setLayout(new GridLayout(4, 5));
```

Similarly, within a `JFrame`, you can establish the same layout with either of the following:

```
this.setLayout(new GridLayout(4, 5));

setLayout(new GridLayout(4, 5));
```

>> **NOTE**
When you use `GridLayout`, you specify rows first and then columns, which is the same approach you take when specifying two-dimensional arrays, as you learned in Chapter 8.

As you add new `Components` to a `GridLayout`, they are positioned in sequence from left to right across each row. Unfortunately, you can't skip a position or specify an exact position for a component. (However, you can add a blank label to a grid position to give the illusion of skipping a position.) You also can specify a vertical and horizontal gap measured in pixels, using two additional arguments. For example, Figure 14-14 shows a `JDemoGridLayout` program that uses the following statement (shaded in the figure) to establish a `GridLayout` with three horizontal rows and two vertical columns, and horizontal and vertical gaps of five pixels each:

```
private GridLayout layout = new GridLayout(3, 2, 5, 5);
```

Five JButton Components are added to the JFrame's automatically retrieved content pane. Figure 14-15 shows the result. The Components are placed into the pane across the rows. Because there are six positions but only five Components, one spot remains available.

```
import javax.swing.*;
import java.awt.*;
public class JDemoGridLayout extends JFrame
{
    private JButton b1 = new JButton("Button 1");
    private JButton b2 = new JButton("Button 2");
    private JButton b3 = new JButton("Button 3");
    private JButton b4 = new JButton("Button 4");
    private JButton b5 = new JButton("Button 5");
    private GridLayout layout = new GridLayout(3, 2, 5, 5);
    public JDemoGridLayout()
    {
        setLayout(layout);
        add(b1);
        add(b2);
        add(b3);
        add(b4);
        add(b5);
        setVisible(true);
        setSize(200, 200);
    }
    public static void main(String[] args)
    {
        JDemoGridLayout frame = new JDemoGridLayout();
    }
}
```

Figure 14-14 The JDemoGridLayout class

Figure 14-15 Output of the JDemoGridLayout program

> **NOTE** With GridLayout, you can specify the number of rows only, you can use 0 for the number of columns and let the layout manager determine the number of columns, or you can use 0 for the number of rows, specify the number of columns, and let the layout manager calculate the number of rows. Even when you do not specify rows or columns, the components placed in a GridLayout are in fixed rows and columns, filling the available space. When you use FlowLayout, Java determines the rows and columns, but components are not placed in rigid rows, and they retain their "natural" size—that is, the minimum size they need so that their contents are fully visible.

USING CardLayout

The **CardLayout manager** generates a stack of containers or components, one on top of another, much like a blackjack dealer reveals playing cards one at a time from the top of a deck. Each component in the group is referred to as a card, and each card can be any component type—for example, a JButton, JLabel, or JPanel. You use a CardLayout when you want multiple components to share the same display space.

A card layout is created from the CardLayout class using one of two constructors:

» CardLayout() creates a card layout without a horizontal or vertical gap.

» CardLayout(int hgap, int vgap) creates a card layout with the specified horizontal and vertical gaps. The horizontal gaps are placed at the left and right edges. The vertical gaps are placed at the top and bottom edges.

For example, Figure 14-16 shows a JDemoCardLayout class that uses a CardLayout manager to create a stack of JButtons that contain the labels "Ace of Hearts", "Three of Spades", and "Queen of Clubs". In the class constructor, you need a slightly different version of the add() method to add a component to a content pane whose layout manager is CardLayout. The format of the method is:

```
add(aString, aContainer);
```

In this statement, aString represents a name you want to use to identify the Component card that is added.

```
import javax.swing.*;
import java.awt.*;
import java.awt.event.*;
public class JDemoCardLayout extends JFrame
    implements ActionListener
{
    private CardLayout cards = new CardLayout();
    private JButton b1 = new JButton("Ace of Hearts");
    private JButton b2 = new JButton("Three of Spades");
    private JButton b3 = new JButton("Queen of Clubs");
    public JDemoCardLayout()
    {
        setLayout(cards);
        add("ace", b1);
        b1.addActionListener(this);
        add("three", b2);
        b2.addActionListener(this);
        add("queen", b3);
        b3.addActionListener(this);
        setSize(200, 100);
        setVisible(true);
    }
}
```

Figure 14-16 The JDemoCardLayout class (*continued*)

```
public void actionPerformed(ActionEvent e)
{
    cards.next(getContentPane());
}
public static void main(String[] args)
{
    JDemoCardLayout frame = new JDemoCardLayout();
}
}
```

Figure 14-16 (*continued*)

> **NOTE** The example in Figure 14-16 uses the Strings only as placeholders in the add() method calls. However, the Strings are required; the class compiles but does not execute if you do not include them. Containers with a CardLayout manager can use these Strings to identify specific cards; you can use any names you want within your programs. More details are available at *http://java.sun.com*.

In a program that has a CardLayout manager, a change of cards is usually triggered by a user's action. For example, in the JDemoCardLayout program, each JButton can trigger the actionPerformed() method. Within this method, the statement next(getContentPane()) flips to the next card of the container. (The order of the cards depends on the order in which you add them to the container.) You also can use previous(getContentPane());, first(getContentPane());, and last(getContentPane()); to flip to the previous, first, and last card, respectively. You can go to a specific card by using the String name assigned in the add() method call. For example, in the application in Figure 14-16, the following statement would display the "Three of Spades":

```
cards.show(getContentPane(), "three");
```

> **NOTE**
> If the user continued to click the card buttons in Figure 14-17, the cards would continue to cycle in order.

Figure 14-17 shows the output of the JDemoCardLayout program when it first appears on the screen, after the user clicks the button once, and after the user clicks the button a second time. Because each JButton is a card, each JButton consumes the entire viewing area in the container that uses the CardLayout manager.

> **NOTE**
> Explore the JTabbedPane class at *http://java. sun.com*; the class operates like a container with a CardLayout, but folder-type tabs are in place for the user to select the various components.

Figure 14-17 Output of JDemoCardLayout when it first appears on the screen, after the user clicks once, and after the user clicks twice

USING ADVANCED LAYOUT MANAGERS

Just as professional Java programmers are constantly creating new Components, they also create new layout managers. You are certain to encounter new and interesting layout managers during your programming career; you might even create your own.

For example, when `GridLayout` is not sophisticated enough for your purposes, you can use `GridBagLayout`. The **GridBagLayout manager** allows you to add `Components` to precise locations within the grid, as well as to indicate that specific `Components` should span multiple rows or columns within the grid. For example, if you want to create a `JPanel` with six `JButtons`, in which two of the `JButtons` are twice as wide as the others, you can use `GridBagLayout`. This class is difficult to use because you must set the position and size for each component. `GridBagLayout` is more complicated to use than `GridLayout`; more than 20 methods are associated with the class. To use a `GridBagLayout` effectively, you must customize one or more of the `GridBagConstraints` objects that are associated with its components. Visit *http://java.sun.com* for details on how to use this class.

Another layout manager option is the **BoxLayout manager**, which allows multiple components to be laid out either vertically or horizontally. The components do not wrap, so a vertical arrangement of components, for example, stays vertically arranged when the frame is resized. The Java Web site can provide you with more details.

»TWO TRUTHS AND A LIE: LEARNING MORE ABOUT LAYOUT MANAGERS

1. The `FlowLayout` manager is the default manager class for all content panes.
2. The `BorderLayout` manager can directly hold only up to five components.
3. The `GridLayout` manager arranges components in rows and columns.

The false statement is #1. The `BorderLayout` manager is the default manager class for all content panes.

USING THE `JPanel` CLASS

Using the `BorderLayout`, `FlowLayout`, `GridLayout`, and `CardLayout` managers would provide a limited number of screen arrangements if you could place only one `Component` in a section of the layout. Fortunately, you can greatly increase the number of possible component arrangements by using the `JPanel` class. A

```
java.lang.Object
   !--java.awt.Component
        !--java.awt.Container
             !--javax.swing.JComponent
                  !--javax.swing.JPanel
```

Figure 14-18 The inheritance hierarchy of the `JPanel` class

JPanel is a plain, borderless surface that can hold lightweight UI components. Figure 14-18 shows the inheritance hierarchy of the `JPanel` class. You can see that every `JPanel` is a `Container`; you use a `JPanel` to hold other UI components, such as `JButtons`, `JCheckBoxes`, or even other `JPanels`. By using `JPanels` within `JPanels`, you can create an infinite variety of screen layouts.

To add a component to a `JPanel`, you call the container's `add()` method, using the component as the argument. For example, Figure 14-19 shows the code that creates a `JFrameWithPanels` class that extends `JFrame`. A `JButton` is added to a `JPanel` named pane, and two more JButtons are added to another JPanel named pane2. Then pane and pane2 are added to the JFrame's content pane.

```java
import javax.swing.*;
import java.awt.*;
public class JFrameWithPanels extends JFrame
{
    private final int WIDTH = 250;
    private final int HEIGHT = 120;
    private JButton button1 = new JButton("One");
    private JButton button2 = new JButton("Two");
    private JButton button3 = new JButton("Three");
    public JFrameWithPanels()
    {
        super("JFrame with Panels");
        setDefaultCloseOperation(JFrame.EXIT_ON_CLOSE);
        JPanel pane = new JPanel();
        JPanel pane2 = new JPanel();
        Container con = getContentPane();
        con.setLayout(new FlowLayout());
        con.add(pane);
        con.add(pane2);
        pane.add(button1);
        pane.setBackground(Color.BLUE);
        pane2.add(button2);
        pane2.add(button3);
        pane2.setBackground(Color.BLUE);
        setSize(WIDTH, HEIGHT);
        setVisible(true);
    }
    public static void main(String[] args)
    {
        JFrameWithPanels panel = new JFrameWithPanels();
    }
}
```

Figure 14-19 The JFrameWithPanels class

Figure 14-20 shows the output of the JFrameWithPanels program. Two JPanels have been added to the JFrame. Because this application uses the setBackground() method to make each JPanel's background blue, you can see where one panel ends and the other begins. The first JPanel contains a single JButton and the second one contains two JButtons.

Figure 14-20 Output of the JFrameWithPanels application

When you create a JPanel object, you can use one of four constructors. The different constructors allow you to use default values or to specify a layout manager and whether the JPanel is double buffered. If you indicate **double buffering**, which is the default buffering strategy, you specify that additional memory space will be used to draw the JPanel offscreen when it is updated. With double buffering, a redrawn JPanel is displayed only when it is complete; this provides the viewer with updated screens that do not flicker while being redrawn. The four constructors are as follows:

» JPanel() creates a JPanel with double buffering and a flow layout.

» JPanel(LayoutManager layout) creates a JPanel with the specified layout manager and double buffering.

» JPanel(Boolean isDoubleBuffered) creates a JPanel with a flow layout and the specified double-buffering strategy.

» JPanel(LayoutManager layout, Boolean isDoubleBuffered) creates a JPanel with the specified layout manager and the specified buffering strategy.

>> **NOTE** When you employ double buffering, the visible screen surface is called the **primary surface**, and the off-screen image is called the **back buffer**. The act of copying the contents from one surface to another is frequently referred to as **block line transfer**, or **blitting**, because of the acronym "blt," pronounced "blit." Double buffering prevents "tear-ing," the visual effect that occurs when you see parts of different images because the redrawing rate is not fast enough. As with most beneficial features, double buffering has a cost: additional memory requirements.

For example, the following statements create a JPanel that uses a named BorderLayout manager:

```
BorderLayout border = new BorderLayout();
JPanel myPanel = new JPanel(border);
```

The following statement accomplishes the same thing as the previous two, combining both statements by using an anonymous layout manager:

```
JPanel myPanel = new JPanel(new BorderLayout());
```

After a JPanel has been created, you can set its layout manager using the setLayout() method. The next two statements have the same result as the last two:

```
JPanel myPanel = new JPanel();
myPanel.setLayout(new BorderLayout());
```

>> **NOTE** When a JPanel will have a layout other than FlowLayout, specifying the layout manager when you create the JPanel is preferable for performance reasons. If you create the JPanel first and change its layout later, you automatically create an unnecessary FlowLayout object for the original instantiation.

You add components to a JPanel with the add() method—the same method you use to add components to a content pane. Figure 14-21 shows a JDemoManyPanels program in which the JFrame contains four JPanels and 12 JButtons that each display a single spelled-out number so you can better understand their positions. The automatically supplied content pane for the JFrame is assigned a BorderLayout, and each JPanel is assigned either a GridLayout or FlowLayout and placed in one of the regions (leaving the north region empty). One or more JButtons are then placed on each JPanel. Figure 14-22 shows the output as the user adjusts the borders of the JFrame to change its size. Using the code as a guide, be certain you understand why each JButton appears as it does in the JFrame.

```
import javax.swing.*;
import java.awt.*;
public class JDemoManyPanels extends JFrame
{
  // Twelve buttons
    private JButton button01 = new JButton("One");
    private JButton button02 = new JButton("Two");
    private JButton button03 = new JButton("Three");
    private JButton button04 = new JButton("Four");
    private JButton button05 = new JButton("Five");
    private JButton button06 = new JButton("Six");
    private JButton button07 = new JButton("Seven");
    private JButton button08 = new JButton("Eight");
    private JButton button09 = new JButton("Nine");
    private JButton button10 = new JButton("Ten");
    private JButton button11 = new JButton("Eleven");
    private JButton button12 = new JButton("Twelve");

  // Four panels
    private JPanel panel01 = new JPanel(new GridLayout(2, 0));
    private JPanel panel02 = new JPanel(new FlowLayout());
    private JPanel panel03 = new JPanel(new FlowLayout());
    private JPanel panel04 = new JPanel(new GridLayout(2, 0));

    public JDemoManyPanels()
    {
        setLayout(new BorderLayout());
        add(panel01, BorderLayout.WEST);
        add(panel02, BorderLayout.CENTER);
        add(panel03, BorderLayout.SOUTH);
        add(panel04, BorderLayout.EAST);

        panel01.add(button01);
        panel01.add(button02);
        panel01.add(button03);

        panel02.add(button04);
        panel02.add(button05);
        panel02.add(button06);

        panel03.add(button07);

        panel04.add(button08);
        panel04.add(button09);
        panel04.add(button10);
        panel04.add(button11);
        panel04.add(button12);
```

>> NOTE
If you were creating a program with as many buttons and panels as the one in Figure 14-21, you might prefer to create arrays of the components instead of so many individually named ones. This example does not use an array so you can more easily see how each component is placed.

Figure 14-21 The JDemoManyPanels class (*continued*)

```
        setSize(400, 250);
        setVisible(true);
    }
    public static void main(String[] args)
    {
        JDemoManyPanels frame = new JDemoManyPanels();
    }
}
```

Figure 14-21 (*continued*)

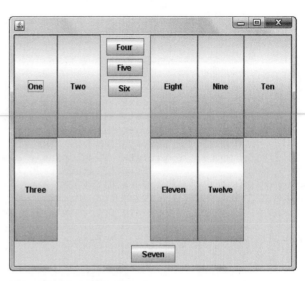

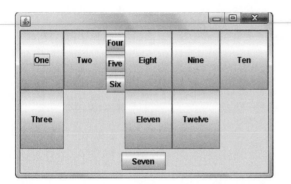

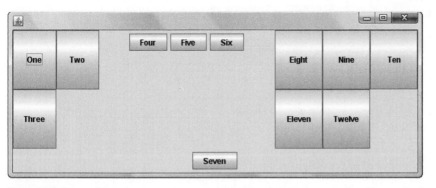

Figure 14-22 Output of the JDemoManyPanels program: three views as the user adjusts the JFrame borders

» NOTE
Swing containers
other than JPanel
and content panes
generally provide
Application Program
Interface (API)
methods that you
should use instead
of the add()
method. See the
Java Web site at
http://java.sun.com
for details.

GridLayout provides you with rows and columns that are similar to a two-dimensional array. Therefore, it particularly lends itself to displaying arrays of objects. For example, Figure 14-23 contains a Checkerboard class that displays a pattern of eight rows and columns in alternating colors. The JPanel placed in the content pane has a GridLayout of eight by eight. Sixty-four JPanels are declared, and in a loop, one by one, they are instantiated and assigned to a section of the grid (see shaded statements). After each set of eight JPanels is assigned to the grid (when x is evenly divisible by 8), the first and second color values are reversed, so that the first row starts with a blue square, the second row starts with a white square, and so on. Within each row, all the even-positioned squares are filled with one color, and the odd-positioned squares are filled with the other. Figure 14-24 shows the output.

```java
import java.awt.*;
import javax.swing.*;
public class Checkerboard extends JFrame
{
    private final int ROWS = 8;
    private final int COLS = 8;
    private final int GAP = 2;
    private final int NUM = ROWS * COLS;
    private int x;
    private JPanel pane = new JPanel
        (new GridLayout(ROWS, COLS, GAP, GAP));
    private JPanel[] panel = new JPanel[NUM];
    private Color color1 = Color.WHITE;
    private Color color2 = Color.BLUE;
    private Color tempColor;
    public Checkerboard()
    {
        super("Checkerboard");
        setDefaultCloseOperation(JFrame.EXIT_ON_CLOSE);
        add(pane);
        for(x = 0; x < NUM; ++x)
        {
            panel[x] = new JPanel();
            pane.add(panel[x]);
            if(x % COLS == 0)
            {
                tempColor = color1;
                color1 = color2;
                color2 = tempColor;
            }
            if(x % 2 == 0)
                panel[x].setBackground(color1);
            else
                panel[x].setBackground(color2);
        }
    }
```

Figure 14-23 The Checkerboard class (*continued*)

```
    public static void main(String[] args)
    {
        Checkerboard frame = new Checkerboard();
        final int SIZE = 300;
        frame.setSize(SIZE, SIZE);
        frame.setVisible(true);
    }
}
```

Figure 14-23 (*continued*)

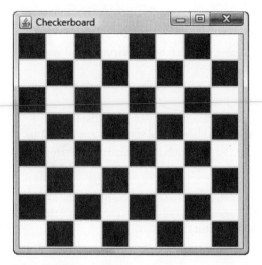

Figure 14-24 Output of the Checkerboard application

>> **NOTE** When creating the Checkerboard class, you might be tempted to create just two JPanels, one blue and one white, and add them to the content pane multiple times. However, each GUI component can be contained only once. If a component is already in a container and you try to add it to another container, the component will be removed from the first container and then added to the second.

>> TWO TRUTHS AND A LIE: USING THE JPanel CLASS

1. A JPanel is a plain, borderless surface that can hold lightweight UI components.

2. To add a component to a JPanel, you call the component's add() method, using the JPanel as the argument.

3. Different JPanel constructors allow you to use default values or to specify a layout manager and whether the JPanel is double buffered.

The false statement is #2. To add a component to a JPanel, you call the container's add() method, using the component as the argument.

CREATING JScrollPanes

When components in a Swing UI require more display area than they have been allocated, you can use a JScrollPane container to hold the components. A **JScrollPane** provides scroll bars along the side or bottom of a pane, or both, so that

```
java.lang.Object
   !--java.awt.Component
         !--java.awt.Container
               !--javax.swing.JComponent
                     !--javax.swing.JScrollPane
```

Figure 14-25 The inheritance hierarchy of the JScrollPane class

the user can scroll initially invisible parts of the pane into view. Figure 14-25 displays the inheritance hierarchy of the JScrollPane class.

The JScrollPane constructor takes one of four forms:

» JScrollPane() creates an empty JScrollPane in which both horizontal and vertical scroll bars appear when needed.

» JScrollPane(Component) creates a JScrollPane that displays the contents of the specified component.

» JScrollPane(Component, int, int) creates a JScrollPane that displays the specified component and includes both vertical and horizontal scroll bar specifications.

» JScrollPane(int, int) creates a JScrollPane with both vertical and horizontal scroll bar specifications.

When you create a simple scroll pane using the constructor that takes no arguments, as in the following example, horizontal and vertical scroll bars appear only if they are needed; that is, if the contents of the pane cannot be fully displayed without them:

```
JScrollPane aScrollPane = new JScrollPane();
```

To force the display of a scroll bar, you can use class variables defined in the ScrollPaneConstants class, as follows:

```
ScrollPaneConstants.HORIZONTAL_SCROLLBAR_AS_NEEDED

ScrollPaneConstants.HORIZONTAL_SCROLLBAR_ALWAYS

ScrollPaneConstants.HORIZONTAL_SCROLLBAR_NEVER

ScrollPaneConstants.VERTICAL_SCROLLBAR_AS_NEEDED

ScrollPaneConstants.VERTICAL_SCROLLBAR_ALWAYS

ScrollPaneConstants.VERTICAL_SCROLLBAR_NEVER
```

For example, the following code creates a scroll pane that displays an image named picture, a vertical scroll bar, and no horizontal scroll bar:

```
JScrollPane scroll = new JScrollPane(picture,
    ScrollPaneConstants.VERTICAL_SCROLLBAR_ALWAYS,
    ScrollPaneConstants.HORIZONTAL_SCROLLBAR_NEVER);
```

Figure 14-26 shows a `JScrollDemo` class in which a label with a large font is added to a panel. The scroll pane named `scroll` includes the panel and two scroll bars.

```java
import javax.swing.*;
import java.awt.*;
public class JScrollDemo extends JFrame
{
    private JPanel panel = new JPanel();
    private JScrollPane scroll = new JScrollPane(panel,
        ScrollPaneConstants.VERTICAL_SCROLLBAR_ALWAYS,
        ScrollPaneConstants.HORIZONTAL_SCROLLBAR_ALWAYS);
    private JLabel label = new JLabel("Event Handlers Incorporated");
    private Font bigFont = new Font("Arial", Font.PLAIN, 20);
    private Container con;
    public JScrollDemo()
    {
        super("JScrollDemo");
        setDefaultCloseOperation(JFrame.EXIT_ON_CLOSE);
        con = getContentPane();
        label.setFont(bigFont);
        con.add(scroll);
        panel.add(label);
    }
    public static void main(String[] args)
    {
        final int WIDTH = 180;
        final int HEIGHT = 100;
        JScrollDemo aFrame = new JScrollDemo();
        aFrame.setSize(WIDTH, HEIGHT);
        aFrame.setVisible(true);
    }
}
```

Figure 14-26 The `JScrollDemo` application

The `JScrollDemo` object in the program in Figure 14-26 is purposely set small enough (180 × 100) so that only part of the label it contains is visible at a time. A user would slide the scroll bars to view the entire "Event Handlers Incorporated" label. Figure 14-27 shows the output.

Figure 14-27 Output of the `JScrollDemo` application

>> **NOTE**
The viewable area in a `JScrollPane` is called a **viewport**.

A CLOSER LOOK AT EVENTS AND EVENT HANDLING

In Chapter 13, you worked with ActionEvents and ItemEvents that are generated when a user works with a widget that is part of one of your programs. Like all Java classes, events are Objects. Specifically, events are Objects that the user initiates, such as key presses and mouse clicks.

The parent class for all event objects is named EventObject, which descends from the Object class. EventObject is the parent of AWTEvent, which in turn is the parent of specific event classes such as ActionEvent and ComponentEvent. Figure 14-28 illustrates the inheritance hierarchy of these relationships.

```
java.lang.Object
  |--java.util.EventObject
       |--java.awt.AWTEvent
            |--java.awt.event.ActionEvent
            +--java.awt.event.AdjustmentEvent
            +--java.awt.event.ItemEvent
            +--java.awt.event.TextEvent
            +--java.awt.event.ComponentEvent
                 |--java.awt.event.ContainerEvent
                 +--java.awt.event.FocusEvent
                 +--java.awt.event.PaintEvent
                 +--java.awt.event.WindowEvent
                 +--java.awt.event.InputEvent
                      |--java.awt.event.KeyEvent
                      +--java.awt.event.MouseEvent
```

Figure 14-28 The inheritance hierarchy of event classes

You can see in Figure 14-28 that ComponentEvent is itself a parent to several event classes, including InputEvent, which is a parent of KeyEvent and MouseEvent. The family tree for events has roots that go fairly deep, but the class names are straightforward and they share basic roles within your programs. For example, ActionEvents are generated by components that users can click, such as JButtons and JCheckBoxes, and TextEvents are generated by components into which the user enters text, such as a JTextField. MouseEvents include determining the location of the mouse pointer and distinguishing between a single- and double-click. Table 14-3 lists some common user actions and the events that are generated from them.

User Action	Resulting Event Type
Click a button	ActionEvent
Click a component	MouseEvent
Click an item in a list box	ItemEvent
Click an item in a check box	ItemEvent
Change text in a text field	TextEvent
Open a window	WindowEvent
Iconify a window	WindowEvent
Press a key	KeyEvent

Table 14-3 Examples of user actions and their resulting event types

Because ActionEvents involve the mouse, it is easy to confuse ActionEvents and MouseEvents. If you are interested in ActionEvents, you focus on changes in a component (for example, a JButton on a JFrame being pressed); if you are interested in MouseEvents, your focus is on what the user does manually with the mouse (for example, clicking the left mouse button).

When you write programs with GUIs, you are always handling events that originate with the mouse or keys on specific Components or Containers. Just as your telephone notifies you when you have a call, the computer's operating system notifies the user when an AWTEvent occurs; for example, when the mouse is clicked. Just as you can ignore your phone when you're not expecting or interested in a call, you can ignore AWTEvents. If you don't care about an event, such as when your program contains a component that produces no effect when clicked, you simply don't look for a message to occur.

When you care about events—that is, when you want to listen for an event—you can implement an appropriate interface for your class. Each event class shown in Table 14-3 has a listener interface associated with it, so that for every event class, such as <name>Event, there is a similarly named <name>Listener interface.

》NOTE
There is no currently active prewritten, built-in Java class named Event (although there was one in Java 1.0); the general event class is AWTEvent.

》NOTE Remember that an interface contains only abstract methods, so all interface methods are empty. If you implement a listener, you must provide your own methods for all the methods that are part of the interface. Of course, you can leave the methods empty in your implementation, providing a header and curly braces but no statements.

» NOTE Every `<name>Event` class has a `<name>Listener`. The `MouseEvent` class has an additional listener, the `MouseMotionListener`.

Every `<name>Listener` interface method has the return type `void`, and each takes one argument: an object that is an instance of the corresponding `<name>Event` class. Thus, the `ActionListener` interface has a method named `actionPerformed()`, and its header is `void actionPerformed(ActionEvent e)`. When an action takes place, the `actionPerformed()` method executes, and `e` represents an instance of that event.

» NOTE In Chapter 13 you learned that interface methods such as `actionPerformed()`, which are called automatically when an appropriate event occurs, are called event handlers.

Instead of implementing a listener class, you can extend an adapter class. An **adapter class** implements all the methods in an interface, providing an empty body for each method. For example, the `MouseAdapter` class provides an empty method for all the methods contained in `MouseListener`. When you extend an adapter class, you need to write only those methods you want to use, and you do not have to bother creating empty methods for all the others.

» NOTE If a listener has only one method, there is no need for an adapter. For example, the `ActionListener` class has one method, `actionPerformed()`, so there is no `ActionAdapter` class.

Whether you use a listener or an adapter, you create an event handler when you write code for the listener methods; that is, you tell your class how to handle the event. After you create the handler, you must also register an instance of the class with the component that you want the event to affect. For any `<name>Listener`, you must use the form `object.add<name>Listener(Component)` to register an object with the `Component` that will listen for objects emanating from it. The `add<name>Listener()` methods, such as `addActionListener()` and `addItemListener()`, all work the same way. They register a listener with a `Component`, return `void`, and take a `<name>Listener` object as an argument. For example, if a `JFrame` is an `ActionListener` and contains a `JButton` named `pushMe`, then the following statement registers this `JFrame` as a listener for the `pushMe` `JButton`:

```
pushMe.addActionListener(this);
```

Table 14-4 lists the events with their listeners and handlers.

Event	Listener(s)	Handler(s)
ActionEvent	ActionListener	actionPerformed(ActionEvent)
ItemEvent	ItemListener	itemStateChanged(ItemEvent)
TextEvent	TextListener	textValueChanged(TextEvent)
AdjustmentEvent	AdjustmentListener	adjustmentValueChanged (AdjustmentEvent)
ContainerEvent	ContainerListener	componentAdded(ContainerEvent) componentRemoved(ContainerEvent)
ComponentEvent	ComponentListener	componentMoved(ComponentEvent) componentHidden(ComponentEvent) componentResized(ComponentEvent) componentShown(ComponentEvent)
FocusEvent	FocusListener	focusGained(FocusEvent) focusLost(FocusEvent)
MouseEvent	MouseListener MouseMotionListener	mousePressed(MouseEvent) mouseReleased(MouseEvent) mouseEntered(MouseEvent) mouseExited(MouseEvent) mouseClicked(MouseEvent) mouseDragged(MouseEvent) mouseMoved(MouseEvent)
KeyEvent	KeyListener	keyPressed(KeyEvent) keyTyped(KeyEvent) keyReleased(KeyEvent)
WindowEvent	WindowListener	windowActivated(WindowEvent) windowClosing(WindowEvent) windowClosed(WindowEvent) windowDeiconified(WindowEvent) windowIconified(WindowEvent) windowOpened(WindowEvent)
MouseWheelEvent	MouseWheelListener	mouseWheelMoved(MouseWheelEvent)

Table 14-4 Events with their related listeners and handlers

AN EVENT-HANDLING EXAMPLE: KeyListener

You use the **KeyListener interface** when you are interested in actions the user initiates from the keyboard. The KeyListener interface contains three methods: keyPressed(), keyTyped(), and keyReleased(). For most keyboard applications in which the user must press a keyboard key, it is probably not important whether you take resulting action when a user first presses a key, during the key press, or upon the key's release; most likely, these events occur in quick sequence. However, on those occasions when you don't want to take action while the user holds down the key, you can place the actions in the `keyReleased()` method. It is best to use the `keyTyped()` method when you want to discover which character was typed. When the user presses a key that does not generate a character, such as a function key (sometimes called an **action key**), `keyTyped()` does not execute. The methods `keyPressed()` and `keyReleased()` provide the only ways to get information about keys that don't generate characters. The `KeyEvent` class contains constants known as **virtual key codes** that represent keyboard keys that have been pressed. For example, when you type "A", two virtual key codes are generated: Shift and "a". The virtual key code constants have names such as `VK_SHIFT` and `VK_ALT`. See the Java Web site for a complete list of virtual key codes.

Figure 14-29 shows a `JDemoKeyFrame` class that uses the `keyTyped()` method to discover which key the user typed last. A prompt in the north border area asks the user to type in the text field in the center area. With each key press by the user, the `keyTyped()` method changes the label in the south border area of the frame to display the key that generated the most recent `KeyEvent`. Figure 14-30 shows the output after the user has typed several characters into the text field.

```java
import javax.swing.*;
import java.awt.*;
import java.awt.event.*;
public class JDemoKeyFrame extends JFrame
    implements KeyListener
{
    private JLabel prompt = new JLabel("Type keys below:");
    private JLabel outputLabel = new JLabel("Key Typed:");
    private JTextField textField = new JTextField(10);
    public JDemoKeyFrame()
    {
        setTitle("JKey Frame");
        setDefaultCloseOperation(JFrame.EXIT_ON_CLOSE);
        setLayout(new BorderLayout());
        add(prompt, BorderLayout.NORTH);
        add(textField, BorderLayout.CENTER);
        add(outputLabel, BorderLayout.SOUTH);
        addKeyListener(this);
        textField.addKeyListener(this);
    }
    public void keyTyped(KeyEvent e)
    {
        char c = e.getKeyChar();
        outputLabel.setText("Last key typed: " + c);
    }
```

Figure 14-29 The `JDemoKeyFrame` class (*continued*)

```
    public void keyPressed(KeyEvent e)
    {
    }
    public void keyReleased(KeyEvent e)
    {
    }
    public static void main(String[] args)
    {
        JDemoKeyFrame keyFrame = new JDemoKeyFrame();
        final int WIDTH = 250;
        final int HEIGHT = 100;
        keyFrame.setSize(WIDTH, HEIGHT);
        keyFrame.setVisible(true);
    }
}
```

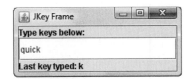

Figure 14-30 Output of the JDemoKeyFrame application after the user has typed several characters

Figure 14-29 (continued)

»TWO TRUTHS AND A LIE: A CLOSER LOOK AT EVENTS AND EVENT HANDLING

1. ActionEvents are generated by components that users can click, TextEvents are generated by components into which the user enters text, and MouseEvents are generated by mouse actions.

2. Every <name>Listener interface method has a return type that refers to an instance of the corresponding <name>Event class.

3. An adapter class implements all the methods in an interface, providing an empty body for each method.

The false statement is #2. Every <name>Listener interface method has the return type void, and each takes one argument: an object that is an instance of the corresponding <name>Event class.

USING AWTEvent CLASS METHODS

In addition to the handler methods included with the event listener interfaces, the AWTEvent classes themselves contain methods. You use many of these methods to determine the nature of and facts about an event in question. For example, the ComponentEvent class contains a getComponent() method that returns the Component involved in the event. You use the getComponent() method when you create an application with several components; the getComponent() method allows you to determine which Component is generating the event. The WindowEvent class contains a similar method, getWindow(), that returns the Window that was the source of the event. Table 14-5 lists some useful methods for many of the event classes. All Components have these methods:

» addComponentListener()

» addFocusListener()

» addMouseListener()

» addMouseMotionListener()

Class	Method	Purpose
`EventObject`	`Object getSource()`	Returns the `Object` involved in the event
`ComponentEvent`	`Component getComponent()`	Returns the `Component` involved in the event
`WindowEvent`	`Window getWindow()`	Returns the `Window` involved in the event
`ItemEvent`	`Object getItem()`	Returns the `Object` that was selected or deselected
`ItemEvent`	`int getStateChange()`	Returns an integer named `ItemEvent.SELECTED` or `ItemEvent.DESELECTED`
`InputEvent`	`int getModifiers()`	Returns an integer to indicate which mouse button was clicked
`InputEvent`	`int getWhen()`	Returns a time indicating when the event occurred
`InputEvent`	`boolean isAltDown()`	Returns whether the Alt key was pressed when the event occurred
`InputEvent`	`boolean isControlDown()`	Returns whether the Ctrl key was pressed when the event occurred
`InputEvent`	`boolean isShiftDown()`	Returns whether the Shift key was pressed when the event occurred
`KeyEvent`	`int getKeyChar()`	Returns the Unicode character entered from the keyboard
`MouseEvent`	`int getClickCount()`	Returns the number of mouse clicks; lets you identify the user's double-clicks
`MouseEvent`	`int getX()`	Returns the x-coordinate of the mouse pointer
`MouseEvent`	`int getY()`	Returns the y-coordinate of the mouse pointer
`MouseEvent`	`Point getPoint()`	Returns the `Point Object` that contains the x- and y-coordinates of the mouse location

Table 14-5 Useful event class methods

You can call any of the methods listed in Table 14-5 by using the object-dot-method format that you use with all class methods. For example, if you have an `InputEvent` named `inEvent` and an integer named `modInt`, the following statement is valid:

```
modInt = inEvent.getModifiers();
```

You use the `getModifiers()` method with an `InputEvent` object, and you can assign the return value to an integer variable. Thus, when you use any of the handler methods from Table 14-4, such as `actionPerformed()` or `itemStateChanged()`, they provide you with an appropriate event object. You can use the event object within the handler method to obtain information; you simply add a dot and the appropriate method name from Table 14-5.

When you use an event such as `KeyEvent`, you can use any of the event's methods. Through the power of inheritance, you can also use methods that belong to any class that is a super-class of the event with which you are working. For example, any `KeyEvent` has access to the `InputEvent`, `ComponentEvent`, `AWTEvent`, `EventObject`, and `Object` methods, as well as to the `KeyEvent` methods.

UNDERSTANDING X- AND Y-COORDINATES

Table 14-5 refers to x- and y-coordinates of a mouse pointer. A window or frame consists of a number of horizontal and vertical pixels on the screen. Any component you place on the screen has a horizontal, or **x-axis**, position as well as a vertical, or **y-axis**, position in the window. The upper-left corner of any display is position 0, 0. The first, or **x-coordinate**, value increases as you travel from left to right across the window. The second, or **y-coordinate**, value increases as you travel from top to bottom. Figure 14-31 illustrates the screen coordinate positions.

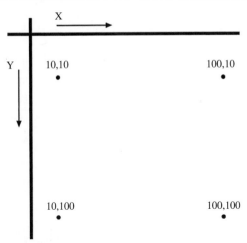

Figure 14-31 Screen coordinate positions

»TWO TRUTHS AND A LIE: USING AWTEvent CLASS METHODS

1. You use many of the `AWTEvent` class methods to determine the nature of and facts about an event.
2. The `getSource()` method returns the `Object` involved in an event and the `getComponent()` method returns the `Component` involved in an event.
3. The methods `isAltDown()` and `isShiftDown()` are `ActionEvent` methods.

The false statement is #3. The methods isAltDown() and isShiftDown() are KeyEvent methods.

HANDLING MOUSE EVENTS

Even though Java program users sometimes type characters from a keyboard, when you write GUI programs you probably expect users to spend most of their time operating a mouse. The **MouseMotionListener interface** provides you with methods named mouseDragged() and mouseMoved() that detect the mouse being rolled or dragged across a component surface. The **MouseListener interface** provides you with methods named mousePressed(), mouseClicked(), and mouseReleased() that are analogous to the keyboard event methods keyPressed(), keyTyped(), and keyReleased(). With a mouse, however, you are interested in more than its button presses; you sometimes simply want to know where a mouse is pointing. The additional interface methods mouseEntered() and mouseExited() inform you when the user positions the mouse over a component (entered) or moves the mouse off a component (exited). The **MouseInputListener interface** implements all the methods in both the MouseListener and MouseMotionListener interfaces; although it has no methods of its own, it is a convenience when you want to handle many different types of mouse events. Tables 14-6 and 14-7 show the methods of the MouseListener and MouseMotionListener classes, respectively.

Method	Description
void mouseClicked(MouseEvent e)	Invoked when the mouse button has been clicked (pressed and released) on a component
void mouseEntered(MouseEvent e)	Invoked when the mouse pointer enters a component
void mouseExited(MouseEvent e)	Invoked when the mouse pointer exits a component
void mousePressed(MouseEvent e)	Invoked when a mouse button has been pressed on a component
void mouseReleased(MouseEvent e)	Invoked when a mouse button has been released on a component

Table 14-6 MouseListener methods

> **NOTE** Many of the methods in Tables 14-6 and 14-7 also appear in tables earlier in this chapter. They are organized by interface here so you can better understand the scope of methods that are available for mouse actions. Don't forget that because MouseListener, MouseMotionListener, and MouseInputListener are interfaces, you must include each method in every program that implements them, even if you choose to place no instructions within some of the methods.

Method	Description
void mouseDragged(MouseEvent e)	Invoked when a mouse button is pressed on a component and then dragged
void mouseMoved(MouseEvent e)	Invoked when the mouse pointer has been moved onto a component but no buttons have been pressed

Table 14-7 MouseMotionListener methods

NOTE The `MouseWheelListener` interface contains just one method named `mouseWheelMoved()`, and it accepts a `MouseWheelEvent` argument.

Each of the methods in Tables 14-6 and 14-7 accepts a `MouseEvent` argument. A **`MouseEvent`** is the type of event generated by mouse manipulation. Figure 14-32 shows the inheritance hierarchy of the `MouseEvent` class. From this diagram, you can see that a `MouseEvent` is a type of `InputEvent`, which is a type of `ComponentEvent`. The `MouseEvent` class contains many instance methods and fields that are useful in describing mouse-generated events. Table 14-8 lists some of the more useful methods of the `MouseEvent` class, and Table 14-9 lists some fields.

```
java.lang.Object
  |
  +--java.util.EventObject
        |
        +--java.awt.AWTEvent
              |
              +--java.awt.event.ComponentEvent
                    |
                    +--java.awt.event.InputEvent
                          |
                          +--java.awt.event.MouseEvent
```

Figure 14-32 The inheritance hierarchy of the `MouseEvent` class

Method	Description
`int getButton()`	Returns which, if any, of the mouse buttons has changed state; uses fields `NOBUTTON`, `BUTTON1`, `BUTTON2`, and `BUTTON3`
`int getClickCount()`	Returns the number of mouse clicks associated with the current event
`int getX()`	Returns the horizontal x-position of the event relative to the source component
`int getY()`	Returns the vertical y-position of the event relative to the source component

Table 14-8 Some useful `MouseEvent` methods

Field	Description
`static int BUTTON1`	Indicates mouse button #1; used by `getButton()`
`static int BUTTON2`	Indicates mouse button #2; used by `getButton()`
`static int BUTTON3`	Indicates mouse button #3; used by `getButton()`
`static int NOBUTTON`	Indicates no mouse buttons; used by `getButton()`
`static int MOUSE_CLICKED`	The "mouse clicked" event
`static int MOUSE_DRAGGED`	The "mouse dragged" event
`static int MOUSE_ENTERED`	The "mouse entered" event
`static int MOUSE_EXITED`	The "mouse exited" event

Table 14-9 Some useful `MouseEvent` fields

Figure 14-33 shows a `JMouseActionsFrame` application that demonstrates several of the mouse listener and event methods. `JMouseActionsFrame` extends `JFrame` and, because it implements the `MouseListener` interface, it must include all five methods—`mouseClicked()`, `mouseEntered()`, `mouseExited()`, `mousePressed()`, and `mouseReleased()`—even though no actions are included in the `mousePressed()` or `mouseReleased()` methods.

```
import javax.swing.*;
import java.awt.*;
import java.awt.event.*;
public class JMouseActionsFrame extends JFrame implements MouseListener
{
    private final int MAX = 20;
    private final int STARTX = 10;
    private final int STARTY = 20;
    private int x, y;
    private String message[] = new String[MAX];
    private int msgCount = 0;

    public JMouseActionsFrame()
    {
        setTitle("Mouse Actions");
        setDefaultCloseOperation(JFrame.EXIT_ON_CLOSE);
        addMouseListener(this);
    }

    public void mouseClicked(MouseEvent e)
    {
        int whichButton = e.getButton();
        String msg;
        if(msgCount == MAX)
            clearScreen();
        message[msgCount] = "You pressed the mouse.";
        if(whichButton == MouseEvent.BUTTON1)
            msg = "button 1.";
        else if(whichButton == MouseEvent.BUTTON2)
            msg = "button 2.";
        else msg = "button 3.";
        message[msgCount] = message[msgCount] +
            " You used " + msg;
        message[msgCount] = message[msgCount] +
            " You are at position " +
        e.getX() + ", " + e.getY() + ".";
        if(e.getClickCount() == 2)
            message[msgCount] = message[msgCount] +
                " You double-clicked";
        else
            message[msgCount] = message[msgCount] +
                " You single-clicked";
        ++msgCount;
        repaint();
    }
```

Figure 14-33 The JMouseActionsFrame application (*continued*)

```
    public void mouseEntered(MouseEvent e)
    {
        if(msgCount == MAX)
            clearScreen();
        message[msgCount] = "You entered the frame";
        ++msgCount;
        repaint();
    }
    public void mouseExited(MouseEvent e)
    {
        if(msgCount == MAX)
            clearScreen();
        message[msgCount] = "You exited the frame";
        ++msgCount;
        repaint();
    }

    public void mousePressed(MouseEvent e)
    {
    }

    public void mouseReleased(MouseEvent e)
    {
    }

    public void paint(Graphics g)
    {
        final int SIZE = 20;
        super.paint(g);
        x = STARTX;
        y = STARTY;
        for(int a = 0; a < msgCount; ++a)
            g.drawString(message[a], x, y += SIZE);
    }

    public void clearScreen()
    {
        msgCount = 0;
        for(int a = 0; a < MAX; ++a)
            message[a] = " ";
        repaint();
    }
    public static void main(String[] args)
    {
        JMouseActionsFrame mFrame = new JMouseActionsFrame();
        final int WIDTH = 750;
        final int HEIGHT = 300;
        mFrame.setSize(WIDTH, HEIGHT);
        mFrame.setVisible(true);
    }
}
```

Figure 14-33 (*continued*)

The `JMouseActionsFrame` application in Figure 14-33 displays messages as the user generates mouse actions. In the first unshaded section of the application, a named constant is declared to hold the maximum number of messages that can appear on-screen at any time. Named constants are also declared for the starting x- and y-coordinate position of the messages. The messages are drawn using the `drawString()` method, which takes a `String` argument and x- and y-position coordinates. Next, three fields are declared: integers to hold the mouse position x- and y-coordinates, and an array of 20 `String`s to hold messages that inform the user of the mouse actions taken. An integer is declared to count the number of messages displayed so that the capacity of the `String` array is not exceeded.

In the first shaded section of Figure 14-33, the constructor sets a frame title by passing it to the parent of `JMouseActionsFrame`, sets a close operation, and enables the frame to listen for mouse events.

In Figure 14-33, most of the action occurs in the `mouseClicked()` method (the second unshaded area in the figure). The method constructs descriptive messages to place in the array of messages that appear on the screen. The same actions could have been placed in the `mousePressed()` or `mouseReleased()` method because the statements could be placed in the frame just as well at either of those times. Within the `mouseClicked()` method, the `getButton()` method is used to determine which mouse button the user clicked. If 20 messages have been displayed on the screen, a `clearScreen()` method is called. Then a `String` is built in the next available spot in the array; it contains information about the action that generated the method call. The `msgCount` variable is increased so that the next time the method is called, a message will be stored in the next available array location. The last statement in the method calls `repaint()`, which calls `paint()`.

The `MouseEvent` generated when the `mouseClicked()` method executes is named e. The e object is used several times within the method. First, e is used with the `getButton()` instance method in the first line of the `mouseClicked()` method; it returns an integer that, later in the method, is compared to the `MouseEvent` fields, `BUTTON1` and `BUTTON2`, to determine which button message to display. Later, e is used with `getX()` and `getY()` so that the coordinates at which the user clicks can be displayed. Finally, e is used with `getClickCount()`, returning the number of clicks generated.

In Figure 14-33, messages are also generated in the `mouseEntered()` and `mouseExited()` methods, so that the user is notified when the mouse pointer has "entered"—that is, passed over the surface area of—the `JFrame`, the component that is listening for actions.

Using a loop, the `paint()` method displays as many messages as have been stored in locations indicated by the x- and y-coordinates. The y-coordinate value is increased by 20 on each pass through the loop so that subsequent messages appear lower on the frame.

The `clearScreen()` method, which is called after 20 messages have been generated, sets each `String` in the array of messages to a blank and repaints the screen with 20 blank lines so that a new set of 20 messages can begin.

NOTE The first executable statement within the paint() method in the JMouseActionsFrame class is super.paint(g);. This statement is a call to the paint() method that is part of the parent class (JFrame), and it passes the local Graphics object (named g) in this method. If you remove this statement, the JFrame surface is not repainted, and the surface appears to be transparent, revealing the items that were on your screen before the application started. You will learn more about the paint() method in Chapter 15.

The main() method at the end of the class creates one instance of the JMouseActionsFrame class and sets its size and visibility.

Figure 14-34 shows one execution of the JMouseActionsFrame application. At this point, the user has generated several mouse actions. Of course, in your own applications you might not want only to notify users of their mouse actions; instead, you might want to perform calculations, create files, or generate any other programming tasks.

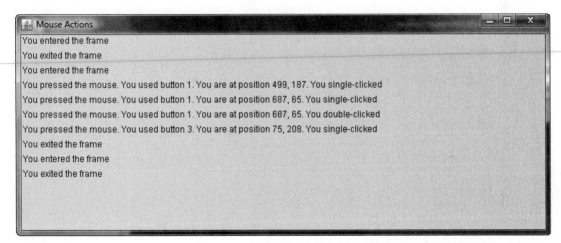

Figure 14-34 Typical execution of the JMouseActionsFrame application

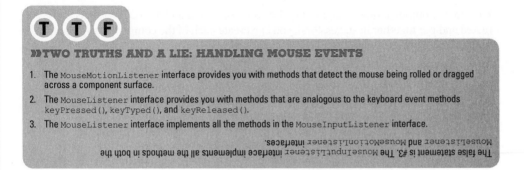

»TWO TRUTHS AND A LIE: HANDLING MOUSE EVENTS

1. The MouseMotionListener interface provides you with methods that detect the mouse being rolled or dragged across a component surface.
2. The MouseListener interface provides you with methods that are analogous to the keyboard event methods keyPressed(), keyTyped(), and keyReleased().
3. The MouseListener interface implements all the methods in the MouseInputListener interface.

The false statement is #3. The MouseInputListener interface implements all the methods in both the MouseListener and MouseMotionListener interfaces.

USING MENUS

Menus are lists of user options; they are commonly added features in GUI programs. Application users are used to seeing horizontal menu bars across the tops of frames, and they expect to be able to click those options to produce drop-down lists that display more choices. The horizontal list of JMenus is a JMenuBar. Each JMenu can contain options, called JMenuItems, or can contain submenus that also are JMenus. For example, Figure 14-35 shows a JFrame that illustrates the use of the following components:

» A JMenuBar that contains two JMenus named File and Colors.

» Three items within the Colors JMenu: Bright, Dark, and White. Dark and White are JMenuItems. Bright is a JMenu that holds a submenu. You can tell that Bright is a submenu because an arrow sits to the right of its name, and when the mouse hovers over Bright, two additional JMenuItems appear: Pink and Yellow.

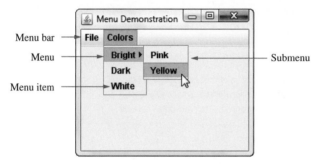

Figure 14-35 A horizontal JMenuBar that holds two JMenus

You create a JMenuBar much like other objects: by using the new operator and a call to the constructor. For example:

```
JMenuBar mainBar = new JMenuBar();
```

To create the output shown in Figure 14-35, a series of JMenu and JMenuItem objects were created and put together in stages. First, you can create each of the components you see in the menus in Figure 14-35 as follows:

» You can create the two JMenus that are part of the JMenuBar:

```
JMenu menu1 = new JMenu("File");
JMenu menu2 = new JMenu("Colors");
```

» The three components within the Colors JMenu are created as follows:

```
JMenu bright = new JMenu("Bright");
JMenuItem dark = new JMenuItem("Dark");
JMenuItem white = new JMenuItem("White");
```

» The two JMenuItems that are part of the Bright JMenu are created as follows:

```
JMenuItem pink = new JMenuItem("Pink");
JMenuItem yellow = new JMenuItem("Yellow");
```

Once all the components are created, you assemble them.

» You add the JMenuBar to a JFrame using the setJMenuBar() method as follows:

```
setJMenuBar(mainBar);
```

Using the setJMenuBar() method assures that the menu bar is anchored to the top of the frame and looks like a conventional menu bar. Notice that the JMenuBar is not added to a JFrame's content pane; it is added to the JFrame itself.

» The JMenus are added to the JMenuBar using the add() method. For example:

```
mainBar.add(menu1);
mainBar.add(menu2);
```

» A submenu and two JMenuItems are added to the Colors menu as follows:

```
menu2.add(bright);
menu2.add(dark);
menu2.add(white);
```

» A submenu can contain its own JMenuItems. For example, the Bright JMenu that is part of the Colors menu in Figure 14-35 contains its own two JMenuItem objects:

```
bright.add(pink);
bright.add(yellow);
```

Figure 14-36 shows a complete working program that creates a frame with a greeting and the JMenu shown in Figure 14-35.

```
import javax.swing.*;
import java.awt.*;
import java.awt.event.*;
public class JMenuFrame extends JFrame implements
    ActionListener
{
    private JMenuBar mainBar = new JMenuBar();
    private JMenu menu1 = new JMenu("File");
    private JMenu menu2 = new JMenu("Colors");
    private JMenuItem exit = new JMenuItem("Exit");
    private JMenu bright = new JMenu("Bright");
    private JMenuItem dark = new JMenuItem("Dark");
    private JMenuItem white = new JMenuItem("White");
    private JMenuItem pink = new JMenuItem("Pink");
    private JMenuItem yellow = new JMenuItem("Yellow");
    private JLabel label = new JLabel("Hello");
    public JMenuFrame()
```

Figure 14-36 The JMenuFrame class (*continued*)

```
   {
       setTitle("Menu Demonstration");
       setDefaultCloseOperation(JFrame.EXIT_ON_CLOSE);
       setLayout(new FlowLayout());
       setJMenuBar(mainBar);
       mainBar.add(menu1);
       mainBar.add(menu2);
       menu1.add(exit);
       menu2.add(bright);
       menu2.add(dark);
       menu2.add(white);
       bright.add(pink);
       bright.add(yellow);
       exit.addActionListener(this);
       dark.addActionListener(this);
       white.addActionListener(this);
       pink.addActionListener(this);
       yellow.addActionListener(this);
       add(label);
       label.setFont(new Font("Arial", Font.BOLD, 26));
   }
   public void actionPerformed(ActionEvent e)
   {
       Object source = e.getSource();
       Container con = getContentPane();
       if(source == exit)
          System.exit(0);
       else if(source == dark)
          con.setBackground(Color.BLACK);
       else if(source == white)
          con.setBackground(Color.WHITE);
       else if(source == pink)
          con.setBackground(Color.PINK);
       else con.setBackground(Color.YELLOW);
       repaint();
   }

   public static void main(String[] args)
   {
       JMenuFrame mFrame = new JMenuFrame();
       final int WIDTH = 250;
       final int HEIGHT = 200;
       mFrame.setSize(WIDTH, HEIGHT);
       mFrame.setVisible(true);
   }
}
```

Figure 14-36 (*continued*)

In the application in Figure 14-36, each JMenuItem becomes a source for an ActionEvent, and the JFrame is assigned the role of listener for each. The actionPerformed() method determines the source of any generated event. If the user selects the Exit option from the File menu, the application ends. If the user selects any of the colors from the Colors menu, the background color of the JFrame is altered accordingly.

USING JCheckBoxMenuItem AND JRadioButtonMenuItem OBJECTS

The JCheckBoxMenuItem and JRadioButtonMenuItem classes derive from the JMenuItem class. Each provides more specific menu items as follows:

» JCheckBoxMenuItem objects appear with a check box next to them. An item can be selected (displaying a check mark in the box) or not. Usually, you use check box items to turn options on or off.

» JRadioButtonMenuItem objects appear with a round radio button next to them. Users usually expect radio buttons to be mutually exclusive, so you usually make radio buttons part of a ButtonGroup. Then, when any radio button is selected, the others are all deselected.

The state of a JCheckBoxMenuItem or JRadioButtonMenuItem can be determined with the isSelected() method, and you can alter the state of the check box with the setSelected() method.

Figure 14-37 shows a JMenuFrame2 application in which two JCheckBoxMenuItems and three JRadioButtonMenuItems have been added to a JMenu. Figure 14-38 shows how the menu looks when the application executes.

```
import javax.swing.*;
import java.awt.*;
import java.awt.event.*;
public class JMenuFrame2 extends JFrame
{
    private JMenuBar mainBar = new JMenuBar();
    private JMenu menu1 = new JMenu("File");
    private JCheckBoxMenuItem check1 = new
        JCheckBoxMenuItem("Check box A");
    private JCheckBoxMenuItem check2 = new
        JCheckBoxMenuItem("Check box B");
    private JRadioButtonMenuItem radio1 = new
        JRadioButtonMenuItem("Radio option 1");
    private JRadioButtonMenuItem radio2 = new
        JRadioButtonMenuItem("Radio option 2");
    private JRadioButtonMenuItem radio3 = new
        JRadioButtonMenuItem("Radio option 3");
    private ButtonGroup group = new ButtonGroup();
```

Figure 14-37 The JMenuFrame2 application (*continued*)

```
    public JMenuFrame2()
    {
        setTitle("Menu Demonstration");
        setDefaultCloseOperation(JFrame.EXIT_ON_CLOSE);
        setLayout(new FlowLayout());
        setJMenuBar(mainBar);
        mainBar.add(menu1);
        menu1.add(check1);
        menu1.add(check2);
        menu1.addSeparator();
        menu1.add(radio1);
        menu1.add(radio2);
        menu1.add(radio3);
        group.add(radio1);
        group.add(radio2);
        group.add(radio3);
    }

    public static void main(String[] args)
    {
        JMenuFrame2 frame = new JMenuFrame2();
        final int WIDTH = 150;
        final int HEIGHT = 200;
        frame.setSize(WIDTH, HEIGHT);
        frame.setVisible(true);
    }
}
```

Figure 14-37 (*continued*)

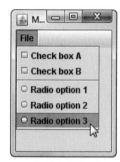

Figure 14-38 Execution of the
JMenuFrame2 application

USING addSeparator()

The shaded statement in Figure 14-37 calls the addSeparator() method. This method adds a horizontal line to menus in order to visually separate groups for your users. In Figure 14-38, you can see that the separator falls between the JCheckBoxMenuItems and the JRadioButtonMenuItems because that's the order in which the shaded addSeparator() method call was made in Figure 14-37. The separator does not change the functionality of the menu; it simply makes the menu more visually organized for the user.

USING setMnemonic()

A **mnemonic** is a key that causes an already-visible menu item to be chosen. You can use the setMnemonic() method to provide a shortcut menu key for any visible menu item. For example, when you add the following statement to the JMenuFrame2 constructor in Figure 14-37, the menu appears as in Figure 14-39:

```
menu1.setMnemonic('F');
```

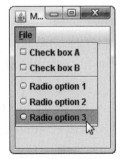

Figure 14-39 The File menu with a mnemonic applied

The mnemonic for the File menu is set to 'F', so the 'F' in *File* is underlined. When a user presses Alt+F on the keyboard, the result is the same as if the user had clicked File on the menu: the menu list is opened and displayed.

You should use a different mnemonic for each menu item that has one; if you use the same mnemonic multiple times, only the first assignment works. Usually, you use the first letter of the option; for example, 'F' for *File*. If multiple menu items start with the same letter, the convention is to choose the next most prominent letter in the name. For example, 'X' is often chosen as the mnemonic for *Exit*.

An **accelerator** is similar to a mnemonic. It is a key combination that causes a menu item to be chosen, whether or not it is visible. For example, many word-processing programs allow you to press Ctrl+P to print from anywhere in the program. Only **leaf menu items**—menus that don't bring up other menus—can have accelerators. (They are called "leaves" because they are at the end of a branch with no more branches extending from them.) See *http://java.sun.com* for more details.

»TWO TRUTHS AND A LIE: USING MENUS

1. The horizontal list of JMenus at the top of a JFrame is a JMenu.
2. Each JMenu can contain options, called JMenuItems, or can contain submenus that also are JMenus.
3. You add a JMenuBar to a JFrame using the setJMenuBar() method.

The false statement is #1. The horizontal list of JMenus at the top of a JFrame is a JMenuBar.

YOU DO IT

USING BorderLayout

Using layout managers in the containers in your applications allows flexibility in arranging the components that users see on the screen. In this section, you will create a JFrame that uses a BorderLayout and place components in each region. In the following sections, you will observe how the same components appear when other layout managers are used.

To create a JFrame that uses BorderLayout with a button in each region:

1. Open a new file in your text editor, and then type the following first few lines of a program that demonstrates BorderLayout with five objects:

```
import javax.swing.*;
import java.awt.*;
public class JBorderLayout extends JFrame
{
```

2. Instantiate five JButton objects, each with a label that is the name of one of the regions used by BorderLayout:

```
private JButton nb = new JButton("North");
private JButton sb = new JButton("South");
private JButton eb = new JButton("East");
private JButton wb = new JButton("West");
private JButton cb = new JButton("Center");
```

3. Write the constructor that sets the JFrame's layout manager and adds each of the five JButtons to the appropriate region. Also set the size, visibility, and default close operation for the JFrame.

```
public JBorderLayout()
{
    setLayout(new BorderLayout());
    add(nb, BorderLayout.NORTH);
    add(sb, BorderLayout.SOUTH);
    add(eb, BorderLayout.EAST);
    add(wb, BorderLayout.WEST);
    add(cb, BorderLayout.CENTER);
    setSize(250, 250);
    setVisible(true);
    setDefaultCloseOperation(JFrame.EXIT_ON_CLOSE);
}
```

4. Add a main() method that instantiates a JBorderLayout object and include a closing curly brace for the class:

```
public static void main(String[] args)
{
    JBorderLayout jbl = new JBorderLayout();
}
}
```

5. Save the file as **JBorderLayout.java**, then compile and execute it. The output looks like Figure 14-40. Each `JButton` entirely fills its region. (If you click the `JButtons`, they appear to be pressed, but because you have not implemented `ActionListener`, no other action is taken.)

Figure 14-40 Output of the `JBorderLayout` program

6. So you can observe the effects of changing the size of the viewing area, use your mouse to drag the right border of the `JFrame` to increase the width to approximately that shown in Figure 14-41. Notice that the center region expands, while the east and west regions retain their original size.

Figure 14-41 Output of the `JBorderLayout` program after the user drags the right border to increase the width

7. Experiment with resizing both the width and height of the `JFrame`. Close the `JFrame` when you finish.

USING FEWER THAN FIVE COMPONENTS WITH THE BorderLayout MANAGER

When you use `JBorderLayout`, you are not required to place components in every region. For example, you might use only four components, leaving the north region empty. Next, you will remove one of the objects from the `JBorderLayout` `JFrame` to observe the effect.

To create a `Container` that uses `BorderLayout` with only four objects:

1. Open the **JBorderLayout.java** file in your text editor. Immediately save it as **JBorderLayoutNoNorth.java**.

2. Change the class name to **JBorderLayoutNoNorth**. Also change the constructor name and the two instances of the class name in the `main()` method.

3. Remove the declaration of the "North" button, and within the constructor, remove the statement that adds the "North" button to the `JFrame`.

4. Save the file and compile it, then run the program. The output appears as shown in Figure 14-42. The center region occupies the space formerly held by the north region.

5. Experiment with removing some of the other components from the `JBorderLayoutNoNorth` program.

Figure 14-42 Output of the `JBorderLayoutNoNorth` program

USING `FlowLayout`

Next, you will modify the `JBorderLayout` program to demonstrate how the same components appear when using `FlowLayout`.

To demonstrate `FlowLayout`:

1. Open the **JBorderLayout.java** file in your text editor, and immediately save it as **JFlowLayoutRight.java**.

2. Change the class name from `JBorderLayout` to **JFlowLayoutRight**. Also change the constructor name and the references to the name in the `main()` method.

3. Within the constructor, change the `setLayout()` statement to use `FlowLayout` and right alignment:

   ```
   setLayout(new FlowLayout(FlowLayout.RIGHT));
   ```

4. Alter each of the five `add()` statements so that just the button name appears within the parentheses and the region is omitted. For example, `add(nb, BorderLayout.NORTH);` becomes the following:

   ```
   add(nb);
   ```

5. Save the file, then compile and execute it. Your output should look like Figure 14-43. The components have their "natural" size (or preferred size)—the minimum size the buttons need to display their labels. The buttons flow across the `JFrame` surface in a row until no more can fit; in Figure 14-43 the last two buttons added cannot fit in the first row, so they appear in the second row, right-aligned.

Figure 14-43 Output of the `JFlowLayoutRight` program

6. Experiment with widening and narrowing the `JFrame`, and observe how the components realign. Then close the `JFrame`.

USING `GridLayout`

Next, you will modify a `JFrame` to demonstrate `GridLayout`.

To demonstrate `GridLayout`:

1. Open the **JFlowLayoutRight.java** file in your text editor and save the file as **JGridLayout.java**.

2. Change the class name from `JFlowLayoutRight` to **JGridLayout**. Change the constructor name and the two references to the class in the `main()` method.

3. Within the constructor, change the `setLayout()` statement to establish a `GridLayout` with two rows, three columns, a horizontal space of two pixels, and a vertical space of four pixels:

```
setLayout(new GridLayout(2, 3, 2, 4));
```

4. Save the file, then compile and execute it. The components are arranged in two rows and three columns from left to right across each row, in the order they were added to their container. Because there are only five components, one grid position still is available. See Figure 14-44.

5. Close the program.

Figure 14-44 Output of the `JGridLayout` program

USING CardLayout

Next, you will create a CardLayout with five cards, each holding one of the JButtons used in the previous examples.

To demonstrate CardLayout:

1. Open the **JGridLayout.java** file in your text editor and save the file as **JCardLayout.java**.

2. Change the class name from JGridLayout to **JCardLayout**. Also change the constructor name and the two references in the main() method.

3. Within the constructor, change the setLayout() statement to establish a CardLayout:

   ```
   setLayout(new CardLayout());
   ```

4. Change the five add() statements that add the buttons to the content pane so that each includes a String that names the added component, as follows:

   ```
   add("north", nb);
   add("south", sb);
   add("east", eb);
   add("west", wb);
   add("center", cb);
   ```

5. Save the file, then compile and execute it. The output looks like Figure 14-45. You see only the "North" JButton because, as the first one added, it is the top card. You can click the button, but no actions take place because you have not implemented ActionListener.

6. Close the program.

Figure 14-45 Output of the JCardLayout program

VIEWING ALL THE CARDS IN CardLayout

Next, you will modify the JCardLayout program so that its buttons can initiate events that allow you to view all five JButtons you add to the content pane.

To view all the cards in CardLayout:

1. Open the **JCardLayout.java** file in your text editor and save the file as **JCardLayout2.java**.

2. Change the class name, constructor name, and two main() method references from JCardLayout to **JCardLayout2**.

3. At the top of the file, add the import statement that adds the classes and methods that allow the class to respond to events:

   ```
   import java.awt.event.*;
   ```

4. At the end of the class header, insert the following phrase so the JFrame can respond to button clicks:

   ```
   implements ActionListener
   ```

5. Instead of an anonymous layout manager, you need to create a `CardLayout` manager with an identifier that you can use with the `next()` method when the user clicks a button. Immediately after the five `JButton` declaration statements, insert the following statement:

```
CardLayout cardLayout = new CardLayout();
```

6. Within the constructor, change the `setLayout()` statement so it uses the named layout manager:

```
setLayout(cardLayout);
```

7. At the end of the constructor, add five statements that allow each of the buttons to initiate an `ActionEvent`:

```
nb.addActionListener(this);
sb.addActionListener(this);
eb.addActionListener(this);
wb.addActionListener(this);
cb.addActionListener(this);
```

8. After the constructor's closing curly brace, add an `actionPerformed()` method that responds to user clicks. The method uses the `next()` method to display the next card (next button) in the collection.

```
public void actionPerformed(ActionEvent e)
{
    cardLayout.next(getContentPane());
}
```

9. Save, compile, and run the program. The output looks the same as in Figure 14-45: you see only the "North" `JButton`. However, when you click it, the button changes to "South", "East", "West", and "Center" in succession. Close the `JFrame` when you finish.

USING A MENU BAR AND `JPanels`

Next, you will create an application for Event Handlers Incorporated that uses a menu bar that contains multiple user options, and that uses separate `JPanels` with different layout managers to organize components.

To create the `EventSelector` application:

1. Open a new file in your text editor and enter the following first few lines of the `EventSelector` class. The class extends `JFrame` and implements `ActionListener` because the `JFrame` contains potential user mouse selections.

```
import javax.swing.*;
import java.awt.*;
import java.awt.event.*;
public class EventSelector extends JFrame implements ActionListener
{
```

2. Figure 14-46 shows the format of the main menu. Create a `JMenuBar` and its two `JMenus` as follows:

```
private JMenuBar mainBar = new JMenuBar();
private JMenu menu1 = new JMenu("File");
private JMenu menu2 = new JMenu("Event types");
```

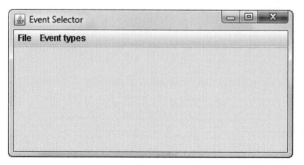

Figure 14-46 The menu bar for the `EventSelector` application

3. Next, create the items that will appear within the menus. The File menu contains an Exit option. The Event types menu contains two submenus: Adult and Child. Each of those submenus contains more options. For example, Figure 14-47 shows the expanded Adult event types menu.

```
private JMenuItem exit = new JMenuItem("Exit");
private JMenu adult = new JMenu("Adult");
private JMenu child = new JMenu("Child");
private JMenuItem adultBirthday = new JMenuItem("Birthday");
private JMenuItem anniversary = new JMenuItem("Anniversary");
private JMenuItem retirement = new JMenuItem("Retirement");
private JMenuItem adultOther = new JMenuItem("Other");
private JMenuItem childBirthday = new JMenuItem("Birthday");
private JMenuItem childOther = new JMenuItem("Other");
```

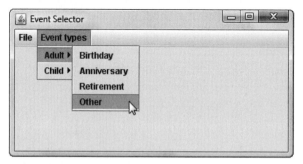

Figure 14-47 The Adult menu

4. Declare several other components that will be used to show how JFrames are composed:

```
private JPanel birthdayPanel = new JPanel();
private JPanel otherPanel = new JPanel();
private JLabel birthdayLabel = new
    JLabel("Birthday events are our specialty");
private JLabel otherLabel = new
    JLabel("We have lots of ideas for memorable events");
private JPanel buttonPanel = new JPanel();
private JRadioButton radButton1 = new
    JRadioButton("Formal events");
private JRadioButton radButton2 = new JRadioButton("Casual events");
```

5. Write the constructor for the JFrame. Set the title, the default close operation, and the layout. Call separate methods to compose the menu, to add the necessary action listeners to the menu items, and to lay out the JFrame's components. These tasks could be performed directly within the constructor, but you can place them in separate methods to better organize the application.

```
public EventSelector()
{
    setTitle("Event Selector");
    setDefaultCloseOperation(JFrame.EXIT_ON_CLOSE);
    setLayout(new FlowLayout());
    composeMenus();
    addActionListeners();
    layoutComponents();
}
```

6. Add the composeMenus() method. Set the main menu bar and add two menus to it. Then add one option to the first menu and two submenus to the second menu. Finally, add four items to the first submenu and two items to the other one.

```
public void composeMenus()
{
    setJMenuBar(mainBar);
    mainBar.add(menu1);
    mainBar.add(menu2);
    menu1.add(exit);
    menu2.add(adult);
    menu2.add(child);
    adult.add(adultBirthday);
    adult.add(anniversary);
    adult.add(retirement);
    adult.add(adultOther);
    child.add(childBirthday);
    child.add(childOther);
}
```

7. Add the `addActionListeners()` method, which makes the `JFrame` become a listener for each menu item:

```
public void addActionListeners()
{
    exit.addActionListener(this);
    adultBirthday.addActionListener(this);
    anniversary.addActionListener(this);
    retirement.addActionListener(this);
    adultOther.addActionListener(this);
    childBirthday.addActionListener(this);
    childOther.addActionListener(this);
}
```

8. The `layoutComponents()` method arranges all the components that appear in the content pane. The `birthdayPanel` object contains a single label. The `otherPanel` object contains a label and another panel (`buttonPanel`) in a grid. The `buttonPanel` contains two radio buttons. For this demonstration, the radio buttons are not functional, but in a more complicated application, an `addActionListener()` method could be applied to them. Also, in a more complicated application, you could continue to place panels within another panel to achieve complex designs.

```
public void layoutComponents()
{
    birthdayPanel.setLayout(new FlowLayout());
    otherPanel.setLayout(new GridLayout(2, 1, 3, 3));
    birthdayPanel.add(birthdayLabel);
    otherPanel.add("other", otherLabel);
    otherPanel.add("buttons", buttonPanel);
    buttonPanel.add(radButton1);
    buttonPanel.add(radButton2);
    add(birthdayPanel);
    add(otherPanel);
}
```

9. Add an `actionPerformed()` method that responds to menu selections. Different background colors are set depending on the user's choices.

```
public void actionPerformed(ActionEvent e)
{
    Object source = e.getSource();
    Container con = getContentPane();
    if(source == exit)
        System.exit(0);
    else if(source == childBirthday || source == childOther)
        con.setBackground(Color.PINK);
    else
        con.setBackground(Color.WHITE);
    if(source == adultBirthday || source == childBirthday)
    {
```

```
        birthdayPanel.setBackground(Color.YELLOW);
        otherPanel.setBackground(Color.WHITE);
    }
    else
    {
        birthdayPanel.setBackground(Color.WHITE);
        otherPanel.setBackground(Color.YELLOW);
    }
    repaint();
}
```

10. Add the `main()` method, which instantiates an `EventSelector` object and sets its size and visibility. Add a closing curly brace for the class.

```
public static void main(String[] args)
{
    EventSelector frame = new EventSelector();
    final int WIDTH = 400;
    final int HEIGHT = 200;
    frame.setSize(WIDTH, HEIGHT);
    frame.setVisible(true);
}
}
```

11. Save the application as **EventSelector.java**, then compile and run it. Make various selections and observe the effects. Figure 14-48 shows the running application after the user has made some selections. Dismiss the frame.

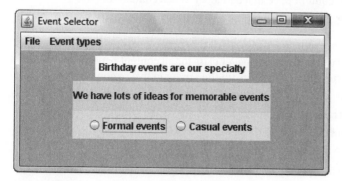

Figure 14-48 The `EventSelector` application

12. Experiment by making changes to the `EventSelector` application. For example, some menu selections could change the `JFrame` background to a different color, and others could add a new `JLabel` to the `JFrame` content pane.

DON'T DO IT

» Don't forget that the content pane is operating behind the scenes when you use a top-level container and that, depending on the operations you want to perform, you might need to get a reference to it.

» Don't forget that when you create a custom `Color` object, 0 represents the darkest shade and 255 represents the lightest.

» Don't forget to set a layout manager if you do not want to use the default one for a container.

» Don't use `add()` to place a `JFrame`'s menu bar. You must use the `setMenuBar()` method to place a menu bar correctly.

» Don't use the same mnemonic for multiple menu items.

KEY TERMS

A **top-level container** is one at the top of a containment hierarchy. The Java top-level containers are `JFrame`, `JDialog`, and `JApplet`.

A **containment hierarchy** is a tree of components that has a top-level container as its root (that is, at its uppermost level).

A **content pane** contains all the visible components in a top-level container's user interface.

A **menu bar** is a horizontal strip that is placed at the top of a container and that contains user options.

A **glass pane** resides above the content pane in a container. It can contain tool tips.

The **`getContentPane()` method** returns a reference to a container's content pane.

The **`Color` class** defines colors for you to use in your applications.

The **`BorderLayout` manager** is the default manager class for all content panes. When you use the `BorderLayout` manager, the components fill the screen in five regions: north, south, east, west, and center.

The **`FlowLayout` manager** arranges components in rows across the width of a `Container`; when the current row is filled, additional `Components` are placed in new rows.

A `Component`'s **preferred size** is its default size.

The **`GridLayout` manager** divides a container surface into a grid.

The **`CardLayout` manager** generates a stack of containers or components, one on top of another.

The **`GridBagLayout` manager** allows you to add `Components` to precise locations within the grid, as well as to indicate that specific `Components` should span multiple rows or columns within the grid.

The **`BoxLayout` manager** allows multiple components to be laid out either vertically or horizontally. The components do not wrap, so a vertical arrangement of components, for example, stays vertically arranged when the frame is resized.

A **JPanel** is a plain, borderless surface that can hold lightweight UI components.

Double buffering is the default buffering strategy in which JPanels are drawn offscreen when they are updated and displayed only when complete.

The **primary surface** is the visible screen surface during double buffering.

The **back buffer** is the offscreen image during double buffering.

A **block line transfer**, or **blitting**, is the act of copying the contents from one surface to another.

A **JScrollPane** provides scroll bars along the side or bottom of a pane, or both, so that the user can scroll initially invisible parts of the pane into view.

The **viewport** is the viewable area in a JScrollPane.

An **adapter class** implements all the methods in an interface, providing an empty body for each method.

You use the **KeyListener interface** when you are interested in actions the user initiates from the keyboard. The KeyListener interface contains three methods: keyPressed(), keyTyped(), and keyReleased().

An **action key** is a keyboard key that does not generate a character.

Virtual key codes represent keyboard keys that have been pressed.

The **x-axis** is an imaginary horizontal line that indicates screen position.

The **y-axis** is an imaginary vertical line that indicates screen position.

The **x-coordinate** is a value that increases as you travel from left to right across a window.

The **y-coordinate** is a value that increases as you travel from top to bottom across a window.

The **MouseMotionListener interface** provides you with methods named mouseDragged() and mouseMoved() that detect the mouse being rolled or dragged across a component surface.

The **MouseListener interface** provides you with methods named mousePressed(), mouseClicked(), and mouseReleased() that are analogous to the keyboard event methods keyPressed(), keyTyped(), and keyReleased().

The **MouseInputListener interface** implements all the methods in both the MouseListener and MouseMotionListener interfaces.

A **MouseEvent** is the type of event generated by mouse manipulation.

Menus are lists of user options.

A **mnemonic** is a key that causes an already visible menu item to be chosen.

An **accelerator** is a key combination that causes a menu item to be chosen, whether or not it is visible.

A **leaf menu item** is a menu item that does not bring up another menu.

CHAPTER SUMMARY

» Every top-level container has a content pane that contains all the visible components in the container's user interface. The content pane can contain components and other containers. Whenever you create a top-level container, you can get a reference to its content pane using the `getContentPane()` method.

» The `Color` class defines 13 colors for you to use in your applications. It can be used with the `setBackground()` and `setForeground()` methods of the `Component` class to make your applications more attractive and interesting. You also can create more than 16 million custom colors.

» A layout manager is an object that controls the size and position of components inside a `Container` object. The layout manager that you assign to the window determines how the components are sized and positioned within the window. The `BorderLayout` manager is the default manager class for all content panes; when you use it, the components fill the screen in five regions: north, south, east, west, and center. The `FlowLayout` manager arranges components in rows across the width of a `Container`. When you create a `GridLayout` object, you indicate the numbers of rows and columns you want, and then the container surface is divided into a grid. The `CardLayout` manager generates a stack of containers or components, one on top of another.

» A `JPanel` is a plain, borderless surface that can hold lightweight UI components.

» A `JScrollPane` provides scroll bars along the side or bottom of a pane, or both, so that the user can scroll initially invisible parts of the pane into view.

» The parent class for all event objects is named `EventObject`. `ActionEvents` are generated by components that users can click, such as `JButtons` and `JCheckBoxes`, and `TextEvents` are generated by components into which the user enters text, such as a `JTextField`. `MouseEvents` include determining the location of the mouse pointer and distinguishing between a single- and double-click. When you want to listen for an event, you implement an appropriate interface for your class. For every event class, such as <name>Event, there is a similarly named <name>Listener interface. Instead of implementing a listener class, you can extend an adapter class. An adapter class implements all the methods in an interface, providing an empty body for each method.

» In addition to the handler methods included with the event listener interfaces, the `AWTEvent` classes themselves contain methods. You use many of these methods to determine the nature of and facts about an event in question.

» The `MouseMotionListener` interface provides you with methods named `mouseDragged()` and `mouseMoved()` that detect the mouse being rolled or dragged across a component surface. The `MouseListener` interface provides you with methods named `mousePressed()`, `mouseClicked()`, and `mouseReleased()` that are analogous to the keyboard event methods `keyPressed()`, `keyTyped()`, and `keyReleased()`. The additional interface methods `mouseEntered()` and `mouseExited()` inform you when the user positions the mouse over a component (entered) or moves the mouse off a component (exited). The MouseInputListener interface implements all the methods in both the MouseListener and MouseMotionListener interfaces.

» Menus are lists of user options. You use JMenuBar, JMenu, JMenuItem, and other classes in menu creation.

REVIEW QUESTIONS

1. If you add fewer than five components to a BorderLayout, _____ .

   a. any empty component regions disappear

   b. the remaining components expand to fill the available space

   c. both a and b

   d. none of the above

2. When you resize a Container that uses BorderLayout, _____ .

   a. the Container and the regions both change in size

   b. the Container changes in size, but the regions retain their original sizes

   c. the Container retains its size, but the regions change or might disappear

   d. nothing happens

3. When you create a JFrame named myFrame, you can set its layout manager to BorderLayout with the statement _____ .

   a. myFrame.setLayout = new BorderLayout();

   b. myFrame.setLayout(new BorderLayout());

   c. setLayout(myFrame = new BorderLayout());

   d. setLayout(BorderLayout(myFrame));

4. Which of the following is the correct syntax for adding a JButton named b1 to a Container named con when using CardLayout?

   a. con.add(b1);   c. con.add("Options", b1);

   b. con.add("b1");   d. none of the above

5. You can use the _____ class to arrange components in a single row or column of a container.

   a. FlowLayout   c. CardLayout

   b. BorderLayout   d. BoxLayout

6. When you use _____ , the components you add fill their region; they do not retain their default size.

   a. `FlowLayout`

   b. `BorderLayout`

   c. `FixedLayout`

   d. `RegionLayout`

7. The statement _____ ensures that components are placed from left to right across a `JFrame` surface until the first row is full, at which point a second row is started at the frame surface's left edge.

   a. `setLayout(FlowLayout.LEFT);`

   b. `setLayout(new FlowLayout(LEFT));`

   c. `setLayout(new FlowLayout(FlowLayout.LEFT));`

   d. `setLayout(FlowLayout(FlowLayout.LEFT));`

8. The `GridBagLayout` class allows you to _____ .

   a. add components to precise locations within the grid

   b. indicate that specific components should span multiple rows or columns within the grid

   c. both a and b

   d. none of the above

9. The statement `setLayout(new GridLayout(2,7));` establishes a `GridLayout` with _____ horizontal row(s).

   a. zero

   b. one

   c. two

   d. seven

10. As you add new components to a `GridLayout`, _____ .

    a. they are positioned left-to-right across each row in sequence

    b. you can specify exact positions by skipping some positions

    c. both of the above

    d. none of the above

11. A `JPanel` is a _____ .

    a. `Window`

    b. `Container`

    c. both of the above

    d. none of the above

12. The _____ class allows you to arrange components as if they are stacked like index or playing cards.

    a. `GameLayout`

    b. `CardLayout`

    c. `BoxLayout`

    d. `GridBagLayout`

13. `AWTEvent` is the child class of _____ .

    a. `EventObject`   c. `ComponentEvent`

    b. `Event`   d. `ItemEvent`

14. When a user clicks a `JPanel` or `JFrame`, the action generates a(n) _____ .

    a. `ActionEvent`   c. `PanelEvent`

    b. `MouseEvent`   d. `KeyboardEvent`

15. Event handlers are _____ .

    a. abstract classes   c. listeners

    b. concrete classes   d. methods

16. The return type of `getComponent()` is _____ .

    a. `Object`   c. `int`

    b. `Component`   d. `void`

17. The `KeyEvent` method `getKeyChar()` returns a(n) _____ .

    a. `int`   c. `KeyEvent`

    b. `char`   d. `AWTEvent`

18. The `MouseEvent` method that allows you to identify double-clicks is _____ .

    a. `getDouble()`   c. `getDoubleClick()`

    b. `isClickDouble()`   d. `getClickCount()`

19. You can use the _____ method to determine the `Object` in which an `ActionEvent` originates.

    a. `getObject()`   c. `getOrigin()`

    b. `getEvent()`   d. `getSource()`

20. Which of the following is true in a standard menu application?

    a. A `JMenuItem` holds a `JMenu`.   c. A `JMenuBar` holds a `JMenu`.

    b. A `JMenuItem` holds a `JMenuBar`.   d. A `JMenu` holds a `JMenuBar`.

EXERCISES

1. Create a JFrame and set the layout to BorderLayout. Place a JButton containing the name of a politician in each region (left, center, and right; or west, center, and east). Each politician's physical position should correspond to your opinion of his or her political stance. Save the file as **JPoliticalFrame.java**.

2. Create 26 JButtons, each labeled with a single, different letter of the alphabet. Create a JFrame to hold five JPanels in a five-by-one grid. Place six JButtons within each of the first four JPanels and two JButtons within the fifth JPanel of the JFrame. Add a JLabel to the fifth JPanel. When the user clicks a JButton, the text of the JLabel is set to "Folder X", where X is the letter of the alphabet that is clicked. Save the file as **JFileCabinet.java**.

3. Create a JFrame that holds four buttons with the names of four different fonts. Display a demonstration JLabel using the font that the user selects. Save the file as **JFontFrame.java**.

4. Create a JFrame that uses BorderLayout. Place a JButton in the center region. Each time the user clicks the JButton, change the background color in one of the other regions. Save the file as **JColorFrame.java**.

5. Create a JFrame with JPanels, a JButton, and a JLabel. When the user clicks the JButton, reposition the JLabel to a new location in a different JPanel. Save the file as **JMovingFrame.java**.

6. Create a class named JPanelOptions that extends JPanel and whose constructor accepts two colors and a String. Use the colors for background and foreground to display the String. Create an application named JTeamColors with GridLayout. Display four JPanelOptions JPanels that show the names, in their team colors, of four of your favorite sports teams. Save the files as **JPanelOptions.java** and **JTeamColors.java**.

7. Write an application that lets you determine the integer value returned by the InputEvent method getModifiers() when you click your left, right, or—if you have one—middle mouse button on a JFrame. Save the file as **JLeftOrRight.java**.

8. a. Search the Java Web site at *http://java.sun.com* for information on how to use a JTextArea. Write an application for the WebBuy Company that allows a user to compose the three parts of a complete e-mail message: the "To:", "Subject:", and "Message:" text. The "To:" and "Subject:" text areas should provide a single line for data entry. The "Message:" area should allow multiple lines of input and be able to scroll if necessary to accommodate a long message. The user clicks a button to send the e-mail message. When the message is complete and the Send button is clicked, the application should display "Mail has been sent!" on a new line in the message area. Save the file as **JEMail.java**.

b. Modify the `JEMail` application to include a Clear button that the user can click at any time to clear the "To:", "Subject:", and "Message:" fields. Save the file as **JEMail2.java**.

9. a. Create an application for Event Handlers Incorporated that uses a graphic interface to capture data about an event from a user and writes that data to a random access output file. The data required includes the host's name, the date, and the number of guests. For simplicity, this application accepts event dates for the current month only, so the date field is an integer. Assume that only one event can be scheduled for a day, so that the day can be the key field. Allow the user to enter data one record at a time and to click a button to save it. Save the class as **CreateRandomEventFile.java**. Figure 14-49 shows the input screen into which the user has typed data for the first record.

Figure 14-49 Data entry screen for the `CreateRandomEventFile` application

b. Create an application that displays one stored event record at a time using a graphic interface. Save the file as **ReadRandomEventFile.java**.

10. Create a `JFrame` for the Summervale Resort. Allow the user to view information about different rooms available, dining options, and activities offered. Include at least two options in each menu and display appropriate information when the user makes a choice. Figure 14-50 shows a sample menu. Save the file as **SummervaleResort.java**.

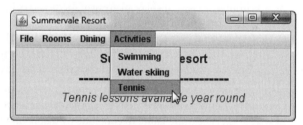

Figure 14-50 Typical execution of the `SummervaleResort` application

DEBUGGING EXERCISES

Each of the following files in the Chapter.14 folder on your Student Disk has syntax and/or logic errors. In each case, determine the problem and fix the program. After you correct the errors, save each file using the same filename preceded with Fix. For example, DebugFourteen1.java will become FixDebugFourteen1.java.

a. DebugFourteen1.java   c. DebugFourteen3.java

b. DebugFourteen2.java   d. DebugFourteen4.java

GAME ZONE

1. a. Create a Mine Field game in which the user attempts to click 10 panels of a grid before hitting the "bomb." Set up a four-by-five grid using `GridLayout` and populate the grid with `JPanel`s. Set the background color for all the `JPanel`s to `Color.BLUE`. Randomly choose one of the panels to be the bomb; the other 19 panels are "safe." Allow the player to click on grids. If the player chooses a safe panel, turn the panel to `Color.WHITE`. If the player chooses the bomb panel, turn the panel to `Color.RED` and turn all the remaining panels white. If the user successfully chooses 10 safe panels before choosing the bomb, display a congratulatory message. Save the game as **MineField.java**.

   b. Improve the Mine Field game by allowing the user to choose a difficulty level before beginning. Using a `BorderLayout`, place three buttons labeled "Easy", "Intermediate", and "Difficult" in one region and place the game grid in another region. Require the user to select a difficulty level before starting the game, then disable the buttons. If the user chooses "Easy", the user must select only five safe panels to win the game. If the user selects "Intermediate", require 10 safe panels, as in the original game. If the user selects "Difficult", require 15 safe panels. Save the game as **MineField2.java**.

2. a. Create a game that helps new mouse users improve their hand-eye coordination. Within a `JFrame`, display an array of 48 `JPanel`s in a `GridLayout` using eight rows and six columns. Randomly display an X on one of the panels. When the user clicks the correct panel (the one displaying the X), remove the X and display it on a different panel. After the user has successfully "hit" the correct panel 10 times, display a congratulatory message that includes the user's percentage (hits divided by clicks). Save the file as **JCatchTheMouse.java**.

   b. Review how to use the `GregorianCalendar` class from Chapter 4, then revise the `JCatchTheMouse` game to conclude by displaying the number of seconds it took the user to click all 10 Xs. When the application starts, create a `GregorianCalendar` object and use the `get(Calendar.SECOND)` and `get(Calendar.MINUTE)` methods with it to get the `SECOND` and `MINUTE` values at the start of the game. When the user has clicked all 10 Xs, create a second `GregorianCalendar` object and get the `SECOND` and `MINUTE` values at the end of the game. If the user starts and ends a game during the same minute, then the playing time is simply the difference between the two `SECOND` values. Make sure your application times the game correctly even if the start and stop times do not occur during the same `MINUTE`. Save the file as **JCatchTheMouseTimed.java**.

   c. In the `JCatchTheMouseTimed` game described in Game Zone exercise 2b, the timer does not work correctly if the user happens to play when the hour, day, or year changes. Use *http://java.sun.com* to find out how to use the `GregorianCalendar` class method `getTimeInMillis()`, then modify the game to measure playing time accurately, no matter when the user plays the game. Save the file as **JCatchTheMouseTimed2.java**.

3. The game Corner the King is played on a checkerboard. To begin, a checker is randomly placed in the bottom row. The player can move one or two squares to the left or upward, then the computer can move one or two squares left or up. The first to reach the upper-left corner wins. Design a game in which the computer's moves are chosen randomly. When the game ends, display a message that indicates the winner. Save the game as **CornerTheKing.java**.

4. Create a target practice game that allows the user to click moving targets and displays the number of hits in a 10-second period. Create a grid of at least 100 `JPanels`. Randomly display an X on five panels to indicate targets. As the user clicks each X, change the label to indicate a hit. When all five Xs have been hit, randomly display a new set of five targets. Continue with as many sets as the user can hit in 10 seconds. (Use *http://java.sun.com* to find how to use the `GregorianCalendar` class method `getTimeInMillis()` to calculate the time change.) When the time is up, display a count of the number of targets hit. Save the file as **JTargetPractice.java**.

5. You set up the card game Concentration by placing pairs of cards face down in a grid. The player turns up two cards at a time, exposing their values. If the cards match, they are removed from the grid. If the cards do not match, they are turned back over so their values are hidden again, and the player selects two more cards to expose. Using the knowledge gained by the previously exposed cards, the player attempts to remove all the pairs of cards from play. Create a Java version of this game using a `GridLayout` that is four rows high and five columns wide. Randomly assign two of the numbers 0 through 9 to each of 20 `JPanels`, and place each of the 20 `JPanels` in a cell of the grid. Initially, show only "backs" of cards by setting each panel's background to a solid color. When the user clicks a first card, change its color and expose its value. After the user clicks a second card, change its color to the same color as the first exposed card, expose the second card's value, and keep both cards exposed until the user's mouse pointer exits the second card. If the two exposed cards are different, hide the cards again. If the two turned cards match, then "remove" the pair from play by setting their background colors to white. When the user has matched all 20 cards into 10 pairs, display a congratulatory message. Save the game as **JConcentration.java**.

6. Create a Mine Sweeper game by setting up a grid of rows and columns in which "bombs" are randomly hidden. You choose the size and difficulty of the game; for example, you might choose to create a fairly simple game by displaying a four-by-five grid that contains four bombs. If a player clicks a panel in the grid that contains a bomb, then the player loses the game. If the clicked panel is not a bomb, display a number that indicates how

many adjacent panels contain a bomb. For example, if a user clicks a panel containing a 0, the user knows it is safe to click any panel above, below, beside, or diagonally adjacent to the cell, because those cells cannot possibly contain a bomb. If the player loses by clicking a bomb, display all the numeric values as well as the bomb positions. If the player succeeds in clicking all the panels except those containing bombs, the player wins and you should display a congratulatory message. Figure 14-51 shows the progression of a typical game. In the first screen, the user has clicked a panel, and the display indicates that one adjacent cell contains a bomb. In the second screen, the user has clicked a second panel, and the display indicates that three adjacent cells contain bombs. In the last screen, the user has clicked a bomb panel, and all the bomb positions are displayed. Save the game as **MineSweeper.java**.

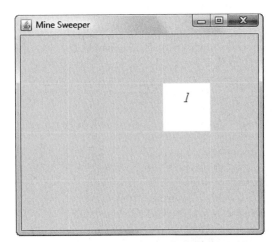

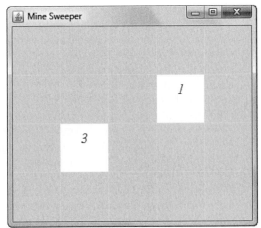

Figure 14-51 Typical progression of MineSweeper game

7. Create the game Lights Out using a five-by-five grid of panels. Randomly set each panel in the grid to a dark color or light color. The object of the game is to force all the panels to be dark, thus turning the "lights out." When the player clicks a panel, turn all the panels in the same row and column, including the clicked panel, to the opposite color. For example, if the user clicks the panel in the second row, third column, then darken all the light-colored panels in the second row and third column, and lighten all the dark-colored panels in that row and column. When all the panels in the grid are dark, all the lights are out, so display a congratulatory message. Save the game as **LightsOut.java**.

8. The game StopGate is played on a checkerboard with a set of dominoes; each domino is large enough to cover two checkerboard squares. One player places a domino horizontally on the checkerboard, covering any two squares. The other player then places a domino vertically to cover any other two squares. When a player has no more moves available, that player loses. Create a computerized version of the game in which the player places the horizontal pieces and the computer randomly selects a position for the vertical pieces. (Game construction will be simpler if you allow the player to select only the left square of a two-square area and assume the domino covers that position plus the position immediately to the right.) Use a different color for the player's dominoes and the computer's dominoes. Display a message naming the winner when no more moves are possible. Figure 14-52 shows a typical game after the player (blue) and computer (black) have each made one move, and near the end of the game when the player is about to win—the player has several moves remaining, but the computer has none. Save the file as **StopGate.java**.

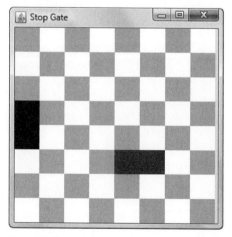 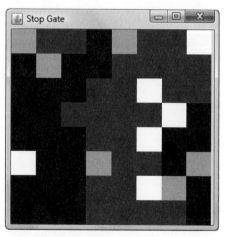

Figure 14-52 A typical game of StopGate just after play begins and near the end of the game

TOUGH QUESTIONS

1. In this chapter you learned there is no built-in `ActionAdapter` class. If there was one, what would the code look like?

2. Describe some general guidelines for developing professional GUI applications.

UP FOR DISCUSSION

1. If you are completing all the programming exercises in this book, you know that working programs require a lot of time to write and test. Professional programs require even more hours of work. In the workplace, programs frequently must be completed by strict deadlines; for example, a tax-calculating program must be completed by year's end, or an advertising Web site must be completed by the launch of the product. Programmers often find themselves working into the evenings or on weekends to complete "rush" projects. How do you feel about having to do this? What types of compensation would make the hours worthwhile for you?

2. Suppose your organization asks you to develop a code of ethics for the Information Technology Department. What would you include?

15

GRAPHICS

In this chapter, you will:

Learn about the paint() and repaint() methods
Use the drawString() method to draw Strings
using various fonts and colors
Create Graphics and Graphics2D objects
Draw lines and shapes
Learn more about fonts and methods you can use
with them
Draw with Java 2D graphics

JAVA ON THE JOB, SCENE 15

"What are you smiling about?" your mentor, Lynn Greenbrier, asks as she walks by your desk at Event Handlers Incorporated.

"I liked Java programming from the start," you say, "but now that I'm creating applications with GUI components and color, I'm really having fun."

"If you like what you've done with your programs so far," Lynn says, "just wait until you add colors, shapes, images, and sound. In this chapter and the next, let me show you how to use graphics and multimedia to add some sizzle."

LEARNING ABOUT THE paint() AND repaint() METHODS

When you run a Java program that contains graphics, such as the `JFrame` applications in Chapters 13 and 14, the display surface frequently must be redisplayed, or **rerendered**. Redisplaying a surface is also called **painting**. Painting operations fall into two broad categories based on what causes them:

» **System-triggered painting** operations occur when the system asks a component to render its contents. This happens when the component is first made visible, if it is resized, or if it is damaged. For example, a component becomes damaged when another component that previously covered part of it has been moved, revealing a portion that was not visible.

» **Application-triggered painting** operations occur when the internal state of a component has changed. For example, when a user clicks a button, a "pressed" version of the button must be rendered.

» NOTE
All of the graphics techniques you will learn in this chapter work with `JApplets` as well as `JFrames`. You will learn about `JApplets` in Chapter 16.

No matter which way a paint request is triggered, a `Component`'s **paint() method** is invoked. The header for the `paint()` method is:

```
public void paint(Graphics g)
```

When AWT invokes the `paint()` method, the `Graphics` object parameter is preconfigured with the appropriate state for drawing on the component:

» The `Graphics` object's *color* is set to the component's `foreground` property.

» The `Graphics` object's *font* is set to the component's `font` property.

» The `Graphics` object's *translation* is set such that the coordinate 0, 0 represents the upper-left corner of the component.

» The `Graphics` object's *clip rectangle* is set to the area of the component that needs repainting.

Programs must use this `Graphics` object (or one derived from it) to render output. They are free to change the state of the `Graphics` object as necessary.

You override the paint() method in your programs when you want specific actions to take place when components must be rendered. You don't usually call the paint() method directly. Instead, you call the **repaint() method**, which you can use when a window needs to be updated, such as when it contains new images or you have moved a new object onto the screen. The Java system calls the repaint() method when it needs to update a window, or you can call it yourself—in either case, repaint() creates a Graphics object for you that is the argument to the paint() method. The repaint() method calls another method named update(), which calls the paint() method. The series of events is best described with an example. Figure 15-1 shows a JDemoPaint class that extends JFrame. The frame contains a JButton. The constructor sets a title, layout manager, and default close operation, and it adds the button to the frame. The button is designated as a source for actions to which the frame can respond.

》》NOTE
The update() method clears the background of the Component's content pane as well as calling the paint() method.

```java
import javax.swing.*;
import java.awt.*;
import java.awt.event.*;
public class JDemoPaint extends JFrame implements ActionListener
{
    JButton pressButton = new JButton("Press");
    public JDemoPaint()
    {
        setTitle("Paint Demo");
        setLayout(new FlowLayout());
        setDefaultCloseOperation(JFrame.EXIT_ON_CLOSE);
        add(pressButton);
        pressButton.addActionListener(this);
    }
    public void actionPerformed(ActionEvent e)
    {
        System.out.print("Button pressed. ");
        repaint();
    }
    public void paint(Graphics g)
    {
        super.paint(g);
        System.out.println("In paint method.");
    }
    public static void main(String[] args)
    {
        JDemoPaint frame = new JDemoPaint();
        frame.setSize(150, 100);
        frame.setVisible(true);
    }
}
```

Figure 15-1 The JDemoPaint class

>>**NOTE** In Figure 15-1, the shaded first line of code in the paint() method is super.paint(g);. This statement is a call to the paint() method that is part of JDemoPaint's parent class (JFrame), and it passes the local Graphics object (named g) to this method. Although this program and others in this chapter will work without this statement, omitting it causes errors in more complicated applications. For now, you can get in the habit of including this method call as the first statement in any JFrame's paint() method, using whatever local name you have declared for your paint() method's Graphics argument.

In the JDemoPaint class in Figure 15-1, the actionPerformed() method executes when the user presses the JButton. The method contains a call to repaint(), which is unseen in the class and which automatically calls the paint() method.

The paint() method in the JDemoPaint class overrides the automatically supplied paint() method. The paint() method displays a line of output at the command line—it announces that the paint() method is executing. Figure 15-2 shows a typical execution of the program. The JFrame is first drawn when it is constructed, and the message "In paint method." appears at the command line. When the user clicks the button on the frame, two messages are displayed: "Button pressed." from the actionPerformed() method, and "In paint method." from the paint() method that is called by repaint(). When the user minimizes and restores the frame, paint() is called automatically, and the "In paint method." message is displayed again.

>>**NOTE**
The repaint() method only requests that Java repaint the screen. If a second request to repaint() occurs before Java can carry out the first request, Java executes only the last repaint() method.

>>**NOTE**
Before the built-in paint() method is called, the entire container is filled with its background color. Then the paint() method redraws the contents. The effect is that components are "erased" before being redrawn.

Figure 15-2 Typical execution of JDemoPaint program

>>**NOTE** If you call repaint() alone in a class that is a container, then the entire container is repainted. (The call to repaint() is actually this.repaint();.) This might cause unnecessary paint processing if only part of the container has changed. If you call repaint() with a component, as in pressButton.repaint(), then only that component is repainted.

USING THE setLocation() METHOD

The **setLocation() method** allows you to place a component at a specific location within a JFrame's content pane. In Chapter 14, you learned that a window or frame consists of a number of horizontal and vertical pixels on the screen, and that any component you place on the screen has a horizontal, or x-axis, position as well as a vertical, or y-axis, position. When you allow a layout manager to position components, specific positions are selected for each component.

You can change the position of a component by using the setLocation() method and passing it x- and y-coordinate positions. For example, to position a JLabel object named someLabel at the upper-left corner of a JFrame, you write the following within the JFrame class:

```
someLabel.setLocation(0,0);
```

If a window is 400 pixels wide by 200 pixels tall, you can place a Button named pressMe in the approximate center of the window with the following statement:

```
pressMe.setLocation(400,200);
```

The coordinate arguments can be numeric constants or variables.

> **NOTE** When you use setLocation(), the upper-left corner of the component is placed at the specified x- and y-coordinates. In other words, if a window is 100 by 100 pixels, aButton.setLocation(100,100); places the JButton outside the window, where you cannot see the component.

For example, Figure 15-3 shows a JDemoLocation class that uses a call to the setLocation() method in the actionPerformed() method. The values of the x- and y-coordinates passed to setLocation() are initialized to 0, and then each is increased by 30 every time the user clicks the JButton. The JButton moves 30 pixels down and to the right every time it is clicked. Figure 15-4 shows the JFrame when it starts with the JButton in its default position; after the user clicks the JButton once, moving it to position 0, 0; after the user clicks it a second time, moving it to position 30, 30; and after the user clicks it a third time, moving it to position 60, 60.

```java
import javax.swing.*;
import java.awt.*;
import java.awt.event.*;
public class JDemoLocation extends JFrame implements ActionListener
{
    JButton pressButton = new JButton("Press");
    int x = 0, y = 0;
    final int GAP = 30;
    public JDemoLocation()
    {
        setTitle("Location Demo");
        setLayout(new FlowLayout());
        setDefaultCloseOperation(JFrame.EXIT_ON_CLOSE);
        add(pressButton);
        pressButton.addActionListener(this);
    }
    public void actionPerformed(ActionEvent e)
    {
        pressButton.setLocation(x, y);
        x += GAP;
        y += GAP;
    }
    public static void main(String[] args)
    {
        JDemoLocation frame = new JDemoLocation();
        frame.setSize(150, 150);
        frame.setVisible(true);
    }
}
```

Figure 15-3 The JDemoLocation class

> **NOTE** In the JDemoLocation program in Figure 15-3, if the user continues to click the JButton, it moves off the frame surface. You could add an if statement to prevent continued progression of the setLocation() coordinates.

Figure 15-4 Execution of the JDemoLocation program

>> **NOTE** The setLocation() method can seem difficult to use at first because it works correctly only when it is used after the layout manager has finished positioning all the application's components (or in cases where no layout manager is functioning). In other words, if you try to use setLocation() on a component within its container's constructor, the component will not be repositioned because the layout manager will not be finished placing components.

(T) (T) (F)

>> **TWO TRUTHS AND A LIE: LEARNING ABOUT THE** paint()
AND repaint() **METHODS**

1. Painting can be system triggered (for example, when a component is resized) or application triggered (for example, when a user clicks a button).

2. When the paint() method is called, the Graphics object parameter is preconfigured with the appropriate state for drawing on the component, including the color and font.

3. You override the repaint() method in your programs when you want specific actions to take place when components must be rendered. You usually call the paint() method directly, and it calls repaint().

The false statement is #3. You override the paint() method in your programs when you want specific actions to take place when components must be rendered. You don't usually call the paint() method directly—you call repaint().

USING THE drawString() METHOD

The **drawString() method** allows you to draw a String in a JFrame or other component. The drawString() method requires three arguments: a String, an x-axis coordinate, and a y-axis coordinate.

You are already familiar with x- and y-axis coordinates because you used them with the setLocation() method for components. However, there is a minor difference in how you place components using the setLocation() method and how you place Strings using the drawString() method. When you use x- and y-coordinates with components, such as JButtons or JLabels, the upper-left corner of the component is placed at the coordinate position. When you use x- and y-coordinates with drawString(), the lower-left corner of the String appears at the coordinates. Figure 15-5 shows the positions of a JLabel placed at the coordinates 30, 10 and a String placed at the coordinates 10, 30.

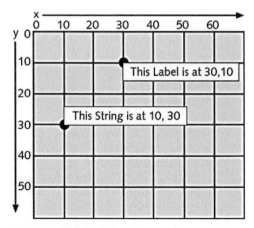

Figure 15-5 Placement of String and JLabel objects on a frame

The drawString() method is a member of the Graphics class, so you need to use a Graphics object to call it. Recall that the paint() method header shows that the method receives a Graphics object from the update() method. If you use drawString() within paint(), the Graphics object you name in the header is available to you. For example, if you write a paint() method with the header public void paint(Graphics brush), you can draw a String within your paint() method by using a statement such as:

```
brush.drawString("Hi", 50, 80);
```

USING THE setFont() AND setColor() METHODS

You can improve the appearance of strings drawn using Graphics objects by using the setFont() method. The setFont() method requires a Font object, which, as you may recall, you create with a statement such as:

```
Font someFont = new Font("TimesRoman", Font.BOLD, 16);
```

Then you can instruct a Graphics object to use the font by inserting the font as the argument in a setFont() method. For example, if a Graphics object is named artist and a Font object is named someFont, the font is set to someFont with the following:

```
artist.setFont(someFont);
```

> **NOTE**
> You learned about the Font class when you changed a JLabel's font in Chapter 13.

Figure 15-6 shows an application that uses the setFont() method with a Graphics object named brush. When the paint() method executes, the automatically created brush object is assigned the bigFont and then used to draw the hello string at position 10, 100. Figure 15-7 shows the output.

```
import javax.swing.*;
import java.awt.*;
public class JDemoFont extends JFrame
{
    Font bigFont = new Font("Serif", Font.ITALIC, 48);
    String hello = "Hello";
    public void paint(Graphics brush)
    {
        super.paint(brush);
        brush.setFont(bigFont);
        brush.drawString(hello, 10, 100);
    }
    public static void main(String[] args)
    {
        JDemoFont frame = new JDemoFont();
        frame.setSize(180, 150);
        frame.setVisible(true);
    }
}
```

Figure 15-6 The `JDemoFont` class

Figure 15-7 Output of the `JDemoFont` program

USING COLOR

You can designate a `Graphics` color with the `setColor()` method. As you learned in Chapter 14, the `Color` class contains 13 constants; you can use any of these constants as an argument to the `setColor()` method. For example, you can instruct a `Graphics` object named `brush` to apply green paint by using the following statement:

```
brush.setColor(Color.GREEN);
```

Until you change the color, subsequent graphics output appears as green.

»TWO TRUTHS AND A LIE: USING THE `drawString()` **METHOD**

1. The `drawString()` method requires three arguments: a `String`, an x-axis coordinate, and a y-axis coordinate.
2. When you use x- and y-coordinates with components, such as `JButton`s or `JLabel`s, the lower-left corner of the component is placed at the coordinate position, but when you use x- and y-coordinates with `drawString()`, the upper-left corner of the `String` appears at the coordinates.
3. The `drawString()` method is a member of the `Graphics` class, so you need to use a `Graphics` object to call it.

The false statement is #2. When you use x- and y-coordinates with components, such as `JButton`s or `JLabel`s, the upper-left corner of the component is placed at the coordinate position, but when you use x- and y-coordinates with `drawString()`, the lower-left corner of the `String` appears at the coordinates.

CREATING Graphics
AND Graphics2D OBJECTS

When you call the paint() method from within an application, you can use the automatically created Graphics object that is passed to it, but you can also instantiate your own Graphics or Graphics2D objects. For example, you might want to use a Graphics object when some action occurs, such as a mouse event. Because the actionPerformed() method does not supply you with a Graphics object automatically, you can create your own.

For example, to display a string when the user clicks a JButton, you can code an actionPerformed() method such as the following:

```
public void actionPerformed(ActionEvent e)
{
   Graphics draw = getGraphics();
   draw.drawString("You clicked the button!", 50, 100);
}
```

This method instantiates a Graphics object named draw. (You can use any legal Java identifier.) The getGraphics() method provides the draw object with Graphics capabilities. Then the draw object can employ any of the Graphics methods you have learned, such as setFont(), setColor(), and drawString().

》NOTE Notice that when you create the draw object, you are not calling the Graphics constructor directly. (The name of the Graphics constructor is Graphics(), not getGraphics().) This operation is similar to the way you call getContentPane(). You are not allowed to call the Graphics or ContentPane constructors because those classes are abstract classes.

》NOTE If you call getGraphics() in a frame that is not visible, you receive a NullPointerException and the program will not execute.

》TWO TRUTHS AND A LIE: CREATING Graphics AND Graphics2D OBJECTS

1. When you call the paint() method from within an application, you must explicitly instantiate a Graphics or Graphics2D object for it to use.
2. The actionPerformed() method does not automatically create a Graphics object, but you can create one to use within the method.
3. When you create a Graphics object, you call the getGraphics() method instead of calling the Graphics constructor directly.

The false statement is #1. When you call the paint() method from within an application, you can use the automatically created Graphics object that is passed to it, but you can also instantiate your own Graphics or Graphics2D objects.

DRAWING LINES AND SHAPES

Just as you can draw `String`s using a `Graphics` object and the `drawString()` method, Java provides you with several methods for drawing a variety of lines and geometric shapes.

You can use the **`drawLine()` method** to draw a straight line between any two points on the screen. The `drawLine()` method takes four arguments: the x- and y-coordinates of the line's starting point and the x- and y-coordinates of the line's ending point. For example, if you create a `Graphics` object named `pen`, then the following statement draws a straight line that slants down and to the right, from position 50, 50 to position 100, 200, as shown in Figure 15-8.

```
pen.drawLine(50, 50, 100, 200);
```

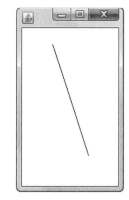

Figure 15-8 A line created with the `drawLine()` method

Because you can start at either end when you draw a line, an identical line is created with the following:

```
pen.drawLine(100, 200, 50, 50);
```

You can use the **`drawRect()` method** and **`fillRect()` method**, respectively, to draw the outline of a rectangle or to draw a solid, or filled, rectangle. Each of these methods requires four arguments. The first two arguments represent the x- and y-coordinates of the upper-left corner of the rectangle. The last two arguments represent the width and height of the rectangle. For example, the following statement draws a short, wide rectangle that begins at position 20, 100, and is 200 pixels wide by 10 pixels tall:

```
drawRect(20, 100, 200, 10);
```

The **`clearRect()` method** also requires four arguments and draws a rectangle. The difference between using the `drawRect()` and `fillRect()` methods and the `clearRect()` method is that the first two methods use the current drawing color, whereas the `clearRect()` method draws what appears to be an empty or "clear" rectangle. For example, the `JDemoRectangles` program shown in Figure 15-9 produces the output shown in Figure 15-10. First, the constructor method sets the background color to blue and sets the layout manager. Then, the `paint()` method sets the drawing color to red, draws a filled rectangle in red, and draws a smaller, "clear" rectangle within the boundaries of the filled rectangle.

```
import javax.swing.*;
import java.awt.*;
public class JDemoRectangles extends JFrame
{
    Container con = getContentPane();
    public JDemoRectangles()
    {
        con.setBackground(Color.BLUE);
        con.setLayout(new FlowLayout());
    }
    public void paint(Graphics gr)
    {
        super.paint(gr);
        gr.setColor(Color.RED);
        gr.fillRect(40, 40, 120, 120);
        gr.clearRect(50, 60, 50, 50);
    }
    public static void main(String[] args)
    {
        JDemoRectangles frame = new JDemoRectangles();
        frame.setSize(200, 200);
        frame.setVisible(true);
    }
}
```

Figure 15-9 The `JDemoRectangles` class

> **» NOTE**
> A rectangle created with the `clearRect()` method is not really "clear"; in other words, it is not transparent. When you create a rectangle, you do not see objects that might be hidden behind it.

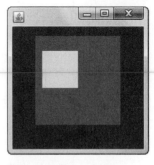

Figure 15-10 Output of the `JDemoRectangles` program

You can create rectangles with rounded corners when you use the **drawRoundRect() method**. The `drawRoundRect()` method requires six arguments. The first four arguments match the four arguments required to draw a rectangle: the x- and y-coordinates of the upper-left corner, the width, and the height. The two additional arguments represent the arc width and height associated with the rounded corners (an **arc** is a portion of a circle). If you assign zeros to the arc coordinates, the rectangle is not rounded; instead, the corners are square. At the other extreme, if you assign values to the arc coordinates that are at least the width and height of the rectangle, the rectangle is so rounded that it is a circle. The `paint()` method in Figure 15-11 draws four rectangles with increasingly large corner arcs. The first rectangle is drawn at coordinates 20, 40, and the horizontal coordinate is increased by 100 for each subsequent rectangle. Each rectangle is the same width and height, but each set of arc values becomes larger, producing rectangles that are not rounded, slightly rounded, very rounded, and completely rounded in sequence. Figure 15-12 shows the program's output. Notice that a rectangle with the same height and width is a square, and a completely rounded square is actually a circle.

> **» NOTE**
> It is almost impossible to draw a picture of any complexity without sketching it first on a piece of graph paper to help you determine correct coordinates.

```
import javax.swing.*;
import java.awt.*;
public class JDemoRoundRectangles extends JFrame
{
    public void paint(Graphics gr)
    {
        super.paint(gr);
        int x = 20;
        int y = 40;
        final int WIDTH = 80, HEIGHT = 80;
        final int HORIZONTAL_GAP = 100;
        gr.drawRoundRect(x, y, WIDTH, HEIGHT, 0, 0);
        x += HORIZONTAL_GAP;
        gr.drawRoundRect(x, y, WIDTH, HEIGHT, 20, 20);
        x += HORIZONTAL_GAP;
        gr.drawRoundRect(x, y, WIDTH, HEIGHT, 40, 40);
        x += HORIZONTAL_GAP;
        gr.drawRoundRect(x, y, WIDTH, HEIGHT, 80, 80);
    }
    public static void main(String[] args)
    {
        JDemoRoundRectangles frame = new JDemoRoundRectangles();
        frame.setSize(420, 140);
        frame.setVisible(true);
    }
}
```

Figure 15-11 The JDemoRoundRectangles class

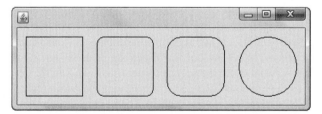

Figure 15-12 Output of the JDemoRoundRectangles program

>>NOTE As with the fillRect() method, you can use the fillRoundRect() method to create a filled rounded rectangle and the clearRoundRect() method to create a clear rounded rectangle.

DRAWING OVALS

It is possible to draw an oval using the drawRoundRect() or fillRoundRect() method, but it is usually easier to use the **drawOval()** and **fillOval() methods**. The drawOval() and fillOval() methods both draw ovals using the same four arguments that rectangles use.

When you supply drawOval() or fillOval() with x- and y-coordinates for the upper-left corner and width and height measurements, you can picture an imaginary rectangle that uses the four arguments. The oval is then placed within the rectangle so it touches the rectangle at the center of each of the rectangle's sides. For example, suppose that you create a Graphics object named tool and draw a rectangle with the following statement:

```
tool.drawRect(50, 50, 100, 60);
```

Suppose that then you create an oval with the same coordinates as follows:

```
tool.drawOval(50, 50, 100, 60);
```

The output appears as shown in Figure 15-13, with the oval edges just skimming the rectangle's sides.

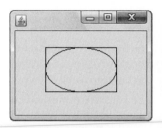

Figure 15-13 Demonstration of the drawOval() method

> **NOTE**
> Your Student Disk contains a JDemoOval.java file that produces the frame in Figure 15-13.

> **NOTE**
> If you draw a rectangle with identical height and width, you draw a square. If you draw an oval with identical height and width, you draw a circle.

DRAWING ARCS

In Java, you can draw an arc using the Graphics **drawArc() method**. To use the drawArc() method, you provide six arguments:

» The x-coordinate of the upper-left corner of an imaginary rectangle that represents the bounds of the imaginary circle that contains the arc

» The y-coordinate of the same point

» The width of the imaginary rectangle that represents the bounds of the imaginary circle that contains the arc

» The height of the same imaginary rectangle

» The beginning arc position

» The arc angle

Arc positions and angles are measured in degrees; there are 360 degrees in a circle. The 0° position for any arc is the three o'clock position, as shown in Figure 15-14. The other 359 degree positions increase as you move counterclockwise around an imaginary circle, so 90° is at the top of the circle in the twelve o'clock position, 180° is opposite the starting position at nine o'clock, and 270° is at the bottom of the circle in the six o'clock position.

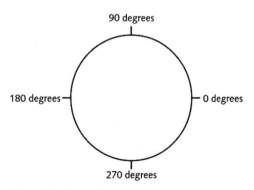

Figure 15-14 Arc positions

The arc angle is the number of degrees over which you want to draw the arc, traveling counterclockwise from the starting position. For example, you can draw a half circle by indicating an arc angle of 180° or a quarter circle by indicating an arc angle of 90°. If you want to travel clockwise from the starting position, you express the degrees as a negative number. Just as when you draw a line, when drawing any arc you can take one of two approaches: either start at point A and travel to point B, or start at point B and travel to point A. For example, to create an arc object using a Graphics object named g that looks like the top half of a circle, the following statements produce identical results:

```
g.drawArc(x, y, w, h, 0, 180);
g.drawArc(x, y, w, h, 180, -180);
```

The first statement starts an arc at the three o'clock position and travels 180 degrees counterclockwise to the nine o'clock position. The second statement starts at nine o'clock and travels clockwise to three o'clock.

The **fillArc() method** creates a solid arc. The arc is drawn, and two straight lines are drawn from the arc endpoints to the center of the imaginary circle whose perimeter the arc occupies. For example, assuming you have declared a Graphics object named g, the following two statements together produce the output shown in Figure 15-15:

```
g.fillArc(10, 50, 100, 100, 20, 320);
g.fillArc(200, 50, 100, 100, 340, 40);
```

>> NOTE
Your Student Disk contains a program named JDemoFillArc.java that produces Figure 15-15.

Each of the two arcs is in a circle that has a size of 100 by 100. The first arc almost completes a full circle, starting at position 20 (near two o'clock) and ending 320 degrees around the circle (at position 340, near four o'clock). The second filled arc more closely resembles a pie slice, starting at position 340 and extending 40 degrees to end at position 20.

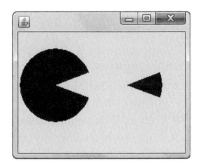

Figure 15-15 Two filled arcs

CREATING SHADOWED RECTANGLES

The draw3DRect() method is a minor variation on the drawRect() method. You use the **draw3DRect() method** to draw a rectangle that appears to have "shadowing" on two of its edges—the effect is that of a rectangle that is lit from the upper-left corner and slightly raised or slightly lowered. The draw3DRect() method requires a fifth argument in addition to the x- and y-coordinates and width and height required by the drawRect() method. The fifth argument is a Boolean value, which is true if you want the raised rectangle effect (darker on the right and bottom) and false if you want the lowered rectangle effect (lighter on the right and bottom). There is also a **fill3DRect() method** for creating filled three-dimensional (3D) rectangles. For example, the program in Figure 15-16 creates two filled 3D rectangles in pink. You can see that the effect on the output in Figure 15-17 is very subtle; the shadowing is only one pixel wide.

```
import javax.swing.*;
import java.awt.*;
public class JDemo3DRectangles extends JFrame
{
    public void paint(Graphics gr)
    {
        super.paint(gr);
        final int WIDTH = 60, HEIGHT = 80;
        gr.setColor(Color.PINK);
        gr.fill3DRect(20, 40, WIDTH, HEIGHT, true);
        gr.fill3DRect(100, 40, WIDTH, HEIGHT, false);
    }
    public static void main(String[] args)
    {
        JDemo3DRectangles frame = new JDemo3DRectangles();
        frame.setSize(180, 150);
        frame.setVisible(true);
    }
}
```

▶▶ NOTE
The 3D methods work best with lighter drawing colors.

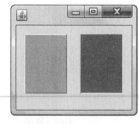

Figure 15-17 Output of the JDemo3DRectangles program

Figure 15-16 The JDemo3DRectangles class

CREATING POLYGONS

When you want to create a shape that is more complex than a rectangle, you can use a sequence of calls to the drawLine() method, or you can use the **drawPolygon() method** to draw complex shapes. The drawPolygon() method requires three arguments: two integer arrays and a single integer.

The first integer array holds a series of x-coordinate positions, and the second array holds a series of corresponding y-coordinate positions. These positions represent points that are connected to form the polygon. The third integer argument is the number of pairs of points you want to connect. If you don't want to connect all the points represented by the array values, you can assign this third argument integer a value that is smaller than the number of elements in each array. However, an error occurs if the third argument is a value higher than the available number of coordinate pairs.

For example, examine the code shown in Figure 15-18, which is a JFrame application that has one task: to draw a star-shaped polygon. Two parallel arrays are assigned x- and y-coordinates; the paint() method draws the polygon. The program's output appears in Figure 15-19.

```
import javax.swing.*;
import java.awt.*;
public class JStar extends JFrame
{
    public void paint(Graphics gr)
    {
        super.paint(gr);
        int xPoints[] = {42, 52, 72, 52,  60, 40, 15,  28, 9,  32, 42};
        int yPoints[] = {38, 62, 68, 80, 105, 85, 102, 75, 58, 60, 38};
        gr.drawPolygon(xPoints, yPoints, xPoints.length);
    }
    public static void main(String[] args)
    {
        JStar frame = new JStar();
        frame.setSize(80, 150);
        frame.setVisible(true);
    }
}
```

Figure 15-18 The JStar class

Figure 15-19 Output of the JStar program

> **NOTE** In Chapter 8, you learned that you can use length for the length of an array. Rather than using a constant integer value, such as 11, in the call to drawPolygon() in Figure 15-18, it is convenient to use the length of one of the coordinate point arrays, as in xPoints.length.

You can use the **fillPolygon() method** to draw a solid shape. The major difference between the drawPolygon() and fillPolygon() methods is that if the beginning and ending points used with the fillPolygon() method are not identical, the two endpoints are connected by a straight line before the polygon is filled with color.

Rather than providing the fillPolygon() method with three arguments, you can also create a Polygon object and pass the constructed object as a single argument to the fillPolygon() method. The Polygon constructor requires an array of x-coordinates, an array of y-coordinates, and a size. For example, you can create a filled polygon using the following statements:

```
Polygon someShape = new Polygon(xPoints, yPoints, xPoints.length);
gr.fillPolygon(someShape);
```

These statements have the same result as the following:

```
gr.fillPolygon(xPoints, yPoints, xPoints.length);
```

In addition, you can instantiate an empty `Polygon` object (with no points) using the following statement:

```
Polygon someFutureShape = new Polygon();
```

You use the **addPoint() method** in statements such as the following to add points to the polygon later:

```
someFutureShape.addPoint(100, 100);
someFutureShape.addPoint(150, 200);
someFutureShape.addPoint(50, 250);
```

It is practical to use `addPoint()` instead of coding the point values when you want to write a program in which you calculate points later or in which the user enters polygon point values. Whether the user does so from the keyboard or with a mouse, points can be added to the polygon indefinitely.

COPYING AN AREA

After you create a graphics image, you might want to create copies of the image. For example, you might want a company logo to appear several times in an application. Of course, you can redraw the picture, but you can also use the **copyArea() method** to copy any rectangular area to a new location. The `copyArea()` method requires six parameters:

» The x- and y-coordinates of the upper-left corner of the area to be copied

» The width and height of the area to be copied

» The horizontal and vertical displacement of the destination of the copy

For example, the following line of code causes a `Graphics` object named `gr` to copy an area 20 pixels wide by 30 pixels tall from the upper-left corner of your `JFrame` (coordinates 0, 0) to an area that begins 100 pixels to the right and 50 pixels down:

```
gr.copyArea(0, 0, 20, 30, 100, 50);
```

»TWO TRUTHS AND A LIE: DRAWING LINES AND SHAPES

1. You can use the `drawLine()` method to draw a straight line between any two points on the screen.
2. You can use methods named `drawRect()`, `fillRect()`, `clearRect()`, `drawOval()`, and `fillOval()` to create a variety of shapes.
3. When you draw an arc, the zero-degree position is at twelve o'clock on an imaginary clock, and the 90-degree position is at twelve o'clock.

The false statement is #3. When you draw an arc, the zero-degree position is at three o'clock, and the degree values increase as you move counterclockwise in a 360-degree circle, so the 90-degree position is at twelve o'clock.

LEARNING MORE ABOUT FONTS AND METHODS YOU CAN USE WITH THEM

As you add more components in your GUI applications, positioning becomes increasingly important. In particular, when you draw Strings using different fonts and do not place the Strings correctly, they overlap and become impossible to read. In addition, even when you define a font such as the following, you have no guarantee that the font will be available on every computer that runs your application:

```
Font myFont = new Font("TimesRoman", Font.PLAIN, 10);
```

If your user's computer does not have the requested font loaded, Java chooses a default replacement font, so you can never be completely certain how your output will look. Fortunately, Java provides many useful methods for obtaining information about the fonts you use.

You can discover the fonts that are available on your system by using the **getAvailableFontFamilyNames() method**, which is part of the GraphicsEnvironment class defined in the java.awt package. The GraphicsEnvironment class describes the collection of Font objects and GraphicsDevice objects available to a Java application on a particular platform. The getAvailableFontFamilyNames() method returns an array of String objects that are the names of available fonts. For example, the following statements declare a GraphicsEnvironment object named ge, and then use the object with the getAvailableFontFamilyNames() method to store the font names in a string array:

```
GraphicsEnvironment ge =
    GraphicsEnvironment.getLocalGraphicsEnvironment();
String[] fontnames = ge.getAvailableFontFamilyNames();
```

Notice in the preceding example that you can't instantiate the GraphicsEnvironment object directly. Instead, you must get a reference object to the current computer environment by calling the static getLocalGraphicsEnvironment() method. Figure 15-20 shows a JFrame that lists all the available font names on the computer on which the program was executed. After the GraphicsEnvironment object is created and the getAvailableFontFamilyNames() method is used to retrieve the array of font names, the names are displayed on the screen using a for loop in which the horizontal coordinate where each font String is drawn is increased by a fixed value, so that five columns are displayed equally spaced across the JFrame surface. After five items are displayed, the horizontal coordinate is set back to 10 and the vertical coordinate is increased so that the next five-column row is displayed below the previous one. The output for one specific computer is shown in Figure 15-21.

```
import javax.swing.*;
import java.awt.*;
public class JFontList extends JFrame
{
    public void paint(Graphics gr)
    {
        super.paint(gr);
        int i, x, y = 40;
        final int VERTICAL_SPACE = 10;
        final int HORIZONTAL_SPACE = 160;
        GraphicsEnvironment ge =
            GraphicsEnvironment.getLocalGraphicsEnvironment();
        String[] fontnames = ge.getAvailableFontFamilyNames();
        for(i = 0; i < fontnames.length; i += 5)
        {
            x = 10;
            gr.setFont(new Font("Arial", Font.PLAIN, 10));
            gr.drawString(fontnames[i], x, y);
            if(i+1 < fontnames.length)
                gr.drawString(fontnames[i + 1], x += HORIZONTAL_SPACE, y);
            if(i+2 < fontnames.length)
                gr.drawString(fontnames[i + 2], x += HORIZONTAL_SPACE, y);
            if(i+3 < fontnames.length)
                gr.drawString(fontnames[i + 3], x += HORIZONTAL_SPACE, y);
            if(i+4 < fontnames.length)
                gr.drawString(fontnames[i + 4], x += HORIZONTAL_SPACE, y);
            y = y + VERTICAL_SPACE;
        }
    }
    public static void main(String[] args)
    {
        JFontList frame = new JFontList();
        frame.setSize(820, 620);
        frame.setVisible(true);
    }
}
```

Figure 15-20 The JFontList class

Figure 15-21 Output of the `JFontList` program

DISCOVERING SCREEN STATISTICS USING THE `Toolkit` CLASS

Frequently, before you can determine the best `Font` size to use, it is helpful to know statistics about the screen on which the `Font` will be displayed. For example, you can discover the resolution and screen size on your system by using the `getScreenResolution()` and `getScreenSize()` methods, which are part of the `Toolkit` class.

The **`getDefaultToolkit()` method** provides information about the system in use. The **`getScreenResolution()` method** returns the number of pixels as an integer. You can create a `Toolkit` object and get the screen resolution using the following code:

```
Toolkit tk = Toolkit.getDefaultToolkit();
int resolution = tk.getScreenResolution();
```

The Dimension class is useful for representing the width and height of a user interface component, such as a JFrame or a JButton. The Dimension class has three constructors:

» The Dimension() method creates an instance of Dimension with a width of 0 and a height of 0.

» Dimension(Dimension d) creates an instance of Dimension whose width and height are the same as for the specified dimension.

» Dimension(int width, int height) constructs a Dimension and initializes it to the specified width and height.

The **getScreenSize() method**, a member of the Toolkit object, returns an object of type Dimension, which specifies the width and height of the screen in pixels. Knowing the number of pixels for the width and height of your display is useful to set the coordinates for the position, width, and height of a window. For example, the following code stores the width and height of a screen in separate variables:

```
Toolkit tk = Toolkit.getDefaultToolkit();
Dimension screen = tk.getScreenSize();
int width = screen.width;
int height = screen.height;
```

DISCOVERING FONT STATISTICS

Typesetters and desktop publishers measure the height of every font in three parts: leading, ascent, and descent. **Leading** is the amount of space between baselines. **Ascent** is the height of an uppercase character from a baseline to the top of the character. **Descent** measures the part of characters that "hang below" the baseline, such as the tails on the lowercase letters g and j. The **height of a font** is the sum of the leading, ascent, and descent. Figure 15-22 shows each of these measurements.

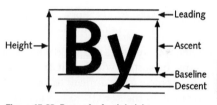

Figure 15-22 Parts of a font's height

» **NOTE**
Leading is pronounced "ledding."

You can discover a font's statistics by first using the Graphics class **getFontMetrics() method** to return a FontMetrics object, and then by using one of the following FontMetrics class methods with the object to return one of a Font's statistics:

» public int getLeading()
» public int getAscent()
» public int getDescent()
» public int getHeight()

» **NOTE** Another method, getLineMetrics(), is more complicated to use, but returns similar font statistics. For more details, see *http://java.sun.com*.

Each of these methods returns an integer value representing the font size in points (one point measures 1/72 of an inch) of the requested portion of the Font object. For example, if you

》NOTE
When you define a Font object, you use point size. However, when you use the FontMetrics get methods, the sizes are returned in pixels.

define a Font object named myFont and a Graphics object named paintBrush, you can set the current font for the Graphics object by using the following statements:

```
paintBrush.setFont(myFont);
int heightOfFont = paintBrush.getFontMetrics().getHeight();
```

Then the heightOfFont variable holds the total height of myFont characters.

》NOTE Notice the object-dot-method-dot-method construction of the getHeight() statement. You can also write two statements if that approach is clearer to you. The first statement declares a FontMetrics object:

```
FontMetrics fmObject = paintBrush.getFontMetrics();
```

The second statement assigns a value to heightOfFont:

```
int heightOfFont = fmObject.getHeight();
```

A practical use for discovering the height of a font is to space Strings correctly as you display them. For example, instead of placing every String in a series vertically equidistant from the previous String with a statement such as the following:

```
pen.drawString("Some string", x, y += INCREASE);
```

(where INCREASE is always the same), you can make the actual increase in the vertical position dependent on the font. If you code the following, you are assured that each String has enough room, and appears regardless of which font is currently in use by the Graphics pen object:

```
pen.drawString("Some string",
    x, y += pen.getFontMetrics().getHeight());
```

When you create a String, you know how many characters are in the String. However, you cannot be certain which font Java will use or substitute, and because fonts have different measurements, it is difficult to know the exact width of the String that appears in a JFrame. Fortunately, the FontMetrics class contains a **stringWidth() method** that returns the integer width of a String. As an argument, the stringWidth() method requires the name of a String. For example, if you create a String named myString, you can retrieve the width of myString with the following code:

```
int width = gr.getFontMetrics().stringWidth(myString);
```

》TWO TRUTHS AND A LIE: LEARNING MORE ABOUT FONTS AND METHODS YOU CAN USE WITH THEM

1. Java is widely used partly because its fonts are guaranteed to look the same on all computers.
2. You can discover the resolution and screen size on your system by using the getScreenResolution() and getScreenSize() methods, which are part of the Toolkit class.
3. Leading is the amount of space between baselines, ascent is the height of an uppercase character from a baseline to the top of the character, and descent measures the part of characters that "hang below" the baseline, such as the tail on the lowercase letter "y."

The false statement is #1. If your user's computer does not have a font you have requested, Java chooses a default replacement font, so you can never be completely certain how your output will look.

DRAWING WITH JAVA 2D GRAPHICS

Drawing operations earlier in this chapter were called using a `Graphics` object—either an automatically generated one that was passed to the `paint()` method or one the programmer instantiated. In addition, you can call drawing operations using an object of the **Graphics2D class**. The advantage of using Java 2D objects is the higher-quality, two-dimensional (2D) graphics, images, and text they provide. The 2D classes don't replace the existing `java.awt` classes; you can still use the other classes and applications that use them.

Features of some of the 2D classes include:

» NOTE
This book cannot cover all of the `Graphics2D` capabilities. For more information, visit *http://java.sun.com*.

» Fill patterns, such as gradients

» Strokes that define the width and style of a drawing stroke

» Anti-aliasing, a graphics technique for producing smoother screen graphics

`Graphics2D` is found in the `java.awt` package. A `Graphics2D` object is produced by casting, or converting and promoting, a `Graphics` object. For example, in a `paint()` method that automatically receives a `Graphics` object, you can cast the object to a `Graphics2D` object using the following code:

```
public void paint(Graphics pen)
{
    Graphics2D newpen = (Graphics2D)pen;
```

The process of drawing with Java 2D objects includes:

» Specifying the rendering attributes

» Setting a drawing stroke

» Creating objects to draw

SPECIFYING THE RENDERING ATTRIBUTES

The first step in drawing a 2D object is to specify how a drawn object is rendered. Whereas drawings that are not 2D can only use the attribute `Color`, with 2D you can designate other attributes, such as line width and fill patterns. You specify 2D colors by using the `setColor()` method, which works like the `Graphics` method of the same name. Using a `Graphics2D` object, you can set the color to black using the following code:

```
gr2D.setColor(Color.BLACK);
```

Fill patterns control how a drawing object is filled in. In addition to using a solid color, 2D fill patterns can be a gradient fill, a texture, or even a pattern that you devise. A fill pattern is created by using the `setPaint()` method of `Graphics2D` with a fill pattern object as the only argument. Classes from which you can construct a fill pattern include `Color`, `TexturePaint`, and `GradientPaint`.

A **gradient fill** is a gradual shift from one color at one coordinate point to a different color at a second coordinate point. If the color shift occurs once between the points—for example, slowly changing from yellow to red—you are using an **acyclic gradient**, one that does not cycle between the colors. If the shift occurs repeatedly, such as from yellow to red and back to yellow again, you are using a **cyclic gradient**, one that does cycle between the colors.

Figure 15-23 shows an application that demonstrates acyclic and cyclic gradient fills. The first `setPaint()` method call sets a gradient that begins at coordinates 20, 40 in LIGHT_GRAY and ends at coordinates 180, 100 in DARK_GRAY. The last argument to the `GradientPaint()` constructor is `false`, indicating an acyclic gradient. After the `Graphics2D` object's paint is applied, a filled rectangle is drawn over the same area. These statements produce the rectangle on the left in Figure 15-24, which gradually shifts from light gray to dark gray, moving down and to the right. The second shaded `setPaint()` statement in Figure 15-23 establishes a new gradient beginning farther to the right. In this statement, the final argument to `GradientPaint()` is `true`, creating a cyclic gradient. As you can see on the right side in Figure 15-24, this rectangle's shading changes gradually across its surface.

> **»NOTE** Later in this chapter, you will learn about the `Rectangle2D.Double` class used to create the rectangles in this application.

```java
import javax.swing.*;
import java.awt.*;
import java.awt.geom.*;
public class JGradient extends JFrame
{
    public void paint(Graphics gr)
    {
        super.paint(gr);
        int x = 20, y = 40, x2 = 180, y2 = 100;
        Graphics2D gr2D = (Graphics2D)gr;
        gr2D.setPaint(new GradientPaint(x, y, Color.LIGHT_GRAY,
            x2, y2, Color.DARK_GRAY, false));
        gr2D.fill(new Rectangle2D.Double(x, y, x2, y2));
        x = 210;
        gr2D.setPaint(new GradientPaint(x, y, Color.LIGHT_GRAY,
            x2, y2, Color.DARK_GRAY, true));
        gr2D.fill(new Rectangle2D.Double(x, y, x2, y2));
    }
    public static void main(String[] args)
    {
        JGradient frame = new JGradient();
        frame.setSize(440, 180);
        frame.setVisible(true);
    }
}
```

Figure 15-23 The JGradient class

Figure 15-24 Output of the JGradient application

SETTING A DRAWING STROKE

All lines in non-2D graphics operations are drawn as solid, with square ends and a line width of one pixel. With the 2D methods, the drawing line is a **stroke**, which represents a single movement as if you were using a drawing tool, such as a pen or a pencil. In Java 2D, you can change a stroke's width using the **setStroke() method**. Stroke is actually an interface; the class that defines line types and implements the Stroke interface is named **BasicStroke**. A BasicStroke constructor takes three arguments:

» A float value representing the line width
» An int value determining the type of cap decoration at the end of a line
» An int value determining the style of juncture between two line segments

BasicStroke class variables determine the endcap and juncture style arguments. **Endcap styles** apply to the ends of lines that do not join with other lines, and include CAP_BUTT, CAP_ROUND, and CAP_SQUARE. **Juncture styles**, for lines that join, include JOIN_MITER, JOIN_ROUND, and JOIN_BEVEL.

The following statements create a BasicStroke object and make it the current stroke:

```
BasicStroke aLine = new BasicStroke(1.0f,
    BasicStroke.CAP_ROUND, BasicStroke.JOIN_ROUND);
```

Figure 15-25 shows a program that draws a rectangle using a very wide stroke. The highlighted statement sets the BasicStroke width to 15 pixels using round endcap and juncture parameters. Figure 15-26 shows the drawn rectangle.

»NOTE
In Chapter 2, you learned that a constant value such as 1.0 is a double by default. You place an "f" after a floating-point constant to indicate that it is a float rather than a double.

```java
import javax.swing.*;
import java.awt.*;
import java.awt.geom.*;
public class JStroke extends JFrame
{
    public void paint(Graphics gr)
    {
        super.paint(gr);
        Graphics2D gr2D = (Graphics2D)gr;
        BasicStroke aStroke = new BasicStroke(15.0f,
            BasicStroke.CAP_ROUND, BasicStroke.JOIN_ROUND);
        gr2D.setStroke(aStroke);
        gr2D.draw(new Rectangle2D.Double(40, 40, 100, 100));
    }
    public static void main(String[] args)
    {
        JStroke frame = new JStroke();
        frame.setSize(180, 180);
        frame.setVisible(true);
    }
}
```

Figure 15-25 The JStroke class

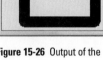

Figure 15-26 Output of the JStroke program

CREATING OBJECTS TO DRAW

After you have created a `Graphics2D` object and specified the rendering attributes, you can create different objects to draw. Objects that are drawn in Java 2D are first created by defining them as geometric shapes using the `java.awt.geom` package classes. You can define the shape of lines, rectangles, ovals, and arcs; after you define the shape, you use it as an argument to the `draw()` or `fill()` methods. The `Graphics2D` class does not have different methods for each shape you can draw.

LINES

Lines are created using the `Line2D.Float` class or the `Line2D.Double` class. Both of these classes have a constructor that takes four arguments. The arguments are the x- and y-coordinates of the two endpoints of the line. For example, to create a line from the endpoint 60, 5 to the endpoint 13, 28, you could write the following:

```
Line2D.Float line = new Line2D.Float(60F, 5F, 13F, 28F);
```

It also is possible to create lines based on points. You can use the `Point2D.Float` or `Point2D.Double` class to create points that have both x- and y-coordinates. For example, you could create two `Point2D.Float` points using the following code:

```
Point2D.Float pos1 = new Point2D.Float(60F, 5F);
Point2D.Float pos2 = new Point2D.Float(13F, 28F);
```

Then the code to create a line might be:

```
Line2D.Float line = new Line2D.Float (pos1, pos2);
```

RECTANGLES

You can create rectangles by using a `Rectangle2D.Float` or a `Rectangle2D.Double` class. As with the `Line` and `Point` classes, these two classes are distinguished by the type of arguments used in their constructors: `float` or `double`. Both `Rectangle2D.Float` and `Rectangle2D.Double` can be created using four arguments representing the x-coordinate, y-coordinate, width, and height. For example, the following code creates a `Rectangle2D.Float` object named `rect` at 10, 10 with a width of 50 and height of 40:

```
Rectangle2D.Float rect = new Rectangle2D.Float(10F, 10F, 50F, 40F);
```

OVALS

You can create `Oval` objects with the `Ellipse2D.Float` or `Ellipse2D.Double` class. The `Ellipse2D.Float` constructor requires four arguments representing the x-coordinate, y-coordinate, width, and height. The following code creates an `Ellipse2D.Float` object named `ell` at 10, 73 with a width of 40 and a height of 20:

```
Ellipse2D.Float ell = new Ellipse2D.Float(10F, 73F, 40F, 20F);
```

ARCS

You can create arcs with the `Arc2D.Float` or `Arc2D.Double` class. The `Arc2D.Float` constructor takes seven arguments. The first four arguments represent the x-coordinate, y-coordinate, width, and height that apply to the ellipse of which the arc is a part. The remaining three arguments are as follows:

» The starting position of the arc

» The number of degrees it travels

» A class field (that represents a constant integer) indicating how it is closed

The starting position is expressed in degrees in the same way as in the `Graphics` class `drawArc()` method; for example, 0 is the three o'clock position. The number of degrees traveled by the arc is specified in a counterclockwise direction using positive numbers. The final argument uses one of the three class fields:

» `Arc2D.PIE` connects the arc to the center of an ellipse and looks like a pie slice.

» `Arc2D.Chord` connects the arc's endpoints with a straight line.

» `Arc2D.OPEN` is an unclosed arc.

To create an `Arc2D.Float` object named `ac` at 10, 133 with a width of 30 and height of 33, a starting degree of 30, 120 degrees traveled, and using the class variable `Arc2D.PIE`, you use the following statement:

```
Arc2D.Float ac = new Arc2D.Float(10,133,30,33,30,120,Arc2D.PIE);
```

POLYGONS

You create a `Polygon` object by defining movements from one point to another. The movement that creates a polygon is a `GeneralPath` object; the `GeneralPath` class is found in the `java.awt.geom` package.

» The statement `GeneralPath pol = new GeneralPath();` creates a `GeneralPath` object named `pol`.

» The `moveTo()` method of `GeneralPath` is used to create the beginning point of the polygon. Thus, the statement `pol.moveTo(10F, 193F);` starts the polygon named `pol` at the coordinates 10, 193.

» The `lineTo()` method is used to create a line that ends at a new point. The statement `pol.lineTo(25F, 183F);` creates a second point using the arguments of 25 and 183 as the x- and y-coordinates of the new point.

» The statement `pol.lineTo(100F, 223F);` creates a third point. The `lineTo()` method can be used to connect the current point to the original point. Alternatively, you can use the `closePath()` method without any arguments.

YOU DO IT

USING THE drawString() METHOD

In the next steps, you will write a class that extends JFrame and that uses the drawString() method.

To use the drawString() method:

1. Open a new text file and begin a class definition for a JDemoGraphics class by typing the following:

```
import javax.swing.*;
import java.awt.*;
public class JDemoGraphics extends JFrame
{
```

2. Declare a String to hold the company name for Event Handlers Incorporated by typing the following:

```
String companyName = new String("Event Handlers Incorporated");
```

3. Add a constructor to set the default close operation:

```
public JDemoGraphics()
{
    setDefaultCloseOperation(JFrame.EXIT_ON_CLOSE);
}
```

4. Type the following paint() method that calls the super() method and uses a Graphics object to draw the companyName String.

```
public void paint(Graphics gr)
{
    super.paint(gr);
    gr.drawString(companyName, 30, 100);
}
```

5. Add a `main()` method that instantiates a `JDemoGraphics` object and sets its size and visibility. Then add the closing curly brace for the class:

```
public static void main(String[] args)
{
    JDemoGraphics frame = new JDemoGraphics();
    frame.setSize(300, 200);
    frame.setVisible(true);
}
}
```

6. Save the file as **JDemoGraphics.java** and then compile and execute it. The program's output appears in Figure 15-27.

7. Close the `JFrame` to end the application.

Figure 15-27 Output of the `JDemoGraphics` program

USING FONTS AND COLORS

Next, you will use your knowledge of fonts and colors to set the color and font style of a drawn `String`.

To add a `Font` and `Color` to your `JDemoGraphics` class:

1. Open the **JDemoGraphics.java** text file in your text editor and immediately save it as **JDemoGraphics2.java**. Change the class name, the constructor name, and the two references in the `main()` method to match.

2. Just after the `companyName` declaration, add a `Font` object by typing the following:

```
Font bigFont = new Font("Boopee", Font.ITALIC, 24);
```

3. Within the `paint()` method after the call to `super()`, type the following statements so the `gr` object uses the `bigFont` object and the color magenta:

```
gr.setFont(bigFont);
gr.setColor(Color.MAGENTA);
```

4. Following the existing `drawString()` method call, type the following lines to change the color and add another call to the `drawString()` method:

```
gr.setColor(Color.BLUE);
gr.drawString(companyName, 60, 140);
```

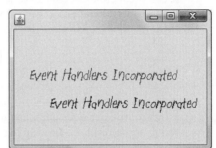

5. Save the file, compile it, and execute it. The program's output appears in Figure 15-28. Although the figure is shown in black and white in this book, notice that the `Strings` on your screen display as magenta and blue text.

6. Close the `JFrame` to end the application.

Figure 15-28 Output of the `JDemoGraphics2` program

> **» NOTE**
> The font that appears in your program might be different, depending on your computer's installed fonts. You can view a list of available fonts on your computer by executing a program similar to the `JFontList` program shown in Figure 15-20.

CREATING YOUR OWN Graphics OBJECT

Next, you will create a Graphics object named pen and use the object to draw a String on the screen. The text of the String will appear to move each time a JButton is clicked.

To write an application in which you create your own Graphics object:

1. Open a new text file in your text editor and type the following import statements for the program:

```
import javax.swing.*;
import java.awt.*;
import java.awt.event.*;
```

2. Start typing the following class that extends JFrame and uses the mouse. The class defines a String, a JButton, a Font, and four integers: two to hold x- and y-coordinates, one to act as a constant size to measure the gap between lines displayed on the screen, and one to hold the size of the JFrame:

```
public class JDemoCreateGraphicsObject extends JFrame
    implements ActionListener
{
    String companyName = new String("Event Handlers Incorporated");
    JButton moveButton = new JButton("Move It");
    Font broadwayFont = new Font("Broadway", Font.ITALIC, 12);
    int x = 10, y = 50;
    final int GAP = 20;
    final int SIZE = 400;
```

3. Type the following constructor, which changes the background color and sets the layout of the Container, adds the JButton, prepares the JFrame to listen for JButton events, sets the close operation, and sets the size of the frame:

```
public JDemoCreateGraphicsObject()
{
    Container con = getContentPane();
    con.setBackground(Color.YELLOW);
    con.setLayout(new FlowLayout() );
    con.add(moveButton);
    moveButton.addActionListener(this);
    setDefaultCloseOperation(JFrame.EXIT_ON_CLOSE);
    setSize(SIZE, SIZE);
}
```

4. Within the actionPerformed() method, you can create a Graphics object and use it to draw the String on the screen. Each time a user clicks the JButton, the x- and y-coordinates both increase, so a copy of the company name appears slightly below and to the right of the previous company name. Type the following actionPerformed() method to accomplish this processing:

```
public void actionPerformed(ActionEvent e)
{
   Graphics pen = getGraphics();
   pen.setFont(broadwayFont);
   pen.setColor(Color.MAGENTA);
   pen.drawString(companyName, x += GAP, y += GAP);
}
```

5. Add a `main()` method to instantiate a `JDemoCreateGraphicsObject` object and give it visibility. Add a closing curly brace for the class.

```
public static void main(String[] args)
{
   JDemoCreateGraphicsObject frame = new
      JDemoCreateGraphicsObject();
   frame.setVisible(true);
}
}
```

6. Save the file as **JDemoCreateGraphicsObject.java** and then compile and run the program. Click the **Move It** button several times to see the `String` message appear and move on the screen.

7. When you finish clicking the button, close the `JFrame` to end the application.

EXAMINING SCREEN COORDINATES

If you run `JDemoCreateGraphicsObject` and click the `JButton` enough times, the "Event Handlers Incorporated" `String` appears to march off the bottom of the `JFrame`. Every time you click the `JButton`, the x- and y-coordinates used by `drawString()` increase, and there is no limit to their value. You can prevent this error by checking the screen coordinates' values to see if they exceed the `JFrame`'s dimensions.

To avoid the error of exceeding the frame's viewing area:

1. Open the **JDemoCreateGraphicsObject** file and immediately save it as **JDemoCreateGraphicsObject2**. Change the class name, constructor name, and the two references to the class in the `main()` method to match.

2. Because the screen size is 400 by 400, you can ensure that at least part of the `String` appears in the frame by preventing the y-coordinate from exceeding a value that is slightly less than 400. Create a constant to hold this limit by adding the following just after the declaration of `SIZE`:

```
final int LIMIT = SIZE - 50;
```

3. In the `actionPerformed()` method, replace the stand-alone call to `drawString()` with one that depends on `LIMIT` as follows:

```
if(y < LIMIT)
   pen.drawString(companyName, x += GAP, y += GAP);
```

4. Add an `else` clause that disables the `JButton` after the x-coordinate becomes too large:

```
else
    moveButton.setEnabled(false);
```

5. Save the file, compile it, and execute it. Now when you click the **Move It** button, the company name moves until the y-coordinate reaches 350, when the `JButton` is disabled; the company name no longer violates the frame's size limits.

6. Close the frame to end the program.

CREATING A DRAWING

Next, you will add a simple line drawing to the `JDemoCreateGraphicsObject2` program. The drawing will appear after the user clicks the `JButton` enough times to disable the `JButton`.

To add a line drawing to a `JFrame`:

1. Open the **JDemoCreateGraphicsObject2** file and immediately save it as **JDemoCreateGraphicsObject3.java**. Change the class name, constructor name, and two references in the `main()` method to match.

2. Replace the current `if...else` structure that tests whether y is less than `LIMIT` in the `actionPerformed()` method. Instead, use the following code, which tests the value of y and either draws the company name or disables the `JButton` and draws a logo. Set the drawing color to black, and create a simple drawing of the Event Handlers Incorporated logo, which is two overlapping balloons with strings attached:

```
if(y < LIMIT)
    pen.drawString(companyName, x += GAP, y += GAP);
else
{
    moveButton.setEnabled(false);
    pen.setColor(Color.BLACK);
    pen.drawOval(50, 170, 70, 70);
    pen.drawLine(85, 240, 110, 280);
    pen.drawLine(110, 280, 90, 320);
    pen.drawLine(90, 320, 110, 340);
    pen.drawOval(100, 200, 70, 70);
    pen.drawLine(135, 270, 120, 290);
    pen.drawLine(120, 290, 130, 310);
    pen.drawLine(130, 310, 110, 340);
}
```

3. Save the file, compile it, and execute it. After the company name moves to the `LIMIT` value, the `JButton` is disabled and the balloon drawing appears, as shown in Figure 15-29.

4. Close the application.

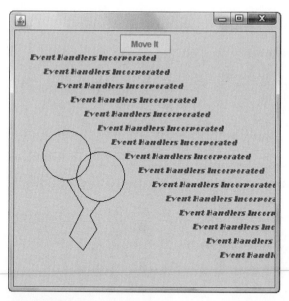

Figure 15-29 The `JDemoCreateGraphicsObject3` program after the `JButton` is disabled

COPYING AN AREA

Next, you will learn how to copy an area containing a shape that you want to appear several times on a JFrame. By copying, you do not have to re-create the shape each time.

To copy an area:

1. Open a new text file in your text editor and then enter the beginning statements for a JFrame that uses the copyArea() method:

```
import javax.swing.*;
import java.awt.*;
public class JThreeStars extends JFrame
{
```

2. Add the following statements, which create a polygon in the shape of a star:

```
int xPoints[] = {42, 52, 72, 52,
                 60, 40, 15, 28, 9, 32, 42};
int yPoints[] = {38, 62, 68, 80,
                 105, 85, 102, 75, 58, 60, 38};
Polygon aStar = new Polygon(xPoints, yPoints, xPoints.length);
```

3. Add a constructor that sets the default close operation:

```
public JThreeStars()
{
    setDefaultCloseOperation(JFrame.EXIT_ON_CLOSE);
}
```

4. Add the following `paint()` method, which sets a color, draws a star, and then draws two additional identical stars:

```
public void paint(Graphics star)
{
    super.paint(star);
    star.setColor(Color.BLUE);
    star.drawPolygon(aStar);
    star.copyArea(0, 0, 75, 105, 80, 40);
    star.copyArea(0, 0, 75, 105, 40, 150);
}
```

5. Add a `main()` method that instantiates a `JThreeStars` object and sets its size and visibility. Add a closing brace to end the class:

```
public static void main(String[] args)
{
    JThreeStars frame = new JThreeStars();
    frame.setSize(200, 300);
    frame.setVisible(true);
}
}
```

6. Save the file as **JThreeStars.java** and then compile the program. When you run the program, the output looks like Figure 15-30.

7. Close the frame to end the application.

8. Modify the program to add more stars in any location you choose, save and compile the program, and then run it to confirm that the stars are copied to your desired locations.

Figure 15-30 Output of the JThreeStars program

USING FontMetrics METHODS TO COMPARE FONTS

Next, you will write a program to demonstrate `FontMetrics` methods. You will create three `Font` objects and display their metrics.

To demonstrate FontMetrics methods:

1. Open a new text file in your text editor and then enter the first few lines of the JDemoFontMetrics program:

```
import javax.swing.*;
import java.awt.*;
public class JDemoFontMetrics extends JFrame
{
```

2. Type the following code to create a `String` and a few fonts to use for demonstration purposes:

```
String companyName =
    new String("Event Handlers Incorporated");
    Font courierItalic = new Font("Courier New", Font.ITALIC, 16),
        timesPlain = new Font("Times New Roman", Font.PLAIN, 16),
        scriptBold = new Font("Freestyle Script", Font.BOLD, 16);
```

3. Add the following code to define four integer variables to hold the four font measurements, and two integer variables to hold the current horizontal and vertical output positions within the `JFrame`:

```
int ascent, descent, height, leading;
    int x = 20, y = 50;
```

4. Within the `JFrame`, you will draw `String`s for "Event Handlers Incorporated" that you position 40 pixels apart vertically on the screen. After each of those `String`s, the `String`s that hold the statistics will be 15 pixels apart. Type the following statements to create constants to hold these vertical increase values:

```
final int INCREASE_SMALL = 15;
final int INCREASE_LARGE = 40;
```

5. Add a constructor as follows:

```
    public JDemoFontMetrics()
    {
        setDefaultCloseOperation(JFrame.EXIT_ON_CLOSE);
    }
```

6. Add the following statements to start writing a `paint()` method. Within the method, you set the `Font` to `courierItalic`, draw the `companyName String` to show a working example of the font, and then call a `displayMetrics()` method that you will write in Step 7. Pass the `Graphics` object to the `displayMetrics()` method, so the method can discover the sizes associated with the current font. Perform the same three steps using the `timesPlain` and `scriptBold` fonts.

```
public void paint(Graphics pen)
{
    super.paint(pen);
    pen.setFont(courierItalic);
    pen.drawString(companyName, x, y);
    displayMetrics(pen);
    pen.setFont(timesPlain);
    pen.drawString(companyName, x, y += INCREASE_LARGE);
    displayMetrics(pen);
    pen.setFont(scriptBold);
    pen.drawString(companyName, x, y += INCREASE_LARGE);
    displayMetrics(pen);
}
```

7. Next, add the header and opening curly brace for the `displayMetrics()` method. The method will receive a `Graphics` object from the `paint()` method. Add the following statements to call the four `getFontMetrics()` methods to obtain values for the leading, ascent, descent, and height variables:

```java
public void displayMetrics(Graphics metrics)
{
    leading = metrics.getFontMetrics().getLeading();
    ascent = metrics.getFontMetrics().getAscent();
    descent = metrics.getFontMetrics().getDescent();
    height = metrics.getFontMetrics().getHeight();
```

8. Add the following four `drawString()` statements to display the values. Use the expression `y += INCREASE_SMALL` to change the vertical position of each `String` by the `INCREASE_SMALL` constant.

```java
    metrics.drawString("Leading is " + leading,
        x, y += INCREASE_SMALL);
    metrics.drawString("Ascent is " + ascent,
        x, y += INCREASE_SMALL);
    metrics.drawString("Descent is " + descent,
        x, y += INCREASE_SMALL);
    metrics.drawString("Height is " + height,
        x, y += INCREASE_SMALL);
}
```

9. Add a `main()` method and include a closing curly brace for the class:

```java
public static void main(String[] args)
{
    JDemoFontMetrics frame = new JDemoFontMetrics();
    frame.setSize(350, 350);
    frame.setVisible(true);
}
}
```

10. Save the file as **JDemoFontMetrics.java** and then compile it. When you run the program, the output should look like Figure 15-31. Notice that even though each Font object was constructed with a size of 16, the individual statistics vary for each Font object.

11. Close the frame to end the program.

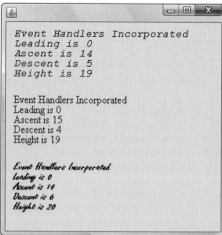

Figure 15-31 Output of the JDemoFontMetrics program

USING FontMetrics METHODS TO PLACE A BORDER AROUND A String

Next, you will use the FontMetrics methods to draw a rectangle around a String. Instead of guessing at appropriate pixel positions, you can use the height and width of the String to create a box with borders placed symmetrically around the String.

To draw a rectangle around a String:

1. Open a new file in your text editor and enter the first few lines of a JBoxAround JFrame:

```
import javax.swing.*;
import java.awt.*;
public class JBoxAround extends JFrame
{
```

2. Enter the following statements to add a String, a Font, and variables to hold the font metrics and x- and y-coordinates:

```
String companyName =
    new String("Event Handlers Incorporated");
Font serifItalic = new Font("Serif", Font.ITALIC, 20);
int leading, ascent, height, width;
int x = 40, y = 60;
```

3. Create the following named constant that holds a number of pixels indicating the dimensions of the rectangle that you draw around the String:

```
static final int BORDER = 5;
```

4. Add a constructor as follows:

```
public JBoxAround()
{
    setDefaultCloseOperation(JFrame.EXIT_ON_CLOSE);
}
```

5. Add the following paint () method, which sets the font, draws the String, and obtains the font metrics:

```
public void paint(Graphics gr)
{
    super.paint(gr);
    gr.setFont(serifItalic);
    gr.drawString(companyName, x, y);
    leading = gr.getFontMetrics().getLeading();
    ascent = gr.getFontMetrics().getAscent();
    height = gr.getFontMetrics().getHeight();
    width = gr.getFontMetrics().stringWidth(companyName);
```

6. Draw a rectangle around the String using the following drawRect () method. In Figure 15-32, the x- and y-coordinates of the upper-left edge are set at x - BORDER, y - (ascent +

leading + BORDER). The proper width and height are then determined to draw a uniform rectangle around the string.

The values of the x- and y-coordinates used in the drawString() method indicate the left side of the baseline of the first character in the String. You want to position the upper-left corner of the rectangle five pixels to the left of the String, so the first argument to drawRect() is 5 less than x, or x - BORDER. The second argument to drawRect() is the y-coordinate of the String minus the ascent of the String, minus the leading of the String, minus 5, or y - (ascent + leading + BORDER). The final two arguments to drawRect() are the width and height of the rectangle. The width is the String's width plus five pixels on the left and five pixels on the right. The height of the rectangle is the String's height, plus five pixels above the String and five pixels below the String.

```
gr.drawRect(x - BORDER, y - (ascent + leading + BORDER),
    width + 2 * BORDER, height + 2 * BORDER);
}
```

7. Add the following main() method and a closing brace for the class:

```
public static void main(String[] args)
{
    JBoxAround frame = new JBoxAround();
    frame.setSize(330, 100);
    frame.setVisible(true);
}
}
```

8. Save the file as **JBoxAround.java**. Compile and execute it. Your output should look like Figure 15-32.

9. Experiment with changing the contents of the String, the x and y starting coordinates, and the value of the BORDER constant. Confirm that the rectangle is drawn symmetrically around any String object.

Figure 15-32 Output of the JBoxAround program

USING DRAWING STROKES

Next, you will create a line with a drawing stroke to illustrate how it can have different end types and juncture types where lines intersect.

To create a line with a drawing stroke:

1. Open a new file in your text editor and then enter the first few lines of a J2DLine JFrame. (Note that you are importing the java.awt.geom package.)

```
import javax.swing.*;
import java.awt.*;
import java.awt.geom.*;
public class J2DLine extends JFrame
{
```

2. Add a constructor:

```
public J2DLine()
{
    setDefaultCloseOperation(JFrame.EXIT_ON_CLOSE);
}
```

3. Enter the following statements to create a `paint()` method, create a `Graphics` environment `gr`, and cast the `Graphics` environment to a `Graphics2D` environment `gr2D`. Create x and y points with the `Point2D.Float` class.

```
public void paint(Graphics gr)
{
    super.paint(gr);
    Graphics2D gr2D = (Graphics2D)gr;
    Point2D.Float pos1 = new Point2D.Float(80, 50);
    Point2D.Float pos2 = new Point2D.Float(20, 100);
```

4. Create a `BasicStroke` object and then create a drawing stroke named `aStroke`. Note that the line width is set to 15 pixels, and the endcap style and juncture style are set to `CAP_ROUND` and `JOIN_MITER`, respectively.

```
BasicStroke aStroke = new BasicStroke(15.0f,
    BasicStroke.CAP_ROUND, BasicStroke.JOIN_MITER);
```

5. Add the following code to create a line between the points `pos1` and `pos2`, and draw the line:

```
    gr2D.setStroke(aStroke);
    Line2D.Float line = new Line2D.Float(pos1, pos2);
    gr2D.draw(line);
}
```

6. Add a `main()` method and the closing curly brace for the class:

```
public static void main(String[] args)
{
    J2DLine frame = new J2DLine();
    frame.setSize(100, 120);
    frame.setVisible(true);
}
}
```

Figure 15-33 Output of the J2DLine program

7. Save the file as **J2DLine.java**, then compile and execute it. Your output should look like Figure 15-33.

8. Experiment by making the `JFrame` size larger and adding more lines to create an interesting design.

WORKING WITH SHAPES

Next, you will use the Java 2D drawing object types to create a JFrame that illustrates sample rectangles, ovals, arcs, and polygons.

To create the JShapes2D JFrame:

1. Open a new file in your text editor and then enter the first few lines of a JShapes2D JFrame:

```
import javax.swing.*;
import java.awt.*;
import java.awt.geom.*;
public class JShapes2D extends JFrame
{
```

2. Add a constructor that sets the default close operation.

```
public JShapes2D()
{
setDefaultCloseOperation(JFrame.EXIT_ON_CLOSE);
}
```

3. Enter the following statements to create a paint() method, create a Graphics environment gr, and cast the Graphics environment to a Graphics2D environment gr2D:

```
public void paint(Graphics gr)
{
    super.paint(gr);
    Graphics2D gr2D = (Graphics2D)gr;
```

4. Create two Rectangle2D.Float objects named rect and rect2. Draw the rect object and fill the rect2 object:

```
        Rectangle2D.Float rect =
          new Rectangle2D.Float(20F, 40F, 40F, 40F);
        Rectangle2D.Float rect2 =
          new Rectangle2D.Float(20F, 90F, 40F, 40F);
        gr2D.draw(rect);
        gr2D.fill(rect2);
```

5. Create two Ellipse2D.Float objects named ellipse and ellipse2. Draw the ellipse object and fill the ellipse2 object:

```
        Ellipse2D.Float ellipse = new
            Ellipse2D.Float(20F, 140F, 40F, 40F);
        Ellipse2D.Float ellipse2 = new
            Ellipse2D.Float(20F, 190F, 40F, 40F);
        gr2D.draw(ellipse);
        gr2D.fill(ellipse2);
```

6. Create two `Arc2D.Float` objects named `ac` and `ac2`. Draw the `ac` object and fill the `ac2` object:

```
Arc2D.Float ac = new
    Arc2D.Float(20, 240, 50, 50, 30, 120, Arc2D.PIE);
Arc2D.Float ac2 = new
    Arc2D.Float(20, 290, 50, 50, 30, 120, Arc2D.PIE);
gr2D.draw(ac);
gr2D.fill(ac2);
```

7. Create a new `GeneralPath` object named `pol`. Set the starting point of the polygon and create two additional points. Use the `closePath()` method to close the polygon by connecting the current point to the starting point. Draw the `pol` object, then end the method with a curly brace:

```
GeneralPath pol = new GeneralPath();
pol.moveTo(20F,320F);
pol.lineTo(40F,380F);
pol.lineTo(100F,400F);
pol.closePath();
gr2D.draw(pol);
}
```

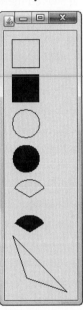

8. Add a `main()` method and the final curly brace for the class:

```
public static void main(String[] args)
{
    JShapes2D frame = new JShapes2D();
    frame.setSize(100, 420);
    frame.setVisible(true);
}
}
```

9. Save the file as **JShapes2D.java**, and compile and execute the program. Your output should look like Figure 15-34. When you are ready, close the window, then experiment with making changes to the program to produce different shapes.

Figure 15-34 Output of the `JShapes2D` program

DON'T DO IT

» Don't forget to call `super.paint()` as the first statement in the `paint()` method when you write a class that extends `JFrame`. Failing to do so can cause odd results, especially when you combine GUI widgets with graphics.

» Don't forget that the `setLocation()` method works correctly only when it is used after the layout manager has finished positioning all the application's components (or in cases where no layout manager is functioning).

» Don't forget that the lower-left corner of a `String` is placed at the coordinates used when you call `drawString()`.

KEY TERMS

When a drawing is **rerendered**, it is repainted or redisplayed.

Redisplaying a surface also is called **painting**.

System-triggered painting operations occur when the system requests a component to render its contents.

Application-triggered painting operations occur when the internal state of a component has changed.

The **paint() method** runs when Java displays a screen; you can write your own paint() method to override the automatically supplied one whenever you want to paint graphics such as shapes on the screen.

You call the **repaint() method** when a window needs to be updated, such as when it contains new images.

The **setLocation() method** allows you to place a component at a specific location within a JFrame's content pane.

The **drawString() method** allows you to draw a String in a JFrame or other component.

The **drawLine() method** draws a straight line between any two points on the screen.

The **drawRect() method** draws the outline of a rectangle.

The **fillRect() method** draws a solid, or filled, rectangle.

The **clearRect() method** draws a rectangle using the background color to create what appears to be an empty or "clear" rectangle.

The **drawRoundRect() method** draws rectangles with rounded corners.

An **arc** is a portion of a circle.

The **drawOval() method** draws an oval.

The **fillOval() method** draws a solid, filled oval.

The **drawArc() method** draws an arc.

The **fillArc() method** creates a solid arc.

You use the **draw3DRect() method** to draw a rectangle that appears to have "shadowing" on two of its edges—the effect is that of a rectangle that is lit from the upper-left corner and slightly raised or slightly lowered.

You use the **fill3DRect() method** to create filled, 3D rectangles.

The **drawPolygon() method** draws complex shapes.

The **fillPolygon() method** draws a solid shape.

The **addPoint() method** adds points to a Polygon object.

The **copyArea() method** copies any rectangular area to a new location.

The **getAvailableFontFamilyNames() method** returns the fonts that are available on your system.

The **getDefaultToolkit() method** provides information about the system in use.

The **getScreenResolution() method** returns the screen resolution on the current system.

The **getScreenSize() method** returns the screen size as a Dimension object.

Leading is one of three measures of a Font's height; it is the amount of space between baselines.

Ascent is one of three measures of a Font's height; it is the height of an uppercase character from a baseline to the top of the character.

Descent is one of three measures of a Font's height; it measures the part of characters that "hang below" the baseline, such as the tails on the lowercase letters g and j.

The **height of a font** is the sum of its leading, ascent, and descent.

You can discover a Font's height by using the Graphics class **getFontMetrics() method** to return a FontMetrics object, and then using one of the following: public int getLeading(), public int getAscent(), public int getDescent(), or public int getHeight().

The FontMetrics class contains a **stringWidth() method** that returns the integer width of a String.

The **Graphics2D class** provides tools for 2D drawing.

Fill patterns control how a drawing object is filled in.

A **gradient fill** is a gradual shift from one color at one coordinate point to a different color at a second coordinate point.

An **acyclic gradient** is a fill pattern in which a color shift occurs once between two points.

A **cyclic gradient** is a fill pattern in which a shift between colors occurs repeatedly between two points.

A **stroke** is a line-drawing feature in Java 2D that represents a single movement as if you were using a drawing tool, such as a pen or a pencil.

The **setStroke() method** changes a stroke's width in Java 2D.

BasicStroke is the class that defines line types and implements the Stroke interface.

Endcap styles apply to the ends of lines that do not join with other lines, and include CAP_BUTT, CAP_ROUND, and CAP_SQUARE.

Juncture styles, for lines that join, include JOIN_MITER, JOIN_ROUND, and JOIN_BEVEL.

CHAPTER SUMMARY

» Painting operations can be system triggered or application triggered. Painting operations are performed by a Component's paint() method, which takes a Graphics argument that renders output. You override the paint() method in your programs when you want specific actions to take place when components must be rendered. The setLocation() method allows you to place a component at a specific location within a JFrame's content pane.

» The drawString() method allows you to draw a String. The method requires three arguments: a String, an x-axis coordinate, and a y-axis coordinate. The drawString() method is a member of the Graphics class, so you need to use a Graphics object to call it. You can improve the appearance of strings drawn using Graphics objects by using the setFont() and setColor() methods.

» When you call the paint() method from within an application, you can use the automatically created Graphics object that is passed to it. However, you can also instantiate your own Graphics or Graphics2D objects, which can employ Graphics methods such as setFont(), setColor(), and drawString().

» Java provides you with several methods for drawing a variety of lines and geometric shapes, such as drawLine(), drawRect(), drawOval(), drawPolygon(), and others. You can also use the copyArea() method to copy any rectangular area to a new location.

» If a user's computer does not have a requested font, Java chooses a default replacement font, so you can never be completely certain how your output will look. You can discover the fonts that are available on your system by using the getAvailableFontFamilyNames() method, which is part of the GraphicsEnvironment class. This class describes the collection of Font objects and GraphicsDevice objects available to a Java application on a particular platform. You can discover the resolution and screen size on your system by using the getScreenResolution() and getScreenSize() methods, which are part of the Toolkit class. The height of every font is the sum of three parts: leading, ascent, and descent. A practical use for discovering the height of a font is to space Strings correctly as you display them.

» You can call drawing operations using a Graphics2D object. The advantage of using Java 2D objects is the higher-quality, 2D graphics, images, and text they provide. With 2D you can designate attributes such as line width and fill patterns.

REVIEW QUESTIONS

1. Repainting of a visible surface is triggered by _____ .

   a. the operating system   c. either of these

   b. the application   d. none of these

2. The method that calls the paint() method for you is _____ .

   a. callPaint()   c. requestPaint()

   b. repaint()   d. draw()

3. The paint() method header requires a(n) _____ argument.

   a. void   c. String

   b. integer   d. Graphics

4. The setLocation() method _____ .

   a. is used to position a JFrame on the screen

   b. is used to set regional and national preferences for an application

   c. takes two integer arguments that represent position coordinates

   d. must be used with every component placed on a JFrame

5. The statement g.drawString(someString, 50, 100); places someString's _____ corner at position 50, 100.

   a. upper-left   c. upper-right

   b. lower-left   d. lower-right

6. If you use the setColor() method to change a Graphics object's color to yellow, _____ .

   a. only the next output from the object appears in yellow

   b. all output from the object for the remainder of the method always appears in yellow

   c. all output from the object for the remainder of the application always appears in yellow

   d. all output from the object appears in yellow until you change the color

7. The correct statement to instantiate a Graphics object named picasso is _____ .

   a. Graphics picasso;

   b. Graphics picasso = new Graphics();

   c. Graphics picasso = getGraphics();

   d. Graphics picasso = getGraphics(new);

8. The statement g.drawRoundRect(100, 100, 100, 100, 0, 0); draws a shape that looks most like a _____ .

   a. square   c. circle

   b. round-edged rectangle   d. straight line

9. If you draw an oval with the same value for width and height, you draw a(n) _____ .

   a. circle   c. rounded square

   b. square   d. ellipsis

10. The zero-degree position for any arc is at the _____ o'clock position.

    a. three   c. nine

    b. six   d. twelve

11. The method you use to create a solid arc is _____ .

    a. solidArc()   c. arcSolid()

    b. fillArc()   d. arcFill()

12. You use the _____ method to copy any rectangular area to a new location.

    a. copyRect()   c. repeatRect()

    b. copyArea()   d. repeatArea()

13. The measurement of an uppercase character from the baseline to the top of the character is its _____ .

    a. ascent　　　　　　　　　　c. leading

    b. descent　　　　　　　　　　d. height

14. To be certain that a vertical series of `Strings` has enough room to appear in a frame, you use which of the following statements?

    a. `g.drawString("Some string",`
       `    x, y += g.getFontMetrics().getHeight());`

    b. `g.drawString("Some string",`
       `    x, y += g.getFontMetrics().getLeading());`

    c. `g.drawString("Some string", x,`
       `    y += g.getFontMetrics().getAscent());`

    d. `g.drawString("Some string",`
       `    x, y += g.getFontMetrics().getDescent());`

15. You can discover the fonts that are available on your system by using the _____ .

    a. `getAvailableFontFamilyNames()` method of the `GraphicsEnvironment` class

    b. `getFonts()` method of the `Graphics` class

    c. `getMyFonts()` method of the `GraphicsFonts` class

    d. `getAllFonts()` method of the `Fonts` class

16. The `getScreenResolution()` method and `getScreenSize()` method _____ .

    a. both return the number of pixels as an `int` type

    b. return the number of pixels as an `int` type and an object of type `Dimension`, respectively

    c. both return an object of type `Dimension`

    d. return the number of pixels as a `double` type and an object of type `Dimension`, respectively

17. A `Graphics2D` object is produced by _____ .

    a. the `setGraphics2D()` method

    b. the `Graphics2D newpen = Graphics2D()` statement

    c. the `Graphics2D = Graphics(g)` statement

    d. casting a `Graphics` object

18. The process of drawing with Java 2D objects includes _____.
   a. specifying the rendering attributes   c. both of the above
   b. setting a drawing stroke   d. none of the above

19. A gradient fill is a gradual change in _____.
   a. color   c. drawing style
   b. font size   d. line thickness

20. With the 2D methods, the drawing line is a _____.
   a. brush   c. belt
   b. stroke   d. draw

EXERCISES

1. Write an application that extends JFrame and that displays your first name in every even-numbered font size from 4 to 24. Save the file as **JFontSizeDemo.java**.

2. Write an application that extends JFrame and that displays your name in blue the first time the user clicks a JButton. The second time the user clicks the JButton, make the first name seem to disappear. (*Hint*: Redraw it using the background color.) At the same time, draw your first name again in a larger font in dark gray. Save the file as **JBlueGray.java**.

3. Write an application that extends JFrame and that displays eight nested rectangles, like those in Figure 15-35. You may use only one drawRect() statement in the program. (*Hint*: Use it in a loop.) Save the file as **JNestedBoxes.java**.

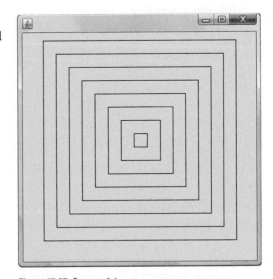

Figure 15-35 Output of the JNestedBoxes program

4. Write an application that extends JFrame and that displays 15 nested circles, like those in Figure 15-36. You may use only one drawOval() statement in the program. Save the file as **JNestedCircles.java**.

Figure 15-36 Output of the JNestedCircles program

5. Write an application that extends JFrame and that displays diagonal lines in a square, like those in Figure 15-37. Save the file as **JDiagonalLines.java**.

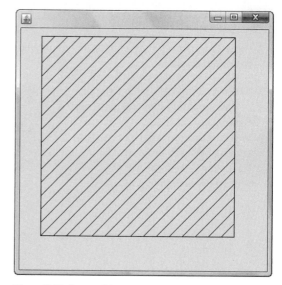

Figure 15-37 Output of the JDiagonalLines program

6. Write an application that extends JFrame and that displays a form for creating an e-mail directory. The form should contain three JLabels that describe three JTextFields for first name, last name, and e-mail address. After the user enters the third item (an e-mail address) and presses Enter, the frame should display the information that was entered.

Use the drawString() method to display a heading line, such as "The e-mail information you entered is: ", followed by the e-mail information. Save the file as **JEmailForm.java**.

7. a. Write an application that extends JFrame and that displays a yellow smiling face on the screen. Save the file as **JSmileFace.java**.

   b. Add a JButton to the JSmileFace program so the smile changes to a frown when the user clicks the JButton. Save the file as **JSmileFace2.java**.

8. a. Use polygons and lines to create a graphics image that looks like a fireworks display. Write an application that extends JFrame and that displays the fireworks. Save the file as **JFireworks.java**.

   b. Add a JButton to the JFireworks program. Do not show the fireworks until the user clicks the JButton. Save the file as **JFireworks2.java**.

9. a. Write an application that extends JFrame and that displays your name. Place boxes around your name at intervals of 10, 20, 30, and 40 pixels. Save the file as **JBorders.java**.

   b. Make each of the four borders display a different color in the JBorders program. Save the file as **JBorders2.java**.

10. Write an application that extends JFrame and that prompts the user to enter his or her name and weight in pounds. After the name and weight are entered, use Graphics2D methods to display the user's name and weight, with the weight displayed in pounds, ounces, kilograms, and metric tons on separate lines. Use the following conversion factors:

    » 1 pound = 16 ounces
    » 1 kilogram = 1 pound / 2.204623
    » 1 metric ton = 1 pound / 2204.623

    Save the file as **JCalculateWeight.java**.

11. Write an application that extends JFrame and that uses the Graphics2D environment to create a GeneralPath object. Use the GeneralPath object to create the outline of your favorite state. Display the state name at the approximate center of the state boundaries. Save the file as **JFavoriteState.java**.

12. Write an application that extends JFrame and that draws a realistic-looking stop sign. Save the file as **JStopSign.java**.

13. Write an application that displays a JFrame that does the following:

    » Turns yellow when the user's mouse enters the frame
    » Turns black when the user's mouse exits the frame
    » Displays a larger circle at the point where the user left-clicks
    » Displays a smaller circle at the point where the user right-clicks

    At most, one circle should appear on the surface of the frame at a time. Save the file as **JMouseFrame.java**.

DEBUGGING EXERCISES

Each of the following files in the Chapter.15 folder on your Student Disk has syntax and/ or logic errors. In each case, determine the problem and fix the program. After you correct the errors, save each file using the same filename preceded with Fix. For example, DebugFifteen1.java will become FixDebugFifteen1.java.

a. DebugFifteen1.java

b. DebugFifteen2.java

c. DebugFifteen3.java

d. DebugFifteen4.java

GAME ZONE

1. a. In Chapter 8, you created a Tic Tac Toe game in which you used a 2D array of characters to hold Xs and Os for a player and the computer. Now create a JFrame that uses an array of nine JButtons to represent the Tic Tac Toe grid. When the user clicks a JButton that has not already been taken, place an X on the button and then allow the computer to place an O on a different button. Announce the winner when either the computer or the player achieves three marks in sequence, or announce that the game was a tie. Figure 15-38 shows a typical game in progress and after the player has won. Save the game as **JTicTacToe.java**.

Figure 15-38 Typical execution of JTicTacToe program

   b. Add a graphic that displays a large letter representing the winning player of the game in Game Zone exercise 1a. Draw a large X, O, or, in case of a tie, an overlapping X and O in different colors. Save the game as **JTicTacToe2.java**.

2. Create an application that plays a card game named Lucky Seven. In real life, the game can be played with seven cards, each containing a number from 1 to 7, that are shuffled and dealt number-side down. To start the game, a player turns over any card. The exposed number on the card determines the position (reading from left to right) of the next card that must be turned over. For example, if the player turns over the first card and its number is 7, the next card turned must be the seventh card (counting from left to right). If the player turns over a card whose number denotes a position that was already turned, the player loses the game. If the player succeeds in turning over all seven cards, the player wins.

Instead of cards, you will use seven buttons labeled 1 through 7 from left to right. Randomly associate one of the seven values 1 through 7 with each button. (In other words, the associated value might or might not be equivalent to the button's labeled value.) When the player clicks a button, reveal the associated hidden value. If the value represents the position of a button already clicked, the player loses. If the revealed number represents an available button, force the user to click it; that is, do not take any action until the user clicks the correct button. After a player clicks a button, remove the button from play. (After you remove a button, you can call `repaint()` to ensure that the image of the button is removed.)

For example, a player might click Button 7, revealing a 4. Then the player clicks Button 4, revealing a 2. Then the player clicks Button 2, revealing a 7. The player loses because Button 7 was already used. Save the game as **JLuckySeven.java**.

3. a. In Chapter 8, you created a game named Secret Phrase in which the user guesses a randomly selected secret phrase by entering one letter at a time. Now create a GUI application that plays the game, allowing users to choose a letter by selecting one of 26 buttons. (*Hint*: Consider creating an array of buttons rather than 26 individually named buttons.)

Disable a letter button once it has been guessed, and after the puzzle is complete, disable all the letters. Figure 15-39 shows a typical execution (1) after the user has guessed an "A", which is in the phrase; (2) after the user has guessed a "D", which is not in the phrase; and (3) after the user has completed the puzzle. Save the file as **JSecretPhrase.java**.

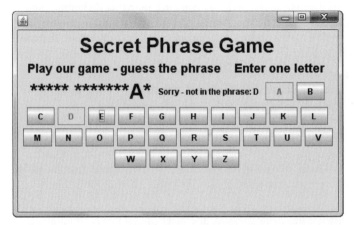

Figure 15-39 Typical execution of JSecretPhrase program

b. Make the `JSecretPhrase` game more like the traditional letter-guessing game Hangman by drawing a "hanged" person piece by piece with each missed letter. For example, when the user chooses a correct letter, place it in the appropriate position or positions in the phrase, but the first time the user chooses a letter that is not in the target phrase, draw a head for the "hanged" man. The second time the user makes an incorrect guess, add a torso. Continue with arms and legs. If the complete body is drawn before the user has guessed all the letters in the phrase, display a message indicating that the player has lost the game. If the user completes the phrase before all the body parts are drawn, display a message that the player has won. Save the game as **JSecretPhrase2.java**.

TOUGH QUESTIONS

1. Write a program that displays two rectangles. Then, in another color, show the overlapping portion whose dimensions you calculate based on the arguments to the original rectangles.

2. Java has a `setIgnoreRepaint()` method that you can use to ignore a repainting request in a graphics program. Why would you do so?

UP FOR DISCUSSION

1. Should you be allowed to store computer games on your computer at work? If so, should you be allowed to play the games during working hours? If so, should there be any restrictions on when you can play them?

2. Suppose you discover a way to breach security in a Web site so that its visitors might access information that belongs to the company for which you work. Should you be allowed to publish your findings? Should you notify the organization? Should the organization pay you a reward for discovering the breach? If they did, would this encourage you to search for more potential security violations? Suppose the newly available information on the Web site is relatively innocuous—for example, office telephone numbers of company executives. Next, suppose that the information is more sensitive—for example, home telephone numbers for the same executives. Does this make a difference?

3. Suppose you have learned a lot about programming from your employer. Is it ethical for you to use this knowledge to start your own home-based programming business on the side? Does it matter whether you are in competition for the same clients as your employer? Does it matter whether you use just your programming expertise or whether you also use information about clients' preferences and needs gathered from your regular job? Suppose you know your employer is overcharging clients and you can offer the same services for less money; does this alter your opinion?

16

APPLETS, IMAGES, AND SOUND

In this chapter, you will:

Learn about applets
Write an HTML document to host an applet
Create a JApplet that contains an init() method
Work with JApplet components
Understand the JApplet life cycle
Understand multimedia and use images
Add sound to JApplets

INTRODUCING APPLETS

An **applet** is a program that is called within another application—often a Web browser. It can contain any number of components, such as buttons, text fields, and pictures. Often, an applet can respond to user-initiated events, such as mouse clicks or keyboard presses. Many of an applet's behaviors come from a Java class named `JApplet`—other behaviors are written by the programmer. The name *applet* means "little application." An applet is like a Java application in several ways:

» You save both applets and applications with a .java file extension.

» You compile both applets and applications into bytecode using the `javac` command, and the bytecode is stored in a file with a .class file extension.

» Both applets and applications can contain any number of methods you define and any number of variables and constants. Both can contain decisions, loops, arrays, and all the other language elements you have learned about in Java.

» Both can (and applets almost always do) contain GUI elements such as buttons and labels, and event listeners that respond to user-initiated actions.

An applet is also different from an application in several ways:

» Unlike applications, applets descend from the `JApplet` class.

» Unlike applications, applets run from another application. You do not use the `java` command to execute an applet.

» Unlike applications, applets do not contain a `main()` method. In this chapter, you will learn about the methods every applet contains.

» Unlike with an application that uses a `JFrame`, you do not set a default close operation for a `JApplet`.

» Applets cannot delete, read, or create files on the user's system.

» Applets cannot run any other program on the user's system.

UNDERSTANDING THE `JApplet` CLASS

To write an applet, you must import the `JApplet` class by using the following statement:

```
import javax.swing.JApplet;
```

When you write an applet, you almost always want to use other components from the `swing` package as well. As an alternative, then, you can import all the classes in the `swing` package using a single `import` statement as follows:

```
import javax.swing.*;
```

`JApplet` is a `Swing` class from which you can inherit to create your own applet. A `JApplet` is a `Component`, and it is also a `Container`. Figure 16-1 shows the relationship among `JApplet`, `Container`, `Component`, and `Object`.

```
java.lang.Object
    |
    +--java.awt.Component
            |
            +--java.awt.Container
                    |
                    +--java.awt.Panel
                            |
                            +--java.applet.Applet
                                    |
                                    +--javax.swing.JApplet
```

Figure 16-1 Inheritance hierarchy of the `JApplet` class

>> **NOTE**
If the `JApplet` class were not already written, you would have to write more than 200 methods to give your `JApplet` all the capabilities of the built-in `JApplet` class. Although you acquire many methods that are already created when you use the `JApplet` class, you can also add any of your own methods, just as you can within Java applications.

RUNNING AN APPLET

To view an applet, it must be called from another document; frequently the document is written in HTML. **HTML**, or **Hypertext Markup Language**, is a simple language used to create Web pages for the Internet. HTML contains many commands that allow you to format text on a Web page, import graphic images, and link your page to other Web pages. You run applets within a page on the Internet, an intranet, or a local computer.

>> **NOTE**   The current version of HTML is **Extensible Hypertext Markup Language (XHTML)**. The differences are minor, although XHTML is stricter. Most Web developers are continuing to use HTML until XHTML matures and some compatibility issues are resolved. You can find more information and tutorials on both HTML and XHTML at *www.w3schools.com*.

You can run an applet in one of two ways:

» You can run an applet in a Web browser, such as Internet Explorer, Firefox, Opera, or Safari. To do so, you open the applet-hosting HTML document in the browser. For example, in Internet Explorer, you click File on the menu bar, click Open, and type the complete path for the HTML document that you created. After you press Enter, the applet appears on your screen. The applet can be run within a page on the Internet or an intranet, but you do not have to connect to the Internet to run an applet in your browser—you can simply use the browser locally.

» You can also view your applet on a local computer by using the **Applet Viewer**, which is a program that comes with the JDK. To do so, you use the `appletviewer` command. The **`appletviewer` command** is part of the Java Development Kit (JDK), which provides a convenient environment in which to test your applets. To run the applet using the command, type `appletviewer` at the command line, followed by the full HTML filename, including the extension. When you press Enter, the Applet Viewer window opens and displays the applet.

NOTE
When you save an HTML file, you can use .html or .htm as a file extension. In some older versions of DOS and Windows, filename extensions were not allowed to be more than three characters. Current Web browsers and servers accept files with .htm and .html extensions. Examples in this book use the four-character .html extension.

»TWO TRUTHS AND A LIE: INTRODUCING APPLETS

1. An applet can contain any number of components, such as buttons, text fields, and pictures, and can respond to user-initiated events, such as mouse clicks or keyboard presses.
2. Applets and applications are similar in that both have .java file extensions and you compile both with the `javac` command.
3. Applets and applications are different in that applets do not use loops and arrays.

The false statement is #3. Applets use all the language constructs in Java.

WRITING AN HTML DOCUMENT TO HOST AN APPLET

When you create an applet, you do the following:

» Write the applet in Java and save it with a .java file extension, just as when you write a Java application.

» Compile the applet into bytecode using the `javac` command, just as when you write a Java application.

» Write an HTML document that includes a statement to call your compiled Java class.

» Load the HTML document into a Web browser (such as Internet Explorer) or run the Applet Viewer program, which in turn uses the HTML document.

Java in general and applets in particular are popular topics among programmers, partly because users can execute applets using a Web browser on the Internet. A **Web browser** is a program that allows you to display HTML documents on your computer screen. Web documents often contain Java applets.

>> **NOTE** Because applets are sent over the Internet and run from other applications, applet code is not trusted. A malicious programmer might try to include code that contains a virus, reads data from your files, or performs other unwanted tasks. Therefore, applet code runs in a constrained area called a sandbox. A **sandbox** is a safe area in which a program can run, much like a real sandbox is an area in a yard where children can play safely.

Fortunately, to run a Java applet, you don't need to learn much HTML; you need to learn only two pairs of HTML commands, called **tags**. The tag that begins every HTML document is **<html>**. Like all tags, this opening tag is surrounded by angle brackets. The html within the tag is an HTML keyword that specifies that an HTML document follows the keyword. The tag that ends every HTML document is **</html>**. The preceding backslash indicates that the tag is a closing tag. The following is the simplest HTML document you can write:

```
<html>
</html>
```

>> **NOTE** Unlike Java, HTML is not case sensitive, so you can use <HTML> in place of <html>. However, this book uses the all-lowercase convention when displaying HTML code. With the growing importance of XML and XHTML, many programmers recommend putting all HTML tags in lowercase because XML and XHTML are case sensitive, even though HTML is not.

The simple HTML document, containing just the pair of html tags, begins and ends and does nothing in between; you can create an analogous situation in a Java method by typing an opening curly brace and following it immediately with the closing curly brace. HTML documents generally contain more statements. For example, to run an applet from an HTML document, you add an <object> and </object> tag pair. Usually, you place three attributes within the <object> tag: code, width, and height. **Tag attributes**, sometimes referred to as arguments, promote activity or describe the features of the tag; with arguments, the HTML tag can do something in a certain way. Note the following example:

```
<object code = "AClass.class" width = 300 height = 200> </object>
```

The three object tag attributes in the previous example are described with their corresponding arguments in the following list:

» code = is followed by the name of the compiled applet you are calling.

» width = is followed by the width of the applet on the screen.

» height = is followed by the height of the applet on the screen.

>> **NOTE** When you assign a height and width to an applet, keep in mind that a browser's menu bar and screen elements (such as the toolbar and the scroll bars) take up some of the screen viewing area for an applet.

The name of the applet you call must be a compiled Java applet (with a .class file extension). The width and height of an applet are measured in pixels. For monitors that display 1024 pixels horizontally and 768 pixels vertically, a statement such as width = 512 height = 384 creates an applet that occupies approximately one-fourth of most screens (half the height and half the width).

Figure 16-2 shows an HTML file that could be used to run a `JApplet` named `JHello`. The applet will be 450 pixels wide by 200 pixels tall.

```
<html>
<object code = "JHello.class" width = 450 height = 200>
</object>
</html>
```

Figure 16-2 The TestJHello.html file

»TWO TRUTHS AND A LIE: WRITING AN HTML DOCUMENT TO HOST AN APPLET

1. You must run applets within a Web page.
2. To view an applet, it must be called from another document, such as one written in HTML.
3. All HTML tags are surrounded by angle brackets.

The false statement is #1. You run applets within a page on the Internet or an intranet; you also can run an applet on a local computer from another program called Applet Viewer.

CREATING A `JApplet` THAT CONTAINS AN `init()` METHOD

The `JApplet` class uses several methods that are invoked by a Web browser when the browser runs an applet. In a Java application, the `main()` method calls other methods that you write, but in contrast, an applet does not contain a `main()` method. With an applet, the browser calls several methods automatically at different times. The following five methods can be called automatically by every applet:

» `public void init()`
» `public void start()`
» `public void paint()`
» `public void stop()`
» `public void destroy()`

You can override any of these methods within a JApplet that you write. If you fail to implement one or more of these methods, your JApplet will use the versions that belong to the parent JApplet class. To create a Java applet that does anything useful, you must code statements within at least one of these methods.

For example, you can create a JApplet using only the init() method. The **init() method** is the first method called in any applet. You use it to perform initialization tasks, such as setting variables to initial values or placing applet components on the screen. In general, tasks that you would place in the constructor for a JFrame in an application are the same types of tasks you place in an init() method in a JApplet.

You must code the init() method's header as follows:

```
public void init()
```

Figure 16-3 shows the JApplet that displays "Hello. Who are you?" on the screen.

```
import javax.swing.*;
import java.awt.*;
public class JHello extends JApplet
{
    JLabel greeting = new JLabel("Hello. Who are you?");
    public void init()
    {
        add(greeting);
    }
}
```

Figure 16-3 The JHello JApplet

After you write this JApplet, you do the following:

» Save this file as JHello.java, and compile it.
» Run the Applet Viewer using the command appletviewer TestJHello.html and the saved file shown in Figure 16-2.

Figure 16-4 shows how the applet appears on your screen. After you view a JApplet, you can click the close button on the Applet Viewer to end the application. Unlike a JFrame, you do not need to set a default close operation with a JApplet.

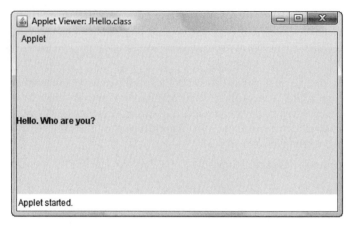

Figure 16-4 Output of the `JHello` `JApplet` when run in the Applet Viewer

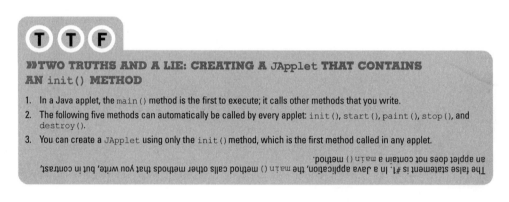

》TWO TRUTHS AND A LIE: CREATING A `JApplet` THAT CONTAINS AN `init()` METHOD

1. In a Java applet, the `main()` method is the first to execute; it calls other methods that you write.
2. The following five methods can automatically be called by every applet: `init()`, `start()`, `paint()`, `stop()`, and `destroy()`.
3. You can create a `JApplet` using only the `init()` method, which is the first method called in any applet.

The false statement is #1. In a Java application, the `main()` method calls other methods that you write, but in contrast, an applet does not contain a `main()` method.

WORKING WITH `JApplet` COMPONENTS

The output in Figure 16-4 is not very attractive. Fortunately, all the techniques that you used with `JFrames` in Chapters 13, 14, and 15 can also be used with `JApplets`. For example, you can do the following:

- 》 Change the font and color of labels
- 》 Use layout managers
- 》 Add multiple GUI components
- 》 Change the background color
- 》 Add listeners for user events

For example, Figure 16-5 shows how you can write a `JApplet` that prompts a user, allows the user to enter text and press a button, and displays output. The `JApplet` also uses color and interesting fonts. The `init()` method sets up the applet surface and enables both the button and text box to generate events to which the `JApplet` can respond.

```
import javax.swing.*;
import java.awt.*;
import java.awt.event.*;
public class JHello2 extends JApplet implements ActionListener
{
    JLabel greeting = new JLabel("Hello. Who are you?");
    Font font1 = new Font("Teen", Font.BOLD, 36);
    Font font2 = new Font("Teen", Font.ITALIC, 48);
    JTextField answer = new JTextField(10);
    JButton pressMe = new JButton("Press me");
    JLabel personalGreeting = new JLabel(" ");
    Container con = getContentPane();
    public void init()
    {
        greeting.setFont(font1);
        personalGreeting.setFont(font2);
        con.add(greeting);
        con.add(answer);
        con.add(pressMe);
        con.setLayout(new FlowLayout());
        con.setBackground(Color.YELLOW);
        pressMe.addActionListener(this);
        answer.addActionListener(this);
    }
    public void actionPerformed(ActionEvent e)
    {
        String name = answer.getText();
        con.remove(greeting);
        con.remove(pressMe);
        con.remove(answer);
        personalGreeting.setText("Hello, " + name + "!   ");
        con.add(personalGreeting);
        con.setBackground(Color.PINK);
        validate();
    }
}
```

Figure 16-5 The JHello2 class that adds a JLabel when the user clicks the JButton

The code in the actionPerformed() method in the JHello2 class shows that after the user clicks the button, the name is retrieved from the text field; the label, button, and text field are removed from the applet surface; and the setText() method sets the JLabel text for personalGreeting to "Hello, " + name + "!   ". Then the personal greeting is added to the JApplet's Container, and the background color is changed. You learned about all of the same methods when you studied JFrames in Chapters 13 and 14. Figure 16-6 shows a typical execution.

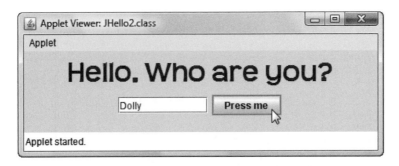

Figure 16-6 Typical execution of the `JHello2` JApplet

The `validate()` method is complex. Even the online Java documentation at *http://java.sun.com* refers to its performance as "voodoo."

In the `actionPerformed()` method in Figure 16-5, the final statement following the addition of the `JLabel` is `validate()`. As you learned in Chapter 14, invoking the `validate()` method after adding one or more `JComponent`s to an applet ensures that the `Components` draw themselves on the screen.

»TWO TRUTHS AND A LIE: WORKING WITH `JApplet` COMPONENTS

1. In an applet, you can change fonts and colors of GUI components just as you can in an application.
2. `JApplet`s can contain an `actionPerformed()` method to respond to mouse clicks.
3. Invoking the `validate()` method in an applet allows it to pass security restrictions.

The false statement is #3. Invoking the `validate()` method after adding one or more `JComponent`s to an applet ensures that the `Component`s draw themselves on the screen.

It isn't necessary to call the `validate()` method every time you add a `JComponent` to a `JApplet`. For example, when you add components in the `init()` or `start()` methods, you do not have to call `validate()`. When you add components in other methods (frequently event-handling methods), you must call `validate()`.

UNDERSTANDING THE `JApplet` LIFE CYCLE

Applets are popular because they are easy to use in Web pages. Because applets execute in a browser, the `JApplet` class contains methods that are automatically called by the browser. You already are familiar with the `paint()` method. In Chapter 15 you learned that the system can request that a component's contents be repainted, or that the application can request repainting. The paint() method is always called after the init() and start() methods execute. It is also called if an applet needs repainting—if, for example, the user covers part of an applet with another open window and then uncovers it. The method works the same way with JApplets as with JFrames. The method header is as follows:

```
public void paint(Graphics g)
```

As you learned in Chapter 15, the paint() method provides you with a Graphics object. If you override the paint() method in your applet, you can use the automatically provided Graphics object to draw shapes and strings.

The other four methods that are automatically called in a JApplet are init(), start(), stop(), and destroy().

THE init() METHOD

You have already seen examples of JApplets that contain init() methods. When a Web page containing a JApplet is loaded in the browser, or when you run the appletviewer command within an HTML document that calls a JApplet, the applet's init() method executes. The init() method might be your version (if you have written one to override the version in the parent class) or the automatically provided version. You should write your own init() method when you have any initialization tasks to perform, such as setting up user interface components.

THE start() METHOD

The **start() method** executes after the init() method, and it executes again every time the applet becomes active after it has been inactive. For example, if you run a JApplet using the appletviewer command and then minimize the Applet Viewer window, the JApplet becomes inactive. When you restore the window, the JApplet becomes active again. On the Internet, users can leave a Web page, visit another page, and then return to the first site. Again, the JApplet becomes inactive and then active. When you write your own start() method, you must include any actions you want your JApplet to take when a user revisits the JApplet. For example, you might want to resume some animation that you suspended when the user left the applet.

THE stop() METHOD

When a user leaves a Web page (perhaps by minimizing a window or traveling to a different Web page), the **stop() method** is invoked. You override the existing empty stop() method only if you want to take some action when a JApplet is no longer visible. You usually don't need to write your own stop() methods.

THE destroy() METHOD

The **destroy() method** is called when the user closes the browser or Applet Viewer. Closing the browser or Applet Viewer releases any resources the JApplet might have allocated. As with the stop() method, you do not usually have to write your own destroy() methods.

Every JApplet has the same life cycle outline, as shown in Figure 16-7. When the applet executes, the init() method runs, followed by the start() method. If the user leaves the JApplet's page, the stop() method executes. When the user returns, the start() method executes. The stop() and start() sequence might continue any number of times until the user closes the browser (or Applet Viewer), which invokes the destroy() method.

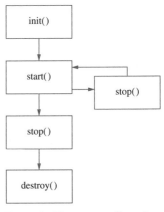

Figure 16-7 The JApplet life cycle

»TWO TRUTHS AND A LIE: UNDERSTANDING THE JApplet LIFE CYCLE

1. The paint() method is always called after the init() and start() methods execute or if an applet needs repainting.
2. When a Web page containing a JApplet is loaded in the browser, the applet's start() method is the first to execute.
3. When a user leaves a Web page, the stop() method executes.

The false statement is #2. When a Web page containing a JApplet is loaded in the browser, or when you run the appletviewer command within an HTML document that calls a JApplet, the applet's init() method is the first to execute.

UNDERSTANDING MULTIMEDIA AND USING IMAGES

Multimedia describes the use of sound, images, graphics, and video in computer programs. Most computers that are sold today are "multimedia ready"—that is, they have CDRW and DVD-RW drives, audio boards, and video capabilities. Java provides extensive multimedia tools, including the following:

» Java programmers can use the Java 2D or the Java 3D Application Programming Interface (API) to create 3D graphics applications.
» The Java Media Framework (JMF) API allows you to add audio and video media to an application.
» Java Sound allows you to play, record, and modify audio files.
» The Java Advanced Imaging API provides image-manipulation capabilities.
» The Java Speech API allows a user to input speech commands and allows an application to produce speech output.

ADDING IMAGES TO JApplets

An **image** is a likeness of a person or thing. Images abound on the Internet in all shapes, colors, and sizes. Image formats supported by Java include:

» Graphics Interchange Format (GIF), which can contain a maximum of 256 different colors

» Joint Photographic Experts Group (JPEG), which is commonly used to store photographs, and is a more sophisticated way to represent a color image

» Portable Network Graphics (PNG), which is more flexible than GIF and stores images in a lossless form. (PNG was originally designed to be a portable image storage form for computer-originated images.)

The Image class provides many of Java's image capabilities; this class loads images that have been stored in one of the allowed Image formats. The Image class, which you can find in the java.awt package, is an abstract class. Because Image is abstract, you must create Image objects indirectly using the getImage() method.

To declare an Image with the name eventLogo, you use the declaration Image eventLogo;. The getImage() method is used to load an Image into the named Image in the applet. One version of the getImage() method can take up to two arguments: a location where the image is stored and its filename. For example, you can create and load the Image named eventLogo with a statement such as the following:

```
eventLogo = getImage(getCodeBase(),"event.gif");
```

>> NOTE The getCodeBase() call returns the Uniform Resource Locator (URL) where the code is located. That is, it finds the directory from which the code is running.

You can use the applet paint() method to display Image object images. The drawImage() method is a Graphics method that uses the following four arguments:

» The first argument is a reference to the Image object in which the image is stored.

» The second argument is the x-coordinate where the image appears on the applet.

» The third argument is the y-coordinate where the image appears on the applet.

» The fourth argument is a reference to an ImageObserver object.

An ImageObserver object can be any object that implements the ImageObserver interface. Because the Component class implements the ImageObserver interface, all Components, including JApplets, inherit this implementation. Usually, the ImageObserver object is the object on which the image appears—in this case, the JApplet. Recall from Chapter 4 that the this reference refers to the current object using a method. Frequently, with the drawImage() method, you use the this reference to indicate that you want the Image drawn on the current JApplet. For example, the code to display the eventLogo image in the upper-left corner of the JApplet is as follows:

```
g.drawImage(eventLogo, 0, 0, this);
```

>> NOTE
Lossless data compression is a set of rules that allows an exact replica of data to be reconstructed from a compressed version. If you have ever worked with a .zip file, you have worked with lossless data compression.

>> NOTE
Recall that an abstract class is one from which you cannot create any objects, but which you can use as an interface or from which you can inherit.

You can use an overloaded version of the `Graphics` method `drawImage()` to output a scaled image. This method takes six arguments. Notice that the first three arguments are the same as those for the four-argument version of the `drawImage()` method. In the overloaded version:

» The first argument is a reference to the `Image` object in which the image is stored.
» The second argument is the x-coordinate where the image appears on the applet.
» The third argument is the y-coordinate where the image appears on the applet.
» The fourth argument is the width of the scaled object.
» The fifth argument is the height of the scaled object.
» The sixth argument uses the `this` reference to implement the `ImageObserver` object.

For example, the following code displays the `eventLogo` image at coordinates 0, 120, using the full width of the `JApplet`, but 100 pixels less than the height:

```
g.drawImage(eventLogo, 0, 120, getWidth(), getHeight() -100, this);
```

Figure 16-8 shows a `JApplet` that draws an image twice. The `JEventImage JApplet` uses an image file named EventHandlers.png, which holds a logo that is originally 328 pixels wide by 104 pixels high. Within the `paint()` method in the `JApplet`, the image is drawn first in its "natural," or original, size in the upper-left corner. Then it is redrawn lower, using a size that is twice its original size. Figure 16-9 shows the contents of the HTML document that displays the applet; the output of the `JEventImage` applet is shown in Figure 16-10.

```
import java.awt.*;
import java.applet.*;
import javax.swing.*;
public class JEventImage extends JApplet
{
    Image eventLogo;
    final int WIDTH = 328;
    final int HEIGHT = 104;
    public void init()
    {
        eventLogo = getImage(getCodeBase(), "EventHandlers.png");
    }
    public void paint(Graphics g)
    {
        super.paint(g);
        // Draw image at its natural size 328 X 104
        g.drawImage(eventLogo, 0, 0, this);
        // Draw the image scaled - twice as large
        g.drawImage(eventLogo, 0, HEIGHT, WIDTH * 2, HEIGHT * 2, this);
    }
}
```

Figure 16-8 The `JEventImage JApplet`

```
<html>
<object code = "JEventImage.class" width = 650 height = 320>
</object>
</html>
```

Figure 16-9 The `TestJEventImage` HTML document

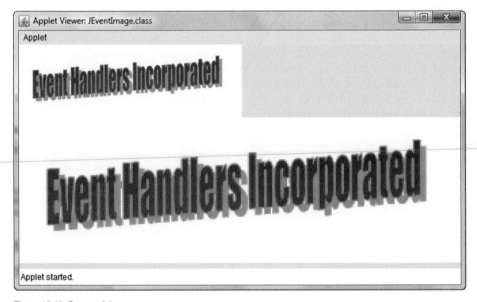

Figure 16-10 Output of the `JEventImage` JApplet

USING `ImageIcons`

You can also use the `ImageIcon` class to create images in your applications and applets. In general, working with the `ImageIcon` class is simpler than working with `Image`. You can use all the `Image` methods with an `ImageIcon`, plus many additional methods. Unlike the `Image` class, you can create `ImageIcon` objects directly. Also, unlike `Images`, you can place an `ImageIcon` on a `Component`, such as a `JPanel`, `JLabel`, or `JButton`, as well as on a `JApplet` or `JFrame`. For example, the following statements create a `JButton` that contains a picture of an arrow:

```
ImageIcon arrowPicture = new ImageIcon("arrow.gif");
JButton arrowButton = new JButton(arrowPicture);
```

You can also use the `paintIcon()` method to display `ImageIcon` images. This method requires four arguments:

» The first argument is a reference to the `Component` on which the image appears—`this` in the following example.

» The second argument is a reference to the `Graphics` object used to render the image—`g` in the following example.

»NOTE
You can examine the EventHandlers .png file in the Chapter.16 folder on your Student Disk.

»NOTE
Behind the scenes, each `ImageIcon` object uses an `Image` object to hold the image data and a `MediaTracker` object to keep track of the image's loading status. As you are aware if you have visited many Web pages, some images can require a good deal of time to load. To improve performance, the `Image get()` methods return immediately while the image continues to load, so that your application does not have to wait before performing other operations.

» The third argument is the x-coordinate for the upper-left corner of the image.

» The fourth argument is the y-coordinate for the upper-left corner of the image.

The code to display the `arrowPicture` ImageIcon using the `paintIcon()` method is:

```
arrowPicture.paintIcon(this, g, 180, 0);
```

You can retrieve an ImageIcon's width and height with methods named `getIconWidth()` and `getIconHeight()`; each returns an integer. Figure 16-11 shows an example of how you can manipulate an ImageIcon's width and height to achieve display effects. In the `JBear` JApplet, an ImageIcon is created using a .gif file. In the `init()` method, the width and height of the ImageIcon are stored in variables named `width` and `height`. In the `actionPerformed()` method, the width and height of the image are doubled with every button click. Figure 16-12 shows the JApplet when it starts, after the user has clicked the button once, and after the user has clicked the button twice.

```java
import java.awt.*;
import java.awt.event.*;
import javax.swing.*;
public class JBear extends JApplet implements ActionListener
{
    private ImageIcon image = new ImageIcon("bear.gif");
    private JButton closerButton = new JButton("Oh my!");
    private int width, height;
    Container con = getContentPane();
    public void init()
    {
        con.setLayout(new FlowLayout());
        closerButton.addActionListener(this);
        con.add(closerButton);
        width = image.getIconWidth();
        height = image.getIconHeight();
    }
    public void actionPerformed(ActionEvent event)
    {
        width = width * 2;
        height = height * 2;
        repaint();
    }
    public void paint(Graphics g)
    {
        super.paint(g);
        g.drawImage(image.getImage(), 0, 0, width, height, this);
    }
}
```

>> NOTE
In the `JBear` JApplet in Figure 16-11, if you eliminate the call to `super.paint()` as the first statement in the `paint()` method, then as you get each new bear image, the previous one remains on the screen "behind" the newer, larger one.

Figure 16-11 The `JBear` JApplet

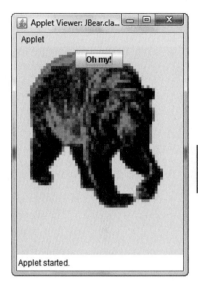

Figure 16-12 Output of the JBear JApplet

In the paint() method in the JBear JApplet, notice that the drawImage() method uses the getImage() method with the image in the following statement:

```
g.drawImage(image.getImage(), 0, 0, width, height, this);
```

An ImageIcon cannot be drawn to scale, but an Image can, so you use the getImage() method to return a scalable Image reference.

≫TWO TRUTHS AND A LIE: UNDERSTANDING MULTIMEDIA AND USING IMAGES

1. Multimedia describes the use of sound, images, graphics, and video in computer programs; most computers that are sold today are "multimedia ready."
2. Image formats supported by Java include GIF, JPEG, and PNG.
3. You can use the Picture class to create images in your applications and applets.

The false statement is #3. You can use the Image or ImageIcon class to create images in your applications and applets; you can even place an ImageIcon on a Component, such as a JPanel or JButton.

ADDING SOUND TO JApplets

Java programs can play audio clips on computers that have speakers and a sound card (which includes most computers that are sold today). Java supports sound using methods from the `Applet` class, rather than `JApplet`. You can use these methods to retrieve and play sound files that use various sound formats. These formats include the Windows Wave file format (.wav), Sun Microsystems Audio file format (.au), and Music and Instrument Digital Interface file format (.midi or .mid).

The simplest way to retrieve and play a sound is to use the `play()` method of the `Applet` class. The `play()` method retrieves and plays the sound as soon as possible after it is called. The `play()` method takes one of two forms:

» `play()` with one argument—The argument is a URL object that loads and plays an audio clip when both the URL object and the audio clip are stored at the same URL.

» `play()` with two arguments—The first argument is a URL object, and the second argument is a folder path name that loads and plays the audio file. The first argument is often a call to a `getCodeBase()` method or `getDocumentBase()` method to retrieve the URL object; the second argument is the name of the audio clip within the folder path that is stored at that URL.

Used with the `codebase` attribute, which indicates the filename of the applet's main class file, the `getCodeBase()` and `getDocumentBase()` methods direct the browser to look in a different folder for the applet and other files it uses. This is necessary when the desired files are in a different location than the Web page containing the applet. By calling `getCodeBase()` in an applet, you get a URL object that represents the folder in which the applet's class file is stored. For example, the following statement retrieves and plays the event.au sound file, which is stored in the same place as the applet:

```
play(getCodeBase(),"event.au");
```

> **»NOTE** The `getDocumentBase()` method returns an absolute URL naming the directory of the document in which the applet is stored. It is sometimes used instead of `getCodeBase()` as a matter of preference. An applet is restricted to reading files only from the server that hosts it.

> **»NOTE**
> Multiple `AudioClip` items can play at the same time, and the resulting sound is mixed together to produce a composite.

To play a sound more than once, or to start or stop the sound, you must load the sound into an `AudioClip` object using the applet's `newAudioClip()` method. `AudioClip` is part of the `java.awt.Applet` class and must be imported into your program. Like the `play()` method, the `getAudioClip()` method can take one or two arguments. The first argument (or only argument, if there is only one) is a URL argument that identifies the sound file; the second argument is a folder path reference needed for locating the file.

The following statement loads the sound file from the previous example into the clip object:

```
AudioClip aClip = new AudioClip(getCodeBase(), "audio/event.au");
```

Here, the sound file reference indicates that the event.au sound file is in the audio folder. After you have created an `AudioClip` object, you can use the `play()` method to call and play the sound, the `stop()` method to halt the playback, and the `loop()` method to play the sound repeatedly.

»NOTE
In the You Do It section, you will create a JApplet that plays a sound.

»TWO TRUTHS AND A LIE: ADDING SOUND TO JApplets

1. Java programs can play audio clips on computers that have speakers and a sound card.
2. Java supports sound using methods from the JApplet class.
3. Sound formats that applets can use include the Windows Wave file format (.wav), Sun Audio file format (.au), and Music and Instrument Digital Interface file format (.midi or .mid).

The false statement is #2. Java supports sound using methods from the Applet class (rather than JApplet).

YOU DO IT

CREATING AN HTML DOCUMENT TO HOST AN APPLET

In this section, you create a simple HTML document that you will use to display the applet you will create in the next section. You will name the applet `JGreet`, and it will occupy a screen area of 450 by 200 pixels.

To create an HTML document to host an applet:

1. Open a new file in your text editor. Type the opening HTML tag:

   ```
   <html>
   ```

2. On the next line, type the opening `object` tag that contains the applet's name and dimensions:

   ```
   <object code = "JGreet.class" width = 450 height = 200>
   ```

3. On the next line, type the applet's closing tag:

   ```
   </object>
   ```

4. On the next line, type the closing HTML tag:

   ```
   </html>
   ```

5. Save the file as **TestJGreet.html**. Just as when you create a Java application, be certain that you save the file as text only and use an .html extension. The .html file extension is required and makes the file easy to identify as an HTML file.

CREATING AND RUNNING A JApplet

Next, you will create the JGreet applet for which you prepared the HTML document.

To create and run the JGreet applet:

1. Open a new text file in your text editor. Enter the following import statements you need for the JApplet. You need the javax.swing package because it defines JApplet, and you need the java.awt package because it defines Container.

```
import javax.swing.*;
import java.awt.*;
```

2. Next, enter the JGreet JApplet. It contains a Container that holds a JLabel. The init() method adds the JLabel to the Container.

```
public class JGreet extends JApplet
{
    Container con = getContentPane();
    JLabel greeting = new JLabel("Greetings!");
    public void init()
    {
        con.add(greeting);
    }
}
```

3. Save the file as **JGreet.java**. Then compile the class. If necessary, correct any errors and compile again.

4. At the command line, type **appletviewer TestJGreet.html** and then press **Enter**. The applet appears on your screen, as shown in Figure 16-13.

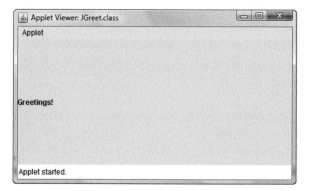

Figure 16-13 The JGreet JApplet

5. Use the mouse pointer to drag any corner of the Applet Viewer window to resize it. Notice that if you increase the window's height, the window is redrawn on the screen and the JLabel is automatically repositioned to remain centered within the window. If you make the window narrower by dragging its right border to the left, the JLabel eventually becomes partially obscured when the window becomes too narrow for the display.

6. Close the Applet Viewer by clicking the **Close button** in the upper-right corner of the window.

RUNNING A JApplet IN YOUR WEB BROWSER

To run the applet using your Web browser:

1. Open any Web browser, such as Internet Explorer. You do not have to connect to the Internet; you will use the browser locally.

2. Click **File** on the menu bar, click **Open** or **Open Page**, type the complete path for the HTML document that you created to access JGreet.class (for example, **C:\Java\Chapter.16\ TestJGreet.html**), and then press **Enter**. You might have to agree to several security messages before you can view the applet. The applet should appear in the browser on your screen. If you receive an error message, verify that the path and spelling of the HTML file are correct.

3. Click the **Close button** in the upper-right corner of the browser to close your Web browser.

CREATING A MORE COMPLICATED JApplet

Next, you will change the font of the text in your JGreet applet, add components, and make other changes to make a more complicated and useful JApplet.

To change the JGreet applet:

1. Open the **JGreet.java** file in your text editor and change the class name to JGreet2. Immediately save the file using the filename **JGreet2.java**.

2. After the declaration of the greeting JLabel, declare a Font object named bigFont by typing the following:

```
Font bigFont = new Font("Times Roman", Font.ITALIC, 24);
```

3. Within the init() method, set the greeting font to bigFont by typing the following:

```
greeting.setFont(bigFont);
```

4. Along with the other declarations, declare two JLabels, two empty JTextFields, and a JButton with the label "View Greeting" by typing the following:

```
JLabel firstLabel = new JLabel("Please enter your first name:");
JLabel lastLabel = new JLabel("Please enter your last name:");
JTextField firstField = new JTextField("",10);
JTextField lastField = new JTextField("",10);
JButton viewButton = new JButton("View Greeting");
```

5. Set the new layout manager to a flow layout with the following statement:

```
FlowLayout flow = new FlowLayout();
```

6. Within the init() method, set a layout manager as follows:

```
con.setLayout(flow);
```

7. Add all the newly created components to the applet by typing the following:

```
con.add(firstLabel);
con.add(firstField);
con.add(lastLabel);
con.add(lastField);
con.add(viewButton);
```

8. On the next line, request focus for the first-name text field by typing:

```
firstField.requestFocus();
```

9. Save the file and compile it.

10. Open the **TestJGreet.html** document you created earlier and change the class name in the object code statement to **JGreet2.class**. Save the file as **TestJGreet2.html**. Execute the **appletviewer TestJGreet2.html** command. The output is shown in Figure 16-14. Confirm that you can type characters into the JTextFields and that you can click the JButton using the mouse. You haven't coded any action to take place as a result of a JButton click yet, but the components should function.

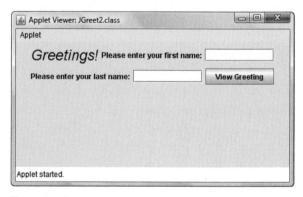

Figure 16-14 The JGreet2 JApplet

11. Close the Applet Viewer window.

MAKING THE JApplet's BUTTON RESPOND TO EVENTS

Next, you will make your applet an event-driven program by adding functionality to the applet. When the user enters a name and clicks the JButton, the JApplet displays a personalized greeting.

To add functionality to your JApplet:

1. Open the **JGreet2.java** file in your text editor and change the class name to **JGreet3**. Immediately save the file as **JGreet3.java**.

2. Add a third import statement to your program by typing the following:

```
import java.awt.event.*;
```

3. Add the following phrase to the class header:

```
implements ActionListener
```

4. Prepare your JApplet for JButton-sourced events by typing the following statement within the init() method:

```
viewButton.addActionListener(this);
```

5. Following the init() method, add the following actionPerformed() method. In the method, declare two Strings—one to hold the user's first name and another for the last name—and then use the getText() method on the JTextFields to retrieve values for these Strings. Using the Strings, display a personalized question for the user.

```java
public void actionPerformed(ActionEvent thisEvent)
{
    String firstName = firstField.getText();
    String lastName = lastField.getText();
    greeting.setText("How are you, " + firstName + " " +
        lastName + "?");
}
```

6. Save the file and compile the program. Edit the file **TestJGreet2.html** to change the class reference to **JGreet3.class**, and then save the file as **TestJGreet3.html**. Run the applet using the **appletviewer TestJGreet3.html** command.

7. Type your name in the JTextFields and then click the **View Greeting** button. The personalized message should appear, similar to the one in Figure 16-15.

Figure 16-15 Typical execution of the `JGreet3` JApplet

8. Drag the mouse to highlight the first or last name (or both) in the Applet Viewer window, and then type a different name. Click the **View Greeting** button. A greeting that uses the new name appears.

9. Close the Applet Viewer window.

UNDERSTANDING THE APPLET LIFE CYCLE

To demonstrate the life cycle methods in action, you can write a `JApplet` that overrides all four methods: `init()`, `start()`, `stop()`, and `destroy()`. When you run this applet, you can observe the number of times each method executes.

To demonstrate the life cycle of a `JApplet`:

1. Open a new text file in your text editor and then type the following `import` statements:

```
import javax.swing.*;
import java.awt.*;
import java.awt.event.*;
```

2. To make the `JApplet` include a `JButton` that the user can click, and to implement an `ActionListener`, type the following header for a `JLifeCycle` applet and include an opening curly brace for the class:

```
public class JLifeCycle extends JApplet implements ActionListener
{
```

3. Declare the following six `JLabel` objects, which display each of the six methods that execute during the lifetime of the applet:

```
JLabel messageInit = new JLabel("init ");
JLabel messageStart = new JLabel("start ");
JLabel messageDisplay = new JLabel("display ");
JLabel messageAction = new JLabel("action ");
JLabel messageStop = new JLabel("stop ");
JLabel messageDestroy = new JLabel("destroy ");
```

4. Declare a `JButton` by typing the following:

```
JButton pressButton = new JButton("Press");
```

5. Declare six integers that hold the number of occurrences of each of the six methods by typing the following code:

```
int countInit, countStart, countDisplay, countAction,
    countStop, countDestroy;
```

6. Start the `init()` method by adding a container and flow layout manager with the following statements:

```
public void init()
{
    Container con = getContentPane();
    con.setLayout (new FlowLayout());
```

7. Add the following statements, which add 1 to `countInit`, place the components within the applet, and then call the `display()` method:

```
    ++countInit;
    con.add(messageInit);
    con.add(messageStart);
    con.add(messageDisplay);
    con.add(messageAction);
    con.add(messageStop);
    con.add(messageDestroy);
    con.add(pressButton);
    pressButton.addActionListener(this);
    display();
}
```

8. Add the following `start()` method, which adds 1 to `countStart` and calls `display()`:

```
public void start()
{
    ++countStart;
    display();
}
```

9. Add the following `display()` method, which adds 1 to `countDisplay`, displays the name of each of the six methods with the current count, and indicates how many times the method has executed:

```
public void display()
{
    ++countDisplay;
    messageInit.setText("init " + countInit);
    messageStart.setText("start " + countStart);
    messageDisplay.setText("display " + countDisplay);
    messageAction.setText("action " + countAction);
    messageStop.setText("stop " + countStop);
    messageDestroy.setText("destroy " + countDestroy);
}
```

10. Add the following `stop()` and `destroy()` methods. Each adds 1 to the appropriate counter and calls `display()`:

```
public void stop()
{
    ++countStop;
    display();
}
public void destroy()
{
    ++countDestroy;
    display();
}
```

11. When the user clicks `pressButton`, the following `actionPerformed()` method executes; it adds 1 to `countAction` and displays it:

```
public void actionPerformed(ActionEvent e)
{
    ++countAction;
    display();
}
```

12. Add the closing curly brace for the class. Save the file as **JLifeCycle.java**. Compile the class.

Take a moment to examine the code you created for JLifeCycle.java. Each method adds 1 to one of the six counters, but you never explicitly call any of the methods except `display()`; each of the other methods is called automatically. Next, you will create an HTML document so that you can test JLifeCycle.java.

To create an HTML document to test JLifeCycle.java:

1. Open a new text file in your text editor and then enter the following HTML code:

```
<html>
<object code = "JLifeCycle.class" width = 460 height = 100>
</object>
</html>
```

2. Save the file as **TestJLifeCycle.html**.

3. Run the HTML document using the following command:

```
appletviewer TestJLifeCycle.html
```

Figure 16-16 shows the output. When the applet begins, the `init()` method is called, so 1 is added to `countInit`. The `init()` method calls `display()`, so 1 is added to `countDisplay`. Immediately after the `init()` method executes, the `start()` method is executed, and 1 is added to `countStart`. The `start()` method calls `display()`, so 1 more is added to `countDisplay`. The first time you see the applet, `countInit` is 1, `countStart` is 1, and `countDisplay` is 2. The methods `actionPerformed()`, `stop()`, and `destroy()` have not yet been executed.

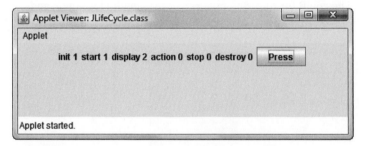

Figure 16-16 The `JLifeCycle JApplet` when it first executes

4. Click the **Minimize** button to minimize the Applet Viewer window and then click the **Taskbar** button to restore it. The applet now looks like Figure 16-17. The `init()` method still has been called only once, but when you minimized the applet, the `stop()` method executed, and when you restored it, the `start()` method executed. Therefore, `countStop` is now 1 and `countStart` has increased to 2. In addition, because `start()` and `stop()` call `display()`, `countDisplay` is increased by 2 and now holds the value 4.

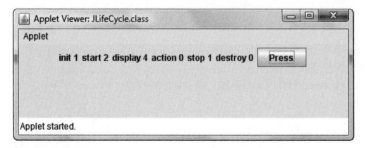

Figure 16-17 The `JLifeCycle JApplet` after minimizing and restoring

5. Minimize and restore the Applet Viewer window again. Now, the `stop()` method has executed twice, the `start()` method has executed three times, and the `display()` method has executed a total of six times, as shown in Figure 16-18.

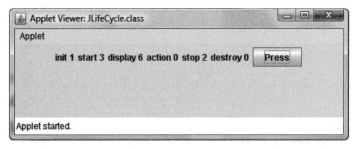

Figure 16-18 The JLifeCycle JApplet after minimizing and restoring twice

6. Click the **Press** button. The count for the actionPerformed() method is now 1, and actionPerformed() calls display(), so countDisplay is now 7, as shown in Figure 16-19.

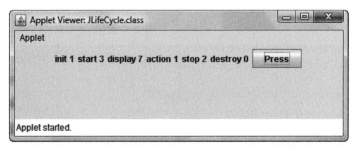

Figure 16-19 The JLifeCycle JApplet after minimizing and restoring twice, and then pressing the button

7. Continue to minimize, maximize, and click the **Press** button. Note the changes that occur with each activity until you can correctly predict the outcome. Notice that the destroy() method is not executed until you close the applet, and then it is too late to observe an increase in countDestroy.

8. Close the Applet Viewer.

DISPLAYING IMAGES
To add an animated image to an applet:

1. Open a new file in your text editor and then enter the first few lines of the JMonkey JApplet:

```
import java.awt.*;
import javax.swing.*;
public class JMonkey extends JApplet
{
```

2. Declare an ImageIcon and initialize it with the monkey.gif file that is stored on your Student Disk. The file contains an animated image of a chimpanzee shaking its head from side to side. Declare variables to hold the width and height of the image, the content pane for the applet, and horizontal and vertical placement positions.

```
private ImageIcon image = new ImageIcon("monkey.gif");
private int width, height;
Container con = getContentPane();
int x = 30;
int y = 30;
```

3. Write the `init()` method to set the layout manager and get the width and height of the image.

```
public void init()
{
    con.setLayout(new FlowLayout());
    width = image.getIconWidth();
    height = image.getIconHeight();
}
```

4. The `paint()` method calls the parent's method, then draws a string and draws the image 20 pixels lower. Add the method shown below and then add a closing curly brace for the class.

```
public void paint(Graphics g)
{
    super.paint(g);
    g.drawString("No, no, no", x, y);
    g.drawImage(image.getImage(), x, y + 20,
        width, height, this);
}
}
```

5. Save the file as **JMonkey.java** and compile it.

6. Write an HTML document to host the applet as follows:

```
<html>
<object code = "JMonkey.class"
    width = 200 height = 150>
</object>
</html>
```

7. Save the HTML document as **TestJMonkey.html**. Run the applet. The output should look like Figure 16-20. On your screen, you will see the animated monkey move.

Figure 16-20 Execution of the JMonkey applet

PLAYING SOUNDS

Next, you will use the `loop()` method and an `AudioClip` to play a sound continually in an applet. You will also create and add a `Graphics2D` object.

To play a sound and add a `Graphics2D` object in a `JApplet` for Event Handlers Incorporated:

1. Open a new file in your text editor and then enter the first few lines of the `JEventSound` `JApplet`:

```
import java.awt.*;
import java.applet.*;
import javax.swing.*;
public class JEventSound extends JApplet
{
```

2. Enter the following statement to declare an `AudioClip` object named `sound`:

```
AudioClip sound;
```

3. Create the `init()` method and an `AudioClip` object to play the event.au sound file by entering the following code:

```
public void init()
{
    sound = getAudioClip(getCodeBase(),"event.au");
}
```

> **▶▶ NOTE**
> You can find the event.au file in the Chapter.16 folder on your Student Disk.

4. Create the following `start()` method. This method uses the `loop()` method to play the event.au sound file continually:

```
public void start()
{
    sound.loop();
}
```

5. Create the following `stop()` method to halt the event.au sound file:

```
public void stop()
{
    sound.stop();
}
```

6. Create a `Graphics` object using `paint(Graphics g)`, and then use a cast to change the graphics context to a `Graphics2D` object. Use the `drawString()` method to create a message that appears on the screen while the `JApplet` plays. Add a closing curly brace for the class.

```
public void paint(Graphics g)
{
    super.paint(g);
    Graphics2D g2D = (Graphics2D)g;
    g2D.drawString("Playing Event Handlers Inc. Event sounds ...",
        10, 10);
}
}
```

7. Save the file as **JEventSound.java** and then compile it.

8. Open a new file in your text editor and then enter the following HTML document to test the `JApplet`:

```
<html>
<object code = "JEventSound.class" width = 300 height = 50>
</object>
</html>
```

9. Save the HTML document as **TestJEventSound.html** and then run it using the **appletviewer TestJEventSound.html** command. The output should look like Figure 16-21. If speakers are installed on your system and they are on, you should also be able to hear sound playing continually.

Figure 16-21 Output of the `JEventSound` JApplet

DON'T DO IT

» Don't forget a matching closing tag for every opening tag in an HTML document.
» Don't forget to use the .class extension with the name of a `JApplet` you want to execute from an HTML document.
» Don't add a `main()` method to a `JApplet`; it will not execute automatically like it does in an application.

KEY TERMS

An **applet** is a Java program that is called from another application.

JApplet is a `Swing` class from which you can inherit to create your own applet.

HTML, or **Hypertext Markup Language**, is a simple language used to create Web pages for the Internet.

Extensible Hypertext Markup Language (XHTML) is an extension of HTML.

Applet Viewer is a program that comes with the JDK and allows you to view applets without using a Web browser.

The **appletviewer command** allows you to view an applet in a viewing program that comes with the JDK.

A **Web browser** is a program that allows you to display HTML documents on your computer screen.

A **sandbox** is a safe area in which a program can run without causing harm to other areas of a system.

Tags are HTML commands.

The tag that begins every HTML document is **<html>**.

The tag that ends every HTML document is **</html>**.

Tag attributes, sometimes referred to as arguments, promote activity or describe the features of an HTML tag.

The **init()** **method** is the first method called in any applet.

The **start()** **method** executes after the init() method, and it executes again every time the applet becomes active after it has been inactive.

In an applet, when a user leaves a Web page (perhaps by minimizing a window or traveling to a different Web page), the **stop()** **method** is invoked.

Within an applet, the **destroy()** **method** is called when the user closes the browser or Applet Viewer.

Multimedia describes the use of sound, images, graphics, and video in computer programs.

An **image** is a likeness of a person or thing.

Lossless data compression is a set of rules that allows an exact replica of data to be reconstructed from a compressed version.

CHAPTER SUMMARY

» An applet is a program that is called within another application—often a Web browser or a program called the Applet Viewer. Applets descend from the JApplet class and do not contain a main() method.

» To view an applet, it must be called from another document written in Hypertext Markup Language (HTML), which is a simple language used to create Web pages for the Internet. When you create an applet, you write it in Java, save it with a .java file extension, compile it, and write an HTML document that includes a statement to call your compiled Java class. You then load the HTML document into a Web browser or run the Applet Viewer program, which in turn uses the HTML document.

» With an applet, the browser calls several methods automatically at different times. The five methods that are included in every applet are init(), start(), paint(), stop(), and destroy(). You can override any of those methods within a JApplet that you write.

» When you write a JApplet, you can add components, use fonts and colors, change the layout manager, and add event listeners, in much the same way you do in a JFrame.

» An applet's paint() method is always called after the init() and start() methods execute. It is also called if an applet needs repainting. When a Web page containing a JApplet is loaded in the browser, or when you run the appletviewer command within an HTML document that calls a JApplet, the applet's init() method executes.

The start() method executes after the init() method, and it executes again every time the applet becomes active after it has been inactive. When a user leaves a Web page (perhaps by minimizing a window or traveling to a different Web page), the stop() method is invoked. The destroy() method is called when the user closes the browser or Applet Viewer.

» Multimedia describes the use of sound, images, graphics, and video in computer programs. Image formats supported by Java include Graphics Interchange Format (GIF), Joint Photographic Experts Group (JPEG), and Portable Network Graphics (PNG). The Image class provides many of Java's image capabilities. You can also use the ImageIcon class to create images in your applications and applets.

» Java programs can play audio clips on computers that have speakers and a sound card. Supported sound formats include the Windows Wave file format (.wav), Sun Audio file format (.au), and Music and Instrument Digital Interface file format (.midi or .mid). The simplest way to retrieve and play a sound is to use the play() method of the Applet class.

REVIEW QUESTIONS

1. An applet is like a Java application in all of the following ways *except* _____ .

    a. you save it with a .java file extension

    b. you compile it into bytecode, creating a file with a .class extension

    c. it can contain decisions, loops, arrays, and all the other language elements of Java

    d. it requires a main() method

2. How is a JApplet different from an application that instantiates a JFrame?

    a. JFrames use graphics.

    b. JApplets run from another program.

    c. JFrames are larger than JApplets.

    d. The user cannot close a JApplet; the program must issue a command to do so.

3. A program that allows you to display HTML documents on your computer screen is a _____ .

    a. search engine   c. browser

    b. compiler   d. server

4. HTML contains commands that allow you to do all of the following except _____ .

    a. add JButtons to JApplets   c. import graphic images to a Web page

    b. format text on a Web page   d. link your page to other Web pages

5. Pairs of HTML commands are called _____ .

    a. tickets   c. tags

    b. labels   d. keywords

6. The name of any applet called using `code` within an HTML document must use the extension _____ .

    a. .exe   c. .java

    b. .code   d. .class

7. Which `JApplet` method can you override in your extended version?

    a. `init()`   c. `paint()`

    b. `stop()`   d. all of the above

8. A `JApplet` is a(n) _____ .

    a. `Container`   c. `Object`

    b. `Component`   d. all of the above

9. The first method called in any `JApplet` is the _____ method.

    a. `init()`   c. `begin()`

    b. `start()`   d. `main()`

10. A `JApplet`'s `init()` method is closest in purpose to a `JFrame`'s _____ .

    a. `main()` method   c. `start()` method

    b. `actionPerformed()` method   d. constructor

11. Which of the following `JApplet` methods is likely to execute the greatest number of times?

    a. `init()`   c. `destroy()`

    b. `start()`   d. `main()`

12. The `paint()` method is automatically called _____ .

    a. before the `init()` method   c. from the `actionPerformed()` method

    b. after the `start()` method   d. never

13. The `start()` method called in any `JApplet` is called _____ .
    a. as the first method when an applet starts   c. when a user revisits an applet
    b. when the user closes the browser   d. when a user leaves a Web page

14. To respond to user events within a `JApplet`, you must _____ .
    a. prepare the applet to accept event messages   c. tell your applet how to respond to events
    b. import the `java.applet.*` package   d. accomplish both a and c

15. When a user leaves a Web page, the `JApplet` method that executes is _____ .
    a. `stop()`   c. `kill()`
    b. `destroy()`   d. `exit()`

16. The term that describes the use of sound, images, graphics, and video in computer programs is _____ .
    a. inheritance   c. art
    b. multimedia   d. graphics

17. Image formats supported by Java include all of the following except _____ .
    a. GIF   c. MIDI
    b. JPEG   d. PNG

18. Unlike using the `Image` class, objects of the `ImageIcon` class _____ .
    a. are harder to work with   c. can be placed on components such as `JButtons`
    b. cannot be extended   d. cannot be created by calling the class constructor

19. The `Applet` class method that retrieves sound is _____ .
    a. `sound()`   c. `record()`
    b. `music()`   d. `play()`

20. The method that plays a sound repeatedly is _____ .
    a. `play()`   c. `repeat()`
    b. `loop()`   d. `continue()`

EXERCISES

For each JApplet you create in the following exercises, create an HTML host document named **Test** plus the JApplet name. For example, the host document for the **JNumberOne.java** file is named **TestJNumberOne.html**.

1. Create a JApplet with a JButton labeled "Who's number one?" When the user clicks the button, display your favorite sports team in a large font. Save the file as **JNumberOne.java**.

2. a. Create a JApplet that asks a user to enter a password into a JTextField and then to press Enter. Compare the password to "Rosebud"; if it matches exactly, display "Access Granted". If not, display "Access Denied". Save the file as **JPasswordA.java**.

   b. Modify the password applet in Exercise 2a to ignore differences in case between the typed password and "Rosebud". Save the file as **JPasswordB.java**.

   c. Modify the password applet in Exercise 2b to compare the password to a list of five valid passwords: "Rosebud", "Redrum", "Jason", "Surrender", or "Dorothy". Save the file as **JPasswordC.java**.

3. Create a JApplet that contains a JLabel and JButton. When the user clicks the JButton, change the font typeface, style, and size on the JLabel. Save the file as **JChangeFont.java**.

4. Create a JApplet that contains a JButton and a JTextField. When the user clicks the JButton, display "Today is ", the date, and the time in the JTextField. Save the file as **JDateAndTime.java**.

5. Create a JApplet that contains two JTextFields, a JButton, and three JLabels. When the user types an employee's first and last names (separated by a space) in a JTextField, the employee's job title displays in a second JTextField. Include two JLabels to describe the JTextFields used for data entry, and include a third JLabel that holds the employee's title or an error message if no match is found for the employee. Use parallel arrays to store the employees' names and job titles. Save the file as **JEmployeeTitle.java**.

6. Create a JApplet that contains two parallel arrays that contain at least five employees' names and jobs. Allow the user to enter either a title or a name and to click a JButton to display the other. Include a JLabel to describe each JTextField. Save the file as **JEmployeeTitle2.java**.

7. Create a JApplet that initially displays a single JButton. When the user clicks the JButton, display a JLabel that prompts the user to enter an integer, a JTextField into which the user can type the integer, and a second JButton that contains the text "Double me". When the user clicks the second button, the integer is doubled and the answer is displayed in the JTextField. Save the file as **JDouble.java**.

8. a. Create a payroll JApplet named JCalculatePay that allows the user to enter two double values: hours worked and an hourly rate. When the user clicks a JButton, gross pay is calculated. Display the result in a JTextField that appears on the screen only after the user clicks the JButton. Save the file as **JCalculatePay.java**.

   b. Modify the payroll applet created in Exercise 8a so that federal withholding tax is subtracted from gross pay based on the following table:

Income ($)	Withholding %
0 to 99.99	10
100.00 to 299.99	15
300.00 to 599.99	21
600.00 and up	28

Save the file as **JCalculatePay2.java**.

9. Write a JApplet that uses the ImageIcon class to place image icon objects on four JButtons. Download any free JPEG or GIF files from the Internet; if necessary, reduce the size of the images to approximately 30 by 30 pixels. Alternatively, you can use the four files named up.jpg, down.jpg, left.jpg, and right.jpg on your Student Disk. Each time a JButton is clicked, display a different message below the JButtons. Save the JApplet as **JButtonIcons.java**.

10. Create a JApplet that paints an ImageIcon the first time its paint() method is called, and then randomly draws small filled ovals in the background color over the image each time a JButton is clicked. The resulting effect is that the image seems to be erased by an increasing number of small overlapping ovals. For example, if you place an ImageIcon at the coordinates contained in variables named startPosX and startPosY, you can create a series of 15-by-10 filled ovals placed randomly on the ImageIcon's surface using the following for loop:

```
for(int count = 0; count < 20; ++count)
{
    int x = (int) (Math.random() * imageWidth) + startPosX;
    int y = (int) (Math.random() * imageHeight) + startPosY;
    g.fillOval(x, y, 10, 10);
}
```

Save your JApplet as **JEraseImage.java**.

11. Create a JApplet for Business Associates, a consulting firm whose motto is "Let Business Associates take care of your business." Include two JButtons: clicking one JButton plays the tune "Taking Care of Business" continuously, and clicking the other stops the music. You can find the business.mid file on your Student Disk. Save the JApplet as **JBusiness.java**.

12. Write an applet that prompts the user for a color name. If it is not red, white, or blue, throw an `Exception`. Otherwise, change the applet's background color appropriately. Create an HTML document to host the `JApplet`. Save the applet file as **RWBApplet.java**.

13. Write a `JApplet` that uses a `JPanel` to show the messages "Mouse Entered Applet!" and "Mouse Exited Applet!" when the mouse enters and exits the applet. Also, when the mouse is clicked on the applet, a message "Clicked Here!" should appear near the clicked location. Save the file as **JMouse.java**.

14. Event Handlers Incorporated wants you to create a `JPartyPlanner` applet that lets a user estimate the cost of an event hosted by the company. Event Handlers uses a sliding fee scale so that the per-guest cost decreases as the total number of invited guests increases. Table 16-1 shows the fee structure.

Number of Guests	Cost per Guest ($)
1–24	27
25–49	25
50–99	22
100–199	19
200–499	17
500–999	14
1000 and over	11

Table 16-1 Cost per guest for events

The applet lets the user enter a number of anticipated guests. The user can click either of two `JButtons`: one to display the fee per person and another to display the fee for the event (the cost per person times the number of guests). The user can continue to request fees for a different number of guests and view the results for any length of time before making another request or leaving the page. When the user leaves the page, erase the last number of requested guests and ensure that the next user starts fresh with a blank `JTextField` that holds the number of guests. Save the file as **JPartyPlanner.java**.

DEBUGGING EXERCISES

Each of the following files in the Chapter.16 folder on your Student Disk has syntax and/or logic errors. In each case, determine the problem and fix the program. After you correct the errors, save each file using the same filename preceded with Fix. For example, DebugSixteen1.java will become FixDebugSixteen1.java. You can test each applet with the TestFixDebugSixteen1.html through TestFixDebugSixteen4.html files on your Student Disk.

a. DebugSixteen1.java

b. DebugSixteen2.java

c. DebugSixteen3.java

d. DebugSixteen4.java

GAME ZONE

1. In Chapter 2, you created a *Mad Libs®* game in which the user entered several words out of context that were then inserted into a rhyme or story, producing humorous effects. Modify the game so that it becomes an applet. In turn, prompt the user for each required word. After all the words are entered, display the completed rhyme or story. Figure 16-22 shows the first and last screens displayed during a typical execution. Save the applet as **JMadLib.java**. Create an HTML document to execute the applet and save it as **TestJMadLib.html**.

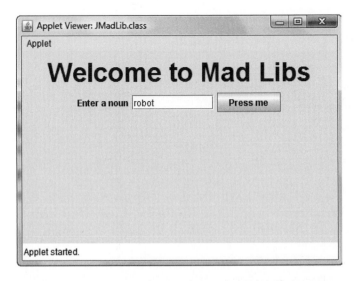

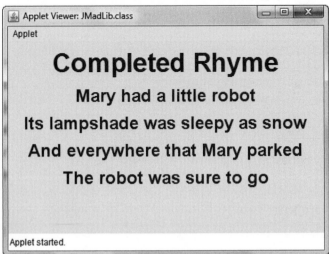

Figure 16-22 First and last screens in a typical execution of JMadLib applet

2. In Chapter 5, you created a Rock Paper Scissors game. Now create it as a `JApplet` in which the user can click one of three buttons labeled "Rock", "Paper", or "Scissors". The computer's choice is still randomly generated. Figure 16-23 shows a typical execution. Save the applet as **JRockPaperScissors.java**. Create an HTML file to execute the applet and save it as **TestJRockPaperScissors.html**.

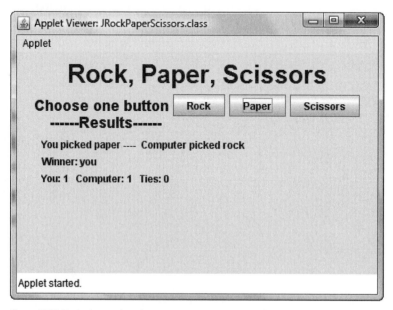

Figure 16-23 Typical execution of `JRockPaperScissors` applet

3. In earlier chapters, you created and used a `Card` class in which each object represents a playing `Card`, and in Chapter 8 you constructed a deck of 52 unique `Cards`. Create a `JApplet` that uses such a deck. Start the player with a $10 stake. Randomly deal a card to the computer and allow the player to make one of four bets:

   » $5 that the player's card will be higher than the computer's card

   » $10 that the player's card will be higher than the computer's card

   » $5 that the player's card will be lower than the computer's card

   » $10 that the player's card will be lower than the computer's card

   After the player makes a bet, deal the player's card and add or subtract the correct amount from the player's winnings based on the results. When the computer's and player's cards are the same value, the computer wins. The game ends when the first of these events happens:

» The player goes broke (the winnings go to $0 or below).

» The player wins $100.

» All 52 cards are exhausted without a winner.

As shown in Figure 16-24, when the player is making a bet, enable four betting buttons. After the player makes a bet, disable the betting buttons while the player examines the outcome, and enable an OK button. When the player is ready to resume play and clicks OK, disable the OK button and enable the four betting buttons. Save the game as **JCardBet.java**. Create an HTML file to execute the applet and save it as **TestJCardBet.html**.

Figure 16-24 Typical execution of JCardBet applet

4. a. In Chapters 9 and 10 you created an Alien class and Martian and Jupiterian classes that descend from it. Add a draw() method for each child class. The draw() method accepts a Graphics object and x- and y- starting coordinates. The method draws the Aliens in any way you choose, using lines, ovals, rectangles, and so on. Using the drawString() method, include a description that names each drawing. Save the files as **Martian.java** and **Jupiterian.java**.

b. Create an applet that instantiates a `Martian` and a `Jupiterian`. In the applet's `paint()` method, draw each type of `Alien`. Save the file as **JDemoAliens.java**. Also create an HTML document to host the applet. Save the file as **TestJDemoAliens.html**. Figure 16-25 shows some sample `Aliens`, but your `Aliens` might look very different.

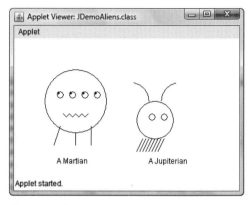

Figure 16-25 Some aliens

c. Create an applet that contains an Alien Hunt game. Place eight numbered buttons in the applet. Randomly assign `Martians` to six of the buttons and `Jupiterians` to two. (*Hint*: You do not need to create an `Alien` array; you can simply create an array that randomly contains 0s and 1s, representing `Martians` and `Jupiterians`.) The object of the game is to find all the `Martians` before finding both `Jupiterians`. When a user clicks a button, display the `Alien` represented by the button. If the user clicks two `Jupiterians` before clicking six `Martians`, the player loses the game. When this happens, display two `Jupiterians` and a message telling the user that Earth has been destroyed. Disable any button after it has been selected. Save the game as **JAlienHunt.java**. Also create an HTML document to host the applet. Save the file as **TestJAlienHunt.html**.

5. a. In Chapter 4, you created a `Die` class that you can use to instantiate objects that hold one of six values. Create a `GraphicDie` class that descends from `Die` but adds a `drawDie()` method that draws a representation of the die on the screen. Design the method so that it accepts a `Graphics` object as well as x- and y-coordinate positions where the drawing should be placed. Create the drawing of a `Die` based on its value and using the `drawRect()` and `fillOval()` methods. Save the file as **GraphicDie.java**.

    b. Create a `JGraphicDie` JApplet that instantiates a `GraphicDie` object. In the `JApplet`'s `paint()` method, pass the method's `Graphics` object and two values to the `GraphicDie` object's `drawDie()` method. Save the file as **JGraphicDie.java**. Also create an HTML document to host the applet. Save the file as **TestJGraphicDie.html**.

    c. In Chapter 8, you created a `FiveDice3` game in which a player's random roll of five dice is compared to the computer's roll and a winner is determined. Now create an applet that plays the game. At each roll, initiated by a player's button click, display the player's five dice and the computer's five dice. Save the file as **JFiveDice.java**. Also create an HTML document to host the applet. Save the file as **TestJFiveDice.html**. Figure 16-26 shows a typical game.

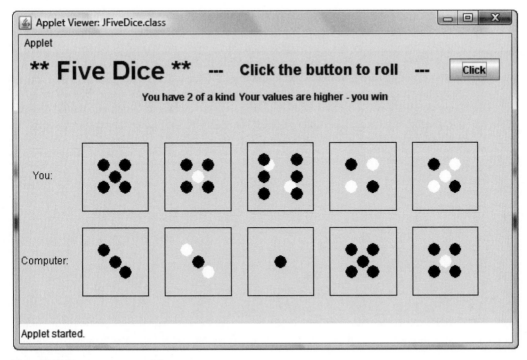

Figure 16-26 The JFiveDice applet

TOUGH QUESTIONS

1. You can write to a file in an application, but not in a standard applet. Why?
2. You can use HTML to write Web pages, so why would you need applets?

UP FOR DISCUSSION

1. Why are applets not as popular in the programming community as applications?
2. Making exciting and professional-looking applets becomes easier once you learn to include graphics images. You can copy graphics images from many locations on the Web. Should there be any restrictions on what graphics you use? Does it make a difference if you are writing programs for your own enjoyment as opposed to putting them on the Web where others can see them? Is using photographs different from using drawings? Does it matter if the photographs contain recognizable people? Would you impose any restrictions on images posted to your organization's Web site?

3. Think of some practice or position to which you are opposed. For example, you might have objections to organizations on the far right or left politically. Now suppose such an organization offered you twice your annual salary to create Web sites for them. Would you do it? Is there a price at which you would do it? What if the organization was not so extreme, but featured products you found mildly distasteful? What if the Web site you designed was not objectionable, but the parent company's policies were objectionable? For example, if you are opposed to smoking, is there a price at which you would design a Web site for a tobacco company, even if the Web site simply displayed sports scores without promoting smoking directly?

WORKING WITH THE JAVA PLATFORM

In this appendix, you will:

Configure Windows to work with the Java SE
   Development Kit
Use Notepad to save and edit source code
Use TextPad to work with Java

»NOTE
For downloading help, visit *http://java.sun.com*.

CONFIGURING WINDOWS TO WORK WITH THE JAVA SE DEVELOPMENT KIT

Several versions of Java are available for free at the Java Web site (*http://java.sun.com*). The official name of the most recent version is Java Platform, Standard Edition 6, often called **Java SE 6** for short. Two version numbers (for example, 1.6.0 and 6) are used to identify this release of the Java Platform. Version 6 is the product version and 1.6.0 is the developer version. The number 6 is used to reflect Java's evolving level of maturity. As new versions containing advanced features emerge, you can download them. Alternatively, you can use the version that comes with this book.

»NOTE
Each new version of Java has a code name. The code name for version 6 is Mustang. The name for version 5 was Tiger and the scheduled name for version 7 is Dolphin.

> **»NOTE** Over the years, Java has been inconsistent in numbering new versions. Before version 6, the standard editions were called JDK 1.0.3, JDK 1.1.2 through 1.1.8, J2SE 1.2.0 through 1.4.2, and J2SE 5.0. With version 6, Java is attempting to simplify the name and number changes. Java sometimes adds a "half step" for minor revisions in a version, such as JDK 1.6.0_05.

»NOTE
The **Java Micro Edition** (ME) is another Java platform, which is used for small devices such as PDAs (personal digital assistants), cell phones, and other consumer appliances.

The different names for Java versions are somewhat confusing, and frequently misused. If you download Java to use with this book, you want to acquire the Java Standard Edition (SE) Development Kit, also known as the **JDK**. Java also supports the **Java Enterprise Edition** (EE), which includes all of the classes in the Java SE, plus a number of classes that are more useful to programs running on servers than on workstations. The Java EE Development Kit is known as **SDK**. The names of the development kits have changed frequently; originally, JDK meant "Java Development Kit," but that interpretation was used with the earliest Java versions and is no longer used officially.

To configure your Windows operating system with the JDK, you must add the Java bin directory to the command path of your operating system (OS). That way, your OS will know where to look for the Java commands that you use.

»NOTE
In Windows XP Professional, you click Start, click Run, type "cmd" in the text box, and then click OK.

One way to update the OS path for Windows Vista, Windows XP, or Windows 2000 is to edit or set the OS path in the autoexec.bat file. This file is automatically executed every time you start your computer. A simpler and less error-prone alternative is to type two commands at the OS prompt when you want to begin a session of working on Java programs. (These two commands are described later in this appendix.)

You do not need to be an operating system expert to issue operating system commands. Learning just a few commands allows you to create and run all the examples in this book.

»NOTE
In Microsoft Windows/95/98/ME, the console window was called the MS-DOS (Microsoft Disk Operating System) prompt. In other versions of Windows, it is the command prompt.

FINDING THE COMMAND PROMPT

Locating the command prompt on your computer depends on which operating system it uses.

» In Windows Vista or XP, click Start, point to All Programs, point to Accessories, then click Command Prompt.

» In Windows 2000, click Start, point to Programs, point to Accessories, then click Command Prompt.

COMMAND PROMPT ANATOMY

The command prompt contains at least a disk drive name followed by a colon, a backslash, and a greater-than sign (for example, C:\>). You might also see folder or directory names within the command prompt just before the greater-than sign, as shown in the following examples:

C:\Documents and Settings>

C:\Documents and Settings\Administrator>

Each directory in the path is separated by a backslash.

CHANGING DIRECTORIES

You can back up one directory level by typing cd for "change directory," followed by two periods:

```
cd..
```

For example, if your OS prompt contains C:\Documents and Settings\Primary> and you type cd.., the command prompt changes to C:\Documents and Settings>. If you type cd.. again, the prompt changes to C:\>, indicating the root directory. Figure A-1 shows this progression.

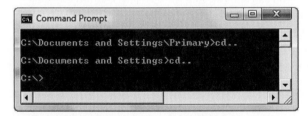

Figure A-1 Results following two cd.. commands

When you have multiple directories to back through, it is easier to use the following command:

```
cd\
```

This takes you immediately to the root directory instead of backing up one level at a time.

At the command prompt, you can change to another disk drive by typing its name and a colon, then pressing Enter. For example, the following command changes the command prompt to refer to the A drive:

```
A:
```

You can change the directory by typing cd followed by the name of the directory. For example, if you have a folder named Java and it contains a folder named Chap.01, you can change the command prompt to the Chap.01 folder by backing up to the root directory and typing the following:

```
cd Java
cd Chap.01
```

As shown in Figure A-2, the command prompt now reads C:\Java\Chap.01>. When you compile and execute your Java programs, you should start from the command prompt where the files are stored.

Figure A-2 Changing to the Java\Chap.01 directory

SETTING THE class AND classpath VARIABLES

When you start a Java session, you might need to set the `class` and `classpath` options. These settings tell the operating system where to find the Java compiler and your classes. If you or someone else has altered your autoexec.bat file to contain these commands, you do not need to type them. Otherwise, every time you want to compile and execute Java programs, you need to type statements similar to the following:

```
path = c:\program files\java\jdk1.6.0_05\bin
set classpath=.
```

After you have typed these statements, you can compile and run as many Java programs as you want without typing these commands again. You must type them again if you close the Command Prompt window or restart your computer.

The first statement sets the path and allows the OS to recognize the `javac` command you use when compiling programs. Consider the following example:

```
path = c:\program files\java\jdk1.6.0_05\bin
```

This example assumes that you are using JDK 1.6.0_05 and that it is stored in the java folder in the program files folder. These are the defaults when you download Java from the Java Web site; if you installed Java in a different location, you need to alter the command accordingly.

The command `set classpath=.` tells Java to find your compiled classes in the current directory when you execute your applications and applets. There must be no space between `classpath` and the equal sign, or between the equal sign and the period.

After you set the path correctly, you should be able to use the `javac` command. If you attempt to compile a Java class and see an error message that `javac` is not a recognized command, either Java was not properly installed or the path command was incorrect. On the other hand, if classes compile successfully but do not execute, you might have entered the `classpath` command incorrectly.

CHANGING A FILE'S NAME

When working through the examples in this book, you will often find it convenient to change the name of an existing file—for example, when you want to experiment with altering code without losing the original version, or if you find that when you previously saved a file, you mistyped a filename so that it did not match the class name within the .java file you created. You can take at least three approaches:

» Open the existing file using the appropriate software application (for example, Notepad), click File on the menu bar, and then click Save As. Select the folder you want, then type a new filename for the file. Now you have two versions—one with the old name and one with the new.

» In Windows, open My Computer and locate the misnamed file. Select the file and then click the filename. (Do not double-click the filename unless you want to open the file.) Now, you can edit the filename by using a combination of the Backspace, Delete, and new character keys. Press Enter when the filename is correct.

» At the command prompt, use the `rename` command. You type `rename`, a space, the old filename, another space, and the new filename. For example, to change a file named xyz.java to abc.java, type the following at the command prompt for the directory containing the existing file:

```
rename xyz.java abc.java
```

COMPILING AND EXECUTING A JAVA PROGRAM

At the command prompt, change from the default drive prompt to the drive where your application is stored. Then change the directory (or folder) to the directory that holds your application.

To compile an application or applet, you type the `javac` command to start the Java compiler, then type a space and the complete name of the .java file—for example, First.java. If the application doesn't compile successfully, the path might not be set correctly to the Java JDK bin directory where the javac.exe file is located. Also, you might have failed to use the same spelling as the Java filename.

When you compile a .java file correctly, the Java compiler creates a .class file that has the same filename as the .java file. Thus, a successful compilation of the First.java file creates a file named First.class. To run a Java application, you use the `java` command and the class name without the .class extension. For example, after an application named First.java is compiled, producing First.class, you execute the program using the command `java First`.

When the program ends, control is returned to the command prompt. If a program does not end on its own, or you want to end it prematurely, you can press Ctrl+C to return to the command prompt.

After you compile a Java program, you can execute it as many times as you want without recompiling. If you change the source code, you must save and compile again before you can see the changed results in an executed application.

» NOTE
When you are testing a Java program, you often issue the commands to compile and execute it many times before you are satisfied with the results. If you press the Up Arrow key at the command line, the previous commands repeat in reverse succession. When you find the command you want to repeat, just press Enter.

USING NOTEPAD TO SAVE AND EDIT SOURCE CODE

You can use the Windows Notepad text editor to save and edit the source code for Java programs. To start Notepad using Windows 2000, click the Start menu, point to Programs, point to Accessories, and click Notepad. To start Notepad using Windows XP, click the Start menu, point to All Programs, point to Accessories, and click Notepad. After you start Notepad, you can enter and edit the code just as you would with any text editor.

Saving source code in Notepad requires that the Java source file be saved with a .java extension. Because Java is case sensitive, you must save a file with the proper capitalization. If the class name of the file and the filename do not match in both spelling and case, you receive an error when you attempt to execute compiled source code. The default extension for Notepad documents is .txt. To create a file with a .java extension, you can use one of the following approaches:

» Use Save As, locate the folder you want, and type the filename. In the Vista operating system, you can simply type the filename. In older Windows operating systems, type the filename with double quotation marks around it, as in "First.java". This ensures that the file is not saved as "First.java.txt". Then click Save.

» Use Save As, locate the folder you want, and type the filename. Click the Save As type list box below the File name list box, select All Files, and then click Save. With this approach, you do not need double quotes around the filename, but you do need to use the Save As type list box.

» Save the file as a .txt file, and then change it to a .java file using one of the techniques outlined in the previous section.

USING TEXTPAD TO WORK WITH JAVA

As an alternative to Notepad, you can use TextPad—a text editor that includes many features helpful to Java programmers. You can download a trial version from *www.textpad.com*. Unlike Notepad, TextPad is not included with Windows; to install TextPad, run the setup file after downloading it from the TextPad Web site, and then respond to the dialog box options. Because you download a trial version, you should purchase TextPad if you decide to use it beyond the trial period. Note that TextPad runs only under the Windows operating system. If you are not using Windows, you can use the text editor that comes with your operating system, or you can search the Web to find a text editor that better suits your needs.

To enter and edit source code in TextPad, you can use the same techniques that you use with any other Windows text editor. In short, you can use the standard Windows shortcut keystrokes and menus to enter, edit, and save your code. You can use the File menu to open and close files. You can use the Edit menu to cut, copy, and paste text, and you can use the Search menu to find and replace text. In addition, TextPad color-codes the source files so it is easier to recognize the Java syntax. TextPad also makes it easier to save Java files with the proper capitalization and extension. To compile the current source code, you can select the Compile Java command from the Tools menu. If the source code does not compile cleanly, TextPad displays a Command Results window, including line numbers that identify the source of problems. With TextPad, you can choose to display line numbers in your code.

KEY TERMS

Java SE 6 is the most recent version of Java. The full, official name is Java Platform, Standard Edition 6.

The **JDK** is the Java Standard Edition Development Kit.

The **Java Enterprise Edition** (EE) includes all of the classes in the Java SE, plus a number of classes that are more useful to programs running on servers.

The **SDK** is the Java EE Development Kit.

The **Java Micro Edition** (ME) is another Java platform, which is used for small devices such as PDAs, cell phones, and other consumer appliances.

B

LEARNING ABOUT ASCII AND UNICODE

The characters used in Java are represented in Unicode, which is a 16-bit coding scheme for characters. For example, the letter A actually is stored in computer memory as a set of 16 zeros and ones as 0000 0000 0100 0001 (a space is inserted after each set of four digits for readability). Because 16-digit numbers are difficult to read, programmers often use a shorthand notation called hexadecimal, or base 16. In hexadecimal shorthand, 0000 becomes 0, 0100 becomes 4, and 0001 becomes 1, so the letter A is represented in hexadecimal as 0041. You tell the compiler to treat the four-digit hexadecimal 0041 as a single character by preceding it with the \u escape sequence. Therefore, there are two ways to store the character A:

» NOTE
For more information about Unicode, go to *www.unicode.org*.

```
char letter = 'A';
char letter = '\u0041';
```

The second option, using hexadecimal, is obviously more difficult and confusing than the first method, so it is not recommended that you store letters of the alphabet using the hexadecimal method. However, you can produce some interesting values using the Unicode format. For example, the sequence '\u0007' is a bell that produces a noise if you send it to output. Letters from foreign alphabets that use characters instead of letters (Greek, Hebrew, Chinese, and so on) and other special symbols (foreign currency symbols, mathematical symbols, geometric shapes, and so on) are available using Unicode, but not on a standard keyboard, so it is important that you know how to use Unicode characters.

» NOTE
Two-digit, base-16 numbers can be converted to base-10 numbers by multiplying the left digit by 16 and adding the right digit. For example, hexadecimal 41 is 4 times 16 plus 1, or 65.

In the United States, the most widely used character set traditionally has been ASCII (American Standard Code for Information Interchange). The ASCII character set contains 128 characters, some of which are shown in Table B-1 with their decimal or numerical code and equivalent character representation. The first 32 characters (values 0 through 31) and the last character (127) are control characters and are nonprintable. You can enter these characters by holding down Ctrl and pressing a letter on the keyboard. For example, the Tab key or ^I (Ctrl+I) produces a character 9, which produces a hard tab when pressed.

You can create any Unicode character by adding eight zeros to the beginning of the ASCII character value. This means that the decimal value of any ASCII character is the same as that of the corresponding Unicode character. For example, 'B' has the value 66 in both character sets. The decimal values are important because they allow you to show nonprintable characters, such as a carriage return, in decimal codes. Also, the numeric values of the coding schemes are used when a computer sorts numbers and strings. When you sort characters in ascending order, for example, numbers are sorted first (because their Unicode values begin with decimal code 48), followed by capital letters (starting with decimal 65), and then lowercase letters (starting with decimal 97).

Table B-1 contains a list of Unicode values for some commonly used characters. For a complete list, see *www.unicode.org/charts*. There you will find Greek, Armenian, Hebrew, Tagalog, Cherokee, and a host of other character sets. Unicode also contains characters for mathematical symbols, geometric shapes, and other unusual characters.

Decimal Value	Explanation	Character
32	Space	
33	Exclamation point	!
34	Quotation mark	"
35	Octothorpe or pound sign	#
36	Dollar sign	$
37	Percent sign	%
38	Ampersand	&
39	Single quote	'
40	Left parenthesis	(
41	Right parenthesis	)
42	Asterisk	*
43	Plus sign	+
44	Comma	,
45	Minus sign or dash	-
46	Period	.

Table B-1 Decimal values, descriptions, and characters for commonly used Unicode values

Decimal Value	Explanation	Character
47	Slash	/
48	Digit zero	0
49	Digit one	1
50	Digit two	2
51	Digit three	3
52	Digit four	4
53	Digit five	5
54	Digit six	6
55	Digit seven	7
56	Digit eight	8
57	Digit nine	9
58	Colon	:
59	Semicolon	;
60	Less-than sign	<
61	Equal sign	=
62	Greater-than sign	>
63	Question mark	?
64	At sign	@
65	Letter A	A
66	Letter B	B
67	Letter C	C
68	Letter D	D
69	Letter E	E
70	Letter F	F
71	Letter G	G
72	Letter H	H
73	Letter I	I
74	Letter J	J
75	Letter K	K
76	Letter L	L
77	Letter M	M
78	Letter N	N

Table B-1 (*continued*)

Decimal Value	Explanation	Character
79	Letter O	O
80	Letter P	P
81	Letter Q	Q
82	Letter R	R
83	Letter S	S
84	Letter T	T
85	Letter U	U
86	Letter V	V
87	Letter W	W
88	Letter X	X
89	Letter Y	Y
90	Letter Z	Z
91	Left square bracket	[
92	Backslash	\
93	Right square bracket	]
94	Circumflex accent	^
95	Underscore	_
96	Grave accent	`
97	Letter a	a
98	Letter b	b
99	Letter c	c
100	Letter d	d
101	Letter e	e
102	Letter f	f
103	Letter g	g
104	Letter h	h
105	Letter i	i
106	Letter j	j
107	Letter k	k
108	Letter l	l
109	Letter m	m
110	Letter n	n

Table B-1 (*continued*)

Decimal Value	Explanation	Character
111	Letter o	o
112	Letter p	p
113	Letter q	q
114	Letter r	r
115	Letter s	s
116	Letter t	t
117	Letter u	u
118	Letter v	v
119	Letter w	w
120	Letter x	x
121	Letter y	y
122	Letter z	z
123	Left curly brace	{
124	Pipe		
125	Right curly brace	}
126	Tilde	~

Table B-1 (*continued*)

C

FORMATTING OUTPUT

In this appendix, you will:

Understand the limitations of the println() method
Use multiplication and division to supply formatting
Use the printf() method
Use the DecimalFormat class

UNDERSTANDING THE LIMITATIONS OF THE println() METHOD

When you display numbers using the println() method in Java applications, it is sometimes difficult to make numeric values appear as you want. For example, suppose you have declared variables named price, taxRate, and totalPrice, as shown in the ComputePriceWithTax application in Figure C-1. As the output shows in Figure C-2, the application correctly calculates a final price of $21.3893. Although this answer is mathematically correct, you might prefer to express the final sale price with tax in dollars and cents—that is, to show the output value rounded to two decimal places.

```java
public class ComputePriceWithTax
{
   public static void main(String[] args)
   {
      double price = 19.99;
      double taxRate = .07;
      double totalPrice = price + (price * taxRate);
      System.out.println("Total price is $" + totalPrice);
   }
}
```

Figure C-1 The ComputePriceWithTax application

Figure C-2 Output of the ComputePriceWithTax application

You encounter another formatting problem when you want to align a column of numeric values. For example, Figure C-3 shows a NumberList application that contains an array of integer values. The application displays the values using a for loop, but as the output in Figure C-4 shows, the numbers are not aligned by the (implied) decimal point as you usually would want numbers to be aligned. Because the println() method displays values as Strings, the displayed values are left-aligned, just as series of words would be. The numeric values are accurate; they just are not attractively arranged.

```
public class NumberList
{
    public static void main(String[] args)
    {
        int[] list = {1, 23, 456, 7890, 987, 65};
        int x;
        for(x = 0; x < list.length; ++x)
            System.out.println(list[x]);
    }
}
```

Figure C-3 The NumberList application

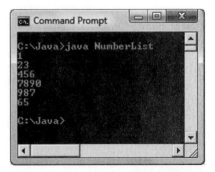

Figure C-4 Output of the NumberList application

» NOTE If you are interested in mathematically correct output, the programs in Figures C-1 and C-3 are adequate. However, to improve the appearance of your output, a number of techniques are available to help you. If you are just starting to learn Java and are not yet comfortable with classes and methods, you might prefer to use multiplication and division to achieve better-looking output, as described in the next section. If you are comfortable using new methods and classes, then you can explore using the printf() method or the DecimalFormat class, as described in later sections of this appendix.

FORMATTING USING MULTIPLICATION AND DIVISION

A simple way to convert a longer number to a fixed number of decimal places involves multiplying, then dividing the number by a fixed value. For example, to convert a value with more than two decimal places to one that contains only two decimal places, you can perform the following steps:

» Multiply the number by 100.
» Remove the decimal portion.
» Divide by 100.

Figure C-5 shows a sample application in which the value 123.45678 is multiplied by 100, giving 12345.678, and truncated to a temporary int with the value 12345. When this value is divided by 100.0 and stored in a double, the result is 123.45, which is the original value reduced to two decimal places. Figure C-6 shows the application's execution.

```
public class TwoPlacesNoRounding
{
   public static void main(String[] args)
   {
      double money = 123.45678;
      System.out.println("Before conversion: " + money);
      int temp;
      temp = (int)(money * 100);
      money = temp / 100.0;
      System.out.println("After conversion: " + money);
   }
}
```

≫NOTE
The eighth line in Figure C-5 performs a cast, forcing a double to become an int. Chapter 2 describes casting.

Figure C-5 The TwoPlacesNoRounding class

Figure C-6 Output of the TwoPlacesNoRounding program

≫NOTE If you decide to use the formatting technique used in the TwoPlacesNoRounding class, you might want to provide a named constant to use for the 100.0 value. You should also provide program comments to explain your intention.

In the output in Figure C-6, you can see that the original value is reduced to two decimal places, without rounding. Rounding requires a simple trick, as shown in the class in Figure C-7. The only changes in this class from the one in Figure C-5 are in the class name and the shaded addition of 0.5 to the money * 100 calculation. Using this trick causes any value not to be rounded when the third position to the right of the decimal point is 4 or less, but to be rounded up when the digit in that position is 5 or more. Figure C-8 shows the program execution.

```
public class TwoPlacesWithRounding
{
    public static void main(String[] args)
    {
        double money = 123.45678;
        System.out.println("Before conversion: " + money);
        int temp;
        temp = (int)(money * 100 + 0.5);
        money = temp / 100.0;
        System.out.println("After conversion: " + money);
    }
}
```

Figure C-7 The `TwoPlacesWithRounding` class

>>**NOTE** Another option for rounding is to use the `Math` class `round()` method. For example, in the program in Figure C-7, the value of `Math.round(money * 100)` would be 12346. The `Math` class is covered in Chapter 4.

```
Command Prompt                              ▢ ▢ ✕

C:\Java>java TwoPlacesWithRounding
Before conversion: 123.45678
After conversion: 123.46

C:\Java>_
```

Figure C-8 Output of the `TwoPlacesWithRounding` program

Using this multiply-and-divide technique to display values has its limitations. For example, the applications in Figures C-5 and C-7 display values to no more than two decimal places, but not to exactly two decimal places. If you change the value of `money` in the `TwoPlacesWithRounding` class to 123.40, it displays as 123.4 both before and after the arithmetic. Although you could determine whether the last digits of values were zeros and then display extra zeros accordingly, this approach is cumbersome. To conveniently achieve output that displays values to a fixed number of decimal places, you should explore the `System.out.printf()` method and the `DecimalFormat` class presented in the next sections.

>>**NOTE**
You can determine whether a number ends with 0 by using the modulus operator (%). In the decimal system, if there is no remainder when a value is divided by 10, then the value ends with 0. Similarly, if there is no remainder when a value is divided by 100, the value ends with two 0s.

USING THE `printf()` METHOD

The **System.out.printf() method** is used to format numeric values. It is a newer Java feature that was first included in the Formatter class in Java 1.5.0. (This is the internal version number of the Java Development Kit; the external version number is 5.0.) Because this class is contained in the java.util package, you do not need to include any import statements to use it. The printf() method allows you to format numeric values in two useful ways:

» By specifying the number of decimal places to display
» By specifying the field size in which to display values

> **» NOTE** C programmers use a printf() function that is very similar to Java's printf() method. Although the printf() method is used in these examples, in Java, you can substitute System.out.format() for System.out.printf(). There is no difference in the way you use these two methods.

When creating numeric output, you can specify a number of decimal places to display by using the printf() method with two types of arguments that represent the following:

» A format string
» A list of arguments

A **format string** is a string of characters; it includes optional text (that is displayed literally) and one or more format specifiers. A **format specifier** is a placeholder for a numeric value. Within a call to printf(), you include one argument (either a variable or a constant) for each format specifier.

The format specifiers for general, character, and numeric types contain the following elements, in order:

» A percent sign (%), which indicates the start of every format specifier.
» An optional argument index, which is an integer indicating the position of the argument in the argument list. The integer is followed by a dollar sign. You will learn more about this option later in this appendix.
» Optional flags that modify the output format. The set of valid flags depends on the data type you are formatting. You can find more details about this feature at the Java Web site.
» An optional field width, which is an integer indicating the minimum number of characters to be written to the output. You will learn more about this option later in this appendix.

» An optional precision, which is a decimal point followed by a number and typically used to control decimal places displayed. You will learn more about this option in the next section.
» The required conversion character, which indicates how its corresponding argument should be formatted. Java supports a variety of conversion characters, but the three you want to use most frequently are d, f, and s, the characters that represent decimal (base-10 integer), floating-point (float and double), and string values, respectively.

For example, you can use the `ConversionCharacterExamples` class in Figure C-9 to display a declared integer and `double`. The `main()` method of the class contains three `printf()` statements. The three calls to `printf()` in this class each contain a format string; the first two calls contain a single additional argument, and the last `printf()` statement contains two arguments after the string. None of the format specifiers in this class use any of the optional parameters—only the required percent sign and conversion character. The first `printf()` statement uses `%d` in its format string as a placeholder for the integer argument at the end. The second `printf()` statement uses `%f` as a placeholder for the floating-point argument at the end. The last `printf()` statement uses both a `%d` and `%f` to indicate the positions of the integer and floating-point values at the end, respectively. Figure C-10 shows the output, in which the strings display with the values inserted in the appropriate places. As Figure C-10 shows, floating-point values are displayed with six decimal positions by default.

```java
public class ConversionCharacterExamples
{
    public static void main(String[] args)
    {
        int age = 23;
        double money = 123.45;
        System.out.printf("Age is %d\n",age);
        System.out.printf("Money is $%f\n", money);
        System.out.printf
            ("Age is %d and money is $%f\n", age, money);
    }
}
```

Figure C-9 The `ConversionCharacterExamples` application

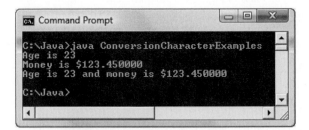

Figure C-10 Output of the `ConversionCharacterExamples` application

Notice that in the `ConversionCharacterExamples` class, the output appears on three separate lines only because the newline character ('\n') has been included at the end of each `printf()` format string. Unlike the `println()` statement, `printf()` does not include an automatic new line.

SPECIFYING A NUMBER OF DECIMAL PLACES TO DISPLAY WITH printf()

You can control the number of decimal places displayed when you use a floating-point value in a printf() statement by adding the optional precision factor to the format specifier. Between the percent sign and the conversion character, you can add a decimal point and the number of decimal positions to display. For example, the following statements produce the output "Money is $123.45", displaying the money value with just two decimal places instead of six, which would occur without the precision factor:

```
double money = 123.45;
System.out.printf("Money is $%.2f\n", money);
```

Similarly, the following statements display 8.10. If you use the println() equivalent with amount, only 8.1 is displayed; if you use a printf() statement without inserting the .2 precision factor, 8.100000 is displayed.

```
double amount = 8.1;
System.out.printf("%.2f",amount);
```

When you use a precision factor on a value that contains more decimal positions than you want to display, the result is rounded. For example, the following statements produce 100.457 (not 100.456), displaying three decimals because of the precision factor.

```
double value = 100.45678;
System.out.printf("%.3f",value);
```

You cannot use the precision factor with an integer value; if you do, your program will throw an IllegalFormatConversionException.

> **NOTE**
> If a numeric value contains more positions than you indicate for its printf() field size, the field size is ignored, and the entire value displays.

SPECIFYING A FIELD SIZE WITH printf()

You can indicate a field size in which to display output by using an optional integer as the field width. For example, the NumberList2 class in Figure C-11 displays each element in an array of integers in a field with a size of 6. Each value is displayed right-aligned in its field; for example, a single digit is preceded by five blank spaces, and a two-digit number is preceded by four blank spaces. Figure C-12 shows the output of the application.

```
public class NumberList2
{
   public static void main(String[] args)
   {
      int[] list = {1, 23, 456, 7890, 987, 65};
      int x;
      for(x = 0; x < list.length; ++x)
         System.out.printf("%6d\n", list[x]);
   }
}
```

Figure C-11 The NumberList2 class

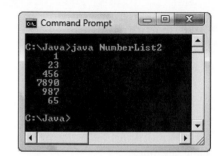

Figure C-12 Output of the NumberList2 class

Throughout this book, you have been encouraged to use named constants for numeric values instead of literal constants, so that your programs are clearer. In the program in Figure C-11, you could define a constant such as:

```
final int DISPLAY_WIDTH = 6;
```

Then the printf() statement would be:

```
System.out.printf("%" + SIZE + "d\n", list[x]);
```

Another, perhaps clearer alternative is to define a format string such as the following:

```
final String FORMAT = "%6d\n";
```

Then the printf() statement would be:

```
System.out.printf(FORMAT, list[x]);
```

With floating-point values, you can combine a field size with a decimal position indicator if you want. For example, to produce four spaces followed by 98.6, you could write the following:

```
double temperature = 98.602;
System.out.printf("%8.1", temperature);
```

In this example, the entire field size displayed is 8; this includes four blanks, the number 98, the decimal point, and the single decimal place digit, 6. (In this case, no rounding occurs because the digit following the 6 is not 5 or greater.)

You can specify that a value be left-aligned in a field instead of right-aligned by inserting a negative sign in front of the width. Although you can do this with numbers, most often you choose to left-align strings. For example, the following code displays five spaces followed by "hello" and then five spaces followed by "there". Each string is left-aligned in a field with a size of 10.

```
String string1 = "hello";
String string2 = "there";
System.out.printf("%-10s%-10s", string1, string2);
```

USING THE OPTIONAL ARGUMENT INDEX
WITH printf()

The **argument index** is an integer that indicates the position of an argument in the argument list of a printf() statement. To separate it from other formatting options, the argument index is followed by a dollar sign ($). The first argument is referenced by "1$", the second by "2$", and so on.

For example, the printf() statement in the following code contains four format specifiers but only two variables in the argument list:

```
int x = 56;
double y = 78.9;
System.out.printf("%1$6d%2$6.2f%1$6d%2$6.2f",x,y);
```

The printf() statement displays the value of the first argument, x, in a field with a size of 6, and then it displays the second argument, y, in a field with a size of 6 with two decimal places. Then, the value of x displays again, followed by the value of y. The output appears as follows:

```
56 78.90     56 78.90
```

USING THE DecimalFormat CLASS

The **DecimalFormat class** provides ways to easily convert numbers into strings, allowing you to control the display of leading and trailing zeros, prefixes and suffixes, grouping (thousands) separators, and the decimal separator. You specify the formatting properties of DecimalFormat with a pattern String. The **pattern String** is composed of symbols that determine what the formatted number looks like; it is passed to the DecimalFormat class constructor.

The symbols you can use in a pattern String include:

- » A pound sign (#), which represents a digit
- » A period (.), which represents a decimal point
- » A comma (,), which represents a thousands separator
- » A zero (0), which represents leading and trailing zeros when it replaces the pound sign

For example, the following lines of code result in value being displayed as 12,345,678.90.

```
double value = 12345678.9;
DecimalFormat aFormat = new DecimalFormat("#,###,###,###.00");
System.out.printf("%s\n", aFormat.format(value));
```

A DecimalFormat object is created using the pattern #,###,###,###.00. When the object's format() method is used in the printf() statement, the first two pound signs and the comma between them are not used because value is not large enough to require those positions. The value displays with commas inserted where needed, and the decimal portion is displayed with a trailing 0 because the 0s at the end of the pattern indicate that they should be used to fill out the number to two places.

When you use the DecimalFormat class, you must use the import statement import java.text.*;. Figure C-13 shows a class that creates a String pattern that it passes to the DecimalFormat constructor to create a moneyFormat object. The class displays an array of values, each in a field that is 10 characters wide. Some of the values require commas and some do not. Figure C-14 shows the output.

```java
import java.text.*;
public class DecimalFormatTest
{
    public static void main(String[] args)
    {
        String pattern = "###,###.00";
        DecimalFormat moneyFormat = new DecimalFormat(pattern);
        double[] list = {1.1, 23.23, 456.249, 7890.1, 987.5678, 65.0};
        int x;
        for(x = 0; x < list.length; ++x)
            System.out.printf("%10s\n", moneyFormat.format(list[x]));
    }
}
```

Figure C-13 The DecimalFormatTest class

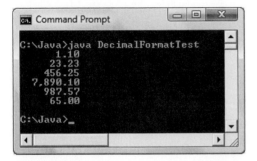

Figure C-14 Output of the DecimalFormatTest program

KEY TERMS

The **System.out.printf() method** is used to format numeric values.

A **format string** in a printf() statement is a string of characters; it includes optional text (that is displayed literally) and one or more format specifiers.

A **format specifier** in a printf() statement is a placeholder for a numeric value.

The **argument index** in a printf() statement is an integer that indicates the position of an argument in the argument list.

The **DecimalFormat class** provides ways to easily convert numbers into strings, allowing you to control the display of leading and trailing zeros, prefixes and suffixes, grouping (thousands) separators, and the decimal separator.

A **pattern String** is composed of symbols that determine what a formatted number looks like; it is passed to the DecimalFormat class constructor.

An **octothorpe** is a pound sign.

D

GENERATING RANDOM NUMBERS

In this appendix, you will:

Understand random numbers generated
by computers

Use the Math.random() method to generate
random numbers

Use the Random class to generate random numbers

UNDERSTANDING RANDOM NUMBERS GENERATED BY COMPUTERS

A **random number** is one whose value cannot be predicted. Many types of programs use random numbers. For example, simulations that predict phenomena such as urban traffic patterns, crop production, and weather systems typically use random numbers. You might want to use random numbers to change your screen's appearance; for example, screen savers often use random numbers so that a changing pattern remains interesting.

»NOTE
Computers are said to be **deterministic**; that is, their output is determined by their input—they are consistent.

Random numbers are also used in many computer game applications. When you play games with human opponents, their choices are often unpredictable (and sometimes even irrational). Computers usually are predictable and rational, so when you play a game against a computer opponent, you frequently need to generate random numbers. For example, a guessing game would not be very interesting if you were asked to guess the same number every time you played.

Most computer programming languages, including Java, come with built-in methods that generate random numbers. The random numbers are calculated based on a starting value, called a **seed**. The random numbers generated using these methods are not truly random; they are **pseudorandom** in that they produce the same set of numbers whenever the seed is the same. Therefore, if you seed a random number generator with a constant, you always receive the same sequence of values. Many computer programs use the time of day as a random number-generating seed. For game applications, this method works well, as a player is unlikely to reset his computer's clock and attempt to replay a game beginning at exactly the same moment in time.

»NOTE
For applications in which randomness is more crucial than in game-playing, you can use other methods (such as using the points in time at which a radioactive source decays) to generate truly random starting numbers.

There are two approaches to generating random numbers in Java. Both techniques are explained in this appendix and summarized in Table D-1.

Method/Class	Advantages
`Math.random()` method	You do not need to create an object.
	You do not need to understand constructors and multiple methods.
`Random` class and its methods	You can generate numbers in the format you need without arithmetic manipulation.
	You can create reproducible results if necessary.

Table D-1 Generating random numbers in Java

USING THE `Math.random()` METHOD

»NOTE
Chapter 4 provides details about Java's `Math` class.

Java's `Math` class provides a `random()` method that returns a `double` value in the range of 0.0 up to, but not including, 1.0. For example, the application in Figure D-1 generates three random numbers and displays them. Figure D-2 shows three successive executions of the program.

```
public class SomeRandomNumbers
{
    public static void main (String[] args)
    {
        double ran;
        ran = Math.random();
        System.out.println(ran);
        ran = Math.random();
        System.out.println(ran);
        ran = Math.random();
        System.out.println(ran);
    }
}
```

Figure D-1 The SomeRandomNumbers class

Figure D-2 Three executions of the SomeRandomNumbers program

The values displayed in Figure D-2 appear to be random, but are not typical of the values you need in a game-playing program. Usually, you need a relatively small number of whole values. For example, a game that involves a coin flip might only need two values to represent heads or tails, and a dice game might need only six values to represent rolls of a single die. Even in a complicated game in which 40 types of space aliens might attack the player, you need only 40 whole numbers generated to satisfy the program requirements.

For example, suppose you need a random number from 1 to 10. To change any value generated by the Math.random() method to fall between 0 and 10, you can multiply the generated number by 10. For example, the last three numbers in Figure D-2 would become approximately 4.79, 1.33, and 6.55. Then, you can eliminate the fractional part of each number by casting it to an int; after this step, every generated number will be a value from 0 to 9 inclusive. Finally, you can add 1 to a value so that it falls in the range from 1 to 10 instead of 0 to 9. In short, the following statement generates a random number from 1 to 10 inclusive, and assigns it to ran:

> **NOTE**
> Chapter 2 describes casting.

```
int ran = 1 + (int)(Math.random() * 10);
```

Suppose that, instead of 1 through 10, you need random numbers from 1 to 13. (For example, standard decks of playing cards have 13 values from which you might want to select.) When you use the modulus operator (%) to find a remainder, the remainder is always a value from 0 to one less than the number. For example, if you divide any number by 4, the remainder is always a value from 0 to 3. Therefore, to find a number from 1 to 13, you can use a statement like the following:

```
int ranCardValue = ((int)(Math.random() * 100) % 13 + 1);
```

In this statement, a randomly generated value (for example, 0.447) is multiplied by 100 (producing 44.7). The result is converted to an int (44). The remainder after dividing by 13 is 5. Finally, 1 is added so the result is 1 through 13 instead of 0 through 12 (giving 6). In short, the general format for assigning a random number to a variable is:

```
int result = ((int)(Math.random() * 100) %
    HIGHEST_VALUE_WANTED + LOWEST_VALUE_WANTED);
```

» NOTE
Chapter 2 describes using the modulus operator.

USING THE Random CLASS

The Random class provides a generator that creates a list of random numbers. To use this class, you must use one of the following import statements:

```
import java.util.*;
import java.util.Random;
```

» NOTE
Instead of 100 as the multiplier, you might prefer to use a higher value such as 1000 or 10,000. For most games, the randomness generated using 100 is sufficient.

You also must instantiate a random number generator object using one of the following constructors:

» Random(), in which the seed comes from the operating system. This constructor sets the seed of the random number generator to a value that is probably distinct from any other invocation of this constructor.

» Random(long seed), in which you provide a starting seed so that your results are reproducible.

After you create a random number generator object, you can use any of the methods in Table D-2 to get the next random number from the generator.

Method	Explanation
nextInt(int n)	Returns a pseudorandom int value between 0 (inclusive) and the specified value *n* (exclusive), drawn from the random number generator's sequence
nextInt()	Returns a pseudorandom int value between 0 (inclusive) and 1.0 (exclusive), drawn from the random number generator's sequence
nextLong()	Returns the next pseudorandom long value from the generator's sequence
nextFloat()	Returns the next pseudorandom float value between 0.0 and 1.0 from the generator's sequence
nextDouble()	Returns the next pseudorandom double value between 0.0 and 1.0 from the generator's sequence
nextBoolean()	Returns the next pseudorandom boolean value from the generator's sequence

Table D-2 Selected Random class methods

For example, Figure D-3 contains an application that declares a Random generator named ran, using the version of the constructor that takes no arguments. This ensures that the results will be different each time the application runs. The program then defines LIMIT as 10, and calls ran.nextInt(LIMIT) three times, displaying the results (see Figure D-4).

```
import java.util.*;
public class SomeRandomNumbers2
{
    public static void main(String[] args)
    {
        Random ran = new Random();
        final int LIMIT = 10;
        System.out.println(ran.nextInt(LIMIT));
        System.out.println(ran.nextInt(LIMIT));
        System.out.println(ran.nextInt(LIMIT));
    }
}
```

Figure D-4 Three executions of the SomeRandomNumbers2 program

Figure D-3 The SomeRandomNumbers2 class

In Figure D-4, each displayed value falls between 0 and LIMIT. Of course, to select values between 1 and LIMIT inclusive, you could add 1 to each result. Even though the three method calls to ran.nextInt(LIMIT) are written identically, you can see that each call results in the retrieval of a new value.

Figure D-5 shows a class using the version of the Random constructor that takes an argument (shaded). In this example, a value between 0 and 7 is generated 15 times. Figure D-6 shows the output when the program is run three times. Although the 15 numbers displayed for each execution constitute a random list, the list is identical in each program execution. You use a seed when you want random but reproducible results. For games, you usually want to use the no-argument version of the Random constructor.

```
import java.util.*;
public class SomeRandomNumbers3
{
    public static void main(String[] args)
    {
        Random ran = new Random(129867L);
        final int TIMES = 15;
        final int LIMIT = 7;
        for(int x = 0; x < TIMES; ++x)
            System.out.print(ran.nextInt(LIMIT) + " ");
        System.out.println();
    }
}
```

Figure D-5 The SomeRandomNumbers3 class

Figure D-6 Three executions of the SomeRandomNumbers3 program

KEY TERMS

A **random number** is one whose value cannot be predicted.

Deterministic is an adjective that describes the predictability and consistency of computer output.

A **seed** is a starting value.

Pseudorandom numbers appear to be random, but are the same set of numbers whenever the seed is the same.

JAVADOC

In this appendix, you will:

Learn about the Javadoc documentation generator
Understand Javadoc comment types
Generate Javadoc documentation

THE JAVADOC DOCUMENTATION GENERATOR

Javadoc is a documentation generator created by Sun Microsystems that allows you to generate Application Programming Interface (API) documentation in Hypertext Markup Language (HTML) format from Java source code. In Chapter 1, you learned that you can place both line and block comments anywhere in a program to provide documentation that can be useful both to yourself and others. A **Javadoc comment** is a special form of block comment that provides a standard way to document Java code. After you write Javadoc comments, they can be interpreted by special utility programs that generate an HTML document. The resulting HTML document provides an attractive format for the documentation when you open it in a browser. Most class libraries, both commercial and open source, provide Javadoc documents. If you have visited the Sun Microsystems Web site to research how to use a class, you most likely have viewed documentation created by the Javadoc utility.

In Chapter 1, you learned that block comments start with /* and end with */ and can span as many lines as necessary, and that Javadoc comments start with /** and end with */. For symmetry, many developers end their Javadoc comments with **/. By convention, asterisks start intermediate lines in a Javadoc comment. This is not required, but it helps you to more easily distinguish comments from code.

Javadoc comments can contain tags. A **Javadoc tag** is a keyword within a comment that the Javadoc tool can process. Tags begin with an at-sign (@) and use a limited vocabulary of keywords. Some commonly used Javadoc tags include:

- » `@author`: Describes the author of a document.
- » `@param`: Describes a parameter of a method or constructor.
- » `@return`: Describes the return type of a method.
- » `@throws`: Describes an exception a method may throw.
- » `@exception`: Describes an exception.

JAVADOC COMMENT TYPES

There are two types of Javadoc comments:

- » Class-level comments that provide a description of a class
- » Member-level comments that describe the purposes of class members

Class-level Javadoc comments provide a description of a class; you place class-level comments above the code that declares a class. Class-level comments frequently contain author tags and a description of the class. Figure E-1 shows a shaded class-level comment in a class.

```
/**
 * @author Joyce Farrell.
 * The Employee class contains data about one employee.
 * Fields include an ID number and an hourly pay rate.
 */
public class Employee
{
    private int idNum;
    private double hourlyPay;
    public Employee(int id, double pay)
    {
        idNum = id;
        hourlyPay = pay;
    }
    int getIdNum()
    {
        return idNum;
    }
    void setIdNum(int id)
    {
        idNum = id;
    }
}
```

Figure E-1 An `Employee` class with class-level comments

Member-level Javadoc comments describe the fields, methods, and constructors of a class. Method and constructor comments may contain tags that describe the parameters, and method comments may also contain return tags. Figure E-2 shows a class with some shaded member-level comments.

```
/**
 * @author Joyce Farrell.
 * The Employee2 class contains data about one employee.
 * Fields include an ID number and an hourly pay rate.
 */
public class Employee2
{
    /**
     * Employee ID number
     */
    private int idNum;
    /**
     * Employee hourly pay
     */
    private double hourlyPay;
    /**
     * Sole constructor for Employee2
     */
    public Employee2(int id, double pay)
    {
        idNum = id;
        hourlyPay = pay;
    }
    /**
     * Returns the Employee2 ID number
     *
     * @return int
     */
    int getIdNum()
    {
        return idNum;
    }
    /**
     * Sets the Employee2 ID number
     *
     * @param id employee ID number
     */
    void setIdNum(int id)
    {
        idNum = id;
    }
}
```

Figure E-2 An `Employee2` class with class-level and member-level comments

> **NOTE** Like all program comments, Javadoc comments can contain anything. However, you should follow the conventions for Javadoc comments. For example, developers expect all Javadoc comments to begin with an uppercase letter and they recommend that method comments start with a verb such as "Returns" or "Sets." For more information, go to *http://java.sun.com/j2se/javadoc/writingdoccomments/#styleguide*.

GENERATING JAVADOC DOCUMENTATION

To generate the Javadoc documentation from your class, you should do the following:

1. Create a folder in which to store your class. For example, you might store the Employee2.java file in a folder named Employee2.

2. Within the folder, you can create a Documents subfolder to hold the documentation that you generate. However, if you omit this step and use the syntax described in Step 3, the folder will be created for you automatically.

3. Go to the command prompt and navigate to the directory that holds the Employee2.java file. (See Appendix A for information on finding the command prompt and changing directories.) From the command prompt, run the following command:

```
javadoc -d Documents *.java
```

The −d is the directory option. If you omit it, all the generated files will be saved in the current directory. By including this option, you indicate that the files should be saved in the Documents directory.

> **NOTE** To see the author's name in the resulting documentation, change the Javadoc command to the following:
> ```
> javadoc -d Documents -author *.java
> ```

> **NOTE** If you are using the jGRASP development environment to create your Java programs, you can execute the Javadoc command with a button click. The jGRASP program is provided on the CD that comes with this book.

4. Navigate to the Documents folder. You will see a number of generated files, including ones that contain lists of all the constants in your class, all the deprecated methods in your class, and so on. (In the Employee2 class, there are no constants or deprecated methods, but you can open the files and view the format that the contents would take if they existed.) The index.html file provides an index of all class interface, constructor, field, and method names; when you double-click it, the file opens in your default browser. Figure E-3 shows how the index.html file for Employee2 appears in Internet Explorer.

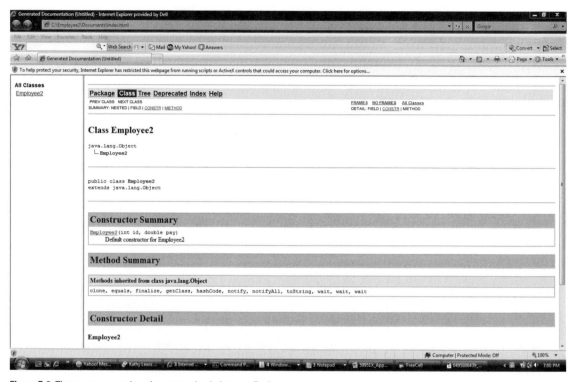

Figure E-3 The `Employee2` class documentation in Internet Explorer

»NOTE
The Javadoc tool will run on .java source files that are stub files with no method bodies. This means you can write documentation comments and run the Javadoc tool when you are first designing classes, before you have written implementations for the class's methods.

If you have searched the Sun Microsystems Web site for Java documentation, the format of the page in Figure E-3 is familiar to you. The class name and other information appear in a font and style consistent with other classes in the Java API. You can see information about the class constructor and the notes that you added in your comments. You see inheritance information—`Employee2` descends directly from `Object`. The format of this documentation is familiar to users, making it much easier for them to find what they need than if each developer created documentation formats independently.

Writing acceptable Javadoc comments requires adherence to some style standards. For example, professionals recommend that multiple @author tags should be listed in chronological order, with the creator of the class listed at the top, and that multiple @param tags should be listed in argument-declaration order. Additionally, Javadoc comments can provide hyperlinks that allow navigation from one document to another. For example, when a class contains a field that is an object of another class, you might want to link to the other class's documentation. For more information, see Sun Microsystems' recommendations at *http://java.sun.com/ j2se/javadoc/writingdoccomments/*.

SPECIFYING VISIBILITY OF JAVADOC DOCUMENTATION

By default, Javadoc documents only `public` and `protected` members of an API. In other words, even if you write Javadoc comments for `private` members, the comments will not appear in the generated documentation unless you take special action to make them visible. Although Figure E-3 shows details about the `Employee2` class's constructor and methods, there is no information about the `private` fields `idNum` and `hourlyPay`. To generate that documentation, you must specify `private` visibility by using the following `javadoc` command:

```
javadoc -d Documents -private *.java
```

Figure E-4 shows the documentation generated by this command. You can see that the newly generated documentation includes a Field Summary section. It lists the fields in alphabetical order preceded by their access specifiers and data types. Each field identifier is followed by the appropriate description that was provided in the Javadoc comment in the source code.

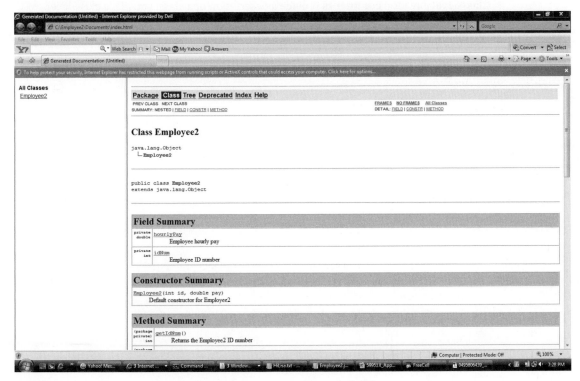

Figure E-4 The `Employee2` class documentation when `private` members are included

You can specify four types of visibility:

- » public—Displays public members only.
- » protected—Displays public and protected members only. This is the default option.
- » package—Displays package classes and members in addition to public and protected members.
- » private—Displays all members.

KEY TERMS

Javadoc is a documentation generator created by Sun Microsystems that allows you to generate Application Programming Interface (API) documentation in Hypertext Markup Language (HTML) format from Java source code.

A **Javadoc comment** is a special form of block comment that provides a standard way to document Java code.

A **Javadoc tag** is a keyword within a comment that the Javadoc tool can process.

Class-level Javadoc comments provide a description of a class; you place class-level comments above the code that declares a class.

Member-level Javadoc comments describe the fields, methods, and constructors of a class.

GLOSSARY

A

abstract class—a class from which you cannot create any concrete objects, but from which you can inherit. Abstract classes usually have one or more empty abstract methods. Contrast with **concrete classes**.

abstract data type—a type whose implementation is hidden and accessed through its public methods.

abstract method—a method declared with the keyword `abstract`. It is a method with no body—no curly braces and no method statements—just a return type, a method name, an optional argument list, and a semicolon. You are required to code a subclass method to override the empty superclass method that is inherited.

abstraction—the programming feature that allows you to use a method name to encapsulate a series of statements.

accelerator—a key combination that causes a menu item to be chosen, whether or not it is visible.

access modifier—defines the circumstances under which a class can be accessed and the other classes that have the right to use a class.

access specifiers—access modifiers.

accessor methods—methods that return information about an object.

accumulating—the process of repeatedly increasing a value by some amount to produce a total.

action key—a keyboard key that does not generate a character.

`actionPerformed(ActionEvent e)` method—a method that defines the actions that occur in response to an event.

actual parameters—the arguments in a method call. Contrast with **formal parameters**.

acyclic gradient—a fill pattern in which a color shift occurs once between two points.

adapter class—a class that implements all the methods in an interface, providing an empty body for each method.

`addActionListener()` method—a method that tells a class to expect `ActionEvents`.

add and assign operator—an operator that alters the value of the operand on the left by adding the operand on the right to it; it is composed of a plus sign and an equal sign (+=).

`add()` method—a method that adds components to a container.

`addPoint()` method—a method that adds points to a `Polygon` object.

aggregation—a type of composition in which a class contains one or more members of another class that would continue to exist without the object that contains them.

Allman style—the indent style in which curly braces are aligned and each occupies its own line; it is named for Eric Allman, a programmer who popularized the style. Contrast with **K & R style**.

ambiguous—describes a situation in which the compiler cannot determine which method to use.

anonymous classes—nested, local classes that have no identifier.

anonymous object—an unnamed object.

`append()` method—a `StringBuilder` class method that lets you add characters to the end of a `StringBuilder` object.

applet—a Java program that is called from within another application, frequently a Web page.

Applet Viewer—a program that comes with the JDK that allows you to view applets without using a Web browser.

appletviewer command—a command that allows you to view an applet in a viewing program that comes with the JDK.

application—a stand-alone, executable program.

application files—files that store software instructions. See also **program files**.

application-triggered painting—painting operations that occur when the internal state of a component has changed. Contrast with **system-triggered painting**.

arc—a portion of a circle.

architecturally neutral—describes the feature of Java that allows a program to run on any platform.

argument index—in a `printf()` statement, an integer that indicates the position of an argument in the argument list.

arguments—data items sent to methods in a method call.

arithmetic operators—operators used to perform calculations with values.

array—a named list of data items that all have the same type.

ArrayList class—a Java class that provides a dynamically resizable container that stores lists of objects.

Arrays class—a built-in Java class that contains many useful methods for manipulating arrays, such as methods to search, fill, compare, and sort arrays.

ascending—describes the order from lowest value to highest.

ascent—one of three measures of a `Font`'s height; it is the height of an uppercase character from a baseline to the top of the character. See also **leading** and **descent**.

assert statement—a statement that creates an assertion.

assertion—a Java language feature that can help you detect logic errors and debug a program.

assignment—the act of providing a value for a variable.

assignment operator—the equal sign (=); any value to the right of the equal sign is assigned to the variable on the left of the equal sign.

associativity—describes the order in which operands are used with operators.

attributes—the characteristics that define an object as part of a class.

B

back buffer—the offscreen image during double buffering.

base class—a class that is used as a basis for inheritance.

BasicStroke—a class that defines line types and implements the `Stroke` interface.

batch processing—processing that involves performing the same tasks with many records, one after the other.

binary data—data stored in machine-readable code that must be read by an application before you can understand it.

binary operators—operators that require two operands.

black box—a device you can use without understanding how it works.

blank `final`—a `final` variable that has not yet been assigned a value.

block—the code between a pair of curly braces.

block comments—comments that start with a forward slash and an asterisk (/*) and end with an asterisk and a forward slash (*/). Block comments can appear on a line by themselves, on a line before executable code, or on a line after executable code. Block comments can also extend across as many lines as needed. Contrast with **line comments**.

block line transfer or **blitting**—the act of copying contents from one surface to another.

Boolean values—true or false values; every computer decision results in a Boolean value.

Boolean variable—a variable of the data type that can hold only one of two values—`true` or `false`.

`BorderLayout` manager—the default manager class for all content panes. When you use the `BorderLayout` manager, the components fill the screen in five regions: north, south, east, west, and center.

`BoxLayout` manager—a layout manager that allows multiple components to be laid out either vertically or horizontally. The components do not wrap, so a vertical arrangement of components, for example, stays vertically arranged when the frame is resized.

bubble sort—a type of sort in which you continue to compare pairs of items, swapping them if they are out of order, so that the smallest items "bubble" to the top of the list, eventually creating a sorted list.

buffer—a memory location that you use to hold data temporarily.

`ButtonGroup`—a UI component that groups several components, such as `JCheckBoxes`, so a user can select only one at a time.

`byte`—the data type that holds very small integers, from –128 to 127.

bytecode—programming statements that have been compiled into binary format.

C

call—to invoke a method.

call stack—the memory location where the computer stores the list of method locations to which the system must return.

called method—a term used to describe the relationship between two methods; a method that is invoked by another.

calling method—a term used to describe the relationship between two methods; a method that invokes another.

camel casing—a naming style in which an identifier begins with a lowercase letter and subsequent words within the identifier are capitalized. Contrast with **Pascal casing**.

capacity—an attribute of an `ArrayList` whose value is the number of items it can hold without having to increase its size. Also, with a `StringBuilder` object, the actual length of the buffer, as opposed to that of the string contained in the buffer.

`capacity()` method—a `StringBuilder` class method that returns the actual length, or capacity, of the `StringBuilder` object.

`CardLayout` manager—a layout manager that generates a stack of containers or components, one on top of another.

cast operator—an operator that performs an explicit type conversion; it is created by placing the desired result type in parentheses before the expression to be converted.

`catch` block—a segment of code that can handle an exception that might be thrown by the `try` block that precedes it.

catch or specify requirement—the Java rule that checked exceptions require catching or declaration.

chaining the stream objects—the act of using a `DataOutputStream` connected to `FileOutputStream`.

`char`—the data type that holds any single character.

`Character` class—a class whose instances can hold a single character value. This class also defines methods that can manipulate or inspect single-character data.

`charAt()` method—a `String` and `StringBuilder` class method that requires an integer argument that indicates the position of the character that the method returns.

checked exceptions—exceptions that a programmer should plan for and from which a program should be able to recover. Contrast with **unchecked exceptions**.

child class—a derived class.

class—a group or collection of objects with common properties.

class client—an application or class that instantiates objects of another prewritten class. See also **class user**.

class definition—a description of attributes and methods of objects instantiated from a class.

class diagram—a visual tool that provides an overview of a class. It consists of a rectangle divided into three sections—the top section contains the name of the class, the middle section contains the names and data types of the attributes, and the bottom section contains the methods.

class-level Javadoc comments—Javadoc comments that provide a description of a class; you place class-level comments above the code that declares a class.

class library—a package.

class methods—static methods that do not have a `this` reference (because they have no object associated with them).

class user—an application or class that instantiates objects of another prewritten class. See also **class client**.

class variables—static variables that are shared by every instantiation of a class.

clean build—a compilation that is created when you delete all previously compiled versions of a class before compiling again.

`clearRect()` method—a method that draws a rectangle using the background color to create what appears to be an empty or "clear" rectangle.

closing a file—the action that makes a file no longer available to an application.

collision—describes a class naming conflict.

`Color` class—a class that defines colors for you to use in your applications.

comes into scope—describes what happens to a variable when it is declared. Contrast with **goes out of scope**.

comment out—the technique of turning a program statement into a comment so the compiler will not execute its command.

`compareTo()` method—a `String` class method used to compare two `Strings`; the method returns zero only if the two `Strings`

refer to the same value. If there is any difference between the `Strings`, a negative number is returned if the calling object is "less than" the argument, and a positive number is returned if the calling object is "more than" the argument.

comparison operator—a relational operator.

compiler—a program that translates language statements into machine code. A compiler translates an entire program before executing it. Contrast with **interpreter**.

compile-time error—an error for which the compiler detects a violation of language syntax rules and is unable to translate the source code to machine code.

composition—describes the relationship between classes when an object of one class is a data field within another class. See also **has-a relationship**.

computer file—a collection of stored information in a computer system.

concatenated—describes values that are added onto the end of another value.

concatenation—the process of joining a variable to a string to create a longer string.

concrete classes—nonabstract classes from which objects can be instantiated. Contrast with **abstract class**.

conditional operator—an operator that requires three expressions separated with a question mark and a colon; the operator is used as an abbreviated version of the `if...else` structure.

confirm dialog box—displays the options Yes, No, and Cancel; you can create one using the `showConfirmDialog()` method in the `JOptionPane` class.

console applications—programs that support character output to a computer screen in a DOS window.

constant—describes a data item whose value cannot be changed during the execution of an application.

constructor—a method that establishes an object.

consume—to retrieve and discard an entry without using it.

container—a type of component that holds other components so you can treat a group of them as a single entity.

containment hierarchy—a tree of components that has a top-level container as its root (that is, at its uppermost level).

content pane—a component that contains all the visible components in a top-level container's user interface.

convenience class—a class that has been designed to make the programmer's job easier.

`copyArea()` **method**—a method that copies any rectangular area to a new location.

counter-controlled loop—a definite loop. Contrast with **event-controlled loop**.

counting—the process of continually incrementing a variable to keep track of the number of occurrences of some event.

cyclic gradient—a fill pattern in which a shift between colors occurs repeatedly between two points.

D

data files—files that consist of related records that contain facts and figures, such as employee numbers, names, and salaries.

data type—describes the type of data that can be stored in a variable, how much memory the item occupies, and what types of operations can be performed on the data.

dead code—unreachable statements.

debugging—the process of locating and repairing a program's error.

`DecimalFormat` **class**—a class that provides ways to easily convert numbers into strings, allowing you to control the display of leading and trailing zeros, prefixes and suffixes, grouping (thousands) separators, and the decimal separator.

decision structure—a logical structure that involves choosing between alternative courses of action based on some value within a program.

decrementing—the act of subtracting 1 from a variable.

default constructor—a constructor that requires no arguments.

default package—the unnamed package in which a class is placed if you do not specify a package for the class.

definite loop—a loop that executes a specific number of times; a counted loop. Contrast with **indefinite loop**.

derived class—a class that inherits from a base class.

descending—describes the order from highest to lowest.

descent—one of three measures of a `Font`'s height; it measures the part of characters that "hang below" the baseline, such as the tails on the lowercase letters g and j. See also **ascent** and **leading**.

deserialization—the process of re-creating an object in computer memory after it is retrieved from a file.

`destroy()` **method**—a method invoked in an applet when the user closes the browser or Applet Viewer.

deterministic—an adjective that describes the predictability and consistency of computer output.

dialog box—a GUI object resembling a window in which you can place messages you want to display.

direct access files—random access files.

directories—elements in a storage organization hierarchy. See also **folders**.

divide and assign operator—an operator that alters the value of the operand on the left by dividing the operand on the right into it; it is composed of a slash and an equal sign (/=).

do-nothing loop—a loop that performs no actions other than looping.

`do...while` **loop**—a loop that executes a loop body at least one time; it checks the loop control variable at the bottom of the loop after one repetition has occurred.

double—a data type that can hold a floating-point value of up to 14 or 15 significant digits of accuracy. Contrast with **float**.

double buffering—the default buffering strategy in which `JPanels` are drawn off-screen when they are updated and displayed only when complete.

Double class—a wrapper class that contains a simple `double` and useful methods to manipulate it.

double-precision floating-point number—a type of value that is stored in a `double`.

draw3DRect() method—a method that draws a rectangle that appears to have "shadowing" on two of its edges—the effect is that of a rectangle that is lit from the upper-left corner and slightly raised or slightly lowered.

drawArc() method—a method that draws an arc.

drawLine() method—a method that draws a straight line between two points on the screen.

drawOval() method—a method that draws an oval.

drawPolygon() method—a method that draws complex shapes.

drawRect() method—a method that draws the outline of a rectangle.

drawRoundRect() method—a method that draws rectangles with rounded corners.

drawString() method—a method that allows you to draw a `String` in a `JFrame` or other component.

dual-alternative if—a decision structure that takes one of two possible courses of action. Contrast with **single-alternative if**.

dummy values—values the user enters that are not "real" data, but just signals to stop data entry.

dynamic method binding—the ability of an application to select the correct subclass method when the program executes. See also **late binding**.

dynamically resizable—describes an object whose size can change during program execution.

E

echoing input—the act of repeating the user's entry as output so the user can visually confirm the entry's accuracy.

editable—describes a component that can accept keystrokes.

element—one variable or object in an array.

empty body—a block with no statements in it.

empty statement—a statement that contains only a semicolon.

encapsulation—the act of hiding data and methods within an object.

endcap styles—styles applied to the ends of lines that do not join with other lines; they include CAP_BUTT, CAP_ROUND, and CAP_SQUARE.

endsWith() method—a `String` class method that takes a `String` argument and returns `true` or `false` if a `String` object does or does not end with the specified argument.

enhanced for loop—a language construct that allows you to cycle through an array without specifying the starting and ending points for the loop control variable.

EOF—the end-of-file condition.

equalsIgnoreCase() method—a `String` class method that ignores case when determining if two `Strings` are equivalent.

equals() method—an `Object` class method that takes a single argument, which must be the same type as the type of the invoking object, and returns a Boolean value indicating whether two object references are equal. The method is overridden in the `String` class to evaluate the contents of two `String` objects to determine if they are equivalent.

equivalency operator—the operator composed of two equal signs that compares values and returns `true` if they are equal.

Error class—a class that represents more serious errors than the Exception class—those from which a program usually cannot recover.

escape sequence—a sequence that begins with a backslash followed by a character; the pair frequently represents a nonprinting character.

event—a result when a user takes action on a component.

event-controlled loop—an indefinite loop. Contrast with **counter-controlled loop**.

event-driven program—a program in which the user might initiate any number of events in any order.

event handler—a method that executes because it is called automatically when an appropriate event occurs.

exception—in object-oriented terminology, an unexpected or error condition.

Exception class—a class that comprises less serious errors than those from the Error class; the Exception class represents unusual conditions that arise while a program is running, and from which the program can recover.

exception handling—an object-oriented technique for managing errors.

exception specification—the practice of using the keyword throws followed by an Exception type in the method header. If a method throws a checked Exception that it will not catch but that will be caught by a different method, you must use an exception specification.

executing—the act of carrying out a program statement.

explicit conversion—the data type transformation caused using a cast operator.

extended—describes classes that have descended from another class.

extends—a keyword used to achieve inheritance in Java.

Extensible Hypertext Markup Language (XHTML)—an extension of HTML.

F

FAQs—frequently asked questions.

fault-tolerant—describes applications that are designed so that they continue to operate, possibly at a reduced level, when some part of the system fails.

field—a data variable declared in a class outside of any method. In reference to storage, a group of characters that has some meaning.

File class—the Java class that provides methods to gather file information.

file pointer, or **file position pointer**—an automatically created variable that holds the byte number of the next file position to be used.

fill patterns—patterns that describe how drawing objects are filled in.

fill3DRect() method—a method that creates filled, three-dimensional rectangles.

fillArc() method—a method that creates a solid arc.

fillOval() method—a method that draws a solid, filled oval.

fillPolygon() method—a method that draws a solid shape.

fillRect() method—a method that draws a solid, or filled, rectangle.

final—the keyword that precedes named constants, which describes superclass methods that cannot be overridden in a subclass, and describes classes in which all methods are final.

finally block—a block of code that executes at the end of a try...catch sequence.

fixed method binding—the opposite of dynamic method binding; it occurs when a subclass method is selected while the program compiles rather than while it is running. See also **static method binding**.

float—a data type that can hold a floating-point value of up to six or seven significant digits of accuracy. Contrast with **double**.

floating-point—describes a number that contains decimal positions.

flowchart—a tool that helps programmers plan a program's logic by writing the steps in diagram form, as a series of shapes connected by arrows.

FlowLayout manager—a layout manager that arranges components in rows across the width of a `Container`; when the current row is filled, additional `Components` are placed in new rows. By default, the components in each row are centered.

folders—elements in a storage organization hierarchy. See also **directories**.

Font class—a Java class that holds typeface and size information.

for loop—a loop that can be used when a definite number of loop iterations is required.

formal parameters—the variables in a method declaration that accept the values from actual parameters. Contrast with actual **parameters**.

format specifier—in a `printf()` statement, a placeholder for a numeric value.

format string—in a `printf()` statement, a string of characters that includes optional text (that is displayed literally) and one or more format specifiers.

fragile—describes classes that are prone to errors.

fully qualified name—describes a filename that includes the entire hierarchy in which a class is stored.

fundamental classes—basic classes contained in the `java.lang` package that are automatically imported into every program you write. Contrast with **optional classes**.

G

garbage value—the unknown value stored in an uninitialized variable.

getAvailableFontFamilyNames() method—a method that returns the fonts that are available on your system.

getContentPane() method—a method that returns a reference to a container's content pane.

getDefaultToolkit() method—a method that provides information about the system in use.

getFontMetrics() method—a method that returns a `FontMetrics` object so you can discover its leading, ascent, descent, and height.

getScreenResolution() method—a method that returns the screen resolution on the current system.

getScreenSize() method—a method that returns the screen size as a `Dimension` object.

getText() method—a method that retrieves the `String` of text in a `Component`.

glass pane—a pane that resides above the content pane in a container. It can contain tool tips.

goes out of scope—describes what happens to a variable at the end of the block in which it is declared. Contrast with **comes into scope**.

gradient fill—a gradual shift from one color at one coordinate point to a different color at a second coordinate point.

Graphics2D class—a class that provides tools for two-dimensional drawing.

GridBagLayout manager—a layout manager that allows you to add `Components` to precise locations within the grid, as well as to indicate that specific `Components` should span multiple rows or columns within the grid.

GridLayout manager—a layout manager that divides a container surface into a grid.

H

has-a relationship—a relationship based on composition.

hash code—a calculated number used to identify an object.

header—the first line of a method; its declaration.

heavyweight components—components that require interaction with the local operating system. Contrast with **light-weight components**.

height of a font—the sum of its leading, ascent, and descent.

high-level programming language—a language that allows you to use a vocabulary of reasonable terms, such as "read," "write," or "add," instead of the sequences of on and off switches that perform these tasks. Contrast with **low-level programming language**.

<html>—the tag that begins every HTML document.

</html>—the tag that ends every HTML document.

HTML, or **Hypertext Markup Language**—a simple language used to create Web pages for the Internet.

I

identifier—the name of a program component such as a class, object, or variable.

if statement—the single-alternative decision statement.

if...else statement—the statement that provides the mechanism to perform one action when a Boolean expression evaluates as true, and to perform a different action when a Boolean expression evaluates as false.

image—a likeness of a person or thing.

immutable—describes objects that cannot be changed.

implementation hiding—a principle of object-oriented programming that describes the encapsulation of method details within a class.

implicit conversion—the automatic transformation of one data type to another. Also called **promotion**.

import statement—a Java statement that allows access to a built-in Java class that is contained in a package.

incrementing—the act of adding 1 to a variable.

indefinite loop—a loop in which the final number of iterations is unknown. Contrast with **definite loop**.

indexOf() method—a String class method that determines whether a specific character occurs within a String. If it does, the method returns the position of the character; the first position of a String begins with zero. The return value is –1 if the character does not exist in the String.

infinite loop—a loop that never ends.

information hiding—the object-oriented programming principle used when creating private access for data fields; a class's private data can be changed or manipulated only by a class's own methods, and not by methods that belong to other classes.

inheritance—a mechanism that enables one class to inherit, or assume, both the behavior and the attributes of another class.

init() method—the first method called in any applet.

initialization—the act of making an assignment at the time of variable declaration.

inlining—an automatic process that optimizes performance in which calls to final methods are replaced with the expanded code of their definitions at each method call location.

inner block—a block contained in an outer block. See also **inside block.**

inner classes—nested classes that require an instance. See also **nonstatic member classes**.

inner loop—a loop that is contained entirely within another loop.

input dialog box—a GUI object that asks a question and provides a text field in which the user can enter a response.

InputStream—an abstract class that contains methods for performing input.

insert() method—a StringBuilder class method that lets you add characters at a specific location within a StringBuilder object.

inside block—a block contained in an outside block. See also **inner block**.

instance—an existing object of a class.

instance methods—methods used with object instantiations. See also **nonstatic methods**.

instance variables—the data components of a class.

`instanceof` **operator**—an operator that determines whether an object that is the operand on the left is a member or descendant of the class that is the operand on the right.

instant access files—files in which records must be accessed immediately.

instantiation—an object; one tangible example of a class.

`int`—the data type used to store integers.

integer—a whole number without decimal places.

`Integer` **class**—a wrapper class that contains a simple integer and useful methods to manipulate it.

integer division—the operation in which one integer value is divided by another; the result contains no fractional part.

interactive applications—programs in which a user communicates with the program by using an input device.

interactive program—an application in which the user makes direct requests, as opposed to one in which input comes from a file.

interface—a construct similar to a class, except that all of its methods must be abstract and all of its data (if any) must be `static` `final`; it declares method headers, but not the instructions within those methods. Also used to describe the part of a method that a client sees and uses—it includes the method's return type, name, and arguments.

interpreter—a program that translates language statements into machine code. An interpreter translates and executes one statement at a time. Contrast with **compiler**.

invoke—to call or execute a method.

is-a relationship—the relationship between an object and the class of which it is a member.

iteration—one loop execution.

J

`JApplet`—a `Swing` class from which you can inherit to create your own applet.

Java—a programming language developed by Sun Microsystems as an object-oriented language used both for general-purpose business applications and for interactive, Web-based Internet applications.

Java API—the application programming interface, a collection of information about how to use every prewritten Java class.

Java ARchive (JAR) file—a file that compresses the stored data.

Java Enterprise Edition (EE)—a Java edition that includes all of the classes in the Java SE, plus a number of classes that are more useful to programs running on servers.

Java Foundation Classes (JFC)—selected classes from the `java.awt` package, including `Swing` component classes.

Java interpreter—the program that checks bytecode and communicates with the operating system, executing the bytecode instructions line by line within the Java virtual machine.

Java Micro Edition (ME)—a Java platform that is used for small devices such as PDAs, cell phones, and other consumer appliances.

Java SE 6—the most recent version of Java. The full, official name is Java Platform, Standard Edition 6.

Java Virtual Machine (JVM)—a hypothetical (software-based) computer on which Java runs.

`java.lang`—the package that is implicitly imported into every Java program and that contains the fundamental classes.

Javadoc—a documentation generator created by Sun Microsystems that allows you to generate Application Programming Interface (API) documentation in Hypertext Markup Language (HTML) format from Java source code.

Javadoc comment—a special form of block comment that provides a standard way to document Java code.

Javadoc tag—a keyword within a comment that the Javadoc tool can process.

JButton—a `Component` the user can click with a mouse to make a selection.

JCheckBox—a UI component that consists of a label positioned beside a square; you can click the square to display or remove a check mark. Usually, you use a `JCheckBox` to allow the user to turn an option on or off.

JComboBox—a UI component that combines two features: a display area showing an option and a list box containing additional options. The display area contains either a button that a user can click or an editable field into which the user can type.

JDK—the Java Standard Edition Development Kit.

JFrame—a container with a title bar and border.

JLabel—a built-in Java `Swing` class that holds text you can display.

JOptionPane—a Java class that produces dialog boxes.

JPanel—a plain, borderless surface that can hold lightweight UI components.

JScrollPane—a pane that provides scroll bars along the side or bottom, or both, so that the user can scroll initially invisible parts of the pane into view.

JTextField—a component into which a user can type a single line of text data.

juncture styles—styles applied to lines that join; they include `JOIN_MITER`, `JOIN_ROUND`, and `JOIN_BEVEL`.

K

K & R style—the indent style in which the opening brace follows the header line; it is named for Kernighan and Ritchie, who wrote the first book on the C programming language. Contrast with **Allman style**.

keyboard buffer—a small area of memory where keystrokes are stored before they are retrieved into a program. Also called the **type-ahead buffer**.

key field—the field in a record that makes the record unique from all others.

KeyListener interface—an interface that provides methods that respond to actions the user initiates from the keyboard. The `KeyListener` interface contains three methods—`keyPressed()`, `keyTyped()`, and `keyReleased()`.

L

late binding—the ability of an application to select the correct subclass method when the program executes. See also **dynamic method binding**.

layout manager—a class that controls component positioning in a UI environment.

leading—one of three measures of a `Font`'s height; it is the amount of space between baselines. See also **ascent** and **descent**.

leaf menu item—a menu item that does not bring up another menu.

length field—a field that contains the number of elements in an array.

length() method—a `String` class method that returns the length of a `String`.

length property—a `StringBuilder` class attribute that identifies the number of characters in the `String` contained in the `StringBuilder`.

lexicographical comparison—a comparison based on the integer Unicode values of characters.

library of classes—a folder that provides a convenient grouping for classes.

lightweight components—components written completely in Java that do not have to rely on the code written to run in the local operating system. Contrast with **heavyweight components**.

line comments—comments that start with two forward slashes (//) and continue to the end of the current line. Line comments can appear on a line by themselves or at the end of a line following executable code. Contrast with **block comments**.

listener—an object that is interested in and reacts to an event.

literal constant—a value that is taken literally at each use.

literal string—a series of characters that appear exactly as entered. Any literal string in Java appears between double quotation marks.

local classes—nested classes that are local to a block of code.

local variable—a variable known only within the boundaries of a method.

logic—describes the order of program statements that produce correct results.

logic error—an error that occurs when a program compiles successfully but produces an error during execution.

logical AND operator—an operator used between Boolean expressions to determine whether both are `true`. The AND operator is written as two ampersands (`&&`).

logical OR operator—an operator used between Boolean expressions to determine whether either expression is `true`. The OR operator is written as two pipes (`||`).

long—the data type that holds very large integers, from -9,223,372,036,854,775,808 to 9,223,372,036,854,775,807.

look and feel—describes the default appearance and behavior of any user interface.

loop—a structure that allows repeated execution of a block of statements.

loop body—the block of statements that executes when the Boolean expression that controls the loop is `true`.

loop control variable—a variable whose value determines whether loop execution continues.

loop fusion—the technique of combining two loops into one.

lossless data compression—a set of rules that allows an exact replica of data to be reconstructed from a compressed version.

low-level programming language—a language that corresponds closely to a computer processor's circuitry. Contrast with **high-level programming language**. Compare with **machine language**.

lvalue—an expression that can appear on the left side of an assignment statement. Contrast with **rvalue**.

M

machine language—circuitry-level language; a series of on and off switches. Compare with **low-level programming language**.

magic number—a value that does not have immediate, intuitive meaning or a number that cannot be explained without additional knowledge. Unnamed constants are magic numbers.

matrix—a two-dimensional array.

member-level Javadoc comments—Javadoc comments that describe the fields, methods, and constructors of a class.

menu bar—a horizontal strip that is placed at the top of a container and that contains user options.

menus—lists of user options.

method—a program module that contains a series of statements that carry out a task.

method call—the act of invoking another method.

method declaration—the header, or first line of a method.

method's type—the method's return type.

mission critical—describes any process that is crucial to an organization.

mnemonic—a key that causes an already visible menu item to be chosen.

modulus operator—the percent sign; when it is used with two integers, the result is an integer with the value of the remainder after division takes place. Also called the **remainder operator**; sometimes called just **mod**.

`MouseEvent`—the type of event generated by mouse manipulation.

`MouseInputListener` **interface**—an interface that implements all the methods in both the `MouseListener` and `MouseMotionListener` interfaces.

`MouseListener` **interface**—an interface that provides methods named `mousePressed()`, `mouseClicked()`, and `mouseReleased()` that are analogous to the keyboard event methods `keyPressed()`, `keyTyped()`, and `keyReleased()`.

`MouseMotionListener` **interface**—an interface that provides methods named `mouseDragged()` and `mouseMoved()` that detect the mouse being rolled or dragged across a component surface.

multidimensional arrays—arrays that contain two or more dimensions.

multimedia—describes the use of sound, images, graphics, and video in computer programs.

multiple inheritance—the capability to inherit from more than one class; Java does not support multiple inheritance.

multiply and assign operator—an operator that alters the value of the operand on the left by multiplying the operand on the right by it; it is composed of an asterisk and an equal sign.

mutator methods—methods that set field values.

N

named constant—a memory location whose declaration is preceded by the keyword `final`, and whose value cannot change during program execution.

NaN—a three-letter abbreviation for "Not a number."

nested—describes the relationship of inner and outer blocks.

nested classes—classes contained in other classes.

nested `if` statements—describes `if` statements when one is contained within the other.

`new` **operator**—an operator that allocates the memory needed to hold an object.

nonstatic member classes—nested classes that require an instance. See also **inner classes**.

nonstatic methods—methods used with object instantiations. See also **instance methods**.

nonvolatile—describes storage that does not require power to retain information. Contrast with **volatile**.

NOT operator—the exclamation point (!); it negates the result of any Boolean expression.

`null` **String**—an empty `String` created by typing a set of quotes with nothing between them.

numeric constant—a number whose value is taken literally at each use.

O

`Object` **class**—a class defined in the `java.lang` package, which is imported automatically every time you write a program and is the base class for all other Java classes.

object-oriented programming—a style of programming that involves creating classes, creating objects from those classes, and creating applications that use those objects. Contrast with **procedural programming**.

objects—instances of a class; objects are made up of attributes and methods.

octothorpe—the pound sign.

one-dimensional array—an array that contains one column of values and whose elements are accessed using a single subscript. See also **single-dimensional array**.

opening a file—the action that creates an object and associates a stream of bytes with it.

operand—a value used in an arithmetic statement.

operator precedence—the rules for the order in which parts of a mathematical expression are evaluated.

optional classes—classes that reside in packages that must be explicitly imported into your programs. Contrast with **fundamental classes**.

outer block—a block that contains a nested block. See also **outside block**.

outer loop—a loop that contains another loop.

OutputStream—an abstract class that contains methods for performing output.

outside block—a block that contains a nested block. See also **outer block**.

overloading—describes using one term to indicate diverse meanings, or writing multiple methods with the same name but with different arguments.

overriding a method—a technique in which you create a method in a child class that has the same name and argument list as a method in its parent class.

overrides—describes what a variable does to another with the same name when it takes precedence over the other variable.

P

package—a named collection or library of classes. See also **class library** and **library of classes**.

paint() method—a method that runs when Java displays a screen; you can write your own paint() method to override the automatically supplied one whenever you want to paint graphics, such as shapes, on the screen.

painting—the act of displaying or redisplaying a surface.

parallel array—an array with the same number of elements as another, and for which the values in corresponding elements are related.

parameters—data items received by a method.

parent class—a base class.

parse—to break into component parts; the process the compiler uses to divide source code into meaningful portions for analysis.

parseDouble() method—a Double class method that takes a String argument and returns its double value.

parseInt() method—an Integer class method that takes a String argument and returns its integer value.

Pascal casing—the style of using an uppercase letter to begin an identifier and to start each new word in an identifier. Contrast with **camel casing**.

passed by reference—describes a variable passed to a method when the address is passed to the method. Contrast with **passed by value**.

passed by value—describes a variable passed to a method when a copy is made in the receiving method. Contrast with **passed by reference**.

passing—the act of sending arguments to a method.

path—the complete list of the disk drive plus the hierarchy of directories in which a file resides.

pattern String—an argument passed to the DecimalFormat constructor that is composed of symbols that determine what a formatted number looks like.

permanent storage devices—hardware storage devices that retain data even when power is lost.

pixels—the picture elements, or tiny dots of light, that make up the image on your video monitor.

point size argument—an argument to the Font constructor that is an integer that represents about 1/72 of an inch.

polymorphism—the feature of languages that allows the same word to be interpreted correctly in different situations based on the context; the act of using the same method name to indicate different implementations.

populating the array—the act of providing values for all of the elements in an array.

postfix ++ or the **postfix increment operator**—an operator that is composed by placing two plus signs to the right of a variable; it evaluates the variable, then adds 1 to it. Contrast with **prefix ++**.

posttest loop—a loop in which the loop control variable is tested after the loop body executes. Contrast with **pretest loop**.

preferred size—a Component's default size.

prefix ++ or the **prefix increment operator**—an operator that is composed by placing two plus signs to the left of a variable; it adds 1 to the variable, then evaluates it. Contrast with **postfix ++**.

prefix and postfix decrement operators—operators that subtract 1 from a variable before and after evaluating it, respectively.

pretest loop—a loop in which the loop control variable is tested before the loop body executes. Contrast with **posttest loop**.

primary key—a unique identifier for data within a database.

primary surface—the visible screen surface during double buffering.

priming read or **priming input**—the first input statement prior to a loop that will execute subsequent input statements for the same variable.

primitive type—a simple data type. Java's primitive types are byte, short, int, long, float, double, char, and boolean.

private access—refers to a field that no other classes can access.

procedural programming—a style of programming in which sets of operations are executed one after another in sequence. Contrast with **object-oriented programming**.

procedures—sets of operations performed by a computer program.

program—a set of instructions that you write to tell a computer what to do.

program comments—nonexecuting statements added to a Java file for the purpose of documentation.

program files—files that store software instructions. See also **application files**.

program statements—similar to English sentences; they carry out the tasks that programs perform.

programmer-defined data type—a type that is created by a programmer and not built into the language.

promotion—an implicit conversion.

prompt—a message that requests and describes user input.

property—an object; an instance variable or field.

protected—a Java keyword that provides you with an intermediate level of security between public and private access. Protected members are those that can be used by a class and its descendants.

pseudocode—a tool that helps programmers plan a program's logic by writing plain English statements.

pseudorandom—describes numbers that appear to be random, but are the same set of numbers whenever the seed is the same.

R

ragged array—a two-dimensional array that has rows of different lengths.

random access files—files in which records can be located in any order.

random access memory (RAM)—temporary, volatile storage.

random number—a number whose value cannot be predicted.

range check—a series of statements that determine within which of a set of ranges a value falls.

range match—the process of comparing a value to the endpoints of numerical ranges to find a category in which the value belongs.

real-time—describes applications that require a record to be accessed immediately while a client is waiting.

record—a collection of fields that contain data about an entity.

redeclare a variable—to attempt to declare a variable twice—an illegal action.

reference—a variable that holds a memory address.

reference to an object—the name for a memory address where the object is held.

reference types—objects that hold memory addresses.

relational operator—an operator that compares two items; an expression that contains a relational operator has a Boolean value.

remainder and assign operator—an operator that alters the value of the operand on the left by assigning the remainder when the left operand is divided by the right operand; it is composed of a percent sign and an equal sign (%=).

remainder operator—the percent sign; when it is used with two integers, the result is an integer with the value of the remainder after division takes place. Also called the **modulus operator**.

remove() method—a method that removes components from a container.

repaint() method—a method you execute when a window needs to be updated, such as when it contains new images.

replace() method—a `String` class method that allows you to replace all occurrences of some character within a `String`.

rerendered—describes a drawing that is repainted or redisplayed.

return statement—a statement that ends a method, and frequently sends a value from a called method back to the calling method.

returning a value—the act of sending a data value from a called method back to the calling method.

robustness—describes the degree to which a system is resilient to stress, maintaining correct functioning.

root directory—the main directory of a storage device, outside any folders.

run-time error—an error that occurs when a program compiles successfully but does not execute.

runtime exceptions—unplanned exceptions that occur during a program's execution. The term is also used more specifically to describe members of the `RuntimeException` class.

rvalue—an expression that can appear only on the right side of an assignment statement. Contrast with **lvalue**.

S

sandbox—a safe area in which a program can run without causing harm to other areas of a system.

scalar—describes simple, primitive variables, such as `int`, `double`, or `char`.

scientific notation—a display format that more conveniently expresses large or small numeric values; a multidigit number is converted to a single-digit number and multiplied by 10 to a power.

scope—in reference to a variable, the portion of a program within which you can refer to the variable.

SDK—a software development kit, or a set of tools useful to programmers; the Java EE Development Kit.

searching an array—the process of comparing a value to a list of values in an array, looking for a match.

seed—a starting value.

semantic errors—the type of errors that occur when you use a correct word in the wrong context in program code.

sequence structure—a logical structure in which one step follows another unconditionally.

sequential access file—a data file in which each record is stored in order, based on the value in some field.

serialization—Java's built-in mechanism for manipulating objects as streams of bytes.

serialized object—an object that is represented as a sequence of bytes and includes the object's data as well as information about the types of data stored in the object.

setCharAt() method—a StringBuilder class method that allows you to change a character at a specified position within a StringBuilder object.

setEditable() method—a method that changes the editable status of a JTextField.

setEnabled() method—a method that makes a component available or dimmed and unavailable.

setFont() method—a method that changes a JLabel's font.

setLength() method—a StringBuilder class method that changes the length of the characters in the String in a StringBuilder object.

setLocation() method—a method that allows you to place a component at a specific location within a JFrame's content pane.

setStroke() method—a Java 2D method that alters a stroke's width.

setText() method—a method that allows you to change the text in a Component that has already been created.

setToolTipText() method—a method that defines the text to be displayed in a tool tip.

short—the data type that holds small integers, from –32,768 to 32,767.

short-circuit evaluation—describes the feature of the AND and OR operators in which evaluation is performed only as far as necessary to make a final decision.

showConfirmDialog() method—a method that displays a confirm dialog box with the options Yes, No, and Cancel.

showInputDialog() method—a method that creates an input dialog box.

signature—a method's name and the number, types, and order of arguments.

significant digits—refers to the mathematical accuracy of a value.

single-alternative if—a decision structure that performs an action, or not, based on one alternative. Contrast with **dual-alternative if**.

single-dimensional array—an array that contains one column of values and whose elements are accessed using a single subscript. See also **one-dimensional array**.

single-precision floating-point number—a type of value that is stored in a float.

sorting—the process of arranging a series of objects in some logical order.

source—a component on which an event is generated.

source code—programming statements written in a high-level programming language.

stack trace history list, or more simply **stack trace**—a list that displays all the methods that were called during program execution.

standard input device—normally the keyboard.

standard output device—normally the monitor.

start() method—a method that executes after the init() method in an applet and executes again every time the applet becomes active after it has been inactive.

startsWith() method—a String class method that takes a String argument and returns true or false if a String object does or does not start with the specified argument, respectively.

state—the values of the attributes of an object.

static—a reserved keyword that means a method is accessible and usable even though no objects of the class exist.

static member class—a type of nested class that has access to all static methods of its top-level class.

static method binding—the opposite of dynamic method binding; it occurs when a subclass method is selected while the program compiles rather than while it is running. See also **fixed method binding**.

`stop()` **method**—a method invoked in an applet when a user leaves a Web page (perhaps by minimizing a window or traveling to a different Web page).

stream—a pipeline or channel through which bytes flow into and out of an application.

`String`—a built-in Java class that provides the means for storing and manipulating character strings.

`StringBuilder` **and** `StringBuffer` **classes**—classes used to store and manipulate changeable data composed of multiple characters. It is an alternative to the `String` class when you know a `String` will be modified.

`String` **class**—a class used to work with fixed-string data—that is, unchanging data composed of multiple characters.

`String` **variable**—a named object of the `String` class.

`stringWidth()` **method**—a `FontMetrics` class method that returns the integer width of a `String`.

stroke—a line-drawing feature in Java 2D that represents a single movement as if you were using a drawing tool, such as a pen or a pencil.

strongly typed language—a language in which all variables must be declared before they can be used.

style argument—an argument to the `Font` constructor that applies an attribute to displayed text and is one of three values: `Font.PLAIN`, `Font.BOLD`, or `Font.ITALIC`.

subclass—a derived class.

subscript—an integer contained within square brackets that indicates one of an array's variables, or elements.

`substring()` **method**—a `String` class method that allows you to extract part of a `String`.

subtract and assign operator—an operator that alters the value of the operand on the left by subtracting the operand on the right from it; it is composed of a minus sign and an equal sign (`-=`).

subtype polymorphism—the ability of one method name to work appropriately for different subclasses of a parent class.

`super`—a Java keyword that always refers to the superclass of the class in which you use it.

superclass—a base class.

`Swing` **components**—UI elements such as dialog boxes and buttons; you can usually recognize their names because they begin with J.

`switch` **statement**—a statement that uses up to four keywords to test a single variable against a series of exact integer or character values. The keywords are `switch`, `case`, `break`, and `default`.

symbolic constant—a named constant.

syntactic salt—describes a language feature designed to make it harder to write bad code.

syntactic sugar—describes aspects of a computer language that make it "sweeter," or easier, for programmers to use.

syntax—the rules of a language.

syntax error—a programming error that occurs when you introduce typing errors into a program or use the programming language incorrectly. A program containing syntax errors will not compile.

`System.out.printf()` **method**—a method used to format numeric values.

system-triggered painting—painting operations that occur when the system asks a component to render its contents. Contrast with **application-triggered painting**.

T

table—a two-dimensional array; a matrix.

tag attributes—arguments that promote activity or describe the features of an HTML tag.

tags—HTML commands.

`this` **reference**—a reference to an object that is passed to any object's nonstatic class method.

thread—the flow of execution of one set of program statements.

throw statement—a statement that sends an `Exception` out of a block or a method so it can be handled elsewhere.

token—a unit of data; the `Scanner` class separates input into tokens.

`toLowerCase()` **method**—a `String` class method that converts any `String` to its lowercase equivalent.

tool tips—popup windows that can help a user understand the purpose of components in an application; a tool tip appears when a user hovers a mouse pointer over the component.

top-level class—the containing class in nested classes.

top-level container—a container at the top of a containment hierarchy. The Java top-level containers are `JFrame`, `JDialog`, and `JApplet`.

`toString()` **method**—an `Object` class method that converts an `Object` into a `String` that contains information about the `Object`. Also, a `String` class method that converts any object to a `String`.

`toUpperCase()` **method**—a `String` class method that converts any `String` to its uppercase equivalent.

try block—a block of code you attempt to execute while acknowledging that an exception might occur.

two-dimensional array—an array that contains two or more columns of values and whose elements are accessed using multiple subscripts. Contrast with **one-dimensional array**.

type-ahead buffer—the keyboard buffer.

type casting—an action that forces a value of one data type to be used as a value of another type.

typeface argument—an argument to the `Font` constructor that is a `String` representing a font. Common fonts have names such as Arial, Century, Monospaced, and Times New Roman.

type-import-on-demand declaration—an import statement that uses the wildcard format to import a package in an application.

type-wrapper classes—a method that can process primitive type values.

U

UI components—user interface components, such as buttons and text fields, with which the user can interact.

unary cast operator—a more complete name for the cast operator that performs explicit conversions.

unary operator—an operator that uses only one operand.

unchecked exceptions—exceptions that cannot reasonably be expected to be recovered from while a program is executing. Contrast with **checked exceptions**.

Unicode—an international system of character representation.

Unified Modeling Language (**UML**)—a graphical language used by programmers and analysts to describe classes and object-oriented processes.

unifying type—a single data type to which all operands in an expression are converted.

unreachable statements—statements that cannot be executed because the logical path can never encounter them; in Java, an unreachable statement causes a compiler error. See also **dead code**.

upcast—to change an object to an object of a class higher in its inheritance hierarchy.

V

validating data—the process of ensuring that a value falls within a specified range.

variable—a named memory location that you can use to store a value.

variable declaration—a statement that reserves a named memory location.

viewport—the viewable area in a `JScrollPane`.

virtual classes—the name given to abstract classes in other programming languages, such as C++.

virtual key codes—codes that represent keyboard keys that have been pressed.

virtual method calls—method calls in which the method used is determined when the program runs, because the type of the object used might not be known until the method executes. In Java, all instance method calls are virtual calls by default.

void—a keyword that, when used in a method header, indicates that the method does not return any value when it is called.

volatile—describes memory that requires power to retain information. Contrast with **nonvolatile**.

W

Web browser—a program that allows you to display HTML documents on your computer screen.

while loop—a construct that executes a body of statements continually as long as the Boolean expression that controls entry into the loop continues to be `true`.

whitespace—any combination of nonprinting characters; for example, spaces, tabs, and carriage returns (blank lines).

wildcard symbol—an asterisk; a symbol used to indicate that it can be replaced by any set of characters. In a Java `import` statement, you use a wildcard symbol to represent all the classes in a package.

window decorations—the icons and buttons that are part of a window or frame.

windowed applications—programs that create a graphical user interface (GUI) with elements such as menus, toolbars, and dialog boxes.

wrapper—a class or object that is "wrapped around" a simpler element.

"write once, run anywhere" (WORA)—a slogan developed by Sun Microsystems to describe the ability of one Java program version to work correctly on multiple platforms.

X

x-axis—an imaginary horizontal line that indicates screen position.

x-coordinate—a value that increases as you travel from left to right across a window.

XHTML—Extensible Hypertext Markup Language, an extension of HTML.

Y

y-axis—an imaginary vertical line that indicates screen position.

y-coordinate—a value that increases as you travel from top to bottom across a window.

INDEX

Note: Boldface page numbers indicate definitions.

& (ampersand), 199, 212
<> (angle brackets), 30
* (asterisk), 17, 160
@ (at sign), 424, 840
\ (backslash), 17, 528
, (comma), 22, 485, 830
{ } (curly braces), 14, 24, 26, 30, 122, 234, 236, 249, 467
$ (dollar sign), 12, 829
= (equal sign), 45, 190
! (exclamation point), 211
/ (forward slash), 17, 30, 528
( ) (parentheses), 11, 13, 15, 30, 235, 311
% (percent sign), 826
. (period), 436, 830
+ (plus sign), 50, 284, 377
# (pound sign), 830
; (semicolon), 30, 125, 161, 191, 219
[] (square brackets), 30
_ (underscore), 12
| (vertical bar), 200–201, 212

A

abs() method, 159
abstract classes, 390, **414–417**, 433, 437–441
abstract keyword, 415
accelerators, **685**
access modifiers
  final access modifier, 96, 97
  inheritance and, 383–384
  package access modifier, 91, 384
  private access modifier, 91, **105**, 435, 845

  protected access modifier, 91, 384, 435, 845
  public access modifier, 12–14, 18, 91, 104, 382–384, 435, 845
AccessACharacter program, 549–551
accessor methods, **108**
accumulating, use of the term, 243
AChildClass program, 401–402
acos() method, 159
action keys, **670**
actionPerformed() method, 608–610, 625, 626, 652, 656, 668, 673, 712–713, 717, 738–741, 771–772, 778
add and assign operator, 243
add() method, 342, 594–595, 643, 644, 650, 657, 659
addActionListener() method, 608, 612
addItem() method, 619
addition (+) operator, **52–53**
addressString variable, 290
addSeparator() method, 684
ADTs (abstract data types), **116**
AgeCalculator program, 163
aggregation, **373**
aGreeting variable, 279
AirlineDialog class, 70–71
Allman style, 14
ambiguity, 144–147
ampersand (&), 199, 212
AND operator, 247, 253
angle brackets (<>), 30
Animal class, 416–420, 423–425, 430, 437
anonymous classes, **166**
AnyClassName class, 16
AParentClass program, 401
append() method, 291, 296

applet(s)
  adding images to, 775–777
  described, **9**, 764–766
  life cycle, 786–790
  overview, 763–806
  running, 765–766, 783
Applet Viewer, 766
application(s). *See also* programs
  analyzing, 10–16
  described, **4–5**, 9
  files, **526**
  running, 19
  writing, 26–28
architectural neutrality, 8
arcs, drawing, **719**, 721–722, 735
areas, copying, 725, 741–742
args identifier, 15
argument(s). *See also* parameters
  constructors requiring, 171–172
  described, **11**, 90
  dialog boxes and, 67
  index, optional, **829–830**
  inheritance and, 379–380, 398–400
  methods that accept, 120–121
  methods that require no, 118
  passing, 11
  sending, to constructors, 147–148
arithmetic operator(s)
  described, **51–52**
  shortcut, 243–245
  using, 74–75
arithmetic statements, writing, 51–52
array(s). *See also* elements; subscripts
  creating, 344–345
  declaring, 310–313
  described, **310**
  initializing, 310–313, 345